INTERNATIONAL ECONOMIC DEVELOPMENT

Theories, Models and Case Studies of Countries Leading the Change

INTERNATIONAL ECONOMIC DEVELOPMENT

Theories, models & case studies
of countries leading the change

Editor
Kishore G. Kulkarni

MATRIX

ISBN: 978-81-910142-3-5

First published 2010

Published by Sanjay Sethi for

MATRIX PUBLISHERS
S 2, Akarshan Bhawan, 4754/23 Ansari Road, Daryaganj, New Delhi 110 002
email: ssethi@matrixpublishers.org
mobile: +91 98100 45161

Lasertypeset by Sai Graphic Design, 8678/XV, Arakashan Road, Paharganj, New Delhi 110 055

Printed at Sanat Printers, Kundli, Haryana

To my Thousands of Amazing Students World Over:
who have made Teaching a Passion rather than a Punishment

Preface

To bring out this book for the students of Economic Development related courses has been a great pleasure. This is not only a product of work done by some of the most remarkable students in my graduate classes, but also it shows that the development field has so many applied topics that need to be explored.

I am a firm believer of the saying, 'Theory is useless if does not shed any light on reality'. This book tries to show that the development oriented economic theory and models can easily be used to shed light on reality. Therefore, this book is a collection of many applications of theories such as Heckscher Ohlin, Harrod Domar, Dutch Disease, Lewis' model, population policies and international trade policy for economic development. All chapters come out of some outstanding work done by graduate students. Our hope is that the book will be useful for development oriented classes all over the world, especially for B.A., B.Com, M. A. and M.Com classes in India and undergraduate and graduate classes in USA. Ph.D. students and general readers can also find this as a lesson in carrying out empirical work.

To complete this book with such a high efficiency and amazing timeliness was not possible without tremendous help from numerous individuals. All the authors took special efforts in completing a publishable chapter which required a lot of research on their part. I appreciate their help in getting this done on a prompt basis. Mr. Sanjay Sethi of Matrix Publishers has been an inspiration for finishing this project on a short notice. His commitment to work and his efficiency are the attributes that are rarely seen in the publishing industry. Ms. Neeru Sood was punctual, hard working and effective reader of the drafts of each chapter. I owe a big thank you to these special individuals. I have been fortunate to have colleagues such as Dr. John Cochran, Dean, School of Business at the Metropolitan State College of Denver and Dean Tom Farer at the Korbel School of International Studies, University of Denver, whose constant encouragement is greatly appreciated.

I also want to profusely thank my wife, Jayashree for pushing me to complete new projects and for understanding the reasons for my slowness in completing the tasks at home. I am grateful to our daughters Dr. Lina and Aditi, who make us proud parents by their tremendous achievements in academics as well as in the gymnastics arena.

If there are any comments, readers are encouraged to contact me by e-mail at kulkarnk@mscd.edu

Denver, Colorado, USA   **KISHORE G. KULKARNI**

Contents

Introduction

Importance of Learning Economic Development and the Basic Theories of How Countries Develop

Kishore G. Kulkarni

This book is made up of 30 articles some of which are authored and co-authored by Prof. Kishore G. Kulkarni in the field of Economic Development in general, and International Economic Growth experiences in particular. It is important to learn and read the economic development theories for several reasons. There has not been a faster growing branch of general economics than the economic development field. While the theoretical growth in the field is impressive, there is also a whole lot of awareness in the profession to recognize that the majority of the world population is deprived of basic necessities and the means of living a regular life. About 25 per cent of world population of roughly seven billion people make less than one US dollar a day and roughly 35 per cent makes less than two US dollars a day. This makes it roughly 2.45 billion people living in a miserable living condition. The newly added population to this world is rarely in the developed world and most of the developed countries have a very small population growth rate. A couple having less than 2 children essentially means that a couple is replaced by fewer individuals and the country experiences a negative population growth. Most of the developed countries have negative population growth and most of the developing countries have a very high population growth rate (roughly 2 per cent a year).

But, given the high base of large numbers, even 2 per cent of the Indian population means roughly twenty million people a year which creates added burden on the resources and the economic development is that much harder to come by. No wonder then the appalling statistics that 80 per cent of the world population holds only 20 per cent of the world resources (which means 20 per cent of the world population mostly in the developed countries, gets 80 per cent of the resources) creating an acute problem of re-distribution. The developed countries' world has a totally different lifestyle than the developing countries which contributes to the majority of the world population. While dualism is one of the characteristics of the developing countries, the meager resources available to survive are the prime reason for such a living condition. Almost all of their income is spent on procuring the bare necessities of food, shelter and clothing. Natural disasters (such as floods) easily ruin their lives by taking away whatever they have and the famous saying that, "an average Indian person is born in poverty, he/she lives in poverty and dies in poverty" is quite evident.

There are limited opportunities to break the social class structure. When a new baby is born, there is a 90 per cent chance that he/she is born in a developing (poor) country. So, we do have some serious facts to consider and the policy decisions to make. The field of economic development would consider these policy options.

Additionally, if importance of any field is measured by the quality of research carried out in it, then economic development field is in the forefront of that achievement. There are many economists who have worked in the development field and have received the most coveted award. In recent years, one of the Indian economists, Prof. Amatya Sen, Gunnar Myrdal, Arthur Lewis, Simon Kuznets, Wassily Leontief, Paul Samuelson, Bertil Ohlin, and Banlgadeshi Mohammed Yunis, all have received Noble Prize for their outstanding work in the field of economic development. Moreover the increased international trade, globalization, awareness of other cultures, improved travel facilities and knowledge of world cultures are the factors that have all added to the fact that economic development awareness is of crucial importance.

Therefore, the next question is what are the ways in which economy can achieve economic development? Economists have paid a lot of attention to questions like this. In fact, the basic explanations popped up with the work of Cambridge University economists such as W.W. Rostow who proposed the *Stages of Economic Growth* and a team of Harrod and Domar who proposed the exact way in which economic development is possible. Added to the existing literature, the work of Arthur Lewis (Princeton University, and Nobel Prize winner), in terms of the Model of Structural Change, can make some interesting path of growth theories for us. We would summarize the main arguments of these theories here and then add to them the most famous contemporary model of economic growth given by Neo-classical economists.

W.W. Rostow was the pioneer in presenting an explanation of the stages in economic growth by arguing that these stages are not only mere explanation of historical development but they have inner logic and continuity which lead them to become the substantial evidence of how economic development normally takes place. The initial stage of economic development is called the stage of 'traditional society' in which the production methods are crude, the main production is in agriculture sector, the technology is primitive and the population is mainly interested in producing the means of survival. There is no manufacturing of course and the cultural development is minimal. There are some tribes and rural areas of the world that can qualify for this stage of the economic development.

The second stage is called the stage of 'Pre-conditions for Take-off'. In this stage as the name suggests some preconditions are met for the take-off such as the manufacturing production starts taking place and industrial sector becomes active if not prominent. In this stage, lower proportion of population relies on the agriculture sector to produce the necessities of life than in case of traditional society, and there is readiness for high level of investment projects not just in the public sector but also in the private sector. In the third stage of development, called the stage of 'Take-off', the real action begins. The vibrant manufacturing and industrial sector starts employing much higher proportion of the population. Improved technology in agricultural sector such as the 'Green Revolution' makes the food production increase by employing lower proportion of population in rural areas. The industrial sector, mainly in mega cities, follows the life style of rich countries at least for some people even if the slums and shanty towns are usual occurrence in urban sector. Production of necessities which includes the utilities such as electricity, telephones, and some luxuries such as refrigerators, and cars is on the rise in this sector. In essence, this is the stage in which most of the emerging market economies are settled in last fifty years or so.

In terms of Rostow's growth stages, fourth stage is the one where most of developed countries are in recent years. It is the prosperity stage. In this stage, the most important sector, from the employment point of view, is the service sector, even if industrial output and mechanization in production is abundant. In this stage, the least important sector is the agriculture as a very small proportion of population sufficiently produces food products with the help of improved technology. While manufacturing uses very modern technology, there is a wide and huge investment in innovation, research and development. Necessities are in abundant supply, while luxuries, even if expensive, have only few supply constraints. The final and the fifth stage of economic growth is called the age of high mass consumption which is rarely reached even by developed countries. Few examples of such growth can be the stage of USA in modern times or top ten countries in the per capita income ranking. Clearly in this stage, the aggregate supply of goods and services is not a major concern but creating the aggregate demand is the primary objective of the economic policy. Marketing, advertising and commercialization are the main avenues of generating higher aggregate demand in such economies. In essence, Rostow argued that if an economy has to grow, it has to go through these specified stages irrespective of the time they may take. Of course as a major criticism of this theory, there is no clear-cut explanation of the reasons why and the how (that is, the process) an economy moves from one stage to the other. In other words, Rostow fails to provide the reason for economic development, if at all, he only explains the stages. The crucial reason for economic growth is provided by the theory of another duo from University of Cambridge, Harrod and Domar.

In Harrod-Domar model, the process of growth is mainly dependent upon the saving rate (saving/GDP or S/Y) of the economy. To arrive at this conclusion, they make the following arguments with needed assumptions:

Suppose Consumption (C), which is the expenditure of consumers on final goods and services, is mainly determined by the national income or GDP (Y).

$$C = cY.$$

Saving (S), in simplistic terms, can be defined as income (Y) that is not consumed therefore,

$$S = Y - C,$$
or, $$S = Y - cY$$

or, $S = (1 - c) Y$

And, if $s = (1 - c)$ then

            $S = sY$ where s can be termed as the saving rate.

Define Investment (I) as the expenditure of producers on a) purchase of machinery, tools and equipment b) construction activities and c) increase in the stock of inventories. Essentially therefore, Investment is the increase in capital stock and if capital stock is represented by letter K then I = change in K.

Assume that capital output ratio (K/Y) of an economy is constant, so that,

j = K/Y where j is the capital output ratio. Then to keep j constant we also know that (change in K/ change in Y) = j. This also shows that change in K = j times change in Y, or I = j x change in Y.

According to Harrod-Domar model, assume further interest rate (r) in the economy is flexible, so that we are guaranteed that Saving (S) = Investment (I). This would give us the concluding argument of Harrod Domar Model that:

            (Change in Y/Y) = s/j or

the percentage change in real GDP = saving rate/capital output ratio of an economy.

Since the right hand side of the above equation is the expression of economic growth, the growth according to Harrod-Domar model directly depends upon the ability of the economy to raise the saving rate (s), (recall that j is constant and therefore cannot be changed). With the popularity of the Harrod-Domar argument in 1950s, many economies put in place policies that would directly affect the saving rate. Increase in saving rate was sought by making worldwide pleas, encouraging domestic residents to save more with numerous saving schemes, and by increasing the real interest rate. Of course the increase in saving was seen as the pre-condition for increased investment, and with few other notable arguments such as the one by Rosenstein-Rodan's Big Push theory, the world was looking at the increased investment activities as the only way to solve the problem of underdevelopment. Indian policies were no exception to this type of thinking. However this advice and its implementation only increased the public investment and the government's control over the economic resources quadrupled in a very short time in many of the developing economies.

Harrod Domar model thus was an excellent attempt to answer the question of how an economy achieves growth. It however left some other questions unanswered: What about institutional factors? International trade? Role of the government? In fact 1970s witnessed more hardship rather than solutions for economic development in almost all developing economies that adopted the Harrod-Domar model prescription.

A different explanation of the process of economic development was offered by Arthur Lewis' model of structural adjustment. In this model a developing economy is basically seen as divided into two major sectors: a) Traditional or agricultural (rural) sector and b) Industrial, urban and manufacturing sector. While the agricultural sector has abundance of labour to the point at which the marginal productivity of labour is close to zero. Hence, taking labour away from this sector makes no difference to the total product. Of course the labor that has employment in this sector has the wage rate close to the subsistence level; hence in the rural sector, people somehow survive, there is no modern technology, no high productivity, no substantive production. In the urban industrial sector, however the age rate is above subsistence level, labour productivity is positive and there is an attractive force from the urban sector for the labour of traditional sector.

The process of structural adjustment begins when the labour starts migrating from rural to urban sector and urban areas grow at a much faster rate than the rural sector. However as the marginal productivity of labour is close to zero in traditional sector, there is no loss of production, but the total product in urban sector increases due to the positive marginal labour productivity. This increased total product, increases the profitability and the capitalists are supposed to reinvest the profits in purchasing higher means of production. This would lead to more production with same labour resources and the economic growth ensues. In general therefore, the Lewis's model predicts that urban sector alone is responsible for economic development. While this model successfully explains the growth of mega-cities and urbanization process in developing countries, it ignores some other structural adjustments such as the role of service sector (a la India economic development in recent years) and role of governmental policy in influencing the development.

While the traditional models discussed so far insisted the economic growth being mainly an endogenous phenomenon they have not paid much attention to the international trade or the role of foreign direct investment or the so called external factors. The Neoclassical model of economic growth started by monumental work of Robert Solow and his colleagues such as Bela Belassa, I.M.D. Little and Jagdish Bhagwati and others emphasizes the importance of globalization, international trade, reduced bureaucracy, more free markets, less regulation and administrative costs in economic development.

In their (Neoclassical) argument, the production function, that shows the relationship between output produced and inputs used, is represented as the one with diminishing marginal returns for individual factors of production (such as Labour (L) and Capital (K)) and it is of homogeneous of degree one which means that if both factors of production are increased by x per cent, then the output will increase by x per cent as well. Hence the main argument is that traditional factors of production will increase the output but with decreasing rate (diminishing returns). The economic development therefore does not come from endogenous factors. The crucial contributor for economic growth however is the 'Solow Residual' which captures all the subjective factors mentioned above. Hence in this model, the growth is caused by external (exogenous) factors rather than internal (endogenous). In 1970s, the Neoclassical model of economic development became so popular that the countries that were tired of trying the usual remedy to develop, enthusiastically, but slowly, adopted neo-classical ideas in their attempt to manage the economy including ofcourse India and China. The results were positive. Economies started growing at a high rate (It can be noted that the fastest growing economies of the world in last five years are China and India) and the neo-classical model made sense to the policy makers and politicians even if it argued for reduced role for both these groups. In general, we are now left with a time dependent history of growth models.

Some new versions of growth models also added some value to the overall explanation of how economies grow. Notable amongst them are such models as the Paul Romer's explanation of technological growth as the precondition for economic growth. In fact, the most recent growth of US economy (in 1990s) was primarily determined by the tremendous technological revolution in computer, communication and information technology, therefore such explanation can make a lot of sense to the economic development literature. Similarly, some extreme views such as International Dependence hypothesis which postulates that developed countries on purpose like to keep up with the arrangement of center and periphery. At the center are the rich economies which get fed by the supply of raw materials and the important ingredients to keep their manufacturing output going. This Marxist view claims that the supply of raw cotton from former colonies of UK mad the cloth mills in Manchester run for a long time and there is no intention on the part of developed world to change this arrangement. In this view, the economic development is going to be hard and almost impossible to be equally distributed in the world. Of course the solution for this is to have developing countries unite and show a uniform resistance to the status quo.

Another interesting explanation of why economic development process is hard to come by is the one offered by 'False Paradigm' Hypothesis. According to this hypothesis, the decision making authorities and those who put forward solutions of development problems are all individuals from developed countries who have no real experience of development. Hence the solutions forwarded by big school graduates form the Western countries scholars are bound to fail. Moreover they work in air-conditioned offices to solve the problems of world poverty and have little interest or ability to come up with workable solutions. Hence they live in a 'False paradigm' or in the dream world which has no solutions for economic development and until we come up with a better substitute there is no hope for the real solution of economic development. While this view has an interesting argument, it fails to realize that the knowledge has power. One does not have to 'test' a poison and the experience can be a good teacher but not for all and not always. Hence there is nothing wrong in thinking about real solutions to world poverty if enough knowledge about it is acquired.

We are therefore left with several explanations of why and how economic development takes place. While all of these explanations were useful to be applied in some countries of the world, there is still a small gap in theory and reality in this area. This book collects some related articles in the areas of growth and development. In Chapter 1, we discuss how to measure economic development and the problems involved in such measurement. While GDP is the most acceptable and widely used measure of economic development we point out some problems in its measurement. Two of the fastest growing economies of the world in recent times are China and India. Even if Chinese economic development strategy has been considered as a miracle in the modern times, the record of the Chinese government for human rights is questionable. India's economic growth has happened in a freer society where the rights to express and freedom of individual opinion is well protected.

1

Applying Simon Kuznets Six Characteristics of Economic Development to South Africa

Brandie Miller

CHAPTER SUMMARY

South Africa rests at the Southern tip of the continent Africa, and has a large population of 49,052,489 (CIA World Fact Book, 2009). South Africa is considered a middle-income country with a copious amount of natural resources; as far back as 1912, the gold and diamond empire was laid out (Rothenberg, 2006). South Africa is a dual economy with two distinct societies: black and white, capitalist and agrarian and a rural impoverished African sector (Worden, 2000, p. 3). South Africa also has a very high unemployment rate at nearly 50 per cent despite a decent size service and industry sector, yet it also has well-developed financial, legal, communications, energy, and transport sectors, a stock exchange that is seventeenth largest in the world, and modern infrastructure supporting an efficient distribution of goods to major urban centers throughout the region (Todaro, 2000).

The economy is still facing many problems including: "poverty, lack of economic empowerment among the disadvantaged groups, and a shortage of public transportation" (CIA World Fact Book, 2009). Many of those problems are stemming from the era of colonialism, but especially from the more recent Apartheid proponents.

Colonialism in South Africa was a time period of exploitation and domination, of shifting political power, and slavery and racism. White settlers attempted to "civilize" South Africans, namely the black South Africans, all while creating a plush life for themselves. The after-effect of colonialism in South Africa is that once independence was gained, the South African economy found itself with many burdens. Rothenberg (2006) reveals that: "the statistics that show today that Africa is underdeveloped are the statistics representing the affairs at the end of colonialism" (p. 100).

Additionally under colonial powers, South Africa's infrastructure was opened to imports-exports by way of railways and roads which all led straight to the sea. Colonialism introduced some elements of capitalism into South Africa such as private property and land ownership, yet colonial powers failed to advance South Africa in human development (Rothenberg, 2006).

Apartheid laws, enforced by the National Party in South Africa were from 1948 to 1994. This time period of South African history was burdened with racial discrimination thus large-scale human right abuses. Moreover, one can explain Apartheid times as the unhappy history of virulent racism (Worden, 2000, p.3).

Major oppositions to Apartheid including: The African National Congress (ANC) and Nelson Mandela, dismantled the regimes by way of protests, insurgencies and western institutions aiding the fall-out through boycotts. A form of democracy was implemented in the 1994 election using the majority rule; ending Apartheid governance (Todaro, 2000).

The end of the Apartheid reign left South Africa with many issues such as poverty, ill health care, housing and education. Moreover, the economy is still struggling from this era, as are the people who suffered the abuses.

This chapter is designed to test Simon Kuznets hypothesis: six characteristics of economic growth on the country South Africa. The purpose is to identify if Kuznets theory has any relevance to the economy of the state of South Africa. Many of the comparisons within each characteristic will include elements of Apartheid ruling, and post-Apartheid ruling.

SIX FAMOUS CHARACTERISTICS OF SIMON KUZNETS

Simon Kuznets defines economic growth as a "long term rise in capacity to supplement increasingly diverse economic goods to its population, this growing capacity based on advancing technology and the institutional and ideological adjustments" (Todaro, 1999, p. 121). Kuznets' three principal components are further described as:

1. The sustained rise in national output is a manifestation of economic growth, and the ability to provide a wide range of goods is a sign of economic maturity.
2. Advancing technology provides the basis or preconditions for continuous economic growth – a necessary but not sufficient condition.
3. To realize the potential for growth inherent in new technology, institutional, attitudinal, and ideological adjustments must be made.

Todaro (1999) cites Kuznets: "Technological innovations without concomitant social innovation is like a light bulb without electricity – the potential exists, but without the complementary input, nothing will happen" (p. 121). The next section of this chapter will detail the six characteristics. Within each characteristic will be the application of Kuznets' theory and its relationship to South Africa, along with critiques.

Characteristic 1: High Rates of Growth of Per Capita Output and Population Growth

Todaro (2000) argues that all developed countries have experienced large multiples of economic growth. Historically the GDP growth in rich countries was 3 per cent with population growth at 1 per cent as opposed to developing countries where the GDP grows by 2.5 per cent and populations grow by 1.5 per cent. It would take more years to double per capita income in developing countries. Without high rates of GDP and per capita GDP, economic growth is impossible. Furthermore, in order for the per capita to grow, the growth in GDP has to be greater than growth in population.

Characteristic 2: High Rates of Increase in Total Factor Productivity

Total Factor Productivity (TFP) can be defined as "the output per unit of all inputs" (Todaro, 2000, p. 122). Furthermore, Todaro (2000) states that the principle of TFP is that efficiency with which "all inputs are used in a production function." Also productivity gains have to be universal: upgradation of existing physical and human resources; more capital and labour to become more productive. Moreover, land reforms or productivity;

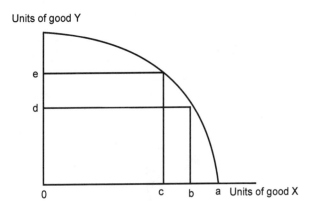

Figure 1.1: The Productions Possibilities Curve

Source: http://faculty.mc3.edu/kbaird/ProductionPossibilities Curve/sld003.htm

fertilizers, and enterprise knowledge of technology should be increased. Increase in total factor productivity (TFP) is the same thing as shift of PPC to the right. *(See: The Production Possibilities Curve in Figure 1.1)*

Applying Kuznets's Theory to Characteristic One and Two: High Rates of Growth Per Capita Output and Population Growth

(Note: This section will analyze characteristic one and two together because of their similarities.)

In the latter part of the apartheid years 1980-93, the real GDP growth rate was an average of 1 per cent while in the post-apartheid time period of 1994-2001, the growth rate increased to 2.8 per cent calculated by TFP *(See:* Figure 1.2*)*. Arndt and Lewis (2000) attribute this increase to the investment in machinery and equipment and trade liberalization. The prominent role of TFP in South Africa's recent growth performance is that GDP growth can generally be sustained as long as there continues to be improvements in technology and efficiency (Arndt and Lewis, 2000). Kuznets would call this "enhanced enterprise knowledge of technology" (Todaro, 2001). Additionally, Table 1.1 below provided by the World Bank shows contributions of labour and capital in South Africa's growth from 1980-2001. Growth was robust from 2004 to 2008 as South Africa reaped the benefits of macroeconomic stability and a global commodities boom, but began to slow in the second half of 2008 due to the global financial crisis' impact on commodity prices and demand. GDP fell nearly by 2 per cent in 2009 (IMF, 2009). Even though South Africa may be robust in exporting and manufacturing, the economy was still affected by the economic crisis the more developed worlds experienced.

Table 1.1: Contributions to Growth, 1989-2001

	1980-93	1994-2001	1980-2001
Real GDP growth (in per cent)	1.0	2.8	1.7
Contributions (in percentage points)			
Capital	0.9	0.6	0.8
Labour	0.1	−0.9	−0.3
TFP	0.0	3.1	1.2

Sources: Statistics South Africa; and author's estimates.

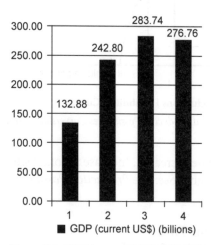

Figure 1.2: GDP (current US$) (billions)

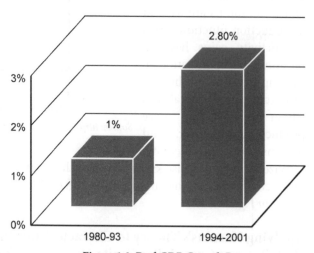

Figure 1.3: Real GDP Growth Rates

It has been shown in the above figures that even though GDP is positive, the rate of GDP growth is decreasing. The second part of Kuznets' first characteristic claims that growth in GDP has to be greater than population growth in order for per capita growth to occur. The fertility rate for South Africa in the year 2000 was the highest in the world at 5.3 children per woman (Lutz, Sanderson and Scherbov, 2004). This rate is projected to decline mostly impart to the HIV/AIDS epidemic dominating the country. Population growth from 2000 to 2008 as the data

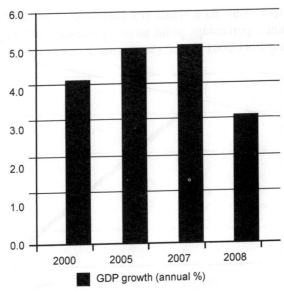

Figure 1.4: GDP Growth Annual (%)

Source: All of the original information for the GDP was taken from the World Bank.

from the IMF shows in Figure 1.5 has been increasing most recently. As with fertility rate, it is also projected to decrease.

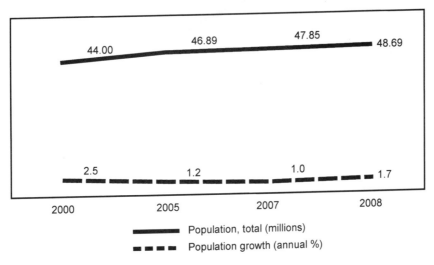

Figure 1.5: Population Growth: 2000-2008

Along with the GPD decreasing, employment shrank during 1994-2001 period, as the positive annual average growth of 0.2 per cent during 1980-93 period was replaced by negative growth of 1.6 per cent (See Figure 1.6). As a result, the contribution to GDP growth of capital and labour together fell from 1 percentage point annually during 1980-93 period to negative 0.3 percentage points during 1994-2001 period (See Figure 1.7).

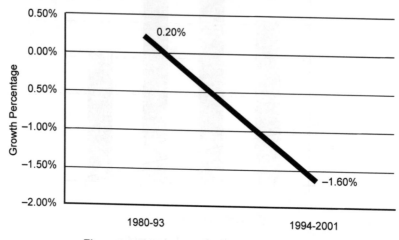

Figure 1.6: Shrinking of Employment, 1980-2001

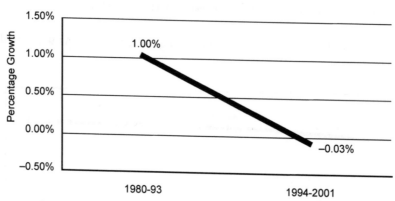

Figure 1.7: Falling of Both Capital and Labor as a Result of Decline in Employment, 1908-2001

Source: Arndt and Lewis, 2000.

Overall it has been estimated that over 1 million jobs have been lost predominantly amongst the artisans and unskilled. This has led to a significant growth in unemployment from 33 per cent in 1996 to 41 per cent in 2001. (See Figure 1.8 and 1.9 respectively)

This increase has disproportionately affected the majority African population with unemployment increasing from 42.5 per cent to over 50 per cent in just five years. The loss of jobs in the formal sector is giving rise to so-called informal sector jobs. These include activities such as hawking, food retailing, home based manufacturing (Chopra and Sanders, 2004, p. 4).

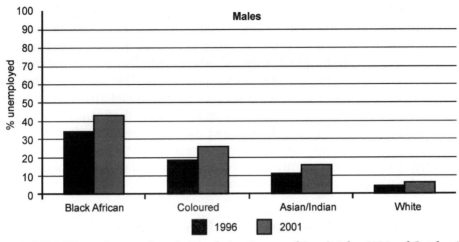

Figure 1.8: Official Unemployment Rates by Population Group and Sex, October 1996 and October 2001

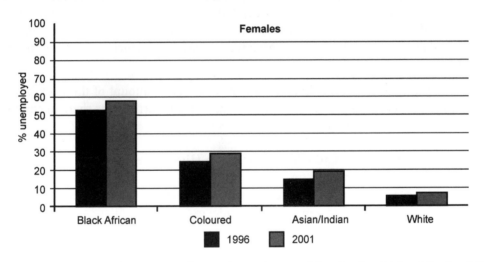

Figure 1.9: Official Unemployment Rates by Population Group and Sex, October 1996 and October 2001

Critiques of Characteristic 1 and 2

High rates of growth of per capita output and population growth are aggregate economic variables. What the first principle does not account for, is how detrimental high rates of population growth can be to an economy. Specifically in South Africa, ethnic divides created from previous Apartheid laws, have profound effects on the suppressed society of black South Africans. Many black South Africans were kept ignorant which greatly contributed to higher rates of population growth by way of a lesser education and information to knowledge and information. In fact, black Africans comprise approximately 75 per cent of the population (Todaro, 2000, p. 200).

The current world is a crowded place with a higher amount of land usage. There may not be enough resources in order to support a large population; as a result, urbanization can occur widening the gaps in standards of living. In order to have an increase in per capita growth, Kuznets argues that total factor productivity will also have to increase. To the contrary, some theorists see TFP as invalid because one cannot quantify the TFP variables. What is more, a push for technological innovations currently is a great strategy for international communication and exchanges. On the other hand, many countries do not have the financial capital to support new technology or, labourers may not have proper training to use technology effectively. Most importantly, the people in South Africa who have access to new technological enterprise is the white minority with the black majority still accepting lower paid work with harsher conditions, mainly in the form of physically intensive labour.

Characteristic 3: A High Rate of Structural Transformation

All developed countries have experienced a high rate of structural transformation. Components of structural transformation include: lower dependence on agricultural sector while shifting to urban-oriented manufacturing and improvements in manufacturing and service sectors (less family owned businesses and a shift towards large corporations) which make the output growth the fastest.

The goal according to Kuznets is to eventually have a higher amount of the workforce in the industrialized sector, making it the most important sector in terms of its share in employment and production (Szirmai, 2005).

Applying Kuznets's Theory to Characteristic 3: High Rates of Structural Transformation

South Africa is a middle-income, rather industrialized nation sharing many characteristics with developing countries. Some examples include: extreme inequities in wealth, division of labour between formal and informal sectors, dependence on commodity exports, and high government intervention (Todaro, 2000, p. 200). Cheap labour was the basis of the economy and it explained much of the growth and dynamics of modern South Africa (Worden, 2000, p. 3).The formal sector is well developed with an emphasis on mining and manufacturing. Mining has been a major part of the South Africa economy since the discovery of gold. There are small agricultural and service sectors, as well as a strong private sector. Additionally, there is an extensive government intervention and corporate ownership. (See Figure 1.10)

Table 1.2

GDP- Composition by Sector	Labour Force	Labour Force- By Occupation
Agriculture: 3.5%	17.32 million economically active (2009 est.)	Agriculture: 9%
Industry: 32.1%	country comparison to the world: 35	Industry: 26%
Services: 64.4% (2009 est.)		Services: 65% (2007 est.)

Source: Worden, 2000.

Economic policy has concentrated on the formal sector, but since mid-1980s the policy has sought to develop the informal sector, focusing on education and training, job creation, and small business assistance since there is such a large unemployment rate (Szirmai, 2005). The CIA Fact book predicts the unemployment rate at 24 per cent in conjunction with the industrial production growth rate at a –7 per cent (See Figure 1.10) (*Note*: Other estimates believe the unemployment rate is upwards of 50 per cent when excluding the informal sector)

Table 1.3

Unemployment Rate	Industrial Production Growth Rate
24%(2009 est.)	–7%
Country comparison to the world: 173	Country Comparison to the world: 125

Common to many countries that are in transition to a developed country, South Africa's agricultural sector demonstrated a sequential shift from 12 per cent of their industry in agriculture in the 1950s, to only 3 per cent in the year 2000 (Szirmai, 2005). (See Figure 1.10) Moreover, this demonstrates how important the service industry is in South Africa. Szirmai (2005) believes that the rapid growth in the service sector can be attributed to the expansion of the government sector.

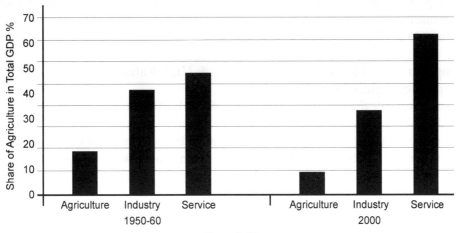

Figure 1.10

Critiques of Characteristic 3

There can be many problems with a large workforce in the industrial sector. Industrializing a nation encourages urbanization of the labour force where significant problems become associated with urbanization; such as slum dwellings and labour abundance. The urban population is 61 per cent of total population (2008) with the rate of urbanization being 1.4 per cent annual rate of change (2005-10 EST) (CIA, 2008). The Laissez-Faire theorists explain that when the supply of labour exceeds the demand, wage rate will fall producing cheap labour in highly exploitative conditions, which is what is occurring with much of the population currently.

Furthermore, when the service sector increases, so do labour intensive jobs. This can create a decrease in productivity unless other means such as financial services and technological change occurs (Szirmai, 2005, p. 109).

Characteristic 4: High Rates of Social and Ideological Transformation

Economic change is associated with social and ideological transformations; attitudes, ideology, more freedom for minorities, and institutions. A transformation in all of these is known as 'modernization' (Todaro, 2000, p. 123). Gunnar Myrdral and Todaro listed four criterias for social transformation (2000). These criteria are:

1) Rationality – Substitution in ideology of consumption, distribution, rationale in production and in thinking. Furthermore, opinions in economics and politics should be rooted in relevant facts.
2) Economic planning – The government needs to take a greater role in creating more coordinated policy change.
3) Social and economic equalization – Granting higher opportunities by creating better equality in: status, incomes, wealth, standards of living, etc.
4) Improved institutions and attitudes – This is necessary in order to create economic mobility and to promote development. Examples include: outmoded land tenure systems, social and economic monopolies, educational and religious structures, systems of administration, and a change in attitudes of workers.

Applying Kuznets's Theory to Characteristic 4: High Rates of Social and Ideological Transformation

Kuznets may attribute the middle-income status of South Africa in part due to the slow rates of social and ideological transformation. Szirmai (2005) refers to authors: Mcgowan and Johnson (1984) with the data that: there is a negative correlation between an index of political instability and growth per capita income in thirty-nine countries in Sub-Sahara Africa. Political instability and a major civil unrest in South Africa have not helped further economic growth. Szirmai (2005) classifies South Africa as a predatory state, where money is taken from the citizens for the benefit of the rulers.

It wasn't until 1994 with the breakdown of Apartheid laws, and the newly elected President Nelson Mandela coming into power, that South Africa first attempted a democratic election. Moreover, debates between the political parties ANC (demanding social and economic equalization by way of redistribution of wealth) and the South Africa Foundation (advocating for privatization, and deregulation of the financial sector to encourage attraction of foreign investment), was there any economic progress (Chopra and Sanders, 2004).

The Apartheid segregation still has rippling effects currently; one can clearly see those in the institution of education as an example. Case in point, the black literacy rate is 33 per cent and over three quarters of the black teachers are unqualified for their jobs (Todaro, 2000, p. 201). The disparities are so extreme between races that the United Nations Development Programme wrote:

"If white South Africa were a separate country, it would rank 24th in the world. Black South Africa would rank 123rd in the world. Not just two different peoples, there are almost two different worlds."

However, there have been some attempts at integration but, as Chopra and Sanders (2004) highlight, "the pressure to become a global city which attracts foreign investment and tourism has severely limited the progress towards urban integration. Despite an extensive and widely publicized process of identifying development nodes that are situated closer to the areas that have concentrations of the poor, nearly all private investment has continued to flow to the richer suburbs. This is largely due to the reluctance and inability of local government to influence market forces – 'the general implication is that income, social class and market forces have replaced race and state control in directing the pattern of urban development.'"

Critiques of Characteristic 4

Myrdral wrote that the government needs to take a greater role in economic planning. However the opposite in South Africa is occurring where the government has too much interference. This is leading to corruption and lack of freedom for the citizens. It is important to note that the citizens who are the most disadvantaged are the black South Africans. This is as a result of their historical inferior status, perpetuated by current high rates of poverty. Additionally, even though many advocates for changing social and ideological perception, transformations can be very impeding upon a culture with deep roots in racism and tradition.

Characteristic 5 : Freer Markets Domestically as well as Ability to Reach to the World Market and World Demand

Freer international trade is seen as a precondition for growth. For instance: raw materials, cheap labour, and lucrative markets. This is made possible by the expansion of modern technology especially in transportation and communication (Todaro, 2000).

Applying Kuznets's Theory to Characteristic 5: Freer Markets Domestically as well as the Ability to Reach to the World Market and World Demand

Prior to 1994, the economy of South Africa was in a decline phase for close to two decades. By the early nineties, the economy was in negative growth with high rates of capital flight and high levels of unemployment (Lewis, 2001). The strategy of primary product export and import substitution had foundered on the rocks of unstable primary product prices, shortage of skilled labour and lack of a large enough domestic market. The situation was compounded by the huge costs of maintaining the Apartheid apparatus (Chopra and Sanders, 2004, p. 4).

Since the 1994 elections, South Africa's external trade liberalization has increased dramatically. Lewis (2001) explains: "Accession to the WTO, negotiation of a free trade agreement with the EU, and discussions over a SADC free trade area collectively mark the growing contribution of trade to the prospects and prosperity of the economy."

One major aspect of the trade agreement South Africa made with the GATT, is reduction in tariffs. Initially there were very positive results especially in regards to protections, however since 1996, the positive rates declined somewhat dramatically. (See Box 1.1 that follows)

	All rates 1990	All rates 1996	All rates 1999	Positive rates 1999
Box 1.1: South African Tariff Changes at a Glance				
Number of tariff lines	12500	8250	7743	2463
Number of different rates (bands)	200	49	47	45
Min rate, %	0	0	0	1
Max rate, %	1389	61	55	55
Unweighted mean rate, %	27.5	9.5	7.1	16.5
Standard deviation, %	n.a.	n.a.	10.0	8.6
Coefficient of variation, %	159.8	134.0	140.3	52.2

Source: 1990 & 1996, Tsikata (1999a): 1888, TRAINS Database (2000).
Note: "Positive rates" includes only non-zero tariff lines, "all rates" include positive rates, zero and "not available" entries.

South Africa has also experienced a major export explosion. Their main exports are in the form of chemicals, metals (iron & steel, non-ferrous metals), metal products, and machinery. Motor vehicles and paper were also important contributors, while food, clothing, and footwear suffered absolute decline in exports (Lewis, 2001). The economy of South Africa also changed prices of imports leading to an improvement in the latter 1990s.

Critiques of Characteristic 5

Free trade is a highly debatable topic in economics. Proponents against free trade believe it is a highly unfair and immoral system of trade benefiting the MDCs almost exclusively by way using the LDCs for their benefit. Some LDCs complain about export instability due to fluctuations in developed countries. As developed countries experience recession, their imports fluctuate creating export instability for LDCs. As was expressed earlier in the paper, South Africa's economy has been negatively affected by the world economic recession since 2008. LDCs also complain about non-availability of financial resources in international financial markets. Commercial lending to LDCs is small and declining. For example, the IMF conditionalties are worrisome for some LDCs due to conditionalties.

Characteristic 6: Limited Spread of Economic Growth to more than 1/3 of the World Population

Economic development cannot be concentrated to only few countries. This is an example of power relationships and dominance of LDCs by MDCs.

Applying Kuznets's Theory to Characteristic 6: Limited Spread of Economic Growth to more than 1/3 of the World Population

Historically, many developing countries did not participate in global trade. South Africa was no exception during the Apartheid reign. However, after the Apartheid was no longer in power, South Africa began re-emerging from 'isolation.' According to Lewis (2001), they have been spending considerable time re-integrating into the world economy.

"Negotiation of a free trade agreement with the EU, discussion over a SADC free trade area and participation in global forums involved in international debates over (for example) the next round of WTO-sponsored global trade negotiations all underscore the growing outward orientation of the South African economy" (p. 21).

The WTO meetings held in Seattle in 1994 were a great opportunity for South Africa and other developing countries to be involved with global trade. There, South Africa was encouraged to create multiple trade alliances for efficiency and for protection purposes.

Since the WTO meetings, South Africa has made much progression using free trade agreements. For example, since 1999, there has been a union between South Africa (SA) and the European Union (EU). This agreement further led to an agreement with Southern African Development Community (SADC), as well as South African Customs Union (SACU) (Lewis, 2001). Other agreements are: Common Market for Eastern and Southern Africa (COMESA)/Preferential Trade Area for Eastern and Southern Africa (PTA), Cross-Border Initiative (CBI), and Bilateral Trade Arrangements (BTA).

African countries contribute a very small share of world trade exports. South Africa contributes a higher amount than other African countries at 0.8 per cent. Even though 0.8 per cent is a small amount world wide, it is a large amount of their GDP. (See Table 1.4 that follows) South Africa also has the highest dependency on trade shares at 60 per cent (Lewis, 2001, p. 35).

Table 1.4

	EU	High-income Asia	Low-income Asia	North America	Rest of southern Africa	Rest of sub-Saharan Africa	South Africa	Rest of World	Total
Shares in World Exports:									
Primary Products	10.2	6.7	15.0	30.8	1.7	7.0	1.3	27.3	100.0
Energy & Mining	7.2	2.6	11.1	5.6	1.5	7.3	2.7	62.1	100.0
Food Processing	30.5	8.2	17.7	18.1	0.6	1.4	1.0	22.5	100.0
Textiles & Apparel	18.7	16.1	41.7	5.0	0.5	0.2	0.3	17.4	100.0
Other Manufacturing	28.8	28.7	11.3	17.9	0.1	0.2	0.7	12.4	100.0
Serices	30.0	13.9	12.4	25.6	0.3	0.8	0.8	16.2	100.0
Total	26.2	21.0	14.2	18.2	0.3	1.1	0.8	18.0	100.0
Share in World Imports:									
Primary Products	32.2	24.6	13.7	10.0	0.3	0.9	0.6	17.7	100.0
Energy & Mining	34.6	31.3	8.9	18.3	0.1	0.1	1.1	5.7	100.0
Food Processing	21.0	25.4	9.1	13.2	0.6	2.3	0.9	27.5	100.0
Textiles & Apparel	26.7	15.4	11.4	24.2	0.3	0.9	0.5	20.7	100.0
Other Manufacturing	21.1	16.0	17.3	22.1	0.3	1.2	1.0	21.1	100.0
Serices	26.7	17.7	8.7	16.5	0.3	0.9	0.8	28.3	100.0
Total	24.1	18.1	13.9	20.0	0.3	1.0	0.9	21.7	100.0

Source: Lewis, Robinson, and Thierfelder (1999), Tables 1–2.

Critiques of Characteristic 6

The 6th Kuznets characteristic follows that economic growth in LDCs is not always attainable. The wealth gap and inequality of income is only increasing, and again, a lack of financial capability can prevent the spread of economic growth internationally. However, with the dismantling of Apartheid powers coupled with the opportunity from the WTO in 1994, South Africa has been able to spread economic growth.

Then again, the second part of Kuznets critique is that the wealth gap will only increase as trade does. As it was mentioned beforehand, South Africa has some of the largest inequalities world wide, and is a dualistic society. There is increasing divergence of the income per capita among countries, and as a consequence the distribution of income is becoming less equal; the ratio of income of the richest 10 per cent of countries to the poorest 10 per cent of countries rose from 10.5 in 1975 to 18.5 in 2005 (World Bank, 2006).

CONCLUSION

The first characteristic is high rates of growth of per capita output and population growth. South Africa's high rates of GDP growth post-Apartheid (1994-2001) were largely due to the shrinking and labour per capita decreased in the same time period. The unemployment rates are extremely high at nearly 50 per cent currently, and are forecasted to only increase. Additionally, population growth is decreasing despite extremely high fertility rates in South Africa.

Kuznets' first characteristic claims that growth in GDP has to be greater than population growth, in order for per capita growth to occur. Despite having high rates of GDP growth in the post-Apartheid boom, GDP is now decreasing and population is increasing. According to the first characteristic, South Africa will not continue to experience growth rates with the population growth being so high.

High rates of increase in total factor productivity is Kuznets' second characteristic. The prominent role of TFP in South Africa's recent growth performance is that GDP growth can generally be sustained as long as there continues to be improvements in technology and efficiency (Arndt and Lewis, 2000). GDP growth rate, calculated by the TFP, showed vast improvements again during the Apartheid boom. However, there continues to be a decrease in TFP.

A high rate of structural transformation is the third characteristic. A middle-income country such as South Africa is capable, and has succeeded in structural changes even with strong government intervention. Modern economic development changes the entire structure of the economy with the decline in the agricultural sector and the increase of industry and service. In particular, the large service sector in South Africa contributes largely to the GDP. The formal sector is well developed, yet the rise in unemployment is creating a vast informal sector as a result of unemployment. Nearly half the population is unemployed, and there is a fear of escalating poverty as urbanization continues especially with the rate of urbanization being 1.4 per cent annual rate of change.

The fourth characteristic and perhaps the most complex one is: high rates of social and ideological change. During the Apartheid reign, racism and especially segregation was in its most blatant and damaging form. Furthermore, the economy was deeply suffering and there was little support from the global sphere. The suppression of the South African people and the economy did not disappear simply overnight from the disbanding of the Apartheid regime and the incoming of President Mandela. It in fact it still hasn't quite recovered. This was a time of major human rights abuses and dramatic political instability.

There has been much economic development occurring in South Africa since 1994, and less attempts at human development and changing of ideals. The disparities in the dualistic economy have profound effects on human development. However, attempts at policy implementation are active. For instance, as of 2000 the government of South Africa embarked upon a five-year 10.5 billion reconstruction and development plan to enhance human development. Examples of how the money is being spent are: reducing unemployment, providing free medical care to pregnant mothers and children less than 6 years of age, and housing projects (Todaro, 2000 p. 201). South Africa has also been working on portraying their country as friendly to the market of foreign and domestic investment.

Simon Kuznets fifth characteristic is freer markets domestically as well as ability to reach to the world market and world demand. Prior to 1994, South Africa had severed ties with the international world market impart of conflicting political interests. In fact domestically, capital fight had a very lofty prevalence too. With Mandela as President he began to reach out for global support and began making connections for global trade purposes. Trade agreements were created and South Africa experienced what was considered a GDP growth 'boom' post 1994. Therefore, South Africa utilized global trade to dramatically increase their economic growth.

Characteristic six limited spread of economic growth to more than one-third of the world population, is very similar to characteristic five in that South Africa has been able to successfully expand their economic growth by creating partnerships with unions and other trade partners. Lewis (2001) states: "Economically, South Africa dominates. It accounts for 71 per cent of SADC GDP and about 22 per cent of its population. South Africa's importance also manifests itself in other ways – particularly in trade and transport." He continues: "The economic structures of the SADC countries also reflect great heterogeneity" (p. 25). Yet, with the current world recession, South Africa's trade is being negatively affected. This may prevent the country from either trading with all partners, or it may limit the amount of trade being done with trade alliances.

Overall, South Africa has experienced high and low development, or what Chopra and Sanders (2004) would call: "combined and uneven development." They have the highest rates of GDP growth of any African country thanks to rich internal resources, and liberalized trade. However, South Africa is still recovering from poverty and deep inequalities. Kuznets conclusion on the economic development may insinuate that even though components of his characteristics are relevant and in some cases dead-on in his theory, South Africa has many milestones still to accomplish before becoming an industrialized country. Furthermore, policy focusing on developing human well-being needs to be a priority. The deep racial divides which the country is still experiencing are hindering development economically as well as in the human sense.

REFERENCES

1. Arndt, C., Lewis, J. D. 2000. The Macro Implications of HIV/AIDS in South Africa: A preliminary assessment. *South African Journal of Economics.* The World Bank. http://www.worldbank.org/afr/wps/wp9.pdf (Accessed: 2nd February 2010)

2. Arora, V. B., Bhundia, A. 2003. Potential output and total factor productivity growth in post-Apartheid South Africa. International Monetary Fund Working Paper. NO.03/178. http://papers.ssrn.com/sol3/papers.cfm?abstract_id=880244 (Accessed: 2nd February 2010)

3. Chopra, M., Sanders, D. 2004. From Apartheid to globalization: health and social change in South Africa. *Hygiea Internationalis.* http://www.ep.liu.se/ej/hygiea/ra/023/paper.pdf (Accessed: 3rd February 2010)

4. Lewis, J. D. 2001. Reform and opportunity: the changing role and patterns of trade in South Africa and SADC. World Bank: Africa Region Working Paper Series No. 14. http://www.essa.org.za/download/wb/Lewis_Trade_AFRWP14.pdf (Accessed: March, 2010)

5. Lutz, W., Sanderson, W. C. and Scherbov, S. 2004. The end of world population growth. International Institute for Applied Systems Analysis.

6. Mihaljek, D., Saxena, S. 2009. Wages, productivity and "structural" inflation in emerging market economies. Participants in the meeting. http://www.bis.org/publ/bppdf/bispap49d.pdf (Accessed: 20th February 2010)

7. Rothenberg, Paula. 2006. *Beyond Borders: Thinking Critically about global issue.* New York, Worth Publishers.

8. Szirmai, Adam. 2005. *Dynamics of socio-economic development: an introduction.* Cambridge United Kingdom, Cambridge University Press.

9. Todaro, Michael. 2000. *Economic Development: Seventh Edition.* New York University, Addison Wesley Longman, Inc.

10. Worden, Nigel. 2000. *The making of modern South Africa: conquest, segregation, and apartheid.* Blackwell Publishing.

11. CIA – The World Fact Book. 20th February 2010. https://www.cia.gov/library/publications/the-world-factbook/geos/sf.html.

2

The Beijing Consensus and Income Distribution in China

Inequality tested by the Kuznets Hypothesis

Enrico Cellini

CHAPTER SUMMARY

Thanks to its miraculous growth, China has emerged as the main developing country in the world and is an example to follow for other LDCs. However, the model sponsored by Beijing has been having a costly dark side for Chinese society: the mantra of the economic growth occurred to the detriment of an equitable distribution of wealth and further increased the rural-urban cleavage affecting the society.

In this chapter, I start by analyzing the antithetic model of growth offered by the Washington consensus and what has been defined as the Beijing consensus. In the first paragraph, I have summarized the basic principles of both and have drawn a balance of the results they have produced. A focus will be put on the reforms and the initiatives that have been responsible of the China's economic growth. Then I have examined the dark side of the Chinese miracle, focusing on the distribution of wealth in Chinese society: through an analysis of the Gini coefficient. As a part of this chapter, I will also examine the ongoing social fractionalization and verify whether the Kuznets hypothesis of inverted U curve applies to the case of China. Finally, I have also looked in detail at the rural-urban cleavage, pointing it as the main cause of the persistent division.

PROBLEMS AND FLAWS OF THE STUDIES ABOUT CHINA

Before starting with examination of the data, some introductory statements should be made. One should always keep in mind when dealing with equality studies on China, that the latter is a nation with the world's largest population, spread over an area that almost equals Europe. The 1.3 billion Chinese are spread across thirty-one provinces and prefectural cities. It is also important to some of the municipalities are classified as rural in China while they would be considered as big cities in the other countries.

When studying China, one should always keep in mind that the large share of "floating" population and the big stake played by non-market transactions may cause complications in the interpretation of the data – in spite of some measures that limit the free migration of people (See the final paragraph of this chapter), it is believed that between 50 and 200 million people are migrant workers that send significant remittances at their native areas, thus altering the official regional statistics. Finally, as the majority of the population lives in the rural areas where a significant proportion of their needs are satisfied by home and self-production, the classical measurement of wealth such as GDP will underestimate the actual production.

In addition to all these problems related to this statistical measurement, most of the times one could find notable discrepancies in the data provided by official Chinese sources such as National Bureau of Statistics and State Statistical Bureau and the international agencies such as World Bank and the OECD. This might be due to the unwillingness of Beijing to disclose all the real and unbiased information publicly which is related to its development leading to the consequent shortage of data that foreigner organizations have to deal with. In this chapter, rather than focusing merely on single charts or numbers, all the propositions will be drawn from general trends reflected unanimously in all the empirical sources that have been found.

CHINA'S MIRACLE AND THE BEIJING "SUPPOSED" CONSENSUS

The Failure of the Washington Consensus

As he himself candidly admitted,[1] John Williamson had no idea that the ten recommendations written by him in 1989 for American congress with respect to ways and means that can be used by the debtor countries to overcome their debt burden and to foster development, would become a sort of mantra for the next fifteen years in the field of economic growth. Through this ten-point list, he was able to capture and summarize the consensus growing in Washington on what a developing country should do. The ten original reforms constituting the list were as follows:

1. Fiscal discipline
2. Re-ordering public expenditure priorities
3. Tax reform
4. Liberalizing interest rates
5. A competitive exchange rate
6. Trade liberalization
7. Liberalization of inward FDI
8. Privatization
9. Deregulation
10. Property rights.

Irrespective of the original content and intent, the term "Washington Consensus" has come to be identified with the different development theories that rely heavily on privatization, liberalization and price stability. They were based on the neoliberal faith on unfettered markets and thus predicated the reduction, or even the minimization, of the role of the state. This approach was broadly adopted for the following years in many developing countries especially in Latin America and Africa.

However, there seems to be a consensus in the literature about the failure of the "Washington Consensus" – in most of the countries it has not been able to ignite the desired growth and in some cases it even turned out to be less productive than the "failed" policies of import substitution of the 1960s and 1970s, which it aimed to replace. The reasons of its failure to a great extent may be traced in its narrow definition and conception of growth. The other reasons were related to its failure to understand the development and developing countries – focusing mainly on the increase of the GDP and neglecting the sustainability and the equality in the developing process. This exposed the LDCs in dangerous conditions which they have not been able to handle. As it has been noted by Stiglitz, most of the times countries have confused the means with the ends – privatization and liberalization have become the ultimate goal to pursue and low inflation was seen as an objective itself. As has been exemplified by a Russian case , this "quest" occurred to the detriment of equality and stability.[2]

The Reform Era in China: Development Takes Off

Scholars generally identify "Reform era" as the period of time that started with the advent of Deng Xiaoping as paramount leader (supreme leader of the communist party and of the country) in 1978 – he started a series of policies aimed to modernize Chinese economy through a gradual abandonment of the collectivist structure inherited by Mao towards a "socialist market economy".

Generally speaking, economic reforms can be divided into different realms, covering different periods of time. The rural sector was the first one to be reformed: the main reason why the reforms started in this branch of economy was that agriculture was not dominated by state-ownership. It was organized under the so-called three tiers of ownership: commune, production brigade and production team. Land and other resources were collectively owned, instead of being state-owned. Farmers were not paid in cash but they were remunerated according to the accumulated work points which they made during the production season and their reward was based on the level of harvest. This organization and ownership structure implied that farmers had little resistance to exhibit acceptance towards privatization and risk-taking if they were allowed to retain more products for their effort.

Then, it was the time of the urban reforms which covered both the production management and distribution systems, focusing on the expansion of enterprise autonomy and the reduction of the government within plan allocations. More freedom had been allowed to the private capital and some concessions were made regarding the rigid system controlling the internal mobility (See further in this chapter) in order to sustain the increasing industrial demand of workforce. The reforms went towards a gradual decentralization of the state-ruled economy and a progressive opening to the market of the system. Decentralization affected several aspects of Chinese economy – before 1978, China's foreign trade was centralized at the national level and was conducted by twelve state-owned foreign trade corporations (FTCs). Along with economic reforms, the FTCs were gradually given greater autonomy and they were made more accountable for their operations. The management of the trade system was also decentralized from the central government to the provincial governments. By the late 1980s, the number of FTCs had soared to more than 5,000.[3]

In addition to domestic reforms, China also adopted an open policy for international trade and investment. It changed from a self-reliance and import substitution development strategy, which emphasized the utilization of domestic resources (labour, capital, and land), to an export promotion strategy. In the meantime, foreign investments were allowed to enter China to transform its inefficient industrial sector and improve competition and technologies. In theory and practice, China's open policy has proved to play an important role in economic growth under economic reforms. Perhaps this is the most significant turn adopted by Beijing that transformed the nature and scope of Chinese economy. Under the open-door policy, China encouraged foreign investment from joint ventures to wholly owned foreign-investment firms. In the 1980s, attracted by the cheap labour and by a internal market of more than 1 billion potential consumers, a lot of foreign investors started to pour investments especially in the South East zone. The more the producers settled down in China, the higher the benefits for more investors to operate there – investments literally started to feed upon each other. The ultimate step of this new liberal approach can be considered the admission of China in the World Trade Organization (WTO) in 2001, more than twenty years after the initial application.

The peculiar characteristic of the strategy put it in action by Beijing is the gradual and systematic implementation of its reforms: its approach is the antithesis of other nations that have followed the Washington Consensus that opted for a sudden and comprehensive changeover to a free-market economy, believing that an increased openness was the panacea for their economic difficulties. China kept its centralized system intact for a long time, for example, while in other developing countries the privatization-mantra promoted by the Washington Consensus led the selling of most of the state-owned enterprises (SOEs) to private investors. In China, these remained under the central control for a more extended period. The devolution from a socialized and autarchic country to a market oriented and industrialized economy did not take place with an abrupt "big-bang": it was a continuous and coherent process lead by a central and political power together with the forces of trade and globalization.

The Path to Development According to Beijing

The path drawn by Xiaoping was followed and further implemented after the end of his mandate in 1993 according to the increased economic and political might that China had been accumulating. The result has been a comprehensive archetype of development that some scholars have identified as the "Beijing Consensus". The combination of active state management and market economics is merely the economic declination of the model – the Beijing Consensus, though, is a more holistic philosophy that affects the whole landscape of international relationships. It contains many ideas that regard the way of conduction politics, an equitable quality of life and a harmonic balance of power in the global scale. Unlike the dogmatic Washington Consensus, Beijing does not believe in a universally-valid way to development. Biejing Consensus is pragmatic and ideological but at the same time, it expresses the message that a country's development path is rooted in its own history, culture and society.

It is closely related to the philosophy that China has chosen to adopt in dealing with other nations in the world political arena – it is the epitome of China's "peaceful rise", the harmonic vision of its own development in a harmonic political context. Thanks to this approach, China has been successfully in portraying itself as a benign force and it has finally attracted other developing countries follow its example.

Is It a Consensus?

The definition itself can be very misleading – the economic model proposed by Beijing is far from being widely recognized as proof of efficiency. Further, it seems quite clear that the economic, political and structural conditions of the Chinese case will be unrepeatable in any other nation from now on – due to its peculiar nature as a nation even before than as an economy, the model is not easily exportable because there cannot be *ceteris paribus* in confronting with China.

Although it is not representative in nature, the consensus is that the path undertaken by China may serve as a model for countries that have been under a regime of autarchy and closeness – it provides a successful example of ways and means to generate economic growth out of a stagnant economy. Quite a few of other Asian states have been fascinated by the Chinese miracle and have tried to adopt some similar reforms. Amongst the different Asian states, the most faithful to the consensus has been Vietnam (the "Moi Doi", or renovation, is the closest application of the Chinese model), but also Nepal, Bangladesh and Sri Lanka have opened their economies to international trade following Beijing.

It is undeniable though, that the Beijing "supposed" Consensus has brought new ideas and principles that are extremely different from the ones coming from Washington. The "miracle" it has been able to carry out is undeniable as well. By referring to Table 2.1, one can notice the astonishing performance of Chinese economy in the thirty years after the launch of the reforms. The GDP in this time window has been growing to an average ratio of 10.26 per cent per year, with only three years when the nation grew at the rate of 8 per cent. Table 2.2 shows how the per capita income has been growing to a similar rate. China's income per capita in 2006 was more than five times higher than it was in 1978. Probably, the most outstanding accomplishment in this realm is the improvement in standard of living. Although different studies suggest different values, it has been estimated that around 300 million Chinese have been pulled out of poverty in this period of time.[4]

Nevertheless, an analysis of the Chinese miracle that keeps into account only the absolute numbers can be very misleading – in order to grow, China had to pay a very high price in terms of equality and social fractionalization.

1. ECONOMIC GROWTH

Table 2.1: China's Growth According to World Bank

	GDP growth (annual %)	GDP per capita growth (annual %)	GINI index
1978	12	10	"
1979	8	6	"
1980	8	6	"
1981	5	4	"
1982	9	8	"
1983	11	9	"
1984	15	14	"
1985	14	12	"
1986	9	7	"
1987	12	10	"
1988	11	10	"
1989	4	3	"
1990	4	2	"
1991	9	8	"
1992	14	13	"
1993	14	13	"
1994	13	12	"
1995	11	10	"
1996	10	9	"
1997	9	8	"
1998	8	7	"
1999	8	7	"
2000	8	8	"
2001	8	8	"
2002	9	8	"
2003	10	9	"
2004	10	9	"
2005	10	10	42
2006	12	11	"
2007	13	12	"
2008	9	8	"

Source: Word Bank, DDP Quick.[5]

Table 2.2

China

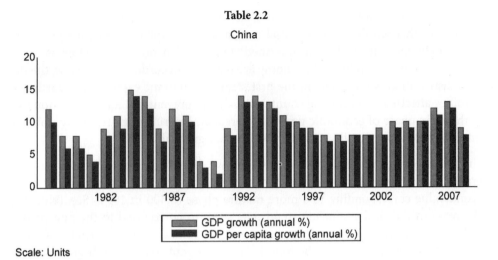

GDP growth (annual %)
GDP per capita growth (annual %)

Scale: Units

Source: Word Bank, DDP Quick Query.[6]

INEQUALITY AND DISPARITY

Income Distribution and the Kuznets Hypothesis

It is widely recognized that before the reform era, the distribution of income in China was rather equal. One of the purpose of the economic reforms, though, was to trickle down the development of the overall economy by allowing some workers to become well-off first – it was believed that, by widening the income disparity, efficiency would have been stimulated and ultimately an increase in general prosperity would have taken place. The implementation of this policy, though correct in theory was more troublesome than expected and China had to pay a very high social price in order to sustain its growth – an uncontrollable rise in inequality.

In the late 1990s, the level of inequality of China, though doubling the OECD countries' average, was still inferior to Brazil, Mexico, South Africa, Russia, Turkey and Venezuela (See Table 2.5). What is really impressive, though, is the velocity at which the inequality has apparently increased – the coefficient increased by 21 per cent in fourteen years between 1980 and 1994 and by 39 per cent in the entire period between 1980 and 2000. As the World Bank database testifies, in 2005, the first decile of the population possessed the 31 per cent of the total income while the last decile of the population owed the 2 per cent of the cake: the last 20 per cent of the population possessed just a 6 per cent of the wealth.

In spite of the incredible performance in terms of per capita income, one should not be tempted to conclude that the economic growth is indicative of everyone being better off economically. In the everlasting debate on the relationship between growth and distribution of wealth, the theory proposed by the Harvard economist Simon Kuznets in 1955 still provides a clear mindset to examine the trend of distribution of wealth. He argued that the relationship between the per capita income and inequality in the distribution of income assumes the form of an inverted U. In other words, with an initial rise in the per capita income, inequality will rise correspondingly, reach its peak at an intermediate level of income and decline as the income levels typical of a mature industrial economy are reached. According to this view, the disparity in wealth distribution is inevitable in the first stage of economic expansion – starting uneven opportunities affecting a developing country which will prevent the equal allocation of wealth during the early phase of economic growth. Thereafter, a period with relatively stable income disparity will follow and, finally inequality will reduce gradually.

Applying his theory to the data related to China we dispose of, one could recognize a steep acceleration in the value of the coefficient from the initial period of reforms (0,330 in 1980) to the second value corresponding to a more mature phase (0,400 in 1994)(See Table 2.3). This steep increase in the Gini coefficient trend may seem to correspond to the first phase of the inverted U-curve proposed by Kuznets. Although the values of the coefficient vary changing the sources, this general trend can be found across different sources, both domestic ones and international ones (See Table 2.4). In the initial years of the last decade, the inequality increase seems to have slowed down – although the Gini coefficient are still slightly increasing, their values seem to be leveling off as predicted by the inverted U curve. Unfortunately, the data that we have does not allow to make definitive formulation on the possibility that China has been facing during the intermediate phase of its path to the development. The 2005 value of 0,42 reported by the World Bank (See Table 2.1) is not enough to celebrate a leveling off of the disparity level.

Applying the Kuznets hypothesis to the Chinese case, Beijing should further promote the development of whole economy in order to proceed to the next level – at that point the "natural" evolution of the process would slow down the disparity and it would be possible to start some redistributing policies. Only further development can represent the basis for a common prosperity. In other words, only if the size of the "cake" grows it can be well distributed in a desirable way.

Nevertheless, it is reasonable to think that an ongoing increase of disparity within an economy and a society cannot be sustained forever – if inequality is not reduced in a society that is already extremely fractioned, economic, social and political risks may be triggered. The dramatic effects related with the combination of vertical growth and increasing inequality should reflect about the possibility to invert the trend. Is it possible to grow and promote an equal society at the same time? The question is legitimized also by the fact that the first stage of increasing inequality had been going on for quite a long time – even if with diminishing intensity, inequality has been growing until 2000, that equals to say more than two decades after the economy took off.

Without necessarily undertaking redistributive measures, Chinese government could ease the artificial barriers that have maintained and fed the main source of disparity – the rural-urban fraction.

2. INCOME DISTRIBUTION

Rural-Urban Disparity

The main factor that has been fostering an imbalanced economic development in Chinese economy is the sharp cleavage between the rural sector and the urban areas. The World Bank in 1997 reported that urban–rural inequality explained over one-third of China's total inequality and over half of inequality growth from the late 1980s to the mid-1990s.[9] Table 2.3 shows how the values of the intra-urban and intra-rural Gini coefficients have been fluctuating but

Table 2.3: Gini Coefficient and Income Disparity

Year	(1) Regional displarity (coefficient-of-variation)	(2) Household income Gini coefficient	(3)	(4)	(5) Urban-rural HH Income ratio
		Rural areas	Urban areas	Nation	
1978	0.974	0.212	0.160		2.570
1979	0.929	0.241	0.160		2.416
1980	0.906	0.241	0.150	0.330	2.497
1981	0.957	0.232	0.150		2.202
1982	0.805	0.246	0.150		1.950
1983	0.777	0.244	0.160		1.821
1984	0.742	0.227	0.190		1.859
1985	0.732	0.304	0.190		2.123
1986	0.704	0.305	0.200		2.166
1987	0.676	0.303	0.230		2.168
1988	0.648	0.310	0.230		2.287
1989	0.622	0.310	0.230		2.200
1990	0.601	0.307	0.240		2.400
1991	0.634	0.313	0.250		2.585
1992	0.649	0.329	0.270		2.797
1993	0.670	0.321	0.300		2.863
1994	0.670	0.342	0.280	0.400	2.715
1995	0.678	0.323	0.280		2.512
1996	0.682	0.329	0.290	0.424	2.469
1997	0.700	0.327	0.300		2.509
1998	0.715	0.336	0.295	0.456	2.509
1999	0.715			0.457	2.649
2000	0.738			0.458	2.787
2001	0.759				

Source: Chang 2002, 337.

Table 2.4: Gini Coefficient Calculated by Domestic and Foreign Experts

Source	Year estimated	Gini coefficient
World Bank	1978	0.300
	1979	0.330
	1981	0.288
	1988	0.382
	1995	0.445
Institute of Economy, Chinese	1988	0.382
Academy of Social Science	1995	0.445
Li Qiang	1996	0.458

Source: Table taken from the 2004 OECD report.[7]

always remained below 0.30 and 0.34. This means that income disparities between individuals, within the rural and urban areas, are not substantially developed. What is really impressive is the nationwide Gini coefficient that appears to be more than 10 percentage point higher than the single intra-urban and intra-rural coefficients. Moreover, unlike the sector coefficients that have fluctuated during the years, the nationwide coefficient shows a consistent increase. The expanding gap between the two sectors is also reflected by the income ratios presented in Table 2.8 – after 1986, the urban income has been always double that of the rural income and the urban/rural ratio has increased almost constantly till reaching 2.90 in 2001.

As the quintessence of developing country, China has a typical dual economy structure where the urban and the rural sectors differ sensibly. That is why many scholars still find it convenient to frame the Chinese growth through structural change model proposed by Lewis. The trend of the distribution of population seems to correspond to the theoretical prediction of the economist: as can be seen in Tables 2.6 and 2.7, urban population has been consistently increasing while rural population is stable, if not decreasing. In 1978, more than eight Chinese out of ten used to live in rural areas; thirty years after, the share of urban inhabitants has almost equaled the one of rural inhabitants (43 per cent of urban population vis-à-vis 57 per cent of rural residents).

Compared with the urban area, the countryside relies heavily on manual work while urban industries on the other hand are endowed with modern machineries that permit to have a higher marginal productivity of labour. Urban sector can extract human labour from the countryside, gaining extra profits that will be re-invested to achieve capital accumulation, further enhancing economic growth. In the case of China though, the "natural" structural shift from a rural centered economy to an industrialized one predicted by the model, seems not to have been completely fulfilled. As the OECD report points out, Chinese economy has been operating on the basis of the separation of rural and urban markets, with dual governance systems hampering the circulation and the most socially efficient allocation of the productive factors.[10] The system has proved to be rigid, to impede the gradual allocation and use of the excessive rural labour.

Table 2.5: Inequality in China in Comparative Perpspective

Country	Gini	Date	Source
China	0.458	2001	China Daily
OEOO average	0.288	Mid-90s	OEOD
Armenia	0.444	1998	WDI
Australia	0.305	Mid-90s	OEOD
Austria	0.266	1997	WDI
Belgium	0.272	Mid-90s	OEOD
Brazil	0.807	1998	WDI
Canada	0.305	1998	LIS
Chille	0.567	1998	WDI
Estonia	0.381	2000	LIS
France	0.278	1994	LIS
Germany	0.252	2000	LIS
Greece	0.336	Mid-90s	OEOD
Hungry	0.244	1998	WDI
India	0.378	1997	WDI
Indonesia	0.317	1999	WDI
Italy	0.342	1995	LIS
Japan	0.260	Mid-90s	OECD
Kazakhstan	0.354	1998	WDI
Kytgyz Republic	0.346	1999	WDI
Korea	0.316	1993	WDI
Mexico	0.531	1998	WDI
Norway	0.256	Mid-90s	OEOD
Paraguay	0.577	1998	WDI
Poland	0.316	1998	WDI
Spain	0.325	1990	WDI
Russia	0.487	1998	WDI
Sourh Africa	0.593	1993-94	WDI
Slovak Republic	0.195	1990	WDI
Silvenia	0.249	1999	LIS
Sweden	0.252	2000	LIS
Turkey	0.491	Mid-90s	OEOD
Ukraine	0.290	1996	WDI
United Kingdom	0.345	1999	LIS
United States	0.368	2000	LIS
Uzbekistan	0.447	1998	WDI
Venezuela	0.495	1998	WDI

Note: This table presents different Gini's measured by income or by expenditure and made as comparable as possible by providers to international standards.
Source: Forster and earson (2002): World Development Indicators (WDI) (2002); Luxembourg Income Study (LIS) (2003).
Source: Table taken from the 2004 OECD report.[8]

It must be noted though, that in the initial phase of the reform era, a series of policies destined to reduce the rural-urban gap had temporarily succeeded in reversing the trend of unequal distribution of wealth. Policies such as increases in procurement prices for agricultural products, the shift from collectivism to new systems of production, the partial relaxation of restrictions on labour mobility led to a boom of agricultural production (in six years, total grain output rose by 108 million tons, that is, from 300 to 408 million tons) and this led to an increase of per capita rural incomes by almost 15 per cent per year.[11] Further, for the first decade of the reforms, townships and villages' enterprises (TVEs) were encouraged at the local level. As a result, the urban-rural ratio decreased from 2.57 in 1978 to 1.82 in 1983 (see Table 2.8). Yet, it was only in this period that the peasantry saw their incomes grow faster than their urban counterparts. Growth in agricultural incomes was almost stagnant in the late 1980s because the government failed to raise agricultural procurement prices permanently and substantially cut back agricultural investments. The situation however improved in the 1990s, even though, rural per capita income still grew slower than urban incomes.

As has been noted by Tao Yang, the reform has not been completed and implemented as it was needed – urban citizens have kept on receiving privileges and welfare policies that are largely unavailable to rural migrants. For example, "child care and education at elementary and middle school are available only to family of urban registration".[12] The institutional barriers and the restraints on the migration have been preventing the income gap to disappear and an equal development to occur.

Causes of the Formation of Inequality

The process of formation of inequality within Chinese society may be explained by several factors, just partially of economic nature. All the factors integrated and feed upon each other, contributing to the present level of income disparity.

The first cause of this fracture is rooted in the historical heritage of Chinese society – the disparity in the development of different sectors has existed for a long time and thus was deeply rooted in the Chinese system at the beginning of the reform era. Starting from the 1950s, Chinese governments have put up two different price systems for industrial and agricultural goods – the collective system set up for agricultural products in the 1950s allowed the state to buy and sell the rural goods at relatively low prices, when compared to the prices of the industrial goods. These two price systems made the farmers' income low and favoured the increase in the difference between the two sectors. Since 1978, the government has started some opening-up policies, starting from east to the west, resulting in a fast economic development especially in the southern eastern regions. As it has been stated before in this chapter, though, the reforms were not comprehensively enforced and the primary sources of inequality were not eliminated.

Further, unlike the consistent increase of the urban population share may suggest, Chinese people have been far from being free to migrate and choose their place to stay – in particular the *Hukuo* system, or registered permanent residence, has represented a severe constraint to internal mobility and an obstacle to a fair and equal distribution of wealth. In 1958, the Chinese government began using the family register system to control the movement of people between urban and rural areas. Individuals were broadly categorized as a "rural" or "urban" worker. A worker seeking to move from the country to urban areas to take up non-agricultural work would have to apply through the relevant bureaucracies. With its large rural population of poor farm workers, *hukou* limited mass migration from the land to the cities to ensure some structural stability.

Not having *Hukou* in urban areas means that migrants receive no education or health benefits and cannot purchase housing, since they cannot register to it. In an empirical study conducted in 2004 about the its economic impact in the previous 20 years, Whalley and Zhang concluded that all the "results point towards a significant role of the Hukou system in preventing movement towards a more equal distribution of income in China".[13] Effectively, the *Hukou* system has operated as an artificial barrier to urban-rural migration in China and has supported large regional wage differentials, which labour markets do not compete away.

As it has already been argued when the application of Lewis model was discussed, China has a dualistic economic structure – the urban and the rural realms differ dramatically and China's overall economy has been operating on the basis of the separation of the labour and goods markets between the urban and the rural markets. As has been pointed in the 2004 OECD report, "dual governance systems exist in the urban and rural areas, impeding circulation and optimization of productive factors".[14] Due to the persisting restrictions, the allocation and the use of the labour surplus of the rural areas has not been optimized.

Chinese dual track development must be mainly explained by same engine of the economic growth itself – the government reforms. Since the opening-up, Beijing has been following a urban-biased line, that granted preferential policies and investments in the coastal cities and the south-east region – this privileged treatment affected foreign investments, taxation and banking and significantly fostered economic growth and technological improvement. Coastal areas rural-urban inequality increased after the initial phase of economic reforms (in the year 2000, urban income was almost three times the rural one, see Table 2.8) as a direct result of government policy that was persistently urban biased. The rural–urban productivity difference was artificially induced by government labour policy which prevented rural people from taking formal urban jobs while much of the urban production capacity was accumulated from resources transferred from the rural and agricultural sector over time.

3. RURAL–URBAN POPULATION TRENDS

Table 2.6: The Shift toward Urbanization

	Rural population (% of total population)	Urban population (% of total)	Rural population growth (annual %)	Urban population growth (annual %)
1978	81	19	1	4
1979	81	19	1	4

1980	80	20	1	4
1981	80	20	0	5
1982	79	21	1	5
1983	78	22	1	5
1984	78	22	0	4
1985	77	23	0	4
1986	76	24	0	5
1987	75	25	0	5
1988	74	26	0	5
1989	73	27	0	5
1990	73	27	0	5
1991	72	28	0	4
1992	71	29	0	4
1993	70	30	0	4
1994	69	31	−0	4
1995	69	31	−0	4
1996	68	32	−0	4
1997	67	33	−0	4
1998	66	34	−0	4
1999	65	35	−0	3
2000	64	36	−1	3
2001	63	37	−1	3
2002	62	38	−1	3
2003	61	39	−1	3
2004	61	39	−1	3
2005	60	40	−1	3
2006	59	41	−1	3
2007	58	42	−1	3
2008	57	43	−1	3

Source: Word Bank, DDP Quick Query[15]

Table 2.7

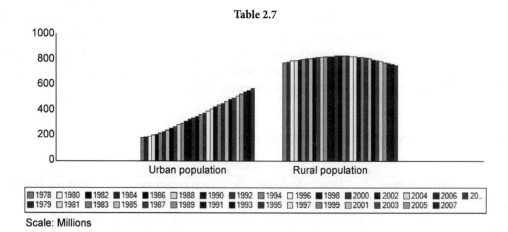

Scale: Millions

Source: Word Bank, DDP Quick Query.[16]

Table 2.8: The Rural-Urban Disparity

Year	Per capita net income of rural households (CNY)	Per capita disposable income of urban households (CNY)	Ratio of incomes (urban/rural)
1978	133.6	343.4	2.57
1979	160.2	387.0	2.42
1980	191.3	477.6	2.50
1981	223.4	491.9	2.20
1982	270.1	526.6	1.95
1983	309.8	564.0	1.82
1984	355.3	651.2	1.83
1985	397.6	739.1	1.86
1986	423.8	899.8	2.12
1987	462.6	1 002.2	2.17
1988	544.9	1 181.4	2.17
1989	601.5	1 375.7	2.29
1990	686.3	1 510.2	2.20
1991	708.6	1 700.6	2.40
1992	784.0	2 026.6	2.58
1993	921.6	2 577.4	2.80
1994	1 221.0	3 496.2	2.86
1995	1 577.7	4 283.0	2.71
1996	1 926.1	4 838.9	2.51
1997	2 090.1	5 160.3	2.47
1998	2 162.0	5 425.1	2.51
1999	2 210.3	5 854.0	2.65
2000	2 253.0	6 280.0	2.79
2001	2 366.4	6 859.0	2.90

Source: China Statistical Year book, 2002, National Bureau of Statistics, China.
Table taken and readapted from 2004 OECD report.[14]

CONCLUSIONS

In the last 32 years, since the reform era was launched by Deng Xiaoping, China has been experiencing an economic miracle: the mixture of market impulse coming from the opening-up of the economy and the heavy governmental interventionism and control over the economy have resulted in a new approach toward the economic development that diverges from the principles proposed by the Washington Consensus. It has proved that economic growth can be ignited and carried out by a heavily state-centered system.

In order to be effective though, the Beijing Consensus requested a high price to be paid in terms of social inequality – throughout these three decades, the inequality has been increasing alongside the average income per capita. Chinese society has been torn in two pieces, the rural sector and the urban one, that have been enhancing their distance going along a dual track development. Kuznets theory forecasts that inequality needs to increase in the first phase in order for the economy to take off. After more than 30 years, it is legitimate to ask when the initial phase should be over and whether it is opportune to invert the trend "artificially", through a series of policies that promote the development of the backward rural sector.

WORKS CITED

1. Williamson, *A short story of the Washington Consensus*, pp. 14-31.
2. Stiglitz, *Is there a post-Washington Consensus Consensus?*, pp. 41-57.
3. Shujie, *Economic growth, income distribution and poverty reduction in contemporary China*, p. 31.
4. Cooper Ramo, *The Beijing Consensus*, p. 11.
5. http://ddpext.worldbank.org/ext/DDPQQ/member.do?method=getMembers&userid=1&queryId=135
6. http://ddpext.worldbank.org/ext/DDPQQ/member.do?method=getMembers&userid=1&queryId=135
7. OECD, *Income Disparities in China: an OECD perspective*, p. 20.
8. Ibidem, 113.
9. Shujie, *Economic growth, income distribution and poverty reduction in contemporary China*, p. 128.
10. OECD, *Income Disparitiies in China: an OECD perspective*, p. 50.
11. Shujie, *Economic growth, income distribution and poverty reduction in contemporary China*, p. 131.
12. Yang, Urban-biased policies and rising income inequality in China, p. 308.
13. Whalley and Zhang, *Inequality Change in China and (Hukou) Labour Mobility Restrictions*, p. 30.
14. OECD, *Income Disparities in China: an OECD perspective*, p. 33.
15. *www.worldbank.org* http://ddpext.worldbank.org/ext/DDPQQ/member.do?method=getMembers&userid=1&queryId=135
16. *www.worldbank.org* http://ddpext.worldbank.org/ext/DDPQQ/member.do?method=getMembers&userid=1&queryId=135
17. OECD, *Income Distribution in China: an OECD perspective*, p. 30.
18. Ibidem, 18.

REFERENCES

1. Cannon, Terry. *China's Economic Growth*. New York: St. Martin Press, 2000.
2. Chang, Gene. "The Cause and the Cure of China's widening income disparity." *China Economic Review*, 2002: pp. 335-340.
3. Chang, Gordon. "The Beijing Consensus won't last" *The Asian Wall Street Journal*. November 9, 2009, p. 19, http://proquest.umi.com/pqdweb?index=9&did=1896376021&SrchMode=2&sid=2&Fmt=3&VInst=PROD&VType=PQD&RQT=309&VName=PQD&TS=1267569435&clientId=48347 (accessed January 14, 2010).
4. Cooper Ramo, Joshua. *The Beijing Consensus* (London: The Foreign Policy Center, 2004) fpc.org.uk/fsblob/244.pd

5. Griffin, Keith and Zhao Renwei. *The distribution of income in China*. New York: St. Martin Press, 1993.

6. *Income Disparitiies in China: an OECD perspective*. Paris: OECD Publications, 2004.

7. Kulkarni, Kishore. "Economic growth and income distribution in Malaysia: A test of the Kusznets inverted hypothesis". In *Reading in international economics*, edited by Kishore G. Kulkarni, pp. 223-241, Delhi: Serials Publications, 2004.

8. Sicular, Terry and others. *Inequality and public policy in China*. New York : Cambridge University Press, 2008.

9. Stiglitz, Joseph. "Is there a post-Washington Consensus Consensus?". In *The Washington Consensus reconsidered: Toward a new global governance*, edited by Narcis Serra and Joseph E. Stoglitz, pp. 41-57, Oxford: Oxford University Press, 2008.

10. Stglitz, Joseph E., Narcis Serra and Shari Spiegel. "Introduction: From the Washigton Consensus towards a new global governance". In *The Washington Consensus reconsidered: Toward a new global governance*, edited by Narcis Serra and Joseph E. Stoglitz, pp. 3-14, Oxford: Oxford University Press, 2008.

11. Todaro, Micheal, and Stephen Smith "Understanding a development miracle: China". In *Economic Development (Tenth edition)*, edited by MIcheal P. Todaro and Stephen C. Smith, pp.193-199, Boston: Pearson Addison Wesley, 2009.

12. Whalley, John, and Shunming. Zhang. "Inequality Change in China and (Hukou) Labour Mobility Restrictions." *National Bureau of Economic Research*, 2004: NBER Working Paper No. 10683.

13. Williamson, John. "A short story of the Washington Consensus". In *The Washington Consensus reconsidered: Towards a new global governance*, edited by Narcis Serra and Joseph E. Stiglitz, 14-31, Oxford: Oxford University Press, 2008.

14. World bank. *http://www.worldbank.org/*. February 22, 2010. http://econ.worldbank.org/WBSITE/EXTERNAL/EXTDEC/0,,menuPK:476823~pagePK:64165236~piPK:64165141~theSitePK:469372,00.html (accessed February 22, 2010).

15. Yang, Dennis Tao. "Urban-biased policies and rising income inequality in China." *The American Economic Review*, Vol. 89, No. 2: pp. 306-309.

16. Yao, Shujie. *Economic growth, income distribution and poverty reduction in contemporary China*. (Routhledge Curzon, 2005).

17. http://0-www.netlibrary.com.bianca.penlib.du.edu/Details.aspx

3 | An Analysis of the Kuznet's Curve

Kyle Barker

CHAPTER SUMMARY

Economic development continues to be an important topic of both academic thought and policy implementation. With 85 per cent of the world's population living in what are considered to be 'developing' countries, economic development is of paramount importance (UNHDR, 2010). Economic growth allows families to escape poverty and improve their quality of life. However, it has long been noted that with economic growth comes an increase in disparity of incomes within a society.

Income equality within a country allows for the stable operation of not only the economy but also the government and many other aspects of life. People who feel that they have an economic stake in a system are far less likely to dissent or generally disrupt the functioning of the state. More important, there is a high correlation between the measure of economic inequality and the rank of a country as measured by the Human Development Index (UNHDR, 2010). This index includes a variety of indicators such as education, labour mobility, and others, all of which are considered to be the keys to a prosperous and healthy life.

Therefore there is a paradox within economic development. In order to better the lives of people through the development of health, education, and other social measures, economic development needs to occur. Yet, economic development will cause an increase in income inequality, which is counter to the ultimate goal of development.

This chapter will look at a hypothesis presented by Simon Kuznet in 1955, which states that the level of income inequality will increase as economic development occurs, but over time this income inequality decrease. The graphical representation of this hypothesis is often referred to as Kuznet's curve, or the Inverted U-curve. This hypothesis will be tested in two ways. First, a cross-sectional analysis of whether there is a significant relationship between levels of gross domestic product (GDP) per capita and levels of inequality with the most recent data available will be looked at. And second, to study if this hypothesis is applicable to a specific historical perspective, this chapter will look at income inequality within Chile from 1971 through 2006.

Chile was chosen as a case study due to its historically significant economic and social policy actions. In 1973, a coup occurred within Chile, allowing for the radical transformation of its economy from a socialist, government-controlled approach to one of almost full liberalization. This allowed the Chilean economy to thoroughly experience the economic ramifications of international trade and investment with little interference from the government, creating an almost ideal study in the implementation of neo-classical economic thought of economic development. If Kuznet's hypothesis is correct, we should be able to see a distinct inverted U-shaped curve for income inequality plotted against time, between 1973 and points later on.

MEASUREMENTS OF INCOME DISTRIBUTION

Income data are collected through the use of surveys within a country (Kulkarni, 2006). This data are collected from a representative sample of households from a given country and then projected over all households. Two main factors affect the dissemination of income data. First, data collection of this sort is dependent on the willingness of participants to accurately represent true household income and the methods employed by the surveying agency. For this reason, data regarding income distribution is not always easily available, also there is no agreement between various agencies that undertake income data surveys. Second, while collection of income data has increased in the last two decades, the collection of such data is still heavily dependent on the willingness of individual governments to agree to such collection or conduct the surveys themselves. For various political and social reasons, not all countries are willing to collect and/or publish such data.

Income data that are collected is used to create a Lorenz curve, named after the statistician Max O. Lorenz who created and first defined this curve in 1905. This curve is a graphical representation of the income distribution within a country, as seen in Figure 3.1. With the percentage of population plotted along the vertical axis and the percentage of income plotted along the horizontal axis, the 45-degree angle line that diagonally bisects the square represents a theoretically perfect distribution of wealth across a population. In other words, at any given point along this 45-degree angle line, the given percentage of the population holds that same percentage of the wealth, i.e. 50 per cent of the population would hold 50 per cent of the wealth within the country. The dotted curve represents that actual income distribution within an economy. The further this curve is away from the diagonal line, the greater the inequality of income distribution is.

To quantify the Lorenz curve, the Gini coefficient was created. This numerical representation of income inequality within an economy is derived from the area between the diagonal line and the curve, divided by the sum of the areas bounded by the diagonal line and the curve and the area below the curve. This equation can be represented as the following, using the areas represented by A and B in Figure 3.1:

$$\text{Gini coefficient} = \frac{A}{A+B}$$

The Gini coefficient will be a number between 0 (theoretically representing perfect equality) and 1 (theoretically representing perfect inequality).

While the Gini coefficient is often used as an easily represented value of income inequality within an economy, it is by no means a perfect representation of the true income distribution. Various Lorenz curves can intersect, which could potentially give different Lorenz curves the same Gini coefficient (Kulkarni, 2006). For example, while the Lorenz curves would represent a more detailed picture of where the wealth within a population is occurring, the Gini coefficient would simply give two identical numeric representations. To account for this discrepancy in the Gini coefficient, many studies have instead used data that breaks the income distribution into quintiles. Since the primary concern is the ratio of the lowest quintile to the highest quintile, these two numbers are looked at for comparison. However, this method is not without its shortcomings either. By taking this approach, researchers ignore what is occurring in the middle of the wealth distribution.

For this chapter, income inequality will be measured using the Gini coefficient. While this is not a perfect representation of income inequality, as explained above, it is the most readily available data and provides an adequate enough picture for this analysis.

KUZNET'S CURVE

In 1955, Simon Kuznet explored whether "inequality in the distribution of income increases or decreases in the course of a country's economic growth" (Kuznet, 1955, p. 1). For his seminal study, Kuznet decided to use a particularly select sample of developed countries, consisting of the United States, between 1929 and 1950; the United Kingdom, between 1880 and 1947; and Germany, between 1875 and 1947 (Kuznet, 1955). Based on this data, Kuznet states that although "a scant sample…the general conclusion suggested is that the relative distribution of income…has been moving towards equality" (Kuznet, 1955, p. 4). Based on this work, a graphical representation of income inequality against time was derived. This representation is an inverted U-shaped curve and is now referred to as the Kuzent's curve (See Figure 3.2).

Kuznet explains his findings as a structural change that occurs within economies that are developing, including a shift from agriculture towards industrialization and urbanization (Kuznet, 1955). He believes that an increasing weight of urban populations, along with the belief that "per capita productivity in urban pursuits increase more rapidly than in agriculture", will lead to increasing income inequality as nations industrialize.

Furthermore, since there is a greater discrepancy between the knowledge and skills of urban and rural workers in developing countries than in developed countries, this will put a price premium on those urban workers in developing countries that possess the necessary skills. In theory, it is believed that as this structural change continues to occur within an economy, more wealth will be concentrated in the urban areas. As owners of the capital used in the industrialization of the economy reap the rewards on their investments in the form of returns , they will continue to re-invest in such industrialization, increasing the demand for industrialized labour, drawing more and more workers from the agriculture sector to the industrial sector. This will serve to further the gap in income distribution between the two sectors.

If the proceeding factors account for the continued widening of income inequality within an economy as it grows, what therefore accounts for second half of the U-shaped curve, the decreasing gap in income inequality? Kuznet hypothesizes two main reasons for the diminishing inequality gap. First, he believes that, colloquially, "the successful great entrepreneurs of today are rarely sons of the great and successful entrepreneurs of yesterday" (Kuznet, 1955, p. 10). In other words, Kuznet believes that as economies industrialize and technology becomes a vital component of economic success, there is increased opportunity for new entrepreneurs to accumulate wealth, rather than the wealth staying in the hands of a relatively small percentage of the population. This also assumes that as an economy develops, initially there may be a concentration of work in one sector, such as textiles or clothing manufacture. However, as that industry grows, advances in the industry will spawn new industries that are needed to support the initial sector's continued growth. For example, delivery services will be needed to transport the manufactured clothing or the machines needed to create the clothing may become domestically produced. This dispersion in number and types of sectors that are supported by the economy will help spread the wealth among different groups of people, lowering the initial income inequality. This assumes that the rate of technology will be such that the supply of labour to operate such technologies will eventually catch up with the demand.

Second, Kuznet believes that there will be an intra-industry shift of workers from lower-income industries to higher-income industries. As the rewards of working within the non-agricultural sector are realized, more people will invest in their own education and skills training to be better suited and better equipped for that type of work. As this occurs, an increase in supply of qualified workers will lower the price premium on skilled workers. This will have the affect of dispersing wealth among a greater pool of people, lowering income inequality.

Kuzent also hypothesizes that legislative and political decisions within an economy will have a large effect on decreasing the gap in income inequality. However, he states that "To discuss this complex of processes is beyond the competence of this paper, but its existence and possible wide effect should be noted and one point emphasized" (Kuznet, 1955, p. 9). Kuznet goes on to conclude that although legislative and political decisions on how to minimize the concentration of wealth in the hands of few would have a great impact on income inequality, such measures should not necessarily be taken as it would also slow down the growth of the economy. He warns that such a view is "a force that would operate in democratic societies even if there were no other counteracting factors" (Kuznet, 1955, p. 10).

Kuznet's work has been considered to some extent as the validation that income inequality is a natural part of economic development. And, if Kuznet's hypothesis holds true, that income inequality will eventually diminish as an economy continues to develop. Therefore, concerning the policy applications of this theory, policy changes that may lessen income inequality but hurt economic growth should not necessarily be undertaken, since the income gap will naturally widen and then retract later on.

ACADEMIC WORK ON KUZNET'S CURVE

There has been a significant amount of academic work written on the subject of Kuznet's curve since he first published an article, "Economic Development and Income Inequality", in 1955. The academic work in the preceding decades of his original publication generally tend to support the conclusions made by Kuznet drew. However, since the 1990s, there has also been a significant amount of academic work that calls into question whether the Kuznet's curve aptly applies to modern economic development. Although fundamentally, the necessary aspects of economic development have not changed in the past half century, the network which governs the world economy has. These changes may have altered the relationship between economic growth and income inequality.

In defending Kuznet's broad generalizations that income inequality grows with economic development and then shrinks in later stages of development, Irving Kravis in 1960, conducted a study of relative inequality among a group of developed and developing countries. His study concluded that there was far less income inequality in developed economies than there was in developing economies. Kravis goes on to state, "We conclude that the explanation of the greater income equality that is found in the developed countries lies in the social and economic conditions that distinguish them from the underdeveloped countries" (Kravis, 1960, p. 416). While this lends some support to Kuznet's hypothesis that inequality within an economy will rise before it falls, it does not give any support to Kuznet's belief that the inherent functioning of the free market system will bring about that eventual decrease in income inequality. Furthermore, comparing countries in which economic development has occurred and countries in which economic development has not occurred, assumes that all countries follow the same trajectory of income equality and economic growth. Kravis's study does not speak about what is happening internally with regards to economic or social policy.

One of the most important papers in support of Kuznet's curve was written by Montek S. Ahluwalia in 1976, titled , "Inequality, Poverty and Development". The conclusions of this paper, along with the recommendations that it promoted, were adopted by the World Bank in the late 1970s (Anand & Kanbur, 1993). In his study, Ahluwalia used a cross-sectional data sample of 60 countries, including 40 developing countries, 16 developed countries and 4 socialist countries (Ahluwalia, 1976). This sample was used to create a multivariate regression analysis comparing the relationship of income inequality to selected variables that reflect aspects of the development process (Ahluwalia, 1976). Although Ahluwalia is very explicit in his paper that this type of analysis can only yield "broad generalizations about the relationship between income distribution and development", he goes on to conclude that there was a "substantial measure of support for the [Kuznet] hypothesis" (Ahluwalia, 1976, p. 1 & 2). Ahluwalia theorized that there are three aspects which are systemically related to the development process. Much as Kuznet concluded, these variables are: intersectoral shifts in the decline of the agricultural sector and the rise of the industrial sector, expansion of the educational and skill characteristics of the population, and a reduction in the rate of growth of the population (Ahluwalia, 1976).

There are particularly two interesting aspects to note from Ahluwalia's study. The first of which is the inclusion of six socialist countries in his study. Kuznet strongly believed that the forces that caused the initial income inequality and then eventual return towards equality were demand side created (Kuznet, 1955). If this is the case, then a free market would be needed to create such conditions. This would not be possible in socialist countries in which strong government policy exists with regards to the operation of the market. In his explanation of the inclusion of socialist countries, Ahluwalia concludes that "A consistent finding in all the equations estimated is that the six socialist countries in the sample display substantially greater equality than is predicted by the cross country regression line" (Ahluwalia, 1976, p. 17).

The second interesting note from Ahluwalia's study is his explanation of the educational characteristics and endowments of the population. Again, in supporting Kuznet's original hypothesis, Ahluwalia believes that education is endogenous to economic growth. As economies develop and there is a shift towards the industrial sector and technology, a premium will be placed on knowledge. This premium will lead to a widening inequality gap until the market is able to educate enough workers to reduce this premium and thus reverse the widening inequality. Ahluwalia states this relationship by saying, "There is clear evidence that education is significantly positively correlated with equality" (Ahluwalia, 1976, p. 14). Yet, in his study, he is not able to show that education is in fact endogenous to growth and not a variable that needs external support from government.

Robert Barro takes a similar approach to Ahluwalia in his 2006 study entitled "Inequality and Growth Revisited" (Barro, 2008). Barro uses a cross-section approach to study both developed and developing nations at the same time, rather than a time-series approach which would look at individual countries over a period of time. In an attempt to mitigate any anomalous data, Barro looks at four separate time periods; 1965–75, 1975–85, 1985–95, and 1995-2003 or 2004, depending on the availability of data (Barro, 2008). He concludes that the Kuznet's curve is present in all the periods, showing that, "Income inequality first rises but subsequently declines with per capita GDP"(Barro, 2008, p. 13). However, Barro includes the caveat that the observed curve does not explain the majority of variation in income inequality across countries or across time periods (Barro, 2008). Meaning, just as Ahluwalia's study showed, that statistically, a Kuznet's curve appears in cross-sectional analyses but these results do not indicate the reasons for the curve or policy implications. This is unlike Kuznet's original full hypothesis which attempts to explain the presence of the curve through the workings of a free market economy.

In 1993, Sudhir Anand and S.M.R. Kanbur, scrutinized the work of Ahluwalia and concluded that his estimates, based on the functional form and data sets used, were lacking in robustness

(Anand & Kanbur, 1993). The paper refutes the findings of Ahluwalia and attacks the income distributions for the 60 developing and developed countries used as "not comparable with respect to income concept, population unit and survey coverage" (Anand & Kanbur, 1993, p. 1). When Anand et al., corrected for the deficiencies that they saw in Ahluwalia's work, they found that the Kuznet's curve failed to materialize. The income inequalities of developed and developing countries did not follow an inverted U-shape trajectory over time.

In a 1999 paper titled "Explaining Inequality the World Round: Cohort Size, Kuznets Curves, and Openness", Matthew Higgins and Jeffrey G. Williamson examine economic inequality from a more recent perspective. Higgins and Williamson describe what they refer to as "weak" and "strong" versions of the Kuznet's curve. The "strong" Kuznet's curve is the basic premise of Kuznet's hypothesis, that is, technology and structural changes within an economy will demand capital and skilled labour more so than unskilled labour. They refer to this as the "strong" version because income inequality is hypothesized to only be effected by the demand for capital and skilled labour, nothing else.

The "weak" version of the Kuznet's curve is predicated on the belief that these demand forces which cause the initial inequality can be offset by state policy and other factors if sufficiently powerful. This is the point that Kuznet acknowledges in his paper but does not explore further. Higgins and Williamson give the example of a strong public policy towards education and the eradication of illiteracy. They believe this would have the affect of taking the premium off the skilled workers, diminishing the increased inequality gap as an economy grows (Higgins & Williamson, 1999). The other factors that Higgins and Williamson look at are cohort size and relative openness of the economy. Cohort size refers to the size of the various generations of workers. They found that if there is a large cohort of very young and very old workers, compared to the cohort size of middle-aged workers, income inequality grew with development until the middle-aged cohort group gained enough workers to offset this effect. At which point, income inequality began to shrink. If the middle-aged cohort group was large to begin with, income inequality was not as pronounced as economic development occurred. Higgins and Williamson concluded that the "strong" version of the Kuznet's curve, which was based solely on market demand, does not exist. However, a "weak" version of Kuznet's curve, encompassing other factors, in this case cohort size, does exist.

In their book titled "Economic Development", Michael Todaro and Stephen Smith give a relatively brief synopsis of Kuznet's hypothesis. Specifically, they note that Kuznet did not "specify the mechanism by which his inverted-U hypothesis was supposed to occur, it could in principle be consistent with a sequential process of economic development" (Todaro & Smith, 2006, p. 212). From the data which Todaro and Smith collected, they draw the conclusion that there is no relationship between countries with varied levels of per capita GDP and degrees of inequality (Todaro & Smith, 2006). However, this conclusion faces the same constraints that previous studies had, that is, the studies both in support of and in defiance of Kuznet's hypothesis. Those constraints being that equality within an economy will only be relative to itself and not levels of equality of other economies. Todaro and Smith also cite a study done by Gary Fields and George

Jakubson that concludes when looking at time series data from numerous developing countries, a Kuznet's curve only appears with the inclusion of Latin American countries (Todaro & Smith, 2006). When these countries are pulled from the sample, the Kuznet's curve fails to materialize. Based on this study, Todaro and Smith question whether the Kuznet's curve is simply a "statistical fluke, resulting from...extraneous historical reasons" (Todaro & Smith, 2006, p. 215).

CROSS SECTIONAL ANALYSIS OF KUZNET'S CURVE

Using available data from the World Bank Group, a population of 68 countries was analyzed to understand if a Kuznet's curve is present today (The World Bank Group, 2010). Since Gini coefficient data is not readily available for all countries each year, data from 2000-2002 was used to gain a statistically significant population. The full list of countries can be seen in Appendix A. The population includes 15 "developed economies" and 53 "emerging and developing economies" (IMF, 2009).

A scatter plot of the cross-sectional analysis can be seen in Figure 3.3. For this graph, the natural log of GDP per capita was used in order to meet the statistical assumption of normality. A polynomial trend line is fit to the points and has an r-square of 0.2265, indicating a fairly significant relationship. This trend line produces a distinctly inverted U-shaped curve. However, because the natural log of GDP per capita was taken, therefore the curve should be interpreted with this in mind. Statistically, both the dependent and independent variables are significant at the 0.05 level and overall, the test shows significance with a p-value of 0.03.

A modern analysis of a cross-sectional look at country's GDP per capita plotted against their Gini coefficient confirms the presence of a Kuznet's curve. This analysis indicates that there is a strong correlation that countries with lower levels of GDP per capita also have lower levels of the Gini coefficient much as countries with higher levels of GDP per capita also have lower levels of the Gini coefficient. However, countries will mid-levels of GDP per capita have higher levels of the Gini coefficient.

Unfortunately, the major deficiencies of this type of analysis still exist. These deficiencies are those that the Barro (2006), Ahluwalia (1976) and Kravis (1960) studies encountered as well. The presence of an inverted U-shaped curve in this data is simply stating that at this point in time, there is trend that economies with lower and higher rates of GDP per capita have lower degrees of income inequality and those economies with moderate rates of GDP per capita have higher rates of income inequality. Although a fairly robust polynomial trend line with an r-square of 0.2265 can be fit to the data points, the correlation between GDP per capita and income inequality is significantly less, with an r-square of 0.0683 (The full regression analysis can be seen in Appendix B). Therefore, this type of analysis speaks nothing of how individual countries progress along their own development path. Also the analysis does not say anything about policies that an economy should or should not pursue. Without any such social, political or even economic context in which to frame this data, the presence of an inverted U-shaped curve, unfortunately, says quite little about economic development.

KUZNET'S CURVE IN CHILE

To gain a more robust understanding of the social, political and economic context in which to frame the Kuznet's curve, let us take a historical perspective of Chile between 1973 and 2006. In 1973, President Salvador Allende and his socialist government were overthrown by a military coup. He was replaced by General Augusto Pinochet who took strong measures to impose a free-market economy upon the nation and to open up the country's economy to international trade (Weyland, 1997). Heavy emphasis was placed on the reduction of the role of the government in all sectors while privatization of industry and business was strongly promoted (Chumacero & Fuentes, 2002).

This drastic transition from a socialist economy to a liberalized, free market economy should be an ideal setting to study if the Kuznet's curve can be applied to a modern developing country. As Simon Kuznet pointed out in his original paper, robust data regarding income distributions over time is difficult to obtain. This is applicable to the case for Chile over the past four decades. The only consistent and reliable source of income data has been from the World Bank. Unfortunately, this data was only collected sporadically over the period in question. Table 3.1 shows the full set of data for Chile (The World Bank Group, 2010).

Table 3.1: Chilean Gini Coefficient and GDP per capita

Year	1971	1980	1989	1990	1994	2000	2006
Gini Coefficient	.4600	.5321	.5788	.5540	.5649	.5590	.5220
GDP per capita, in USD 2000	2359	2501	3013	3070	3917	4880	5882

Note: Data collected from World Development Indicators and CEPAL Statistics, both are compiled by the World Bank Group.

Unfortunately, with such large gaps in the time series data, it is hard to authoritatively state any conclusions. However, with the data that is available, it is apparent that there is a steady increase in economic growth in Chile since 1971 and this is accompanied by an increase in the income inequality for approximately first 20 years and then a gradual decrease in income inequality. A graphical representation is in Figure 3.4.

By plotting the available data points, Chile's income distribution seems to fit the Kuznet's curve over this time period. Since 1970, there has been a consistent growth as represented by the GDP per capita. This line, represented in Figure 3.5, has an obvious upward slope, beginning slowly between 1970 and 1980, but then increasing rapidly since 1990. At the same time, there has been an increase in the Gini coefficient for Chile since 1970, starting at 0.46 and growing to a peak in 1989 of 0.5788. While there was a dip in the Gini coefficient in 1990 and then a rise in 1994, overall, the trend in the Gini coefficient since 1990 has been downward to 0.5220 in 2006. This graph would tend to support Kuznet's hypothesis that as an economy develops there is a tendency for income inequality to widen, but this gap then tends to retract as economic development continues.

SOCIAL, POLITICAL AND ECONOMIC CONTEXT OF CHILE

As with the cross sectional analysis, the appearance of a Kuznet's curve with regards to Chile since 1971 speaks nothing of Chile's internal economic policies, social goals, or any explanation of the widening and then retracting inequality gap. The appearance of the Kuznet's curve only confirms that with economic growth, income inequality will increase, and then at some later point, it will retract. The curve itself gives no indication of any future projections concerning time frames or necessary conditions for the income inequality gap to begin to restrict.

In Kuznet's original paper, he hypothesizes that the income inequality gap will begin to recede as the premium for skilled labor diminishes. This is believed to be at a time within the economy when technology has diffused across the industrial sector and there is no longer a shortage of skilled labour. This is consistent with the view that holds that education is an endogenous part of economic growth. In other words, when a premium is created for skilled workers, people will be motivated to invest in their own education in order to be able to raise their potential wage rate. If Kuznet was correct in his hypothesis, we would most likely see a decrease in the income equality gap, represented by the Gini coefficient. Yet, in the case of Chile, the income inequality gap continued to grow for 17 years under free market conditions. While Kuznet's hypothesis gives no time frame for which the curve should occur, 17 years is long enough for the generation that was born when the free market reforms were implemented to enter the job market by 1989. Unfortunately for Chile, the reduction in income inequality did not occur within this time frame.

It was not until a major social change occurred within the country that the income inequality gap began to lessen. During the 17 year rule of Pinochet's government, it was mainly concerned with implementing neo-classical market reforms, promoting efficiency and competitiveness of markets. Due to this narrow focus, heavy restraints were placed on social programmes in order to maintain price controls and other economic conditions, leading to "the withdrawal of state social protection" (Montecinos, 1997, p. 225). Taxes, which would support such social programmes, were believed to "weaken market incentives, reduce profits and investments, and thus depress growth" (Weyland, 1997, p. 37).

In 1988, General Pinochet and his government were voted from power. The democratically elected President, Patricio Aylwin, took office in 1990 and realigned the focus of the government towards social programmes. Aylwin's government viewed equality enhancing measures as a necessity for achieving social and political stability. However, the President's Secretary General acknowledged that "inequality and poverty would prompt a wave of demands for immediate benefits that would endanger sound economic policy" (Weyland, 1997, p. 38). Rather than wait for a popular uprising, the Aylwin government proactively increased spending on social goods, concentrating on education, health and welfare pensions. However, they only raised social spending by as much as they could generate through implementing a progress tax reform. By doing so, the government was able to increase social spending without breaking from the neo-classical policy measures already in place (Weyland, 1997).

This marked departure from the previous social policy position of the Pinochet government occurs preciously at the time that the Gini coefficient within Chile begins to decline. If this drastic shift in social and political policies is the cause of this decrease in income inequality, it can be said the Kuznet's Curve undoubtedly occurs within a historical context for Chile but that the reasons for such are not due to endogenous features of the economy as Kuznet had originally hypothesized.

EDUCATION POLICIES WITHIN CHILE

Although Kuznet does not address specific social programmes that a government can work on in his original paper, he does argue one of the major factors in the growing income equality gap is caused by the premium placed on skilled workers and the use of technology (Kuznet, 1955). One way to mitigate such skill premiums, and thus reduce the inequality gap, is to create public education programmes.

In the 17 year rule of General Pinochet, government spending on education was dramatically decreased. Unfortunately, again, full data regarding education spending levels in Chile has not been kept by the World Bank Group. However, we know that in 1971, when the Allende's socialist programmes were on great height , government spending on education was 22 per cent of the total government spending. By 1980, seven years after the General Pinochet gained power, government spending on education had decreased to 12 per cent and hit a low of 10 per cent the year when President Aylwin took office. Since that time, government spending on education has gone up to 14 per cent in 1995 and then to 16 per cent in both 2000 and 2006 (See Table 3.2).

Table 3.2: Chilean Government Spending on Education and the Gini Coefficient

Year	1971	1980	1989	1990	1994	2000	2006
Gini Coefficient	.4600	.5321	.5788	.5540	.5649	.5590	.5220
Government Spending on Education, per cent of Govt. Spending	22*	12	-	10	14**	16	16

Note: Data collected from World Development Indicators and CEPAL Statistics, both are compiled by the World Bank Group.
* Education data is incomplete and does not exist for 1971. This statistic is from 1970, but for the sake of comparison is placed in 1971.
** Education data is incomplete and does not exist for 1994. This statistic is from 1995, but for the sake of comparison is placed in 1994 .

While it is difficult to claim a statistically significant relationship between government spending on education and the Gini coefficient with very few data points, there is an apparent association. Kuznet believed that a reduction of income inequality would occur organically within an economy and without government interference. However, with regards to Chile, this claim seems somewhat dubious. The Gini coefficient did increase within the Chilean society as the economy was liberalized and growth began to occur. However, for 17 years, the Chilean economy grew with no downward movement in the Gini coefficient. It was only when concerted efforts were taken to fund social programmes did the inequality gap begin to shrink.

Furthermore, Kuznet's original claims that government interference into the market by implementing social programs would inhibit economic growth does not hold true in the case of Chile either. As can be seen in Figure 3.4, stronger economic growth occurred within the economy after President Aylwin's implementation of social programmes than during General Pinochet's tenure as president. In his account of Chile and its struggle between economic growth and equality, Weyland writes that contrary to neo liberals claim "economic growth per se was not the main cause for the reduction in poverty and misery" (Weyland, 1997, p. 48). He goes on to specifically state that "…new job-training programmes…facilitated the disproportional growth in employment among poorer groups" (Weyland, 1997, p. 48).

CONCLUSION

Economic growth is an integral part of the development of a society and a nation. With 154 emerging and developing countries in the world, there is a great of importance associated with how these countries develop and the income disparity that occurs within these countries (IMF, 2009).

While the Kuznet's curve is present in current cross-sectional analyses and within the economic growth of Chile over the past four decades, this presence alone lends few clues to its meaning. Supporters of the Kuznet's curve will argue that the presence of the curve indicates that governments and economic planners should not be overly concerned with rising levels of income inequality within a society. This is owing to the reason that economic growth occurs and this increased inequality will eventually diminish. In other words, increased income inequality is an intrinsic and necessary part of economic growth and any attempt to mitigate such inequalities will only harm economic growth.

However, the Kuznet's curve alone fails to provide any meaningful policy implications. In isolation, the curve lacks a time frame for which it occurs. Also, it does not give certain levels of GDP per capita or inequality to expect. It speaks nothing of a society's moral appetite, that is, to what extent is income inequality is acceptable or the consequences that the inequality may have on certain social and economic groups. The Kuznet's curve simply states that income inequality will rise with economic growth, and that at some point in the future, those increased levels of income inequality will begin to decrease.

Therefore, governments should be aware that income inequality will most likely rise as economic growth occurs, but whether this increased inequality can be mitigated to some extent through thoughtful and carefully planned social programmes is to be understood. Unlike the governments of the socialist Allende and the radically free market-oriented Pinochet before him, President Aylwin showed that fiscally responsible free market policies and socially responsible welfare programmes are not mutually exclusive. There are no clear or easy answers within economic development and, therefore, governments should be acutely aware of relationship between the prevailing economic development theory and social welfare.

APPENDIX 3.1

Full list of countries with GDP per capita and Gini Coefficients for 2000-2002 (The World Bank Group, 2010)

Country	GDP per capita (constant 2000 US$)	Log of GDP per capita	GINI index	Country	GDP per capita (constant 2000 US$)	Log of GDP per capita	GINI index
Albania	1541.04	3.188	0.3303	Uganda	291.39	2.464	0.4262
Argentina	8094.17	3.908	0.5003	Ukraine	960.23	2.982	0.2821
Bangladesh	400.70	2.603	0.3102	Uruguay	7229.47	3.859	0.4494
Belarus	1871.39	3.272	0.2792	Venezuela	5000.08	3.699	0.4761
Bolivia	1115.98	3.048	0.5819	Yemen, Rep.	550.55	2.741	0.3769
Brazil	3974.82	3.599	0.5639	Angola	639.32	2.806	0.5864
China	1452.28	3.162	0.4153	Austria	24194.81	4.384	0.29148
Congo, Rep.	1163.56	3.066	0.4732	Belgium	22623.28	4.355	0.329658
Costa Rica	4502.40	3.653	0.4723	Canada	23559.50	4.372	0.32562
Croatia	5999.57	3.778	0.2899	Chile	4880.05	3.688	0.5536
Dominican Republic	3013.52	3.479	0.4997	Colombia	2364.27	3.374	0.575
Ecuador	1589.28	3.201	0.5365	Estonia	4106.13	3.613	0.37
Egypt, Arab Rep.	1539.21	3.187	0.3214	Finland	23543.30	4.372	0.2688
El Salvador	2423.67	3.384	0.497	Germany	23114.23	4.364	0.2831
Ethiopia	149.66	2.175	0.2976	Greece	11500.65	4.061	0.34266
Gabon	4033.66	3.606	0.4145	Guatemala	1717.86	3.235	0.5497
Georgia	973.49	2.988	0.4078	Ireland	25329.38	4.404	0.342768
Honduras	1305.19	3.116	0.5671	Italy	19269.02	4.285	0.360331
India	588.99	2.770	0.368	Luxembourg	46456.62	4.667	0.307603
Indonesia	942.57	2.974	0.3941	Macedonia	1785.17	3.252	0.3444
Iran	1924.39	3.284	0.3828	Mauritania	421.32	2.625	0.3904
Kenya	425.74	2.629	0.4768	Mexico	5934.98	3.773	0.5187
Madagascar	246.35	2.392	0.4724	Norway	37472.37	4.574	0.2579
Mongolia	583.82	2.766	0.3303	Panama	3939.22	3.595	0.5656
Nicaragua	842.16	2.925	0.5233	Philippines	977.13	2.990	0.4609
Niger	166.34	2.221	0.4389	Romania	1650.97	3.218	0.3025
Pakistan	605.74	2.782	0.3118	Rwanda	218.02	2.338	0.4668
Paraguay	1360.45	3.134	0.5389	South Africa	3019.95	3.480	0.5777
Peru	2350.66	3.371	0.5197	Spain	14421.94	4.159	0.346612
Poland	5229.63	3.718	0.3492	Sweden	27688.89	4.442	0.25
Romania	2260.22	3.354	0.315	Switzerland	34787.10	4.541	0.33682
Russia	2443.96	3.388	0.3751	Tanzania	266.01	2.425	0.3462
Senegal	522.34	2.718	0.3919	Tunisia	2033.07	3.308	0.4081
Turkey	4690.83	3.671	0.4323	United States	34605.84	4.539	0.4081

APPENDIX 3.2

The full regression analysis run between GDP per capita and income inequality for the 68 economies looked at between 2000 and 2002.

SUMMARY OUTPUT								
Regression Statistics								
Multiple R	0.261342							
R Square	0.0683							
Adjusted R Square	0.054183							
Standard Error	9.474693							
Observations	68							
ANOVA								
	Df	*SS*	*MS*		*F*	*Significance F*		
Regression	1	434.3262	434.3262		4.838221	0.031343		
Residual	66	5924.807	89.76981					
Total	67	6359.134						
	Coefficients	*Standard Error*	*t Stat*	*P-value*	*Lower 95%*	*Upper 95%*	*Lower 95.0%*	*Upper 95.0%*
Intercept	54.31399	6.17628	8.793961	1.01E-12	41.982	66.645	41.982	66.645
X Variable 1	−3.92089	1.78254	−2.1996	0.031343	−7.479	−0.361	−7.479	−0.361

REFERENCES

1. Ahluwalia, M. S. *Inequality, Poverty and Development*. Washington, DC: World Bank, 1976
2. Anand, S. & Kanbur, S., Inequality and Development. *Journal of Development Economics* (41), 19-43, 1993
3. Barro, R. J. *Inequality and Growth Revisited*. Manila: Asian Development Bank, 2008.
4. Chumacero, R. A., & Fuentes, J. R. (2002). On the Determinants of Chilean Economic Growth. Santiago: Banco Central de Chile.
5. Higgins, M. & Williamson, J. G. (1999). Explaining Inequality the World Round: Cohort Size, Kuznets Curves, and Openness. New York: Federal Reserve Bank of New York.
6. IMF. (2009, October). World Economic Outlook. Retrieved February 2010, from International Monetary Fund: *http://www.imf.org/external/pubs/ft/weo/2009/02/weodata/groups.htm#oem*
7. Kravis, I. B. (1960). International Differences in the Distribution of Income. *The Review of Economics and Statistics* Vol. 42, No. 4 , 408-416.
8. Kulkarni, K. G., *Readings in International Economics*. New Delhi: Serials Publications, 2006
9. Kuznet, S. (1955). Economic Growth and Income Inequality. *The American Economic Review*, Vol. 45, No. 1 , 1-28.
10. Montecinos, V. (1997). Economic Reforms, Social Policy and the Family Economy in Chile. *Review of Social Economy*, Vol. LV, No. 2 , 224-234.
11. The World Bank Group. (2010, February). WDI Online. Retrieved February 2010, from World Development Indicators: *http://ddp-ext.worldbank.org/ext/DDPQQ/member.do?method=getMembers&userid=1&queryId=6*
12. Todaro, M. P., & Smith, S. C., *Economic Development*. Boston: Pearson Addison Wesley, 2006.
13. UNHDR. (2010, February). *Human Development Reports*. Retrieved February 2010, from United Nations Development Programme: *http://hdr.undp.org/en/*
14. Weyland, K. (1997). "Growth with Equality" in Chile's New Democracy? Latin American Research Review, Vol. 32, No. 1, 37-67.

4

Testing the Harrod-Domar Model

A Comparative Study of Economic Growth in Haiti and the Dominican Republic

Will Smith

CHAPTER SUMMARY

Recent destruction caused by the January 2010 earthquake in Haiti revealed the country's vulnerability to the world. With more aid flowing into Haiti than ever before, it is important to recognize the connection between aid, savings, and potential economic growth in order to affectively apply economic policy and transport Haiti to a less vulnerable position. Although Haiti shares the island of Hispaniola, with its neighbour the Dominican Republic, there are stark contrasts in economic success between the countries with the divergence starting in 1960. Haiti is the poorest country in the western hemisphere with a meager or non-existent growth rate while the Dominican Republic, still a relatively poor country, has a strong economic growth rate of around 5 per cent and a GDP per capita five times greater than Haiti. This chapter investigates the last 19 years (1990 to 2008) of economic growth in the two countries using the Harrod-Domar Model of economic development.

Section one includes a general history of Haiti and the Dominican Republic ranging from their existence as French and Spanish colonies to the dictatorships of Trujillo and Duvalier; it also emphasizes global perspectives and internal policies that may impact each country's economy. The Harrod-Domar Model is explained in section two, including its background, mathematical calculation, and applicability. The Harrod-Domar Model has become the most widely used economic growth perspective in history due to its simplicity, resiliency, and ability to evolve. This section also contains an introduction to the "financing gap" and describes how aid, savings, and growth are connected. Section three applies the Harrod-Domar/Financing Gap Model to Haiti and the Dominican Republic, searching for insights on Haiti's stagnant growth. Omissions and adaptations, the title of section four, is designed to identify possible reasons for the disjuncture of the Harrod-Domar Model in regards to Haiti. Ideas of aid categorization, political instability, and environmental degradation are discussed. Finally, the conclusion is a summative section that suggests areas for future research.

SECTION 1: HISTORY OF HISPANIOLA

The island of Hispaniola is home to both the Dominican Republic and Haiti. The two poor Caribbean countries share similar stories of colonialism, occupation, political instability, natural resources, and misguided economic policy. The early Spanish settlers used the natives for labour and in the 18th century; recognizing that labour was limited, Spain started to loose interest in the island and focussed on South America. At this time, the French took control over the western part of Hispaniola. The greater wealth of the French allowed them to import slaves from Africa to work in the fields. This influx created a great disparity in the demographics between the two colonies; by the end of the 18th century the western colony of Saint-Dominque was home to over 500,000 black slaves while the Spanish colony of Santo Domingo housed only 60,000. (Silver 2010). After numerous revolts against the French government and the Louisiana Purchase to the United States, France lost the will to maintain control of Saint-Dominque and in 1804 Haiti was established as the world's first sovereign black republic.

Early decisions by Haitian nationals proved costly to their long term economic livelihood. In an attempt to remove structures that resembled past regimes, land was reallocated to small family farms, making it impossible to re-establish abusive plantations. The Haitian government supported subsistence farming and provided little incentive for the production or exportation of cash crops (Diamond 2005). The country's history and fear of slavery led Haiti to close its borders to foreigners. In addition, their unique language, French-Creole, and dark skin made them less attractive to European economic trade than their lighter skinned, Spanish speaking neighbours that declared independence in 1821 (Brean, 2010). By the end of the 19th century, with the help of invested capital from Europe and the United States, the Dominican Republic was starting to develop a market economy, leaving Haiti behind.

A noticeable common characteristic in the history of both countries is political instability. Between 1844 and 1930, the Dominican Republic had fifty presidents and thirty revolutions, during a slightly smaller timeframe, from 1844 to 1915, only one of Haiti's twenty-two presidents was neither assassinated or forced out of office (Brean, 2010). The volatility of the region led to American intervention during World War I. Following U.S. withdrawal – 1924 from the Dominican Republic and 1935 from Haiti – both countries regressed to infighting which led to the rise of two vastly different dictators. Rafael Trujillo controlled the Dominican Republic from 1930 to 1961. Although egotistical to the point that he renamed the capital after himself, he was hard-working and developed the economic infrastructure needed to increase exports.

In Haiti, Francios "Papa Doc" Duvalier rose to power in 1957 and maintained control until 1971. Similar to Truijillo, Duvalier commanded the will of his people; however he had little interest in modernizing the economy and was perhaps best known for allowing Dominicans to purchase Haitians and force them to work on their plantations (Diamond, 2005).

In 1960, we see the beginning of economic statistical deviation between the two countries (See Figure 4.1). In their study in search of the explanatory variables, Jaramillo and Sancak (2007) concluded that 'strong similarities in the initial conditions in the Dominican Republic and Haiti indicate that these cannot explain the divergence in real incomes of the two countries since 1960' (p. 9). The widening gap of GDP per capita apparent in the last fifty years, according to the authors, can be attributed to the Dominican Republic's ability to implement stronger structural measures, stabilization policies, and maintain political stability.

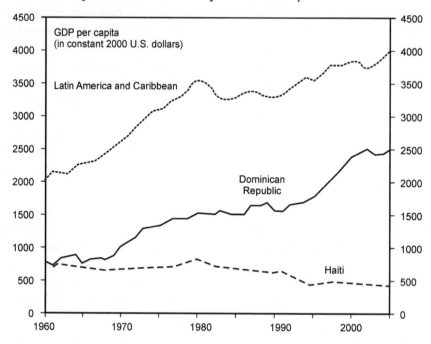

Figure 4.1: Economic Growth in Haiti & Dominican Republic: 1960–2005

Source: Jaramillo and Sancak (2007).

Currently the GDP per capita in the Dominican Republic is five times greater than Haiti's. Real GDP per capita has actually fallen in Haiti by 50 per cent since the 1980s (UN-ECLAC 2005). Haiti is the poorest country in the western hemisphere and globally ranks only in front of parts of Africa. Out of 182 countries listed on the U.N's human development index, Haiti ranks 149th while the Dominican Republic is 90th (Silver 2010). With regards to free trade, both countries have minimal barriers and Haiti's tariff rate is actually lower than all countries in Latin America or the Caribbean, a status that has seen little economic advantage (Jaramillo and Sancak, 2007). Additionally, external support is not new to the region as the IMF initiated its first programme in Haiti in 1958 (Fasano, 2009). The quagmire is, how do we explain the expanding economic imbalance in Hispanolia? Given similar institutions, geography, and political instability what economic framework can help us understand the difference between economic growth in the Dominican Republic and Haiti? To gain insight into this query, we will look to the Harrod-Domar/Financing Gap Model.

SECTION 2: THE HARROD-DOMAR MODEL

During the last 50 years in which the economies of the Dominican Republic and Haiti have drifted apart, the Harrod-Domar model of economic development was the logic most commonly applied to spur economic growth. Published in April 1946, Evsey Domar's original intention was to design a model that would discuss the relationship between short-term recessions and investment in the United States; he genuinely believed that his model 'made no sense for long term growth' (Easterly, 1997). Ironically, the Harrod-Domar model became a resilient model for growth that continues to permeate decisions in development, including strategy sessions in the IMF and World Bank.

Part of the appeal of the model is its simplicity. According to Todaro and Smith (2003), in the Harrod-Domar model 'the mechanisms for growth and development…are simply a matter of increasing national savings and investment' (p. 115). The construction of the Harrod-Domar economic model starts with the assumption that not everything included in a country's GDP (Y) is consumed and that which is saved (S) is set aside at a standard savings rate (s).

$$Y \cdot s = S$$

The theory then focuses on real investments (I) that will adjust capital (K), such as increasing inventory or adding machinery, instead of financial investments such as stocks and bonds. Investment is equal to the change in capital stock.

$$I = K$$

The capital output ratio (j) postulation is fundamental to the model. This constant ratio equals the capital stock (K) divided by gross domestic product (Y). As a constant, whatever adjustment is made to capital stock an equal proportional shift will occur in GDP. For example if the capital output ratio is 3 then a USD 3 increase in capital is always necessary to create a USD 1 increase in GDP.

$$j = \Delta K / \Delta Y$$

Therefore,

$$j \cdot \Delta Y = \Delta K$$

The Harrod-Domar model then looks at the interest rate and assumes fluidity. A dynamic interest rate will create an equilibrium where savings (S) equals investment (I); if savings is greater than investment, the interest rate will decrease to promote spending. In contrast, when savings is less than investment, the interest rate will increase to encourage savings. Therefore, eventually there will be a balance between savings and investment.

$$S = I$$

With this understanding, savings (S) can be substituted for change in capital stock (K) and with the acceptance that savings was a specific savings rate (s) of gross domestic product (Y), the following equation is manufactured.

$$j \cdot \Delta Y = s \cdot Y$$

Restructuring this equation gives us the conclusion of the Harrod-Domar model which is as follows:

$$\Delta Y/Y = s/j$$

As the capital output ratio (j) is constant for a country, generally between two and five, the only way for economic growth to occur (as seen as an increase in the percentage change in GDP (Y)) is through an increase in the savings rate. For instance, if a country has a savings rate of 6 per cent with a capital output ratio of 2, the country can expect a 3 per cent increase in GDP. Increasing the savings rate, and hence the GDP, can be done by: artificially increasing the interest rate, decreasing consumption through heavier taxation thereby increasing prices, increasing foreign direct investment, or borrowing money from international financial institutions. Historically, economic theorists have hypothesized that developing countries are unable to generate the required change internally and must therefore seek external financial support in order to experience growth.

The Harrod-Domar model has been resilient in the past 50 years; its evolution has led to multiple applications and an engrained presence in all the financial development institutions. The first, most straightforward function lies in calculating expected GDP growth. Using the previous example of a country with a savings rate of 6 per cent and a capital output ratio of 2, we can expect GDP growth to be at 3 per cent. This rate, however, does not illustrate an improvement in the general wellbeing or standard of living of the population. To measure change in GDP per capita and thus real, significant economic growth you need to subtract the population growth rate (p) from the expected GDP growth; with a population growth rate of 2 per cent the sample country would have a GDP per capita growth rate of 1 per cent.

$$\Delta Y/Y = s/j - p$$

Example: 6/2% – 2% = 1% GDP per capita growth rate

Setting an economic target is another function possible with the Harrod-Domar model. If a country wishes to grow at a GDP per capita rate over 4 per cent and currently has a population growth rate of 2 per cent with a capital output ratio of 3, the country would need a savings rate greater than 18 per cent.

Example: 18%/3 – 2% = 4% GDP per capita growth rate

For developing countries an 18 per cent savings rate is often unattainable, as such to reach their growth goal they need to obtain outside assistance. Capturing this discrepancy in a gap model, Rosenstein-Rodan (1961) believed that foreign aid must fill in the disparity in order for the country to reach its targeted rate of growth. Their model has since been refined and is now understood as the Financing Gap model, designating a direct one to one connection between aid and savings and a linear relationship between savings and growth (Westerberg). In the given example, if the developing country had a savings rate of 10 per cent, they would need to secure the financial aid necessary to fill their 8 per cent 'financing gap'.

Foreign aid was solidified as the key to economic growth by Rostow (1960) who used the Harrod-Domar model to calculate the investment necessary for a developing country to move into the 'takeoff' stage of his five stages of economic development. "Rostow predicted the recipient country will naturally increase its savings as it takes off, so that after 'ten or fifteen years' the donors can anticipate aid being discontinued" (Easterly, 1997, p. 8). Unfortunately, sustainability for countries was not reached as swiftly as Rostow had imagined and many developing countries were left with an increasing debt. Aid was further rationalized to help underdeveloped countries service their existing loans (Bauer, 1972). This led to the ironic arrangement of more aid flowing to countries that saved inefficiently. The neo-classical economists recognized this 'waste' of resources and declared that foreign aid was necessary, but not sufficient, to produce the desired growth. In the 1980s and 1990s, this group of economists strongly influenced institutions such as IMF; using the Harrod-Domar model to calculate the required financing and the Solow residual to identify the sufficient conditions needed, thus increasing conditionalities present in IMF foreign aid packages.

The evolution of the Harrod-Domar model has enabled it to persevere through the last fifty years, as evident in the recent history of the IMF, European Bank for Reconstruction and Development, and the World Bank. The European Bank for Reconstruction and Development announced in 1995 that it would use the Harrod-Domar model to calculate its investment requirement in client countries. In the World Bank, 90 per cent of country desk economists still calculate the 'financing gap' and the model has been used to expedite a country's recovery from civil war, ameliorate the chaotic transition from communism to capitalism, and to impede the diffusion of macroeconomic crisis. The model is so engrained in the philosophy of the World Bank that it is often continued even when it is apparent it was unsuccessful. For example, total GDP in Guyana fell from 1980 to 1990 even though their savings rate increased and foreign aid stayed strong at 8 per cent of the their GDP. The solution to the problem, according to the World Bank, was to increase external financial assistance to the country (Easterly, 1997).

Empirical studies have produced mixed results on the effect of aid on economic growth. Positive correlations have been found in studies by Dalgard and Hansen (2000), Hansen and Tarp (2000), and Lensink and White (2001). These studies revealed increased growth associated at higher aid flows with, however, a diminishing return on aid. Numerous reports contradict these findings, unveiling weak or even negative relationships between aid, savings, and growth. In concluding his 1990 study, Daniel Snyder noted that 'aid is found to have relatively little influence on domestic savings' (p. 179). William Easterly, in his 1997 study of 88 countries with data spanning from 1965 to 1995, found that 60 per cent exhibited a negative relationship between foreign aid and investment. To explain these divergent findings researchers have investigated variables that are situated within the recipient country – endogenous variables – and practices of the international donors or conditions external to the country – exogenous variables.

In a very influential study, Burnside and Dollar (2000) concluded that aid only stimulates growth in countries with sound economic policies. Their four categories of policy focus were summarized by Lotta Westerberg in her study applying the Harrod-Domar model to Ecuador and included:

1) Microeconomic Policies (For example: Monetary and exchange rate policy)
2) Structural Policies (For example: Impact taxes and other country structures have on encouraging production)
3) Public Sector Management (For example: Extent to which public institutions support private initiatives)
4) Social Inclusion (For Example: including social services that impact the poor and marginalized)

Countries that are experiencing a diminished ratio of less than one to one aid to growth need to review these four categories and strengthen them as needed. Aid switching or 'crowding out' has been hypothesized as another explanation given for seeing minimal growth. First identified in 1970, Griffin argued that foreign aid would 'crowd out' domestic savings by shifting aid to consumption and not savings. By using financial assistance to pay for commonly used commodities, countries are unable to save and therefore invest the influx of credit. Support for this hypothesis, however, is weak at best (Snyder, 1990 and Shields, 2007). Other endogenous variables that have an adverse affect on growth include: export price shocks, poor institutional quality, political instability, and inadequate environmental policy (Radelet, Clemens, and Bhavnani, 2004). Hence, factors within the country make success conditional, making it possible for NGOs to work through the government of some countries (Hondoras, Slovakia) while donors must work around the government in others (Collier and Dollar, 2004).

Factors outside of the country's control also impact the usefulness of aid. Although little empirical research has been done on how the structure of donor practices impacts economic growth, there are theories that state 'participatory' development projects create a stronger correlation between aid and growth because less money is lost to executive overhead and corruption. In addition, there is a belief that multilateral aid may be more effective than bilateral aid (Radelat, Clemens, and Bhavnani, 2004). Furthermore, events such as war and natural disasters may shift the priority of a country's spending and although a hike in aid is likely, external assistance will be used to overcome the humanitarian crisis and not situated into savings. Regardless of the mentioned exogenous and endogenous factors that can inhibit growth, the Harrod-Domar model proved to be resilient, evolving through the years to be the most widely applied theory on economic growth. Let us now turn our attention back to Haiti and the Dominican Republic to search for insights revealed by the Harrod-Domar/Financing Gap Model.

SECTION 3: APPLYING THE HARROD-DOMAR MODEL TO HAITI AND THE DOMINICAN REPUBLIC

In an attempt to gain clarity on the exponential divergence between the economies of Haiti and the Dominican Republic, this chapter will apply the Harrod-Domar/Financing Gap model to the years 1990 through 2008. In place of the savings rate, I will use gross capital formation as a percentage of GDP. Gross capital formation was first used by Kuznets (1934) as he investigated the connection between capital formation and national income. It is defined by the OECD as a measurement of the total value of changes in inventories and acquisitions less disposals of valuables; currently, gross capital formation is used as a measure of total investment in capital (which is the objective of the savings rate). The first challenge is to compare the expected change in GDP per capita produced by the Harrod-Domar model with the recorded percentage change.

Recalling that to calculate the GDP per capita growth rate, the following equation is needed:

$$\Delta Y/Y = s/j - p$$

By substituting in the gross capital formation percentage for s, an assumed capital output ratio of 3 (accepted ratios range from 2 to 5), and plugging the population growth rate for p, we can calculate the expected GDP per capita growth rate. In Haiti for 2008 s = 12.2 per cent and p = 1.7 per cent, therefore we can expect a GDP per capita growth rate of approximately 2.4 per cent.

$$12.2\%/3 - 1.7\% = 2.4\%$$

The recorded percentage change in real GDP for Haiti in 2008 was 1.2 per cent, only half of the expected, indicating a diminishing effect of savings on aid due to endogenous or exogenous variables. Table 4.1 shows the expected GDP per capita growth rate for Haiti in the first column with the recorded rate in the second column. Table 4.2 contains the same information for the Dominican Republic. Data was collected from the United Nations 'UN Data' and the IMF 'World Economic Outlook Database'.

Table 4.1: Haiti – Expected vs. Recorded GDP

	Expected GDP per capita Growth Rate (in %)	Recorded GDP Growth Rate (in %)	Disparity (in %) (Expected - Recorded)
2008	2.40	1.20	1.20
2007	2.30	3.40	−1.10
2006	2.90	2.30	0.60
2005	2.70	1.80	0.90
2004	2.70	−3.50	6.20
2003	3.20	0.40	2.80
2002	2.30	−0.30	2.60
2001	2.40	−1.00	3.40
2000	2.60	0.90	1.70
1999	2.60	2.70	−0.10
1998	2.50	2.20	0.30
1997	2.40	2.70	−0.30
1996	3.00	4.10	−1.10
1995	2.70	9.90	−7.20
1994	0.10	−11.60	11.70
1993	0.60	−4.90	5.50
1992	1.10	−2.30	3.40
1991	3.20	1.30	1.90
1990	2.70	−0.40	3.10
Average	2.34%	0.47%	1.87%

Table 4.2: DR – Expected vs. Recorded GDP

	Expected GDP per capita Growth Rate (in %)	Recorded GDP Growth Rate (in %)	Disparity (in %) (Expected - Recorded)
2008	5.00	5.30	−0.30
2007	5.20	8.50	−3.20
2006	4.60	10.70	−6.10
2005	4.00	9.30	−5.30
2004	3.40	1.30	2.10
2003	3.40	−0.30	3.70
2002	5.50	5.80	−0.30
2001	5.30	1.80	3.50
2000	6.10	5.70	0.40
1999	5.80	6.70	−0.90
1998	6.20	7.00	−0.80
1997	4.40	8.00	−3.60
1996	4.20	7.10	−2.90
1995	4.10	5.50	−1.40
1994	4.50	2.30	2.20
1993	4.30	7.20	−2.90
1992	4.10	10.50	−6.40
1991	3.70	0.90	2.80
1990	4.90	−5.50	10.40
Average	4.67%	5.15%	−0.47%

As evident by the preceding tables, the Harrod-Domar model is a stronger predictor of GDP growth in the Dominican Republic with an average difference between expected and recorded growth at −0.47 per cent. Haiti's statistics illustrate an ineffective translation from investment to growth; on an average the country has a financing gap of 1.87 per cent to get to their expected GDP growth of 2.34 per cent. Financing gaps (indicated by italics on the tables) are common in Haiti, as 14 of the 19 years studied required external financial assistance in order to meet the meager expected growth. The Dominican Republic, in contrast, had financing gaps in only 7 of the 19 years, indicating more efficient use of available resources.

In order for Haiti to close the gap with developed countries they must grow at a much faster rate than either the expected (2.34 per cent) or recorded (0.47 per cent) average rates for Haiti; given the assumption that developing countries are unable to adjust their savings rate to the needed level internally, we can expect to see increased financing gap. If, for example, Haiti targeted a 5 per cent GDP growth rate, the country would, on an average, need to accumulate 4.53 per cent of the needed funds from outside aid. It is not surprising given the stagnant growth of Haiti that they have over four times the outside development assistance (ODA) of the Dominican Republic in 2008. The next examination of the Harrod-Domar model involves the financing gap and the ability for aid to generate growth. According to the model, aid goes into investment one to one and investment drives economic growth. We should, therefore, see a linear relationship between the ODA of a country and their increase in GDP. Figure 4.2 illustrates the relationship between ODA and GDP in Haiti while Figure 4.3 covers the Dominican Republic. The data expressed in Figure 4.2 was gathered from the IMF and the OECD.

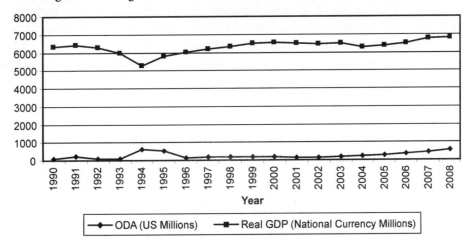

Figure 4.2: Haiti – ODA & GDP

ODA has had little, if any, impact on economic growth in Haiti from 1990 to 2008. Although ODA increased from 105 million US dollars in 1990 to 557 million in 2008, an increase of 430 per cent, the real GDP of the country (measured in national currency) jumped only 7.9 per cent from 6.33 billion to 6.83 billion.

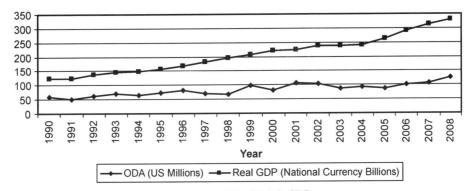

Figure 4.3: DR - ODA & GDP

In the Dominican Republic, we see a strong positive correlation between ODA and economic growth. Although the Dominican Republic receives far less foreign aid than Haiti (127 million to 557 million in 2008), their ability to effectively convert aid to growth significantly surpasses Haiti. ODA in the Dominican Republic jumped from 58 million US dollars in 1990 to 127 million in 2008, an increase of 119 per cent. At the same time, real GDP sharply increased in national currency from 122 billion in 1990 to 331 billion in 2008, an increase of 171 per cent.

We can see from the data that the Harrod-Domar model and its first proposition of a one to one connection between saving and growth is best represented in the Dominican Republic. In addition, the 'financing gap' direct linear connection between aid and savings and, therefore, growth is best modeled in the Dominican Republic. Haiti's economic growth patterns do not correspond to the logic presented in the Harrod-Domar model, as the country has a significant difference between expected and actualized GDP growth, nor does it capture external financial support to catalyze economic growth. The lack of applicability in Haiti, therefore, draws attention to the limitations of the Harrod-Domar model. In the next section these omissions are brought forward and alternative explanations for the stagnant growth in Haiti are discussed.

SECTION 4: OMISSIONS AND ADAPTATIONS OF THE HARROD-DOMAR MODEL

With their history of political stability, absent economic practices, and vulnerability to natural disasters, the first consideration is the type of aid coming into Haiti, a distinction not made in the Harrod-Domar/Financing Gap model. In 2009, the former IMF regional representative in Haiti, Ugo Fasano, purported that authorities in Haiti have 'had a strong track record of delivering on their commitments on structural reforms'. If this is in fact the case, one has to ask if the reforms delivered were appropriate for the development of economic growth.

Insight into the inability of the Harrod-Domar model to accurately predict or explain the economic growth in Haiti comes from a study completed by Radelet, Clemens, and Bhavnani (2004) critiquing current research practices. They state that most research is flawed for two reasons: (1) substance and (2) timing. Often aid, when applied to economic growth, is not differentiated. Certain types of aid, for example food aid, will not directly impact economic growth but are still included in its calculation. Their study suggests the segmentation of aid into humanitarian aid, long term aid, and short term aid. It is possible, if not likely, that Haiti receives a significant percentage of humanitarian and long term aid that diminishes the effects of short term economic specific assistance.

The country's political volatility and susceptibility to natural disasters draws in humanitarian aid that, due to the disaster, actually has a simple negative relationship with growth. Additionally, strengthening needed institutions such as health and education is long term support that does not have an immediate economic payback. The fact that the timeline many studies routinely use is a set for four years, detracts any impact made by this long term aid. Figure 4.4 illustrates the independent expected impact made by each type of aid. The issue for Haiti then may not be disconnect between aid and growth but a lack of distinction between aid that promotes inappropriate expectations.

Political stability is an overarching structure that is too greatly discounted in the Harrod-Domar model. The UN in their investigation of development issues in Haiti came to the conclusion that 'political stability is a requisite for sustained economic development' (p. 22), without the certainty of safety and control economic growth cannot occur. This view is supported in the work of Jaramillo and Sancak (2007) as they focus on institutional quality as one of the cornerstones

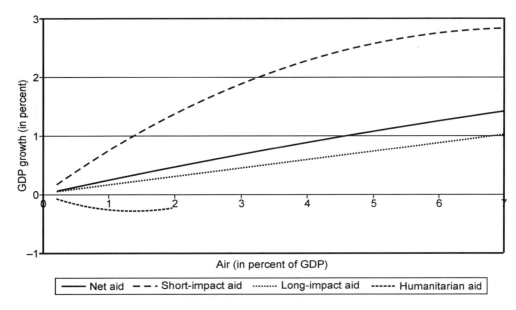

Figure 4.4: Impact of Different Types of Aid on Growth

Source: Radelet, Clemens and Bhavnani (2004).

to lay the groundwork for economic growth. They use the Polity IV database to illustrate the political instability in Haiti (Figure 4.5) and the Dominican Republic (Figure 4.6). These figures designate a relative political order with scores of + 6 or greater identifying democracy and –6 or below identifying autocracy. Dashed lines indicate a time of transition or interruption and letters given include C (political coup), X (autocratic backsliding), A (significant authority initiated change), and S (state failure events).

Since 1945, the Dominican Republic has been relatively more democratic than Haiti with significantly less political coups. If we focus on the 19 years investigated in this study we see a tumultuous pattern of democracy and autocracy in Haiti, leading to uncertain policy and inability to effectively control or impact national outcomes, while the Dominican Republic has been a genuinely coherent democracy.

The final alteration of the Harrod-Domar model pertinent to Haiti is the inclusion of environmental degradation. Deforestation, soil depreciation, and the reliance on wood charcoal as a source of fuel have been identified as one of the main distinctions between Haiti and the Dominican Republic (Diamond, 2005 and Faria and Sanchez-Fung, 2009). Hamilton and Clemens (1999) propose a genuine savings rate – traditional net savings less the value of resource depletion and environmental degradation plus the value of investment in human capital. Their 1993 estimates of genuine savings rate in Haiti and the Dominican Republic widen the divide between the two countries; standard savings calculated in this study showed a disparity of 11 per cent in favour of the Dominican Republic, while the discrepancy expanded using genuine savings rate to 29.4 per cent. The use of genuine savings rate in place of standard or net savings

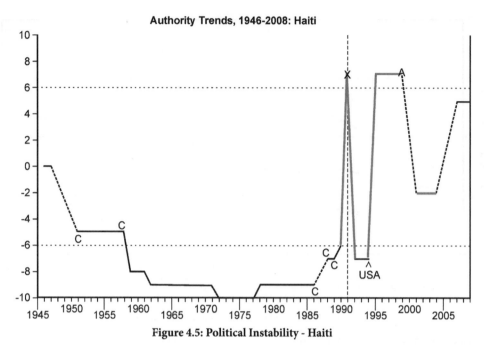

Figure 4.5: Political Instability - Haiti

Source: www.systemicpeace.org/polity/polity4.htm

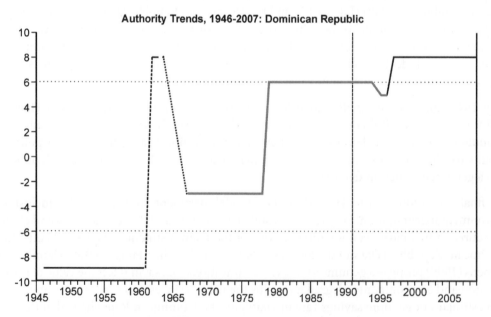

Figure 4.6: Political Instability – Dominican Republic

Source: www.systemicpeace.org/polity/polity4.htm

rate may provide clarification for Haiti's stagnant growth when substituted in the Harrod-Domar Model.

CONCLUSION

Differences in economic growth between Haiti and the Dominican Republic cannot be solely explained with the use of the Harrod-Domar model. Although the model explains and predicts economic growth outcomes in the Dominican Republic, the original model is not useful when applied to Haiti. There is a disconnect between the expected rate of the GDP growth calculated by the Harrod-Domar model and the recorded rate of growth for the country, identifying a significant financing gap to reach the meager expected growth rate of 2.34 per cent.

To close the gap with the Dominican Republic and the rest of Latin America, Haiti must target a much larger growth rate requiring more external aid to fill their financing gap. The accumulation of aid, however, is not a setback in Haiti, as they have over four times the amount of outside financial assistance as the Dominican Republic. Instead, there seems to be an interruption in the transformation from aid to investment to growth in Haiti, evident in a 430 per cent increase in aid from 1990 to 2008 but only a 7.9 per cent increase in real GDP over the same time period.

Factors that influence the efficiency in the use and administration of savings and aid include: elaborated expectations for the type of aid received, continued political instability, and poor environmental practices. In relation to the Dominican Republic, Haitian aid is proportionally more humanitarian and long term, categories of aid that are not correlated with direct economic growth. Much of this aid is designed to overcome the ever changing political structures of the country, dissuading investment and consequently limiting economic growth. Lastly, environmental policies have depleted the available resources in Haiti, rendering economic development difficult. Future studies should focus on sorting different types of aid prior to the research as well as substituting the genuine savings rate for the net savings rate when applying the Harrod-Domar model.

REFERENCES

1. Bauer, Peter Thomas. *Dissent on Development: Studies and Debates in Development Economics*. Cambridge, Massachusetts: Harvard University Press, 1972.
2. Brean, Joseph. "Countries in Contrast: One land, two fates." *Nationalpost.com*. 18 January 2010. http://www.nationalpost.com/news/world/story.html?id=2454507.
3. Burnside, Craig and David Dollar. "Aid, Policies, and Growth." *American Economic Review* 90, No. 4 (2000): 847-868.
4. Collier, Paul and David Dollar. "Development Effectiveness: What have we Learnt?" *Economic Journal* 114, No. 496 (2004): 244-271.
5. Dalard, Carl-Johan and Henrick Hansen. "On Aid, Growth, and Good Policies." *CREDIT Research Paper*, No. 00/17 (2000)
6. Diamond, Jared. *Collapse*. New York: Penguin Group, 2005.
7. Easterly, William. "The Ghost of the Financing Gap: How the Harrod-Domar Growth Model Still

Haunts Development Economics," *World Bank Policy Research Working Paper*, No. 1807 (1997): p. 40.

8. Faria, Joao and Jose R. Sanchez-Fung. "The Economy and the Environment in the Dominican Republic and Haiti: What Explains the Differences?" Discussion Paper, *Kingston upon Thames* (2009): p. 21.

9. Fasano, Ugo. "Haiti's Economic Development Since 2004/05 and Macroeconomic Outlook." Presentation, The American-Haiti Chamber of Commerce, Port-au-Prince, Haiti, 1 July 2009.

10. Hamilton, Kirk and Michael Clemens. "Genuine Savings Rate in Developing Countries," *The World Bank Economic Review* 13, No. 3 (1999): 333-356.

11. Hansen, Henrik and Finn Tarp. "Aid Effectiveness Disputed." *Journal of International Development* 12 (2000): 375-398.

12. Jaramillo, Laura and Cemile Sancak. "Growth in the Dominican Republic and Haiti: Why has the Grass Been Greener on One Side of Hispaniola?" *IMF Working Papers*, No. 07/63 (2007)

13. Kuznets, Simon. *Gross Capital Formation: 1919-1933*. Cambridge, Massachusetts: NBER Books, 1934.

14. Lensink, Robert and Howard White. "Are there Negative Returns to Aid?" *Journal of Development Studies* 37, No. 6 (2001): 42-65.

15. Marshall, Monty (Director). "Polity IV Project." *Center for Systemic Peace*. http://systemicpeace.org/polity/polity4.htm (accessed February 25, 2010)

16. "OECD StatExtracts." *Organization for Economic Co-operation and Development*. http://stats.oecd.org/index.aspx (accessed February 25, 2010)

17. Radalet, Steve, Clemens, Michael and Rikhil Bhavnani. "Aid and Growth: The Current Debate and Some New Evidence." In *The Macroeconomic Management of Foreign Aid*, edited by Peter Isard, 43-60. International Monetary Fund, 2006.

18. Rosenstein-Rodan, Paul. "International Aid for Underdeveloped Contries." *Review of Economics and Statistics* 43 (1961): 107-148.

19. Rostow, Walt Whitman. *The Stages of Economic Growth: A Non-Communist Manifesto*. London: Cambridge, 1960.

20. Shields, Michael. "Foreign Aid and Domestic Savings: The Crowding Out Effect," *Monash Economics Working Papers* 35, No. 7 (2007): p. 15.

21. Silver, Alexandra. "Haiti and the Dominican Republic: A Tale of Two Countries." *Time.com*. 19 January 2010: http://www.time.com/time/world/article/0,8599,1953959,00.html.

22. Snyder, Daniel. "Foreign Aid and Domestic Savings: A Spurious Correlation?" *Economic Development and Cultural Change* 39, No. 1 (1990): 175-181.

23. Todaro, Michael and Stephen Smith. *Economic Development*. Boston: Addison Wesley, 2003.

24. "UN Data." *United Nations*. http://data.un.org/ (accessed 25 February 2010)

25. United Nations Economic Comission for Latin America and the Caribbean-ECLAC. *Haiti: Short and Long-Term Development Issues*. 18 October 2005.

26. Westerberg, Lotta. "Foreign Aid and Economic Growth in Ecuador: A Test of the Harrod-Domar/Financing Gap Growth Model." *Scribd*: http://www.scribd.com/doc/24708419/A-Test-of-the-Harrod-Domar-Financing-Gap-Growth-Model-Ecuador (accessed 20 February 2010)

27. "World Economic Outlook Database." *International Monetary Fund*, 2009: http://www.imf.org/external/pubs/ft/weo/2009/02/weodata/index.aspx.

5

Investigating Economic Growth in LDCs from Child Labour

Shreya Hersh Mehta

CHAPTER SUMMARY

The 20th and 21st centuries have shown that the developed countries' economies have been experiencing profound economic growth due to globalization. The magnitude of these changes and transformations has sparked concerns over the actions taken by least developed nations (LDCs) who are pressured to achieve the same level of economic prosperity. One specific concern has been over the subtleness of allowing child labour as a method of achieving economic growth for LDCs.

It has been heavily debated whether or not child labour contributes to economic growth for LDCs. This chapter investigates the employment of child labour on economic growth in LDCs. This chapter will NOT address morals or ethics on the issue. Rather, this chapter analyzes theoretical economics of trade and labour. It will further investigate the benefits and consequences attributed from child labour on LDCs.

The chapter is divided as follows: (1) Definition of child labour (2) Literature review on contributing factors to child labour (3) Theoretical arguments for trade and labour (4) Empirical case study on India's child labour and its economic impacts on LDCs (5) Concluding remarks on policy reformation.

DEFINITION OF CHILD LABOUR

There is no consensus on the basic definition of child labour. Even within the organization (e.g. the ILO or UNICEF) the concept of 'children's work' has various meanings depending on the organization, or the author, or the topic. 'The definition of *work* is marked by moral attitude, which determines the activities which should or should not count as work. One problem arises from the fact that ILO sees work as an economic activity that contributes to the gross national product'(Liebel, 2004:43-45). For this chapter we will define child labour as a person, age of 15 or younger employed in an economic activity that contributes to the economic welfare of a family, and overall a nation's GDP.

LITERATURE REVIEW ON THE CONTRIBUTING FACTORS TO CHILD LABOUR

According to currently available ILO estimates, 211 million children between the age of of 5 and 14 were 'economically active' in the year of 2000. Statistics show that most of the economically active children are in developing countries where participation rate of the 5 to 14 age group ranges between 15 per cent and 29 per cent. It is estimated that only 4 per cent of all working children are actually engaged in what international conventions call 'unconditional worse' forms of child labour (Cigno, 2005:1).

In recent years, the impact of globalization on the incidence of child labour has started to spark both public and academic debate, and has become an issue because academia, scholars, economists, politicians, and citizens who question whether or not child labour provides economic benefits in developing countries. The prevalent existence of child labour requires a deeper understanding of the determinants of child labour. By doing so, we can also understand its welfare implications.

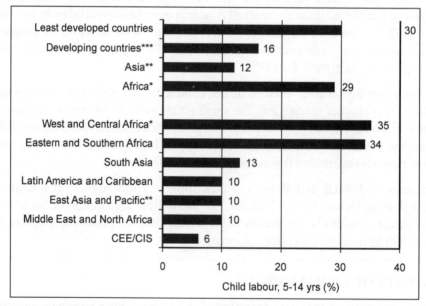

Figure 5.1: Children Aged 5-14 Engaged in Child Labour (%), by Region (1999-2008)

Source: UNICEF SOWC 2010.

Child labour has been argued to be ethically unacceptable, hence scholars argue that 'the arguments in favour of child labour echoed those which defended the slave trade: the assertion that if England were to shorten the working day for the labour of children, others would gain an advantage, paralleled that which insisted that if England were to abandon the sale trade her rivals would seize it' (Seabrook, 2001:1). These scholars also argue that child labour is 'one of the most monstrous of many institutionalised injustices…it is perhaps, the greatest reproach to a model of growth and development that is now uncontested in the world' (Seabrook, 2001:47).

Scholars who counter this viewpoint do not necessarily promote child labour, but rather argue that banning it would have serious impact on the economic welfare of impoverished families. These scholars have been misconstrued as promoting the exploitation of child workers. In contrast, these economists argue that child labour is 'the individual optimization assumption underlying standard economic thinking.'(Cigno, 2005:224). In this case, Cigno argues that public intervention in child labour is *only* justified if there is a coordination failure (i.e. efficiency considerations), or on the grounds of social justice (i.e. equity considerations).

Bearing these concepts in mind, this chapter aims to provide a deeper understanding of why non-exploitive children choose to work and the how their labour impacts the economies of LDCs. This chapter also questions if these economic impacts help LDCs become self-sustaining economies.

The Supply Side

There have been several major contributing factors to child labour. On the micro level, case studies have shown that the fundamental determinants of child labour are often impoverished parents that sent their children to work in order to survive as a family. Even parents, altruistic in nature, must send their children to work in order to secure some type of income. 'There is by now a virtually unanimous view that poverty is the main, although not the only cause, of child labour' (Ahmed, 1999). Second, families on the brink of poverty want to secure income to prevent the possibility of future economic crises. This additional income provided by a child can secure stability for a short run. Third, rural populations in LDCs lack access to credit. 'Poor parents will often face binding credit constraints, and whilst they are unable to borrow money they are able to send their children to work' (Neumayer & Soysa, 2004:44). Fourth, schooling in the developing world has come at a cost for impoverished families. The problem here is that the gains of education are only seen in long term. For parents to pay for tuition, books, uniforms, schooling does not appear to be as worthwhile. As it turns out, all of these factors contribute to temporary work and a temporary desperate need for income. Kaushik Basu so eloquently phrased the supply factors of child labour as detrimental to LDCs. 'It's a failure to recognize that (1) parents do not typically send their children to work out of sloth but out of desperation, and (2) it is possible for children to suffer a worse fate than labour, such as starvation' (Basu, 2001:491). However, they usually translate into more dependency on permanent employment.

On a macro level, developing countries have also been a supplying factor in allowing child labour to exist. As of January 2007, 150 governments were members of the GATT/WTO, obliging member countries to negotiate the reduction of tariffs, eliminate non-tariff barriers, and refrain from discriminatory treatment. As a result, human rights groups have been unable to make recognition of workers' rights, (e.g. prohibiting child labour) a condition for trade under the GATT/WTO agreement. 'Developing countries have opposed such restrictions, arguing that the measures are protectionist and would hinder developing countries from competing with developed countries in the global market. These countries also maintain that such measures would only punish children who are an important source of income for their families' (Jonassen, 2008:18). The WTO controversy indicates developing countries argue that they cannot compete against the developed countries on the world market unless they take advantage of cheap labour. 'Since the developing countries are in the best position to assess their economic circumstances, the argument goes, it should be up to them, and not to their wealthier competitors, to decide what standards to apply'(Jonassen, 2008:26).

As Jonassen noted,

> These economic considerations shade into the political differences between developed and developing countries. Among developing countries, it is common to regard to the solicitude of developed countries for children as a form of hypocrisy that masks self-interested protectionism. The imposition of labour standards in developing countries would raise the price of their exports, diminish their competitiveness, and thereby subsidize the high wages of the developed nations. Whereas the industrial nations historically made ample use of child labour in building up their economies to the point where they could afford restrictions on child labour, the imposition of such laws on countries that have not yet reached that stage of development would condemn them to forever remain economically disadvantaged. (Jonassen 2008:27)

The Demand Side

On the demand side, employers often want children because they are cheaper than adults. Wages for are lowed and non-wage benefits such as medical insurance or pensions are virtually nonexistent. Additionally, children are more likely to tolerate bad working conditions and have a more flexible labour supply. Also, it has been presumed that children have "excellent eyesight, 'nimble fingers,' and small stature in an advantage in such economic activities as in carpet weaving and mining, and therefore seen as more productive workers than adults" (Neumayer & Soysa 2004:45).

Globalization has also impacted the demand side for child labour. For example, trade liberalization in a developing country, which is abundant in unskilled labour, is likely to raise the relative rate of return to unskilled labour, thus reducing the incentive to invest in skills and education. As a consequence, the returns to child labour increase with the substitution effect toward increased supply of child labour (Neumayer & Soysa, 2004:45). Hence, it is essentially free trade that induces countries to a 'race to the bottom.' Barton argues that if all other things being equal, 'investment location decision will be influenced by the relative stringency of labour regulations in various countries.; and this phenomenon should put downward pressure on labour standards in countries concerned about attracting foreign direct investment' (Barton, 2006:189).

'A higher extent of child labour could cut costs to help a country gain a competitive advantage over others. Hence, since all countries face this incentive, increase trade openness could bring about an increased incidence of child labor all over the world. (Neumayer & Soysa, 2004:45). Because of this demand, developing countries continue to have lax labour standards and low wages for their abundant supply of unskilled labour, which provide a haven for foreign investors. 'High-profile cases such as Nike, Reebok, and Adidas show that multinational corporations do at times subcontract to enterprises that employ children' (Neumayer & Soysa, 2004:45).

Theoretical Section

Traditional trade theories, such as the Heckscher-Ohlin (H-O) Theorem provide a foundational understanding of economies in LDCs. The Heckscher-Ohlin Theory argues that even if technology of production of the same goods across countries is exactly the same, trade can still be beneficial, due to the differences in the factor of abundance. The H-O theorem essentially states that a country should open itself to trade and should do so by specializing in the production of that good which is intensive in its abundant factor. The theory states: the two factors of production are capital (k) and labour (l); the two goods are x and y; wage rate is (w) and rental rate is (r); and the two countries are A and B.

Then the assumptions would follow as:

1. If $(k/l)_A > (k/l)_B$, then country A is capital abundant and country B is labour abundant.

2. If $(w/r)_A > (w/r)_B$, then country A is said to be capital abundant and country B is labour abundant.

3. If $(k/l)_x > (k/l)_y$, then good x production is capital intensive, good y is labour intensive.

Therefore, the conclusion is that a mutually beneficial trade would occur if country A specializes in the production of good x because it is capital abundant and its production of good x is capital intensive. Country A should export good x to country B. The vice versa would occur for country B, specializing in the production of good y and exporting good y to country A.

According to the H-O theory, LDCs have been characterized as labour abundant countries. LDCs have a

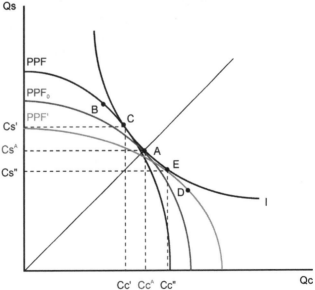

Figure 5.2: The Free Trade Equilibrium in the Heckscher-Ohlin Model

tendency of being far more labour abundant in contrast to developed nations that are capital abundant. Hence, LDCs should specialize in labour-intensive goods and export such labour-intensive goods to the developing world. LDCs' being labour abundant is inclusive of the wide availability of child labour. Because of this abundance of child labour, LDCs have little or no option to use or employ their labour at maximum capacity to produce labour-intensive goods for economic growth and prosperity.

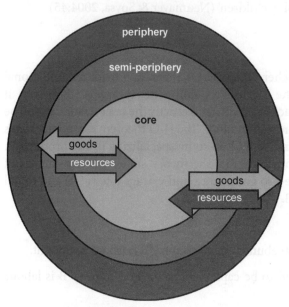

Figure 5.3: The Dependency Theory Model

The Interdependence or Dependency Theory by Theotonio Dos Santos counters the H-O theorem. The Dependency Theory argues that there is no such thing as a mutually beneficial trade relationship between labour abundant countries (LDCs) and capital abundant countries (developed countries). Rather, the theory argues that poor countries *depend* on rich countries for their economic growth. In this case, the rich countries are at the centre of the development system and LDCs are at the periphery. The Dependency theory argues that the world structure is such that the LDCs, "poor," supply raw materials and resources that are labour intensive to the developed, "rich" countries. The developed countries experience a faster growth rate in comparison to the LDCs as a result of using such raw materials. Hence, the economic growth of the developed countries is a pre-condition for the economic development of LDCs.

Santos argued that the entire system of trade and development is flawed because LDCs will be forever dependent on developed countries to experience even minimal economic growth. His solution to breaking this perpetuated cycle is for LDCs to unite and change this economic development structure of dependency. Hence, LDCs are leaving their economies dependent on the growth of developed countries. 'According to dependency or world system theory, foreign investors are the henchmen for lackeys of exploitation of the peripheral and semi-peripheral developing countries to the benefit of the core of the developed world' (Neumayer & Soysa, 2004:46).

At what cost is it purposeful to employ children if it really would not lead to significant economic growth and self-reliance? Should even minimal economic growth in LDCs be a case in favour for child labour? In the next section, the chapter examines how these theories of labour and trade has impacted LDCs when child labour is implemented.

EMPIRICAL SECTION

Case Study: Bhavnagar, India

Child labour has been the subject of a case study on its economic impacts in Bhavnagar, the state of Gujarat, India. The state of Gujarat is one of India's high-income states, ranking fourth in GDP in the nation.

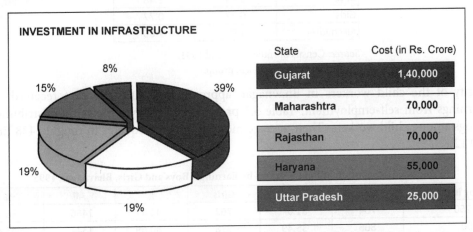

Figure 5.4: 1998 Gujarat ranks #1 in Investment in Infrastructure

The nature of this growth in output and occupations in Bhavnagar has been associated largely with the labour market that is 'unregulated or has the characteristics of an informal labour market' (Swaminathan, 1998:1515). Swaminathan explains that an unregulated or informal labour market has led to an exploitation of workers including children. In Bhavnagar, Gujarat, there have been two specific growing industries in the unregulated labour market: diamond cutting and ship breaking. These two industries have been thriving by avoiding legislation on workers' rights and as a result, have a high number of children employed in the workforce. 'An estimated 100,000 workers engaged in diamond cutting in Gujarat, as many as 15 per cent are child workers' (Swaminathan, 1998:1515).

Table 5.1 Child Work Force Participation, Urban Gujarat, 1987-88 and 1993-94[a]

Category	1987-88	1993-94
Boys, 5-9	0.2	0.6
Boys, 10-14	5.0	4.3
Girls, 5-9	0	0.2
Girls, 10-14	2.5	2.5

Source: National Sample Survey Organisation (1990, 1997).

[a] This includes principal and subsidiary workers.

The 1991 census showed that with a population of 400,000 persons, the literacy rate was higher than the Indian average: 83 per cent (males), 65 per cent (females), and 75 per cent for all persons aged 7 and above. It was estimated that in 1991, 1,655 of the workers in Bhavnagar were children.

Table 5.2: Child Work Force Participation, Urban Gujarat, 1981 and 1991
from the Census of India[a]

Category	1981	1991
Boys	2.94	2.48
Girls	0.77	0.77
All children	1.91	1.66

Source: Census of India, 1981 and 1991.
[a] This refers to the 5-14 age group.

Majority of the child workers in Bhavnagar, approximately 71.5 per cent received wages or earnings from self-employment. Table 5.3 presented as follows shows the distribution of earnings among child workers. Their average monthly income equates to roughly 438 Rupees (USD 12).

Table 5.3: Distribution of Paid Workers by Earnings, Boys and Girls, Bhavnagar, 1995[a]

Earning in Rupees	Boys	%	Girls	%	All	%
Up to 250	704	31.0	762	43.47	1466	36.43
250-500	806	35.49	538	30.69	1344	33.4
500-1000	641	28.23	432	24.64	1073	26.67
100-1500	95	4.18	14	0.80	109	2.71
1500-5600	25	1.08	7	0.41	32	0.79
Total	2,271	100.0	1,753	100.0	4,024	100.0

Source: Census of Child Workers, Shaishav-SPARC.
[a] Of a total of 5,631 workers, only 4,024 were paid a wage; 1,420 were unpaid family workers and 187 were unpaid apprentices.

The Bhavnagar case study reveals how much the distribution of the share of household income was contributed by child workers (See Table 5.4). 'In 86 per cent of the cases, a child's income

Table 5.4: Contribution of Child Workers to Household Income, Boys and Girls, Bhavnagar, 1995[a]

Share of child's earning in total family income	Boys	%	Girls	%	All	%
0-10	435	19.5	567	32.6	1002	25.2
10-20	896	40.1	685	39.4	1581	39.8
20-30	512	22.9	311	17.9	823	20.7
30-40	234	10.5	107	6.2	341	8.6
40-50	102	4.6	46	2.6	148	3.7
50-85	54	2.4	22	1.3	76	2.0
Total	2,233	100.0	1,738	100.0	3,971	100.0

Source: Census of Child Workers, Shaishav-SPARC.
[a] Of a total of 5,631 workers, only 4,024 were paid a wage; 1,420 were unpaid family workers and 187 were unpaid apprentices.

share was less than 30 per cent of the total household income. And in 14 per cent of the cases, child workers contributed more than 30 per cent of the household income. Hence, it is important for advocators and politicians wishing to abolish child labour to recognize that there is an opportunity cost of child labour as it contributes to a family's economic welfare.

Figure 5.5 measures child labour (the participation rate of children aged 10-14) with per capita income in the year 2002 across sixty-nine countries. The overall scatter plot does not show a strong correlation. The outliers show that few countries high levels of per capita income experienced a large employment of children in the workforce.

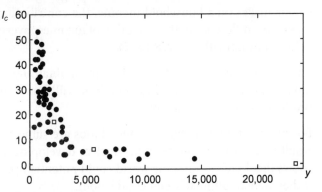

Labour Market Participation Rate of 10-14-year-old Children Against Income Per Capita
Data from Worldbank (2000) for 69 countries with positive participation rates. Squares show averages for economics with low, middle, and high income.

Figure 5.5: Child Labour and Per Capita Income Correlation

The Consequences of Child Labour

The Bhavnagar case study shows that child labour has contributed to economic growth in LDCs. However, this growth has raised questions about its impact over the long-term. Economists have conducted several studies to prove that the employment of children in LDCs has not equated with an increase in overall GDP, or improvement of an impoverished family household's income in the long-term. In Bhavnagar, Gujarat, the city experienced immense economic growth, which contributed to the overall growth of the state in India. But this growth came as a result of deregulating the labour market, and the ruthless employment of children. The prevalence of the expansion of the child labour workforce in Bhavnagar became an un-sustainable solution to aggregate the economic growth of the city, state, and nation as a whole.

Tesfay concluded that Bhavnagar's employment of child labour eventually stagnates.

> The supply of children in a deregulated labour market perpetuates a cycle of poverty in two ways:
> (1) By interfering with the accumulation of human capital, child labour reduces the adulthood labour market productivity of child workers, thereby discouraging economic growth and development.
> (2) By depressing adult wages, child labour results in households becoming more reliant on children as income earning assets. (Tesfay 2003:2)

Other factors also contribute to unsuccessful long-term gains from child labour in LDCs' economies. First, economists have studied the relationship between entering the workforce early and the gaining of apprenticeship skills and earning a higher income. 'Those who started working at a later age were more likely to have higher earnings than those who started working very early' (Swaminathan, 1998:1522). Swaminathan's data revealed that even with years of work, there is no advantage for children to have higher earnings. 'This data disproved the hypothesis that an early entry into the labour force is associated with acquisition of skills, better on–the-job learning, and socialization of work'. (Swaminathan, 1998:1523).

Second, child labour is notorious for keeping wages low. Despite the positive contribution their labour makes on a household income, the contribution is overall small. 'Child labour cannot make a big difference to the reduction of income-poverty of households to which these children belong' (Swaminathan, 1998:1526).

Third, child labour prevents children from obtaining at minimum a basic education. Without a basic quality education, these children will find it difficult to obtain higher skillful, higher productivity, higher paid jobs.

Fourth, children employed in menial jobs are subjected to health hazards, which in turn will result in a harmful long-term productive development for their lifestyle. The following figure shows that LDCs around the world could potentially experience sustainable economic benefits if they were to ultimately end child labour.

Economic Benefits Cited for Ending Child Labor
Banning child labor and educating all children would raise the world's total income by 22 percent, or $4.3 trillion, over 20 years, according to the International Labour Organization (ILO). The principal benefit would be the economic boost that most countries would experience if all children were educated through lower secondary school, plus substantial but less dramatic health benefits. The ILO analysis assumes countries that banned child labor would pay poor parents for their children's lost wages, something critics say is unrealistically expensive.

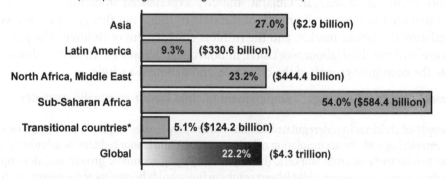

Net Economic Benefits of Eliminating Child Labor
(as a percentage of annual gross national income)

Asia	27.0%	($2.9 billion)
Latin America	9.3%	($330.6 billion)
North Africa, Middle East	23.2%	($444.4 billion)
Sub-Saharan Africa	54.0%	($584.4 billion)
Transitional countries*	5.1%	($124.2 billion)
Global	22.2%	($4.3 trillion)

* Transitional countries — such as Taiwan, Singapore and Malaysia — are no longer considered "developing" but not yet classified as fully industrialized.

Source: "Investing in Every Child," International Programme on the Elimination of Child Labour, International Labour Office, December 2003

Figure 5.6 Economic Benefits Cited for Ending Child Labour

CONCLUDING REMARKS

This chapter demonstrated that because of the paradox between the benefits and consequences arising from child labour, it is highly unlikely that impoverished families will be able to solve the problem. Child labour is not a sustainable long-term solution to secure economic growth for LDCs. However, it is difficult to abolish child labour in reality. Though banning child labour can potentially improve welfare of an LDC, it may also have distributional impact on an economy. In theory, if LDCs banned child labour, there would be a shortage of labour. Basu argues that if adults are substitutes for children, the wages for adults would rise. 'But as adult wages rise, it is possible, given our above assumption, that parents will now want to send their children to work. Hence, the ban may become redundant' (Basu, 1998:413).

The main policy for abolishing child labour is divided into two concepts: (1) Legal interventions (e.g. ILO standards, UN Conventions on the Rights of Children, and WTO safeguard clauses. (2) Collaborative interventions (e.g. the availability of good schools, the provision of free meals, and efforts to bolster adult wages).

In collaborative interventions, the government must take on a welfare-promoting role. Economists and politicians have advocated governments in LDCs to create and promote subsidized human capital programmes. For example, public support for education through schemes such as 'food for education' as implemented in Bangladesh. In the case of Europe, the government provided family allowances and tax rebates if children regularly attend school. 'Even if *legal* intervention in the child labour market is found to be undesirable, this does not mean government should sit back and wait for natural economic growth to gradually remove children from the labor force' (Basu, 1999:1093). Government should intervene in the market to create a variety of incentives, such as providing better and more schools, giving school meals, and improving conditions in the adult labour market, which result in the reduction of child labour.

Economists also argue that legal intervention is necessary. But because capital can move so rapidly from one country to another, policy change will require a multi-country coordinated action. 'The coordination has to be among the developing countries in their own collective interests' (Basu, 1999:496). Hence, at a global level, the WTO is the only organization with the potential to handle labour standards and policies. 'One beneficial effect of such standards could be the help that they can provide to developing nations to make a coordinated improvement in their working conditions, without causing a flight of capital' (Basu, 1998:1116). This is also a contentious topic, as it encourages protectionism, hurting not just workers in the developing world but consumers in the developed nations. Instead, Jagdish Bhagwati argues for 'methods of suasion' stating that the International Labour Organization should be the main international agency to strive towards better labour standards.

It is clear that there is no one solution that can ban child labour and still lead to positive improvements for impoverished families on the micro levels and economic growth for LDCs on the macro level. There needs to be an effective collaborative effort made among international institutions, developing countries' governments, and developed countries' governments to reduce child labour and ensure other means for LDCs to prosper fairly.

REFERENCES

1. Baland, Jean-Marie. "Is Child Labor Inefficient?" *Journal of Political Economy*. Vol. 108, No. 4. 2000.

2. Basu, Kaushik. "Child Labor: Cause, Consequence, and Cure, with Remarks on International Labor Standards." *Journal of Economic Literature*. Vol. 37, No. 3, pp. 1083-1119. 1999.

3. Basu, Kaushik. Van, Pham Hoang. "The Economics of Child Labor." *The American Economic Review*. Vol. 88, No. 3, pp. 412-427. 1998.

4. Jonassen, Frederick B. "A Baby-Step to Global Labor Reform: Corporate Codes of Conduct and the Child." *Minnesota Journal of International Law*. Vol. 17. No. 7. 2008

5. Seguino, Stephanie. "Gender Inequality and Economic Growth: A Cross-country Analysis." *World Development*. Vol. 28. No. 7, pp. 1211-1230. 2000

6. Strulik, Holger. "Child Mortality, Child Labour and Economic Development." *The Economic Journal*. Vol. 114. pp. 547-568. 2004.

7. Swaminathan, Madhura. "Economic Growth and the Persistence of Child Labor: Evidence from an Indian City." *World Development*. Vol. 26. No. 8, pp. 1513-1528. 1998.

8. Tesfay, Nardos Kebreab. "Child Labour and Economic Growth." Department of Economics. University of Saskatchewan. 2003.

9. Cigno, Alessandro. Rosati, Furio C. "The Economics of Child Labour" Oxford University Press. Oxford. 2005.

10. Liebel, Manfred. "A Will of Their Own: Cross Cultural Perspective on Working Children" Zed Books. London. 2004.

11. Seabrook, Jeremy. "Children of Other Worlds: Exploitation in the Global Market." Pluto Press. London. 2001.

6

The Problem of Child Labour in India and Rwanda

Amy Gregory

CHAPTER SUMMARY

Less developed countries (LDCs) struggle with the problem of child labour because of high poverty levels. The characteristics associated with child labour and youth employment consist of poor working conditions, pitifully low wages, and high rates of exploitation. Due to the lack of job opportunities, education does not necessarily ensure a job. LDCs face many hardships with child labour, creating a dependency. The International Labour Organization (ILO) report in 2006 revealed that in 2004, 166 million children between the ages of 5 and 14 were child labourers, which totals to 14 per cent for that age group. About 75 per cent of this age group engages in hazardous work, which can adversely affect their health and safety (Dinopoulos and Zhao, 2007). Children living in the poorest households 'and in rural areas are most likely to be engaged in child labour' (UNICEF, 2008). Labour typically interferes with a child's education and in order to prevent child labour, children's education must be secured. Child labour can be viewed as an epidemic of the global economy (Dinopoulos and Zhao, 2007).

The prevalence of child labour in India and Rwanda remains a constant issue. India faces many challenges with a dependency on child labour. In India, many laws have been passed to abolish child labour, but the issue has not been resolved due to lack of enforcement. A high drop out rate in schools also poses serious problems. Rwanda's story is similar to India, which makes comparing the different countries interesting. Children as young as six years of age, work ten hour shifts in Rwanda. The 1994 genocide put child labour in high demand. The ILO projected that 416,000 children between the age group of 10 to 14 are child labourers. By observing two situations in LDCs, it provides an assessment of different responses for improving the situation. However, regardless of these improvements, both situations need better solutions.

This chapter begins by addressing theories and explanations of child labour. It then analyzes the ongoing problem of child labour in India and Rwanda, including what has been done and what needs to be done to combat this issue. Use of empirical data will reflect the theories and whether they hold up or are inconsistent. It then considers how child labour can be viewed in a positive light, followed by concluding remarks, summarizing the findings in both India and Rwanda.

GENERAL THEORIES AND EXPLANATIONS

What classifies a child as a child labourer? There are various answers, but typically governments and international organizations label child labour as a child between the age group of 5 to 14 that is economically active or gainfully employed when they work on a regular basis contributing toward the output desired by the market. However, consideration must be given to those 'invisible' workers that do unpaid work, such as within the household. Insufficient data on child labour tends to be deficient because of under-reporting and restrictions countries make on child labour, many employers hide information on 'illegal' work done by children (Basu 1999, 1085).

There are different types of child labour. One particular type includes those in sweat shops. These children work in hazardous conditions. For instance, many children work in industries or factories that produce fireworks and matchboxes. One false move and the child could die from an explosion. However, factory owners and managers have low profit margins, and if they were to hire adults to do a child's labour, they would be required to pay a higher wage and would not be able to compete with other factories. By closing these factories, it would worsen the economic situation for these communities (Weiner 1991, 26). Another type revolves around the centuries-old apprenticeship where a father teaches his child how to toil the land in order for the tradition to be carried on. This vocation alternative differentiates from other unhealthy child labour practices.

Table 6.1 represents the participation rates in various countries for children in the age group of 10 to 14.

The ILO projected the data for 2000 and 2010. The first five rows reflect the distribution across the main continental regions of the world. The percentages have been reduced, but the overall numbers have increased. As the table shows, the problem is enormous, in particular for Africa and India (Basu, 1999, 1086), which will be studied further in this essay.

Theories originated by Karl Marx, Alfred Marshall, Arthur Pigou, and John Stuart Mill discuss child labour. Marx outlined a formal model of the cause of child labour. With the rise of new technology, such as machinery, children were employed because of their supple limbs. Therefore, capitalists employed women and children to work with the machinery. Marx noted that since machinery was:

Table 6.1: Participation Rates for Children, 10-14 Years

	1950	1960	1970	1980	1990	1995	2000	2010
World	27.57	24.81	22.30	19.91	14.65	13.02	11.32	8.44
Africa	38.42	35.88	33.05	30.97	27.87	26.23	24.92	22.52
Latin America & Caribbean	19.36	16.53	14.60	12.64	11.23	9.77	8.21	5.47
Asia	36.06	32.26	28.35	23.42	15.19	12.77	10.18	5.60
Europe	6.49	3.52	1.62	0.42	0.10	0.06	0.04	0.02
Ethiopia	52.95	50.75	48.51	46.32	43.47	42.30	41.10	38.79
Brazil	23.53	22.19	20.33	19.02	17.78	16.09	14.39	10.94
China	47.85	43.17	39.03	30.48	15.24	11.55	7.86	0.00
India	35.43	30.07	25.46	21.44	16.68	14.37	12.07	7.46
Italy	29.11	10.91	4.12	1.55	0.43	0.38	0.33	0.27

(*Source*: Basu 1999, 1086)

> Owned by one agent and labour by another, a diminished need for labour would tend to depress wages, so much that (1) it may be worthwhile for the capitalist to use capital liberally and (2) it may be necessary for workers to have their entire family work in order to make ends meet (Basu 1999, 1094).

However, Marshall furthered this theory. He observed that children laboured before the industrial revolution, 'but the moral and physical misery and disease caused by excessive work under bad conditions reached their highest point in the first quarter of the nineteenth century' (Basu, 1999, 1094). He also noted that 'the most valuable of all capital is that invested in human beings' (Basu, 1999, 1094). Controversy arose and people began to ban child labour.

Most early writers favoured bans, restrictions, and interventions on the quantity and quality of child labour. Pigou argued that a ban would cause 'poor families to dip below their subsistence level' and thought that a ban should be 'coupled with social welfare being provided by the state to the neediest families' (Basu, 1999, 1095). Some of the early writers believed in the need for government intervention. Child labour keeps children from receiving an education, which restrains children from benefiting from society. Mill thought that the positive externality of education rested on a parent's shoulders because for a parent not to educate their child is 'a breach of duty not only towards the child, but towards the members of the community generally, who are liable to suffer seriously from the consequences of ignorance and want of education in their fellow citizens' (Basu, 1999, 1095). Mill concluded that 'children and young persons not yet arrived at maturity, should be protected…from being overworked. Labouring for too many hours in the day, or [working] beyond their strength, should not be permitted' (Basu, 1999, 1095). The end result writers argued for relief by government intervention in order to direct children to the classroom and away from work. A ban on child labour was a second-best means of intervention because parents and employers make child employment decisions based on their self-interest, where the child becomes an instrument of their bargain (Basu, 1999, 1095).

Various explanations address child labour's widespread problem in developing countries. Two important assumptions comprise a model of child labour: First, a 'household with a sufficiently high income would not send its children to work' and second 'child and adult labour are substitutes' (Todaro, 2006, 373). It can be argued that children do not work as efficiently as adults, and adults can perform any work that a child can do.

Figure 6.1 below graphs the child labour model. The x-axis contains the supply of labour in adult equivalents and because of the interest in knowing the impact of the demand for labour the graph considers homogeneous units of labour (Todaro, 2006, 373). If a child labourer 'is y times as productive as an adult worker' then the possibility arises that one child might be the productive equivalent of y adult workers (Todaro, 2006, 373). The y-axis represents adult wages. If there are X children in the economy, it will equal yX (Basu, 1999, 1101). By starting with the assumption that all adults work, regardless of wage, gives an inelastic vertical adult labour supply curve called AA'. The adult supply AA' is the number of unskilled adults. If the adult wage were to fall to W:

Then some of the families find they are poor enough that they have to send their children for work. As the wage continues to fall, more families do the same, and labour supply expands along the S-shaped curve, until a wage of WL is reached, at which point all of the children are working. At this point, we are on the vertical line labeled TT', which is the aggregate labour supply of all the adults and all the children together (Todaro, 2006, 374).

As long as the wage rate stays above W, the supply curve remains along AA". As wage rises from W to W, 'one household after another withdraws its children from the labour force; so the total supply of labour keeps decreasing, as shown by the curve CB' (Basu 1999, 1101). The total supply of all sorts of labour plotted against the alternative wages of the adults gives the curve of ACBT. AB consists of only adult labour, and as it moves form B to C it includes more child labour, and from C to T this shows all available labour in the economy (Basu 1999, 1101). However, if the wage falls below WL, the supply curve will be along TT', and in between these points the S-shaped curve lies between the two vertical lines (Todaro, 2006, 374).

With the labour demand curve, D', if demand were to be inelastic to cut AA' at W and cut TT' below WL, then two stable equilibria will be present, labeled E and E'. If there are two equilibria, the bad equilibrium as E', an effective ban on child labour will:

Move the region to the good equilibrium [E]. Moreover, once the economy had moved to the new equilibrium, the child labour ban would be self-enforcing, because by assumption the new wage is high enough for no family to have to send its children to work. If poor families could coordinate with each other and refuse to send their children to work, each would be better off; but in general, with a large number of families, they will be unable to achieve this (Todaro 2006, 375).

Banning child labour, as mentioned previously, might be an irresistible policy when an alternative equilibrium is present, but while families of child labourers will be better off, employers might be worse off because they now have to pay a higher wage (Todaro 2006, 375).

Development policy poses four main approaches to child labour. The first attributes child labour as 'an expression of poverty and recommends an emphasis on eliminating poverty rather than directly addressing child labour' (Todaro, 2006, 375). The second concentrates on strategies to have more children attend school. Compulsory schooling seems to be a good idea, but 'is not an effective solution to child labour' (Todaro, 2006, 375). The third

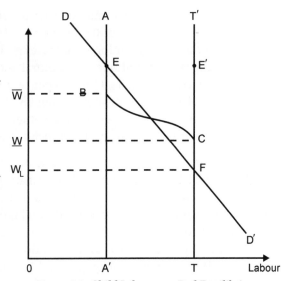

Figure 6.1: Child Labour as a Bad Equilibrium

Source: Basu 1999, 1101.

approach deems child labour as inevitable and stresses measures to regulate it to prevent abuse and 'provide support services for working children' (Todaro, 2006, 375). The fourth focuses on banning child labour. Many countries impose trade sanctions against those that 'permit child labour or at least banning goods on which children work' (Todaro, 2006, 376).

The theories help outline why LDCs have a continual problem with child labour. For countries such as India and Rwanda, they constantly deal with poverty and its effects on its population, resulting in high amounts of child labour. Bans and regulations tend to be unsuccessful because regulation cannot be enforced. The other approaches expand on these theories to illustrate wage rates and the ability adults have to perform the same tasks as most children, but many families rely on their child's income to help support their family.

INDIA

Unemployment plays an important role in the prevalence of child labour. India's unemployment rate at 6.8 per cent reflects the lack of jobs available. The employment rate grows at 2.3 per cent, but the labour force surpasses employment at a rate of 2.5 per cent, showing there are not enough jobs supplied to keep up with the demand for jobs needed. Self-employment makes up 60 per cent of the work force. This includes 30 per cent casual workers and 10 per cent regular employees. About 40 per cent of these employees are employed by the public sector. Also, 90 per cent of the labour force makes up the unorganized sector, which lacks benefits. The unorganized sector bears many problems regulating the minimum wage, partially because children can be employed for less pay since there are not enough jobs (India One Stop).

Child labour in India is a grave and extensive problem. India has the largest number of children employed than any other country in the world (Eco India). Children under 14 constitute 3.6 per cent of the total labour force. Of these children, 9 out of 10 work in rural settings. About 85 per cent engage in traditional agricultural activities, less than 9 per cent work in manufacturing, services, and repairs. Only 0.8 per cent work in factories (Indian Embassy). Around 90 million out of 179 million children, roughly 50 per cent, in the age group of 6 to 14 do not attend school and instead engage in some other form of occupation. However, many families do not report to the census, making it difficult to estimate accurately (Eco India 2008).

Laws have been put in place to fix the problem, but lack regulatory enforcement, which hinders abolishing child labour. The strategy for eliminating child labour began in 1979. The government formed its first committee, the Gurupadswamy Committee, to tackle the issue of child labour. The Gurupadswamy Committee enacted the Child Labour (Prohibition and Regulation Act) in 1986. The act 'prohibits employment of children in certain specified hazardous occupations and processes and regulates the working conditions in others' (Government of India). Following this act, the 1987 National Policy on Child Labour strived to 'adopt a gradual and sequential approach with a focus on rehabilitation of children working in hazardous occupations and processes in the first instance' (Government of India). The action plan drew on three strategies: a legislative action plan, a focus on general developmental programmes for benefiting child labour, and a project-based plan of action. The legislative action plan ensured that children would not be employed in hazardous conditions. The general development programmes focused on alleviating children and families struggling with poverty. Lastly, the project-based plan of action:

Envisages starting of projects in areas of high concentration of child labour. Pursuant to this, in 1988, the National Child Labour Project (NCLP) Scheme was launched in 9 districts of high child labour endemicity in the country. The Scheme envisages running of special schools for child labour withdrawn from work. In the special schools, these children are provided formal/non-formal education along with vocational training, a stipend of Rs.100 per month, supplementary nutrition and regular health check ups so as to prepare them to join regular mainstream schools. Under the Scheme, funds are given to the District Collectors for running special schools for child labour. Most of these schools are run by the NGOs in the district (Government of India).

Under the Committee, the focus remained on improving economic conditions for families because poverty remains the root cause of child labour.

The Scheme was carried out by various independent agencies in 2001. Based on recommendations made since 1988, a tenth plan strategy was devised. Some of the points include:

- Focused and reinforced action to eliminate child labour in the hazardous occupations by the end of the Plan period.
- Expansion of National Child Labour Projects to additional 150 districts.
- Linking the child labour elimination efforts with the Scheme of Sarva Shiksha Abhiyan of Ministry of Human Resource Development to ensure that children in the age group of

5 to 8 years get directly admitted to regular schools and that the older working children are mainstreamed to the formal education system through special schools functioning under the NCLP Scheme.

- Convergence with other Schemes of the Departments of Education, Rural Development, Health and Women and Child Development for the ultimate attainment of the objective in a time bound manner (Government of India).

Eliminating child labour continues to be the largest programme for the Ministry. In order for there to be progress, a holistic and multipronged approach towards poverty and illiteracy will bring about better results.

Under the plan of the National Policy on Child Labour, various other National Child Labour Projects (NCLP) have been launched to eradicate child labour. On 15 August 1994, a programme initiated withdrawing children working in hazardous conditions and to rehabilitate them through special schooling. Under the programme:

A total of two million children are sought to be brought out of work and put in special schools where they will be provided with education, vocational training, monthly stipends, nutrition and health-checks. As a follow-up, a high powered body, the National Authority for the Elimination of Child Labour (NAECL) was constituted on 26 September, 1994 under the Chairmanship of the Minister for Labour, Government of India. The functions of NAECL are:

- To lay down policies and programmes for the elimination of child labour, particularly in hazardous employment;
- To monitor the progress of the implementation of programmes, projects and schemes for the elimination of child labour;
- To coordinate the implementation of child labour related projects of the various sister Ministries of the Government of India (to ensure convergence of services for the benefit of the families of child labour) (Indian Embassy).

The programme established 76 child labour projects that cover 150,000 children. Special schools enroll around 105,000 children. However, more needs to be done to address for unaccounted children. Table 6.2 shows the figures of the state-wide coverage of children under the NCLP.

Much has been done to start the process of abolishing child labour, but child labour still consumes the bulk of India.

The majority of Indian children are illiterate, not enrolled in school, and do not have an education. In August 1985, the Ministry of Education released a *Challenge of Education – A Policy Perspective* review. The 119-page document discussed 'educational restructuring' to universalize elementary education, reduce the school drop out rate, create a network of 'model schools', use new communications technologies in schools, better secondary education, expand non-formal education, delink degrees from jobs, make education more 'socially relevant', and depoliticize the universities (Weiner 1991, 91). However, multiple failures followed in educational development, which were noted in the report. These included:

Table 6.2: Coverage Under National Child Labour Project

State	Districts	Sanctioned Schools	Coverage Children	Actual Schools	Coverage Children
Andhra Pradesh	20	807	43550	610	36249
Bihar	08	174	12200	173	10094
Gujarat	02	040	2000	023	1254
Karnataka	03	100	5000	024	1200
Madhya Pradesh	05	138	9800	087	6524
Maharashta	02	074	3700	024	1200
Orissa	16	430	33000	239	14972
Rajasthan	02	060	3000	054	2700
Tamil Nadu	08	379	19500	307	14684
Uttar Pradesh	04	150	11500	105	7488
West Bengal	04	219	12000	164	8250
Total	**76**	**2571**	**155250**	**1810**	**104615**

Source: Indian Embassy.

1. A quarter of the pupils in primary schools are under-age or over-age and the illiterate population keeps increasing with time.
2. Despite an increased enrollment of girls in primary schools, the situation in many states remains unsatisfactory.
3. About 20 per cent of those in India do not have schools, when most children live within one kilometer of a primary school. The schools themselves are unsatisfactory:
   - 40 per cent of the schools do not have brick or cement buildings
   - 9 per cent have no buildings at all
   - 40 per cent have no blackboards
   - 60 per cent do not have drinking water
   - 70 per cent have no library facilities
   - 53 per cent are without playgrounds
   - 89 per cent lack toilet facilities
   - 35 per cent of the schools have only a single teacher to teach three or four different classes; 'many schools remain without any teacher for varying periods of time and some teachers are not above sub-contracting teaching work to others who are not qualified' (Weiner, 1991, 92).
4. About 60 per cent of children drop out between classes 1 and 5.
5. While the literacy rate increased from 16.7 per cent in 1951 to 36.2 per cent and literacy grew from 60 million to 248 million, the absolute number of illiterates grew from 294 million to 424 million in 1981.
6. The regional variations remain large. Eight states have a literacy rate of five or more percentage points above the national average, but five states have literacy rates of five or more percentage points below the national average.

7. India spends 3 per cent of its gross national product on education, well below the percentage spent in many other developing countries and below the 6 per cent recommended by the Educational Commission.
8. Educational expenses are disproportionately lower in rural areas.
9. Expenditure on elementary education over a successive five-year plan has declined.
10. The goal of universalizing elementary school education remains elusive due to the rapidly increasing population (Weiner, 1991, 91-96).

These problems still persist. The Congress in India advocates to end child labour and establish compulsory education for children up to the age of 14 (Weiner, 1991, 7). Under this law, no child under the age of 14 may work in a factor or mine or occupy oneself in any other hazardous work (Weiner, 1991, 7). Schools still have low attendance, resulting in low literacy rates. The following table illustrates school attendance.

Table 6.3: School Attendance, 1981 (millions)

	Age Group	Total Population			Total Attending School		
		Persons	Male	Female	Persons	Male	Female
Urban	6--9	15.8	8.1	7.7	10.6	5.7	4.9
	10--14	19.3	10.1	9.2	13.8	7.8	6
Rural	6--9	57.4	29.6	27.8	22.9	14.2	8.7
	10--14	66.3	35	31.3	29.3	20.2	9.1
Total		158.8	82.8	76	76.6	47.9	28.7

Source: Weiner 1991, 9.

The school attendance figures account for India's low literacy rate. Less than half of the total population attends school. The table which follows represents the actual population, literacy, and illiteracy rates.

Table 6.4: Population, Literacy, and Illiteracy, 1901-1981 (in millions)

Year	Population	Literates	Illiterates	Increase in Illiterates	Literacy Rate (per cent)
1901	235.1	12.6	222.5		5.4
1911	248.2	14.7	233.5	+ 11.0	5.9
1921	246.7	17.7	229.0	- 4.5	7.2
1931	273.4	26.0	247.4	+ 18.4	9.5
1941	312.0	50.2	261.8	+ 14.4	16.1
1951	353.1	58.9	294.2	+ 32.4	16.7
1961	428.0	102.6	325.5	+ 31.3	24.0
1971	533.5	157.3	376.2	+ 50.7	29.5
1981	665.3	241.0	424.3	+ 48.1	36.2

Source: Weiner 1991, 11.

The Indian government's inability to end child labour and to establish compulsory primary-school education clearly stands out. As the population continues to grow, literacy and illiteracy rates rise as well.

On many occasions, families keep their children involved in child labour instead of letting them attend school. Parents become greedy and do not value their child's education. Parents need to know that their child is more important than the little income that they receive from their labour. Many parents take their children out of school and have them work to help the family. For example, Weiner accounted a father pulling his son out of school to work, but the son rebelled and his parents let him return to school. His father was not so poor that he had to send him to work, but families traditionally do not send their children to school. Many parents 'do not think, but just send their children out to work'(Weiner 1991, 55).

The school system in India does not contribute to bettering a child's education because of its deficiency. According to Weiner, the system 'is good for nothing' and does not build character nor does it prepare children for self-employment (Weiner 1991, 59). On various occasions, teachers do not show up to teach, especially during the farming season. Teachers do not have motivation to teach their pupils because of irregular attendance and parents do not cooperate to keep their children in school (Weiner 1991, 59). Further, a better education in an LDC does not guarantee a higher paid job or any job opportunity whatsoever. India does not have many employment opportunities in general for its population.

RWANDA

Similar to India, Rwanda struggles with its child labour problem but does not have the same hardship with unemployment. Statistics do not show Rwanda's unemployment rate. According to the OECD, it is not a serious problem. Pockets of unemployment exist around unskilled people, and among unskilled labour no shortage of labour exists. To tackle what unemployment remains, the government is in the 'process of creating a vocational training centre with the aim of training people particularly for middle management jobs' (United Nations Development Programme). Part of the government's agenda includes a labour-market reform to tackle deficiencies of skills in the labour force and to integrate Rwanda into the East African Community (EAC) by bringing up its skills levels to that of other communities (United Nations Development Programme). However, the OECD's argument seems unrealistic because the 1994 genocide killed and displaced millions. Instead, one would tend to believe this would result in higher rates of unemployment.

Despite unemployment not being as major of an issue in Rwanda, poverty levels remain high, factoring into child labour rates. Over 60 per cent of individuals live in poverty and about 42 per cent in absolute poverty. The 1994 genocide killed close to a million people, left a quarter of a million orphans, and over two million displaced (Organisation for Economic Co-Operation and Development 2007). This has worsened the poverty situation. The care for orphans distinguishes Rwanda's situation from other developing countries, which creates a greater need for government intervention to eradicate child labour because orphans are easy defenseless targets. Due to poor economic conditions because of armed conflict starting in 1990, those living under the poverty line have risen from 40 per cent in 1985 to over 53 per cent in 1992 (United Nations Development Programme). Currently, 57 per cent of the population lives below the poverty line (Organisation for Economic Co-Operation and Development 2007).

Poverty and child labour go hand-in-hand, but Rwanda has a high demand for child labour. According to a 2006 ILO global report on child labour, 49.3 million children are economically active in Sub-Saharan Africa. At 26.4 per cent, the region has the highest percentage of children between the age group of 5 to 14 who are already working. For Rwanda, the 2002 housing and population consensus states that 353,550 children or 13 per cent are involved in child labour. Within this consensus, it found that 47 per cent are boys, and the other 53 per cent are girls. This includes economically active children, which range from 30-41 per cent. The majority of children work in the agricultural and rural areas, but 'research has also found children in quarry work, coltan mines, brick making, sand harvesting, petty trade, commercial sex work, sugar cane and tea plantations, pottering, and domestic service' (Kisambira, 2009).

Rwanda's child labour law sets the minimum labour age at 16, but does not apply to children working in subsistence agriculture (UNHCR, 2009). Children under the age of 16 are:

Prohibited from working between the hours of 7 p.m. and 5 a.m. or from performing any work deemed hazardous or difficult as determined by the Ministry of Labour, and must have at least 12 hours of rest between work shifts. Subject to the aforementioned provisions and restrictions, children may be employed in light work at 14 years with parental consent. The Ministry of Labour can also make exceptions to allow children 14 to 16 years to work in a company or in apprenticeships. By law, however, the Ministry of Labour will only grant exceptions for light work that will not harm children's health or education (UNHCR, 2009).

The law also prohibits forced labour. The government continues to implement the National Plan of Action against Child Labour, which was developed with assistance from ILO-IPEC under the USDOL-funded Global Child Soldiers Project. It includes a five year plan of activities, such as the development and implementation of 'a national child labour survey and the development of a child labour monitoring system' (Organization for Economic Co-operation and Development, 2007). In 2008, the ministry of public service of labour in Rwanda announced its national policy on the elimination of child labour (NPEC). The policy states that a child is any person younger than the age of 18.

Rwanda combats child labour in various ways. The government of Rwanda continues to:

Participate in the 4-year, Kenya, Uganda, Rwanda, and Ethiopia Together (KURET) project, funded by USDOL at USD 14.5 million and by World Vision at USD 5.8 million. Implemented by World Vision, the International Rescue Committee, and the Academy for Educational Development, the KURET Project aims to withdraw or prevent a total of 30,600 children from exploitive labour in HIV/AIDS-affected areas of these four countries through the provision of educational services (UNHCR, 2009).

Rwanda's initiatives have positive results, but lack regulatory enforcement because the genocide left Rwanda severely scattered. Many non-governmental agencies work with the government in Rwanda assisting with child-headed households to help sensitize their needs. Local authorities help place children in foster homes and government-led facilities. The government 'supports 12 centers throughout the country that provide street children with shelter and help meet their basic needs' (UNHCR, 2009).

Education in Rwanda has started to emerge as an important factor. Until the 1950s, Rwanda did not have public schools and secondary education was only attainable at schools funded by Catholic missionaries. After its independence, Rwanda expanded its educational programmes. In 1989, education accounted for 25.4 per cent of its total government expenditure. However, the Catholic Church still plays a major role in Rwanda's education system. In 2000, projected adult illiteracy rates stood at 33 per cent (males, 26.3 per cent; females, 39.4 per cent). Education remains free and compulsory for children between 7 and 13, but the law lacks enforcement (Encyclopedia of the Nations). The number of kindergarten schools continues to be low and have few available urban centers. Primary schools have a higher demand, with continual increases in enrollment since 1994. Secondary schooling intake increased by 13.9 per cent since 1997/1998 to 2002/2003 due to the government's efforts to increase the number of students in secondary schools. The following table represents the school enrollment and literacy rates in Rwanda.

Table 6.5: School Enrollment and Literacy Rates 1980-2002 in Rwanda

	Rwanda	Sub-Saharan Africa	World
Net Primary Enrollment Both Sexes	X	X	X
1980	X	X	X
1997-1999	91%	X	X
Net Secondary Enrollment 1997-1999			
Female	X	X	X
Male	X	X	X
Gross Tertiary Enrollment 1996-1999	1%	X	X
Adult Literacy Rate, 2002			
Female	63%	55%	75%
Male	75%	71%	86%
Youth Literacy Rates (ages 15-24), both sexes			
1980	58%	55%	80%
2002	85%	79%	87%

Source: World Resources Institute 2003.

"X" represents missing information that is unavailable. Thus, the Table 6.5 reflects that the government's success can be noted in Rwanda's literacy rates and enrollment percentage increases.

The Positive Side of Child Labour

Families influence their children to partake in child labour. Instead of going to school, families stress the importance of learning a trade. A child becomes skilled in the factory, whether making firecrackers or another trait. If a father works in a certain factory, he might want his son to work there as well, which is similar to that of agriculture. The father brings his son to work in the field and thinks that if there is unemployment on the land, why not bring the son to the factory? By training the son, he assures his future in order for him to support the family. It models an apprenticeship. If a father waited for his child to be older, the work might not be available and does not guarantee an income.

Many families rely on their child's income from child labour. Child labour is an economic problem that must be dealt with accordingly, but without causing hardship to the families of the child labourer. Without various industries that employ child labour, these families might not have any source of income. By abolishing child labour, it would upset the industries, 'which are a major source of income in the area not only for the children, but also for the adults' (Weiner, 1991, 25). The government needs to consider that abolishing jobs would not be practical, but would upset many families and only fulfill the theoretical issue at hand.

Many examples of child labour can be discussed to show why child labour tends to be necessary in these poverty stricken LDCs. For instance, a boy shining shoes in India might not have eaten for days, and the payment he gets for shining a passerby's shoes would provide enough money to buy food for him and his family. If child labour were abolished altogether, this child might not have any opportunity to make any money to allow him and his family to eat (Kulkarni, 2010).

CONCLUSION

Less developed countries cannot fall out of the dependency cycle of child labour and poverty. The scarcity of job opportunities and willingness of children to work in hazardous conditions for incredibly low wages contributes to the unending cycle. Without regulatory agencies to enforce laws that abolish child labour, the cycle will continue.

The theories carried out by Marx, Marshall, Pigou, and Mill explain why LDCs have trouble combating child labour. Children's bodies make it easier for them to work with machinery and perform activities that an adult's body might not be able to do. However, all philosophers agree that bans and restrictions must be in place, despite whether they are enforced. A child's self-interest must be accounted for.

Wage rates factor into the equation of child labour's prevalence in LDCs. Lower wages tend to be associated with higher rates of child labour because adults will not work for low wages. However, if wages were to be higher, adults would work instead of children and the need for child labour would decrease.

When looking at India and Rwanda, vast differences arise in how child labour is dealt with in the two countries. India's problem with child labour suffers greatly because the unemployment rate continues to rise. Many action plans exist, but have not been carried out. The education system fails in many respects. Teachers are not motivated to teach and families cannot let their children attend because families depend on their child's income to help provide for their family. However, children should be allowed to attend school and not be withdrawn when families do not necessarily need the extra income. Education might not help guarantee a better job opportunity, but many families focus on their self-interests and not what seems best for their child.

Rwanda's situation differs greatly from that of India because of the 1994 genocide that killed about a million people and displaced many others. Children became orphans and child labourers. Many NGOs and the government have devised projects to combat child labour and help educate children. Rwanda enforces and regulates its laws more than in India as well. Regardless of Rwanda having a slightly better situation than India, more governmental regulation is needed to combat child labour because orphans have become easy targets for child labour.

When debating about abolishing child labour, the alternative of child labour as a positive aspect needs to be considered. Without allowing child labour, many families would be unable to support themselves. Families depend on their children and need the income. If a child contributes minimally, it might make a world of a difference to that family to help feed them.

Distinguishing between various types of child labour is important. Abusive labour practices, such as those where children compile matchboxes or fireworks, need to be abolished because their safety must be a priority. However, the more vocational and family-oriented work of children differs greatly because children are not in danger. If unemployment rates were to be lowered, more heads of households would be able to support their families.

Overall, child labour has many flaws. Solutions must be developed in order to eradicate child labour. Unfortunately, the situation seems to progressively worsen because LDCs do not have the resources to create better jobs and opportunities. Without regular strict enforcement to better the situation, LDCs will continue to address the cyclical effect of child labour and poverty.

REFERENCES

1. Basu, Kaushik. "Child Labor: Cause, Consequence, and Cure, with Remarks on International Labor Standards." *Journal of Economic Literature*, No. XXXVII, (1999): 1083-1119.
2. Dinopoulos, Elias and Laixun Zhao. "Child Labor and Globalization." *University of Florida*. Jan 2007. Journal of Labor Economics. Accessed 26 Feb 2010. http://bear.warrington.ufl.edu/Dinopoulos/PDF/ChildLaborandGlobalization.pdf

3. Eco India. "Child Labour." 2008. Accessed 12 Feb 2010. http://www.ecoindia.com/views/labour.html.

4. Encyclopedia of the Nations. "Rwanda - Education." Accessed 20 Feb 2010. http://www.nationsencyclopedia.com/Africa/Rwanda-EDUCATION.html.

5. Government of India. "National Child Labour Project." *Ministry of Labour and Employment.* Accessed 12 Feb 2010. http://labour.nic.in/cwl/ChildLabour.htm.

6. Indian Embassy. "Child Labor and India." *Embassy of India Policy Statements.* Accessed 12 Feb 2010. http://www.indianembassy.org/policy/Child_Labor/childlabor.htm.

7. India One Stop. "India's Employment Perspective." http://www.indiaonestop.com/unemployment.htm. Accessed 12 Feb 2010.

8. Kisambira, Timothy. "Child Labor is a Threat to Rwanda's Vision 2020." *Gender.* 10 Apr 2009. East African Community. Accessed 19 Feb 2010. http://www.eac.int/gender/index.php?option=com_content&view=articl e&id=57&catid=57.

9. Kulkarni, Kishore G. Personal Interview. 22 Feb 2010.

10. Organisation for Economic Co-Operation and Development. "Rwanda." 2007. Accessed 15 Feb 2010. http://www.oecd.org/dataoecd/27/19/38562991.pdf.

11. The World Bank. "Rwanda: Poverty Reduction and Sustainable Growth." *Poverty Net.* Accessed 19 Feb 2010. http://web.worldbank.org/WBSITE/EXTERNAL/TOPICS/EXTPOVERTY/EXTPA/0,,contentMDK:20204620~isCURL:Y~menuPK:435735~pagePK:148956~piPK:216618~theSitePK:430367,00.html.

12. Todaro, Michael P and Stephen C. Smith. *Economic Development.* 9th ed. Boston: Pearson Addison Wesley, 2006.

13. UNHCR. "2008 Findings on the Worst Forms of Child Labor - Rwanda." *Refworld.* 10 Sep 2009. Accessed 19 Feb 2010. http://www.unhcr.org/refworld/country,,USDOL,,RWA,456d621e2,4aba3ec624,0.html.

14. UNICEF. "Child Protection from Violence, Exploitation and Abuse." 06 Mar 2008. Accessed 12 Feb 2010. http://www.unicef.org/protection/index_childlabour.html.

15. United Nations Development Programme. "Rwanda." *Poverty Reduction.* Accessed 15 Feb 2010. http://www.undp.org.rw/Poverty_Reduction.html.

16. Weiner, Myron. *The Child and the State in India.* Princeton, NJ: Princeton University Press, 1991.

17. World Resources Institute. "Population, Health, and Human Well-Being—Rwanda." *Earth Trends Environmental Information.* 2003. Accessed 20 Feb 2010. http://earthtrends.wri.org/pdf_library/country_profiles/pop_cou_646. pdf.

7 | Family Planning in China

Svetlana Shegai

CHAPTER SUMMARY

The unprecedented population growth in the world poses a serious issue for its inevitable impact on the well-being of the humanity. In 2010, the UN estimates the earth's population to be over 6.8 million people, adding 80 to 90 million persons per year. 97 per cent of the net population increase takes place in the developing world. By 2050, the number is projected to rise to 9.2 billion with over 90 per cent of that population being in less developed countries. The major causes of demographic change today are lower mortality rates and higher birth rates.

Population growth has long been a subject of the on-going debate. Some experts assert it is not a problem per se and other issues such as underdevelopment, depletion of resources, their unequal distribution and subordination of women should be addressed. However empirical evidence supports the argument of population growth being a real problem. Michael Todaro and Stephen Smith point out to the potentially negative consequences of population growth that fall under seven categories. It impedes economic growth, exacerbates inequality and poverty, restricts educational opportunities, harms the health of mothers and children, increases food insecurity, degrades environment and contributes to international migration. The following major solutions to deal with accelerating growth are suggested: addressing underlying socioeconomic causes of under-development, promoting family-planning policies and programmes, using the example of China's one child per family law and curbing rich countries' appetites for world resources. The present chapter will specifically dwell on the one-child policy in the People's Republic of China. The chapter will attempt to review the policy from the times the idea emerged till the present day when it is one of the nation's key policies. It will look at how the state has pushed population planning further and faster than any other developing country and has achieved 'striking fertility declines almost unique in the annals of demographic history' (Draper Fund Report, 1980). It will consider the historical context stipulating the inception of the policy and how the policy was accepted and resisted by citizens. The chapter will also attempt to apply the economic theory of fertility to the China's context. Finally, the chapter will discuss international community's reaction to the implementation of the one-child law as well as some of the economic and social costs that China is bearing as a result of the policy.

THE PEOPLE'S REPUBLIC OF CHINA

Located in East Asia, China is the world's third largest country by area and is largest by population with over 1.3 billion people, making every fifth person on the planet a resident of this country. China gave birth to one of the world's earliest and most continuous civilizations and has a long and rich cultural tradition. Today it is one of the world's politically most fascinating, complicated, dynamic and significant nations. China is a multi-ethnic country with 56 ethnic groups who account for 8 per cent of the population (Xizhe, 2000). Established in 1949, the republic was politically and economically weak. In the present times, being the fastest growing economy in the world with the GDP of 4.9 trillion US dollars, China is overtaking the second biggest economy – Japan (World Bank, 2009) and becoming an increasingly influential actor on the world arena. *The Economist* calls relationships between China and the U.S. probably the most important relationships of today's world, and even more of tomorrow's. Below is the review of how China initiated and has been implementing one of the fundamental national programmes to overcome economic backwardness and become one of the world powers.

EMERGENCE OF FAMILY PLANNING IDEAS

Almost all Asian cultures are known for their strong family values. For many families in Asia, wealth is in their children who are often regarded as social, cultural and financial assets. That had been true for China for centuries. In the early years of the Republic however social scientists began to associate poverty, low levels of healthcare and education attainment as well as food problems with overpopulation. The idea of family-planning began to circulate in political discourse as early as the 1930s but was condemned by the Chinese pro-natalist traditions and the communist ideology (Scharping, 2003).

The Maoist government saw the county being more powerful with a larger population and therefore encouraged child-bearing. Against such backdrop, birth control was a taboo subject and abortions were punishable. However food shortages and economic crisis stipulated the imperative to reconsider the then policies pertinent to family planning. The Great Chinese Famine in 1958-61 took the lives of approximately 36 million people (Applebaum, 2008). No starvation of such a magnitude occurred in China afterwards and yet, in 1978, with the population estimated at 962,052,000 (UNFPA, 1979) there were approximately 200 million food-insecure people. Moreover, by the mid-1980s, nearly 150 million peasants and up to 25 million of city residents totaling to 50 per cent of the labour force were underemployed (Scharping, 2003). There were also a number of social challenges such as inadequate provision of housing, healthcare, education for the ever-growing number of school-age children that the nation had to grapple with.

Finally, there were implications of excessive population growth on the environment which were manifested in water and land resource scarcity, air and soil pollution, deforestation, erosion and desertification (Qu and Li, 1994). In the light of these issues, birth-control campaigns were viewed as a partial solution. The first campaign of 1954-1958 restricted families to four children and was mostly tied to educational work of the Women's Federation and the health clinics which began to propagate late marriage, promote new preventive techniques, offer contraceptive counselling and render abortions and sterilizations in a few special cases. Initially launched in one rural province, the campaign expanded further to all the densely populated areas in the countryside and eventually to cities. The second campaign of 1962-1968 proclaimed 'One child isn't too few, two are just fine, three are too much' (Scharping, 2003). The elements of the first campaign remained but were complemented by liberalization, free performance of abortions and distribution of contraceptives free of charge. The third birth-control campaign of 1971-1975 interfered in family-planning further imposing age restriction for marriages: 23-25 years for women and 25-28 years for men, plus a birth-spacing rule of four or five years between the first and the second child (ibid.). Unlike the preceding campaigns, the third one was successful in halving the total fertility rate.[1] All of these efforts were aimed at boosting economy but were justified as measures to improve health in the eyes of the citizens.

INTRODUCTION OF ONE-CHILD POLICY

In 1979, the Chinese government lead by Deng Xiaoping introduced a single-child policy that has been implemented by the State Family Planning Commission, the Ministry of Public Health, the China Family Planning Association, the All-China Women's Federation and a number of non-governmental organizations. At the 1982, Fifth National People's Congress, the Constitution was amended to include family-planning as one of the major state policies (Zhenming, 2000). One child per family is a population control policy that officially limits married urban couples to one child but exempts ethnic minorities, parents without own siblings and rural families. The latter are allowed to apply to have a second child if the first one is a girl or the child has a physical disability, mental illness or retardation. If a family lost their child, as in the Sichuan earthquake, the family is endorsed to have a second child (BBC News, 2008). Chinese citizens returning from abroad are also permitted to have an extra child (Qiang, 2006). The policy does not apply to the Special Administrative Regions of Hong Kong and Macau.

Government officials claim the policy is a great success as it has prevented at least 400 million births since 1980. The crude birth rate dropped from 33.43 in 1970 per thousand to 14.00 in 2009 (CIA, 2010), the population growth rate decreased from 2.58 per cent to 0.58 per cent while the fertility rate declined from 5.81 to 1.73 children per woman (UN, 2007).

Family planning programmes were promoted by three Chinese concepts of 'late, long, few' implying lateness in marriage and childbirth, spacing of children and reduction in family size (UNFPA, 1979). Each major movement or policy, particularly back in the 1970s, was supported by an incentive. To ensure the effectiveness of the 'one-child', the government used a range of techniques from propagandizing at personal communication level to social pressure and criticism (Schima, 1978). Young couples, for instance, received information on contraception at marriage, press was abundant with stories on the benefits of planned births and late marriage for the individual, the family and the state. Today China is providing one-child families with a package of substantial incentives. These include preferential access to housing, schools, farm land and health services, monthly bonuses, extension of maternity leaves or better financial conditions for paid maternity leave, paid nursing or caretaking leave, preference in recruitment for non-agricultural jobs and army, extra pension for employees and insurance for old peasants, higher subsidized food ration, preference in credit, relief and economic assistance, reduced procurement quotas of low-priced grain and other products, less collective fees, exemption from or reduction of compulsory labour and many others (Scharping, 2003).

Along with incentives, economic, administrative and disciplinary sanctions are imposed in a number of cases including having an unauthorized child, early marriages, illegitimate or early pregnancies and disregard for spacing requirements for second children. In urban areas, disobedient parents are fined up to six times their annual income – fines euphemistically called 'social service expenditures' which are an important source of revenue for local government in rural areas (Demick, 2009). In rural areas it is tantamount to income deductions. Overall, sanctions constitute fines, privately paid medical and maternity expenses, no bonus payments, suspended job promotion and demotion, possible discharge from work, possible revocation of business license or holding provisional registration, abrogation of leases of state, suspended medical insurance and social welfare benefits for unauthorized children, no subsidized grain rations, reduction of land allotments, higher procurement quotas for low-priced agricultural products, public criticism and more (Scharping, 2003).

ACCEPTANCE OF THE ONE-CHILD POLICY

One of the major arguments for the single-child policy is that depopulation will result in improving the quality of life today as well as for the future generations. The current economic growth in China is perhaps the strongest evidence for the validity of the argument. According to the Pew Research Center Report 2008, 86 per cent of the citizens are content with the direction the country is heading towards and the nation's booming economy. One-child policy is generally accepted by 76 per cent of the population. It can be explained to a certain extent by the economic theory of fertility.

Economic Theory of Fertility

The seeds of this theory were planted by British classical economist Thomas Malthus who maintained that the age at the marriage and frequency of coition during marriage, because abstinence was the predominant way of birth control, were the major determinants of fertility.

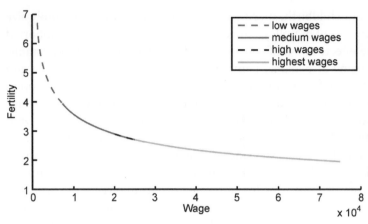

Figure 7.1 : Economic Theory of Fertility

Source: Larry Jones and Mich`ele Tertilt 2008.

Modern economic theory of fertility is based on neoclassical theory of household and consumer behaviour as well as the principles of economy and optimization. According to the traditional theory of consumer behaviour, satisfaction derived from consuming goods, which are determined by a person's set of preferences (utility function), will depend on the income and price variables. Gary Becker and Robert Barro translate this into childbearing analysis: children are considered as a special good and fertility is an economic response to the family's demand. So the desired number of children is expected to vary directly with the household income. Michel Todaro and Stephen Smith note the argument may not hold valid for weak economies which can be assumed the theory is applicable to the rising China.

According to them, it can be expressed as follows:

$$Cd = f(Y, Pc, Px, tx), x=1, …, n$$

where Cd is the demand for surviving children
        Y is the household income
        Pc is the difference between anticipated costs (mostly opportunity costs such as a mother's time)
        Px is the prices of all other goods
        tx is the tastes for goods relative to children.

So as wages grow up, parents may prefer 'quality' over 'quantity'. It can be manifested in spending more on each child and providing better health care and education which will lead to a smaller number of children. Becker and Barro argue that fertility depends positively on the world interest rate, the degree of altruism and the growth of child-survival probabilities. A negative correlation can be observed between increasing technical progress and social security and fertility rates. There is ample empirical evidence that support the theory. In early stages of economic development, in most countries women averaged six to seven births during their reproductive years, but in country after country, as development advances, this number falls to two or even fewer births per woman (Macunovich, 2003). As a whole, fertility rates today are higher in poor countries than in rich ones. Below is the specific example given by Larry Jones and Mich`ele Tertilt who use the U.S. Census Data on lifetime fertility and occupations to show a negative cross-sectional relationship between income and fertility in the U.S.

Table 7.1: A Negative Cross-sectional Relationship Between Income and Fertility in the US

Birth cohort	Fertility	Annual income in 2000 Dollar	Number of observations
1826-1830	5.59	4,154	452
1836-1840	5.49	5,064	1,960
1846-1850	5.36	6,173	4,520
1856-1860	4.9	7,525	7,241
1866-1870	4.5	9,173	7,347
1876-1880	3.25	11,182	3,203
1886-1890	3.15	13,631	6,644
1896-1900	2.82	16,616	8,462
1906-1910	2.3	20,255	11,812
1916-1920	2.59	24,690	46,908
1926-1930	3.11	30,097	97,143
1936-1940	3.01	36,688	44,428
1946-1950	2.22	44,723	62,210
1956-1960	1.8	54,517	71,517

Their 2008 study shows a clear relationship between fertility and income and the relationship has been stable over time. It therefore suggests fertility decline can be explained almost exclusively by increasing income.

Economic Theory of Fertility Applied in China

The economic theory of fertility holds valid for the China's context. Higher labour employment due to growth in industry and manufacturing in China is concomitant with increasing incomes and consumer spending. Asian Development Bank reports that per capita GDP has grown at an average annual rate of more than 8 per cent over the last three decades leading to a dramatic decline in poverty (2007). China's improved livelihood standards mean higher expenditures on education, medical care and daily life of the offspring.

Economic growth is also offering opportunity costs of childbirth: growing incomes and expanding labour market are attracting people, particularly youth of reproductive age, to transfer from the agricultural sector to the industrial section and focus on career-building. The situation is likening to the one in many developed countries where the number of families is dropping and the family size is shrinking to a large extent because raising children is becoming so time-consuming and expensive that working women either delay childbirth or forego it completely. Zhenming points out to another factor impacting fertility – migration to urban, industrialized regions. Having young children or being pregnant significantly decreases the odds of finding better-paid jobs. Finally, he states the cost of marriage, that is almost ten times the cost in the 1980s, is another factor deferring nuptials. Of note is the fact that giving birth and raising children outside wedlock are both subject to fines and societal stigma. Thus, Zhenming concludes the time spent on childrearing means lost money and career opportunities.

RESISTANCE TO THE ONE-CHILD POLICY

Despite reflecting modern day family trends and being generally accepted, there is also resistance to the one-child policy. In rural regions, where 56 per cent of the population resides (Embassy of the People's Republic of China in the US, 2007), the birth planning policy is considerably less popular – under 25 per cent of peasants support the one-generation policy. The late 1980s and the 1990s saw a large number of attacks, wounding and even murdering of the policy executors throughout the provinces. These days, conflict may take a form of riots but most Chinese avoid such clashes. Instead they find cunning strategies to get around the child ban. These include falsification of documentation such as medical certificates claiming the first child is chronically ill, misreporting ethnic status (Scharping, 2003) or resorting to fertility drugs whereby a woman bears twins, triplets or more (BBC News, 2007). Back in the 1980s, China had to deal with the problem of 'floating population'. Those were people who left their home communities to live in 'excess-birth floating villages' and thus avoided the registration of 'illegal' children (Aird, 1990). By 1988, floating population was estimated at some 50 million nationally, a decade later the figure doubled (Changmin, 2000). The strategies were devised not only by citizens but also by grassroots cadres. By the end of the 1980, the erosion of the statistical reporting system was a major problem as it involved gross discrepancies and exaggerations (White, 2006).

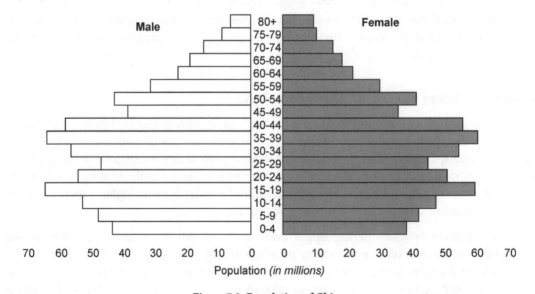

Figure 7.2: Population of China

Gender Imbalance

The loopholes above could be explained by the real economic and cultural need for more than one child especially in rural areas. It can also be attributed to cultural preference for boys. Since a married woman is traditionally expected to move to her husband's household, aging parents with limited savings depend on their children, especially sons who are considered to carry on the family line and provide for their senility. This gender preference has dramatically shifted the gender balance in the country as a result of increasing rates of abortions. The premature pregnancy termination has become accessible since 1979 when China started manufacturing and importing ultrasound B machines. In 1999, China was producing 10,000 ultrasound machines. Initially intended to evaluate women's health and pregnancies, the technology turned into a way to identify gender and terminate the life of a foetus in case it was a girl. Recognizing the peril of gender selective abortions, the Ministry of Health and the Birth-Planning Commission repeatedly banned the misuse of ultrasound machines. Today, families and doctors performing gender screening are legally liable. However people still find ways to circumvent the rules through corruption, bribery and personal relations. As a result, in 2006, male to female ratio was 100 to115. In 2009, about 126 boys were born per 100 girls – the highest gender gap in the world. Among second-born children, the ratio is even higher reaching 149 males per 100 females (Zhu, Lu and Hesketh, 2009). China is thus becoming a 'nation of bachelors' with the official statistics predicting as many as 40 million single men by 2020. Such serious demographic crisis gives rise to prostitution, sex crimes and wife-buying. Some experts relate this gender imbalance with growing crime rates. Reaching adolescence, boys idle and frustrated turn to crime 'without specific motives, often without forethought' (New York Times, 2008).

COMPARISON AGAINST SEVEN NEGATIVE CONSEQUENCES OF POPULATION GROWTH

1. *Economic growth:* Rapid population growth negatively affects per capita income particularly in countries which rely on the agricultural sector and experience pressures on land and natural resources. As mentioned earlier, the single-child policy was a measure taken by the Chinese government to grapple with economic backwardness.

2. *Poverty and inequality:* At the beginning of the economic reform in 1978, the World Bank estimated China's poverty – living under 1 US dollar – at over 60 per cent with most of the vulnerable population living in remote areas. According to the UNDP Report 2009, almost 16 per cent of the Chinese citizens lived on 1.25 US dollars a day in 2007, while over 36 per cent of the total population lived on 2 USD per day. Back in the 1970s and 1980s, the nation was characterized by inequalities. These days with the rapid economic growth and social development, inequalities in the country are deepening. It is primarily expressed in income disparities between urban and rural areas and across provinces. Non-income gap is widening as well and constitutes unequal access to medical services and education. The Gini coefficient in China in 2007 was measured at 41.5 (UNDP, 2009). There is a high risk that these inequalities can ultimately undermine sustainable growth.

Table 7.2

	Urban	Rural
Average per capita income (yuan/year)	1,789	441
Infant mortality rate/1000	14	72
Life expectancy (years)	72	64

Source: The National Health Survey in 1993 and the 1990 Population Census

3. *Education:* As a whole, large size families with low incomes are constrained in providing adequate education for their children. Overpopulation dilutes educational expenditures and lowers quality. According to the 1990 census, there were over 204 million illiterate people in China accounting for more than 18 per cent of the total population. The average number of years of schooling was 5.45 years which can be explained by young people quitting schools in search for jobs (Xizhe, 2000). In 2007, the percentage of illiterate persons has decreased to 6.7 per cent (Human Development Report, 2009).

4. *Health:* High fertility harms the health of mothers and children. It increases the health risks of pregnancy and closely spaced births have been shown to reduce birth weight and increase child mortality rates. Chinese women used to describe childbirth as a time when they had 'only one foot on earth, the other in hell' (Ren-Ying, 1989). In 2007, maternal death rate was at 41 per 100,000 (UNICEF). In 1979, the infant mortality rate was 31.41 per 1000 live births in cities and 45.52 in the countryside (Yan and Chen, 1990).

5. *Food:* Increasing population aggravates food shortages. Population growth causes over 90 per cent of additional LDC food needs channeling a large proportion of aid to food relief. During the food crisis in 1958-61, the crude death rate in China peaked to 25.58 deaths per 1000 (Yao and Yin, 1994). As mentioned above, food crisis was one of the main reasons behind birth-control campaigns.

6. *Environment:* Population growth is placing tremendous stress on the natural environment and resources. China's population growth significantly contributes to the depletion of land, forest, grassland, water, mineral and energy resources. Increasing demand for and consumption of these resources result in pollution of air, soil and water as well as irreversible damage to ecosystems (Geping and Jinchang, 1994). Despite nationwide nature conservation programmes, environmental problems are among the most pressing problems in the country.

7. *International Migration:* Population growth is considered to be one of the causes of both legal and illegal international migration. Todaro and Smith indicate, unlike the first six consequences, some economic and social costs of international migration fall on host countries which are mostly in the developed world. International migration has therefore entered a political dimension. Despite China's rising per capita income, there is still a large number of job seekers. Moreover, China is encouraging labour outflow as a means to reduce unemployment pressures (UN, 2001). University of Sussex and the World Bank estimate there were approximately six million international Chinese migrants in 2000 (cited from OECD Note). According to OECD, the actual number is most likely considerably higher.

Thus, China's overpopulation clearly entails the seven negative consequences argued by Todaro and Smith. Despite improvements in each of the category, Chine continues to struggle with the abovementioned issues.

Dependency Ratio

There is a distinct bulge in the youth and elderly population globally but particularly in the developing world. Such demographic imbalance leads to the economic dependency burden, implying people who are not in labour force need financial support by those who work. Dependency ratio is calculated as follows:

One of the variables in the dependency ratio is persons over 65 years old. The proportion of elderly population in China has soared from 4.9 per cent in 1982 to 11 per cent in 2007 (Peng and Ping, 2000). The distribution of the elderly is uneven, reaching up to over 21 per cent in some areas such as Shanghai (BBC News, 2009). Today people older 65 constitute over 130 million people of the total population rendering China the largest graying nation. Experts predict the accelerating ageing will continue and estimate the figure will rise to over 35 per cent by 2050 and consume more than 10 per cent of the national income. The ageing tendency in China is virtually inevitable, unless dwindled by mortality, because those who will be the elderly in the middle of the next century have already been born. Peng and Ping maintain China is not ready for such a rapid demographic transition due to the lack of resources and capacity to adequately provide for the senior citizens as opposed to developed countries who have established good social security and service systems. Moreover, in 1996 the Chinese government passed the law on the Protection of the Rights and Interests of the Elderly which reads, 'the elderly shall be provided for mainly by their families, and their family members shall care for and look after them' (ibid.). In this light, a phenomenon known as 'four-two-one' is daunting many single young people because one person is to support both parents and four grandparents. Despite China's economic growth, many citizens financially struggle with the four-two-one problem, unable to ensure quality of life for the people in their twilight years. And if a family is childless, the senescent citizens may find themselves destitute.

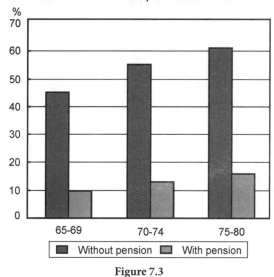

Figure 7.3

Source: Tabulations of the 2006 China Health and Nutrition Survey.

The bar chart clearly shows almost half of the elderly aged 65-69 per cent is not supported by social programmes while 60 per cent of people between 75-80 years old are almost exclusively dependent on their children (OECD Policy Brief). Well-to-do families can afford to resort to the services of private nursing homes transferring to them the responsibility of looking after their relatives. Such tendency is causing much resentment as it is being perceived as neglect and culturally unacceptable. Like in many Asian societies, senior age people are venerated and traditionally being looked after by their offspring.

Another side of the dependency burden is related to children under 15 years old. Before the implementation of the one-child policy (1964, for instance), children made up 73 per cent (Yongping and Xizhe, 2000). In 1990, the child dependency ratio dropped to 0.42 (ibid.). As per the UN Human Development Index Report 2009, children constitute about 27.7 per cent of the overall population. Despite the obvious decline the figure is still high compared to 18 per cent in the developed world (Todaro and Smith, 2006). The decreasing number of children leads to social negative effects. One of them is known as the 'little emperors and empresses'. There is always a tendency for parents of only children to become child-centered.

Chinese sociologists and government officials are concerned it is becoming increasingly true for the country where children now are often labeled as 'little emperors' – generations of spoilt, self-absorbed individuals with poor social communication and cooperation skills. It appears younger people relate with more difficulty not only to each other but also to older people. According to the 1992 Beijing Multidimensional Longitudinal Survey, almost half of the elderly interviewed agreed that young people had less respect to the elderly (Peng and Ping, 2000). So, while people of older age dot on their children and rely on them as they age, youth's perception is changing revealing more trends of neglect and irreverence. Egocentrism among only children is not the only problem. Studies indicate many children suffer from mental and behaviour problems that psychologists attribute to the absence of siblings (BBC News, 2004). Of note is the fact that some multinational corporations are capitalizing on China's one-child policy (New York Times, 1995). Chinese parents' trend to over-indulge the little ones was one of the reasons why World Disney has opened a large number of outlets throughout the country and Mickey's Corner is selling high-priced toys, accessories, and children's wear.

Thus, almost 39 per cent of the Chinese population is not economically active and causes a strong dependency ratio. It exerts a great pressure on the economy with a potentially negative impact on the future economic growth. The high dependency ratio also reveals dire social consequences.

Criticism of the Policy

China's birth-control programme is one of the most sensitive issues both at international and national level. It has evoked diverse reactions ranging from a medal for meritorious work granted by the UN to the Chinese Birth-Planning Commission in 1983 to repeated accusations of violations of human rights. John Aird, a former senior research specialist on China at the US Bureau of Census, calls it the most draconian slaughter of the innocents since the times of King Herod for coercion, forced sterilization and abortion, infanticide, and abandonment of undesired children. China has also been accused of imposing severe penalties including extortionate fines, destruction of property, imprisonment and even torture. Presidents Ronald Reagan, George H.W. Bush and George W. Bush used the 'Kemp-Kasten amendment' which bans the use of US aid to 'support or participate in the management of a programme of coercive abortion or involuntary sterilization' overseas (Smith, 2004).

At the conception of the one-child policy, coercive tactics ranged from stern propaganda and verbal pressure to denial of food and drinking water to violent sterilization and abortion of unauthorized children. In 1983, coercion reached the peak when sterilization was found to be the principle 'technical measure' and the government launched a mass campaign sterilizing one of the spouses in each family with more than one child. 1983 saw about 25 million sterilizations, almost 80 per cent were female (Aird and White, 2006). From a government perspective, the mandatory sterilization was advantageous over other birth control techniques – it was permanent and as such did not require further monitoring of unauthorized pregnancies nor propagandizing to have abortions. By the end of that year, civic unrest, particularly in rural regions, cadre frustration and harsh criticism shifted the campaign (ibid.).

The first deliberate infanticide in foreign media was reported by the *Wall Street Journal* describing obstetricians giving injections to pregnant women to have stillbirths, deliver nonviable babies or killing infants immediately after the delivery if the woman did not have a permission slip from her workplace. Doctors who allowed unauthorized children to survive were punished by demotion, salary reduction and loss of their jobs (ibid.). According to Aird, there have been some 379 million coercive birth-control 'operations' between 1971 and 1985 alone.

Part of the China's approach to family planning was the introduction of the eugenics law. The *New York Times* reports that a number of Chinese provinces enforced sterilization if either of the prospective groom or bride were found to be mentally challenged. In case sterilization was evaded, the couple had to do abortion. Gansu Province in northwestern China in 1988 became the first to adopt a law of eugenics. Seven years later, concerned by the opposition abroad, the law relaxed and was renamed into the Law on Maternal and Infant Health. The Law still aims at 'improving of the quality of the population' and makes pre-marital tests to detect carriers of hereditary disease voluntarily (Chinese Ministry of Health, 2005).

CONCLUSION

The People's Republic of China recognized the problem of the rapid demographic change back in the 1930s. It was aggravated by a myriad of economic hardships, food crisis and environmental problems. After launching three birth-control campaigns, the Chinese government resolved to introduce the one-child policy in 1979. The national government still believes it is the only viable way of controlling the country's population. Officially, the policy helped prevent over 400 million births. However the costs, both economic and social, are potentially very high. Some of them are already obviously manifested: the world's largest gender gap, the break with traditional family norms, the increasing dependency ratio with a rapidly ageing population, the spoiled generation of 'little emperors and empresses' are among the few to mention.

Experts predict such negative social consequences of the one-child policy can hurt China's economy in the future unless these issues are effectively addressed today. The Chinese government has been praised by supporters of the policy and awarded by the UN but it has also been opposed internally and highly castigated by NGOs and Western countries for gross human rights violations. Had not China accomplished such fertility declines she would have been equally criticized. In my view, China is a good example of determination to deal with overpopulation for the developing world. However, the means such as violence, forced abortions and sterilizations that China is employing to implement the policy can never be justified. There are certainly other alternative techniques such as empowering women through greater education and economic opportunities that China can utilize. Hopefully, maturing of the government in that respect as well as attention and pressure on the part of the international community will change the situation. Despite being exemplary, I believe LDCs will not be able to put into effect this type of family-planning exactly the way China has been implementing it for the absence/lack of strongly controlling governments and depressed economies. However LDCs could certainly imitate China's resolution to stabilize population growth since it is so intrinsically related to the economic growth and ultimately to the well-being for all.

NOTE

1. Fertility rate is the average number of children that would be born to a woman over her lifetime.

REFERENCES

1. Aird, J. (1990) *Slaughter of the innocents: coercive birth control in China*. Washington, D.C.: The AEI Press. pp. 1, 33, 73, 91.
2. Applebaum A. (2008, August 12). When China Starved. *The Washington Post*. Retrieved 9 February 2010 from *http://www.washingtonpost.com/wp-dyn/content/article/2008/08/11/AR2008081102015.html*
3. Asian Development Bank (2007, August 9). *Reducing Inequalities in China requires inclusive growth*. Retrieved 13 February 2010 from *http://www.adb.org/media/Articles/2007/12084-chinese-economics-growths/*
4. BBC News (2000, September 25). *China steps up 'one child' policy*. Retrieved 09 February 2010 from *http://news.bbc.co.uk/2/hi/asia-pacific/941511.stm*
5. BBC News (2008, June 6). *Baby hope for earthquake parents*. Retrieved 11 February 2010 from *http://news.bbc.co.uk/2/hi/asia-pacific/7440480.stm*
6. BBC News (2007, May 25). *Chinese challenge one-child policy*. Retrieved 11 February 2010 from *http://news.bbc.co.uk/2/hi/asia-pacific/6694135.stm*
7. BBC News (1999, June 9). *China losing fight to eradicate poverty*. Retrieved 14 February 2010 from *http://news.bbc.co.uk/2/hi/asia-pacific/364804.stm*
8. Becker G. and Barro R. (1985). Working Paper No. 1793 Cambridge, MA: National Bureau of Economic Research. p. 2.
9. Central Intelligence Agency World Factbook 2010. China. Birth Rate. Retrieved 09 February 2010 from *https://www.cia.gov/library/publications/the-world-factbook/geos/ch.html*
10. Demick B. (2009, September 20). *Los Angeles Times*. Retrieved 27 February 2010 from *http://www.latimes.com/news/nationworld/world/la-fg-china-adopt20-2009sep20,0,618775*
11. Ding Q. and Hesketh T (2006, August 19) Family size, fertility preferences, and sex ratio in China in the era of the one child family policy: results from national family planning and reproductive health survey. *British Medical Journal*. Retrieved 13 February 2010 from *http://www.bmj.com/cgi/content/abstract/333/7564/371*
12. Draper Fund Report (1980, March) No 8. *Birth planning in China*. Washington, D.C.: Population Crisis Committee. pp.1, 3, 13, 15.
13. Embassy of the People's Republic of China in the United States of America. *NBS: China's rural population shrinks 2007*. Retrieved 11 February 2010 from *http://www.china-embassy.org/eng/xw/t374790.htm*

14. Geping Q. and Jinchang L. (1994). *Population and the environment in China.* Boulder, CO: L. Rienner Publishers. pp. 1, 126.

15. Jones L. and Tertilt M. (2008) *Fertility theories: can they explain the negative fertility-income relationship?* pp 9, 54.

16. Kane P. and Choi C. (1999, October 9). China's one child family policy. *British Medical Journal* Retrieved 09 February 2010 from *http://www.ncbi.nlm.nih.gov/pmc/articles/PMC1116810/#B5*

17. Moe K. (2003) *Women, family, and work: writings on the economics of gender.* Oxford, U.K. Malden, Mass.: Blackwell. p.103.

18. Organization for Economic Co-operation and Development Policy Brief February 2010. Economic Survey of China 2010

19. Pew Research Center (2008, July 22). *The Chinese celebrate their roaring economy, as they struggle with its costs.* Retrieved 11 February 2010 from *http://pewglobal.org/reports/display.php?ReportID=261*

20. Qiang G. (2006) Are the rich challenging family planning policy? *China Daily.* Retrieved 11 February 2010 from *http://www.chinadaily.com.cn/china/2006-12/28/content_770107.htm*

21. Scharping T. (2003). *Birth control in China, 1949-2000: population policy and demographic development.* New York: Routledge. pp.30, 36, 48-49, 125, 132, 137, 141, 226.

22. The New York Times (1991, August 15). *Some Chinese provinces forcing sterilization of retarded couples.* Retrieved 27 February 2010 from *http://www.nytimes.com/1991/08/15/world/some-chinese-provinces-forcing-sterilization-of-retarded-couples.html?pagewanted=1*

23. The New York Times (2008, July 11). *Abortion and crime: the flip side.* Retrieved 14 February 2010 from *http://freakonomics.blogs.nytimes.com/2008/07/11/abortion-and-crime-the-flip-side/*

24. The Economist (2010, February 4). *As China and America square off in the latest round of recriminations, how bad are relations really?* Retrieved 14 February 2010 from *http://www.economist.com/world/united-states/displaystory.cfm?story_id=15452683*

25. Todaro M. and Smith S. (2006). *Economic development.* Boston: Pearson Addison Wesley. pp 272, 283, 292-293.

26. UN Data. Retrieved 08 February 2010 from *http://data.un.org*

27. UN Human Development Report 2009. *Overcoming barriers: human mobility and development*

28. UNICEF Statistic. Retrieved 14 February 2010 from *http://www.unicef.org/infobycountry/china_statistics.html*

29. United Nations (2001). *International migration: emerging opportunity for the socio-economic development of the ESCAP region.* Social Policy Paper No. 6 p.9.

30. UN World Population Prospects Report. *The 2006 Revision.* Department of Economic and Social Affairs Population Division.

31. Wei W., Lu L., Hesketh T (2009). China's excess males, sex selective abortion, and one child policy: analysis of data from 2005 national intercensus survey 09 April 2009. *British Medical Journal.* Retrieved 13 February 2010 from *http://www.bmj.com/cgi/content/abstract/338/apr09_2/b1211*

32. White T. (2006). *China's longest campaign: birth planning in the People's Republic, 1949-2005.* Ithaca, N.Y.: Cornell University Press. pp.145, 183.

33. Xizhe P. and Zhigang G. (2000). *The changing population of China.* Oxford, Malden: Blackwell Publishers, pp 1, 52, 61, 67, 78, 79, 86, 88, 130.

8

Seigniorage and Hyperinflation

The Cases of Peru and Bolivia

Colleen Farr

CHAPTER SUMMARY

Since the collapse of the Bretton Woods monetary system in 1973, countries have been free to individually control their own domestic money supplies. Money is not required to be backed by any supply of precious metals, and money can be created at the will of the monetary authorities, or in some cases, at the will of governments. Modern money supply functions smoothly for three reasons. First, money supply includes 'legal tender', which is made up of legally printed coins and bills. The legality of these coins and bills induces public confidence in the system, which is the second reason that modern money supply functions smoothly. The third reason is that there is an inherent responsibility of monetary policy to keep money supply growth at a reasonable rate. However, the lack of outside control in this system can lead to economic crisis. Because money supply no longer needs to be backed by a supply of precious metals, governments who have control over their monetary authorities can gain tremendous profit in printing excessive amounts of domestic currency. The profit that governments gain from printing currency is called 'seigniorage'. Excessive greed for seigniorage, and hence, excessive money creation, can lead to hyperinflation. This type of 'runaway inflation' causes economic collapse, poverty, and political chaos.

In the years immediately after World War I and World War II, Austria, Germany, Poland, Russia, and Hungary all experienced hyperinflation as a result of greed for seigniorage. These countries are often called the 'classical' examples. More recent experiences with hyperinflation have occurred in Latin America, including Brazil, Chile, Argentina, Peru, and Bolivia, and in Asia, including Indonesia, Malaysia, and the Philippines. Zimbabwe's inflation and money supply growth rates are currently out of control. Zimbabwe has claimed the title of the worst hyperinflationary episode in history, experiencing rates of inflation as high as 231 million percent. It has recently printed a 100 trillion dollar note (CNN,

2009). Other countries, such as the Democratic Republic of the Congo, Eritrea, Kenya, and Venezuela, are also currently on the brink of hyperinflation, experiencing consistently *high* levels of annual inflation in the 15 to 34 per cent range (CIA, 2010).

In this chapter, we will investigate two Latin American episodes of hyperinflation, one in Bolivia between 1984 and 1985, and one in Peru between 1988 and 1990. These countries were chosen because of their relatively short periods of hyperinflation and their success in halting runaway inflation rates. These countries also show similarities to the classical hyperinflation experiences in Europe in their origins and methods of bringing inflation levels down. This is in contrast to other more recent hyperinflationary experiences in Latin America, Asia, and elsewhere. After comparing the experiences of Bolivia and Peru, this chapter will draw simple conclusions regarding policy implications for current and future cases of hyperinflation.

HYPERINFLATION

While there is no formal definition for 'hyperinflation', economists generally agree that the term refers to a very large and rapid increase in price level. More specifically, an economy is said to hyperinflate when inflation is greater than 50 per cent per month. However, hyperinflations almost never stabilize around that rate, but rather, 'race uncontrollably past the 50 per cent mark into stratospheric, inconceivable rates of inflation' (Langdana, 2002, 115). In Germany in 1923, for example, the average price level increased by a factor of 20 billion (Langdana, 2002, 115).

In 1956, economist Phillip Cagan proposed a theory of the causes of hyperinflation which is widely accepted today. Specifically, Cagan studied the relationship between the quantity of money and the price level during the hyperinflations that took place in Austria, Germany, Hungary, Poland, and Russia during the early 1920s and in Greece and Hungary during the mid 1940s (Cagan, 1956, 25). Hyperinflation, he explained, begins in the month the rise in prices exceeds 50 per cent and ends in the month before the monthly rise in prices drops below that amount and stays below for at least a year (Cagan, 1956, 25).

Based on his empirical study, Cagan noted two important trends. First, 'the ratio of the quantity of money to the price level – real cash balances – [tends] to fall during hyperinflation as a whole but [fluctuates] drastically from month to month', and second, 'the rates at which money and prices [rise] [tend] to increase and in the final months preceding currency reform [reach] tremendous heights' (Cagan, 1956, 86). This second pattern holds the key to hyperinflation, but the first observation is essential in helping explain the second. Cagan's explanation of the first observation is as follows. Fluctuations in real cash balances result from the variables that determine the demand for real cash. Individuals cannot alter the amount of money in circulation, but collectively they can alter the value of their cash by spending or hoarding money, thereby biding prices up or down, respectively (Cagan, 1956, 86). During hyperinflations, there is a cost of holding money, 'which is equal to the rate of depreciation in the real value of money, or equivalently, the rate of rise in prices' (Cagan, 1956, 86). Cagan argues that at the beginning of a hyperinflationary period, issuing money on a grand scale does not immediately lead to extreme flight from the currency because of individuals' lingering confidence in its future value. Therefore, there is a lag whereby the expected price change rates do not keep pace with the rapidly increasing actual price change rates (Cagan, 1956, 88). In the later months of a hyperinflationary period, however, there is a shorter lag in expected rates behind actual rates, which can be argued is a response of individuals' expectations regarding continual inflation (Cagan, 1956, 88).

What explains the sudden increase in money supply? Cagan argues that issuing money on a large scale is a major source of funds for government expenditures. This revenue gained from printing money is called 'seigniorage'. The inflation caused by new money issue depreciates the value of the currency, and therefore places an 'inflation tax' on cash balances. The real revenue of the inflation tax is the product of the rate of rise in prices (the tax rate) and the real cash balances (the tax base) (Cagan, 1956, 88). This is a simple way to raise government funds. There also exists a rate of money issue that yields maximum revenue. Authorities issue money at increasing rates to take advantage of expectation lags and collect more money than they could while issuing money at a constant rate. In other words, governments respond to rates of inflation by accelerating rates of money issue (Cagan, 1956, 89).

Cagan concludes that hyperinflation can be explained almost entirely in terms of the demand for money, and this explanation places crucial importance on the supply of money. This implies that wage increases and foreign-exchange rate depreciation during hyperinflationary periods are effects of the rise in prices. Most importantly, during hyperinflationary periods, authorities issue money in order to raise revenue to cover costs of their budget deficits (Cagan, 1956, 91).

LITERATURE REVIEW

More recent literature on the causes of hyperinflation tends to extend Cagan's basic theory, focusing on the stability of hyperinflation and on money-financed budget deficits as a cause of hyperinflationary periods. Thomas J. Sargent and Neil Wallace (1973) study Cagan's same countries' experiences with hyperinflation, and argue that in explaining hyperinflations, one cannot regard money creation as exogenous with respect to inflation. Instead, 'the monetary authorities [seem] to make money creation respond directly and systematically to inflation, which [is] probably an important reason that hyperinflations [develop]' (Sargent and Wallace 1973, 350).

Similarly, Rodney Jacobs (1977) and Miguel Kiguel (1989) argue that the supply of money during hyperinflationary periods is not exogenous, but dependent on government behaviour. Both authors find that 'hyperinflation is the natural outcome of continued reliance on currency issue to finance a large portion of government expenditures' (Jacobs, 1977, 295). Also, Jacobs argues, like Cagan, that to maintain any volume of real revenue from money issue, a government has to respond to changes in the price level by changing the rate of money issue. Therefore, hyperinflation is seen as 'an attempt by governments to extract an excessive level of real income from the economy through the inflation tax'. As prices increase in response to increases in the money stock, higher and higher levels of money issue are resorted to in order to maintain the desired level of real revenue' (Jacobs, 1977, 295). For example, in China, between 1927 and 1937, the Chinese government ran a deficit of nearly 25 per cent of expenditures, which they typically financed through the sale of domestic and foreign bonds. However, when the Japanese invaded China in 1937, the Chinese government was faced with huge increases in military expenditures and no tax system capable of financing such increases. Because bond markets would not absorb any new bond issues, the Chinese government resorted to issuing currency as a method of financing the war (Jacobs, 1977, 294). A similar situation occurred in Germany after World War I, and by 1923, 99 per cent of German government expenditures were financed by the issue of currency (Jacobs, 1977, 295).

Robert J. Barro (1972) and Leonardo Auernheimer (1976) focus on the 'stability' of hyperinflation. Issuing money, they argue, will bring governments revenue (seigniorage) as long as the rates of increase in money supply do not exceed revenue-maximizing rates, which differ by country. When the rate of money supply increase is greater than the revenue-maximizing rate, hyperinflation becomes unstable and revenue begins to decline. If governments continue to increase rates of money creation, this will most likely lead to an almost complete flight from money, and 'any benefit derived from inflationary finance would vanish' (Barro, 1977, 989). Barro claims that inflationary finance occurs at great cost to individuals. This cost, or the 'welfare cost', he argues, comes from increased frequency of monetized transactions, in which individuals spend now to avoid higher future costs, and individuals' increased use of non-monetary forms of payment, which have higher transactions costs (Barro, 1977, 797). Finally, Barro calculates actual welfare costs and finds that for inflation rates between 2 and 5 per cent per month, the estimated welfare cost is between 3 and 7 per cent of income. For the 25 to 50 per cent per month range, the estimated welfare cost is between 11 and 22 percent of income, which is typical of hyperinflationary economies. When the inflation rate rises between 100 and 150 per cent per month, which is the range, he calculates, in which hyperinflation becomes unstable, the estimated welfare cost is between 22 and 38 per cent of income (Barro, 1977, 994).

EFFECTS OF HYPERINFLATION

Hyperinflations are among the most traumatic of economic disasters. They change lives, policies, and entire generations. Almost inevitably, hyperinflations 'result in the total overhaul of the incumbent government' (Langdana, 2002, 115).

Once the monetization of an unsustainable deficit begins, a country experiences a series of stages which culminate in complete economic collapse. In the beginning, monetization of the debt creates a rise in prices, signaling consumers to 'buy now' to beat future price increases. This creates excess demand for goods, driving prices further upward. As the cost of living increases, workers demand higher wages. As firms succumb to workers' demands, the higher wages push prices up further. This creates a 'wage-spiral', in which wages and prices mutually drive each other higher. In anticipation of higher prices, suppliers hoard goods, creating artificial shortages and, again, rapidly increasing prices to meet high demand. At this point, public confidence in the monetary system completely plummets.

Governments facing high levels of inflation typically own a number of inefficient and unprofitable State Owned Enterprises (Langdana, 2002, 116). Most of these enterprises, which can include government-owned steel, power, transportation, mining, and oil companies, rely on state subsidies, tax credits, and guaranteed prices for 'sub-standard, globally uncompetitive output' (Langdana, 2002, 117). As inflation mounts, state owned enterprises demand increases subsidies and supports under threat of national strikes, which could cripple the economy. Forced to cave to industry pressures, governments resort to printing more money to finance these expenditures. This is often the 'fatal dose of money creation that becomes the proverbial last straw' (Langdana, 2002, 117). With these added doses of money, inflation rages out of control and races upward. Prices may double or triple in the period of several hours. Stores close periodically throughout the day to change their prices.

As investor and consumer confidence completely deflate, capital rapidly flows out of the country and individuals convert their domestic savings and earnings, denominated in the failing currency, into 'hard currencies' such as the Dollar, Euro, Pound, or Yen, or into precious metals, such as gold, to maintain some of their purchasing power.

Individuals who fail to convert can completely lose their life savings. (In an attempt to stop this 'haemorrhage', the government can instate capital controls, which usually prove to be unsuccessful as illegal secondary markets in hard currency and precious metals develop rapidly). As individuals convert their currency, the exchange rate increases, devaluing the domestic currency, and making crucial imports like food, medicine, and fuel unaffordable (Langdana, 2002, 118). The poorest individuals in society can no longer afford even the most basic food items. In extreme cases of hyperinflation, as the domestic currency continues to depreciate and eventually becomes worthless, the domestic economy can deteriorate into a barter economy where goods are traded on informal markets. The paper upon which money is printed can even be worth more than the denomination inked on its front. Currency becomes more useful as wallpaper or as fire kindling, as was the experience in Germany in 1923 (Langdana, 2002, 118).

REMEDIES FOR HYPERINFLATION

The model of hyperinflation presented above takes a 'monetarist' perspective. In other words, excessive money creation to finance large budget deficits is the main cause of hyperinflation. Therefore, remedies that stem from this perspective, so called 'orthodox' remedies, attempt to fix the underlying causes of inflation as seen from this point-of-view: unsustainable budget deficits, and excessive amounts of money circulating in the domestic economy. It should be noted here that other perspectives about the causes of hyperinflation do not take unsustainable budget deficits and excessive currency to be the underlying causes of hyperinflation. Hence, remedies for runaway inflation that stem from other points-of-view are often contradictory to orthodox remedies. This essay will CHK focus on orthodox remedies only.

Consider an IS-BB-LM model in which the commodity market, the money market, and the foreign trade markets are all in equilibrium at point E (See Graph 8.1). Due to some circumstances such as a war or a regime shift to populism, government expenditure rises. Expenditures could include war financing, massive infrastructure projects, or ill-conceived expansionary fiscal policy (Langdana, 2002, 116). This rise in expenditure shifts the IS curve up to the IS_1 level. However, at point D on the IS_1 curve, there is a deficit in the balance of payments. This is the first condition of most hyperinflationary periods.

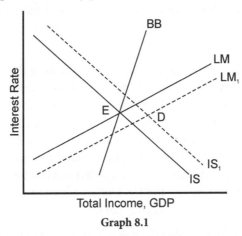

Graph 8.1

To finance such a deficit under normal circumstances, a government would sell bonds in the bond market, shifting the BB curve right to create a new equilibrium at point D. However, as governments consistently run large deficits, and the deficit/GDP ratio increases toward an upper bound (usually 5 per cent for developed countries), further bond financing becomes impossible. Governments that sell too many bonds are seen as irresponsible, and investors will not take the risk in lending those governments funds through bond purchase. Another possible reason for the inability to sell bonds would be a generally poor international economic environment. Even if a country can no longer "roll over" its debt by selling bonds, it is still responsible for paying interest and principal payments on that debt. The only way forward for some countries is to 'monetize' the debt by printing currency (Langdana, 2002, 116). Expansionary monetary policy shifts the LM curve downward to the LM_1 level, throwing the entire model further out of balance (the degree of which is determined by the offset coefficient), and 'setting the stage for unmitigated money creation to finance giant runaway budget deficits' (Langdana 2002, 116). Once hyperinflation sets in, there are several steps that a government can take to remedy the problem, should it choose to do so. Given that unsustainable deficits are the underlying cause of the need to create new money and the resulting hyperinflation, two things need to be addressed: the unsustainable deficit, and the huge amounts of new money in circulation.

In order to control high levels of inflation, first, the unsustainable deficit needs to be brought back to a sustainable range through large, difficult government spending cutbacks. This tightening of expenditures carries with it a shift in market curves back towards equilibrium levels. Spending cutbacks could involve significant cuts in government employee salaries, cuts to pension programs, reductions in subsidies and tax breaks for large (often state-owned) enterprises, and importantly in many cases, privatization of formerly inefficient state-owned enterprises (Langdana, 2002, 116). IMF loans often require these types of measures as conditions on present and future debt assistance. In the wake of financial crisis, these measures can be difficult to implement, as they typically lead to high unemployment and poor economic growth in the years immediately after their implementation. For that reason, some countries choose less orthodox methods of stabilization. Many economists argue, however, that sharp reductions in fiscal deficits are *always* a critical element in a stabilization programme (Reinhart and Savastano, 2003, 23).

The second puzzle to solve is the problem of massive amounts of domestic currency circulating in the economy. There are several solutions to this problem, though they are often considered only temporary, and without expenditure reductions and fiscal discipline, are ineffective. First, a country can 'index' its currency. In other words, it can link the number of currency units necessary to fulfill obligations to a specified price index. Second, a country can introduce a new currency, where some amount of the old, hyperinflated currency (for example, one million units) is now equal to one unit of the new currency. Often, governments choose to 'peg' their new currency to some harder currency, like the US Dollar, allowing the exchange rate to fluctuate along with the hard currency (Langdana, 2002, 121).

These solutions, as noted above, are only effective in the context of fiscal discipline. Additionally, strong monetary discipline is needed, along with monetary autonomy. Central Banks must be completely independent of policymakers, and thus able to reject any influence to print excessive currency by irresponsible governments. Another method to create monetary discipline is a constitutional and legislative directive that includes a specified upper limit on inflation and budget deficits, with penalties for failure to comply (Langdana, 2002, 122). To give an example, this type of policy was used successfully in New Zealand.

THE CASE OF BOLIVIA

Causes of Hyperinflation in Bolivia

Bolivia is one of the few cases in the last 50 years of a 'true' hyperinflation, applying Cagan's 1956 definition. By this definition, Bolivia's hyperinflationary period lasted from April 1984 to September 1985. During that time, prices rose at a rate of 20,000 per cent, and peaked between June and August 1985 at an annualized rate of 60,000 per cent (Sachs, 1987, 279). The origin of Bolivia's hyperinflation is similar to the 'classical' hyperinflations that occurred in Europe, Russia, and China in the Post World War I and II years. As with these earlier hyperinflations, 'the Bolivian hyperinflation was caused by public budget deficits financed by an inflationary increase of the monetary base' (Bernholz, 1995, 227). In other words, a rise in need for seigniorage and consequential money creation led to the outbreak of hyperinflation. Bolivia is unique, however, in that its hyperinflation did not arise in the aftermath of a foreign or civil war or a political revolution (Sachs, 1987, 279). Rather, Bolivia's hyperinflation emerged in the context of 'several less-dramatic shocks hitting the country during a period of intense political instability' (Sachs, 1987, 279). In the years between 1979 and 1985, Bolivia underwent a series of coups, electoral stalemates, and interim governments, culminating in 13 different heads of state between 1978 and 1989 (CIA, 2010).

By the end of 1980, several factors contributed to Bolivia's economic instability. These included the worsening of the international economic environment, with high interest rates, falling commodity prices, and tight credit. Bolivian access to financial markets completely dried up, and the World Bank and IMF ceased lending to the country. The annual inflation rate reached 300 per cent, and the economy was in sharp decline in October 1982, when President Siles Zuazo took power as the head of a leftist government (real GNP fell by 6.6 per cent in 1982) (Sachs, 1987, 279). At the same time, the government represented a coalition on the political left that pressed for increases in social spending and public sector employment, and that lacked a tax base to raise revenues to increase spending in such a manner.

There are three fundamental aspects that explain the appearance of Bolivian hyperinflation. First, the cutoff of international lending and the rise in international interest rates in the early 1980s forced the Bolivian government to meet higher debt-servicing costs and drops in international lending with an increase in the inflation tax. In the early 1980s, Bolivia's GNP was approximately equal to USD 3.6 billion. It had been accepting resource transfers of nearly USD178 million in 1980. By 1983, net transfers *away* from Bolivia of USD190 million signified a 10 per cent shift of GNP (Sachs, 1987, 280). Loans that foreign banks had extended to Bolivia's state-owned corporations, which amounted to 3 per cent of Bolivia's long-term debt in 1970, amounted to 31 per cent of that debt in 1980 (Campbell, 1995, 403). In 1981, government authorities permitted a capital flight of nearly USD 600 million. A drop in tin prices in 1982 caused a decline in export revenues of five per cent of GDP. By 1983, net international reserves had declined to –USD 256.7 million (Pastor, 1992, 214). A second important aspect of Bolivian hyperinflation was that as inflation increased after 1981, the tax system collapsed. Central government revenues fell from about 9 per cent of GNP in 1981 to about 1.3 per cent of GNP in early 1985 (Sachs, 1987, 280).

The third and most important cause of Bolivian hyperinflation in 1984 and 1985 was that as the government lost income from international lenders and its own failing tax system between 1981 and 1985, it was forced to monetize its debt. Bolivia resorted to increasing levels of seigniorage to finance its public expenditures and maintain its total levels of income (Campbell, 1995, 400). Rather than shrinking government expenditures, the government chose to increase seigniorage through runaway inflation because much of the burden of such inflation fell on the public rather than on the government (Campbell, 1995, 400). As fiscal revenues fell (from 9.4 per cent of GDP in 1981 to 2.7 per cent in 1984), a jump in seigniorage from 1981 to 1982 (from 1.7 per cent of GDP to 13.3 per cent) expanded total government income from 12.9 per cent of GDP in 1981 to 18.6 per cent of GDP in 1982.

As is consistent with Cagan's model, however, 'assuming that expectations of inflation adjust slowly to actual inflation, and that the demand for real money balances is a function of expected inflation, a permanent increase in the seigniorage needs of the government (as occurred after 1981) will produce an inflation rate that rises over time while the stock of real money balances declines' (Sachs, 1987, 280). The increase in seigniorage between 1981 and 1984 was followed closely by a sharp increase in inflation (See Figure 8.1). As the real monetary base declined, the government increased the monetary expansion rate to keep the level of seigniorage from falling.

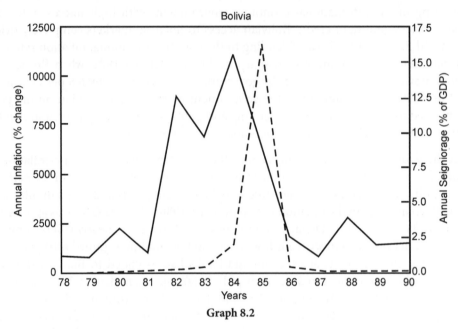

Graph 8.2

Source: Kiguel and Liviatan 1995, 377.

From 1982 to 1985, the real monetary base fell from an average monthly level of 10,807 pesos to 3,524 pesos. During the same period, the Bolivian government was forced to increase the average monthly monetary expansion rate from 12.3 per cent in 1982 to 48.4 per cent in the first eight months of 1985. In 1984 and 1985, government income as a percentage of GDP was 19.4 per cent and 21.8 per cent, respectively, as it successfully maintained a stream of revenue from seigniorage (Campbell, 1995, 404). Between April 1984 and September 1985, hyperinflation ensued, averaging 12,000 per cent during 1985 (The Economist, 1989). (For yearly seigniorage statistics, see Table 8.1 in appendix.)

Effects of Hyperinflation in Bolivia

President Zuazo came into power in 1982 with the support of the labour movement. Zauzo opted for policies that sought to deal with the crisis he inherited while still pleasing his supporters. He raised export taxes, restricted imports, and protected real wages through 100 per cent indexation and adjustments for price increases (Pastor, 1990, 215). As prices continued to rise, wages continued to increase, causing a wage-spiral. The government continued to monetize its expenditures, and capital flowed out of the country. Bond issuing became impossible, a result of the international financial crisis and perceptions of risk. Foreign exchange earnings represented only 15 per cent of government revenues by 1983 (Chavez, 1985, 1). Bolivians shifted their savings and earnings into dollars, a process called dollarization, in order to maintain purchasing power (Campbell, 1995, 400). On the black market in 1985, a dollar was worth 120,000 pesos, but official exchange rates valued a dollar at only 50,000 pesos. Bank deposits fell from around USD 600 million in 1983 to only USD 10 million in May 1985 (Chavez, 1985, 1).

By February 1985, hyperinflation was out of control, at a monthly rate of over 180 per cent and increasing rapidly (Pastor, 1990, 212). Life in Bolivia was in shambles. Minimum monthly wages were around USD 80.70, while a medium-sized chicken cost USD 7 and a dozen eggs cost USD 2. For those who could afford to stay overnight, hotel bills were paid with suitcases of money (Chavez, 1985, 1). In relating his experience in Bolivia in 1985, economist Jeffrey Sachs described the daily, human experience of hyperinflation as 'an extraordinary and terrifying thing to see... People [were] in disarray, enterprises [were] barely functioning. People...[were] getting paid with huge stacks of money... and running to the market to try to turn the soon-to-be worthless paper into some physical commodities'. He noted that on the streets, 'one felt that anything could happen, that society could descend to civil war.... Obviously, it was a society at the edge of the precipice' (PBS, 2000). In the final months of hyperinflation, the economic situation deteriorated to such an extent that President Zuazo was forced to hold early elections in July 1985. His successor, Victor Paz Estenssoro, took over in August 1985 and in September 1985 announced a sweeping stabilization programme. Ten days later, Bolivia's hyperinflation came to an abrupt halt (Campbell, 1995, 404).

Remedies for Hyperinflation in Bolivia

Ten days after Victor Paz Estenssoro* announced his broad stabilization programme, Bolivia's hyperinflation abruptly ended. The new administration market, a clear regime change. Estenssoro's programme, called the New Economic Policy, was ambitious and went beyond macroeconomic reform to include fiscal reform, trade liberalization, elimination of price controls, and privatization. On the fiscal side, the government committed to an immediate reduction in the deficit through sharp increases in public sector prices, especially in oil. For example, gas taxes were increased from a ceiling price of 3 cents per liter to 28 cents per liter (Campbell, 1995, 405). Also, the government froze public sector wages, and revamped the tax system to broaden the tax base and raise tax revenue. The government restricted central bank financing, adopting a policy of outright refusal to spend more than is made in revenue and effectively balancing the budget on a day-to-day basis. In sticking with this rule, at one point the government had to delay public sector wage payments for almost a month (Campbell, 1995, 405). Bolivia also suspended principal and interest payments to commercial bank creditors,

---

* President Estenssoro flew in Harvard-trained hyperinflation specialist, Jeffrey Sachs, to help create a stabilization plan.

despite IMF urgings to continue payments. However, in 1986, Bolivia signed an IMF standby agreement, and held meetings to reschedule payments of government debt owed to international creditors (Sachs, 1987, 281). By 1987, Bolivia had successfully proven its commitment to reform through policies that appealed to lenders-free convertibility of foreign exchange, elimination of price controls, elimination of trade quotas, removal of restrictions on private wages, hiring and firing, among others, and began receiving payments of between USD 200 million and USD 300 million from the International Development Association and the Inter-American Development Bank.

On the monetary side, Bolivia adopted a 'managed' or 'dirty' float of the exchange rate. The stabilization programme had legalized the parallel, 'black' foreign exchange market, eliminating any significant differences between the parallel market and official exchange rates. It also held daily auctions of foreign exchange, in which the central bank controlled the exchange rate, but made no commitment to hold it constant (Campbell, 1995, 406). In August 1985, immediately following the stabilization decree, the exchange rate rose to 1,000,000 pesos per dollar, 'and when the stabilization programme appeared to be failing, rose further to 2,000,000' pesos per dollar. The 'fixing of the exchange rate had the effect of stabilizing prices immediately' (Campbell, 1995, 406). Campbell and Sachs both attribute this to the use of the dollar as a unit of account and the store of value. 'Prices were either set implicitly or explicitly in dollars, with transactions continuing to take place in peso notes, at prices determined by the dollar prices converted at the spot exchange rate. Therefore, by stabilizing the exchange rate, domestic inflation could be made to revert immediately to the US dollar inflation rate' (Sachs, 1987, 281). In 1987, Bolivia introduced a new 'Boliviano' to replace the old Peso Boliviano (the 'peso') at a rate of one million to one.

Bolivia's successful remedies for hyperinflation fit the orthodox model well. For a long time, the IMF hailed Bolivia as the 'good boy' among a group of Latin American 'bad boys'. (For most of the 1980s and 1990s, Latin American countries, such as Argentina and Brazil, struggled with persistently high levels of inflation and recurring periods of hyperinflation. Some of their less orthodox policies for stopping inflation were not favourable in the eyes of the IMF, who promoted the ageless orthodox medicine for balance-of-payments crises and inflation: devaluations and budget cuts).

THE CASE OF PERU

Causes of Hyperinflation in Peru

The origins of the Peruvian Hyperinflation of 1988 to 1990 are similar to those of Bolivia and the classical hyperinflations in Europe. One fact that sets Peru apart from the classical hyperinflations is that inflation in Peru was consistently high for several years before its hyperinflationary episode began. Rates varied from 66 to 163 per cent per year between 1980 and 1987 (Kiguel and Liviatan, 1995, 383). Despite this slight difference, Peru fits Cagan's model in that its increasing deficits were financed through money creation, and 'a rise in seigniorage led to the outbreak of hyperinflation' (Kiguel and Liviatan, 1995, 383) (See Graph 8.3). Between 1988 and 1990, inflation rates in Peru reached over 7,500 per cent. The origins of hyperinflation in Peru, like Bolivia, lie in the budgetary deficits the country ran since 1979. After several years of unsuccessful economic reforms between 1980 and 1985, center-leftist Alan García won the presidency in 1985. His attempts at economic reforms also proved unsuccessful, and his populist policies further increased national debt and exacerbated the inflationary situation in Peru. Between 1980 and 1988 Peru's economy was in poor shape. Its economic growth and trade balances were generally negative between 1981 and 1988, its external debt increased consistently from USD 6 billion in 1980 to USD 12 billion in 1988, and its external reserves fell into negative figures by 1988 (Pastor, 1992, 93).

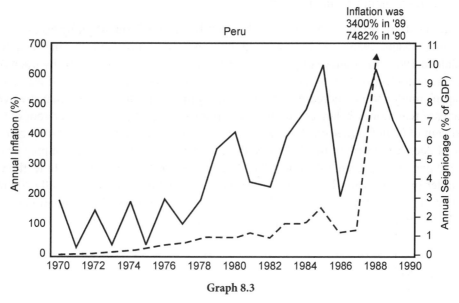

Graph 8.3

Source: Kiguel and Liviatan 1995, 384.

Peru's Hyperinflation from 1970-1990

There are three fundamental aspects that explain the rise of Peruvian hyperinflation. First, Peru experienced a decline in external financing and no policies to create alternative sources of foreign exchange to pay its debts. Its anti-IMF, anti-imperialist rhetoric isolated Peru from the international financial community, which deemed Peru an 'ineligible borrower' in August 1986. The government's policy of increasing imports while holding down prices through a fixed exchange rate, which was meant to reduce inflation, proved unsuccessful. The government allowed imports to rise from USD 1.8 billion in 1985 to USD 3.2 billion in 1987. Export revenues fell by more than 10 per cent, which transformed a 1985 trade surplus of USD 1.2 billion into a deficit of more than USD 500 million in 1987. Net international reserves fell from USD 1.4 billion in 1985 to USD 81 million by 1988 (Pastor, 1992, 99).

Second, the populist Peruvian government used massive fiscal expansion policies, increasing public sector deficit from 2.4 per cent of GDP in 1985 to 6.5 per cent in 1987 (Pastor, 1992, 101). In an attempt to reactivate the economy, government increased real wages, reduced taxes, and increased subsidies. Tax revenue fell from 12.4 per cent of GDP in 1985 to 7.4 per cent in 1988 (Pastor, 1992, 101). At the same time, Peru gained little revenue from domestic or foreign investment. Despite García's attempts to negotiate with private investors, the private sector remained wary after a failed government attempt to gain profits from a mandatory bond-purchasing scheme. García also attempted to nationalize banks in 1987, a policy that failed to be implemented but inevitably spooked foreign investors (Pastor, 1992, 104). By 1989, Peru's deficit equaled nearly 16 per cent of its national income (Reid, 1989, 1). (For trends in Peru's budget deficit, see Figure 8.2 in appendix).

Third, and most importantly, the Peruvian hyperinflation was brought on by excessive money creation in 1985 and 1986, used to finance increasing expenditures and international debts. In the middle of 1985, the money supply growth rate increased by 100 per cent. By the middle of 1987, money supply growth rate increased by 200 per cent (Ventura, 2000, 3). This is consistent with Cagan's model, where increases in money supply produce inflation rates that rise over time and decrease real money balances. In 1985, seigniorage jumped from 2.45 per cent of GDP to 9.86 per cent of GDP (Kiguel and Liviatan, 1995, 382). To keep up with its seigniorage needs in the face of decreasing real money balances, Peru increased its rate of money supply growth by nearly 750 per cent between 1988 and 1990 (Ventura, 2000, 3). In July 1989 alone, the Central Bank, under pressure from the García government, printed money equal to USD 200 million[*] (Reid, 1989, 1). Seigniorage remained high through the end of Peru's hyperinflationary period, and by 1990, inflation exceeded 7, 450 per cent (Kiguel and Liviatan, 1995, 384).

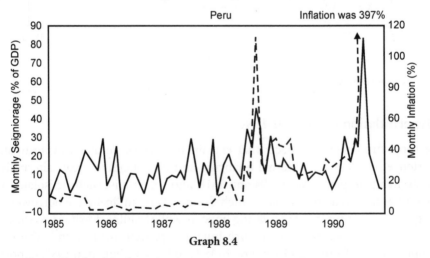

Graph 8.4

Source: Kiguel and Liviatan 1995, 387.

---

[*] The Chairman of the Central Bank, Pedro Coronado, resigned as a result of this decision, which he opposed.

Effects of Hyperinflation in Peru

Peru is somewhat different than Bolivia because it experienced slow increases in inflation for over ten years before its episode of hyperinflation began. However, as prices began to rise in the mid 1980s, García's government increased wages as per policy. Inherent in his populist policies was a desire to appease state-owned enterprises with increased subsidies and protections. As it printed money, gaining seigniorage to finance these expenditures, the public slowly began to convert Intis into dollars. This process of dollarization was similar to that which occurred in Bolivia several years earlier. US dollars were sold on the black market, and curbside, for 65,000 Intis in 1990. The state of Peru's economy and fear of holding Intis for longer than needed even spawned a new profession. 'Cambistas' worked the streets offering instant exchange for US dollars (Brooke, 1990, 1). In August 1990, the government introduced a 5 million note Inti.

The crumbling Peruvian economy took a toll on this already poverty-stricken country. For Peruvians, who generally earned less than USD 100 per month, food prices rose far beyond their reach (Riding, 1988, 1).The value of national wages dropped by more than two-thirds in 1989, and living standards decreased significantly along wage values. Development workers claimed that months of hyperinflation took a toll on malnutrition and infant mortality (Reid, 1989, 2). Inflation effectively 'made Peru a land of impoverished millionaires' (Brooke, 1990, 2). Inflation-generated poverty also increased the flow of new recruits to Peru's left-wing guerilla groups like the Marxist T'upac Amaru Revolutionary Movement and the Maoist Sendero Luminoso (Shining Path) (Reid, 1989, 2). As Peruvians struggled to survive, they may have feared these guerilla groups more than they feared abject poverty. Sendero Luminoso alone was responsible for nearly 22,000 deaths between 1980 and 1990 and nearly USD 20 billion worth of damage to Peru's infrastructure (Radu, 1992, 17). With an economy in crisis, these groups gained more strength. As the country stood on the brink of revolution in July 1990, Peruvians turned to a presidential candidate without party ties or political experience in the hope of successful economic reforms. Alberto Fujimori took office on 28 July 1990, and his first priority was to implement a dramatic economic shock programme which effectively halted hyperinflation in 1991 (Palmer, 1996, 70).

Remedies for Hyperinflation in Peru

President Fujimori inherited an economic and social 'basket case' when he took power in 1990. However, within a year, Fujimori implemented drastic measures to successfully break the hyperinflation cycle in Peru. Fujimori's orthodox strategy for stopping hyperinflation was comparable to that of Bolivia and the classical hyperinflations. The government made a notably strong commitment to fiscal discipline. It maintained a comprehensive programme aimed at long term growth, which also included privatization and trade liberalization (Kiguel and Liviatan, 1995, 391). In its commitment to balancing its budget, Peru created a 'cash committee', which was responsible for keeping payments in line with revenues under strict laws. Peru's tight fiscal policy was positively affected by increasingly higher revenues. During the hyperinflationary period, tax revenues had almost completely collapsed. In response, Fujimori levied emergency taxes, eliminated tax exemptions, and drastically increased public sector prices. For example, the price of gas increased twentyfold, from 41,800 Intis to 1,200,000 Intis per gallon. This threw the country into what Peruvians called 'fujushock', the effect of dealing with tripling or quadrupling prices of basic items such as bread, milk, and cooking gas (Brooke, 1990, 2).

On the monetary side, the Peruvian government committed to restraining monetary growth. A new currency, the 'Nuevo Sol' was put into use, replacing the Inti at a rate of 1 Nuevo Sol per 1,000,000 Intis. The government also made a concerted effort to regain the acceptance of international financial lenders, approaching the IMF and other lending agencies throughout the stabilization process. The government decided not to use the exchange rate as a nominal anchor, but allowed the Nuevo Sol to float freely against the dollar. As in the classical hyperinflations, the exchange rate was stabilized quickly. However, a stable exchange rate did not succeed, as it did in Bolivia, in stabilizing prices in the long-run. While hyperinflation ceased, Peruvian inflation was stubborn, and remained generally high into the mid-1990s at levels around 4 per cent per month (Kiguel and Liviatan, 1995, 391). Kiguel and Liviatan argue that this had to do with the country's relatively longer initial struggle with *high* inflation rates before the outbreak of hyperinflation. The high degree of dollarization and subsequent legalization of dollar bank deposits which occurred in Peru during inflationary periods resulted in a failure to expand the real monetary base during and after the stabilization period. Because money demand did not recover during the stabilization period, the system was vulnerable to a resumption of inflation (Kiguel and Liviatan, 1995, 399).

Notwithstanding, 'the comprehensiveness of [Fujimori's] programmes…, [the] thoroughness of stabilization attempts, and the adherence to fiscal discipline indicate that [Peru's] basic strategy was comparable to the one that succeeded in stopping hyperinflation in Bolivia' (Kiguel and Liviatan, 1995, 391). Fujimori's economic success is often overlooked by his record of political violence and human rights abuses. However, in stopping hyperinflation and making a clear break from populism, Fujimori's orthodox policies were successful.

CONCLUSIONS

It is clear that Bolivia and Peru show similarities in both the origins of and remedies for their hyperinflations. These two experiences also support Cagan's classical model of causes of hyperinflation, as well as the success of orthodox models in remedying hyperinflation. However, all hyperinflations are *not* equal. Bolivia and Peru are unique in the Latin American experience and in the modern hyperinflation experience in general. While they might be successful in halting hyperinflation, IMF-supported macroeconomic stabilization policies have been shown, in many cases, to reduce economic growth and increase poverty in the short-run. Bolivia and Peru even showed poor economic growth and increases in poverty levels in the years following their stabilization programmes. Peru's inflation rate remained stubbornly high into the mid 1990s. Some scholars argue that stabilization policy effectiveness might lie in the origins of hyperinflation, a country's economic, social and political history, and/or a country's ability to adapt and strategy for adaptation to long periods of high inflation. Countries that are better able to adapt to such circumstances, through dollarization or other means, may find it more difficult to stabilize prices after a period of hyperinflation. As many development scholars have noted, policies should take into consideration every country's unique history and current situation.

This conclusion has implications for countries currently facing economic crises, high inflation rates, or hyperinflation. Zimbabwe and the Democratic Republic of the Congo face hyperinflation in the context of decades of political and social unrest and war. Venezuela's high inflation rates may be a consequence of its current policy regime. Kenya, Eritrea, and other poor African countries facing high inflation rates may be hesitant to expose their populations to the economic shocks involved in combating inflation. In these cases, governments should use case studies and the experiences of countries in Latin America, Asia, and Europe to consider the costs and benefits of different types of stabilization programmes. Rather than implement mass-produced macroeconomic policies for recovery, governments should carefully consider their own country's unique history and economic, social, and political situation, and create policies for economic recovery and long-run growth that fit its needs.

REFERENCES

1. Auernheimer, Leonardo. 1976. 'The Effects of Inflationary Finance on Stability: A Theoretical Analysis'. In *Southern Economic Journal* 42 (3): 502-507.
2. Barro, Robert J. 1972. 'Inflationary Finance and the Welfare Cost of Inflation'. In *The Journal of Political Economy* 80 (5): 978-1001.
3. Bernholz, Peter. 1995. 'Hyperinflation and Currency Reform in Bolivia: Studied from a General Perspective'. In *Great Inflations of the Twentieth Century: Theories, Policies, and Evidence.* Ed. Pierre L. Siklos. Hants, UK: Edward Elgar Publishing Limited.
4. Brooke, James. 1990. What's Hawked at Curbside? Dolares. *New York Times,* July 4, Late Edition.
5. Brooke, James. 1990. Peru Rocked by Hyperinflation: Fujimori Government Ushers in New Economic Shock Program. *Daily News of Los Angeles,* August 12.
6. Cagan, Phillip. 1956. 'The Monetary Dynamics of Hyperinflation'. In *Studies in the Quantity Theory of Money.* Ed. Milton Friedman. 25-91. Chicago: University of Chicago Press.
7. Campbell, Colin D. 1995. 'Seigniorage and Bolivia's Runaway Inflation, 1982-1985'. In *Eastern Economic Journal* 21 (3): 399-407.
8. Cardoso, Eliana A. 1989. 'Hyperinflation in Latin America'. In *Challenge* (January-February): 11-19.
9. Carstens, Agustin and Luis I. Jacome H. 'Taming the Monster'. In *Finance and Development* 42 (4): 26-30.
10. Chavez, Lydia. 1985. Hyper-inflation Traumatizes Bolivia. *New York Times, 8* April, Late Edition, East Coast.
11. Chossudovsky, Michel. 1992. 'Under the Tutelage of IMF: The Case of Peru'. In *Economic and Political Weekly* 27 (7): 340-248.
12. CIA World Factbook. 2010. 'Bolivia'. CIA World Factbook Online. Available: https://www.cia.gov/library/publications/the-world-factbook Accessed: 2/28/2010.
13. CIA World Factbook. 2010. 'Country Comparison: Inflation Rate'. CIA World Factbook Online. Available: https://www.cia.gov/library/publications/the-world-factbook/rankorder/2092rank.html?countryName=Congo,%20Democratic%20Republic%20of%20the&countryCode=cg&regionCode=af&rank=214#cg Accessed: 2/28/2010.

14. CNN. 2009. Zimbabwe to print first $100 trillion note. *CNN World Online,* January 16, World Edition Online. Available: http://www.cnn.com/2009/WORLD/africa/01/16/zimbawe.currency/index.html Accessed: 2/28/2010

15. The Economist. 1989. The Case for Hyperinflation. *The Economist,* 13 May.

16. The Economist. 1993. Commitment, Competence, and Consensus. *The Economist,* 13 November.

17. de Holanda Barbosa, Fernando. 'Hyperinflation: Inflation Tax and the Economic Policy Regime.' Graduate School of Economics of the Getulio Vargas Foundation.

18. Jacobs, Rodney L. 1977. 'Hyperinflation and the Supply of Money.' In *Journal of Money, Credit, and Banking* 9 (2): 287-303.

19. Kiguel, Miguel A. 1989. 'Budget Deficits, Stability, and the Monetary Dynamics of Hyperinflation.' In *Journal of Money, Credit, and Banking* 21 (2): 148-157.

20. Kiguel, Miguel A. and Nissan Liviatan. 1995. 'Stopping Three Big Inflations: Argentina, Brazil, and Peru.' In *Reform, Recovery and Growth: Latin America and the Middle East.* Ed. Rudiger Dornbusch and Sebastian Edwards. 369-414. Chicago: University of Chicago Press.

21. Kiguel, Miguel A. and Pablo Andres Neumeyer. 1995. 'Seigniorage and Inflation: The Case of Argentina.' In *Journal of Money, Credit, and Banking* 27 (3): 672-682.

22. Langdana, Farrokh K. 2002. *Macroeconomic Policy: Demystifying Monetary and Fiscal Policy.* Boston: Kluwer Academic Publishers.

23. Mann, Arthur J. and Manuel Pastor Jr. 1989. 'Orthodox and Heterodox Stabilization Policies in Bolivia and Peru: 1985-1988.' In *The Journal of Interamerican Studies and World Affairs* 31 (4): 163-192.

24. Margolis, Mac. 1988. Bolivia Shifts From Hyperinflation to Stability. *The Washington Post,* 17 May.

25. Palmer, David Scott. 1996. 'Fujipopulism and Peru's Progress.' In *Current History* 95: 70-75.

26. Pastor, Jr. Manuel. 1990. 'Bolivia: Hyperinflation, Stabilization, and Beyond.' In *The Journal of Development Studies* (February): 211-236.

27. Pastor, Jr. Manuel. 1992. 'Peruvian Economic Policy in the 1980s: From Orthodoxy to Heterodoxy and Back.' In *Latin American Research Review* 27 (2): 83-117.

28. PBS. 2000. 'Commanding Heights: Interview with Jeffrey Sachs.' PBS Online. Available: http://www.pbs.org/wgbh/commandingheights/shared/minitext/int_jeffreysachs.html#3 Accessed: 2/28/2010.

29. Radu, Michael. 1992. 'Can Fujimori Save Peru?' In *The Bulletin of the Atomic Scientists* (July/August): 1621.

30. Reid, Michael. 1989. Rebels Gain as Economy Worsens: Peru, a Downward Spiral. *Christian Science Monitor,* 2 August.

31. Reinhart, Carmen M. and Miguel A. Savastano. 2003. 'The Realities of Modern Hyperinflation.' In *Finance and Development* (June): 20-23.

32. Riding, Alan. 1988. South America's Basket Case: Hyperinflation, Extremist Violence in Peru-Some Warn Anarchy Near. *Houston Chronicle,* 4 December.

33. Sachs, Jeffrey. 1987. 'The Bolivian Hyperinflation and Stabilization.' In *The Americna Economic Review* 77 (2): 279-283.

34. Sargent, Thomas J. and Neil Wallace. 1973. 'Rational Expectations and the Dynamics of Hyperinflation.' In *International Economic Review* 14 (2): 328-350.

35. Ventura, Jaime Pedro. 2000. 'Money Demand and Inflation in Peru, 1979-1991.' In *Federal Reserve Bank of Cleveland, Economic Commentary*: 1-4.

APPENDIX

Table 8.1: Sources of Government Income in Bolivia, 1977-1991

Year	Fiscal Revenues	Seigniorage	Net Transfers on Debt	US Grants and Credits	Total Government Income
1977	11.7%	3.1%	8.7%	1.0%	24.5%
1978	11.4	1.5	4.7	1.6	19.2
1979	9.3	1.2	1.9	.8	13.3
1980	9.6	3.5	2.8	.6	16.4
1981	9.4	1.7	1.5	.3	12.9
1982	4.8	13.3	−0.1	.5	18.6
1983	3.3	10.6	−2.7	.9	12.1
1984	2.7	18.4	−2.3	.6	19.4
1985	7.1	16.7	−3.0	1.1	21.8
1986	11.2	2.7	2.7	2.4	19.1
1987	11.4	2.6	1.9	2.5	18.4
1988	11.0	3.7	0.8	1.6	17.1
1989	11.0	2.0	2.5	2.4	17.8
1990	12.0	2.6	−0.2	2.1	16.5
1991	13.1	2.3	0.5	2.9	18.8

Source: Campbell 1995, 401.

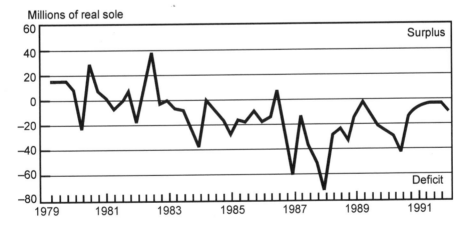

Figure 8.1: Peru's Federal Budget Balance, 1979-1991

Source: Ventura 2000, 4.

9

Sun, Sand and Deindustrialization

Employing the Dutch Disease Model to Tourism-Dependent Saint Lucia and Dominica

Lisa Caputo

CHAPTER SUMMARY

The Caribbean has become increasingly reliant on tourism as their agricultural and manufacturing sectors languish. This chapter applies the Dutch Disease model, a theory commonly used to describe the economic impact of an export boom, to two small states in the Caribbean. By employing several variables to measure the economic effects of the tourism boom, this chapter suggests Saint Lucia shows signs of Dutch Disease while Dominica's slower tourism boom and emphasis on the agricultural and manufacturing sectors has allowed the island to create a disparate path.

It is nearly a cliché to remind the reader that tourism is the fastest growing industry on the globe. Tourism accounted for 6 per cent of goods and services throughout the globe in 2003 (UNWTO, 2009). The labour-intensive industry has undoubtedly generated employment, income, foreign investment and the production of improved infrastructure for less developed countries (LDCs). Because of these positive attributes, tourism was included in 80 per cent of the poverty reduction strategies for low-income countries in 2006 (Overseas Development Institute, 2007, 1). While myriad reports demonstrate the positive opportunities available for those focusing on tourism, few have considered the structural change that may occur due to the dramatic effects it will have on the economy. This study will apply the Dutch Disease model to the nations of Saint Lucia and Dominica to determine if the islands are indeed deindustrializing due to their rising tourism sectors.

It has been well documented that tourism can cultivate growth in an economy and generate employment. The Overseas Development Institute estimates tourism has grown 7 to 12 per cent per year in most developing nations over the past ten years[1] (Overseas Development

Institute, 2007, 1) and is responsible for 2 to 6 per cent of all jobs in Africa alone (Overseas Development Institute, 2007, 1). Some nations, however, do run the risk of over relying on tourism, which may engender an economic disadvantage in the long run. Many government and development agencies have viewed tourism as a panacea of development, wrongly leading nations to avoid diversifying their exports.

Tourism is a highly variable industry, capriciously declining during an economic downturn, global terrorism threats, increases in oil prices and changing perspectives of the destination. Haiti, for example, was a tourism-dependent nation that suffered due to an erratic change in interest. Haiti's tourism industry was accountable for most of the nation's foreign capital and employing tens of thousands of Haitians in 1980. Due to a mislead American media, public opinion of the nation changed in the early 1980's, diminishing the industry until became nearly 'nonexistent' by 1983 (Farmer, 2003, 213).

This chapter will first discuss the causes and characteristics of Dutch Disease, an economic model describing the domestic changes that may occur as a nation moves from a manufacturing or agricultural concentration towards deindustrialization. The study will then apply this model to Saint Lucia and Dominica, two Caribbean nations increasingly dependent on their tourism sectors.

THEORETICAL FRAMEWORK

Dutch Disease

Coined by *The Economist* in 1977, Dutch Disease describes the side effects an export boom may have on an economy. The term refers to the experience of the Netherlands after the demand for their natural gas suddenly increased as a reaction to the rise in oil prices. The once fortuitous export boom created a sudden influx of foreign exchange reserves as well as raising the cost of production, leading to inflation and the eventual deindustrialization of the Dutch manufacturing sector (Corden, 1984, 360).

Drawing from Salters's 1959 'dependent economy' model (Corden and Neary, 1982, 825), Corden (1984) and Corden and Neary (1982) pioneered the Dutch Disease model in the late seventies and early eighties in an attempt to explain the economic reaction of an export boom. It assumes the nation of interest has a small, open economy with labour able to move freely (Corden and Neary 1982, 825). Additionally, the theory assumes there are three sectors of study[2]: the lagging sector (L), the booming sector (B) and the non-tradable sector (N) (Corden, 1984, 360). As may be assumed, the booming sector is experiencing high growth and contains the export of study; the lagging sector is experiencing a decline and is often representative of the manufacturing or agricultural sector (Corden, 1984, 360). The lagging and booming sectors are traded internationally with prices determined by the world market. The non-tradable sector consists of goods and services produced for consumption or use within the domestic economy, such as retail or construction work and thus have prices determined by the demand within the nation's borders (Corden 1984, 360). The Dutch Disease model predicts two concurrent economic reactions to the export boom that would disturb the regular distribution of income and potentially lead to deindustrialization (Corden and Neary, 1982, 825).

According to Corden and Neary, the growing demand of B increases both income and the demand of labour, engendering a rise in wage rate (Corden and Neary, 1982, 827). Because we assume labour can move freely, workers voluntarily move from L and N towards the higher wage available in B, engendering a *resource movement effect*. Workers leave L to enter B, leading to a declining output by B, causing *direct deindustrialization* (Corden, 1984, 361). Similarly, the migration of workers from N to B creates a decrease in output of N. The domestic demand for N, however, rises as incomes rise; this raises prices in N, causing a *real appreciation* (Corden 1984, 361). Further, the movement of workers from L to N further harms the abilities of L, leading to *indirect deindustrialization* (Corden 1984, 361). Figure 9.1 demonstrates this movement of labour.

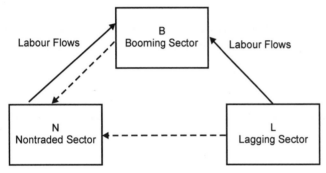

Figure 9.1: Movement of Labour in Dutch Disease

As earnings from B are circulated through the economy, incomes increase creating a rise in the demand for goods and services in the *spending effect*. The demand for goods from N and L rises. This leads to an eventual increase in the prices of non-traded goods (Corden, 1984, 360) as the prices for N are determined on a domestic level. Remembering prices for L is determined by world demand, increasing domestic demand will not impact prices (Kenell, 2008, 5). In response to the rising prices within the non-traded sector, labour will transfer out of B and L towards N (Corden, 1984, 360). The appreciation of the real exchange rate increases the cost of production, further hampering L's ability to compete in world market's prices (Kenell, 2008, 5).

The context of Dutch Disease is not only applicable to boom in natural resource exports. Several studies have also found associations between the influx of foreign aid and Dutch Disease, potentially providing insight on how historically aid has not encouraged economic growth (Arellano et al., 2009, 100). Acosta, Lartye, and Mandelman's 2009 study is the latest in a string of research connecting remittances with an appreciation of the real exchange rate due to rising non-tradable prices and the neglect of the manufacturing sector (Acosta et al., 2009, 114).

Dutch Disease and Tourism

Because the nature of the tourism industry is extremely unique, Copeland (1991) notes 'a straightforward application…is not possible' (Copeland, 1991). Thus, it is necessary to modify some characteristics of the booming sector (B), or the tourist sector. As opposed to the studied exports in B that are shipped to the customer in the classic Dutch Disease model, consumers travel *to* the good in tourism. Tourists spend hours or days in their destination consuming a bundle of goods and services for the non-tradable sector, such as restaurant meals, transportation and communication services, as opposed to a single item from the booming sector. Tourists therefore enjoy the unpriced scenery, climate, or historical sight while consuming goods from N, redefining these goods as 'partially tradable' (Copeland, 1991). This consumption pattern leads to a direct increase in the price of these non-traded goods, causing an appreciation in the real exchange rate. (Copeland, 1991).

Is Dutch Disease a Disease at All?

While long-term risk exists in deserting a manufacturing sector for an emerging sector that may be increasingly vulnerable over time, the increased demand of a nation's exports is generally an opportunity to advance an economy.

Several international trade theories recommend producing and exporting goods that fit best with an economy. Ricardo theorized that a nation should produce the item that the nation has the absolutely advantage in (Kulkarni, 2010). The 1912 Heakscher-Ohlin theory suggests that a nation should specialize in the export that best employs the nation's 'abundant factor' (Kulkarni, 2010). Thus, it has been proved in various models that developed countries should specialize in labour-intensive goods that they essentialy have an advantage in producing. Dutch Disease should be viewed as a model to explain economic and structural change rather than to identify a problem or failure. *The Economist* succinctly discusses the situation of Dutch Disease in 1982, 'To refer to a vast, valuable energy resource as the source of a *disease* sounds rather ungrateful' (*The Economist, 1982).*

Empirical Research

Several variables will be measured to determine if the nations have indeed paralleled the effects discussed in the Dutch Disease model.

First, inflation will be measured by examining the currency and Consumer Price Index (CPI). This study will also investigate changes in output and incomes within the agricultural, manufacturing, and non-tradable sectors to determine if a decline in the lagging sector has occurred. Lastly, movement of labour between sectors will be monitored. A nation impacted by Dutch Disease would likely witness a move away the manufacturing/agricultural sector to work in the non-tradable service sector.

THE CARIBBEAN

The islands that make up the Caribbean have a long history of isolation, being 'islands in both the physical and metaphorical senses'(Gossling, 2003, 3). Because of high transport costs and small domestic market, the nations of the Caribbean have become increasingly dependent on the tourism market rather than manufacturing. Because of the close proximity to the United States and its beautiful scenery, tourism took off in the 1950's shortly after the introduction of the jet. Today, development agencies and governments have encouraged the redirection of money and labour from the agricultural market towards the tourism industry (Conway, 193). Since then, tourism has become an opportunity to attract foreign capital, generate employment and improve infrastructure while developing a comparative advantage in the hemisphere. Approximately 25 per cent of all income in the Caribbean can be attributed to tourism (Gossling, 2003, 4), making it the most tourist-dependent region on the globe (Gossling, 2003, 4).

SAINT LUCIA

Saint Lucia is a mountainous island largely dependent on tourism and agriculture. As of 2005, 21 per cent of the population of the island lived under the poverty, a number that has been steadily increasing since 1997 (St. Lucia 2005, 19). While the unemployment rate remains high at 15 per cent , women especially experience difficulty finding jobs (St. Lucia 2005, 19). As the agricultural sector languishes, policy makers and government officials have encouraged the explosive growth of tourism on the island.

Tourism in Saint Lucia

Large, all-inclusive hotels and spas with names such as The Ginger Lily, Almond Morgan Bay and Cinnamon Villa owned by multinational corporations such as Sandals, Holiday Inn and Hilton, characterize the once-isolated Saint Lucia. Over the past fifty years, Saint Lucia has taken a 'hands off' approach to tourism, allowing larger, and mainly foreign, tourism industries establish themselves on the island (Wilkenson, 2004 88), attracting nearly 300,000 tourists in 2004 (UNWTO, 2008). While the island has attracted more foreign direct investment than would be otherwise possible, the nation experiences a 50 per cent leakage rate of profits to foreign investors (Wilkenson, 2003, 94). As demonstrated in Figure 9.2, tourism has been growing steadily since the 1960's, and is estimated to grow.

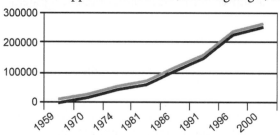

Figure 9.2: Tourist Arrivals in Lucia

Source: Wilkenson 2003, 92, (UNWTO 2005).

Economic Indicators

Following the Dutch Disease model, an economic boom in Saint Lucian tourism should increase the money supply, causing inflation. The Saint Lucian Consumer Price Index indicates a sharp level of inflation; the Government of Saint Lucia reports the CPI has risen from USD 111.5 in 1987 to USD 187.10 in 2005 (GOSL, 2006). Food prices have especially risen, from USD 105 to USD 197 in the same period of time (GOSL, 2006).

Saint Lucia and Dominica, as well as six other Caribbean nations, use the Eastern Caribbean Dollar. While this may not be a telling indicator when contrasting inflation between the two countries, it should be noted that the currency has steadily devalued from USD 2.01 Eastern Caribbean Dollar per SDR in 1968 to USD 3.85 Eastern Caribbean Dollar per SDR in 2005 (IMF, 1998) (IMF, 2006). This indicates inflation has occurred within the eight economies that utilize the currency.

Labour Force

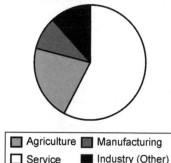

Agriculture ☐ Manufacturing
☐ Service ■ Industry (Other)

Figure 9.3: Percentage of GDP by Sector – 1980

Assuming the economic boom in the tourism sector has increased the income of the sector and thus raised wage rates, the Dutch Disease model would predict a change in the employment structure. Workers are likely to leave the manufacturing and agricultural sectors to receive higher wages in the booming sector of tourism. It has been estimated that wages are significantly higher for Saint Lucians in the tourism industry. For example, Wilkenson (2003) cites a 1992 study estimating the annual wage for an average hotel worker was more than USD 4,000 (Wilkenson, 2003, 100), as compared with the average per capita income in 1992 of $1,930 according to the CIA World Factbook (1992).

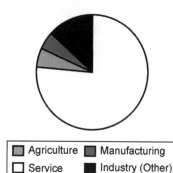

Agriculture ■ Manufacturing
☐ Service ■ Industry (Other)

Figure 9.4: Percentage of GDP by Sector – 2005

Paralleling this information, the International Labour Organization (ILO) estimates there has been a significant drop in agricultural employment within the decade between 1994 and 2004 (ILO, 2008). Conversely, employment in the non-tradable sector, such as retail, sales, construction, real estate and hotel and restaurant sales, witnessed increasing employment numbers in the same time period (ILO, 2008). This trend indicates labour has left the lagging sector (L) for the higher wage rates in the booming sector (B).

Table 9.1 reviews the structural change in Saint Lucian employment.

**Table 9.1: Employment Trends in Saint Lucia Select Economic Sectors
(Percentage of Workforce)**

	1994	1998	2004
Agriculture	23%	21%	12%
Manufacturing	12%	9%	7%
Hotels / Restaurants	9%	9%	10%
Construction	7%	7%	7%
Wholesale and Retail Trade	12%	16%	16%
Real Estate	1%	2%	4%

Source: ILO 2008.

Manufacturing and Agricultural Sectors

As discussed in the theoretical framework, output and exports from the manufacturing and agricultural sectors are expected to decline as the cost of production rises due to inflation as well as a decrease in employees. The data agrees with the Dutch Disease model, as the service sector has increased its contribution to GDP and output; the opposite is true for the manufacturing and agricultural sectors. The service sector has jumped from 62 per cent to 76 per cent of the GDP between 1980 and 2005 (World Bank, 2005). In the same amount of time, the agricultural sector has experienced a substantial drop from 14 per cent to just 5 per cent of the GDP (World Bank, 2005). Manufacturing also witnessed a drop of 10 per cent to 5 per cent in the same period (World Bank, 2005).

The Dutch Disease model cannot wholly explain this structural change. Saint Lucia's main export in the agricultural sector has been bananas since sugar prices dropped after World War II. By 1964, 85 per cent of the island's exports were bananas (Wilkenson, 2003, 91). The banana industry continued to be of great importance until the World Trade Organization ended a preferential trade policy between the island and the European Union in 1993 (Timms, 2006, 40). As demonstrated in Figure 9.4, the banana export has since fallen from approximately USD 70 million in 1992 to just USD 16.3 million eleven years later

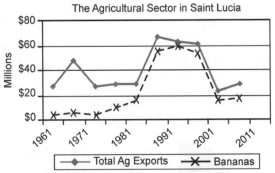

Figure 9.5: Demonstrates This Structural Change in the Economy from 1980 to 2005

Source: World Bank 2004.

(FAOSTAT). While many would assume the deterioration of the banana trade policy was the sole contributor to the fall of Saint Lucian agriculture, it is important to note other agricultural crops that were not impacted by the WTO ruling, such as cocoa and non-agricultural goods, have also fallen (Timms 2006, 40). Timms notes, for example, non-agricultural goods dropped from USD 2.8 million in 1994 to 0.5 million in just eight years (Timms, 2006, 40). Further, it must be noted government-funded agricultural extensions have also been reduced (Timms, 2006 40), potentially increasing the cost of production and limiting increases in technology used to produce the agriculture.

The lack of agricultural production is also evident in changes in the island's terms of trade. According to the World Bank, total exports[3] have taken a tumble, going from USD 48 million in 1983 to $120 million a decade later and then receding to $70 million in 2003 (Timms, 2006, 41). Imports, on the other hand, have followed a steady trajectory, from USD 107 million in 1983 to over USD 400 million in 2003 (Timms, 2006, 41). Food imports have nearly tripled, rising from USD 24 million in 1983 to USD 71 million in 2003 (Timms, 2006, 41). Table 9.2 illustrates this trend.

Table 9.2: Trends in Trade for Saint Lucia (in Millions)

	1983	1993	2003
Exports	$48	$120	$70
Imports	$107	$300	$401

Source: Timms 2006, 41.

Despite recent government attempts to diversify the economy by increasing the capacity of the manufacturing sector, high costs of production, the lack of manufacturing skills and high wage rates have not provided an incentive for corporations to establish operations in Saint Lucia (Wilkenson 2003, 94). K. Dwight Venner, the former Director of Finance and Planning for Saint Lucia, succinctly discusses the nation's economy in Wilkenson (2003):

While there has been growth and modernization, the all round development of the economy has lagged as it is still structurally unbalanced and not capable of self-sustaining growth. To put it in the jargon of the economist it is open, vulnerable and dependent (Wilkenson, 2003, 93)

Discussion

Saint Lucia has undergone several changes paralleling the symptoms of Dutch Disease. The nation has experienced inflation as demonstrated though their rising CPI, a decrease in output and profitability in their manufacturing and agricultural sectors and a migration of labourers out of the lagging sectors into the non-tradable sector. While the decrease in the agricultural sector has largely been due to the WTO ruling restricting free trade, the reduction in other agricultural goods not impacted by the imposing tariffs as well as the decrease in the manufacturing sector is sufficient evidence that tourism contributed to direct deindustrialization in Saint Lucia.

DOMINICA

Dominica is quite a different island all together. Economically, the nation leaves much to be desired; with a 15 to 25 per cent unemployment rate, 27 per cent of the population lives in extreme poverty (Patterson and Rodriguez 2003, 61). The social networks of the Dominicans, however, make life a bit richer as they enjoy a high life expectancy and low infant mortality. Dominicans also often gather food and building materials from the earth, which is not measured by GDP (Patterson and Rodriguez, 2003, 61). Their relation with the land can also be seen in their government policies, as 20 per cent of the island has been set aside as national parks and protected areas (Patterson and Rodriguez, 2003, 61)

Tourism in Dominica

While the government maintains agriculture is the 'backbone' of their economy (Wilkenson, 2004, 86), Dominica has been including tourism more often in their economic plans as they receive tourists on a steady but increasing trajectory. Unlike Saint Lucia, Dominica has resisted development programmes encouraging large-scale tourism (Wilkenson, 2004, 85), preferring to foster the development of local, small-scale businesses (Brohman, 1996, 56). The island markets itself as the 'Nature Island of the Caribbean,' promoting its rainforest, volcanic beaches, waterfalls, hiking trails, diverse wildlife and the only remaining Carib Territory in the Caribbean.

Because of Dominica's effort to promote 'natural, cultural and historical' sights rather than changing its environment to appease those looking for the typical beach-orientated vacation (Wilkenson, 2004, 85), tourism is more gradual and less intense than other Caribbean islands. While tourism has increased significantly – stay-over visitors have increased 100 times (Patterson and Rodriguez, 2003, 65) – most tourists are from other Caribbean nations (60 per cent) and most stay in private residences (54 per cent) as opposed to large-scale, corporate resorts. As demonstrated in Figure 9.6, the island received near 70,000 tourists in 2004 (UNWTO).

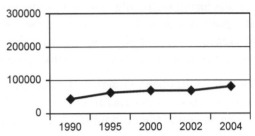

Figure 9.6: Tourist Arrivals in Dominica

Economic Indicators

As previously noted, a nation inflicted by Dutch Disease would experience a high level of inflation due to the vast influx of foreign capital. As previously noted, the Eastern Caribbean Dollar is used for both Saint Lucia and Dominica, as well as other nations in the Caribbean, making it a difficult variable to contrast the two nations with. It should be noted, however, the Eastern Caribbean Dollar has steadily dropped, from USD 2.01 Eastern Caribbean Dollar per SDR in 1968 to USD 3.85 Eastern Caribbean Dollar per SDR in 2005 (IMF, 1998) (IMF, 2006), indicating inflation. According to the Consumer Price Index, inflation in Dominica was the second lowest in all of the Caribbean between 2002 and 2006 (Government of the Republic of Dominica, 2008). According to the Government of the Republic of Dominica, inflation has slowly increased from 0.18 per cent in 2002 to 1.68 per cent in 2005 (Government of the Republic of Dominica, 2008). These statistics reveal there is little inflation occurring in Dominica.

Labour Force

As previously noted, one would assume an economic boom in the tourism sector has increased the income of the non-tradable sector and thus raised wage rates, a nation inflicted with the theoretical Dutch Disease would likely see a change in the employment structure. Workers are likely to leave the manufacturing and agricultural sectors to receive higher wages in other areas.

The International Labour Organization estimates between the years 1991 and 2000 reveal a slightly different picture than the clear deindustrialization in Saint Lucia. The numbers suggest most industries within the non-tradable sector (hotels, restaurants, wholesale and retail trade, and real estate) have experienced growth (ILO, 2008). Interestingly, while agricultural employment has dropped from 30 per cent to 20 per cent, manufacturing has stayed at the same levels throughout the decade (ILO, 2008). These changes indicate a slight movement in priorities towards the non-tradable sector and away from agricultural industry, but the change is not as dramatic as seen in Saint Lucia (ILO, 2008). Table 9.3 displays the structural change in employment in Dominica.

Table 9.3: Employment Trends in Dominica Select Economic Sectors
(Percentage of Workforce)

	1991	2001
Agriculture	30%	20%
Manufacturing	7%	7%
Wholesale and Retail Trade, Hotels and Restaurants	15%	20%
Construction	11%	9%
Real Estate	3%	4%

Source: ILO 2008.

The Manufacturing and Agricultural Sectors

To further measure the possibility of deindustrialization it is necessary to measure the contribution trends of the manufacturing, service and agricultural sectors. According to the World Bank, services have increased by 20 per cent in the past 15 years, from 48 per cent in 1980 to 58 per cent in 2005. Agriculture has fallen from 30 per cent in 1980 to just 18 per cent of GDP fifteen years later (World Bank, 2005), largely paralleling the employment trends previously mentioned. Industry increased its share of GDP in the same time period, from 20 per cent to 23 per cent (World Bank, 2005), as well as manufacturing increased by 4 per cent (World Bank, 2005). Figure 9.8 illustrates the increasing contributions of the service sector and manufacturing to GDP, as well as the decreasing share from agriculture.

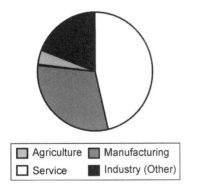

Agriculture   Manufacturing
Service   Industry (Other)

Figure 9.7: Percentage of GDP by Sector – 1980

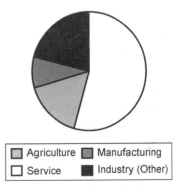

Agriculture   Manufacturing
Service   Industry (Other)

Figure 9.8: Percentage of GDP by Sector – 2005

Source: World Bank 2006

This difference between the two nations lie in Dominica's diversified manufacturing and industry sector. The nation has found the offshore service sector, which includes banking and online gaming, is another industry that allows the nation a specific niche (Patterson and Rodriguez, 2003, 64). These services do not involve high transport costs or importing inputs, making it an excellent opportunity for the island to diversify its exports.

The steady pace in manufacturing and service is evident in Dominica's terms of trade. According to the World Bank, total exports[4] have steadily increased from USD 22 million in 1980 to a reasonable USD 47 in 2005 (World Bank, 2006). As opposed to Saint Lucia, imports have actually decreased from USD 92 million in 1980 to USD 60 million (World Bank, 2006). This trend in imports may be a reflection of the nation's improved and increasing manufacturing and service sector.

Table 9.4: Trends in Trade for Dominica (In Millions)

	1980	1990	2005
Exports	$22	$54	$47
Imports	$92	$80	$60

Source: World Bank 2006.

Discussion

Although Dominica has greatly expanded its service sector, there are no signs of deindustrialization. The nation has experienced a low inflation rate, an increase in manufacturing, and diversification of their service sector. The nation has also not demonstrated migration trends displayed by nations affected by Dutch Disease.

CONCLUSIONS

This study successfully fulfilled its intention of determining if two nations with increasing tourism industries, Saint Lucia and Dominica, were following the Dutch Disease model. It is concluded Saint Lucia's explosive tourism industry has indeed led to direct deindustrialization, while Dominica's subtle approach to tourism has provided them with a different path.

The case studies of the two nations were contrasting. Saint Lucia has focused on attracting large, foreign corporations to the nation, which has allured large numbers of tourists. Although a WTO ruling, mandating tariffs of their main export, bananas, led to a dramatic drop in production and output in the agricultural sector, other agricultural products as well as the manufacturing sector has dropped in the past two decades. Labour has shifted to the non-tradable sector and inflation has risen since 1987. The variables suggest Saint Lucia has inadvertently limited their economy as they expand their tourism market, paralleled the symptoms of Dutch Disease.

Dominica, on the other hand, has experienced a growing dependence on tourism as well but has not experienced the labour migration, notable inflation or a substantial decrease in their alternate sectors. Evidence suggests their low-impact approach to tourism has allowed them to *diversify* their economy by growing their tourism market.

As Caribbean nations increasingly favour tourism as the most fitting opportunity for development, research determining the impacts on the economy is essential. As the Dutch Disease model explains, the economic reaction to an export boom may lead to deindustrialization, potentially limiting their future competitiveness.

NOTES

1. Reliable data has not been released regarding tourism growth after the 2009/2010 financial recession.
2. For the purpose of this study we will borrow the terminology for Sectors from Corden's 1984 *Booming Sector and Dutch Disease Economics: Survey and Consolidation.*
3. 'Exports' do not include tourism.
4. 'Exports' does not include tourism.

REFERENCES

1. Acosta, Pablo A., Emmanuel K.K. Lartey and Federico S. Mandelman. 2009.
2. Remittances and Dutch Disease. *Journal of International Economics* 79: 102–116.
3. Arellano, Cristina, Ales Bulir, Timothy Lane and Leslie Lipschitz. 2009. The dynamic implications of foreign aid and its variability. *Journal of Development Economics* 88: 87–102.
4. Brohman, John. 1996. New Directions for Tourism in Third World Development. *Annals of Tourism Research* 23: 48–70.
5. Capo, Javier, Antoni Riera Font and Jaume Rossello Nadal. 2007. Dutch Disease in Tourism Economies: Evidence from the Balearics and the Canary Islands. *Journal of Sustainable Tourism* 15: 615–627.
6. Central Intelligence Agency. 'CIA World Factbook 1992.' *University of Missouri St. Louis.* Available: http://www.umsl.edu/services/govdocs/wofact92/
7. Chao, Chi-Chur, Bharat R. Hazari, Jean-Pierre Laffargue, Pasquale M. Sgo and Eden S. H. Yu. 2006. Tourism, Dutch Disease and Welfare in an Open Dynamic Economy. *The Japanese Economic Review* 54: 501–515.
8. Conway, Denis. 2004. 'Tourism, environmental conservation and management in local agriculture in the Caribbean.' In *Tourism in the Caribbean,* ed. David Timothy. Duval, 186–202. London: Routledge.
9. Copeland, Brian R. 1991. Tourism, Welfare and Deindustrialization in a Small Open Economy. *Economica* 58: 515–529.
10. Corden, W. Max. 1984. Booming sector and Dutch Disease economies: survey and consolidation. *Oxford Economic Papers* 36: 359–80.
11. Corden, W. Max and J. Peter Neary. 1982. Booming sector and deindustrialization in small open economy. *Economic Journal* 92: 825–48.
12. Duval, David Timothy. 2004. 'Trends and circumstances in Caribbean tourism.' In *Tourism in the Caribbean,* ed. David Timothy Duval, 3–22. London: Routledge.
13. Floating on Gas.' January 30, 1982 *The Economist*: 4.

14. Food and Agriculture Organization (FAO). 'FAOSTAT.' Available: http://faostat.fao.org/

15. Gossling, Stefan. 2003. 'Tourism and Development in Tropical Islands: Political Ecology Perspectives.' In *Tourism and Development in Tropical Islands,* ed. Stefan Gossling, 1–38. Cheltenham, UK: Edward Elgar Publishing.

16. Government of the Republic of Dominica. 2008. 'Dominica's Cost Of Living Figures

17. Grossly Exaggerated.' *Government of the Republic of Dominica.* Available: http://www.dominica. gov.dm/cms/index.html?q=node/244

18. Government of Saint Lucia (GOSL). 2007. 'Consumer Price Index 1987–2006.' *Government of Saint Lucia.* Available: http://www.stats.gov.lc/pri121.htm

19. International Monetary Fund. 2006. *International Financial Statistics.* Washington, DC: International Monetary Fund.

20. International Monetary Fund. 1998. *International Financial Statistics.* Washington, DC: International Monetary Fund.

21. Kairi Consultants Limited. 'St. Lucia Country Poverty Assessment 2005/2006.' *The Caribbean Development Bank.* Available: http://www.caribank.org/titanweb/cdb/webcms.nsf/AllDoc/0D12B 24D6A68362387257338006F5DF3?OpenDocument

22. Kenell, Lena. 2008. Dutch Disease and Tourism: The Case of Thailand. *Lund University.* Available: biblioteket.ehl.lu.se/olle/papers/0002903.pdf

23. Mitchell, Jonathan. 2007. 'Can tourism offer pro-poor pathways to prosperity? June 2007 Briefing Paper.' *Overseas Development Institute.* Available: www.odi.org.uk/resources/download/84.pdf

24. Patterson, Trista and Luis Rodriguez. 2003. 'The Political Ecology of Tourism in the Commonwealth of Dominica.' In *Tourism and Development in Tropical Islands,* ed. Stefan Gossling, 60–87. Cheltenham, UK: Edward Elgar Publishing.

25. Timms, Benjamin. 2006. Caribbean Agriculture – tourism linkages in a neoliberal world. *International Development Planning Review* 28: 35–56.

26. United Nations World Tourism Organization (UNWTO). 'International Tourism Arrivals.' *United Nations World Tourism Organization.* Available: http://unwto.org/facts/eng/pdf/indicators/ITA_ Americas.pdf.

27. Wilkenson, Paul F. 2004. 'Caribbean tourism policy and planning.' In *Tourism in the Caribbean,* ed. David Timothy Duval, 80–98. London: Routledge.

28. Wilkenson, Paul F. 2003. 'Tourism Policy and Planning in St. Lucia.' In *Tourism and Development in Tropical Islands,* ed. Stefan Gossling, 88–101. Cheltenham, UK: Edward Elgar Publishing.

29. World Bank. 2005. *World Bank.* 'Dominica at a Glance.' Available: http://go.worldbank.org/ YB2ATM3HY0.

30. World Bank. 2005. *World Bank.* 'St. Lucia at a Glance.' Available: http://go.worldbank.org/ YB2ATM3HY0.

10 | Neoclassical or Keynesian Economic Model

Which Way to Economic Development in Nigeria?

Omolade Ogunye

CHAPTER SUMMARY

Since the early nineteen hundreds, economists have proposed more than nine theories of economic development including the Harrod-Domar theory, Lewis' model of structural change, and W.W. Rostow's theory. However this chapter will focus on comparing the neoclassical model of economic development and the Keynesian proposal/Big push hypothesis. Many developing countries like Nigeria adopted the Keynesian proposal/ Big push hypothesis in their economic development strategies and have not seen much improvement while certain countries have experienced progress. While it is not expected that Nigeria like its fellow African states will become prosperous capitalist societies overnight, the constant lagging of these countries in the area of economic development has become a cause for concern. This is an empirical study of both models of economic development and which is theoretically more suitable for the Federal Republic of Nigeria independent of politics. The chapter will first present a brief theoretical review of both the neoclassical and Keynesian models, and then the Development Plans in Nigeria since its independence will be reviewed. Finally, the more adaptable model will be identified and recommendations that may aid in the crafting of better economic development policies will be made.

Economic development can be defined as the increase in the standard of living of a nation's population with sustained growth from a simple, low-income economy to a modern, high-income economy. The economic development of a country depends on the quantity and quality of its resources, the states of technology and the efficient deployment of resources in both the production and consumption processes.

Nigeria became a modern political entity in 1914 after its amalgamation by the British and remained a British colony from 1868 until 1 October 1960 when it gained its independence. It then embarked on a number of political transitions. First, it was an independent federation under the Commonwealth, then on 1 October 1963, it became a republic but still remained in the commonwealth. Its government was first modeled as a parliamentary democracy fashioned after the British system between 1960 and 1965 before it came under military rule in January 1966 when the civilian government was overthrown in a *coup d'état*. On 1 October, 1979, a new civilian government based on the presidential system was created and existed until 13 December, 1983. From 1983 till 1999, a sequence of military dictators controlled the coffers of the country until power was peacefully handed over to a civilian government.

According to the CIA World fact book, 68 per cent of the Federal Republic of Nigeria's 150 million-strong population is literate (July 2009). The country has thirty-six administrative states and a federal capital territory in Abuja, although Lagos remains the main hub of diplomatic, media, commercial, and banking activities. By 2007 estimate, 70 per cent of the Nigerian population live below the poverty line despite 51.04 million being in the workforce. Unemployment rate is estimated at 10.8 per cent. While the country has begun to reform its banking sector and money-laundering controls according to the International Monetary Fund's specifications, the most common problems experienced in Nigeria by investors are the country's reputation as a major money-laundering centre, erratic electricity supply, weakened rule of law, and its corruption and criminal activity. (CIA World Factbook)

Like many other developing economies that adopted the Keynesian model of economic development which proposes that government has a greater involvement in the economy and become large employers of the nation's heavy industries, financial projects, and institutions in their countries, there are characteristics that distinguish Nigeria from developed countries. These include duality in several aspects of its society such as urban and rural communities; industrial and agricultural sectors; private (albeit very small) and public sectors; and skilled and unskilled (very large) labour. Also, the government sector is the largest producer of goods and employer of labour due to its ownership of major industries such as steel, transportation, and cement. This heavy government control then leads to high taxes and bulky administrative machinery.

THE ROOTS OF NIGERIA'S ECONOMIC CRISIS

To understand the solutions to a problem, one must understand the causes of the problem. In the case of Nigeria, that means going back to studying the nature of pre-colonial society, contact with imperialist forces and its effect on various aspects of the nation. There is a near consensus on the fact that colonialism in Nigeria as in other former colonies inhibited and distorted all aspects of pre-colonial society as it previously existed. According to Ihonvbere, since first contact with the Royal Niger Company (RNC) in 1851, 'the natural processes of state and class formation, and possibilities of improvement on indigenous technology and industrial patterns were either destroyed, deformed, or recomposed to serve alien interests and support the imposed…economic and administrative structures in the service of colonial…subjugation and exploitation'. (Ihonvbere, 1994)

STUDYING CONTEMPORARY REASONS FOR UNDERDEVELOPMENT

It cannot be argued that Nigeria's problem is a lack of resources as the country is currently Africa's second largest oil producer and ninth largest producer in the world, and has the tenth largest proven oil reserves. In addition, it has a vast possession of natural resources such as arable land, cocoa, tin, and iron ore among many others. However, its history of economic stagnation, declining welfare and social instability, has undermined development for most of the past 30 years. Because the major reason for underdevelopment is low rates of productivity, Nigeria's problem must lie in its use of its factors of production; land, labour, capital, and enterprise.

Julius Ihonvbere writes that the period of 'military rule in Nigeria has not only suffocated civil society, but has also entrenched a culture of repression, corruption, privatization of public office, official irresponsibility, arrogance, and non-accountability to the public.' (Ihonvbere, 1994) He also notes that Nigeria should take an example from the disintegration of the Soviet Union as a superpower and as a nation; the lesson being that 'what happened in Eastern Europe demonstrates the failure of the practice of socialism in a global economy dominated by capitalist interests, and the encumbrances imposed on growth and development by a heavy bureaucracy…' (Ihonvbere, 1994)

THEORETICAL SECTION

NEOCLASSICAL ECONOMICS

Swiss Leon Walras, Austrian Carl Menger, and English William Jevons are three economists who worked independently, but are credited collectively with the rise of neoclassical economics in the 1870s. Their individual works based on the theory of utility maximization and marginal utility being proportional to price were a challenge to classical economists such as Adam Smith and David Ricardo whose cost-based theories of value were the long accepted norm.

Neoclassical economists argue that the consumer is a rational self-interested individual who always makes an optimum response to changing price signals. Although it was perceived as believing that demand was the sole determinant of price, Alfred Marshall's work reinforced the importance of supply in the market. For neoclassical economists, day to day fluctuations of the marketplace and interactions such as that between prices and quantities were the essence of economic life. The central point of this model of economics was to understand the general laws of supply and demand and the utility-maximizing consumer. They came to the conclusion that the typical market would have a unique and stable equilibrium (a long-run concept).

One of the major problems with neoclassical economics was 'the obsession with relative price movements'. While its assumptions necessary to the proof of stability in the individual market were valid, it made the mistake of using these assumptions for the whole economy. Leon Walras avoided discussing the stability issue in his work by using intellectual devices such as 'auctioneer' or 'recontracting' to refer to the idea that what happened when the system was not at its equilibrium could be ignored. Alfred Marshall does not discuss it in his work. (Martinussen, 1997)

The idea of general equilibrium implied that if all prices were at equilibrium values, then everything on the macroeconomic level would be fine; hence, if there were macroeconomic disequilibria, then some prices were out of line with others, and the answer would lie in relative price movements where the price of goods in excess supply should fall, and the price of goods in excess demand should rise. So, the unsolvable problem laid in the variety of possible relative price problems and the reality that prices of different goods moved relative to one another.

The Great Depression which began in the United States with the stock market crash of 29 October 1929 threw neoclassical economics into a major crisis and showed that the economists' great confidence in the adaptability of a free market economy was unfounded. This devalued reputation prepared the groundwork that would usher in the great acceptance of John Maynard Keynes' revolution in economic theory.

Neo-classical economists such as Bela Belassa, Jagdish Bhagwati, and Robert Solow argue that economic development is impossible if government sector has heavy interference in the economy as evidenced through:

a) High bureaucracy
b) More control
c) Heavy taxation
d) Administrative drawbacks
e) Protectionism from free trade

The neoclassical model is an extension of the Harrod-Domar model with the inclusion of productivity growth. They assume that capital is subject to diminishing returns, and economic growth declines because at some point the amount of new capital produced is barely enough to make up for the amount of existing capital lost due to depreciation.

Gross Domestic Product (GDP) $(Y) = A. K^a. L^{1-a}. e^u$.

This is the assumed relationship between input and output of the economy and is also called production function. The production function is a degree of homogeneity.

A = constant term
K = capital stock
L = labour employment
a = degree of increase in output when K is changed
e^u = all other inputs than K and L that cause increase in GDP.

They are called residual contributions or solow residual.

If a constant (say 5 per cent) increase in K and L is made, $0 < 8 < 1$.

Then GDP (Y) will increase by 5 per cent as well.

This production function also recognizes diminishing marginal returns from the use of K and L. So, the real growth comes from all the inputs that are neither capital nor labour but cause an increase in the country's GDP.

This model has been criticized for encouraging completely free markets as excessive deregulation and privatization has its own perils. In addition, because almost everything is included in solow residual, solow residual is invisible and renders the theory largely unclear in many ways.

Keynesian Economics

When in 1936, British economist John Maynard Keynes published *The General Theory of Employment Interest and Money*, a book that was a product of the crisis in economic theory produced by the Great Depression, economics in the period after was dubbed 'The Keynesian Revolution'. Keynes' policy recommendations had been used in several countries such as the United States, Sweden, France, and Germany prior to the publication of the book, but Keynes work was still influential because it 'bridged the gulf between practical ideas and pure neoclassical theory and…(created) a new general theory of economics'. (Bleaney, 1985)

Keynesian economics as laid out in The General Theory concentrates on the short-run dynamics of capitalism. Essentially, what J.M. Keynes did was an examination of what would happen if the economic system was pushed away from its general equilibrium – a question that neoclassical economists had systematically avoided. In the book's first chapter which is a single paragraph, Keynes states his main conclusion: that his theory is the general theory of output and employment as opposed to neoclassical theory which is only a special case that can be applied to situations of full employment.

In challenging neoclassical thought, Keynes argues that the problem of deficient effective demand cannot be solved through adjustments in the labour market where excess supply will manifest itself. Because labour is exchanged for money and not directly for the products of their labour, workers can easily engineer a cut in their money wage, but this would reduce prices of goods by lowering marginal costs in a competitive market. Hence, the neoclassical argument that excess supply of labour would be fixed by a fall in real wage is proven incorrect since cutting money wage is simple, but cutting real wage is not.

Keynes further argued that even if a fall in real wages resulted from this process, the level of demand would not be raised due to the undesirable impact of decreasing prices on entrepreneurial expectations and the real burden of firms' debts. Hence, price changes in the market where the symptoms of a demand deficiency appear would not solve the problem. In addition, Keynes accuses the neoclassical economic model of never abandoning the early nineteenth century concept of Say's Law according to which supply creates its own demand. However, the downfall of Keynesian theory is that it adopts the 19th century assumption of competitive markets, and does not investigate the structure of 20th century capitalist economies.

Keynesian economics advocates a mixed economy consisting of a dominant private sector, but with a large presence of government and public sector. During the latter part of the Great Depression, World War II, and the post war economic expansion from 1945–1973, the model was adopted in many nations, however it lost some influence following the stagflation of the 1970s. Since the 1940s, the government sector of many developing countries has become very active in economic development due to the traditional growth model of Keynes. The advent of the global financial crisis in 2007 has caused a resurgence in Keynesian thought. (Bleaney, 1985)

MODIFICATIONS OF THE KEYNESIAN MODEL

While the Keynesian model has now been criticized by many economists since its decline, there have been modifications to it such as the Big Push hypothesis, the Harrod-Domar model, and Okun's law.

a. ***Big Push Hypothesis:*** Austrian economist, Paul Rosenstein-Rodan's model was developed from Allyn Young's 1928 article titled 'Increasing Returns and Economic Progress' which was developed from Adam Smith's 1776 work. Rosenstein-Rodan argued that a deliberate creation of extensive investment programmes in countries with a large surplus workforce in agriculture that sought industrialization. In the big-push logic, anything that stimulates demand will do, whether a large public spending programme, foreign aid, discovery of minerals, or a rise in the world price of a natural resource. (Sachs, Warner, 1999)

b. ***Harrod-Domar Model:*** This model is used to explain an economy's growth rate in terms of savings rate and capital productivity. Developed independently by Sir Roy F. Harrod in 1939 and Evsey Domar in 1946, the model which was originally meant to explain the business cycle shows that because labour is abundant in developing countries but physical capital is not, economic development will be slow. Developing countries do not have adequate average income to enable high rates of saving, and therefore accumulation of the capital stock through investment is low. Harrod-Domar model is usually applicable to modern countries with fixed saving rates.

Recognize that Y represents GDP, K represents capital stock, S is total saving, s is the savings rate, I represents investment (purchase of machinery, tools, and equipment, construction activities or increase in inventories), and δ represents the rate of depreciation of the capital stock. The Harrod–Domar model assumes that:

$Y = f(K)$	1: Output is a function of capital stock.
$\dfrac{dY}{dK} = c \Rightarrow \dfrac{dY}{dK} = \dfrac{Y}{K}$	2: The marginal product of capital is constant; the production function exhibits constant returns to scale. This implies capital's marginal and average products are equal.
$f(0) = 0$	3: Capital is necessary for output.
$sY = S = I$	4: Saving = the product of the savings rate (s) and output = Investment (I)
$\Delta K = I - \delta K$	5: The change in the capital stock = Investment – the depreciation of the capital stock.

$$c = \frac{dY}{dK} = \frac{Y(t+1)-Y(t)}{K(t)+sY(t)-\delta K(t)-K(t)}$$

$$c = \frac{Y(t+1)-Y(t)}{sY(t)-\delta \frac{dK}{dY} Y(t)}$$

$$c\left(sY(t)-\delta \frac{dK}{dY} Y(t) \right) = Y(t+1)-Y(t)$$

$$cY(t)\left(s-\delta \frac{dK}{dY} \right) = Y(t+1)-Y(t)$$

$$cs - c\delta \frac{dK}{dY} = \frac{Y(t+1)-Y(t)}{Y(t)}$$

$$s\frac{dY}{dK} - \delta \frac{dY}{dK}\frac{dK}{dY} = \frac{Y(t+1)-Y(t)}{Y(t)}$$

$$sc - \delta = \frac{\Delta Y}{Y}$$

Therefore, according to the Harrod-Domar model, a higher saving rate is the precondition for economy's growth. To raise saving rate, there must be:

a. Increase in interest rate;
b. Lower conspicuous consumption by increasing taxes on luxury goods;
c. Borrowing in the international financial market;
d. Efforts to attract foreign direct investment (FDI).

It must be noted that this model has been criticized on the grounds of being too constrained and ignoring the role of institutions, government, culture, and work habits of the people. In addition, it has been blamed for assuming that economic growth and economic development are the same thing (where economic growth is the process of acquiring new resources and producing at a higher level than was previously possible, economic development is using available resources more efficiently). Hence, the model has also been accused of implying that developing countries should borrow more money in order to prompt domestic economic growth. Still, in the 1950s, this model was most influential in the making of economic development policy.

c. *Okun's Law:* This law has been accepted as an empirical fact which predicts that a 3 per cent increase in GDP will cause a 1 per cent reduction rate in unemployment. (Prachnowy, 1993)

EMPIRICAL SECTION

DEVELOPMENT PLANNING IN NIGERIA

Development or economic planning is a deliberate direction by government's policies to coordinate economic decision making in order to influence the nation's principal economic variables to achieve pre-determined economic objectives. Planning for economic development essentially means attempting to speed up the process of social and economic development by ensuring the greatest volume and the best possible allocation of resources for economic growth in order to reach the goals set by the people through their governments. through direct and indirect means (Onimode et al., 2004).

Development planning is popular in developing countries because it is perceived as the best strategy for transforming their economies and narrowing the gap between them and advanced industrial economies. Nigeria's planning experience dates back to the1940s when the British Colonial Office requested the colonies to prepare development plans that would assist it in disbursing the Colonial Development and Welfare Funds. In response to this request, the administration in Nigeria prepared the Ten Year Plan of Development and Welfare from 1945 till 1955 but the plan was halted in 1950 due to the challenges faced when attempting to measure development over a long period in a country experiencing frequent structural changes. Hence, they decided to divide the plan period into two 5-year periods with the second plan covering the sub-period 1956 till 1960.

Since 1960, Nigeria has created and commenced three other development plans that were formulated within the framework of an improved system of national accounts, covered the operations of both public and private sectors of the economy, and had their projects related to a number of well expressed economic targets. Planning in Nigeria has been within the framework of a mixed economy similar to those in advanced western economies and very different from the pervading models in Soviet countries. While the contributions of the private sector were recognized, the main instrument for achieving the objectives of each plan would be public sector investment programmes.

The 1962-1968 Plan was the first serious effort to relate planning to national objectives and goals, and so it has been argued that the previous plans were not plans because in actuality they were a series of projects that had not been coordinated or related to any overall economic target. However, the implementation of the 1962-1968 Plan was stalled in 1966 by the military coup in 1966 and the subsequent Biafra civil war; during this time, the annual capital budgets were used as the main instrument of allocating developmental resources and control. The 1962-1968 National Development Plan had goals such as:

a.   Achieve an average economic growth rate of 4 per cent or more;
b.   Achieve an increase in per capita consumption by about 1 per cent per year;
c.   Achieve self-sustaining growth no later than the end of the Third or Fourth National Plan;
d.   Attain a modernized economy which was consistent with the democratic, political, and social aspirations of the people including a more equitable distribution of income among the people and the various regions; create more jobs and opportunities in non-agricultural occupations.

When the political crises of 1966 occurred, the planners believed that the nation had been provided with an opportunity to set new goals and objectives of national planning that would fire the nation's imagination and provide a motive for social action and development activities. And so, the Second National Development Plan aimed to establish Nigeria as:

a. A united, strong and self-reliant nation;
b. A great and dynamic economy;
c. A just and egalitarian society;
d. A land of bright and full opportunities for all citizens; and
e. A free and democratic society.

By setting these as goals, the planners made it more difficult to quantify and measure the achievement of the Plan, and pursued policies that were not strictly economic. However, these goals were deemed so pertinent that they were retained in the Third Plan with seven not-so-new short-term objectives being added to them. These included:

a. Increase in per capita income;
b. More equitable distribution of income;
c. Reduction in the level of unemployment;
d. Increase in the supply of high level manpower;
e. Diversification of the economy;
f. Balanced development; and
g. Indigenization of economic activity.

There was no specific planning machinery for the realization of the Ten Year Plan, instead it was deemed 'a disjointed set of individual projects grouped under departmental headings which reflected the administrative structure of the colonial government rather than any coordinated sectoral division of the economy'. The National Economic Council consisting of the Prime Minister, regional premiers, and some federal and regional ministers was established in 1955 to discuss development policies and common economic problems. Because they handled other responsibilities, they could not meet frequently and so they created the Joint Planning Committee, chaired by the Economic Advisor to the Federal Government. In addition, the Economic Planning Unit located in the Federal Ministry of Economic Development and the regional ministries of Economic Planning. (Clarke, 1963)

The National Development Plan for 1962-1968 was created under these agencies, and this was the first of its kind in the country. However, there were many problems to be encountered. First, there was an inadequate number of the economists, statisticians, and other technical staff required to draw up a comprehensive plan, and so foreign experts who did not fully understand the country's political and social history and might not be committed to the country's vision were entrusted with the plan. Also, because government was decentralized with regions possessing a considerable amount of power, different levels of planning units would prepare plans independent of each other and employ different methods. Furthermore, the regional prejudices and ethnic mistrust that had long existed served to create rivalries that hindered exchange of ideas as well as coordination of the plan.

When the political crisis occurred in 1966, implementation of the Plan was disrupted and some of the planning institutions such as the National Economic Council and its creation the Joint Planning Committee were eliminated and replaced by the National Economic Planning Advisory Group in 1966 to review the economy's progress since independence in 1960, make projections into the future and tender recommendations about the direction of long-rub economic policies, as well as identify points that required modification of existing policies. This newly created agency did not have a large impact partly because of the country's situation as well as its short-lived existence. (Olaloku et al., 1979)

The following year, thirteen states were created to replace the five existing regions, and Advisory Group could not shoulder the responsibility of planning for all the governments, especially since they lacked institutional machinery and manpower resources for economic planning. Hence, the federal government through the Federal Ministry of Economic Development and its Economic Planning Unit took over the responsibility of coordinating national efforts in the Development Plan. In addition, the Central Planning Office was created in 1971 under the same parent ministry to become the official planning institution and to create the Third National Development Plan for 1975 to 1980 which included such goals as a GDP target growth of 9 per cent every year in real terms and a 6 per cent annual per capita income growth rate.

To ensure that all sectors in the economy were given adequate consideration in creating the Plan, a National Economic Advisory Council was established in 1972 to advise the government on planning matters. The Joint Planning Board consisting of members from the federal and state ministries, the Central Bank of Nigeria, and the Nigerian Institute of Social and Economic Research was created to harmonize the economic policies and development activities of the federal and state governments, and Plan Implementation Committees at both the federal and state level were established. With this, state planning authorities had a lesser role to play in the formulation of the Third National Development Plan.

On 26 March 1992, the National Planning Commission was established by Decree 12 as issued by the military head of state Ibrahim Babangida at that time and later amended by Act 71 in the aborted 1993 constitution. The commission has the mandate to determine and advise the thirty-six governments of the federation on matters relating to the country's development and overall management of the economy.

Starting in 2003, the National Economic Empowerment Development Strategy (NEEDS), an economic reform programme designed to raise quality of life for the nation's citizens through various means including macroeconomic stability, deregulation, liberalization, privatization, transparency, and accountability was launched by the National Planning Commission. The government hopes that NEEDS will create 7 million new jobs, diversify the economy, boost non-energy exports, increase industrial capacity utilization, and improve agricultural productivity. It is also hoped that NEEDS will address the lack of basic amenities such as the lack of fresh water for household use and irrigation, erratic power supply, and dilapidated infrastructure among others.

In 2003, the Olusegun Obasanjo administration launched the Nigeria Vision 2020 which is aimed at transforming Nigeria into one of the 20 largest economies in the world, as well as consolidation of its leadership role in Africa and as a significant player in the global economic and political arena. Of the many parameters that would be used by the government to measure the success of the plan, one of them was to build 'a sound, stable and globally competitive economy with a GDP of not less than USD 900 billion and a per capita income of not less than USD 4000 per annum'. Another was to build a health sector that 'supports and sustains a life expectancy of not less than 70 years and reduces to the barest minimum the burden of infectious diseases such as malaria, HIV/AIDS and other debilitating diseases'.

Upon assuming power in 2008, the Nigerian president Umaru Yar'Adua laid out a Seven Point Action Plan which he planned to implement during his tenure as president. This agenda emphasized power and energy production; food security and agriculture; mass transportation; land reform; security; and qualitative and functional education. By doing this, he was further reinforcing the country's commitment to the United Nations' Millennium Development Goals as well as the Nigeria Vision 2020. (http://www.nassnig.org)

In order to attain the Nigeria Vision 2020, the current administration through the National Planning Commission has created national technical working groups that consist of about twenty technical experts in each of the 28 designated fields. In addition, ten special interest groups comprising women, people with disabilities, media, labour, and youth were created with the responsibility of developing objectives that would serve the interests of each group. To further develop the development plan, the following committees were created;

a.   The National Council on Vision 2020: the highest committee which has the President as its Chairman.
b.   The National Steering Committee: This committee is charged with developing the template for Vision 2020 strategic plan, its implementation guidelines, monitoring, and evaluation strategy. It consists of about 70 members from both public and private sectors in an attempt to ensure that lower agencies and government branches prepare and implement their component of the Vision.
c.   The National Technical Working Group: comprises about 25 experts in specified fields drawn from both public and private sectors who will undertake specific studies or research work to provide data necessary for the working groups' report.
d.   The Stakeholder Development Committee: includes officials from state governments, federal ministries, departments and agencies as well as other key institutions who are expected to provide information that will feed into the Plan.
e.   The Economic Management Team: with its chairman and vice-chairman already serving as members of the National Council and National Steering Committee, this committee serves as a think-tank and a link for both committees.

The Vision document is to be developed in the following stages (Figure 10.1).

• Stage 1: Building a Solid Foundation for Vision (2008–2010)

In this stage, the first two components of the framework – the National Council on Vision 2020 and the National Steering Committee on Vision 2020 should be established by the end of April 2007. The National Council should undertake an immediate review of all current strategy and related documents including the President's Seven Point Agenda, and other relevant documents

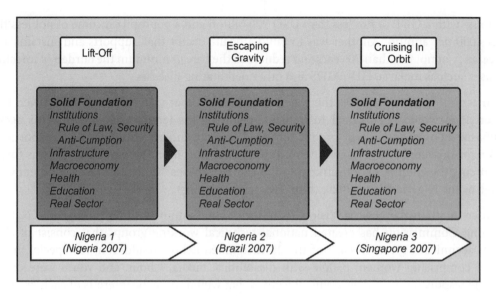

Figure 10.1: Stages of the Vision 2020 Development Plan

Source: Nigeria Vision 2020.

and prepare a statement of national priorities that will form the core elements of the country's development plans and budgets during the period 2008 to 2010 and constitute the foundation for Vision 2020. The statement of national priorities should set specific targets to be achieved by 2010. The steering committee will also refine the Vision 2020 framework and develop guidelines for its development process.

• Stage II: Achieving the Millennium Development Goals Enroute to Vision 2020 (2011–2015)

By the end of January 2008, the steering committee should have set up the technical working groups, one in each of the key areas of national priority and all stakeholder groups will establish their Vision 2020 Committees. Under the overall direction of the S, the NTWGs will work closely with the Stakeholder Visioning Committees to develop detailed action plans and implementation strategies and commence implementation of Stage I of the Vision. At the same time Stakeholder Committees will begin the development of the next two stages of their Vision document. Stage II should focus on achieving all the MDGs by 2015 as a general guide. Stakeholder committees will determine their areas of focus in accordance with their progress on the MDGs.

• Stage III: Becoming a Top 20 Economy by 2020

In stage III, the National Steering Committee will develop detailed key goals and targets that must be met in order to achieve convergence with the projected positions of the top 20 economies. These goals and targets will be cascaded into sectors and sub-national levels. The working groups will provide support in the form of data and methodologies as well as capacity building in their areas of specialty. They will also collate and harmonize the various stakeholder action plans and strategies into the National action plan and strategy for Vision 2020. (Nigeria Vision2020. http://www.nv2020.org/?Iparameters)

CAN THERE BE ECONOMIC DEVELOPMENT IN NIGERIA?

While there are pessimists such as Simon Kuznet who believe that there can be no solution to the problem of underdevelopment because developed countries have been growing faster than poor countries despite development efforts, there are optimists who believe that the technological growth occurring in developing countries such as China and India is a proof that there is a better understanding of development and a chance for development.

Despite the goals set by the Nigerian government, albeit under several military leaders as well as civilian leaders, the nation is still perceived by the larger international society as a relatively weak state characterized by political instability, corruption, and poor macroeconomic management although it has been in the process of important economic reform since civilian leadership in 1999. As Nigeria's former military rulers did not diversify the economy, there is an excessive reliance on the capital-intensive oil sector (despite the nation being a labour abundant country), which provides 80 per cent of the nation's GDP, 95 per cent of its foreign exchange earnings, and about 65 per cent of government revenue. The nation which was previously a large exporter of food now imports some of its food products since its agricultural sector could not keep up with the rapid population growth.

The term resource curse is the term that has been coined by the economists to refer to the coexistence of vast wealth in natural resources and extreme personal poverty in developing countries such as Nigeria. The nation's workforce/human capital of 47,330,000 (12th in the world) was ranked 151st out of 177 countries in the United Nations Development Index in 2004. Outside of the energy sector, Nigeria's economy is highly inefficient, and its non-energy-related infrastructure is inadequate.

However, since 2003, things have been on the upswing. In 2003, Goldman Sachs Investment Bank listed Nigeria in its Next 11 or N-11 list; this refers to countries such as Bangladesh, Mexico, South Korea, and Egypt who have been deemed as 'having a high potential of becoming the world's largest economies along with Brazil, Russia, India, and China' based on the criteria of macroeconomic stability, political maturity, openness of trade and investment policies, and quality of education.

According to the Economist Intelligence Unit and the World Bank, Nigeria's GDP at purchasing power parity nearly doubled from USD 170.7 billion in 2005 to USD 292.6 billion in 2007 while GDP per capita increased from USD 692 per person in 2006 to USD 1,969. In addition, the United Nations placed the nation in the list of countries that have attained a medium level of human development due to its increased literacy rate (72 per cent of its population is literate) and increased GDP per capita. (Human Development Report, 2009) In 2009, the International

Monetary Fund predicted a growth rate of 8.3 per cent in its GDP which is currently the 37th highest in the world.

Recently, the country has become home to one of the fastest growing telecommunications markets in the world with major emerging cell phone market operators in Africa such as MTN, Virgin, and Nigerian native-owned Globacom establishing their largest and most profitable companies in various urban centers in the country. The government has recently begun exploring space as the country has a space satellite which is monitored at the Nigerian National Space Research and Development Agency Headquarters in the federal capital territory, Abuja.

In addition, there is a fast developing financial services sector, with a mix of local and international banks, asset management companies, brokerage houses, insurance companies and brokers, private equity funds and investment banks. It also has a manufacturing industry in various cities in the country such as Lagos, Onitsha, and Kano which produces goods such as leather and textiles, car assembly for the French car manufacturer Peugeot and English truck company Bedford, clothes, as well as processed food and beverages. The Nigerian movie industry called 'Nollywood' has also made huge strides and generates a large amount of revenue as it produces the highest number of movies annually in the world, surpassing even Hollywood and Bollywood.

In essence, although slow, the country is beginning to reduce its dependence on oil, diversify its economy, and reform its financial system, and the international community is recognizing these efforts.

CONCLUSION: ADOPTING A MODEL OF ECONOMIC DEVELOPMENT

Having briefly reviewed the theories proposed by the neoclassical and Keynesian economic models for development, this chapter will attempt to select the one that will be most adaptable for the growth of the Nigerian economy. Recognizing that each development plan created in Nigeria has been largely unsuccessful and that the underlying theory of flexible price in the neoclassical model has been overturned, it is debatable that either of the two models can provide an effective development path for the nation.

History has shown that while most African countries created ambitious plans for a rapid, perhaps unrealistic pace of economic development right after attaining independence from their colonial rulers, not much has been achieved in the past decades. (Cheru, 1990) Adjibolosoo points out that development economists have pointed out major problems of economic development in Africa and propounded theories to deal effectively with these problems. (Adjibolosoo, Harrison; 1994) Developing countries have attempted to do this in national development plans and annual budgets, while helpful developed countries have concentrated their assistance efforts on tackling the problems, however not much development has resulted. He then asks the question, '...whether the diagnosis of the African problem has been wrong or whether some other pertinent factor(s) might be lacking.'

Adopting a neoclassical model of development and allowing the market to regulate itself is too risky a model for the fragile economy of a developing country that is newly reforming its economy and bureaucratic system. First, the model assumes that the consumer is a rational, utility maximizing individual who would respond to changing price signals and also assumes that the market will take care of itself. In a developing economy whose financial systems are not as advanced, it is arguable that the market should not be left unregulated as the economy which is already dependent on foreign economies may never rebound from the crash of its own market.

If the Keynesian model of economic development which recommends an increased amount of government-led policies is adopted, considering Nigeria's history with such plans and its myriad problems such as insufficient personnel, bulky administrative departments, and inadequate technology, are those development plans feasible? Also, has the culture of corruption which Adjibolosoo wrote of as pervading and permeating the fabric of Nigeria's administrative and bureaucratic structures since its independence, become so strong that the nation cannot effectively use the old Keynesian advice of heavy government involvement?

'Africa continues to be in search of a development paradigm that would eradicate abject poverty from Africa...in pursuit of that goal, a series of theories and concepts have been advanced and tried to no avail. Most of them have been grounded in Western political and development traditions that failed to take cognizance of Africa's cultural and historical background' (Onimode et al., 2004). Onimode et al. argue that Western experts refer to the structural adjustment programme of the Bretton Woods institutions which are reminiscent if social and political institutions left to African countries by their colonial rulers as a prescription for all countries despite economic, socio-cultural, and historical backgrounds.

Professor Adebayo Adedeji, a previous Nigerian Minister for Economic Development and Reconstruction, former UN Under-Secretary-General, and Executive Secretary of the UN Economic Commission for Africa (ECA) advocates African indigenous alternative paradigms for development. Under his leadership at the ECA, the commission created an African Alternative Framework to Structural Adjustment Programme for Economic Recovery and Transformation (AAF-SAP) that won the consent of African Ministers of Finance and Planning Development at the 1989 Summit meeting of what is now the AU and the General Assembly of the UN in December of the same year.

Adedeji's framework recommends that a society can only develop with the mobilization of its people and African leaders should demonstrate political will and begin a process that puts the individual at the centre of development so that the process would strengthen African capacity and desire for self-reliance. It implies that for a country to succeed, good leadership, sound economic policy reforms, and capacity-building policies are the most important requirements in crafting effective policies.

After reviewing both policies, this chapter will defer to the conclusion of Adedeji. While it is arguable that the false paradigm hypothesis is untrue because one does not need to experience certain conditions to be knowledgeable of it and subsequently provide solutions, the failure or incomplete success of many African countries to work despite the scores of proposed development theories speaks volumes of the application of Western answers to the Nigerian question.

REFERENCES

1. Atser, Godwin. The Punch Magazine. *IMF predicts 9 per cent GDP growth rate for Nigeria.* http://www.punchng.com/articl.aspx?theatric=Art20090229153046.
2. Bleaney Michael F. *The Rise and Fall of Keynesian Economics.* New York: St. Martin's Press. 1985.
3. Cheru, F. *The Silent Revolution in Africa.* London: Zed Books. 1990.
4. Clarke P.B. *Economic Planning for a Country in Transition: Nigeria* in E.E. Hagen (ed.) Planning Economic Development. 1963.
5. Ezeala-Harrison F, Adjibolosoo S.K. (eds.) *Perspectives on Economic Development in Africa.* Connecticut: Praeger Publishers. 1994.
6. Human Development Report 2009. http://hdr.undp.org/en/
7. Ihonvbere J.O. *Nigeria: The Politics of Adjustment and Democracy.* New Jersey: Transaction Publishers. 1994.
8. Martinussen, John. *Society, State and Market: A Guide to Competing Theories of Development,* London: Zed Books. 1997.
9. Nigeria Vision 2020. http://www.nv2020.org/?IParameters
10. Olaloku F.A., Adejugbe A, Fajana F.O. et al. *Structure of the Nigerian Economy.* New York: St. Martin's Press. 1979.
11. Onimode Bade et al. *African Development and Governance Strategies in the 21st Century. Looking Back to Move Forward: Essays in honor of Adebayo Adedeji at 70.* London: Zed Books. 2004.
12. The National Assembly of the Federal Republic of Nigeria. http://www.nassnig.org/
13. Prachowny, Martin. *Okun's Law: Theoretical Foundations and Revised Estimates.* The Review of Economics and Statistics, Vol. 75, No. 2, p. 331-336. MIT Press. May 1993.
14. Sachs, Jeffrey D., Warner A.M. *The Big Push, Natural Resource Booms and Growth* in the Journal of Development Economics. Vol. 59, p.43–76. 1999.

11

The Effects of Currency Devaluation on the Balance of Trade

An Analysis of the J-Curve Effect and Kulkarni Hypothesis

Stephanie Dybsky

CHAPTER SUMMARY

Can a country improve its balance of trade (BOT)[1] account through an exchange rate devaluation? Many empirical analyses, both multi-country panel regressions and econometric models applied to individual countries, have been conducted into how exchange rate changes affect the BOT account of developing and developed countries.[2] Importantly, analysts have found that the effects of currency devaluation vary depending upon the time period (e.g. short or long term) assessed. Results have also shown that similar trends exist among developing countries in terms of the influence of monetary policies on domestic currency devaluation.

In the decades proceeding 1973, all exchange rates functioned on a fixed system. With the disintegration of the Bretton Woods agreement, however, after 1973 each country was able to control its money supply. Nations were no longer obligated to have precious metals, such as gold and silver, as stock to back or increase their modern money supply.[3] Additionally, the system granted governments a new sense of power over their country's entire economy; governments could select any value for their domestic currency and could peg their currency against any other. Most developed countries opted to follow an open exchange rate system and many developing countries chose to use a fixed exchange rate system.

Studies show that developing countries that selected to implement a fixed exchange rate system have incurred BOT deficits and additional economic problems. Governments have adopted monetary policies to counter their deficits. With the results of such monetary policies, specialists have developed the J-curve Hypothesis, the Marshall-Lerner Condition, and the Kulkàrni Hypothesis.

This chapter is divided into four sections. Section 1a explores significant monetary policies utilized in open and fixed exchange rate systems. Section 1b explains the J-curve Effect and the Kulkarni Hypothesis. Section 2 offers a literature review of two different studies undertaken to test the J-curve Hypothesis. Section 3 provides a case study of Zambia with the application of the J-curve Hypothesis and Kulkarni Hypothesis. Section 4 offers conclusions and recommendations.

Thus, this chapter examines the effects of currency devaluation on a country's balance of trade in the short and long term. Based on our literature review, it has been found that the J-curve Hypothesis was relevant for Chile, Ecuador, and Uruguay, which means that the BOT of each country improved in the long run. Dissimilarly, it was also discovered that the J-curve was not relevant for Argentina, Brazil, Argentina, and Colombia because their BOT deficits did not improve even in the long term. Additionally, the analysis showed that the J-curve and the Kulkarni Hypothesis were relevant for Ghana and Zambia.

SECTION 1A – THEORETICAL ANALYSIS OF FIXED VS. OPEN EXCHANGE RATE SYSTEMS

Today, we define the exchange rate in American terms as the number of domestic units per unit of foreign currency. This implies that as the exchange rate increases, the domestic currency depreciates. 'Devaluation' only occurs when the government implements policy to depreciate the currency under a fixed exchange rate system. In the case of currency in an open exchange rate system, as followed by developed countries, the currency depreciates or appreciates as determined by the foreign exchange market.[4]

The foreign exchange market is determined by the supply of foreign exchange curve and the demand of foreign exchange curve (shown in Figure 11.1). The demand of foreign exchange curve is downward sloping because as the exchange rate increases and the domestic currency looses value, imports decrease and domestic residents demand lower amounts of foreign exchange. Similarly, an increase in the exchange rate causes domestic exports to increase and foreign residents to supply higher quantities of foreign exchange. Thus, the supply of foreign exchange curve is upward sloping from left to right. In a 'freely floating' or open exchange rate system, the exchange rate will always be in equilibrium (point S in Figure 11.1) due to the 'Paradox of Flexibility'. This paradox states that if a price (or exchange rate) is free to move up and down, then it will stay at one level: the equilibrium point. [5]

Economists recognize that governments that oversee a fixed exchange rate system will maintain an exchange rate below equilibrium. For example, governments of many developing countries will fix the exchange rate at $ER2$ (Figure 11.1), creating a shortage (from $Q2$ to $Q3$) of foreign exchange in the domestic market. The fixed exchange rate allocates more purchasing power to importers, who are often the governments themselves. At the same time, the fixed exchange rate hurts exporters by inflating export prices in foreign markets.[6] Thus, the government is vulnerable to acquiring large deficits, or a BOT deficit, by setting the exchange rate below equilibrium.

To counteract the foreign exchange shortages, governments are forced to adopt policies that will lower the quantity of foreign exchange demanded by domestic residents. For example, governments of many developing countries implement high import tariffs and import quotas. Additionally, governments put limitations on residents' travel abroad or restrict foreign exchange available for travel abroad. Lastly, governments place bans on the purchase of foreign financial real assets.

When the shortage of foreign exchange becomes uncontrollable, a parallel market[7] for currency transactions develops. Often, parallel exchange rates deviate significantly from official rates. In this case, evasion becomes endemic and illegal markets for goods and foreign currencies expand, defeating the very purpose of monetary controls. Although the nature of illegal markets precludes collection of detailed and reliable data, these markets appear to be common phenomena in developing countries. [8]

More specifically, blacks markets generally develop in conditions of excess demand for a commodity subject to legal restrictions of sale, official price ceilings, or both. In a large majority of developing countries, transactions in foreign exchange are subject to both kinds of restrictions. Typically, the exchange rate is officially pegged by the central bank and only a small group of intermediaries is permitted to engage in currency transactions. Purchases of foreign currencies by domestic agents are, in principle, restricted to uses judged by the authorities to be "essential" for economic development, such as imports of capital goods. Consequently, some of the supply of foreign exchange is diverted and sold illegally – at a market price higher than the official price – to satisfy the excess demand.[9]

In addition to setting the exchange rate below equilibrium, after 1973, governments of many developing countries took advantage of seigniorage. Seigniorage is the name economists give to the real resources a government earns when it prints money that it spends on goods and services.[10] When their governments were expanding money supplies continually to extract high levels of seigniorage, developing countries experienced inflation and even hyperinflation. Some currencies experienced such high depreciation rates that they became 'soft currencies', indicating that they had almost zero value outside of their own domestic markets. [11]

There has been growing recognition over the past several years that widespread exchange and trade restrictions in developing countries have been ineffective in preserving reserves or in supporting an overvalued exchange rate.[12] Studies show that, to respond to the rising demand for foreign exchange and other issues faced by economies with fixed exchange rate systems, governments are eventually forced to increase the exchange rate (or devalue the domestic currency). An increase in exchange rate or a devaluation of the domestic currency is known to reduce the shortage of foreign exchange, causing a surplus in the BOT account.[13]

SECTION 1B – THEORETICAL ANALYSIS OF THE J-CURVE EFFECT AND KULKARNI HYPOTHESIS

As mentioned, in the occurrence of BOT deficits, governments of many developing countries devalue their currency to facilitate BOT improvement. Devaluation improves the BOT by increasing the real price of foreign imports and reducing the real price of exports in foreign markets. The traditional trade literature observes that the effect of exchange rate devaluations on the BOT is dependent on the price elasticity of a country's imports and exports. The Marshall-Lerner condition – created by Alfred Marshall and Abba Lerner in the early 1900s – states that 'if initially the balance of trade is zero and if supply elasticities are infinite, then the absolute values of export and import demand elasticities have to be at least large enough to add up to unity[14] to have an exchange rate devaluation bring about the surplus in BOP'. [15] Elasticity is positively affected by the number of available substitutes (e.g. the more substitutes, the higher the elasticity) and the amount of time after the exchange rate devaluation (e.g. the more time passed, the higher the elasticity).

The relationship between the trade balance and the real exchange rate has attracted the attention of economists for some time. There is a popular belief that this relationship differs through time. That is, the short-run and the long-run responses of the BOT will be different. [16] This is attributable to the fact that elasticities are quite dependent upon the time period; in the short run, the elasticities are small and the Marshall-Lerner condition is less likely to be satisfied, leading to a further BOT deficit. This notion is popularly called 'the perverse reaction' of the BOT to the exchange rate change.

On the other hand, in the long run, elasticity values are high and the Marshall-Lerner condition is satisfied, leading to a surplus in the BOT.[17] In other words, it is sometimes observed that a country's BOT worsens immediately after a real currency depreciation and begins to improve only some months or even years later. If the current account initially worsens after depreciation, its time path has an initial segment reminiscent of a 'J', as shown in Figure 11.2. Consequently, economists have come to call this patterned effect the "J-curve Hypothesis".[18]

The J-curve effect is attributed to a lagged adjustment of quantities to changes in relative prices. For example, if there is a depreciation of the domestic currency, then the increased competitiveness in the domestic prices leads to exporting more and importing less, thereby improving the BOT. This is known as the volume effect. At the same time, the depreciation increases the import unit value and results in a deterioration of the BOT, which is referred to as the value (price) effect. The value effect prevails in the short-run – whereas the volume effect dominates in the long-run – which causes the time path of the trade balance depicted by the J-curve phenomenon.[19]

As explained, the J-curve Hypothesis argues that once the elasticity values become large enough to add up to unity over the longer term, the BOT begins yielding a surplus. In practice, however, it is quite possible that one devaluation is followed by another devaluation in the short term.[20] As a consequence, in the short term, the BOT will incur a further deficit, due to continuous devaluations, before improving and gaining a surplus. This phenomenon is referred to as the

"Kulkarni Hypothesis": continuous currency devaluations will lead to higher BOT deficits. Given the occurrence of the Kulkarni Hypothesis, it can be concluded that devaluation is not necessarily the solution to improving the BOT of any country. In other words – while the J-curve Hypothesis is a comparative static analysis – in reality, dynamic events of the J-curve occur after *every* devaluation.[21] The next section provides a number of case studies which test the relevance of the J-curve Hypothesis and Kulkarni Hypothesis.

SECTION 2 – LITERATURE REVIEW LEVEL

In the literature on international economics, many studies have been conducted to examine the J-curve hypothesis in US and other countries. In his textbook *International Economics*, Dominick Salvatore, Chair of the Economics Department at Fordham University, provides a case study (recreated in Table 11.1) that supports the Marshall-Lerner condition and confirms the J-curve effect. Table 11.1 presents the absolute value of the estimated short run and long run elasticities for the imports and exports of manufactured goods of industrial countries.[22] As indicated by the impact elasticities, the foreign exchange market seems to be unstable over a six-month adjustment period (in the short run), thus confirming the J-curve effect. For a one-year adjustment period, the short-run elasticities indicate that the Marshall-Lerner condition is met for most countries, though just barely. Dissimilarly, in the long run (e.g. over many years), the unweighted average of the sum of the import and export price elasticities is 1.92 for the seven largest industrial countries, 2.07 for the smaller industrial countries, and 2.00 for all 14 countries. Although focused primarily on developed countries, Salvatore's conclusions are still relevant to my analysis and provide important insight into the J-curve theory.[23]

Southeastern Louisiana University economics professor Yu Hsing found a mixture of results regarding the J-curve through his analysis of seven different Latin American countries. For Chile, Hsing found that real depreciation is negatively affected by real depreciation (and own real income). This result suggests that after real depreciation, there would be a trade deficit initially, then a trade surplus afterward, thus offering evidence of a J-curve.[24]

For Ecuador, Hsing concluded that real depreciation (and higher own real income) would improve the BOT and, like Chile, Ecuador's results support for the J-curve Hypothesis. Hsing uncovered evidence for the J-curve through his test of Uruguay as well. With real depreciation, the Uruguay's BOT deteriorated in the first quarter and improved afterwards. Therefore, real depreciation for Uruguay's currency would lead to deterioration in the BOT in the first four quarters and a subsequent improvement in the BOT.[25]

Interestingly, Hsing also found evidence that does *not* support the J-curve Hypothesis. For example, from 1997 to 2002 the Brazilian real per US dollar (USD) experienced real depreciation, declining from 1.16 to 2.63. Brazil's BOT improved from a deficit of 20,658 million to a surplus of 22,369 million, and the ratio of exports to imports rose from 75.61 per cent to 112.03 per cent. From 2002 to 2007, the real per USD experienced real appreciation and transitioned from 2.63 to 1.43. However, the BOT continued to increase from 22,369 million to 39,112 million, and the ratio of exports to imports changed little from 112.03 per cent to 112.38 per cent. Hsing's analysis suggests that there is no J-curve for Brazil, which is consistent with their experience of no real difference between the long and short run adjustments.[26]

Hsing also found no evidence of the J-curve effect when examining Argentina. From 2001 to 2002, Argentina's real exchange rate in terms of the peso per USD depreciated considerably from 1.039 to 2.57. As a result, the BOT improved from 3,509 million to 46,926 million, and the ratio of exports to imports increased from 112.71 per cent to 212.28 per cent. From 2002 to 2007, the peso per USD experienced real appreciation from 2.570 to 1.910. The BOT declined to 34,866 million, and the ratio of exports to imports decreased to 121.21 per cent. Given these figures, there is lack of support for a J-curve for Argentina due to positive adjustments in the short run and negative adjustments in the long run.[27]

Finally, Hsing's analysis of Columbia also showed no evidence supporting the J-curve Hypothesis. The real effective exchange rate for Columbia increased from 82.54 in 1990 to 128.08 in 1997, 84.89 in 2003, and 103.65 in 2006. The BOT deteriorated from a surplus of 708 billion in 1990 to a deficit of 7,197 billion in 1997, a deficit of 1,071 billion in 2003, and a deficit of 7,885 billion in 2006. Hsing concluded that the real appreciation from 84.89 to 103.65 hurt net exports significantly. Thus, Hsing's investigation shows that there is lack of evidence of a J-curve for Colombia due to positive adjustments in the short run and negative adjustments in the long run.[28]

International economics professor Kishore G. Kulkarni's *Readings in International Economics* (Second Edition) includes a case study of Ghana that supports the J-curve Hypothesis and Kulkarni Hypothesis. After the devaluation of its domestic currency (the cedi) in the early 1980s, Ghana successfully increased its exports and its economy experienced growth for six consecutive years after 1984. However, during these years, the import account continued to increase even faster than export earnings as the purchasing power of consumers increased, yielding the BOT path shown in Figure 11.3. Figure 11.3 shows that even if the devaluation of the cedi was an important step, the benefits were somewhat eroded by the worsening of the BOT.[29]

The results of Kulkarni's study (recreated in Table 11.2) reflect the BOT and exchange rate changes Ghana experienced from 1983 to 1990. As reflected, with the exception of 1988, in all of these years, the BOT deficit increased despite the large decline in the value of the cedi. One of the predominant reasons for the continuous deficits in the BOT is the series of currency devaluations.[30]

Based on the data presented, Kulkarni concluded that devaluation does not necessarily solve a deficit in the BOT of any country. This concept is referred to as the Kulkarni Hypothesis. In light of this evidence, Kulkarni suggests that changing real prices must go hand in hand with other policies that lead to structural adjustment. Further, the structural adjustment that is needed should be in the form of export composition change.[31]

SECTION 3 – A CASE STUDY OF ZAMBIA

Since Zambia's independence in 1964, its economy has been dominated by the production and exportation of a single primary product: copper. Although other minerals are mined in Zambia, copper has remained the major source of export earnings. Soon after independence, copper earnings helped to develop infrastructure, public services, and import-substituting industries. However, in the 1970s, copper prices fell and Zambia's growth – which was founded on the high world prices of copper – slumped. Real GDP per capita declined and copper's contribution to government revenues fell.[32]

The drop in copper prices had a profound effect on the entire Zambian economy. The government reduced its expenditure on economic and social infrastructure since the fall in copper earnings affected tax revenues. The reduction in public expenditure on social services led to a deterioration in the quality of life between 1970 and 1996.[33] Such deterioration led to consistent insecurity and the capital flight of billions of dollars from the mid-1970s onward. Those residents who could not shift their resources abroad defended themselves from state action in other ways, such as tax evasion, the use of parallel markets, currency substitution, smuggling, and shifting into activities over which the government had little control.[34]

With the advancement of widespread economic disruption, the government turned to international financial institutions, the International Monetary Fund (IMF) and the World Bank. Between 1972 and 1982, the government negotiated a number of programmes with the IMF. For example, the 1983/1985 Structural Adjustment Programme (SAP) was framed around the auctioning of foreign exchange. The exchange rate was thus emphasized as important in inducing structural adjustment. This adjustment was meant to correct for the misalignment in the real exchange rate and eliminate the parallel market for foreign exchange that had developed.[35]

The auctioning system was short-lived primarily due to mismanagement. At the time, the Bank of Zambia (BOZ) saw inflation as being driven by rising costs. As a result, the BOZ sought to appreciate the exchange rate by selling foreign exchange in amounts that were in excess to the amount of foreign exchange available. The intervention in the foreign exchange market by the BOZ resulted in the following. Firstly, private traders lost confidence in government commitments, which they found not to be credible, hence creating a huge demand for foreign exchange.[36]

Secondly, as a result of the huge demand created by the unfulfilled promises for foreign exchange, the exchange rate depreciated instead of appreciating as was initially intended. Thirdly, the BOZ incurred significant losses by intervening. By agreeing to sales of foreign exchange that it did not have, the BOZ set up a forward market. However, given the depreciating domestic currency (the Zambian kwacha), the BOZ had to buy foreign exchange at a higher price than the price at which it sold it. Thus, the intervention by the BOZ in the foreign exchange market contributed to the misalignment or disequilibrium in the real exchange rate.[37]

In May 1987, the government abandoned the reform programme and replaced it with a home-grown programme: the New Economic Recovery Programme (NERP). The NERP only lasted for two years. In June 1989, the government returned to the IMF/World Bank programme due to mounting donor and domestic pressure. Through the IMF/World Bank programme, a number of liberalization measures were reintroduced, such as decontrolling the prices of most goods, trade reforms, and tight monetary and fiscal policies.[38]

In the initial period, the IMF/World Bank programme registered some progress. However, with a transfer of political power in 1991, the Movement for Multiparty Democracy (MMD) took control of the economy and did away with the IMF/World Bank programming. The MMD instituted the Economic Reform Programme (ERP), which emphasized economic liberalization and privatization. The MMD removed all price controls, devalued the kwacha, and rapidly liberalized external trade and payment systems.[39]

Table 11.3 reflects the progression of the kwacha from independence in 1964 to December 1996. Based on the data in Table 11.3, it is clear that from independence until 1985, Zambia had a fixed exchange rate regime. The fixed exchange rate was not maintained by an active intervention in the foreign exchange market as is the standard in market economies; instead, the exchange rate was fixed more or less by degree and a series of administrative controls were instituted to deal with any possible excess demand for foreign currency.[40] For example, the government implemented high tariffs, ranging from zero to 150 per cent. Also, foreign imports were controlled through the implementation of government-issued import licenses.[41]

Due to the existence of exchange controls from the time of independence, coupled by external macroeconomic imbalance, a black market for foreign exchange existed alongside the official market. The existence of a black or parallel market (as explored in Section 1a) is an indication of real exchange rate misalignment – or an exchange rate set below the market rate equilibrium. In the black market, the exchange rate was freely floating. The parallel market was by and large illegal in Zambia, except prior to the auctioning system between 1987 and 1988.[42] The black market was made 'quasi-legalized' during this time period because of the implementation of export retention schemes and 'own funds' import licenses.[43]

Due to the illegal nature of the parallel market for most of its existence, information on size and volume of transactions is not available. Nonetheless, the importance of the parallel market is illustrated by the size of the premium. Between 1971 and 1993, for which the data is available, the average premium was 193 per cent. The downward trend in the premium began after 1988 and finally disappeared after market unification in December 1992.[44]

Even after the unification in 1992, the kwacha has continued to depreciate (as shown in Figure 11.4). As of last year (2009), the Kwacha was valued at 5,237.40 per USD. Importantly, though, Zambia's BOT has greatly improved since the 1990s. As shown in Table 11.4, the BOT was in deficit in 1998 at –153. From there, the BOT decreased further to –342.1 in 2001 before beginning to increase the following year. By 2004, the BOT had jumped to a positive balance of 117.6 and continued to increase for the next two years. In fact, by 2006, the BOT had increased to 1293.1. Even though the BOT had since decreased to 401.7 as of 2008, the BOT has still come a long way since its negative balances in the late 1990s.

The results provided support the J-curve effect of Zambia: after the devaluation of the kwacha, the elasticity values became large enough to add up to unity. In the long run, this led to the fulfillment of the Marshall-Lerner condition and a BOT surplus. As illustrated in Figure 11.4, the devaluation of the kwacha caused the BOT to follow a J-shaped curve, decreasing in the short term (e.g. a few years) and increasing in the long term (e.g. several years). Although these time periods are a bit longer than those observed in the example provided by Kulkarni on Ghana, they show the effect of currency devaluation on the BOT overall.

The results from the Zambian economy also support the Kulkarni Hypothesis; the devaluation of the kwacha led to further deficits in the BOT before surpluses in the BOT were gained. As can be observed in Table 11.4, in all of the years preceding 2002, the BOT deficit increased despite the tremendous decline in the Kwacha. With this in mind, it is concluded that devaluation cannot guarantee an improvement in the BOT of any country.

SECTION 4 – CONCLUSION AND RECOMMENDATIONS

This chapter described the historical development of open and fixed exchange rate systems after the early 1970s. Still today, governments of many developing countries, such as Venezuela and Eritrea, strictly control domestic residents' use of foreign currency by limiting access and availability.[45] Such countries usually suffer from severe economic problems, leading to the development of parallel markets and large BOT deficits.

To counter BOT deficits, countries often choose to devalue their currency. The evidence examined showed that currency devaluations eventually led to an improvement in the BOT accounts for Chile, Ecuador, and Uruguay, supporting the existence of the J-curve Hypothesis. On the other hand, evidence from the economies of Brazil, Argentina, and Colombia counters the J-curve Hypothesis.

Examining the progression of the BOTs of Ghana and Zambia, I have concluded that, immediately after devaluation, often times, a country's BOT incurs further deficits before reaching surpluses. The initial deteriorations of the trade account are attributed to the inelasticity of import and export prices in these two countries. As more time passes, however, demand becomes more elastic and the Marshall-Lerner condition is eventually fulfilled, leading to BOT surpluses.

In light of this conclusion – also referred to as the Kulkarni Hypothesis – further research is recommended. Due to the evidence provided in section 2 and since devaluation cannot guarantee the betterment of the BOT, governments interested in improving their BOT deficits should evaluate their options carefully before utilizing devaluation. If governments opt to do so, they may find that other structural adjustments need to be instituted hand-in-hand with currency devaluation, in order to guarantee the improvement of the BOT.

APPENDIX

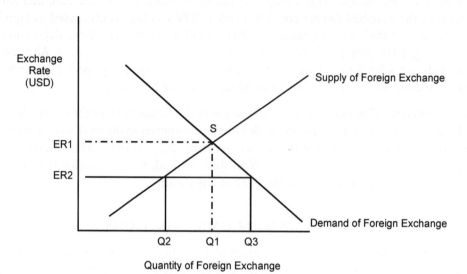

Figure 11.1: Supply and Demand Curves of Foreign Exchange

Source: Kishore Kulkarni, *Readings in International Economics*, 2nd ed., 2006, Serials Publications, New Delhi, Figure 4, p. 43.

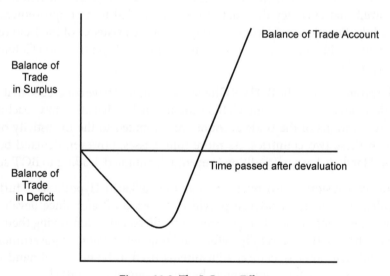

Figure 11.2: The J-Curve Effect

Source: Paul R. Krugman and Maurice Obstfeld, *International Economics, Theory & Policy*, 8th ed., 2009, Pearson Education, Inc. Boston, MA.

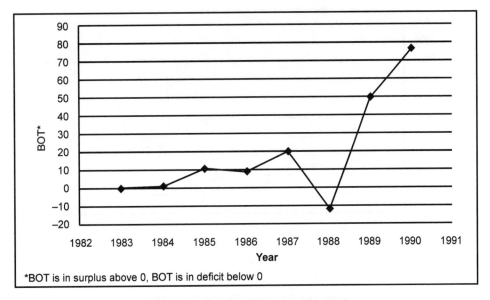

Figure 11.3: J-curve of Ghana (1983-1989)

Source: Kishore Kulkarni, *Readings in International Economics*, 2nd ed., 2006, Serials Publications, New Delhi, Figure 4, p. 48.

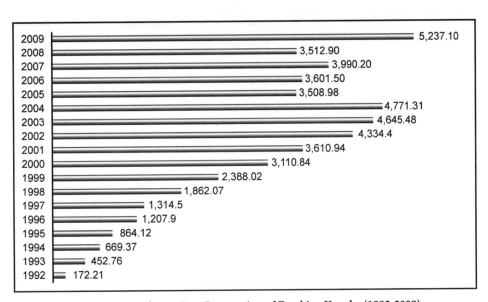

Figure 11.4: Exchange Rate Progression of Zambian Kwacha (1992-2009)

Source: International Monetary Fund, *International Financial Statistics Yearbook*, 2006, Publication Services, Washington, DC.

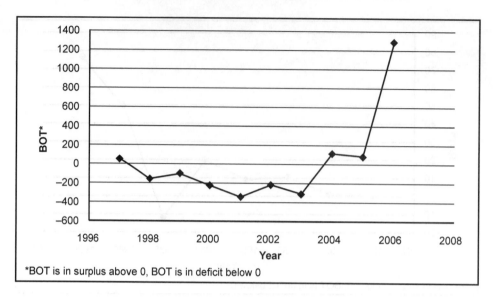

Figure 11.5: J-Curve of Zambia (1997-2006)

Source: International Monetary Fund, *International Financial Statistics Yearbook*, 2006, Publication Services, Washington, DC.

Table 11.1: Estimated Price Elasticities of Exports & Imports

	Short Run	Long Run	Short Run	Long Run
US	1.06	1.06	0.48	1.67
Japan	0.72	0.97	1.01	1.61
Germany	0.77	0.77	–	1.41
France	0.49	0.6	0.48	1.25
UK	0.75	0.75	–	0.31
Italy	0.94	0.94	0.56	0.64
Canada	0.72	0.72	0.4	0.71
Austria	0.36	0.8	0.71	1.37
Belgium	–	0.7	0.59	1.55
Denmark	0.93	1.14	1.13	1.13
Netherlands	1.22	1.22	0.49	0.89
Norway	0.01	0.71	0.74	1.49
Sweden	–	0.94	0.73	1.59
Switzerland	0.25	0.25	0.42	0.73

Source: Dominick Salvatore, *International Economics*, 7th ed., 2001, John Wiley & Sons, Inc., Table 16.2, p. 568.

Table 11.2: BOT and Exchange Rate Change of Ghana (1983-1990)

Year	Exports	Imports	BOT
1983	10.22	10.31	0.09
1984	19.39	20.47	1.08
1985	33.49	44.11	10.62
1986	78.00	87.00	9.00
1987	143.00	163.00	20.00
1988	206.00	174.00	−12.00
1989	275.00	325.00	50.00
1990	298.00	375.00	77.00

Source: Kishore Kulkarni, Readings in International Economics, 2nd ed., 2006, Serials Publications, New Dehli, Table 2, p. 49.

Table 11.3: Exchange Rate Policy Episodes of Zambia (1965-1996)

Period	Policy
1964-1971	Kwacha fixed to the British Pound.
1971-1975	Kwacha fixed to the USD.
1976-1983	Kwacha pegged to the SDR, devalued occasionally.
1983-1985	Kwacha pegged to weighted average of a basket of currencies of Zambia's 5 trade partners. Kwacha allowed to adjust within a narrow range.
1985(Oct)-1987(Jan.)	Dual exchange rate system: auction determined and below auction rate.
1987(Jan.)-1987(Mar.)	Kwacha at fixed rate to USD; then to a basket of currencies of Zambia's trade partners; Rate allowed to float within band of K9-K12 50/USD.
1987(Mar.)-1987(May)	Dual exchange rate system: official rate and auction-determined rate.
1987(May)-1990(Feb.)	Kwacha at fixed rate with occasional devalutions.
1990(Feb.)-1991(Apr.)	Dual exchange rate system.
1991(Oct.)	MMD assumed office with promise to accelerate liberalization process.
1992(Early)	Weekly devaluations of kwacha announced.
1993(June)	BOZ to determine exchange rate.
1994(Jan.)	Exchange Control Act was repealed.
	All capital controls were abolished, making kwacha fully convertible.
1994(Dec.)	The OGL system was abolished
1996	BOZ used rates determined by the average daily retail rates of commercial banks.
KEY: BOZ: Bank of Zambia, K: Zambian Kwacha, MMD: Movement for Multiparty Democracy.	
OGL: Open General License System of Zambia, SDR: Special Drawing Rights, USD: United States Dollar.	

Source: Beatrice Kalinda Mkenda, "Long-run and Short-run Determinants of the Real Exchange Rate in Zambia," April 2001, Working Papers in Economics no. 40, Goteborg University <http://gupea.ub.gu.se/dspace/bitstream/2077/2888/1/gunwpe0040.pdf>.

Stephanie Dybsky

Table 11.4: Balance of Trade of Zambia (1998-2008)

Year	Balance of Trade
1998	−153
1999	−98
2000	−221
2001	−342.1
2002	−214.8
2003	−306
2004	117.6
2005	86,1
2006	1293.1
2007	983.1
2008	401.7

Source: International Monetary Fund, *International Financial Statistics Yearbook*, 2008, Publication Services, Washington, DC.

NOTES

1. BOT = exports − imports
2. Olugbenga Onafowora, "Exchange rate and trade balance in East Asia: is there a J-curve?" Nov. 2003, *Economics Bulletin*, Vol. 5., No. 18 pp. 1-13, Susquehanna University.
3. Kishore Kulkarni, 8 Feb. 2010, Lecture.
4. Kishore Kulkarni, *Readings in International Economics*, 2nd ed., 2006, Serials Publications, New Delhi, p. 42.
5. Kulkarni, p. 42-43.
6. Kulkarni, p. 44.
7. The expressions 'parallel', 'fragmented', 'informal', 'black' (which has an illicit connotation), and 'curb' markets are often used interchangeably in trade literature.
8. Pierre-Richard Agenor, "Parallel Currency Markets in Developing Countries: Theory, Evidence and Policy Implications," Nov. 1992, *Essays in International Finance*, No. 188, Princeton University, Princeton, New Jersey, p. 1-3.
9. Agenor, p. 3-5.
10. Krugman and Obstfled, p. 626.
11. Kulkarni, 8 Feb. 2010.
12. Agenor, p. 1.
13. Kulkarni, 8 Feb. 2010.
14. Unity = Total of 1
15. Kulkarni, p. 41.
16. Jungho Baek, Won W. Koo and Kranti Mulik, "The J-Curve Phenomenon: Myth or Reality?" 2006, 12 Feb. 2010 <http://ageconsearch.umn.edu/bitstream/21382/1/sp06ba05.pdf>, p. 3.
17. Kulkarni, p. 41.
18. Krugman and Obstfeld, p. 447.

19. Baek, p.3.
20. Kulkarni, p. 44.
21. Kulkarni, p. 44-49.
22. Dominick Salvatore, *International Economics*, 7th ed., 2001, John Wiley & Sons, Inc, p. 568.
23. Salvatore, p. 568.
24. Yu Hsing, "A Study of the J-Curve for Seven Selected Latin American Countries," 2008, *Global Economy Journal*,8(4), p. 6.
25. Hsing, p. 6.
26. Hsing, p. 1.
27. Hsing, p. 1-2.
28. Hsing, p. 2.
29. Kulkarni, p. 47-48.
30. Kulkarni, p. 48-49.
31. Kulkarni, p. 48-49.
32. Beatrice Kalinda Mkenda, "Long-run and Short-run Determinants of the Real Exchange Rate in Zambia," April 2001, Working Papers in Economics no. 40,Goteborg University, p. 5.
33. Mkenda, p. 5-6.
34. Catharine B. Hill and Malcolm F. McPherson, *Promoting and Sustaining Economic Reform in Zambia,* 2004, Harvard University Press, p. 43-44.
35. Mkenda, p. 6-9.
36. Mkenda, p. 9-11.
37. Mkenda, p. 11.
38. Mkenda, p. 6.
39. Mkenda, p. 7-8.
40. Mkenda p. 7-9.
41. Hill, p. 239-240.
42. Miguel A. Kiguel, J. Saul Lizondo and Stephen A. O'Connell, *Parallel Exchange Rates in Developing Countries*, 1997, Houndmills, Basingstoke, Hampshire: Macmillan Press, New York, St. Martin's Press.
43. Mkenda, p. 13.
44. Mkenda, p. 13.
45. *Central Intelligence Agency (CIA).* 'Country Comparison: Inflation Rate (Consumer Prices)'. 20 Feb. 2010. <https://www.cia.gov/library/publications/the-world-factbook/geos/er.html>.

REFERENCES

1. Achy, Lahcen. 'Equilibrium Exchange Rate and Misalignment in Selected MENA Countries'. MPRA Paper No. 4799. Lahcen ACHY. Free University of Brussels (Belgium) and INSEA (Morocco) < http://mpra.ub.uni-muenchen.de/4799/1/MPRA_paper_4799.pdf >.
2. Agenor, Pierre-Richard. 'Parallel Currency Markets in Developing Countries: Theory, Evidence and Policy Implications'. Nov. 1992. *Essays in International Finance*. No.188. Princeton University. Princeton, New Jersey.
3. Baek, Jungho, Koo, Won W. and Mulik, Kranti. 'The J-Curve Phenomenon: Myth or Reality?' 2006 <http://ageconsearch.umn.edu/bitstream/21382/1/sp06ba05.pdf>. [Abbreviated 'Baek']
4. Bahmani-Oskooee, Mohsen. 'Devaluation and the J-Curve: Some Evidence from LDCs'. August

1989. *The Review of Economics and Statistics*. Vol. 71, No. 3, pp. 553-554. The MIT Press < http://0-www.jstor.org.bianca.penlib.du.edu/stable/pdfplus/1926918.pdf>.

5. Bremmer, Ian. *The J Curve: A New Way to Understand Why Nations Rise and Fall*. 2006. New York: Simon & Schuster.

6. Central Intelligence Agency (CIA). 'Country Comparison: Inflation Rate (Consumer Prices).' 2010 <https://www.cia.gov/library/publications/the-world-factbook/geos/er.html>.

7. Hill, Catharine B. and McPherson, Malcolm F. *Promoting and Sustaining Economic Reform in Zambia*. 2004. Harvard University Press. [Abbreviated 'Hill']

8. Hsing, Yu. 'A Study of the J-Curve for Seven Selected Latin American Countries.' 2008. *Global Economy Journal*. 8(4).

9. International Monetary Fund, *International Financial Statistics Yearbook*, 2006, Publication Services, Washington, DC. [Abbreviated 'IMF']

10. Kiguel, Miguel A., Lizondo, J. Saul and O'Connell, Stephen A. *Parallel Exchange Rates in Developing Countries*. 1997. Houndmills, Basingstoke, Hampshire: Macmillan Press. New York. St. Martin's Press.

11. Krugman, Paul R. and Obstfeld, Maurice. *International Economics, Theory & Policy*, 8th ed. 2009. Pearson Education, Inc. Boston, MA. [Abbreviated 'Krugman']

12. Kulkarni, Kishore. *Readings in International Economics*. 2nd ed. 2006. Serials Publications, New Delhi. [Abbreviated 'Kulkarni']

13. Li, Xiangming. 'Trade Liberalization and Real Exchange Rate Movement'. IMF Staff Papers. Vol. 51, No. 3 (2004). pp. 553-584 Published by: Palgrave Macmillan Journals on behalf of the International Monetary Fund <http://0www.jstor.org.bianca.penlib.du.edu/stable/pdfplus/30035962.pdf>.

14. Mkenda, Beatrice Kalinda. 'Long-run and Short-run Determinants of the Real Exchange Rate in Zambia'. April 2001. Working Papers in Economics no. 40. Goteborg University <http://gupea.ub.gu.se/dspace/bitstream/2077/2888/1/gunwpe0040.pdf>.

15. Onafowora, Olugbenga. 'Exchange rate and trade balance in East Asia: is there a J-curve?' November 2003. *Economics Bulletin*. Vol. 5. No. 18 pp. 1-13. Susquehanna University <http://www.accessecon.com/pubs/EB/2003/Volume5/EB-03E00003A.pdf>.

16. Salvatore, Dominick. *International Economics*. 7th ed. 2001. John Wiley & Sons, Inc.

12 | The Demographic Transition in Cambodia

Rebecca Muhs

CHAPTER SUMMARY

The demographic transition is a popular theory used to explain the changing rates of mortality and fertility in developed and developing countries. The developing country Cambodia was thrown into chaos by the Khmer Rouge just when the country was starting its demographic transition. The Cambodian genocide greatly impacted both mortality and fertility rates in the country. The population rebounded and eventually resumed its demographic transition. Cambodia has gained economic benefits from its demographic transition most recently seen in the rapid economic growth rates. Ultimately, the country will need to find new ways to support its economic growth and production as the demographics stabilize within the country.

While many books, articles and one famous movie focus on the facts and atrocities of the Khmer Rouge during the Cambodian genocide, the continuing demographic consequences of the events from the 1970s earn far less attention. Current scholarly debates focus on the authenticity and relevance of the justice tribunals and prosecution of war criminals. There is sincere desire to move on from the past and no longer be defined by the horrors of the genocide within the Cambodian population.

The country is now one full generation past the genocide, and we can still see its continuing impact on the country. In this chapter, I look at how the genocide impacted the demographic transition and what these impacts meant for the most recent decade of economic growth. This chapter contains just one thread of a much larger debate on the impacts of population growth and economic development.

This chapter is divided into two major sections. The first section will focus on the overall theory of the demographic transition, and the second section will focus on the Cambodian experience of the demographic transition.

First, I will explain the demographic transition and its three phases. Then, I will speak on whether the transition only occurred in 19th century Western Europe. Third, I include a brief literature review of current areas of research on demographic transitions. Then, I will explore the Malthusian principle of population and why it has proven incorrect. Fifth, I look at how Galor and Weil incorporate technological changes into the demographic transition.

I begin with a review of Cambodia's recent history in the second section. This sets the background for our discussion on demographic indicators in Cambodia. After defining our demographic measurement tools, I review a series of demographic indicators for Cambodia from 1960 to 2010. Various graphs will be used to illustrate changing birth rates, death rates, population growth rates, life expectancies and dependency ratios. Then I discuss how the demographic changes have influenced the recent decade of rapid economic growth in Cambodia.

DEMOGRAPHIC TRANSITION

The demographic transition theory tries to capture the process of countries moving from periods of high mortality and fertility rates to today's low mortality and fertility rates. The theory first tried to explain why many developed countries essentially experienced the same changes of rates within their own populations (Todaro, 2006, p.275). The Office of Population Research at Princeton University in New Jersey, USA first formally formulated and published the demographic theory 1944 (Kirk, 1996, p. 363). Demographers isolated three phases of the demographic transition theory.

Phase 1 of the demographic transition theory covers most of human history. Populations lived tough and demanding lives. Life expectancies were short. Women gave birth to high numbers of children, but many children did not survive childhood. The population died much earlier than they do today. The population grew very slowly. Overall, young people dominated the population (Lee, 2003, p.167). High rates of births and deaths characterize phase 1.

The actual demographic transition starts when a nation's mortality rates begin to steadily decline. Fertility rates remain high. This time represents the shift from phase 1 to phase 2. The transition from phase 1 to phase 2 started in northwest Europe in the early 1800s. Mortality rates begin to decline in response to improvements in preventative and public health, improvements in vaccines, nutrition, hygiene and sanitation (Lee, 2003, p.170). The reduction in mortality rates was accompanied by an increase in the life expectancy (Shah, 1998, p.43). Overall characteristics of phase 2 include low mortality and high fertility rates.

Fertility rates began to decline in Europe between 1890 and 1920. Some of the decline in fertility rates is attributed to the decline in mortality (Lee, 2003, p.173), but the lower fertility rates in this phase are also thought to be partly influenced by modernization and development. The combination of low birth and death rates minimizes the population growth rate (Todaro, 2006, p. 275). Developed countries are now in phase 3 of the demographic transition. Examples of small population growth rates developed countries from 1990-2010 include: Germany, 0.08 per cent; United Kingdom, 0.45 per cent; United States, 1.01 per cent; and Sweden, 0.46 per cent (UN World Population Prospects). Phase 3 continues today.

The theory of demographic transition is still in full force today. The greatest strength of the demographic transition theory lies in its ability to predict a transition in every modernizing society. Unfortunately, the transition theory cannot predict the exact thresholds needed for birth rates to fall (Kirk, 1996, 365). The theory does not give concrete steps for countries to take in order to reap the benefits of falling death and birthrates. The theory describes past events but cannot prescribe actions to take to influence future events.

Developing Countries and the Demographic Transition

The demographic transition occurred not only in developed countries but also in developing countries. Changes due to the transition came later to developing countries and areas outside of Europe. Developing countries experienced higher birth and death rates than developed countries, and changes to these rates would come later than the European transition (Lee, 2003, 169). While phase 2 of the demographic transition began in Europe in the mid 1800s, the same phase did not begin in developing countries until the 1940s (Todaro, 2006, 276).

Mortality rates in developing countries fell faster than rates in 19th century Europe. This was mostly due to 'the application of highly effective imported modern medical and public-health technologies'. (Todaro, 2006, p. 277) Since developing countries had higher birth rates to begin with, the swift decline in mortality rates left phase 2 of the demographic transition with population growth rates well over 2 per cent a year (Todaro, 2006, p. 277).

Phase 3 of the demographic transition looks different in some developing countries than it did in developed countries. There are two main groups, and both groups experienced declining death and birth rates. The second group of developing countries has not had the same drop of birth and death rates. Yes, they did decline but not to the same levels as developed countries. Death rates have not fallen as far due to the prevalence of poverty and low standards as living. Additionally, the AIDS epidemic stems a further drop in death rates. Birth rates have also not dropped as far due to the low standards of living in these countries (Todaro, 2006, p. 277).

LITERATURE REVIEW

Since the demographic transition theory was presented in the mid 1940s, it has become the central focus of many population debates and demographic research. There is a plethora of information and scholarly research on the subject. One recent area of intense focus is demographic transitions in East Asian countries and the resulting consequences of aging populations.

In the David E. Bloom, David Canning and Jaypee Sevilla authored *The Demographic Dividend* 2003 Chapter 3 of this RAND publication looks at the interaction between population shifts and economic growth. The section on East Asia explains how these countries have taken economic advantage of declining birth rates. The East Asian demographic transition was one of the quickest in the world ad spanning less than 75 years. Countries have taken advantage of their growing workforces, but they must pay attention to the impending issues of an aging population. These countries hold some of the highest life expectancies in the world and must be ready to tackle the challenges this presents (Bloom, 2003, pp. 43-48). Challenges can include funding larger pension schemes and offering health systems.

Zhongwei Zhao and Fei Guo, contributors and editors of *Transition and Challenge,* attempt to analyze China's rapid demographic transition. They look at how the transition has affected China and presented new challenges in areas of poverty, life expectancies, population ageing and migration. They are concerned not only for the impact the demographic transition has had upon China itself but what this means for the international community. (Zhao, 2007).

Ronald Lee, Andrew Mason, and Timothy Miller use the demographic transition in Taiwan to examine increases in personal savings and a rise in total capital per worker. They look at what an aging population needs and demands in regards to personal savings, wealth transfer and future support. Aging populations need to support the growing group of old and elderly persons (Lee, 2000, p. 194).

MALTHUS' ARGUMENT

No discussion of population, population growth rates and capita per income can be complete without inclusion of Thomas Malthus. Malthus argued in his 1798 publication 'An Essay on the Principle of Population' population growth rates would not be able to continue growing unchecked. The natural order of the world and its inherent properties would constrain the growth. Malthus grounded his theory in two truths. First, humans require food to survive. Second, men and women will continue to experience passion for one another, and therefore children will continue to be born. The growing population would require a growing amount of food to survive. Ultimately, the population's power to continue growing is more powerful than the earth's ability to create food to support the human race (Malthus, 1798, p. 4).

Malthus believed unless there was a shortage of food to curb the population growth a country would grow at an exponential rate and double in size every 30 to 40 years. Food production cannot grow at the same mathematical rate as population, and food supply growth is limited by the availability of land (Todaro, 2006, pp. 277-278). While the population grows at an exponential rate, food production only grows at an arithmetical rate (Malthus, 1798, p. 4). Food production would never be able to keep at par with the growing population. One side would have to give in to the other, and the side giving in must be the population.

As the total number of workers increased with the growing population, the total land available to workers remained the same. This would cause diminishing returns of marginal product outputs to the total food production. Workers would produce less and less food. The aggregate output of food supplies could not keep up with the growing population's food demands. Since agriculture is the predominant production and means of output, per capita income is defined as the per capita food production. Per capita incomes fall as they cannot keep pace with demands. The population growth rate stabilizes as a population hovers around the subsistence level of per capita income (Todaro, 2006, p. 278).

Malthus also held that a small population could maintain a high standard of living. Ultimately, the 'passion of the sexes' would cause the population to grow. Standards of living would fall with the growth of larger population as resources become scarcer. The population size could be controlled by either preventive checks or positive checks (Galor, 2000, p. 807). The main example of preventive checks on population growth would be birth control or as Malthus put it 'moral restraint'. Malthus argued to keep humans from living at subsistence levels and misery, they must restrain their own growth. A large proportion of the population must participate (Malthus, 1798, p. 5). This argument for preventive checks is seen as one of the very first for the modern day birth control movement (Todaro, 2006, p. 278). If the population failed to restrain themselves from growing, then Malthus argued positive checks would be inevitable. Positive checks might be manmade such as deadly conflict over scarce resources. Positive checks can be from mother earth such as famine and illness. Either way, the population cannot grow unchecked (Todaro, 2006, pp. 279-280).

'Since population could potentially grow more rapidly than the economy, it was always held in check by misery and vice, which were therefore the inevitable human lot. Economic progress could help only temporarily since population could soon grow to its new equilibrium level, where misery and vice would hold it in check' (Lee, 2003, p.169).

MALTHUSIAN POPULATION TRAP THEORY

Modern economists took Malthus' theory of high population growth rates forcing societies to live at subsistence levels and created the Malthusian Population Trap Model. While Malthus did not specifically create the graph or the traps, the traps are attributed to his theories of population growth and economic development. Economists use Malthusian traps to describe what will happen to countries who allow their population growth rate to exceed their income growth rate. The Malthusian population traps are also referred to as the low-level equilibrium population traps. Populations will be forced to survive on less and less income as their population's growth rate increases in the midst of decreasing marginal product outputs (Galor, 1999, p. 150).

'The Malthus model implies that there exists a negative feedback loop whereby, in the absence of changes in the technology or in the availability of land, the size of the population will be self-equilibrating. More significantly, even if available resources do expand, the level of income per capita will remain unchanged in the long run; better technology or more land will lead to a larger, but not richer population.' (Galor, 1999, p. 150)

CRITIQUES OF MALTHUSIAN THEORY

Todaro and Smith find two major faults with Malthus' theory. The first problem is Malthus does not consider or account for technology's impact on the income growth rate. He was correct in acknowledging that there is a set quantity of land to work on. We cannot grow more earth to work on. Unfortunately for his theory, he had no foresight into the technological progress that would allow labourers to increase land's productivity (Todaro, 2006, p. 280).

Frederick Engels also focused on this point in his criticism of Malthus, 'the productive power at mankind's disposal is immeasurable. The productivity of the soil can be increased ad infinitum by the application of capital, labour, and science'. (Engels, 1844, p. 2) We may no longer believe that there is an infinite amount of supplies land can produce, but Engels was correct in noting capital, labour and technology can greatly increase man's production off the land.

Todaro and Smith point to the second fault in the theory. The theory underlying the Malthusian traps holds there is a positive relationship between the national rate of population growth and the national per capita income. 'According to this assumption, at relatively low levels of per capita income, we should expect to find population growth rates increasing with increasing per capita income.' (Todaro, 2006, p. 281) Research on this matter finds no direct relationship between the national rate of population growth and the national level of per capita income in LCDs (Todaro, 2006, p. 281).

Todaro and Smith believe what matters most in regards to population growth is how income is distributed not the national rate of per capita income. Population growth rates are more likely influenced by social and economic institutions within a country (Todaro, 2006, p. 281).

The state of world today is an evidence to prove that Malthus was wrong. The world's population has increased by six times since Malthus penned 'An Essay on the Principle of Population'. Food production and consumption are at higher levels while overall there has been both an increase in standard of living and longevity (Sen, 2003, p. 1).

Even if Malthus has been proved wrong in regards to technology and measurements at the national and local level of per capita income, Malthus' concerns about the earth's ability to sustain the human race is a contemporary topic. Some economists and demographers believe Malthus' analysis was correct but his timing was wrong (Shah, 1998, p. 42). The pressure the human race puts on the earth's environment might still result in a Malthusian catastrophe.

THE THREE REGIMES AND THE ROLE OF TECHNOLOGY

The three phases of the demographic transition have been further expanded on to incorporate the advancement of technology and its impact on the economic development of countries. Galor and Weil (1999 and 2000) argue that three regimes dominate the relationship between population growth, technological change, and the economic development of Western Europe. The regimes in the natural occurring order are: the Malthusian regime, the Post-Malthusian regime and the Modern Growth regime (Galor, 2000, p.806). These regimes match up with the three stages of the demographic transition in Western Europe.

The Malthusian regime started with civilization and lasted until the mid 1800's. Malthus completed his theory on population growth just as Western Europe started to emerge from the trap he described. The framework Malthus constructed accurately reflected history leading up to his time. If compared to modern times, the technological progress and population growth then were minuscule. Income per capita barely grew, and there was a positive correlation between the income per capita and population growth (Galor, 1999, p. 150). The population was able to grow in incremental amounts due to small increases of income (Lagerlof, 2003, p. 775).

In the absence of technology or its growth, the population's size will be self-equilibrate. Land constraint can be overcome with rapid technological progress. This will also allow wages and the income per capita to rise (Galor, 1999, p. 152).

There are two important points with respect to the growth of Europe's population. First, population growth happened alongside the industrialization movement that swept through Western Europe. Second, with the shift to the industrial sector, incomes increased. Population growth occurred with growth in economic prosperity (Shah, 1998, p. 43).

There is an increase in both population and per capita income during the Post-Malthusian regime, and the relationship between the two remains positive (Lagerlof, 2003, p. 775). Income per capita continued to grow throughout the period albeit at a smaller rate than during the Modern Growth regime. The Malthusian regime's direct relationship between income per capita and population growth continued (Galor, 1999, p. 150). The acceleration in pace of the technological progress is what separates the Malthusian and Post-Malthusian regimes (Weisdorf, 2004, p. 456).

The Modern Growth regime follows the Post-Malthusian regime. Per capita income and technology levels continue to climb. This is the first time we see a negative correlation between the income per capita rate and the population growth rate (Galor, 1999, p. 150).

Galor and Weil examined the impact of increasing levels of technology on child rearing:

> Increased technological progress initially has two effects on population growth. On one hand, improved technology eases households' budget constraints, allowing them to spend more resources on raising children. On the other hand, it induces a reallocation of these increased resources toward child quality. In the Post-Malthusian Regime, the former effect dominates, and so population growth rises along with output growth. Eventually, however, more rapid technological progress due to the increase in the level of human capital triggers a demographic transition: the return to child quality continues to rise, the shift away from child quantity becomes more significant, population growth declines, and output growth rises (Galor, 1999, pp. 152-153).

Technology causes a growth in wages. Parents can invest these wages in their children. This will lead to a trade-off where parents start choosing to focus on the quality of their children instead of the quantity of children they will have. They can invest more money in the health and wellbeing of their children. Due to advancements in medical care and health, these children are more likely to survive to adulthood. Parents then can substitute having many children with the hope that only a few will survive to adulthood with having a few children and knowing they will make it to adulthood.

A UNIQUE HISTORY

Cambodia's unique history contains a completed transformation of the economic, political and social structures and all within the past 60 years. Cambodia first gained its independence from French colonial rule in 1953. Although Cambodia attempted to stay neutral of the regional conflicts in the 1950s and 1960s, eastern Cambodian provinces were drawn into the Vietnamese conflicts of the 1960s. In 1970, the Cambodian military led by General Lon Nol deposed Cambodia's ruling Prince Sihanouk. Meanwhile, a communist insurgency was growing within Cambodia. The insurgency took power in 1975, and the Khmer Rouge then had control of the country it renamed the Democratic Kampuchea (US Department of State, 2010).

The estimates widely range on the number of Cambodians killed during the Khmer Rouge rule from 1975–1978. A median estimate is 1 million deaths. The deaths resulted mainly from forced labour and starvation but also a lack of medical care and wholesale execution.

Any industry operating within the country was either taken over by the state or abandoned altogether (Curtis, 1998, p. 5). The country's remaining infrastructure was destroyed. The agriculture system became a communal commodity. There were no banks and no currency. The Vietnamese invaded in mid 1978 and eventually gained control of the capital city Phnom Penh in early January 1979 (US Department of State, 2010). The international community responded with international humanitarian assistance. Once the threat of famine passed, the United States instituted a political and economic embargo against the Vietnamese military involvement in the country. 'The embargo effectively isolated Kampuchea from the non-socialist world and deprived the Cambodian people of all but minimal levels of international humanitarian and development assistance.' (Curtis, 1998, p. 5).

Vietnam fully withdrew from Cambodia in 1990. The UN took over a large portion of Cambodia's administration in 1992 to help enforce the ceasefire and resettle refugees. Many refugees were still living in camps on the Cambodia-Thai border. Cambodia held its first elections in 1993 (US Department of State, 2010). The population and economy suffered greatly during Cambodia's tumultuous past. The country does appear to be on a new trajectory and healing from its past.

MEASURING POPULATION AND THE DEMOGRAPHIC TRANSITION IN CAMBODIA

The makeup of the country's population matters. Each country's makeup is specific and impacts the economic situation and prospects of a country. A country with a relatively young population has a greater need for schools. If the population is mostly composed of people in working ages, then there is a large supply for the labour force. A country with an older population will have a greater need for medical services and pension systems (Haupt, 2004, p. 5).

In order to examine the demographics of Cambodia, I must lay out definitions for the different demographic indicators used. The *total population* is the aggregate number of persons living in the country. The *crude birth rate* is calculated from the total live births divided by the total population. It is then multiplied by 1,000. This represents the number of live births per 1,000 of the population (Haupt, 2004, p. 13). The *crude death rate* is comprised of the total deaths in one year per 1,000 of the population (Haupt, 2004, p. 25). The *population growth rate* measures the population's increase or decrease over a given year. The rate is expressed as a percentage of the year's change divided by the total population. Population growth rates do incorporate net migration rates (Haupt, 2004, p. 44). This chapter does not focus on migration but the birth and death rates.

The population pyramid is one method to look at the size and proportions of the population. Each horizontal line represents the total number of persons in the age range. Each line is also broken down by sex (Haupt, 2004, p. 7). The *age-dependency ratio* is a measurement of the total number of individuals aged 0-14 and 65 plus divided by the total number of individuals aged 15 to 64. The population aged 15 to 64 are generally considered to be economically productive while those aged below 15 and above 64 are considered to be economically dependent (Haupt, 2004, p. 6).

All numbers used in these tables, graphs and population pyramids are taken from the UN's World Population Prospects 2008 Revision Database or the World Bank's Data Catalogue. If data came from the Population Prospects Database, then it is from the medium variant.

Birth and Death Rates

The sudden dips in the crude birth rate and the peak in the crude death rate can be directly attributed to the time of the Khmer Rouge. Cambodia's death rate was declining before the Khmer Rouge. The death rate almost doubled in the late 1970s from its rates in the late 1960s. After the Vietnamese invaded Cambodia, the death rate began to instantly decline. Cambodians were no longer forced to work to exhaustion. They had more access to food and medical care than during the time of the Khmer Rouge. By 1983, the death rate returned to the same level as prior to the conflict. The rate has continued to decline albeit much more gradually than in the immediate post-conflict era.

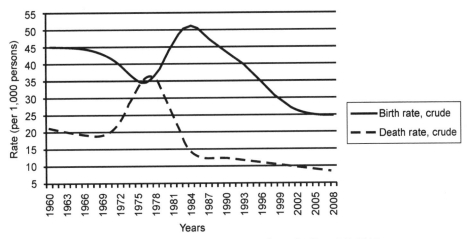

Figure 12.1: Birth and Death Rates of Cambodia, 1960-2008

Cambodia's birth rate was declining as well before the Khmer Rouge took control over the country. Birth rates fell even lower. This is understandable for several reasons. First, men and women were working under a huge amount a stress. Their lives were at stake. It is understandable that having sex and procreating were not a priority then. Second, studies have found that it is much more difficult for a woman to conceive and carry a baby to term when she is malnourished and overworked (Walque, 206, pp. 224-225).

Once the Khmer Rouge was out of power, Cambodia's birth rate not only recovered to pre-conflict levels but increased higher. The women of marriage age during the Khmer Rouge had simply delayed marriage until after the conflict. Women married at higher rates and started having babies. Cambodia had its very own baby boom in the early 1980s (Walque, 2006, p. 225). The peace settlement, a switch to multiparty politics and free market economics accompanied Cambodia's second smaller baby boom in 1990 (World Bank, 2009, p. 29).

POPULATION GROWTH RATE

Most developing countries including Cambodia were beginning to enter phase 2 of the demographic transition in the mid 20th century. Falling death rates were coupled with high birth rates. This meant there would be a growing population growth rate. The Fig. 12.2 shows how the population growth rate in Cambodia was increasing prior to the conflict. The high death rates and low birth rates caused the population growth rate to plummet in the 1970s. Instead of adding people to the population each year and growing, Cambodia was losing numbers from its total population.

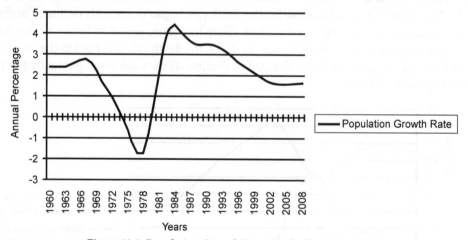

Figure 12.2: Population Growth Rate Cambodia, 1960-2008

The population growth rate rebounded after the end of the Khmer Rouge and increased to a higher level than before the conflict. This is fueled in part by the baby boom referenced earlier. The impact of the second baby boom can also be seen in the slight uptick of the growth rate during its decline from the peak in 1983. The growth rate finally declined below 2 per cent in 2000. It has stayed fairly constant in the 21st century.

AGE OF THE POPULATION

The age of a population can be quite important in regards to what services are demanded or what labour sources are available for the economy. Cambodia had a very youthful population for a long time. The high percentage of youth put an extra burden on the working ages. The graph below provides a brief snapshot of the proportion of the total population made up by the youth ages (0-14) and working ages (15-64).

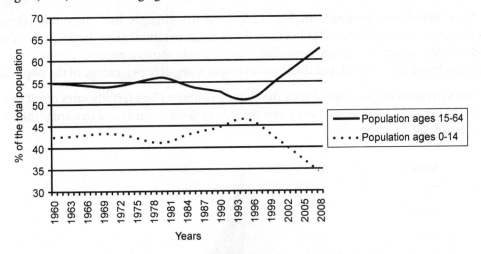

Figure 12.3: Population Age Percentage Cambodia, 1960-2008

The older non-working group (age 65+) is a small percentage of the total population at about 2 per cent. I chose not to include them in the graph above because it distorted the graph. The older age group should now begin to be a bigger percentage of the total population since the life expectancies for Cambodians are increasing.

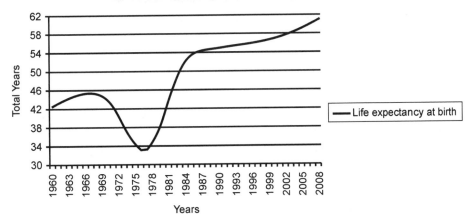

Figure 12.4: Life Expectancy at Birth Cambodia

The increased life expectancies result from lower death rates and by improving health standards. We can still see the impact of the Khmer Rouge on life expectancies. Similarly to the birth, death and population rates, the life expectancies are able to rebound and improve after the end of the conflict.

POPULATION PYRAMIDS

The three population pyramids in Fig. 12.5 show the changes in Cambodia's population structure over the past 50 years. The horizontal axis in the pyramids gives the percent of the total population the age and sex group represent. The male side shows a negative percent. This must be done to build the pyramid, but does not represent a negative percentage of the population.

The 1960s pyramid is quite typical for a developing country. High fertility rates result in a large base of the pyramid. High death rates cause the side to slope inwards and upwards. The 65 years and older age good is very small.

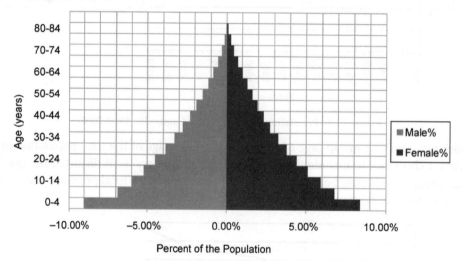

Figure 12.5: Population of Cambodia by Age and Sex, 1960

The first noticeable item in the 1985 population pyramid is the extremely large base of 0 to 4 year olds. This is the first baby boom. The second item, although less noticeable, is the difference between the male and female side from the 30-34 age bracket and higher. We see in this pyramid women were more likely than men to survive the genocide (Walque, 2006, p. 224).

The 2010 pyramid contains UN projected numbers for 2010. You can see the baby booms working their way through the pyramid. The first baby boom is now part of the working aged population. The second baby boom has just entered the working age population as well.

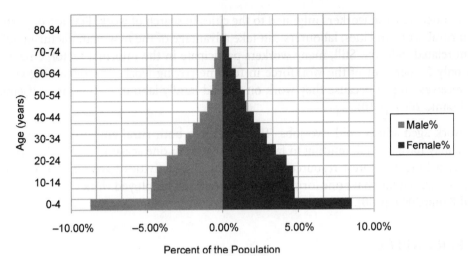

Figure 12.6: Cambodia Population by Age and Sex, 1985

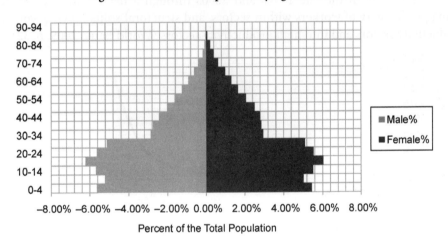

Figure 12.7: Population of Cambodia by Age and Sex, 2010

MEASURING CURRENT LABOUR FORCE

There is currently a high level of labour force participation in Cambodia. The rate measured 87 per cent in 2007. The unemployment rate in 2007 was 3.5 per cent. Unemployment is defined in Cambodia as those not working but available to work and seeking work in the last week. Employment has also been shifting in between sectors. Labourers have moved from agricultural to industrial and then to service sectors. The total participation in the agricultural sector has declined from 75 per cent in 1994, to 70 per cent in 2001 and finally down to 58 per cent in 2007. The share of total participation in the two other sectors has increased as well. While only 5 per cent of the workforce was involved with the industry sector in 1994, 15 per cent worked in the industry sector in 2007 (World Bank, 2009, p. 30).

Large numbers of rural workers migrated to the cities in search of work. Few job opportunities exist in rural areas. In cities, labourers can take advantage of the new manufacturing jobs and tourism related industry. Still, many workers participate in the informal sector. One estimate places only 25 per cent of the workforce in fulltime paying work. The remaining workforce either receives no pay because they work on unpaid family labour, or they are self-employed (World Bank, 2009, p. 30).

Many work aged adults hold two jobs. This applies to both rural and urban workers. Rural workers may have one job tending to farming activities in one season. There other job can be to collect fishing and forest resources once the farming activities have finished for the year. Urban labourers might have one formal job but sustain self-employed work to earn extra money (World Bank, 2009, p. 30).

GDP PER CAPITA

Per capita GDP grew in the late 1990s and 2000s through a decreasing dependency ratio, increasing productivity of workers within sectors, and structural shifts moving workers out of low productivity sectors and into high productivity sectors (World Bank, 2009, p. 32).

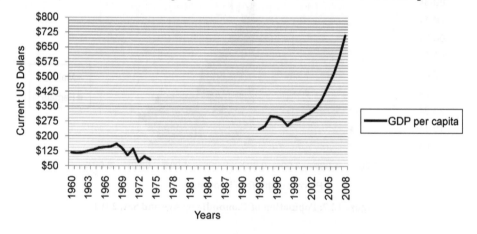

Figure 12.8: GDP Per Capita Cambodia, 1960-2008

The graph above tries to convey Cambodia's growing GDP per capita rate. There is a segment of the data missing due to the conflict and post-conflict economic environment. The Khmer Rouge eliminated currency and incomes. Not only did they not track the data, there was no data to track. Most of the international communities chose to ignore and embargo Cambodia's economy after the Vietnamese took control. I could not find any reliable data from this time period. The recent GDP per capita growth reference in the preceding paragraph identifies easily with the sharp increase on the right side of the graph.

The improvements of living standards witnessed from 1998 to 2004 came about from the structural transformations. The World Bank reports:

Between 1998 and 2000, this reallocation of employment share from low-productivity agriculture to higher productivity industry contributed 6.5 percentage points of the 8.3 per cent annual growth rate in GDP per capita; between 2000 and 2004, this continued inter-sectoral shift in employment (with industry and, now, services both gaining share from agriculture) contributed 13.5 percentage points (offset by the negative effects of other factors which brought net growth in per capita GDP down to 6.4 percentage points per annum). (World Bank, 2009, p. 32)

The impact of the lower dependency ratio was slightly reduced by a higher unemployment rate, but demographics helped contributed 0.8 percentage points per year to the growth in GDP per capita (World Bank, 2009, p. 32).

Most recently (2004-2007) the increase in productivity has fueled increases to the GDP per capita. It is thought that acceleration in productivity within the three sectors of agriculture, industry and service have added a total of 6.9 percentage points to the 10.2 per cent of the annual growth rate. Lower dependency ratios and increased employment continue to make a contribution during this time period by adding 2.9 points per year to the annual growth of GDP per capita (World Bank, 2009, pp. 32-33).

The changing demographic structure has played an important role in Cambodia's recent economic growth. The shift first became important in 2000 when the dependency ratio started rapidly decreases. The ratio decreased by a quarter between 2000 and 2007. In 1998, it took 100 working age adults to support 86 dependents. The number of dependents dropped to 61 in 2007 (World Bank, 2009, p. 33).

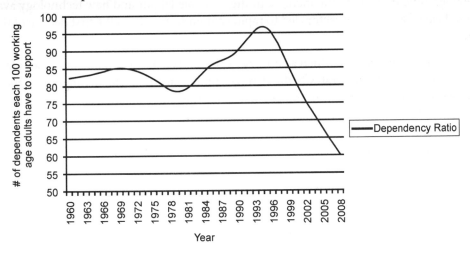

Figure 12.9: Dependency Ratios Cambodia, 1960-2008

THE FUTURE OF ECONOMIC GROWTH

The lowered dependency ratio will continue to benefit Cambodia in the near future. Unfortunately, the demographics will be unable to continue to benefit Cambodia's economic growth the same way it has for the past decade. The increased number of workers are allowed for an increase in productivity. The numbers of workers will most likely stabilize along with the dependency ratios. Therefore, Cambodia cannot rely on the same increase in productivity to drive economic growth as it has over the past ten years.

Future growth rates of GDP per capita will need to come from other areas. Growth can come from continued structural transformation. Productivity can increase from improvements to the value-added per worker in each sector (World Bank, 2009, p. 34). The previous improvement in productivity came from the sheer increase in the number of workers. Sectors need to look at how they can increase the productivity of their current workers instead of relying on increased productivity from more workers.

CONCLUSION

The Cambodian genocide interrupted the beginning of the demographic transition in Cambodia. Instead of experiencing continued declines in the mortality rates of the 1960s, the mortality rate increased in the 1970s and early 1980s. Fertility rates plummeted as well but increased once the genocide was over. The demographic transition did resume at the conclusion of the conflict. Ultimately, it appears the demographic transition was put on hold during shortly before and throughout the genocide.

Only in the past decade has Cambodia been able to reap the economic benefits associated with the demographic transition. The increase in the available labour and new technology available to the industrial and service sectors led to rapid economic growth in the first decade of the 21st century.

In conclusion, the process by which a country experiences a decline in mortality rates followed later by a decline in fertility rates is the demographic transition. The demographic transition is a widely accepted theory about how populations grow and transition. Malthus' principle on population held growing populations would be kept in check by the availability of food supplies. He did not foresee the transformations technology would bring to production. Populations were no longer trapped. These technological advances allowed populations to continue growing. Along with advances in medical care and health, the mortality rates in all countries have declined. This has eventually led to decline in fertility rates as well. Although developed countries progressed through the demographic transition first, developing countries have experienced the transition as well.

The developing country Cambodia suffered through genocide in the 1970s and lost about one million people from its population. The effects of the genocide are visible in graphs depicting death rates, birth rates, population growth rates, life expectancies, and population pyramids. Cambodia did resume its demographic transition. The lowered dependency ratios and increase in the number of workers have fueled recent rapid economic growth. There are doubts on whether Cambodia will be able to sustain this growth. In a future research, I would like to examine in greater details how the demographic transition has impacted standards of living and whether much of Cambodia's recent economic growth has transferred to the poor.

REFERENCES

1. Bloom, David E., David Canning, Jaypee Sevilla, and Population Matters. 2003. *The demographic dividend: A new perspective on the economic consequences of population change.* Santa Monica, Calif.: Rand.

2. Curtis, Grant. 1998. *Cambodia reborn? The transition to democracy and development.* Washington, DC: Brookings Institution.

3. Engels, Frederick. 1844. Outlines of a critique of political economy. *DeutschFranzösische Jahrbücher.*

4. Galor, Oded, and David N. Weil. 1999. From Malthusian Stagnation to Modern Growth. *The American Economic Review* 89, (2) (May): 150-54.

5. Galor, Oded, and David N. Weil. 2000. Population, technology, and growth: From Malthusian stagnation to the demographic transition and beyond. *The American Economic Review* 90, (4) (Sep.): 806-28.

6. Haupt, Arthur, and Thomas T. Kane. 2004. *Population handbook.* 5th ed. Washington DC: Population Reference Bureau.

7. Kirk, Dudley. 1996. Demographic transition theory. *Population Studies* 50, (3) (Nov.): 361-87.

8. Lagerlöf, Nils-Petter. 2003. From Malthus to modern growth: Can epidemics explain the three regimes? *International Economic Review* 44, (2) (May): 755-77.

9. Lee, Ronald. 2003. The demographic transition: Three centuries of fundamental change. *The Journal of Economic Perspectives* 17, (4) (Autumn): 167-90.

10. Lee, Ronald, Andrew Mason, and Timothy Miller. 2000. Life cycle saving and the demographic transition: The case of Taiwan. *Population and Development Review* 26, (Supplement: Population and Economic Change in East Asia): 194-219.

11. Malthus, Thomas. 1798. An essay on the principle of population. (1998).

12. Sen, Armatya. 2003. Population: Delusion and reality. *Asian Affairs on Global Issues.*

13. Shah, Anup. 1998. *Ecology and the crisis of overpopulation: Future prospects for global sustainability.* Cheltenham, England; Northampton, MA: Edward Elgar.

14. Todaro, Michael P., and Stephen C. Smith. 2006. *Economic development.* The Addison-Wesley series in economics. 9th ed. Boston: Pearson Addison Wesley.

15. United Nations Population Division. World Population Prospects: The 2008 Revision Database. 2009. United Nations Department of Economic and Social Affairs. Available from: *http://esa. un.org/unpp/index.asp*

16. US Department of State. 2010. Background note: Cambodia. [cited 05/20 2010]. Available from: *http://www.state.gov/r/pa/ei/bgn/2732.htm.*

17. Walque, Damien de. 2006. The socio-demographic legacy of the Khmer Rouge period in Cambodia. *Population Studies* 60, (2) (Jul.): 223-31.

18. Weisdorf, Jacob L. 2004. From stagnation to growth: Revisiting three historical regimes. *Journal of Population Economics* 17, (3) (Aug.): 455-72.

19. World Bank. 2009. *Sustaining rapid growth in a challenging environment: Cambodia country economic memorandum.* Available from: *http://siteresources.worldbank.org/INTCAMBODIA/ Resources/293755-1181597132695/kh_growth_report2009full.pdf.*

20. World Bank. 2010. World Bank Data Catalogue: Cambodia data [database online]. Available from: *http://data.worldbank.org/country/cambodia.*

21. Zhao, Zhongwei, and Fei Guo. 2007. *Transition and challenge: China's population at the beginning of the 21st Century.* Oxford; New York: Oxford University Press.

13

Economic Development and Income Inequality in Brazil

A Test of Kuznets' U-Curve Hypothesis

Sarah Roth

CHAPTER SUMMARY

Understanding the nature of economic development plays an important role in today's economics. Not only is it important for policy makers *within* a country in alleviating poverty, maintaining stability, and continuing growth but also understanding the development process is important to international institutions to allocate aid effectively. In 1955, Simon Kuznets proposed a hypothesis that connected economic growth to income inequality. He argued that as a country developed, income disparities would first increase and then decrease at some later stage of development. While this hypothesis is still debated among scholars, it calls attention to an important aspect of economic development – how growth is distributed. Disparity of distribution stagnates prospective growth as well as shakes social stability.

Experiencing albeit erratic patterns of growth during the twentieth century, Brazil presents a fascinating case study of economic development. Large in both size and population, the country has struggled to shrink the gap between the top and bottom income groups as well as alleviate poverty. High increases in gross domestic product have reduced absolute poverty in Brazil but inequities persist. Despite being the tenth largest economy in the world, Brazil maintains one of the highest levels of inequality in the world.

This chapter will test Kuznets' Inverted-U Hypothesis using Gini coefficients from Brazil since 1981 to investigate how economic development has affected income disparities in the last 30 years.

Studying the patterns of evolution in income distribution during economic development are of obvious importance lest we wrongly conclude that increases in per capita mean that all people (or even the majority of people) are better off (Kulkarni, 2006). In reality, 'a significant impact of economic growth on poverty alleviation is eroded by high income inequality' (Khasru and Jalil, 2002, i). Traditionally economists have used Gross Domestic Product (GDP) or Per Capita Income (PCI) levels to measure a country's economic growth. While these numbers are universally utilized and essential measures in understanding economic development, they fail to illuminate the whole picture in the sense that these measures fail to consider the distribution of production.

One of the most influential theories concerning economic development and income distribution is Simon Kuznets' Inverted-U hypothesis. According to Kuznets, as a country experiences modern economic growth, income inequality worsens initially, but, that once a country reaches a certain stage of development, the income inequality declines. Although, Kuznets hypothesis continues to be disputed, his hypothesis still has major policy implications for those concerned with economic development in less developed countries (LDCs).

As the largest national economy in Latin America and the tenth largest economy in the world, Brazil's rapid growth throughout the twentieth century makes for a fascinating case study. The country has experienced high levels of economic growth meanwhile the incidence of poverty persists in Brazil due to a highly skewed income distribution (Thomas, 2006).

In the first part of this chapter, I will explore some of the negative impacts uneven income distribution has on a society. Subsequently, I will explain and examine Kuznets Inverted – U Hypothesis first by honing our understanding of two main components of the hypothesis: the Lorenz Curve and gini coefficients. Next, I will apply Kuznets' hypothesis to the case of Brazil using a longitudinal plot of changes in the distribution of income as measured by the gini coefficient. Finally, this chapter will conclude with suggestions for ameliorating income distribution inequality in Brazil.

THEORY

Problems with High Inequality

Aside from normative social justice issues surrounding highly unequal distribution of assets in a society, other problems arise in countries with high levels of income disparity including issues associated with the economic efficiency, social instability, and environmental degradation.

Economic

Excessive inequality restrains economic growth. According to the World Bank, 'Brazil is a highly urbanized country where the gap between the rural and urban areas is persistent' (2004, 7). High levels of inequality prevent a larger percentage of people within that population from credit qualification. When people cannot borrow money they cannot expand their businesses or properly educate their children. Further, high rates of inequality lowers the overall savings rate of a country. Capital flight also occurs through the elites' expenditures on imported goods. Both the low savings rate and lack of investment do not add to the country's productive resources;

in fact, 'they represent significant drains on these resources' (Todaro and Smith, 2006, 208). Unequal land distribution, problematic in Brazil, further exacerbates economic inefficiency. When inequality is high, these factors can result in lower average income and a lower rate of economic growth (Galor and Zaeira, 1993).

Social

Extreme income disparity undermines social stability. Excessive levels of inequality induces poverty. Furthermore, in countries, such as Brazil, weak social mobility perpetuates cycles of increasing inequality (World Bank, 2004). High levels of inequality can also 'strengthen the political power of the rich which facilitates rent-seeking behaviour like excessive lobbying, large political donations, bribery and cronyism which further diverts resources from productive purposes' (Todaro and Smith, 2006, 208). Unequal distribution of incomes can also sway the poor to support populist policies that may cause civil strife such as those in Bolivia, Venezuela, El Salvador, and Iran. These political upheavals not only can cause loss of life but set back economic growth and development.

Some have hypothesized about the 'erosion of social capital in the form of respect for rules and trust in strangers or institutions' (World Bank, 2004, 8). Furthermore, there is substantial international evidence that high levels inequality are associated to a number of costs to society, namely induced levels of violence and crime (World Bank, 2004). Measures of social capital find that community involvement is greater in more equal societies.

Environmental

Brazil's rich natural resource endowment has been vital to economic development. However the depletion of these resources disproportionately affects the poor. According to Torras, intragenerational inequality may actually exacerbate environmental degradation. On one hand the worsening could be a result of the 'environment-poverty' trap where the poor exploit resources unsustainably to meet there subsistence needs. Or on the other hand, a greater still proportion of the environmental degradation can be explained by the wealthy members of societies' ability to avoid the consequences of environmental degradation by passing off the negative externalities on the poor (2003). In Brazil, natural resources constitute a much higher proportion of the assets of the poor than the rich. Thomas states that 'uncontrolled deforestation, soil erosion, and water pollution deprive poor Brazilians of income sources' (2006, 23). He further argues that urban degradation also affects the poor disproportionately; inadequate water and sewage, in particular, take a heavy toll on health (2006, 70).

The Lorenz Curve and the Gini Coefficient

The Lorenz Curve is a measure of the inequality of income distribution for a given population. The graphical representation as shown in Figure 13.1 shows the relationship between the cumulative population as arranged from richest to poorest and their corresponding income.

The horizontal axis gives the cumulative population and the vertical axis gives corresponding cumulative income. The 45 degree diagonal represents a perfectly equal distribution of income. In other words, 10 per cent of the population earns 10 per cent of the cumulative income, 50 per cent of the population earns 50 per cent of the income and all recipients have exactly the same income.

The more unequal the distribution of income in a given population the greater the separation between the diagonal and the Lorenz curve. In the extreme case where one person received 100 per cent of the income, the Lorenz curve would be formed by the horizontal and vertical axis on the lower right side of the figure. Hence, the inequality of income in a population group can be visually assessed from the Lorenz Curve (Campano and Salvatore, 2006).

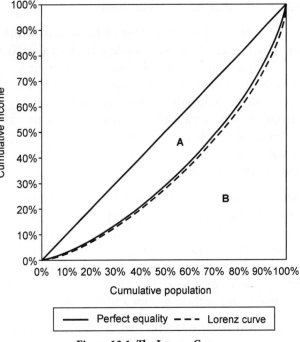

Figure 13.1: The Lorenz Curve

While the Lorenz curve visually represents income inequality, the gini coefficient gives a measurable index of inequality. Developed in 1912 by Italian statistician Corrado Gini, this widely used measure of income inequality is derived from the Lorenz curve. The gini coefficient is the ratio of the area between the diagonal and the Lorenz curve and the triangle area below the diagonal. Or reconsidering Figure 13.1, Gini coefficient = Area A/(Area A + Area B).

A higher Gini coefficient represents higher inequality of income. A perfectly unequal distribution of income would have a Gini value of 1 where as a perfectly equal distribution would have a gini value of 0. Countries with highly unequal income distributions have a Gini value generally between 0.50 and 0.70. While the Gini coefficient for countries with relatively equal income distribution lies between 0.20 and 0.35 (Todaro and Smith, 2006).

As Kuznets' Hypothesis uses the Gini coefficient to measure changes in income distribution over time, it is important to understand the difficulties that arise when attempting to calculate income disparities. Longitudinal studies such as Kuznets' hypothesis require a consistent definition of income which can be very different country to country or even in the same country from period to period (Campano and Salvatore, 2006). Income can be particularly difficult to measure in developing nations among poorer populations where wages may not be the main source of income. Most countries attempt to rectify the issue through household consumption surveys which may be sporadic and inconsistent over time due to lack of resources in the country.

Kuznets' Inverted- U Hypothesis

In 1955, Simon Kuznets published his seminal work *Economic Growth and Income Inequality* in The American Economic Review. In this paper Kuznets characterized the long term changes of distribution of income. He found that income distribution tends to worsen during periods of economic growth only to improve during later stages. A time series plot of changes income distribution (such as the Gini coefficient) will result in the pattern of growth characterized by the Inverted-U shown in Figure 13.2.

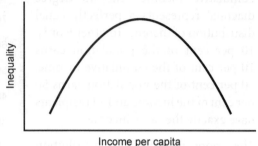

Figure 13.2: Kuznets Inverted U-Curve

Kuznets argues that 'there are at least two groups of forces that make for increasing inequality in the distribution of income. The first group relates to the concentration of savings in the upper-income brackets. Other conditions being equal, the cumulative effect of such inequality of savings would be the concentration of an increasing proportion of income yielding assets in the hands of the upper groups further increasing the income shares of these groups and their descendents' (Kuznets, 1955, 7).

The second group of forces that cause increasing inequality in the income distribution relates to the structural changes that happen as a country develops economically. Economic growth in countries is characterized by the shift away from agriculture, a process usually referred to as industrialization or urbanization. The Lewis Model of Structural Change further illuminates in part the increase in income disparity.

Prior to industrialization, the agricultural sector has an excess supply of labour which makes the wage rate in this sector close to zero. Moreover, the marginal product of labour in the rural sector equals zero. The industrial sector differs not only in the sense that wage rates are higher than subsistence level but also in that the marginal product of labour is positive and higher than the marginal product of labour in the agricultural sector. The higher wage rates in the industrial sector attract labour from the traditional sector. 'As the per capita productivity increases more rapidly in urban pursuits than in agricultural sectors then inequality in the total income distribution should increase' (Kuznets, 1955, 8).

The wage rate in the modern sector remains higher than that in the traditional sector, but gradually decreases as more and more people migrate to industry. As people leave the agricultural sector, the wage rate will rise until the marginal revenue product of labour curves for the two sectors cross. At this point migration will stop and the income distribution will be more equal. While this logic seems plausible 'it suffers from rigor' (Campano and Salvatore 2006, 109).

Empirical Studies on the U-Curve Hypothesis

The validity of Kuznets' hypothesis remains a question of empirical evidence. In his work, Kuzents admits to the lack the empirical data in the field and in doing so makes a call to arms to collect more and better data especially for developing countries. He emphasizes the importance of the field of study:

Since this distribution is a focal point at which the functioning of the economic system impinges upon the human beings who are living members of society and for whom and through whom society operates, it is an important datum for understanding the reactions and behaviour patterns of human beings as producers, consumers, and savers. It follows that better knowledge and comprehension of the subject are indispensable, not only in and of itself but also as a step in learning more about the functioning of society – in both the long and short run.

A better understanding of the distribution of income, particularly in developing nations, affects strategies for growth, public policy options, and how international institutes effectively deliver aid (1995, 27).

Both empirical evidence to support Kuznets' hypothesis and to oppose the hypothesis have been found. Cross-country studies and studies that use income ratios as the measure of inequality tend to support the hypothesis. Studies that use a one country longitudinal study as well as those that analyze Gini coefficients in a cross country study tend not to support the hypothesis. Additionally theoretical models based on dual sector system (traditional/modern or urban/rural) support the hypothesis.

Regardless, the pattern of increasing then declining inequality is not necessary for economic development. Countries such as Taiwan, South Korea, Costa Rica, and Sri Lanka have seen growth accompanied by decreasing disparities. Further, long periods of growth do not necessarily imply an increase in inequality. Latin America stands out as the global region which traditionally has the highest levels of inequality yet many of the countries in Latin America are middle income countries. According to Todaro and Smith, inequality seems to be a stable part of a country's socio-economic make-up, altered significantly only as a result of substantial upheaval (2006, 215).

ECONOMIC DEVELOPMENT IN BRAZIL

There are many factors that characterize the Brazilian Economy. Brazil is the fifth largest county in both geographical area and population (approx. 192 million). The population of Brazil is highly urbanized with about 82 per cent of the population living in urban areas (Thomas, 2006). Rich in natural resources, Brazil houses the largest tropical forests. Brazil also has large and well-developed agricultural, mining, manufacturing, and service sectors, outweighing that of all other South American countries.

Commonly described as a world of difference, Brazil presents a fascinating study of economic development. At times cited as an example of a country that has experienced 'growth without development', Brazil's case study presents some of the complexities involved in economic development. In Brazil, 'world-competitive industry coexists with stagnant, protected sectors. Modern agriculture coexists with low productivity traditional practices' (Todaro and Smith 2006, 27). These strengths and weakness of the Brazilian economy leads to erratic growth with substantial swings over time as seen in Figure 13.3.

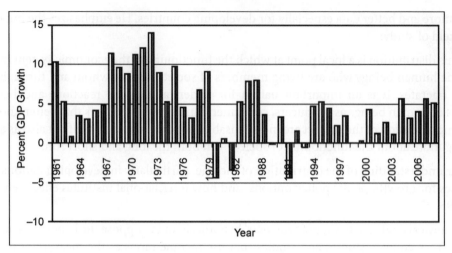

Figure 13.3: GDP Growth (Annual %) in Brazil 1961 to 2008

Source: http://data.un.org/Search.aspx?q=Brazil+datamart%5bWDI%5d

Brazil maintains one of the highest levels of inequality in the world. In the mid twentieth century Brazil had one of the highest growth rates in the world while other development indicators lagged (Thomas, 2006). A 2003 World Bank study found three main reasons to explain this phenomenon. Regressive public spending, inequality in education, and the high wage rate differential for skilled workers all contribute to income disparity.

While Brazil has made significant progress to remedy unequal education distribution in the country, the primary school completion rate is only 71 per cent. Focus is now shifting to secondary education where wage potential rises, helping to alleviate poverty and boosting labour productivity and production. Further changes must be made in the university system as well. The design of the current system favours the upper middle class and fails to benefit the poor and thus further maintains the status quo of income inequality.

Disparities in assets such as education and health lead to even more unequal labour market outcomes. Wage differentials by skill level in Brazil are approximately 50 per cent higher than in the United States. A Brazilian worker who has completed secondary education earns, on an average, about 3.7 times as much as a worker who has completed one to four years of schooling (Thomas, 2006, 35). Moreover, high levels of taxes and mandatory benefits discourage formal sector hiring. Overall tax burden has increased from about 25 per cent in the decade from 2003 to 2004 translating into as many as half of Brazil's labour force working in the informal sector (Todaro and Smith, 2006, 28).

A third major factor affecting Brazil's high level of inequality is the distribution of public spending. Brazil spends one fifth of its gross domestic product on social programmes and transfers including public pensions. While its ratio of national spending is high for a middle income country only a small margin of that spending reaches the poor in Brazil. In 2000, the poorest 20 per cent in Brazil received only 1.7 per cent of monetary social transfers (Thomas,

2006, 36). The pension system in Brazil accounts for over half of social spending in Brazil yet it disproportionately benefits the relatively wealthy. Recent pro-poor social programmes like Bolsa Escolar and Bolsa Família have begun to address some of the inequities inherent in the Brazilian system. These conditional cash transfer programmes attempt to alleviate income disparities in several ways by providing direct funding to families who send their children to school and bring their family in for regular checkups.

KUZNETS' HYPOTHESIS: TESTING THE BRAZILIAN CASE

Now we will examine the data available from 1981 to 2008 to determine whether Brazil's economic development fits Kuznets' Inverted-U Hypothesis. The explosive growth in Brazil's economy in the 1960's and 1970's certainly saw a rise in income disparity from a Gini coefficient of 0.53 to 0.578 during the decade. During the 1980's and 1990's the Gini coefficient continued to rise in Brazil, spiking in 1989 at 0.628. Since then the Gini coefficient has slowly leveled off around the high rate of 0.55.

From Figure 13.4, it is difficult to conclude whether or not Brazil fits Kuznets' hypothesis. Looking at the data the present Gini value of 0.54 is still larger than higher inequality value of 0.53 in the 1960's at the beginning of Brazil's economic boom. We see a large spike of Gini values in the late 1980's in part explained by the debt crisis experienced by many Latin American countries during that time. Increases in inequality during this time could be due to inflationary effects on the poor. The stabilization of the debt problem in the country surely contributed to a stabilization of the Gini coefficient. Still it is disconcerting that despite large growth inequality values remain high in Brazil. Perhaps Brazil's economic development has yet to reach the turning point of income inequality and is still in the upper portion of the U-Curve. Future data can provide further insight on how economic development affects income disparity in Brazil.

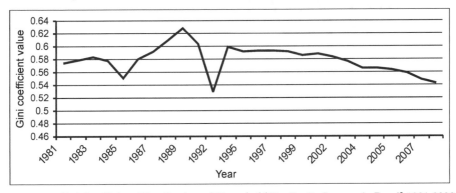

Figure 13.4: Gini Coefficient Distribution of Household Per Capita Income in Brazil 1981-2008

Inflation and Debt Crisis

Past development strategies of import substitution, subsidies to capital, directed credit, and excessive borrowing to cover fiscal deficits resulted in the debt crisis of the 1980s and 1990s neutralized and even reversed decades of progress in Brazil (Thomas 2006, 20). In attempt to repay outstanding loans the government printed more money leading to hyper inflation over 2000 per cent in 1994 (see Table 13.2 and Figure 13.5). Negative effects of inflation and higher macroeconomic volatility on equality include: depressed wages, especially for unskilled workers due to their lower levels of organization, and lower capital investment, which is an important mechanism to reduce poverty long term (Gottschalk, 2006, 51). Table 13.1 shows the declining rates of GNI per capita Income during the early 1980's. Moreover, one can see from Figure 13.4, a correlated spike in Gini value during the 1980s.

Stabilization and Liberalization

The gradual decrease in Gini coefficients can be attributed at least in part to economic stabilization in Brazil during the late 1990s. Where other government leaders had failed in prior years, President Fernando Henrique Cardoso's fiscal policy, *Plano Real*, finally stabilized Brazil's hyperinflation problems. Within two years of implementation, Brazil's inflation rate was in the single digits. Cardoso also began gradually exposing Brazil's industry to global competition further opening Brazil's economy. These plans encouraged economic growth through trade liberalization. After its share of exports decreased during the 1980's, it increased again to 54 per cent by 2000. Finally, the Cardoso government deepened and broadened the scope of the privatization drive. Thought to be worth of USD 190 billion, the sale of the state's 159 public enterprises could bring considerable hard currency to the treasury, while increasing the overall effectiveness of the state and the economy (Font 2003, 28).

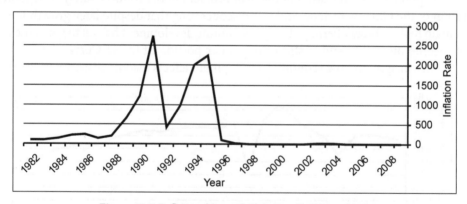

Figure 13.5: Inflation (Annual %) in Brazil 1981 to 2008

Source: http://data.un.org/Search.aspx?q=Brazil+datamart%5bWDI%5d

Policy Recommendations for Income Redistribution

Improved Social Spending

Conditional cash transfer programmes have a great number of potential effects for reducing poverty within a country. These programs have existed since the 1970's, however they have become much more visible in the last eight years. Reaching over 11 million families in Brazil,

Table 13.1: Gini Coefficients for Brazil 1981–2008

Year	GNI Per Capita, Atlas Method (current USD)	Gini Coefficient
1981	1,850	0.574
1982	1,900	0.579
1983	1,730	0.584
1984	1,640	0.578
1985	1,570	0.551
1986	1,720	0.58
1987	1,850	0.592
1988	1,990	0.609
1989	2,510	0.628
1990	2,540	0.604
1992	2,670	0.529
1993	2,700	0.599
1995	3,740	0.592
1996	4,470	0.593
1997	5,060	0.593
1998	4,880	0.592
1999	4,130	0.586
2001	3,870	0.588
2002	3,310	0.583
2003	3,070	0.576
2004	2,970	0.566
2004	3,330	0.566
2005	3,970	0.564
2006	4,820	0.559
2007	6,060	0.548
2008	7,350	0.542

Sources: www.sedlac.com, http://data.un.org/Search.aspx?q=Brazil+datamart%5bWDI%5d

Table 13.2: Inflation Rates in Brazil: 1994 to 2008

Year	1994	1995	1996	1997	1998	1999	2000	2001	2002	2003	2004	2005	2006	2007	2008
Inflation Rate (Annual %)	2,251.70	93.5	17.1	7.6	4.2	8.5	6.2	9	10.6	13.7	8	7.2	6.2	3.7	5.9

Source: http://data.un.org/Search.aspx?q=Brazil+datamart%5bWDI%5d

these programme provide direct funds to moderately poor to the extreme poor (families making less than USD R50 per month) and make members comply with key human development investments (Thomas, 123). Although criticism has been generated surrounding the policy due to the increase in public spending, a study by dos Santos et al. concluded that the income-transfer assistance programmes have undoubtedly been important in reducing the level of income inequality in the Brazilian economy (2009, 615).

Land Reform

Along with income, the high inequity of assets such as land creates economic inefficiencies too. In Brazil, it is estimated that the top 5 per cent of farms comprise 69.3 per cent of the farmland in Brazil (Todaro and Smith, 30). Land distribution also affects sustainable development. The needs of the present supercede the needs of future generations leading to more inequality as time passes. Natural resources are a major share of the assets of the poor and a major contributor to their livelihoods. Considering the resource richness of Brazil, land reform requires serious attention.

Maintaining Macroeconomic Stability

As one can see from the test of Kuznets' hypothesis, macroeconomic volatility increased inequality significantly in Brazil during the 1980s. When inflation was brought under control in 1994-1995, the poverty rate declined by one fifth. Macroeconomic volatility leads to higher poverty, and slows down long-term trends in improvements of social indicators…the consequences to the poor are therefore far reaching (Gottschalk, 2006, 58). Continued stable growth helps alleviate poverty. While not all 'boats may rise' equally as a result of this growth continued investment by the Brazilian government in health and education for the poorer members of society can help combat income disparities in Brazil.

CONCLUSION

The general consensus of Kuznets' hypothesis has resulted in opposing conclusions of its validity, however it remains a common tool in evaluating a country's economic development. The results of testing Kuznets' U-Curve hypothesis were inconclusive. The data from the last 30 years in Brazil saw a rise in income inequality as a result of economic growth, it has yet to see a significant decline. Rather the Gini values in Brazil remain relatively high for a middle income country.

The causes of income inequality as well as the remedies are complex issues. Addressing ineffective institutions and their inherent inequalities is essential to reversing disparity in Brazil. Recognizing distribution and inclusion as a part of growth and protecting future generations' access to resources will be important to Brazil's development. Despite being a country of great differences Brazil remains hopeful for the future.

REFERENCES

1. *Brazil: Inequality and economic development.* Vol. 2 vols. Washington DC: World Bank, 2003.

2. Campano, Fred, Dominick Salvatore, and Inc ebrary. *Income distribution.* New York: Oxford University Press, 2006.

3. CEDLAS (Universidad Nacional de La Plata) and The World Bank. Socio-economic database for latin america and the caribbean. *http://www.depeco.econo.unlp.edu.ar/sedlac/eng/index.php* (accessed 5/20, 2010)

4. Dos Santos, Vladimir Faria, Wilson Da Cruz Vieira, and Bricio Dos Santos Reis. 2009. 'Effects of Alternative Policies on Income Redistribution: Evidence from Brazil'. *Development Policy Review* 27, no. 5: 601-616. *Academic Search Complete*, EBSCOhost (accessed May 21, 2010)

5. Ebrary, Inc. *Inequality and economic development in brazil.* A world bank country study. Washington, DC: World Bank, 2004.

6. Font, Mauricio A. *Transforming brazil :A reform era in perspective.* Lanham, MD: Rowman & Littlefield, 2003.

7. Galor, Oded, and Joseph Zeira. 1993. 'Income Distribution and Macroeconomics'. *Review of Economic Studies* 60, No. 202: 35. *Business Source Premier*, EBSCOhost (accessed May 21, 2010).

8. Gottschalk, Ricardo and Patricia Justino. *Overcoming inequality in latin america :Issues and challenges for the twenty-first century.* Routledge studies in development economics. Vol. 45. London; New York: Routledge, 2006.

9. Khasru, Syed Munir, and Mohammad Muaz Jalil. 2004. 'Revisiting Kuznets Hypothesis: An Analysis with Time Series and Panel Data'. *Bangladesh Development Studies* 30, No. 3-4: 89-112. *EconLit*, EBSCOhost (accessed May 21, 2010).

10. Kulkarni, Kishore. International Economics: Selected writings of Prof. Kishore G. Kulkarni. Ed. *Indian Journal of Economics and Business.* Second ed. Darya Ganj, New Delhi: Serials Publications, 2006.

11. Kuznets, Simon. 1955. 'Economic Growth and Income Inequality'. *American Economic Review* 45, No. 1: 1. *Business Source Premier*, EBSCOhost (accessed May 21, 2010).

12. Thomas, Vinod, World Bank, and Inc ebrary. *From inside brazil.* Washington, DC: Stanford Economics and Finance, 2006.

13. Todaro, Michael P. and Stephen C. Smith. *Economic development.* The Addison-Wesley series in economics. 9th ed. Boston: Pearson Addison Wesley, 2006.

14. Torras, Mariano. *Welfare, Inequality, and Resource Depletion : A Reassessment of Brazilian Economic Growth.* Alternative voices in contemporary economics. Aldershot, Hants, England; Burlington, Vt.: Ashgate, 2003.

15. World Bank. World development indicators 2009. *http://data.un.org/Default.aspx* (Accessed on: 05/20, 2010).

14 | Fine-Tuning Fertility

Population Policies and Economic Development in Singapore

Ashley Marks

CHAPTER SUMMARY

Population explosion has been a subject of much discussion in recent past. While the world population is ready to reach 7 billion, the developed economies are experiencing a slower population growth than the developing economies. This chapter looks at the overall picture of population explosion and considers the population policy as adopted by Singapore in recent years. Besides an extensive literature survey, we also use some modern demographic concepts to measure the population's impact on economic development.

The twentieth century saw tremendous population growth and demographic change. Between 1900 and 2000, the world population increased nearly four-fold (from 1.6 billion to over 6 billion) (Mason, 1). The United Nations estimates that, at current rates, the population will reach 9.2 billion by 2050 (Todaro and Smith, 273). East Asian populations have been among the fastest-growing in the world, accompanying the rapid industrialization and modernization that began in the 1960s. This rapid growth has aroused growing concern over the likely environmental impact and economic effects, prompting international population conferences and multilateral strategies to curb population growth (Mason, 1). East Asian governments were among the first active proponents of population control policies aimed at reducing fertility – these policies were some of the most controversial and aggressive in history. As a result, East Asia has seen unprecedented demographic change, fertility rates dropping more quickly than in any other region (Mason, 1). As Tsui notes, in the span of a single generation, the average completed family size fell by more than 50 per cent (414). At this rate, the demographic transition in East Asia will have been completed by 2025, taking a total of 75 years, compared to the several hundred it took Europe (418).

The small island city-state of Singapore, in particular, has achieved exceptional results. Singapore's fertility declined almost 70 per cent over a 20-year period (Graham, 221), and the median age at marriage increased by almost 7 years (Tsui, 414) – more than any other country in the region. As the 2002 figures shown in Table 14.1. Singapore's levels of fertility, infant mortality, and life expectancy are the most advanced in Southeast Asia (Wong and Yeoh, 4).

Table 14.1

Countries	Total Fertility Rate (per woman)	Infant Mortality Rate (per 1000)	Life Expectancy	
			Male	Female
Brunei Darussalam	2.7	6.0	74	76
Cambodia	4.9	74.0	54	59
Indonesia	2.5	40.0	65	69
Lao PDR	5.6	82.0	57	61
Malaysia	3.1	8.0	70	75
Myanmar	2.7	88.0	54	59
Philippines	3.5	30.0	65	72
Singapore	1.7	3.0	76	80
Thailand	2.0	21.0	70	75
Viet Nam	2.5	34.0	67	71
SOUTH-EAST ASIA	**2.7**	**41**	**65**	**70**

Source: ESCAP, 2002 in Wong and Yeoh, 4.

Today, Singapore's figures are even more progressive, with a Total Fertility Rate (TFR) of 1.3 births per woman, an Infant Mortality Rate of 2 per 1,000 live births, and a life expectancy of 81 years (Population Reference Bureau).

With a total land area of 587.6 square kilometers (Saw, 1), population control has been a primary focus of Singapore's development strategy. Its interventionist population policies have come to characterize Singapore's unique development experience, boosting it to the level of developed countries and sending it flying through the demographic transition. These policies evolved according to the perceived needs of Singapore's rapidly developing economy – first, to reduce fertility and stop population growth; second, to improve the quality and competitiveness of the population; and third, to reverse the fertility trends caused by earlier policies and rekindle population growth. This 'fine-tuning of fertility' (Graham, 230) has created a new sort of population problem for Singapore, one that will have important implications for its future development.

THEORETICAL FRAMEWORK

Population Growth and Economic Development

The relation between population growth and economic development has become the subject of much debate and attention over the past 50 years. A lack of empirical evidence and the difficulty of accurately measuring population impacts continue to make the nature of this relationship unclear. What is evident, however, is that, whether positive or negative, population growth and demographic change impact economic growth – and vice versa (Mason, 4). From one point of view, population growth poses serious consequences for quality of life and development, as the number of people exceeds the planet's capacity to support them. With 75 million new people born each year (Todaro and Smith, 274), this means fewer resources, greater health risks, less quality education, as well as lesser degrees of individual opportunity, choice, and dignity. The large majority (97 per cent) of these people are being born in developing countries, most of which are unable to meet even the basic needs of the current population. High population growth also means a higher proportion of young people, and thus a higher dependency ratio – requiring greater provision of necessities and services and putting significant strain on the smaller working age population to provide for them. This pressure on the provision of basic services reduces public expenditure on productive assets and national savings, both important factors for economic growth (Furuoka, 2).

In his 1798 *Essay on the Principle of Population*, Thomas Malthus argued that when population growth exceeds production output, and thus GDP growth, this results in a lower income per capita that fixes near subsistence level, creating a population-poverty trap (Todaro and Smith, 287). To avoid this, he advocated that states institute 'preventive checks' on population growth, such as family planning services and other forms of population policy (288). This population crisis viewpoint became the prevailing paradigm concerning development during the 1960s and 1970s. Alarmist writings declared rapid population growth not only a major obstacle to economic development, but an imminent threat to our very survival. The 1967 Statement on Population issued by UN Secretary-General U Thant stated:

'The population problem must be recognized as a principle element in long-range national planning if governments are to achieve their economic goals and fulfill the aspirations of their people; …lasting and meaningful peace will depend to a considerable measure upon how the challenge of population growth is met'. (Tsui, 423)

East Asian governments, enjoying the benefits of new economic growth, embraced the population problem argument (Mason, 5). In the 1950s, India and China had been the first to adopt major population control policies, and in the 1960s, other Asian countries began enacting policies of their own (Tsui, 415).

In the 1980s, the other side of the population debate began to emerge, the World Bank and other scholars positing less alarmist predictions and arguing that some population growth may, in fact, be beneficial for economic growth (Mason, 6). Indeed, some countries have since proven Malthus wrong, achieving high economic growth alongside a rising population (Furuoka, 1). Population growth can contribute by expanding the workforce, creating what is called a 'demographic bonus'due to the changing population age structure (Mason, 9). If managed properly, mitigating the unemployment problem, this could result in higher overall productivity – essential to stimulate the economy and fuel growth. It can encourage growth at first by allowing for lower production costs, due to an abundance of labour, and later facilitate greater specialization and larger returns to human capital and knowledge expansion

(Furuoka, 1). This 'population revisionist' position views free markets and human ingenuity as natural corrections to all problems arising from population growth (Todaro and Smith, 298). National security and military power, many have argued, are also dependent on a large and youthful population and growth is, therefore, essential for national prosperity and survival (299; Wong and Yeoh, 12).

According to the literature, the impact of population growth seems to depend greatly on the social, political, and economic context of a particular state (Mason, 6). Slower growth, and the ability to manage this growth with strong institutions and effective policies, is more ideal for developing economies. Rapid population growth, however, is an inherent part of the demographic transition. It took most current developed, high-income economies several hundred years to reduce their fertility to near replacement levels and thus mitigate their population problem. Today's developing economies are experiencing population growth more acutely and working to transition more rapidly than ever before.

The Demographic Transition

As defined by Todaro and Smith, the Demographic Transition is the process by which fertility rates decline to replacement levels and the population stabilizes at low rates of birth and death (283). This happens in four main stages. The first stage, called the High Stationary phase, is

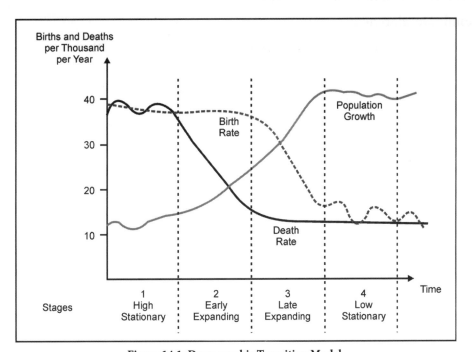

Figure 14.1: Demographic Transition Model

Source: GeographyFieldwork.com

characterized by high rates of both fertility and mortality, such that the population size remains stable, albeit living at rather low standards and in poor conditions. Stage two is the Early Expanding phase, where improvements in public health, nutrition, and higher income due to nascent economic growth cause a reduction in mortality rates and increased life expectancy. During this stage, however, fertility remains high, resulting in a sharp and rapid increase in population. In the Late Expanding, or third phase, greater economic and social development, characterized by improved social services, education, and rising female participation in the workforce, causes a sharp decline in fertility and population growth slows. Finally, in phase four, birth and death rates converge once again and the population is stationary, reproducing at the level of replacement. The model below demonstrates the transition clearly.

As the demographic transition model suggests, population change is a natural result of economic and social development. As a natural phenomenon, however, this process takes time, since fertility behaviour is governed by cultural customs and norms that are slow to change (Coale, 22). Many rapidly industrializing countries, however, have taken proactive measures to speed up this process, reaching replacement levels in a matter of decades. As Graham examines, once replacement-level fertility is reached, it is seemingly irreversible. And, as demonstrated in the case of Singapore, this can have major implications for a country's continued development.

COUNTRY ANALYSIS: SINGAPORE

Economic Development

Singapore, along with Taiwan, Japan, Indonesia, South Korea, and Thailand, is considered a 'miracle country', having achieved tremendous levels of growth and social transformation at an unprecedented rate (Tsui, 413). Between 1960 and 1995, Singapore rapidly rose to the level of developed economies, growing at an average annual rate of 9.1 per cent, and effectively positioned itself as a global competitor in finance and trade (Toh, 186). By the 1990s, the small entrepôt economy had transformed itself into an industrialized, technology-driven economy with a capital surplus, virtually no external debt, and a stable currency. During this period, Singapore's total trade to GDP ratio was more than 300 per cent (187) and it saw its real GDP per capita increase more than eight-fold.

After its expulsion from the Malaysian union in 1963, Singapore embarked on a rigorous open-economy policy, inviting foreign companies to establish production bases there and taking advantage of the skills, expertise, and technologies they brought with them (186). By the late 1960s, the city-state had abandoned its earlier Import Substitution Industrialization policies and shifted to an aggressive export-oriented strategy, exploiting its comparative advantage in cheap production and labour (Saw, 5). In 1970, real GDP growth hit a record high of 13.4 per cent. By the end of the decade, competition for cheap labour in the region had increased (Graham, 222) and the economy shifted again towards the production of hi-tech, higher value products for the world market. This period saw a rapid expansion of the manufacturing sector, which comprised 21.2 per cent of GDP by 1977 (Saw, 5). At the same time, Singapore's infrastructure was developed to place itself as an international financial and information center, attracting substantial foreign investment (Toh, 186). Savings also increased dramatically during this period, from 10.6 per cent of GDP in 1960 to 50.3 per cent in 1995, and Singapore soon boasted one of the highest savings rates in the world (188), contributing substantially to its continued economic growth.

Singapore's development experience is distinctive, not only because of its rapid nature, but because of the policies that made this possible. After Singapore's independence from Malaysia in 1965, the government, led by Prime Minister Lee Kuan Yew and the People's Action Party (PAP), embarked on a series of interventionist policies aimed at expediting social and economic transformation (Saw, 2). This comprehensive development program supported the progressive economic measures with an education system, public housing, modern sanitation, water supply, and modern medical services to meet the needs of an industrializing society (3-4). Singapore was also one of the first countries in the region to incorporate a targeted population control program as an integral part of its development strategy. These population policies had clear economic objectives and would play an influential role in Singapore's economic, social, and demographic development.

Demographic History

Singapore's early population growth was primarily due to immigration from China, Malaysia, and India, now the three major ethnic groups composing roughly 77 per cent, 14 per cent, and 8 per cent of the population, respectively (Yap, 644). By 1947, 56 per cent of the population was Singapore-born, and in 1957, the crude birth rate (CBR) peaked at 42.7 births per 1,000 population (United States) – a TFR of more than six children per woman (Yap, 644). In the 1960s, the government took control of the national family planning program, in existence since 1949, and the TFR dropped under five children per woman in 1965. As a result of rapid economic development and the highly successful population policies discussed below, the TFR

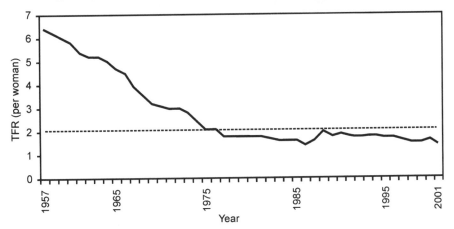

Figure 14.2: Total Fertility Rate 1957-2001

Source: Yap, 645.

had dropped to replacement level by 1975 – Singapore having achieved in 18 years what took Japan three decades (Saw, 184) – and continued to drop, fluctuating below replacement since 1977.

These sharp rises and falls in total fertility are attributed to the population policies implemented at that time, economic factors, as well as cultural factors such as the zodiac years of the Tiger and Dragon and their respective auspiciousness for childbirth (Yap, 644; Wong and Yeoh, 17). Today, Singapore's TFR is at an all-time low of 1.3 average total births per woman, with a birth rate of only 10 per 1,000 population per year (Population Reference Bureau). This low rate of birth coupled with increasing life expectancy has shifted the population age structure towards a greater – though diminishing, as the population pyramid below shows – proportion of productive-age residents.

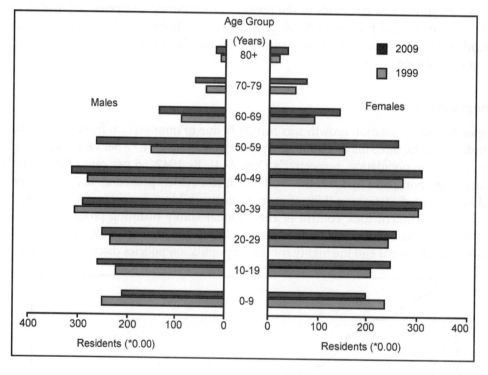

Figure 14.3: Age Group

Source: Statistics Singapore.

What is clear, as we will see, is that while population policies were highly influential on fertility and demographic trends in the 1960s and 1970s, other factors have taken precedence in determining behaviour and maintaining below-replacement fertility ever since.

Population Policies

Singapore's population policies were framed to support its economic development (Tsui, 418), first in line with the belief that population growth would preclude or reverse economic gains, and later to reverse the trend of zero growth those policies had created. The policies were proactive and explicit, involving a carefully planned mix of messaging, social services, as well as monetary and social incentives and disincentives. These 'beyond family planning' policies accelerated Singapore's demographic transition in a way that family planning alone would never have done, while also setting in motion Singapore's current population dilemma. These policies can be separated into three main phases, characterized by Wong and Yeoh and others as the anti-natalist period, the 'eugenics' period, and the pro-natalist period (6).

Anti-Natalist Period (1966-1982)

During the 1960s, following the prevailing paradigm, the Singaporean government became increasingly concerned with its rapid population growth. It feared that its economic achievements 'would be swallowed up by an unsustainably large population' (Wong and Yeoh, 6), threatening living standards and the newly independent state's political stability. As Minister of Health Yong Nyuk Lin said,

> Family planning is therefore a matter of national importance and indeed, one of urgency for us. Our best chance for survival in an independent Singapore is stress on quality and not quantity'. (Saw, 52)

In 1966, the Singapore Family Planning and Population Board (SFPPB) was established and given the monumental task of population control and fertility reduction, with zero population growth as its goal (Wong and Yeoh, 7). This would be achieved through a variety of modern contraceptive methods, publicity campaigns, and practical incentives and disincentives to influence smaller families (Saw, 60). Campaign slogans encouraged families to 'Stop at Two' and 'Take Your Time to Say Yes' to marriage and childbirth (Wong and Yeoh, 7). By 1970, these programmes had already proven successful, gaining over 150,000 new contraceptive users and bringing the CBR down to 22.1 births per 1,000 – a 25 per cent decrease (Saw, 67). In 1970, abortion and sterilization were legalized as a 'second line of defense' against unwanted pregnancies and were further liberalized in 1974, making them readily available on demand and affordable (Saw, 74-105). Although this saw some immediate results in abortion and sterilization rates, it did not achieve the results the government wanted.

In 1972, the government began instituting a series of population incentives and disincentives to further encourage the two-child norm by raising the cost of bearing more than two (118). These measures included priority registration in primary schools to children whose parents had been sterilized, 7 days of paid sick leave and reimbursement of delivery fees for voluntary sterilization, no paid maternity leave for third or subsequent births, increased delivery fees for each additional birth, elimination of income tax deductions for all but the first two children, and no extra consideration for large families in public housing (Wong and Yeoh, 7; United States; Saw, 118). During this time, there were also strict controls on immigration and citizenship.

Temporary residence was granted only to those with certain skills and expertise deemed useful for Singapore's economic progress, and work permit holders were required to obtain official permission to marry a Singaporean citizen and undergo pregnancy tests every six months (129).

By 1975, Singapore had achieved replacement level and was heading towards stabilization at zero population growth, projected to occur around 2040 (Saw, 209). This was seen by the government as essential in order to sustain a certain quality of life and continued socio-economic development in a country of such small land area and with so few natural resources.

Eugenics Period (1983-1987)

In the 1980s, however, Singapore's government began growing concerned with its low rate of population growth, fearing the future economic impacts of a shrinking, less qualified workforce. Due to the rise in female labour force participation, female University graduates were marrying later, or not at all, meaning that fewer educated women were having children (Wong and Yeoh, 8). At the same time, fertility among the less educated remained relatively high. This resulted in what Lee Kuan Yew called 'lop-sided' reproduction and the gradual decrease in workforce quality, which he identified in 1983 as a serious social problem that would jeopardize Singapore's long-term competitiveness in the global economy. This caused a shift in population policies that focused on improving the quality of the workforce to meet the 'future requirements of multinational industries' (Graham, 221). These policies accompanied what the government called the 'second industrial revolution'– the switching of production to hi-tech manufacturing and services – and the emphasis turned to 'offering a highly educated and skilled workforce to the foreign investor' (222).

In 1984, new policies were enacted to 'lighten' the responsibilities of the educated, in order to selectively encourage their fertility while penalizing that of the poor and uneducated (Yap, 652). These included preferential school admission for children of female university graduates, enhanced tax relief for educated mothers with three or more children, a cash incentive of S$ 10,000 for lesser-educated women who were sterilized after one or two children – and a penalty of repayment of the same amount for those who gave birth to a third child – and increased delivery fees for three or more children among lesser-educated women. The Social Development Unit was also established in 1984 to act as a matchmaker among University graduates (653). Immigration policy also began to relax during this period in order to make up for the reduction in births and to facilitate the acquisition of skilled and educated workers (Yap, 645). Foreigners were increasingly encouraged to take up permanent residence and obtaining citizenship was made easier for those with a certain level of educational attainment.

Due to the fertility patterns among Singapore's different ethnic groups, these policies had clear 'discriminatory overtones' (Wong and Yeoh, 10). The Chinese majority has had the lowest fertility rates in the country, and is also the most highly educated segment of the population, whereas the inverse has been true of the Malay minority. As such, population policies seemed directed at sustaining the Chinese majority to the detriment of Singapore's ethnic minorities. Highly controversial and unpopular, these policies were quickly abandoned or modified in 1985.

Pro-Natalist Period (1987 to present)

At the end of the 1980s, government concern shifted again to the changing age structure of the population. Consistent with the demographic transition, Singapore's birth and mortality rates had decreased to the level of many developed, high-income countries and life expectancy had nearly reached 74 years (United States). Projections at the time estimated that the elderly would comprise 25 per cent of the population by 2025, posing serious problems for social services and economic productivity. In 1987, therefore, the New Population Policy (NPP) was instituted, a 'cautiously pro-natalist' policy with a new slogan: 'Have Three or More Children If You Can Afford It' (Wong and Yeoh, 11-12). The NPP continued to give benefits to higher-educated mothers, while also making funds available to cover delivery and hospital charges for a third child. It provided housing grants for young couples, and required pre-abortion and sterilization counseling for men and women with less than three children (Yap, 655). The poor and lowly-educated, on the other hand, received a cash grant for merely accepting family planning, not necessarily sterilization. These measures were accompanied by an extensive publicity campaign, targeting married couples and singles with messages like 'Children – Life would be empty without them', promoting the joys of having children and a family (Wong and Yeoh, 12).

New incentives were launched in 2001 aimed at creating a 'total environment conducive to raising a family'and increasing the affordability of raising children (Yap, 655). These were in response to Prime Minister Goh Chok Tong's concern over the falling TFR, estimating a population decline of almost 16 per cent by 2050, and more than a 25 per cent reduction in the resident workforce, if the TFR continued at this level with no immigration. The new incentives included childcare subsidies, tax relief for third or subsequent children, priority for large families in school enrollment and public housing, marriage and paternity leaves, extended sick leave for civil servants to care for sick children, 8 weeks of paid maternity leave for a third child, and up to four years of unpaid maternity leave (Yap, 656; United States; Wong and Yeoh, 14). The Children Development Co-Savings Scheme, or 'Baby Bonus Scheme', was also announced in 2001, whereby the government matched the amount parents saved in a Child Development Account, which could be used to offset fees for all children in the family. This sought to reduce the financial obstacles to having children, while continued publicity campaigns promoted the 'immaterial benefits' of having a family.

As the graph below shows, however, the TFR fell even further in 2001 despite, as Wong and Yeoh note, the monetary generosity of the NPP (15). Efforts continued over the following years to incite Singaporeans to get married earlier and have more children, including a 'Singapore' campaign in 2003 providing avenues for people to 'express their love'.Singapore's demographic transition had, however, already reached what most consider to be the point of no return – a point which has thus far not proven reversible. As far as Singapore's government is concerned, this constitutes an urgent population crisis and imminent economic downfall.

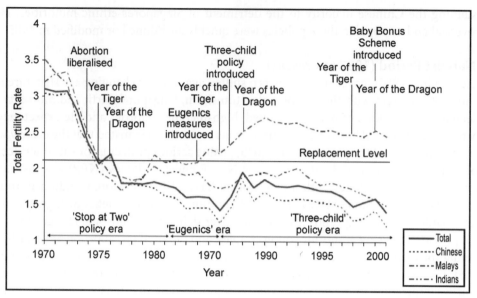

Figure 14.4

Source: Wong and Yeoh, 9.

Impact on Development

Singapore's population policies and economic development have been mutually reinforcing – at least, Graham points out, until 1987 (229). Working in the same direction, the rapid growth of the economy fueled the rapid demographic transition, accelerated even further by strong, determined government action (Mason, 27). These demographic changes then created opportunities for even more rapid growth, shifting the age structure in favour of the more productive age groups and lowering the dependency ratio (13). This, combined with the growing participation of women and rising wages, contributed to a swiftly growing labor force – jobs for which were readily available, thanks to the economy's continued growth and development (15). Singapore's savings and investment increases were also impacted by demographic changes, as lower fertility and increased life expectancy make saving more likely (28). This, in turn, resulted in higher government investment in human resources, such as education and health services, the benefits of which lead to more economic growth and greater social development (18). As wealth, individualism, and opportunity increased, the opportunity cost of having children – particularly for women – rose, as well (Graham, 229).

As a result, Singapore is now faced with the problems of sustained below-replacement fertility and a population no longer responding as they once did to the government's efforts to influence their fertility choices. This has resulted in a projected population decrease of 10 per cent by 2050 if current birth and death rates persist (Population Reference Bureau). With a life expectancy now of 81 years, this also means a steadily ageing population, which implies a decrease in the savings rate, as pensions are withdrawn to support the elderly post-retirement, and it implies decreasing productivity and growth as the size of the productive population becomes progressively smaller. The graph below clearly demonstrates Singapore's diminishing elderly support ratio, or the number of productive-age residents per elderly resident:

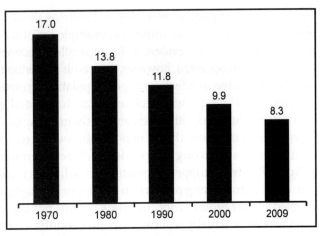

Singapore's predicament not only demonstrates the difficulty in reversing the demographic transition once it has begun – a cautionary tale for interventionist governments elsewhere – but also shows that fertility change is not a matter simply manipulated and controlled through

Figure 14.5

Source: Statistics Singapore.

economics and monetary incentive, as the government has largely and mistakenly assumed. As Graham points out, fertility is a private decision and,

> 'Changes in fertility behavior are thus most likely to come about as a response to changes in the perceived costs and benefits of childbearing, which are, in turn, closely related to cultural specifications of fertility behavior'. (230)

To reverse Singapore's population trend will, therefore, require significant cultural change, which the government is not likely to achieve so rapidly.

CONCLUSION

Over the past 50 years, Singapore has experienced phenomenal economic and social development, sailing through the demographic transition at a rate never before possible. This has been largely attributed to the rigorous population policies enacted by the government to take control of Singapore's evolving population problem. These early policies were extremely successful, Tsui notes, thanks to their health-related focus through family planning, strong political support, absence of religious opposition, substantial and sustained public funding, and effective partnership between the public and private sector in implementing policy measures (418). Singapore's government recognized the important effects of population growth on economic development, 'fine-tuning' fertility in order to meet economic objectives. What it may have underestimated, however, is economic growth's impact on fertility and the difficulty in reversing the demographic transition once it has begun. Efforts to reverse its policies, in order to ensure continued economic advancement, have been largely ineffective and have resulted in a new kind of population problem for Singapore – one characterized not by 'explosion' and resource shortages, but by dwindling productivity and decline.

Singapore's experience, accelerating and utilizing the demographic transition towards economic objectives, can serve as an important example for other developing economies. The benefits of Singapore's policies are evident in its unparalleled economic achievements. This successful and rapid transition occurred, however, as a result of having the right social, political, and economic context. The adverse effects of rapid population growth were minimized because of effective policies that kept pace with technological change and global economic trends and developed means of production to effectively absorb the growing workforce. The adequate provision of social services and rising wealth and opportunity swiftly set the demographic transition in motion, a natural process occurring independently of the government's population control measures. These policies effectively stopped population growth in its tracks, giving way to a 'demographic bonus' caused by an increasing proportion of the working age population. This lower dependency ratio enabled greater productivity and rising income per capita. The question remains, however, as to whether this is actually replicable in other country contexts, and Singapore's situation presents an important warning for countries implementing similar interventionist policies – too much success too fast can have significant, possibly detrimental long-run impacts. When it comes to development, the effects of economic growth on demographic and cultural change cannot be underestimated.

The full scope of the relationship between population and economic development, however, is not yet fully understood. Perhaps the 'population revisionists' are right, and human ingenuity is the solution for this population problem, as well. Perhaps what is needed in Singapore is not significant cultural change as Wong and Yeoh would suggest, shifting the context of reproduction and allowing for alternatives to the 'normal' family paradigm (21). Rather, what might be needed in Singapore is a shift in government policy and resources away from exhorting increased fertility, towards inciting innovation and greater technological change. While it may not be possible to reverse the demographic transition the government has impelled, it seems premature to thus seal Singapore's fate. The relationship between economic development and population growth is a dynamic one and will assuredly present new challenges and solutions as time goes on.

REFERENCES

1. Coale, Ansley J. 'Demographic Transition'. *Social Economics*. London: MacMillan Reference, 1989. 16-24. *Google Books*. Web. 18 May 2010. <http://books.google.co.in/books?hl=en&lr=&id=PTmXshBmTUAC&oi=fnd&pg=PA16&dq=demographic+transition&ots=wv_VeczQPu&sig=lXIxCQX6wIsjexuctmcHc2EUhTo#v=onepage&q=demographic%20transition&f=false>.

2. Furuoka, Fumitaka. 'The Relationship between Population and Economic Growth in Asian Economies'. *ASEAN Economic Bulletin* (2005). *AllBusiness.com*. Web. 10 May 2010. <http://www.allbusiness.com/accounting/873005-1.html>.

3. Graham, Elspeth. 'Singapore in the 1990s: Can Population Policies Reverse the Demographic Transition?' *Applied Geography* 15.3 (1995): 219-32. Print.

4. Mason, Andrew. 'Population and Economic Growth in East Asia'. *Population Change and Economic Development in East Asia: Challenges Met, Opportunities Seized*. Stanford: Stanford UP, 2001. 1-32. Print.

5. Peebles, Gavin, and Peter Wilson. *Economic Growth and Development in Singapore: past and Future.* Cheltenham: Edward Elgar, 2002. Print.

6. *Population Reference Bureau.* Web. 5 May 2010. <http://www.prb.org/Datafinder/Geography/Summary.aspx?region=160&region_type=2>.

7. Saw, Swee-Hock. *Population Control for Zero Growth in Singapore.* Singapore: Oxford UP, 1980. Print.

8. 'Statistics Singapore - Key Annual Indicators'.*Statistics Singapore.* Web. 20 May 2010. <http://www.singstat.gov.sg/stats/charts/popn-area.html#popnB>.

9. Todaro, Michael P., and Stephen C. Smith. *Economic Development.* Boston: Pearson Addison Wesley, 2009. Print.

10. Toh, Mun Heng. 'Savings, Capital Formation, and Economic Growth in Singapore'. *Population Change and Economic Development in East Asia: Challenges Met, Opportunities Seized.* Stanford: Stanford UP, 2001. 185-208. Print.

11. Tsui, Amy Ong. 'Population Policies and Family Planning Programs in Asia's Rapidly Developing Economies'. *Population Change and Economic Development in East Asia: Challenges Met, Opportunities Seized.* Stanford: Stanford UP, 2001. 413-44. Print.

12. United States. Library of Congress. Federal Research Division. *Country Studies.* Library of Congress. *Country Studies.* Web. 3 May 2010. <http://www.country-studies.com/singapore/population.html>.

13. Wong, Theresa, and Brenda S.A. Yeoh. 'Fertility and the Family: An Overview of Pro-natalist Population Policies in Singapore'. *Asian MetaCentre Research Paper Series* 12 (2003). Print.

14. Yap, Mui Teng. 'Fertility and Population Policy: the Singapore Experience'. *Journal of Population and Social Security* 1 (2003): 643-58. Print.

15 | Same Strategy, Different Results
Import Substitution and Export-Oriented
Industrialization in East Asia and Latin America

Stuart King

CHAPTER SUMMARY

The literature and analysis of economic development in the post-war period has been thorough and intensive. However, few academic studies have combined the theoretical assumptions of economic development models with the equally important social and political characteristics of development. This chapter was motivated by the desire to compare the varying degrees of economic development between the regions of East Asia and Latin America, while identifying underlying constructs that help illuminate why and how East Asia has experienced a greater level of economic development as compared to Latin America's trend of poor performance. Central to this study is the emphasis on the social, cultural, and political elements of development that are often unacknowledged in the base assumptions of economic theory. To evaluate this research question, thorough explanations of the theoretical models of Import Substitution Industrialization and Export-Oriented growth are provided, followed by statistical analyses of each region's performance since the end of World War II. Areas of interest include growth rates in Gross Domestic Product (GDP) and GDP per capita, high-tech exports as a percentage of GDP, respective levels of inequality between the two regions as measured by the Gini coefficient, and levels of inflation.

Using this data, the hypothesis that Latin America has experienced a comparatively lower level of economic development is confirmed by its perpetual inability to connect its economic policy with its social and political policies. In contrast, East Asia is shown to have successfully implemented an economic growth strategy based on high productive spending and selective domestic industry subsidies focused on technology upgradation.

These cohesive-capitalist characteristics granted East Asia a level of economic and political stability necessary to achieve elevated economic development and growth, a conclusion confirmed by statistical research.

ECONOMIC DEVELOPMENT – A BRIEF WITH RESPECT TO EAST ASIA AND LATIN AMERICA

Economic development is broadly defined as the increase in a country's production output due to greater employment of its resources. Throughout modern history, economic theorists have debated over as to how a country actually achieves economic development and eventually experiences economic growth. Recognizing such development and growth is not necessarily the hard part, but understanding why and how are the key questions with which economists have struggled.

Both East Asia and Latin America provide excellent case studies on economic development in the post-War II era. The focal research question is why East Asia and Latin America have different degrees of economic development given the similarity of their respective economic development strategies of Import Substitution Industrialization (ISI), followed by Export Orientation (EO) and open markets. Whereas on the surface, each region adopted the same growth strategies in the broadest sense of the terms above, this chapter works to prove that East Asia has experienced an elevated level of economic development compared with Latin American countries for reasons that stretch beyond the pure definition of the economic models described. The findings in this chapter also help illuminate each respective region's growth prospects into the future.

This chapter has been divided into three sections: (1) theoretical section, (2) empirical section, and (3) summary and conclusions. The theoretical section addresses the economic models most pertinent to this study by defining and elaborating on how the Import Substitution Industrialization model leads to greater economic development. In this section, protectionist arguments will be detailed including the infant industry argument of prohibitive trade, as well as several common barriers to trade often imposed by developing countries. In addition, the export-led growth model will also be identified and explained, with special emphasis given to the role of the neoclassical model of economic development. Finally, this section will conclude with an analysis of three variables of economic development.

The empirical section will evaluate the development strategies employed by both East Asia and Latin America since the end of World War II. The main objective of this section is to identify the differences of domestic institutions and public policies that have influenced the varying degrees of development within each region, and use statistical references to support these findings. Recognizing important trends over the past half-century will help illuminate why certain countries, and entire regions, have performed better from a cross-sectional perspective. In addition, a statistical study of the Gross Domestic Product (GDP) of South Korea and Mexico is used to further contrast the different growth trends of the two regions of study.

The summary and conclusion section will help synthesize the theoretical and empirical data presented in the preceding sections to confidently arrive at test results and findings for the ISI and EO models of economic development.

THEORETICAL SECTION

The topic of economic development in East Asia and Latin America has been thoroughly covered by economists since the early 1970s. There has been a profession-wide search for answers as to why East Asia was able to adopt the same strategy of Import Substituting in the 1950s and 1960s as that of Latin America, yet produce much greater economic development. For this reason, journal articles and even books have been devoted to evaluating the use of domestic industry protectionism as a tool for economic development.

The Import Substitution Industrialization (ISI) model of economic development was widely adopted by developing countries after World War II on the perception that economic development could be achieved by limiting imports in order to nurture a domestic manufacturing sector. Generally speaking, for a country to develop this potential comparative advantage in manufacturing, it was believed that some level of protection was necessary for the domestic industry to take root. Other reasons included, trade protection became popular in the developing world in the post-war period included export pessimism, overvalued currencies, and a political preference for industrialization (Bhagwati, 1988: 89-92).

An important argument for this model is the *Infant Industry Argument*, originally proposed by Friedrich List in 1847. According to this argument, complete protection of an 'infant' (undeveloped) domestic industry is both necessary and justified. If foreign competition can be removed by imposing prohibitive tariffs or other non-tariff barriers to trade, the infant industry will grow much faster and easier. Therefore, the short-term reduction in economic welfare is justified by the increased growth experienced in the long run. The graphical explanation for this argument is explained in Figure 15.1.

We see that before protective measures are enforced, the production equilibrium is defined at point M, and the consumption equilibrium is located at point T. The country will therefore export quantity ZM of good X, and import quantity ZT of good Y. The triangle TZM is the 'Trade Triangle' for this economy. However, if protection is given to the domestic infant industry production of good Y by imposing an import tariff, the price of good Y will increase and the rest of the world (ROW) price ratio, $(P_X/P_Y)_{ROW}^1$, will decrease to $(P_X/P_Y)_{ROW}^2$. Since $(P_X/P_Y)_{ROW}^1$ is greater than $(P_X/P_Y)_{ROW}^2$, the new budget line will be flatter and the general equilibrium will shift. The production equilibrium will now be at point W and the consumption equilibrium will be at point J, with the new, smaller Trade Triangle being JKW. This decrease in economic welfare, defined as a leftward shift of CIC_1 to CIC_2, is the short-term effect of infant industry protection. However, supporters of the infant industry argument claim that as the domestic industry is sheltered from foreign competition and undergoes rapid growth, the long-term effects will cause the production possibilities curve (PPC_1) to shift outwards and to the right.

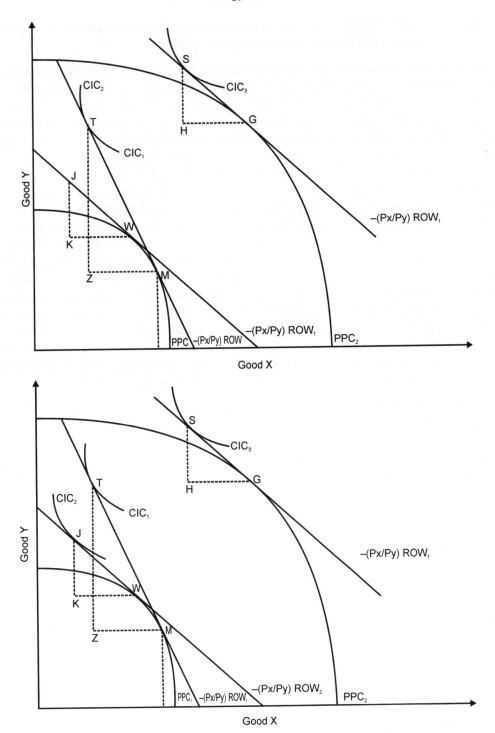

Figure 15.1: Infant Industry Argument

This movement of PPC_1 to PPC_2 shifts the consumption equilibrium to point S on CIC_3 and the economy now experiences a higher degree of economic welfare.

The infant industry argument is supported by the fact that: (1) high capital costs force new industries to start business on a small scale, (2) the expected economies of scale from production take time to develop, and (3) new industries lack the trade connections and consumer goodwill needed to be successful right from the start (Griffiths, 1975: 70). Krugman and Obstfeld echo these arguments as to why infant industry protection is a viable and positive theory with the *imperfect capital markets justification* and the *appropriability argument*. The imperfect capital markets justification states that most developing countries do not have the set of mature financial institutions necessary to supply the new sectors with needed investment, thus protection is needed to raise domestic profits so they can be re-invested for rapid growth. The appropriability argument defends protection due to the high start-up costs incurred by domestic firms and the uncompensated intangible benefits produced by the pioneering firms (2006: 246). In general, however, economists agree that export subsidies are a better form of assistance than industry preference and development. Just because an industry is 'infant' does not mean that it will and it should be granted protection by its government. Only if it can be demonstrated that the rate of return on an infant-industry investment exceeds the social or private return on an alternate investment by a wide margin should that investment be made (Griffiths, 1975: 71-72). Once the industry obtains the level of technological mastery and increased productivity necessary to be competitive in the global market, its level of protection should decrease and firms should begin exporting their products to aid technological development within that industry.

Continuing our study of trade protectionism, it is relevant to examine the economic effects of an ad valorem non-prohibitive tariff imposed by a large country, the most common form of trade protection. A country is either large or small depending on its portion of total global trade of a particular good. This concept is product-specific and has no relation to the geography or population of a country. Because a small country has only a small portion of the total trade of a good, and trade policies enforced by a small country will have no effect on the world price of that good, it is not necessary to elaborate on the economic effects of an import tariff imposed by a small country as there is no optimal tariff for a small country. A large country, however, has a large portion of the total world trade of a good and 'can, by its own actions, affect the price at which it buys or sells a traded good…by using a tariff or an export tax to restrict trade' (Vousden, 1990: 84).

There are multiple effects of an ad valorem non-prohibitive import tariff imposed by a large country on both the domestic and foreign markets. 'A tariff serves to improve a country's terms of trade by restricting demand for imports, thereby driving down their market-clearing world price. The optimal tariff for a large country is arrived at by trading off this terms-of-trade gain against the domestic distortion cost of the tariff' (Vousden, 1975: 103). In addition, a tariff imposed by a large country may have a negative impact on income distribution in the foreign country, which could cause a reduced supply of foreign exports, shifting the world supply curve to the left and increasing the home country's market cost of imports (Vousden, 1975: 86-87).

The typical effects of a non-prohibitive, ad-valorem tariff imposed by a large country are seen in Figure 15.2.

The first effect is that consumers now have to pay a higher price and consume a lower quantity than before the import tariff. In figure 15.2, P_0 represents the domestic equilibrium market price, and P_1 is the world price of the good X before the large country imposes the import tariff. At P_1, the quantity demanded (Q_1) is greater than the quantity supplied (Q_2) and the country imports quantity $Q_2 Q_1$. After the tariff is enforced, the world price increases to P_2 and the consumers now demand quantity Q_3 while only quantity Q_4 is domestically supplied, so the quantity imported becomes $Q_4 Q_3$. This upward movement of the price results in a loss of consumer surplus, measured as the area $P_1 DK$ minus area $P_2 MK$. The total loss of consumer surplus is therefore area $P_1 P_2 MD$, or the blue, green, pink, and purple colored areas in Figure 15.2. Another economic effect of the import tariff is a gain of producer surplus. The producer surplus is represented by the area of the triangle below the market price but above the domestic supply curve. As the price increases from P_1 to P_2, there is a gain of producer surplus measured by the area $P_1 P_2 SG$, or the light blue coloured area in Figure 15.2. There is also an increase in government revenue caused by the import tariff. The tariff revenue per import multiplied by the quantity imported calculates the total gain of government revenue. This is defined in Figure 15.2 by $P_1 P_2$ (or TS) multiplied by $Q_4 Q_3$ (or TR) to represent area TSMR, the pink area.

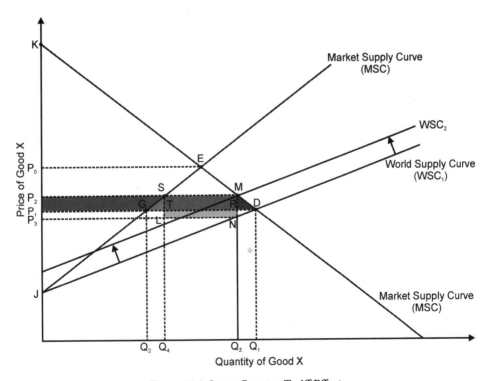

Figure 15.2: Large Country Tariff Effect

Triangles GST (green area) and RMB (purple area) represent loss of consumer surplus that is unaccounted for by another sector's gain, commonly known as deadweight losses. However, if a large country can successfully shift some burden on its import tariff onto foreign producers it can justify the tariff and has improved its terms of trade.

The burden on foreign producers is recognized by considering the price that foreign producers would have accepted for quantity Q_3 had there not been an import tariff. That price is P_3 in the graph above. The difference between P_1 and P_3 is considered the burden transferred to foreign producers per unit of import by the large country. Therefore, area LTRN represents the total burden the large country is able to shift onto foreign producers by charging an import tax. If area LTRN is greater than the combined areas of the deadweight losses (GST + RMD) then the large country policy makers have successfully imposed an 'optimal tariff'. However, this result is considered a 'beggar-thy-neighbor' policy as it has negative economic consequences on the foreign countries. If area LTRN is less than the combined areas of GST and RMD, then even the large country cannot justify imposing an import tariff.

In sum, the following six effects are expected of a non-prohibitive, ad-valorem import tariff. First, there will be a decrease in the quantity of imports into the home country. Second, consumer surplus will decline. Third, producer surplus will rise. Forth, government revenue will rise from the tariffs. Fifth, there will result an uncompensated loss of consumer surplus. And sixth, foreign producers will bear part of the tax burden imposed by the large home country (Kulkarni, 2006: 296).

Lerner's Symmetry explains another consequence of an import tariff imposed by a large country. This theory concerns import and export taxes and is grounded in the Heckscher-Ohlin (H-O) Theorem of international trade. According to Lerner's Symmetry, import taxes will tend to 'drive the economy away from producing export goods to producing import-competing goods' (Kulkarni, 2006: 297). As is seen in Figure 15.2, an import tariff will cause the domestic price of that good to increase. An increase in the relevant price will thus attract more factors of production from elsewhere in the economy to increase the output of that good. The argument is made that by protecting the production of scarce goods, an import tariff will actually move the domestic market away from producing and exporting goods, a nation has a comparative advantage (Kulkarni, 2006: 297). This is a negative economic effect for both the domestic and world economy.

An additional economic effect of an import tariff by a large country is the reduction of foreign wealth. Since an import tariff will reduce the quantity of goods supplied by foreign producers, foreign producer surplus will decline. Because exports generate the wealth to purchase imports, if foreign nations cannot sell their goods they will not be able to generate the money necessary to buy the home country's exports, resulting in decreased demand and profit for the home economy (Kulkarni, 2006: 297).

Countries can also engage in various forms of protectionism by promoting non-tariff barriers to trade. There are many types of non-tariff barriers to trade including voluntary export restrictions (VER), domestic content requirements (DCR), countervailing duties (CD) and anti-dumping provisions, but the most common non-tariff barrier to trade is an import quota policy, which is a government imposed quantitative restriction or limit on a country's imports (Deardorff and Stern, 1998). The economic effects are exactly the same as an ad valorem import tariff policy and can be seen in Figure 15.3.

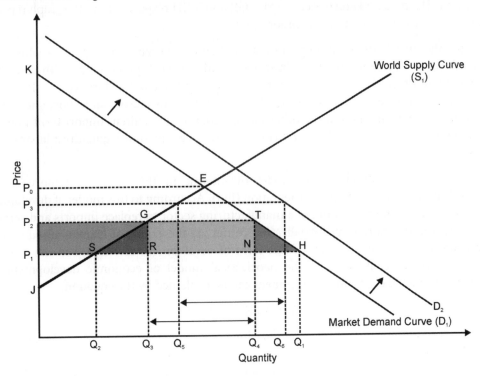

Figure 15.3: Economic Effects of a Quota Policy

The domestic market equilibrium price is denoted by P_0, and the world price before the import quota is imposed is located at P_1. At P_1, the quantity demanded is Q_1, while the quantity supplied by local producers is Q_2. Therefore the quantity imported before the import quota is Q_2Q_1, or SH.

After the import quota has been enforced, there are four economic effects that take place. First, consumer surplus will decline. This decline is measured by the consumer surplus before the quota minus the consumer surplus after the quota, or area KP_1H minus KP_2T. The loss of consumer surplus is then identified as P_1P_2TH, or all the colored areas combined in Figure 15.3. The second effect is an increase in producer surplus measured by subtracting the producer surplus before the quota from the producer surplus after the quota. As can be seen above, the rise in producer surplus is calculated by subtracting area JP_1S from JP_2G. The increase in producer surplus is therefore area P_1P_2GS, the light blue area in Figure 15.3. Thirdly, the government will gain by charging an import-licensing fee to those who wish to import and sell the good. The total revenue generated by charging an import-licensing fee is calculated by multiplying the price per license (P_1P_2) by the quantity imported (RN). The governmental gains by imposing an import quota are therefore represented by the area GRNT, the yellow area in the graph. Finally, the domestic economy will have to absorb deadweight losses caused by the import quota. Deadweight losses are consumer surplus losses that are not compensated by another sector's gain. The pink and green areas, areas SGR and TNH respectively, in the graph represent the deadweight losses caused by the import quota.

The main difference between an import quota and an ad valorem import tariff is whether the policy will cause a price or quantity adjustment. Under import quota policy, with an increase in demand (shift from D_1 to D_2), we see that the price of the good will increase to P_3, and the import quantity will remain the same ($Q_3Q_4 = Q_5Q_6$). For this reason, an import quota is said to cause a price adjustment. On the other hand, under an ad valorem import tariff policy, an increase in demand will cause the *quantity* of imports to go up, thus a quantity adjustment has taken place.

The other economic development model of interest to this study is Export-Oriented Industrialization, or simply Export Orientation (EO). According to this model of development, instead of focusing on the creation of a manufacturing sector to replace imports and serve the domestic sector, the path to industrialization comes via the export of manufactured goods to foreign consumers. Characteristics of this form of development are echoed in the economic theories of neo-mercantilism and the neoclassical model of economic development. The neoclassical model of economic development can be explained by the equation:

$$Y = A \cdot K^a \cdot L^{1-a} \cdot e^{ut}$$

Where A represents a constant set of inputs which make some addition to GDP (Y); K denotes the capital stock of a country; L represents the labour resources of that country; e^u refers to technological change or changes from exogenous resources (also known as the Solow Residual); t coincides to the time period under evaluation; and a (alpha) designates the degree increase in GDP when the capital stock (K) or labour resources (L) change. Due to the production function homogeneous of degree one regarding the capital and labour stock, the neoclassical theory of development concludes that major economic growth must come from e^{ut}, which is changed by improvement in technology, reduced role of the government, freer trade, etc. EO industrialization and its strong emphasis on increase international trade flows is an economic policy strongly supported by many East Asian countries starting as far back as the 1960s, but many economists differ in the explanation for their success. Unpacking the unique characteristics of the East Asian countries and comparing them with the nations of Latin America will help identify the facets of economic development tied to varying development theories that have manifested themselves over the past half-century.

Now that a theoretical explanation of Import Substitution and the economic effects of trade protectionism as well as export-led growth have been explained it is important to identify the three variables of economic development often considered when evaluating a country. These three variables of development are state power, the power to mobilize society, and the entrepreneurial power of capital. State power refers to the degree of autonomy or separation of the state from society, and the power of the state to tax, spend, and direct resources to their most effective use. The power to mobilize society is determined by the capacity of the government to influence powerful actors within society (military, judicial, business elites) to support the state's project of economic development. Entrepreneurial power of capital concerns the social and economic elites' perception of their own interests tied to the interests of the country as a whole, in which entrepreneurs will engage in investments that benefit society as a whole. The presence and inter-relation between these three variables of development (state power, power to mobilize society, and entrepreneurial power of capital) often help explain a state's strategic approach to domestic institutional expansion and its subsequent levels of economic performance and strength. Countries with high rankings in each variable are considered cohesive capitalist development regimes; states with moderate levels of power are classified as multi-class fragmented development regimes; and nations lacking significant levels in all three variables are known as neo-patrimonial development regimes (Kohli, 2004: 9-12). The understanding of each of these variables of development will prove useful when evaluating the regional performance of East Asia and Latin America in the postwar period, despite of the similarity between the two development strategies.

EMPIRICAL SECTION

In the post-World War II era, many countries and regions sought to promote rapid economic development through the domestic industry protections mentioned above. East Asia and Latin America are no exception. Each region adopted trade protectionist measures in an attempt to build domestic industry, reduce foreign imports, and bolster domestic demand. After 1985, most developing countries abandoned high tariffs, removed import quotas, and in general, opened

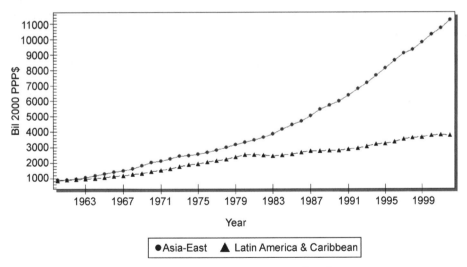

Figure 15.4: Cross Domestic (PPP)

Source: International Futures.

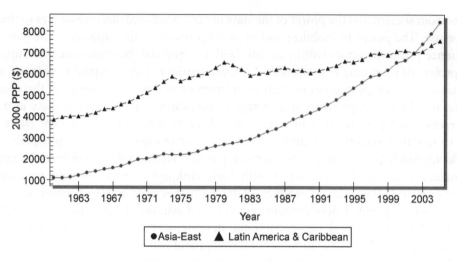

Figure 15.5: GDP per capita (PPP)

Source: International Futures.

their economies to import competition. Debate as to which development strategy, ISI or EO, was responsible for the positive economic gains experienced still continues as not all economies experienced increased or continued growth. The respective figures of Gross Domestic Product growth for East Asia and Latin America are used to illustrate the differing levels and speeds of economic growth and development that each region has experienced since 1960. In constant 2000 dollars, East Asia has seen a marked rise in its GDP and GDP per capita (PPP), diverging from Latin America's level of GDP in the mid-1960s and even surpassing Latin America's GDP per capita in the early 2000s. Why has each region experienced such different levels of economic development over the past half century despite pursing similar growth strategies? The answer lies in their varying success of state planning.

The great economic success of East Asia – Japan, Taiwan, South Korea, Malaysia, Singapore, and Hong Kong – has often been referenced as the 'Asian Miracle'. These countries are commonly classified as cohesive-capitalist economic development regimes due to their high levels of state power, power to mobilize society, and entrepreneurial power of capital. After World War II, many developing countries believed the best way to catch up to the developed world was to engage in Import Substitution Industrialization (ISI) to reduce foreign dependency through local production. East Asian countries followed the ISI approach as well by adopting a national strategy based on resisting foreign ownership and building strong domestic institutions.

The Japanese in many ways can be credited for their first-mover accomplishments in combination of state power and entrepreneurial power of capital by designing powerful domestic companies that would naturally lend themselves to become powerful international companies in the future. In aggregate, East Asian countries resisted foreign investment and created competitive support systems that promoted economies of scale through the formation of an oligopoly system that concentrated power between only a few firms within a sector. This led to a high level of coordination between the selected companies, including R&D support and technology transfer. Guaranteed loans from domestic banks were granted to the selected firms with the idea of promoting performance-based competition between the companies (this type of selective subsidizing is now prohibited by the WTO). Emphasis must be given to the political cohesion and stability manifested in this region. David Brady and Michael Spence correctly identify the importance of a strong ruling system that was able to shift policy to accommodate the new interests created by sustained economic development. In both Japan and South Korea, small changes to public policy regarding industry subsidies and protection, as well as concessions in electoral institutions, were not always economically efficient in isolation, but absolutely vital to protect stability and long-term growth (2009: 214-216).

In the 1960s, Asian politics began to embrace a burgeoning welfare state. Asia's ability to pursue specific policy reforms, like those mentioned above and in regard to welfare state spending, is largely due to the clear separation of state and societal actors (Haggard, 1986: 344). On a national level, Asian states began to develop productive social services of healthcare and education using the state's economic surpluses. The strong emphasis on human capital spending led to a reduction in the labour and middle classes' capacity to demand non-productive goods (wages, pensions, social security), which further empowered the state to continue its developmental strategy. It was during this time period (1960s–1980s) that Asian states began the subtle shift towards building up domestic manufacturing, while congruently encouraging exports. Asian states did so by establishing a realistic exchange rate, while liberalizing imports and creating export incentives such as subsidies, trade restrictions, and credit allocations (Haggard, 1986: 350-351; Narula 2002: 12). The shift to an outward economic orientation is a strategy to speed up industrialization and development by exporting goods in which the country has a comparative advantage (Export Orientation). Towards the end of the 1970s, the Asian countries became friendlier towards FDI, but they continued to maintain a strong course of domestic capacity building. Much of their success in doing so came from national geo-political cohesion that helped mobilize the society behind the state project.

East Asia's ease of transition to export-oriented industrialization can also be attributed to its strong emphasis on technology upgradation (see chart of high-tech exports as a percentage of GDP). Asia initially adopted import substitution models in simple labour-intensive consumer goods, but swiftly began exporting these goods (export substitution) while moving towards more sophisticated and capital-intensive sectors (Weiss and Jalilian, 2003: 1). East Asian development strategies can be categorized into one of three models, in which all include heavy technology upgradation. The autonomous strategy's main objective was to upgrade the domestic industry by using selective restrictions on FDI and technology imports, while using subsidies and incentives to target sectors seeking to promote competitiveness in exports (similar to the strategy described above). The strategic FDI dependent strategy, which was adopted after the autonomous strategy, attempted to attract FDI and then make a strong push to upgrade to higher value activities. The last strategy, the passive FDI dependent strategy, encouraged FDI even more, but relied on market forces to promote upgradation processes (Narula, 2002: 7). Taiwan in the 1980s and 1990s, is a good example of this move up the value chain, as it sought to

Table 15.1: High Tech Exports as
% of GDP

	East Asia	Latin America
1988	21.03	0.017
1989	21.62	4.751
1990	21.40	5.051
1991	21.36	4.495
1992	21.87	6.11
1993	22.23	5.497
1994	23.14	6.013
1995	24.29	6.219
1996	23.92	7.277
1997	24.31	7.918
1998	24.36	9.727
1999	25.34	12.27
2000	27.41	15.00
2001	25.54	14.77
2002	24.72	13.79
2003	24.98	11.85
2004	25.22	11.45
2005	24.44	11.55
2006	23.64	11.09

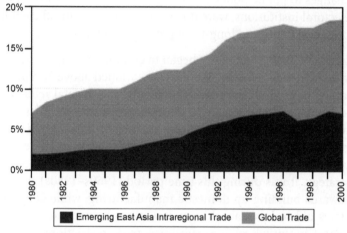

Figure 15.6: Emerging East Asia: Share of Global Trade

Source: International Futures   *Source*: World Bank, *East Asia Integrates* June 2003.

incorporate greater innovation and specialization into its computer manufacturing industry to not simply assembly computer products, but design and attach their own brand names as well.

Latin America, on the other hand, has experienced a different evolution of its national strategy that has significantly compromised its level of economic development. Similar to East Asia, Latin America adopted infant industry protective measures following WWII in hopes of quickly developing its domestic industry. Albert Hirschman identifies the origins of domestic market growth through ISI in devastating wars, balance-of-payment difficulties, growth of the domestic market, and official development strategies, all of which were present at some point in both East Asia and Latin America since the 1950s (1968). However, contrary to East Asia, Latin America did not have a state strategy to create economies of scale and strong business sector leaders. Instead, Latin America opted to open its economy to inflowing Foreign Direct Investment (FDI). Inward FDI is often a developing country's most efficient option given its limited resources, but the attraction of FDI that leads to technology transfer and economic development are often hampered by domestic characteristics (i.e. weak intellectual property rights) (Schneider, 2004). The emergence of multinational corporations (MNCs) did not result in expected cooperation and coordination with domestic businesses, reducing Latin America's absorptive capacity and minimizing the important transfer of technology and high skills to the local economy. Rajneesh Narula discusses the weakness in Latin America's ISI approach centered on FDI stating, 'The benefits of FDI only occur when there is domestic investment, and where the domestic investment has the ability to internalize the externalities from FDI' (2002: 30). Latin America did not engage in the proper level of domestic investment that Narula is referencing in order to develop the necessary high tech infrastructure and technology needed to effectively apply the spillover knowledge.

Ben Schneider and David Soskice extend the concept of varieties of capitalism (Hall & Soskice) to coin a third form of capitalism used to describe Latin American economies, known as Hierarchical Market Economy (HME) (2009). Given Latin America's strong push for inward FDI to help spur development, large multinationals built upon hierarchical systems had little incentive to engage in technology innovation or R&D due to the lack of domestic market competition and weak intellectual property rights (an element popularized by Douglass North as being vital for economic growth and development). MNC and conglomerate partnerships were common in Latin America, as MNCs saw conglomerates as an easy way to mobilize and pool resources, tap into political capacity, or for general project expertise (Schneider, 2004: 15). Furthermore, in the 1980s and 1990s many multinationals began to move out of the manufacturing sector to more protected, non-tradeable or service sectors to seek shelter from international competition.

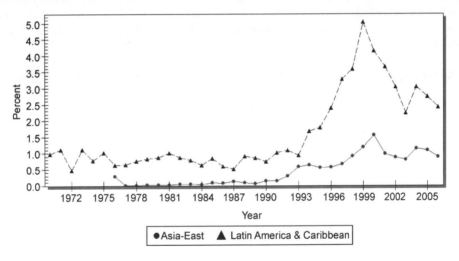

Figure 15.7: Foreign Direct Investment (% GDP)

Source: International Futures.

Central to Latin America's development regime is the political co-dependence between state and social elites. This can be seen by the atomistic labour relationship characteristic to the region. Due to high political contestation, Latin American economies had little capacity to use labour as a resource by investing in training and preventing competitive wage bargaining. Labour markets in Latin America have been often 'characterized by the paradox of high labour turnover despite employment rigidities and protections' (Schneider, 2004: 9). In addition, a common theme in Latin America is that the lack of high-skill labour is a self-perpetuating phenomena, as workers don't invest in acquiring skills because high-skill, high wage jobs do not exist, and firms do not invest in production processes requiring high skills because skilled workers are scarce. Schneider's analysis reflects the reality of employment volatility in Latin American because governments have historically been forced to pursue high non-productive spending on wages, social security, and pensions to appease powerful entitlement groups. In the postwar, ISI period, this resulted in a lack of money to spend on productive goods such as healthcare, education, and infrastructure to help reinforce domestic institutions and companies. In contrast to Asia, Latin American countries were forced to consistently buy off competing forces (military, business elites, unions) rather than direct them. These social and political characteristics hampered Latin America in transitioning from import substitution to export-orientation, as Hirschman describes,

> [I]t has to do, once again, with the distribution of power in Latin American societies. To stage an export drive, an industrialist must frequently make special investments in research, design, and packaging; he must assemble a specialized sales force, delegate considerable authority, launch an entirely different advertising campaign; in short he incurs special risks and new overhead costs which will be recoverable only over a comparatively long period of successful exporting. Therefore, an industrialist will consider exporting only when he can be sure either that the basic institutions and policies which vitally affect his foreign operations are highly stable or, as a minimum, that his interest will be given the most serious attention when these institutions and policies are altered (1968: 28).

Jeffrey Sachs echoes this fundamental characteristic of Latin America with his theory of the populist policy cycle endemic to Latin American economies. Latin America's relatively high levels of income inequality (see Gini Coefficient table) have forced political regimes to pursue overly expansionary macroeconomic policies that lead to high inflation and severe balance of payments crisis. Furthermore, the constant political turmoil that has plagued Latin American states has seen ascension of government regimes intent on quickly raising the living standards of urban workers, only to see GNP and real wages rise and then fall in the midst of depleting foreign reserves and explosive inflation (1989). The following tables identify the stark differences in income inequality as measured by the Gini coefficient, and Latin America's extreme inflation volatility (particularly between 1970 and the mid-1990s), and Latin America's perpetual current account deficit that has made the region susceptible to high foreign debt.

Without a gradual outward oriented shift, Latin America suffered through a prolonged period of ISI, until it emerged in the 1980s as an open economy. Narula now classifies Latin America's economic policy as the 'New Economic Model' (NEM), which includes policies oriented towards export-led growth and increase cross-border specialization and competition with the simultaneous promotion of economic growth through FDI and international trade. Policy makers hoped that trade liberalization would rapidly increase overall trade, but for a number of reasons, the supposed increase in efficiency and growth never took place. Undisciplined finance and budgetary systems were exposed to world price and exchange rate fluctuations, and the underdevelopment of domestic industry forced economies to remain dependent on commodity

Table 15.2				Table 15.3		
Gini Coefficient				**Inflation (%)**		
	East Asia	**Latin America**			**East Asia**	**Latin America**
1993	24.85	56.99		1965	6.593	15.78
1995	33.2	59.03		1966	5.08	17.68
1996	43.44	53.91		1967	4.199	15.6
1998	31.53	53.02		1968	5.555	12.78
2002	32.8	55.14		1969	5.488	7.115
2004	46.9	52.96		1970	7.951	9.421
				1971	6.521	16.76
Current Account (Billion$)				1972	5.187	28.74
	East Asia	**Latin America**		1973	11.33	45.19
1976	−0.31	−5.667		1974	23.23	42.79
1977	10.92	−9.517		1975	12.26	84.89
1978	15.45	−14.8		1976	9.658	157.2
1979	−12.89	−19.3		1977	8.229	75.36
1980	−16.06	−29.8		1978	4.64	66.26
1981	−0.644	−42.8		1979	4.381	65.21
1982	9.128	−41.26		1980	8.712	50.71
1983	22.69	−7.853		1981	5.647	70.56
1984	35	−1.268		1982	3.085	85.13
1985	38.1	−2.736		1983	2.111	141.7
1986	82.49	−16.87		1984	2.375	209.1
1987	93.72	−9.051		1985	2.095	265.4
1988	88.92	−9.732		1986	0.791	102.6
1989	63.01	−7.952		1987	0.875	152.9
1990	53.42	−0.877		1988	2.435	389.6
1991	72.95	−17.22		1989	3.755	1189
1992	114.8	−33.55		1990	3.525	1832
1993	120.9	−45.51		1991	3.813	234.1
1994	133.2	−51.24		1992	2.536	400
1995	104	−37.73		1993	2.891	796.9
1996	49.79	−38.83		1994	3.588	861.1
1997	125.5	−65.6		1995	2.213	40.54
1998	193	−89.46		1996	1.538	20.05
1999	170.4	−55.29		1997	2.186	11.4
2000	159.4	−47.23		1998	1.015	8.312
2001	123	−52.83		1999	-0.46	7.69
2002	165.6	−15.63		2000	-0.4	7.511
2003	210.4	8.994		2001	-0.19	5.947
2004	284.7	21.65		2002	-0.61	9.886
2005	361.9	37.68		2003	0.252	11.56
2006	446.8	46.68		2004	0.903	6.61
Source: International Futures				2005	0.343	6.559

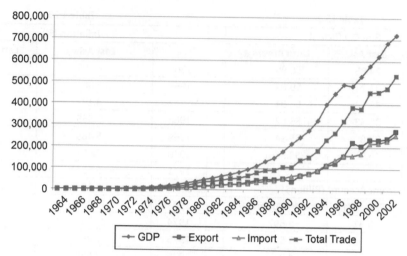

Figure 15.8: South Korea (1964-2003)
Gross Demestic Product and Trade Flows (Billions of Won)

Source: IMF International Financial Statistics.

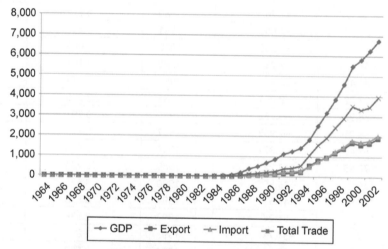

Figure 15.9: Mexico (1964-2003)
Gross Demestic Product and Trade Flows (Billions of Pesos)

Source: IMF International Financial Statistics.

exports. Krugman and Obstfeld point out that 'growth rates in Brazil and other Latin American countries have actually been slower since the trade liberalization of the late 1980s than they were during import-substitution industrialization' (2006: 251). In addition, we see that the combined effects of weak labour (as defined by Mancur Olsen's free-rider problem with large groups) and increased exposure to high levels of trade and capital follows has created an environment of lower government welfare commitments (Rudra, 428). Furthermore, the preservation of state ownership of major industry sectors has enhanced inefficiencies.

To confirm the assumption that greater openness to international trade (increase in import and export activity) leads to higher economic welfare, a time-series (1964–2003) correlation analysis was conducted for Mexico and South Korea respectively. As expected, both countries had correlation coefficient values in the 99th percentile, leading us to conclude that GDP growth and growth in import and export trade (total trade) have a strong positive correlation. From our study, we see that both imports and exports (as identified in the following graphs) increased in tandem over the past half century for the two countries in focus, a result potentially in conflict with the generic assumptions of export-led industrialization and growth. However, it must be noted that according to the basic theories of international trade (i.e. Heckscher-Ohlin model) international trade is mutually beneficial as both countries (in a two country, two good model) engage in international trade. In addition, the role of value-adding inputs (imports) needed for the production of goods and services intended for foreign exports is very important to enhance economic development. As observed in the following graphs (See Figure 15.8 and 15.9), South Korea is noted to have engaged in higher levels of international trade nearly a decade earlier than Mexico, a common theme between East Asian countries and Latin American states.

SUMMARY AND CONCLUSIONS

Has the transition to freer trade, capital flows, and open markets been easy? In a word: no. As evident from the financial crises of Mexico (1994), East Asia (1997), and Argentina (2001) among others, greater exposure to the international market comes with risk. Given the negative consequences of suffering through a currency or financial crisis, many emerging and developing economies have switched from net capital and debt importers to suppliers of finance to the developed world. Federal Reserve chairman, Ben Bernanke, is most famous for terming this phenomenon the 'Global Savings Glut' and the culprit of the US current account deficit (2005). It must also be noted that many emerging markets, and mature markets for that matter, still maintain some levels of trade protection. Many free-trade advocates complain about China's nontariff barriers to trade (i.e. onerous property rights), and Krugman has recently advocated for imposing an across-the-board 25 per cent import tariff on China to force it to revalue the renminbi (2010). In addition, the global economic crisis of 2008 saw the subtle reversion from trade liberalization to new innovative protectionist behavior, further confirming the apparent allure of trade protectionism as a means to spur economic growth. If Asia's 'quick rebound and sunny optimism' is any indication of the role of outward oriented growth in development rhetoric, then economic policymaking will heed the empirical validation of export-led development guided by proactive government policy over trade protectionism (Sally 2010).

In the famous work *Economic Backwardness in Historical Perspective*, Alexander Gerschenkron (1962) identifies a presumable 'catch-up advantage' for less developed countries in the ability to apply and use technologies developed in other countries that would allow a country to pursue rapid development. Whereas this strategy can be effectively applied (i.e. China), research into Latin American development regimes in the postwar period suggests that this approach is potentially too simplistic if the country lacks mature domestic institutions. In the case of East

Asia, strong political leadership to pursue a development strategy that harnessed both domestic and international forces helped propel those countries to high levels of economic success and welfare, as proven by our empirical research. Latin American economies began very similar to East Asia, but soon found that the marriage of state and society made it impossible to shift their attention outward, causing a prolonged period of ISI that further embedded the inefficiencies of infant industry protectionism. It becomes obvious that the varying state structures and institutional mixes within a region play a more decisive role in promoting higher levels of economic development. Bhagwati is very clear that it is not a question of whether government interaction has occurred in the successful Far East economies, or even in the unsuccessful economies of Latin America, but rather how some economies have more effectively engaged in positive strategic decision-making (1988: 98). This report has worked to prove that economic success is not purely the result of the development regime pursued, but rather a delicate balance between private and public interests.

NOTE

International Futures' region descriptions for East Asia and Latin America & Caribbean:

East Asia – China, Hong Kong, Japan, North Korea, South Korea, Mongolia and Taiwan

Latin America and Caribbean – Argentina, Belize, Bolivia, Brazil, Chile, Colombia, Costa Rica, Cuba, Dominican Republic, Ecuador, El Salvador, Guatemala, Guyana, Haiti, Honduras, Jamaica, Mexico, Nicaragua, Panama, Paraguay, Peru, St. Lucia, St. Vincent and the Grenadines, Suriname, Trinidad & Tobago, Uruguay and Venezuela

REFERENCES

1. Jagdish Bhagwati, *Protectionism* (London: The MIT Press, 1988).
2. David Brady and Michael Spence, 'Leadership and politics: a perspective from the Growth Commission,' *Oxford Review of Economic Policy* 25, no. 2 (2009): 205-218.
3. Ben Bernanke, "Remarks by Governor Ben S. Bernanke: The Global Saving Glut and the US Current Account Deficit," The Federal Reserve Board, March 10, 2005, http://www.federalreserve. gov/boarddocs/speeches/2005/200503102/ (accessed May 4, 2010).
4. Alan V. Deardorff and Robert M. Stern, *Measurment of Nontariff Barriers* (Ann Arbor: The University of Michigan Press, 1998).
5. Brian Griffiths, *Invisible Barriers to Invisible Trade* (London: Trade Policy Research Center, 1975).
6. Stephan Haggard, 'The Newly Industrializing Countries in the International System,' *World Politics* 38, no. 2 (January 1986): 343-370.
7. Albert O. Hirschman, 'The Political Economy of Import-Substituting Industrialization in Latin America,' *The Quarterly Journal of Economics* 82, no. 1 (February 1968): 1-32.
8. Atul Kohli, State-Directed Development: Political Power and Industrilaization in the Global Periphery (Cambridge: Cambridge University Press, 2004).
9. Paul Krugman, 'Taking on China,' *The New York Times*: Opinion, March 14, 2010, http://www. nytimes.com/2010/03/15/opinion/15krugman.html?src=me (accessed May 4, 2010).
10. Paul Krugman and Maurice Obstfeld, International Economics: Theory & Policy, 7th Edition (Boston: Pearson Education, 2006).

11. Kishore G. Kulkarni, *Readings in International Economics: Selected Writings of Prof. Kishore G. Kulkarni*, 2nd Edition (Darya Ganj, New Delhi: Serials Publishings, 2006).

12. Rajneesh Narula, *Switching from import substitution to the 'New Economic Model' in Latin America: A case of not learning from Asia*, Working Paper (Paris: Latin American/Caribbean and Asia/Pacific Economics and Business Association, 2002).

13. Nita Rudra, 'Globalization and the Decline of the Welfare State in Less-Developed Countries,' *International Organization* 56, no. 2 (2002): 411-445.

14. Jeffrey Sachs, *Social Conflict and Populist Policies in Latin America*, Working Paper (Cambridge: National Bureau of Economic Reserach, 1989).

15. Razeen Sally, 'International trade and emerging protectionism since the crisis,' East Asia Forum, February 17, 2010, http://www.eastasiaforum.org/2010/02/17/international-trade-and-emerging-protectionism-since-the-crisis/ (accessed May 4, 2010).

16. Ben Ross Schneider, *Varieties of Semi-Articulated Capitalism in Latin America*, Working Paper (Chicago: American Political Science Association, 2004).

17. Ben Ross Schneider and David Soskice, 'Inequality in developed countries and Latin America: coordinated, liberal and hierarchical systems,' *Economy and Society*, February 2009: 17-52.

18. Neil Vousden, *The Economics of Trade Protection* (New York: Cambridge University Press, 1990).

19. John Weiss and Hossein Jalilian, *Industrialization in an age of globalization: some comparisons between East and South East Asia and Latin America*, Working Paper No.16 (LAEBA, 2003).

20. World Bank, East Asia Integrates Report, June 2003, http://go.worldbank.org/BX8SU370U0 (accessed May 3, 2010).

16 | A Dual Sector Model of Bangladesh

Witt Gatchell

CHAPTER SUMMARY

In the article *Economic Development with Unlimited Supplies of Labour*, Sir Arthur Lewis discusses the dualistic nature of developing country economies. The Dual Sector Model states that developing countries' economies are comprised of two main sectors: the rural agricultural sector and the urban industrial sector. The traditional agriculture sector is the largest and, at first, employs a majority of the workforce. It is characterized by low productivity, low incomes, low savings and considerable underemployment. In contrast, the modern industrial sector features higher wage rates than the agricultural sector, higher marginal productivity, and an initial demand for more workers.

The agricultural sector has a limited amount of land to cultivate. This causes the marginal productivity of each additional farmer to be zero due to the law of diminishing marginal returns. Because land is static, adding additional workers does not increase output. The additional labour that is not contributing to output can be called surplus labour. The industrial sector, which is mostly located in the largest cities, is able to absorb the excess labour because it requires a large, relatively unskilled workforce in order to produce commodities.

The model predicts that workers will migrate from the rural areas to urban centres because of the higher wages paid by the industrial sector. Since labour productivity is so low in the agriculture sector, losing workers will not have a negative impact on output. As productivity in the industrial sector grows, due to the surplus generated by the large inexpensive workforce, the owners of capital will reinvest the profit generated in more industrial production. This cycle constitutes economic development because workers are earning higher wages, increasing saving, and the industrial sector is expanding causing economic growth.

Policy makers in developing countries have used the implications of the Dual Sector Model to justify policies that extract the excess labour from the rural sector and transfer it to the urban sector. However, the model is not without criticism. Some have noted that it unrealistically assumes that labour is unlimited in quantity and that the profit generated by the increased productivity of the industrial sector will be reinvested within the country. Furthermore, it does not take into account any of the deleterious effects of migration, such as, the decreasing living standards of people in urban areas. Agricultural productivity may also not remain static as changes in technology can cause a decrease in necessary labour and an increase output, creating a much larger surplus workforce that predicted.

Despite the short falls of the Dual Sector Model, Lewis still provides a solid framework for understanding economic development in developing countries with specific characteristics, namely a large agricultural labour force such that the marginal productivity of workers nears zero. Accordingly, the model can act as a policy guide for governments looking to increase economic growth under this condition.

The existence of a large agricultural sector is a reality for many developing countries. It is the case in many developing countries that a migration from rural to industrialized urban areas occurs as a result of industrial expansion. However, this migration does not always lead to capital accumulation and economic development.

This chapter suggests that the Dual Sector Model can be used to describe economic growth in Bangladesh. The model is applied to Bangladesh to describe economic growth between 1978 and 2008. Bangladesh is an ideal country to test the model because it has a large population that, in the mid-1970, was primarily employed in agriculture. Since then the country has experienced a large-scale migration to urban areas and large growth in industrial production. According to the model, as workers move from the agricultural sector to the industrial sector Bangladesh should experience an increase in economic output. At the same time, agricultural production should remain constant. Eventually, an equilibrium will be reached when marginal productivity in the industrial sector is equal to that in the agricultural sector.

The chapter is organized as follows: Section 1 discusses the Lewis Dual Sector Model in detail; Section 2 applies the model Bangladesh between 1978 and 2008; Section 3 offers some conclusion and explanations for the results.

THE LEWIS DUAL-SECTOR DEVELOPMENT MODEL

Writing in 1954, Sir Arthur Lewis sought to describe the mechanism that drives the economic development. The Dual Sector Model described in *Economic Development with Unlimited Supplies of Labour* was a great contribution to the field of development economics. The Harrod-Domar Model had placed national savings as paramount to achieving economic development. However, how a developing country could increase its national savings remained a mystery. As Lewis put it, 'The central problem in the theory of economic development is to understand the process by which a community which was previously saving and investing 4 or 5 per cent of its national income or less, converts itself into an economy where voluntary saving is running at about 12 to 15 percent of national income or more'. (Lewis, 1954:155).

In order for economic development to occur, a country needs to increase the size of the industrial or capitalist sector of the economy. It is assumed that as domestic saving increases, domestic investment in the capitalist sector will also increase. Capitalist production results in the creation of surplus and if that is invested into new productive capabilities that increases economic output. As overall economic activity increases, workers earn a higher wage and have access to more goods and services. In order for this to occur, producers need to have access to capital to expand production and hire additional workers.

The Dual Sector Model makes the classical economic assumption of an unlimited supply of labour available at a subsistence wage. For certain developing countries, this assumption may be close to true. An unlimited supply of labour is said to exist in those countries where the population is so large relative to capital and natural resources, that there are large sectors of the economy where the marginal productivity of labour is negligible, zero, or even negative (Lewis, 1954:140).

This excess labour usually exists in the agricultural sector where many different families own and work small plots of land. These family holdings are so small that if some members of the family obtained employment elsewhere the remaining members could cultivate the land just as well (of course they would have to work harder: the argument includes the proposition that they would be willing to work harder in these circumstances) (Lewis, 1954:141). The excess labour that is employed in agriculture but that is contributing no marginal productivity could better be used in other sectors where the marginal productivity of additional workers is higher.

Excess labour exists in other sectors of the economy as well. Lewis identifies several other sources of labour including women entering into the workforce, excess wage labourers, and population growth. All of these sources combined ensure that in an over-populated economy, an enormous expansion of new industries or new employment opportunities will not lead to any shortage of unskilled labour becoming apparent in the labour market (Lewis, 1954:145).

If unlimited labour is available, while capital is scarce, we know from the Law of Variable Proportions that capital should not be spread thinly over all the labour (Lewis, 1954: 145). The capitalist sector should utilize labour until the marginal productivity of each additional unit of labour equals zero. However, there is no labour available at zero cost; capitalist production will only utilize labour until the marginal productivity is equal to the current wage. Figure 16.1 illustrates this principle.

The horizontal axis measures the quantity of labour and the vertical axis its marginal product. There is assumed to be a fixed amount of capital. OW is the current wage. If the marginal product of labour were zero outside the capitalist sector, OR ought to be employed. However, the capitalist sector will pay to employ only OM in the capitalist sector. WNP is the capitalists' surplus. OWPM is the wages earned by workers in the capitalist sector (Lewis, 1954:146).

Economies are understood in terms of the relationship between two sectors. The capitalist sector is the part of the economy which uses reproducible capital, and pays the owners of capital for the privilege. Capital is primarily controlled and used by capitalists who hire workers and purchase raw materials in order to produce a final product. The final product is sold at a price that is higher than the combined cost of all the inputs. The difference between the cost of the inputs and the sale price is profit or surplus value. This surplus value is assumed to be reinvested by the capitalist to expand industrial production.

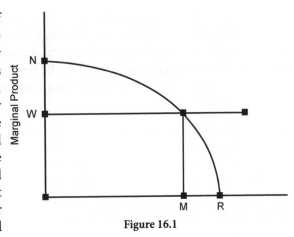

Figure 16.1

The subsistence sector of the economy encompasses all other types of production that do not use reproducible capital. This includes the agricultural sector that is producing only for consumption. This definition excludes agricultural production that is carried out on a large scale in an industrial fashion. Output per worker is less in the subsistence sector because it is not 'fructified' or used to create surplus value by capital (Lewis, 1954: 147). As more capital becomes available due to reproduction, more workers are drawn into the capitalist sector from the subsistence sector, and marginal output increases.

Both of these sectors can be subdivided into many parts and geographic locations. There is not one island of expanding capitalist employment surrounded by a sea of surplus workers. Instead, countries in the first stages of development are characterized by many tiny islands of capitalist production. Capital is not thinly diffused throughout the economy; it is highly concentrated at a number of points, from which it spreads outward (Lewis, 1954:148).

Although it is divided, the capitalist sector is connected through the mechanisms of competition, which tends to equalize the earnings on capital. The competitive principle does not demand that the same amount of capital be employed at each location or that average profit per unit of capital be the same, only that the marginal profit be the same (Lewis, 1954:148). However, even if marginal profits were the same all around, some industries will yield diminishing returns, having cornered the market early. Even developed countries experience uneven capital distribution in the capitalist sector. It is inevitable that a country will experience heavily developed patches of the economy, surrounded by economic darkness (Lewis, 1954:148).

The wage paid by the expanding capitalist sector is determined by what workers can earn in the subsistence sector. In economies where the majority of people are farmers working their own land, the minimum wage labour can have is set by the average product of the farmer. A farmer would not leave the family farm to seek employment if the wage is worth less than they would be able to consume if they remained at home (Lewis, 1954:149).

Earnings in the subsistence sector set a floor to wages in the capitalist sector, but in practice wages are usually higher than this. This may be due, in part, to the higher cost of living in urban areas. It may be a result of the psychological stress of moving from one's home and family to an unfamiliar city. Alternatively, it could be the result of workers in the capitalist sector acquiring tastes and social prestige, which have conventionally to be recognized by higher real wages (Lewis, 1954:150).

The key to the process of economic development is what is done with the surplus generated by capitalist production. If capital is reinvested in creating new capital, the capitalist sector expands, taking more people into capitalist employment and out of the subsistence sector. The surplus is then larger still, capital formation is still greater, and so the process continues until the labour surplus disappears (Lewis, 1954:152). Figure 16.2 shows the marginal productivity of labour schedule for capitalist production.

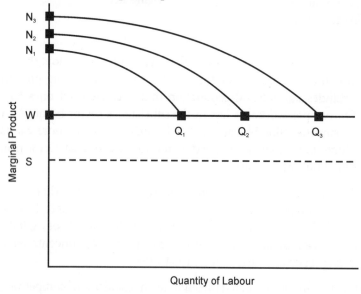

OS is the average subsistence earnings and OW is the capitalist wage. WN_1Q_1 represents the surplus in the initial stage of development. If the surplus capital generated in production is reinvested, the amount of fixed capital increases. The schedule of marginal productivity of labour is expanded to WN_2Q_2. Further reinvestment raises the schedule to WN_3Q_3. This process continues until there is no more surplus labour.

Figure 16.2

The model is the same whether the rise in the marginal productivity of labour is caused by reinvested capital or improvements in technical process. This is because the application of new technical knowledge usually requires new investment, and whether the new knowledge is capital-saving (and thus equivalent to an increase in capital) or labour-saving (and thus equivalent to an increase in the marginal productivity of labour) makes no difference to the diagram (Lewis, 1954:153). In this analysis, the growth of productive capital and the growth of technological knowledge are treated as a single phenomenon. Technological change outside the capitalist sector can however be fundamentally important because it would raise level of wages and reduce the capitalist surplus.

The central fact of economic development is capital accumulation. Rapid industrialization is preceded by an increase in domestic savings. The model assumes that the reason for people saving more is that they have larger incomes. Savings increase relative to the national income because the incomes of the savers increase relative to the national income. During the process of economic development, income distribution is altered in favour of the saving class.

Practically all saving is done by people who receive profits or rents. Workers savings are very small. The major source of savings is profits generated from capitalist production. It is not important how profits are distributed in the economy. The question becomes how to increase profits as a percentage of national income (Lewis, 1954:157).

In a country's early stage of development the national income, consist almost entirely of subsistence income. Most of the labour force is employed in the agricultural sector. Assuming that there is no population growth and that the marginal product of labour is zero, subsistence income remains constant throughout the expansion. The excess labour in the subsistence sector can move to the expanding capitalist sector without reducing output. This process increases the capitalist surplus and the income of workers in the capitalist sector as a proportion of national income (Lewis, 1954:158).

The argument up to this point can be summarized as follows. In many economies, an unlimited supply of labour is available at a subsistence wage. The main sources from which workers come as economic development proceeds are subsistence agriculture, casual labour, petty trade, domestic service, women entering the workforce, and increases in the population. If the country is overpopulated relatively to its natural resources, the marginal productivity of labour is negligible. The subsistence wage at which this surplus labour is available for employment may be determined by a conventional view of the minimum required for subsistence; or it may be equal to the average product per worker in subsistence agriculture plus a margin (Lewis, 1954:189).

In such an economy, employment expands in the capitalist sector as capital formation occurs. Capital formation and technical progress result not in raising wages, but in raising the share of profits in the national income. The reason why savings are low in developing countries is not that people are poor; it is because capitalist profits are low relative to national income. As the capitalist sector expands, profits grow and an increasing proportion of national income is re-invested.

Since the capitalist sector has access to an unlimited pool of labour at a set cost, it can hire as many additional workers as needed without fear of rising wages. Given a fixed supply of capital in the initial stage of modern-sector growth, the demand for labour is determined by labour's declining marginal product. Because profit-maximizing capitalist sector employers are assumed to hire labourers to the point where their marginal physical product is equal to the real wage.

Assuming all the profits are reinvested, the capital stock increases. The larger capital stock causes total production in the economy to increase. This causes an increase in the demand for labour.

This process of capitalist sector self-sustaining growth and employment expansion is assumed to continue until all surplus rural labour is absorbed into the new capitalist sector. When this occurs, additional workers can only be withdrawn from the agricultural sector only at a higher cost of lost food production because the declining labour-to-land ratio means that the marginal product of rural labour is no longer zero. Thus, the labour supply curve becomes positively sloped as modern-sector wages and employment continue to grow. The structural transformation of the economy will have taken place, with the balance of economic activity shifting from traditional rural agriculture to modern urban industry.

Lewis' Dual Sector Model reflects the historical experience of economic growth among Western countries. Western Europe and the United States experienced economic growth as a result of the structural shift from primarily agricultural production to industrial production. Workers from rural areas migrated to urban centers for work in factories. The capitalist sector absorbed the labour and expanded requiring more labour until all the rural labour was absorbed. However, several assumptions that the model makes are not applicable to many contemporary developing countries.

The model implicitly assumes that the rate of labour transfer and employment creation in the modern sector is proportional to the rate of modern-sector capital accumulation. The faster the rate of capital accumulation, the higher the growth rates of the modern sector and the faster the rate of new job creation. The model does not consider that capitalists may invest profits in more sophisticated laboursaving capital equipment rather than just duplicating the existing capital, assuming they even reinvest profits in the domestic economy at all. Labour saving technology requires less input from workers and therefore reduces the demand for workers.

The second problematic assumption the model makes is that surplus labour exists in rural areas while there is full employment in the urban areas. In reality, there is often little surplus labour in rural area, especially during harvest season. Empirical research conducted in developing countries tends to show that there is little excess rural labour in many developing countries (Smith and Todaro, 2009).

The third assumption is that there exists a competitive modern-sector labour market that guarantees the continued existence of constant real urban wages up to the point where the supply of rural surplus labour is exhausted. Prior to the 1980s urban labour markets and wage determination in almost all developing countries was the tendency for these wages to rise substantially over time, both in absolute terms and relative to average rural income, even in the presence of rising levels of open modern-sector unemployment and low or zero marginal productivity in agriculture (Smith and Todaro, 2009). Competitive forces in developing country labour markets are often distorted by institutional factors such as union bargaining, civil service wage scales, and multinational corporations hiring practices.

The model also excludes social and physical conditions of migration to urban centers. When a massive portion of the population moves to urban centers, infrastructure and social relationships are strained. Industrial production in reality does not absorb all the excess labour from rural areas. Excess labour exists in urban centers as well. As a result, slums have become a constant feature of large urban areas in developing countries.

Furthermore, due to the mobility of capital in the modern international economy, profits generated in one country may be moved to another instead of reinvested. The model is often criticized on the points discussed above. However, it does offer a way to explain the mass migration to urban areas that has occurred in many developing countries. It also describes how the capitalist sector can be used as the engine for economic growth. While this migration has huge and often negative non-economic impacts, it has increased the labour force available for industrial production.

In many developing countries, forms of industrial production have employed a significant amount of urban workers. This has increased overall profit in the economy and increased general welfare to some degree, albeit not as much as predicted by the model. This analyzes the effectiveness of the model at predicting economic outcomes in Bangladesh.

DUAL-SECTOR DEVELOPMENT IN BANGLADESH

This section applies the Dual Sector Model to the contemporary experience of a contemporary developing country. The model predicts that labour in a developing country, which is primarily engaged in rural agriculture, will migrate to urban industrial areas in search of higher labour. As more workers move into the industrial sector, it will continue to expand and absorb more workers. At the same time, agricultural productivity should remain constant even as workers leave for higher wages offered in the industrial sector. Migration should continue until all the surplus rural labour is absorbed.

To test the Dual Sector Model economic data from Bangladesh over the period from 1978 to 2008 is examined. Bangladesh is an ideal place to test the model because it started with a large agriculture based subsistence sector and has been gradually developing its urban industrial sector. There has been a large-scale migration of the population from the rural farming areas to population centers. The country is a prime example of a developing economy experiencing structural change from primarily rural agriculture to industrial.

Bangladesh gained independence from Pakistan in 1971. Before liberation, Bangladesh produced mostly agricultural goods such as jute and rice. The brutal war for independence left the primarily subsistence economy completely devastated. After liberation, Bangladesh became a parliamentary democracy. However, a nationwide famine in 1973 and 1974 led to a frustrated population and a socialist revolution. Beginning in early 1975, the country became a socialist republic.

The government took immediate control over industrial and agricultural production by nationalizing all private industries. The countries main export, jute, was eventually replaced in world markets by synthetic materials and the country suffered a severe decrease in exports. Economic planning failed to deliver promised economic stability and the economy suffered a lack of basic foods due to supply disruptions.

In the mid-1970s Bangladesh had large population of unskilled workers, who were primarily employed in agriculture. The government, realizing that the socialist economic model was failing to produce the desired result, began to slowly allow private ownership of industry. The government continued the slow release of private industry until, in 1990, the socialist government was overthrown and a new parliamentary democracy was established.

Since Bangladesh's elections in 1991, the government has expanded private industry further. The country's GDP has been growing by five to six per cent every year since 1996 (CIA, 2010). The industrial sector has expanded as a percentage of GDP from 20.6 per cent in 1980 to 28.7 per cent in 2009 (CIA, 2010). Bangladesh is one of the most populous countries in the world with a population of nearly 160 million and an estimated workforce is 72.5 million. The labour sector is still primarily employed in agriculture; however, there has been a population shift. In 1989, 64 per cent of the workers were employed in the agriculture sector, by 2008 the percentage had dropped to 45 per cent (CIA, 2010).

Bangladesh is an economy in the midst of structural change. The rapid industrialization that has occurred since the early 1990s offers a unique view into an economy evolving from a primarily subsistence rural agricultural society to one that has a thriving industrial sector. The conditions within the country make it an ideal place to test whether industrialization has grown due to migration to urban areas and contributed to the economic well being of the population as a whole.

In order to test if the Dual Sector Model can describe the Bengali economy, several trends should be present in the historical data. First, the country should experience a migration of the rural population into urban areas. Second, if agricultural workers truly have a marginal productivity of zero, the agricultural sectors output should remain relatively constant even as workers leave. Furthermore, agricultural worker output should be rising as there are less workers doing the same amount of work. Third, as workers move to the industrial sector and wages increase, the general level of saving in the country should rise. Fourth, if profit and savings generated from industrial production is being reinvested in the country, the industrial sector should be expanding at an increasing rate. Finally, if this type of structural change from an agricultural based society to an industrial society truly leads to economic development, the standard of living of the average Bengali should be rising.

The conditions within Bangladesh meet the main assumption of the Dual Sector Model very well. The countries large population relative to it's limited land and capital mean that there exists an unlimited supply of labour. Industrial production will never be able to absorb all the excess labour that exists within the economy. This condition makes Bangladesh ideal to test the model. Next, we look at empirical evidence from the period between 1978 and 2008.

Over the last several decades, Bangladesh has experienced a massive migration from rural areas into urban centers. A higher urban wage rate and the pressure of population on scarce land have caused the migration. Arable land per person has been decreasing steadily over the period. In 1978, only 12.9 per cent of the population lived in urban areas. Chart 16.1 shows the rapid urbanization that has taken place between 1978 and 2008. While a majority of the population still lives in rural areas, the trend is towards urbanization.

In 2007, 12.7 per cent of the population lived in urban areas of more than 1 million people. Rural workers have been moving to urban areas in search of higher wages. According to the model, workers that move to urban areas are employed in the industrial sector. As the urban population increases, there should be a higher percentage of the work force engaged in industry. This however has not been the case in Bangladesh. Chart 16.2 shows sector employment starting in 1984, when data collection began. The data shows that while agricultural employment has been slowly declining, industrial employment has not been rising significantly. Instead, there has been a large increase in service industry employment. This may be due to the lack of a large formal industrial sector. Bangladesh's main industrial products are cotton textiles and jute. Labour saving technology in production method in these industries may be causing low employment in the industrial sector while still increasing output.

Rural workers are moving to urban areas in search of

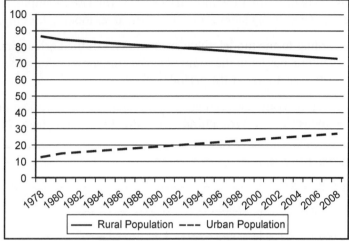

Chart 16.1: Population Location (Percentage of Total Population)

Source: World Data Bank, *http://databank.worldbank.org*

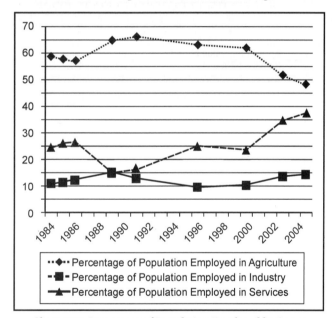

Chart 16.2: Percentage of Population Employed by Sector

Source: World Data Bank, *http://databank.worldbank.org*

jobs, but not always in the industrial sector. The services sector has grown substantially in Bangladesh absorbing many of the displaced agricultural workers. Industrial sector employment remains relatively flat over the period. The Dual Sector Model did not account for laboursaving technology in the industrial sector and therefore does not account for a rise in employment anywhere other that the industrial sector. The rise in employment in the services sector is the result of a growing labour force in urban areas looking for employment.

According to the model, the loss of workers in the agricultural sector should not be affecting agricultural output in the country. Chart 16.3 shows value added to GDP by the agricultural and industrial sectors over the period.

Agriculture is also decreasing as a percentage of GDP while industry is rising. Chart 16.4 shows that industrial and agricultural value added as a percentage of total GDP.

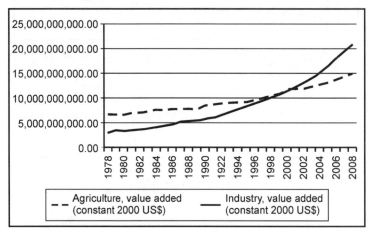

Chart 16.3: Value Added by Sector

Source: World Data Bank, *http://databank.worldbank.org*

Chart 16.3 shows that the value added by the industrial sector has been increasing over the period. Furthermore, the convex slope of the line suggests that the value added by the industrial sector has been increasing at a faster rate. Chart 16.4 shows that, as a percentage of GDP, industry value added surpassed agricultural value added in 1999. This chart shows the structural change Bangladesh underwent, from a primarily agricultural economy to primarily industrial.

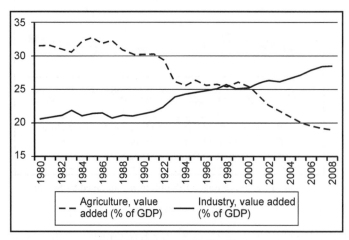

Chart 16.4: Value Added by Sector

Source: World Data Bank, *http://databank.worldbank.org*

According to the model, the value added by agriculture should remain constant, however because of technological advancement in agricultural production, it has risen over the period. The growth may be the result of the Green Revolution which greatly increased agricultural output.

The Dual Sector Model holds fairly well to this point. The data shows that there has been a shift from employment in the rural agricultural sector to the urban industrial sector. Agricultural output has not remained flat, however, in has not decreased. Workers migrating to large urban areas may not be primarily employed in the industrial sector, however employment has been created in the services sector. The industrial sector has become the engine for growth in the economy, expanding at an increasing rate.

The model further states that since there are less farmers working, the same amount of land agriculture value added by worker should increase over the period. Chart 16.5 shows value added per worker in the agricultural sector.

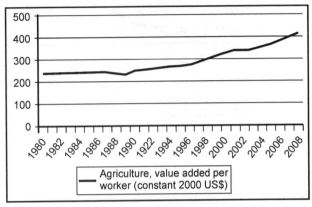

Chart 16.5

Agriculture value added per worker has risen since 1980. This implies that workers have been leaving the agriculture sector. As workers leave, the ones left behind are working harder and their value added per worker rises.

Source: World Data Bank, *http://databank.worldbank.org*

The industrial sector in Bangladesh has expanded between 1978 and 2008. In terms of industrial output, Chart 16.3 shows that the industrial sector has increased at a rapid pace. Agriculture has also expanded, however, at a slower rate. It is difficult to discern whether industrial expansion is a result of domestically generated profit being reinvested, or if it is the result of Foreign Direct Investment. Furthermore, workers who have emigrated from Bangladesh in search of employment contribute a significant portion of savings in Bangladesh by sending home remittances.

According to the model, the rise in wages due to industrial employment should raise the level of national savings. Furthermore, the profit generated in the industrial sector is assumed to be reinvested, increasing the capital stock. Chart 16.6 shows Gross domestic Savings as a percentage of GDP.

Savings increase as a percentage of GDP. In real terms, domestic savings have increased even more dramatically. Chart 16.7 shows Gross Domestic Savings in terms of dollars.

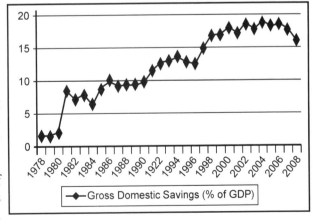

Chart 16.6

Source: World Data Bank, *http://databank.worldbank.org*

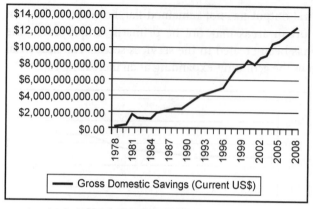

Chart 16.7

Source: World Data Bank, *http://databank.worldbank.org*

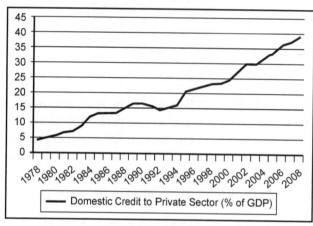

Chart 16.8

Source: World Data Bank, *http://databank.worldbank.org*

Since 1978, domestic savings have increased dramatically. This in itself is not an evidence that increased savings are being used for industrial expansion. It is difficult to know how much of these savings have been reinvested into industry. However, it does appear that the structural change from a subsistence economy to one where services and industry account for a major portion of economic activity has led to a large increase in domestic savings.

Assuming the financial system is functioning efficiently, domestic credit should be funneled to private industry. Banks acting as financial intermediaries should be using the increased domestic savings to increase investment in private industry. Chart 16.8 shows the flow of domestic saving to the private sector as a percentage of GDP over the period 1978 to 2008.

Domestic savings are being mobilized for investment at an increasing rate. Savings are being used to fund industrial expansion as predicted by the model.

We can now see that, for Bangladesh, the Dual Sector Model explains the reality in the country fairly well. There has been a significant population migration from the rural areas to urban centers. Surplus labour from the countryside, which was adding no marginal product to agriculture, has been better used by industry in urban areas. Agricultural production has not suffered from the loss of labour. In fact, agricultural production has increased because of new technologies.

The industrial sector has grown as a percentage of total GDP while the agriculture sector has been declining. However, this increase in the size of the industrial sector has not led to an increase in employment in the sector. It appears that technological advances in industrial production have caused industrial employment to stay stagnant. The rise of the services sector has employed most of the surplus labour moving into urban centers.

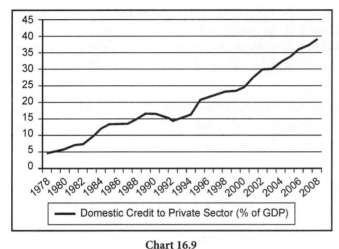

Chart 16.9

The rise in domestic savings predicted by the model has occurred over the period. Domestic savings have also been increasingly driving private industry. However, there remains a major question; is industrial expansion, fueled by surplus labour from rural areas, increasing domestic saving and an expanding industrial sector really leading to economic development. In strictly economic terms, it is clear that the structural change has increased Bangladesh's GDP and general economic welfare. However, it is not as clear that the economic growth translates into a better standard of life for Bengalis.

Bangladesh remains an extremely impoverished country, despite the growth in GDP. Increasing urbanization is a major issue as workers form huge slums on the outskirts of industrial centers. The cheap labour supplied by rural workers has not led to an increase in wages, and much of the population is living well below the poverty line. In 2008, the GDP per capita was USD1500 compared to the world average of USD10,500 (CIA, 210). 36 per cent of the population lives below the national poverty line. The country still lacks major services and infrastructure. Industrial expansion has increased national wealth however; corruptions and inefficiencies within the country have caused that wealth to be squandered.

While economic welfare and GDP have risen in the country, the quality of life in Bangladesh remains relatively unchanged and in some cases even worse. The surplus generated by the industrial sector has failed to 'trickle down' to the average worker in the society.

CONCLUSION

Lewis' Dual Sector Model explains a developing country's economic growth in terms of a structural transition between two sectors. Developing countries are characterized by a large rural subsistence sector. Workers in this sector are primarily engaged in agriculture. It is typically characterized by low wages, an abundance of labour, and low productivity through a labour intensive production process. In contrast, the urban industrial sector is defined by higher wage rates than the agricultural sector, higher marginal productivity, and a demand for more workers initially.

Production in the industrial sector is assumed to be capital intensive. Investment and capital formation in the manufacturing sector are possible over time as capitalists' profits are reinvested in the capital stock. Since there is a fixed amount of land, the marginal product of each additional agricultural worker is assumed to be zero. Workers in rural areas will begin to move to urban areas in search of the higher wages offered by the industrial sector. As the migration occurs agricultural output will remain constant and the additional workers will increase profit for capitalists. The profits will be reinvested in for the expansion of production and will need more workers. This will continue until the marginal productivity of agricultural workers is equal to that of industrial workers.

The model fits the reality in Bangladesh. Rural workers have been moving to urban areas in search of higher wages. Employment in the agricultural sector has been decreasing and output has not suffered as a result. The industrial sector has been expanding at an increasing rate and is driving economic growth. Profit generated from production is increasingly being used to fund new domestic ventures.

However, Lewis' did not consider the effect that labour saving technology would have on employment in the industrial sector. Employment in this sector remained flat over the period while industrial output continued to grow. This caused the rise of a third sector, services,which is now rapidly becoming the largest in Bangladesh.

Furthermore, the model also does not account for the deleterious effects of mass migration into urban areas. Slums are a persistent concern in Bangladesh and the industrial sector has proven unable to supply jobs for a majority of the workers.

The model can act as a good framework to depict the migration from rural to urban areas in developing countries. It also appears that increased employment in the industrial sector does increase savings in the economy as a whole. It is also the case that in Bangladesh, when domestic savings increased, there was a large increase in investment in private industry. The model needs to be updated to take into account labour saving technology in the industrial sector, the detrimental effects of mass migration, and how the service sector grows into a developing economy.

Bangladesh may never reach the equilibrium predicted by the model where marginal productivity of agricultural workers is equal to that of industrial workers. However, the industrial sector is the engine for economic growth. It has an unparalleled ability to generate surplus value in the economy. Policy makers in the country need to design a framework where the surplus generated translates into increasing wages for the agricultural, industrial, and services sector in order for the quality of life to increase.

REFERENCES

1. W. Arthur, Lewis. 'Economic Development with Unlimited Supplies of Labour', *The Manchester School*, Vol. 22, No. 2 (1954), pp. 139-191.
2. Lawrence B. Lesser. 'Economic Reconstruction after Independence'. *A Country Study: Bangladesh.*
3. James Heitzman and Robert Worden (editors). *Library of Congress Federal Research Division* (September 1988).
4. CIA World Fact Book 2010.
5. Todaro, Micheal P., and Stephen C. Smith. Economic Development. 9th ed. Addison Wesley, 2005.

17 | The Factor Price Equalization Theorem and NAFTA

A Case Study of Mexico and Free Trade

Deborah Rakowski

CHAPTER SUMMARY

Paul A Samuelson has made some great contributions in the field of economics. One of his most well known contributions is the Factor Price Equalization Theorem. The main conclusion from this theorem is that developed countries should trade with developing countries since developed countries are capital abundant and developing countries are labour abundant. The North American Free Trade Agreement is the best modern day example of trade between a developed country and a developing country, the United States and Mexico. Mexico has opened its borders to trade and has seen benefits yet has not developed as quickly as was predicted. I begin my research by focusing on trade theories in general, then focusing on the FPE theorem specifically. Next, I examine Mexico and the trends which are appearing within its borders. Finally I apply the FPE theorem to the NAFTA agreement and make several conclusions. After applying the FPE Theorem to NAFTA, we will see that there is only small evidence to show that the wage rental rates are equalizing in these two countries. This could be for several reasons, some of which are discussed in this chapter, however it may simply be too soon to gather this evidence since all barriers to trade were only recently removed. Secondly, it cannot be said that NAFTA is the reason for this factor price equalization, since there are many outside factors.

INTERNATIONAL TRADE – A VITAL STEP IN ECONOMIC DEVELOPMENT

International trade is a vital step in the economic development of a country. There have been many arguments which prove that when a developing country opens its borders to international trade, the country will grow economically. It is this growth which pushes for social development and allows a country to provide for its people. However, if a country opens its borders to free trade, it also opens itself to risks in the exchange of both goods and factors. Therefore, international trade is a balance of open trade and protectionism. Economists from all backgrounds have debated this issue and provided theories as to what occurs within a country when it opens its borders. Paul A. Samuelson of M.I.T. won the Nobel Prize for his contributions to economics. The most fundamental theorem he contributed was the Theorem of Factor Price Equalization. This theorem can provide the fundamentals of trade between a capital abundant country and a labour abundant country, which is largely the situation that occurs when a developed country trades with a developing country. One of the best modern day examples of this type of trade is North American Free Trade Agreement between Canada, the Untied States, and Mexico. In this chapter, I will be focusing on the factor price equalization theorem and applying it to NAFTA. I will begin by taking a deeper look into the theorem and the work of Paul Samuelson. Second, I focus on Mexico and its trade history. A survey of NAFTA will follow, focusing on the role of Mexico and the United States in this agreement. Finally, I will conclude with how NAFTA has affected the Mexican economy and if the FPE Theorem can be clearly demonstrated within the agreement.

THE FPE THEOREM

Summary of Trade Theories

Several economists have weighed in on this issue of trade. One of the first was Adam Smith who in his book, *The Wealth of Nations* proposed international divisions of labour and specialization. In this book, he outlined the theory of absolute advantage, which stated that if a country, for example Mexico, is able to produce a product, such as cars, with fewer units of technology of production than a second country, such as the United States, then Mexico has an absolute advantage in the production of cars. The same is true for the United States, which might have an absolute advantage in the production of car parts. In this case, a mutually beneficial trade will occur if Mexico specializes in the production of cars and exports them to the United States, while the United States specializes in the production of car parts and exports them to Mexico. Adam Smith's theory of absolute advantage is the foundation for international trade.

David Ricardo expanded the theory of absolute advantage to a situation in which the first country has an absolute advantage in the production of both goods. For example, the United States might have an absolute advantage in the production of both cars and car parts. In this case, a mutually beneficial trade is still possible. To discover which product the US should export, some mathematical calculations must be made. First, one must calculate the number of labour units which are needed to produce one car in both the US and Mexico. Second, the same calculation must be done for one car part in both countries. Once these numbers are derived, the labour costs are compared for each country. If Mexico has a comparative advantage in the production of cars, then this country should produce only cars and export them to the United States. Likewise, if the United States has a comparative advantage in the production of car parts, then car parts should be produced in the US and exported to Mexico. This scenario would create a mutually beneficial trade between both countries. However, as pointed out by Samuelson this model assumes that labour is the only input transferrable between industries. He stated that 'if labour worked alone at constant returns, this [model] would give us the constant-cost case of classical comparative advantage. If in addition, the laws of knowledge were everywhere the same, so that the simple labour production functions were the same everywhere, there would be no difference in production costs (no comparative advantages!) and no international trade would occur'. Therefore, with only one input, trade would not even occur. (Samuelson, 1971, 367)

Eli Heckscher and Bertil Ohlin solved this issue and in their theory included differences in factor endowments. They proposed that even if the technology of production for cars is exactly the same for cars in both the United States and Mexico, mutually beneficial trade can still be found. Factor endowments can be defined in two ways. Suppose that the United States and Mexico have two factors of production, capital and labour. The first definition of factor endowments is factor quantities which is the ratio of capital over labour in both the United States and Mexico. If the capital labour ratio is smaller in Mexico, then they are said to be labour abundant and the United States is said to be capital abundant. The second definition takes into account the prices of each factor, capital and labour. The price of capital can be defined as the rental rate and the price of labour can be defined as the wage rate. The wage rate divided by the rental rate is called the wage rental ratio. This ratio can be derived for both the US and Mexico. If the wage rental rate is smaller in Mexico than the US, then Mexico is said to be labour abundant and the US is capital abundant.

Therefore, when comparing the capital labour ratios for cars and car parts, if the capital labour ratio for cars is smaller than the capital ratio for car parts, then cars are labour intensive and car parts are capital intensive. International trade is mutually beneficial if the labour abundant country specializes in the labour intensive product. In this case, Mexico should specialize in cars and export them to the United States. The same is true for the capital abundant country. The United States should specialize in the production of car parts and export them to Mexico. From the H-O Theorem, the conclusion can be made that since developing countries are labour abundant, they should specialize in labour intensive goods and export them to developed countries, which are capital abundant.

Paul Samuelson expanded on the H-O Theorem to summarize a pre-trade and post-trade situation in a country. He stated that if the wage rental ratio for Mexico was smaller than the wage rental ratio for the United States, before trade, then Mexico is a labour abundant country. As trade begins between the United States and Mexico, according to the H-O theorem, Mexico should specialize in the production of cars and the United States should specialize in the production of car parts. Each country should export their product to the other in a mutually beneficial trade. Each theory has come to this conclusion thus far. Samuelson took these theories one step further by saying that under the assumption of full employment of resources, for Mexico to produce more cars resources have to come from the lower production of car parts. However, the lower production of car parts releases capital faster than labour since car parts are capital intensive. The higher production of cars needs labour faster than capital since cars are labour intensive. Therefore, the wage rate will increase and the rental rate will decrease in Mexico after trade begins, causing the wage rental rate to increase. The opposite is true for the United States. Since the United States is producing car parts, a capital intensive product, resources have to come from the lower production of cars. The lower production of cars releases labour faster than capital causing the wage rate to decrease and the rental rate to increase. As trade continues, the wage rental rates for Mexico and the Unites States will reach equilibrium. This theory is called the Factor Price Equalization Theorem.

The creator of this theorem, Paul Samuelson, has written many articles concerning this argument for free trade. In one of his first articles, written in 1948, Samuelson explains his theorem in detail. After reviewing the arguments against the probability that FPE exists, Samuelson states that 'not only is factor-price equalization possible and probable, but in a wide variety of circumstances, it is inevitable' (Samuelson, 1948, 169). Before we draw any conclusions based on this theory, we must look further into the logic of the theory to determine its validity.

The FPE Theorem

To begin his argument, Samuelson 'drew upon earlier insight of Heckscher and Ohlin to show that under standard neo-classical assumptions, 'trade in goods would be a proxy for trade in factors and the effect would be to equalize the relative factor-price ratios of both countries'. (Puttaswamaiah, 20) As discussed earlier, the H-O theorem is the basis for factor price equalization. The validity of this theorem depends on a capital abundant country, such as the United States, trading with a labour abundant country, such as Mexico. If these two countries were to trade capital intensive goods with labour intensive goods, the wage rental rates in both countries would eventually reach equilibrium. The conclusion can then be drawn that the wage rate of the capital abundant country would decrease slightly and the wages in the labour abundant country would increase slightly, until the wage rental rates became equal.

To fully understand the theorem, there are several assumptions which must first be made before coming to a conclusion. In his papers, Samuelson used the example of Europe and the Americas trading food and clothing to prove his theorem. In his hypothesis, to prove that the wage rates are raised, Samuelson began by assuming the following:

1. There are but two countries, America and Europe.
2. They produce but two commodities, food and clothing.
3. Each commodity is produced with two factors of production, land and labour. The production functions of each commodity show 'constant returns of scale', in the sense that changing all inputs in the same proportion changes output in that same proportion, leaving all 'productivities' essentially unchanged. In short, all production functions are mathematically 'homogeneous of the first order' and subject to Euler's theorem.
4. The law of diminishing marginal productivity holds: as any one input is increased relative to other inputs, its marginal productivity diminishes.
5. The commodities differ in their labour and land intensities. Thus, food is relatively 'land using' or 'land intensive', while clothing is relatively 'labour intensive'. This means that whatever the prevailing ratio of wages to rents, the optimal proportion of labour to land is greater in clothing than in food.

6. Land and labour are assumed to be qualitatively identical inputs in the two countries and the technological production functions are assumed to be the same in the two countries.
7. All commodities move perfectly freely in international trade, without tariffs or transport costs, and with competition effectively equalizing the market price-ratio of food and clothing. No factors of production can move between countries.
8. Something is being produced in both the countries of both commodities with both factors of production. Each country may have moved in the direction of specializing on the commodity for which it has a comparative advantage but it has not moved so far as to be specializing completely in one commodity. (Machlup, 734, Stiglitz, 182)

All of these assumptions constitute the hypothesis of the theorem. The conclusion states:

'Under these conditions, real factor prices must be exactly the same in both countries (and indeed the proportion of inputs used in food production in America must equal that in Europe, and similarly for clothing production)'. (Stiglitz, 182)

He begins his argument with discussing the production-possibility curves of Europe and America (Figure 17.1). The ratio before trade can be seen at point C for America and point c for Europe. With free trade, they will end up at point B for America and point d foe Europe. Now suppose all barriers to commodity trade are stripped away. The relative price of food falls in Europe and rises in America. This causes America to move in the direction of increased food production and decreased clothing production and to barter food exports for clothing imports. 'The final equilibrium price ratio settles down between the initial limits at just that level where there is a perfect quantitative meshing of international reciprocal demands' (Stiglitz, 171). The slopes of points B and d become equal. As this equalization occurs, relative marginal costs in each country are adjusted to the new market price and further specialization ceases.

Samuelson goes on to prove this theory mathematically. He also follows up this proof with several papers which combat several critiques of his theory. An important note is that in all of his writings, he assumes that both countries engaging in trade have the same technical possibilities

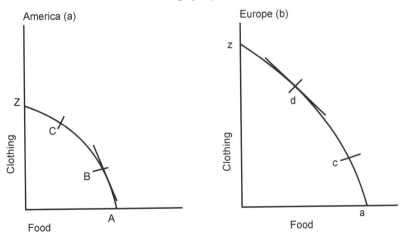

Figure 17.1

for all commodities. He follows this by stating there are three qualifications to his theoretical argument. They are as follows:

1. Goods to not move without transport costs, and to the extent that commodity prices are not equalized it, of course follows that factor prices will not tend to be fully equalized.
2. There are many reasons to doubt the usefulness of assuming identical production functions and categories of inputs in the two countries.
3. It is dangerous to draw sweeping practical conclusions concerning factor-price equalization (Stiglitz, 195).

There are several critiques of Samuelson's work, some of which surround these qualifications. For example, the theory does not account for the skill level of the labour in each country. This was best demonstrated in the Leontief paradox. The results of this study found that a capital abundant country, the United States exports labour intensive commodities and imports capital intensive commodities. Several explanations have been offered to account for this deviation from H-O Theory. The first explanation, offered by Leontief himself, stated that the paradox does not account for the skilled labour force in the United States. Second, it did not account for the fact that labourers could possibly be more efficient.

Theorem Conclusions

There can be at least four conclusions drawn from the FPE Theorem and international trade theories in general. The first is that international trade is a perfect substitute for factor movement. Second, labour abundant countries will benefit from international trade by raising the wage rate. International trade, under the less than full employment of labour assumption, would create jobs in developing countries. Lastly, the import of capital intensive goods in the developing world will be cost effective. These conclusions are debated by economists but have proven to be true in most simple situations. Samuelson expands these conclusions specifically for the FPE Theorem. He lists the following four conclusions:

1. So long as there is partial specialization, with each country producing something of both the goods, factor prices will be equalized, absolutely and relatively by international trade.
2. Unless initial factor endowments are too unequal, commodity mobility will always be a perfect substitute for factor mobility.
3. Regardless of initial factor endowment even if factors were mobile they would, at worst, have to migrate only up to a certain degree, after which commodity mobility would be sufficient for full price equalization.
4. To the extent that commodity movements are effective substitutes for factor movements, world productivity is, in a certain sense, optimal; but at the same time the imputed real returns of labour in one country and of land in the other will necessarily be lower, not only relatively but also absolutely, than other autarky. (Samuelson, 1948, 169)

Jagdish Bhagwati provided a sound analysis for the Factor Price Equalization Theorem. He stated, 'In short, the approach to the FPE theorem was not that it defined reality; rather it was

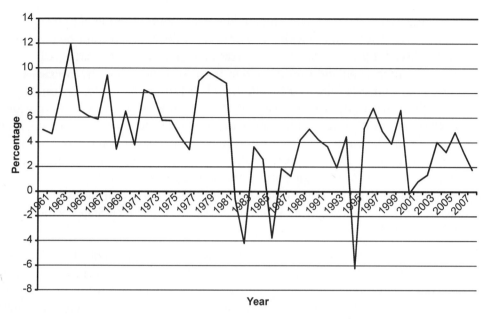

Fig. 17.2: GDP Annual Growth Rate

that the theorem provided the researcher with the necessary clues as to why it did not. By contrast, the tendency today is to regard FPE as in inescapable destiny: with the (unskilled) proletariat facing an inevitable immiseration or, at minimum, a heavy drag on the rise of its real wages. But it is time to remind ourselves that the original view of the FPE theorem was correct: its assumptions are indeed extraordinarily demanding. It is not therefore a compelling, or adequate, guide to real-world phenomena'. (Bhagwati, 1994, 242)

NAFTA AND FPE

The best modern day example for which we can apply the factor price equalization theorem is the North American Free Trade Agreement. Since the United States can be considered a capital abundant country and Mexico a labour abundant country, a closer look into the trade between these two countries will prove if the FPE Theorem can be found in the free trade between a developed country and a developing one. Before any conclusions can be made on the validity of the FPE theorem in this trade agreement, a synopsis on the countries involved and the trade agreement is needed.

Synopsis of Mexico and Its Economy

Mexico is a country with a population of over 111 million people, growing at the rate of 1.3 per cent (Mexico Country Profile). Mexico is the most populous Spanish speaking country in the world and the second most populous country in Latin America, after Portuguese speaking Brazil. Approximately 76 per cent of the population lives in urban areas, with 22 million people living in or around Mexico City, making this city the largest concentration of population in the Western Hemisphere. The trend in Mexico The heading of the figure to come below it and also give a sourcehas been for people living in rural areas to migrate to urban areas in search of jobs. Much of the remaining population resides along the US-Mexican border. (Mexico Country Profile) Mexico has a GDP of USD 1.482 trillion, ranked 12th in the world. Per capita income is around one third that of the United States at USD 13,500. Mexico is a growing economy, but with fluctuating growth rates as seen in Figure 17.2 (Mexico Data). Income distribution remains highly unequal, with the very poor Indians of rural areas rubbing shoulders with the very rich. Mexico, however, lies in a very strategic geographic location. As one of the three largest countries in North America, it borders the United States and is just south of Canada, making trade between these two powerful and developed countries easily accessible. Mexico is also the harbor for people moving from Central America to the United States, which has both positive and negative effects on the Mexican economy.

Mexico has many natural resources including: petroleum, silver, copper, gold, lead, zinc, natural gas, and timber. The agricultural products produced by Mexico include: corn, wheat, soybeans, rice, beans, coffee, fruit, tomatoes, beef, poultry, dairy products, and wood products which account for 4 per cent of GDP. Industry in Mexico accounts for 31 per cent of GDP and includes food and beverages, tobacco, chemicals, iron and steel, petroleum, mining, textiles, clothing, motor vehicles, and consumer durables. Services include: commerce and tourism, financial services, and transportation and communication and make up 64 per cent of Mexico's GDP.

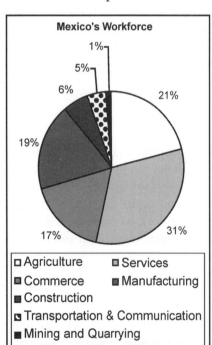

Fig. 17.3: Mexico's Workforce

The workforce represents a similar make up as shown in Figure 17.3. The latest estimates show that the workforce in Mexico is around 45.5 million or 40 per cent of the total population (Mexico Country Profile).

Mexico currently has free trade agreements with over 50 countries and is seen as one of the most open economies in the world. 90 per cent of Mexican trade is under free trade agreements with these numerous countries. (CIA – The World Factbook) Total exports from Mexico equal USD 229 billion with the US receiving 80 per cent of these exports. Canada accounts for 3.6 per cent of exports and Germany at 1.4 per cent. The top exported commodities include: manufactured goods, oil and oil products, silver, fruits, vegetables, coffee and cotton. (CIA – The World Factbook) Mexican imports totaled USD 234 billion in 2009 and include commodities such as: metalworking machines, steel mill products, agricultural machinery, electrical equipment, car parts for assembly, repair parts for motor vehicles, aircraft, and aircraft parts. The US is also the top import partner with 48 per cent of imports coming from just north of the border. China is second with 13.5 per cent, Japan 4.8 per cent, South Korea 4.6 per cent, and Germany 4.1 per cent. Mexico is also a constructive member of the World Trade Organization (WTO) and participates in the G-20 and OECD (Organization for Economic Cooperation and Development).

Clearly, Mexico relies heavily on the United States for foreign trade. This reliance goes beyond trade, however. With a recent rise in immigration of Mexicans to the Untied States for cheap labour, the Mexican economy is growing yet relying heavily on these wages sent from family member abroad. Mexico's economy is strongly linked to the business cycle in the US which was recently demonstrated in the effects that the economic slowdown in the US has had on the Mexican economy. However, as a developing country, Mexico has made great strides to open its economy to free trade, despite the three currency crisis's it has endured.

Mexico's move towards free trade began in the 1980s when it unilaterally liberalized foreign trade and investment policies (Hanson 3). Before that time, a fundamental element of Mexico's industrial strategy was, and still is, the maquiladora program. (Maquiladora is Spanish for 'miller's portion' for processing other people's grain.) This programme was initiated in 1966, partly to compensate for the elimination of the braceros programme that allowed Mexican farm workers temporary entry into the US. Its objective was to stimulate the establishment of labour-intensive, in-bond export processing plants along the northern border region, by offering them tax-free access to imported inputs and machinery, as well as exemption from sales tax and income taxes. In addition, development banks and some public entities, as well as private banks, granted subsidized financial support for industrial activities. This strategy, on the whole, proved to be successful (Moreno-Brid, 10). It transformed Mexico from a largely agrarian society to an urban, semi-industrial society. Maquiladoras continue to play a large role in Mexican trade. These factories import nearly all the needed materials from the United States and export the finished products back to the US. In 1995, exports by maquiladoras accounted for 40.2 per cent of all Mexican exports to the United States (Hanson, 9). These factories are also responsible for transplanting the unskilled labour from the Southern regions of Mexico to the Mexican states that line the US/Mexico border. This is the first clear example of the transfer of a factor of production, occurring within the same country but in close proximity to the country's border.

The Beginnings of NAFTA

The North American Free Trade Agreement (NAFTA) was implemented on 1 January 1994. The agreement was meant to gradually eliminate all barriers to trade between Canada, Mexico, and the United States. Mexican President Carlos Salinas was in power at the time of NAFTAs' implementation. The signing of NAFTA was seen to be his single contribution to Mexico's progress. Conceiving NAFTA, negotiating it with Washington and then Ottawa, and securing its ratification in all three countries were monumental tasks that occupied five to six years of his term. (Preston, 186) The agreement brought down 'the knotted net of regulations that protected Mexican business form foreign competition, opening up vast new markets to the countries entrepreneurs but also forcing them to change their ways. (Preston, 186) The

Salinas government originally sought a trade pact with Washington because it needed foreign investment. The country had given investors the three things they need most: political stability, a growing market, and predictable, intelligently managed macroeconomic policies (Orme, xix). Even with these three things, however, the government could not guarantee access to the US market, or the long term survival of Salinas's reforms. Both of these problems were solved by NAFTA. President Salinas sold the agreement to his constituents as a spur to economic growth. In a way, he oversold it, in that Mexicans saw NAFTA as 'a panacea for many of the country's economic ills.' (Weintraub, 1997, 14)

Since the initial signing of NAFTA, trilateral trade between NAFTA countries has been steadily increasing. Free trade between the three countries has been encouraged continually, with all remaining duties and quantitative restrictions eliminated as scheduled on 1 January 2008 (NAFTA). Mexico experienced a trade boom as a result of NAFTA as well as an inflow of foreign direct investment. According to the US Treasury Department, NAFTA has also been very good for the United States. To sell NAFTA to the American people, President Bush focused on the increase of jobs NAFTA would create due to the increase of exports (Weintraub, 1997, 14). As a result of the trade agreement, in 2009, total goods exported from the United States totalled USD 334 billion and imports were USD 401 billion. The US Department of Treasury also reports that trade with Mexico been steadily increasing since the implementation of NAFTA. This is true for both imports and exports. As of 2008, all restrictions against trade have been removed. The US government continues to produce positive propaganda saying that NAFTA has been a positive agreement for all parties involved. It seems clear that the country with the most to gain from this agreement is Mexico, and with only two years past since the removal of all trade barriers, it may be too soon to tell if this agreement is really making the impact the politicians touted it would.

Evidence of FPE in NAFTA

Paul Samuelson proposed that with free trade in place, the wage rental ratio of both countries would eventually become equal. To see if this theorem is true, the best measurement is to look at the wage rates in both Mexico and the United States. If this is in fact the truth, we should see the wage rates in Mexico increasing and the wage rates for unskilled labour in the United States decreasing. To begin, it is worth noting that the wages in Mexico differ by region. Since most of the maquiladoras are in Northern Mexico along the US/Mexico border, the wage rates are much higher there than in Southern Mexico. These maquiladoras are the largest producers of low-skilled, labour intensive exports. (Morales, 89) As of 2008, exports from these maquiladoras represented 45.5 per cent of all Mexican exports. Excluding oil exports, and taking into account only manufacturing exports, maquiladoras account for 55.6 per cent of total value. This clearly demonstrates that the 'dynamism of Mexican exports has remained anchored in cheap assembly production'. (Morales, 89) Mexico has an abundance of cheap labour and is employing this labour to increase exports. The wage rates in Mexico are closely correlated to these factories also and their proximity to the US market. For example, in 1980, before any trade reforms, 46 per cent of Mexico's manufacturing labour force was located around Mexico City while only 21 per cent was located around the US/Mexican border. In 1998, four years after the implementation of NAFTA, Mexico City's employment share was only 23 per cent while the Border States held 34 per cent. (Hanson, 11). This shift in employment represents the migration of Mexicans to employment in the North, a shift which is largely due to NAFTA.

Table 17.1 shows the patterns of US-Mexican trade. The data shows that Mexico is exporting mainly middle to low wage/capital goods and importing middle to high wage/capital goods. This proves to be in line with the FPE theorem. However, this study goes on to show that the removal of trade protection has a negative impact on the wage of Mexican workers relative to their US counterparts. A 10 per cent reduction in tariff and quota protection appears to have been associated with reductions in relative wages of 3 to 4 per cent. However, trade liberalization

Table 17.1: Patterns of US-Mexican Trade

Industry	Wage level	Capital intensity
Mexican manufacturing net exporting industries		
Food products	Low	Middle
Beverages	Middle	Middle
Apparel	Low	Low
Footwear	Low	Low
Furniture	Low	Low
Potter, china	Low	Middle
Glass and glass products	High	High
Nonmetallic minerals	Middle	Middle
Nonferrous metals	High	High
Electrical machinery	Low	Low
Transportation equipment	Middle	Middle
Mexican manufacturing net importing industries		
Miscellaneous foods	Middle	Middle
Textiles	Low	Middle
Wood	Low	High
Pulp, paper	Middle	Middle
Printing, publishing	Middle	Middle
Basic chemicals	High	High
Pharmaceuticals	High	High
Miscellaneous chemicals	Middle	Low
Tires and tubes	Middle	Low
Plastics	Low	Low
Iron and steel	High	High
Metal products	Middle	High
Nonelectrical machinery	Middle	Middle

Source: Annual surveys of manufactures.

allowed for imports of new capital and technology and induced productivity growth which may have yielded increases in the relative wage (Montenegro, 333). Figure 17.4, (Country Statistical Profiles) however shows the increase in wage rate in both countries from the implementation of NAFTA. This could be due to the openness of trade or possibly inflation.

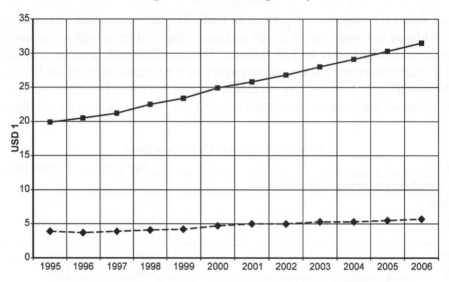

Fig. 17.4: Labour Compensation Per Hour, Total Economy

Hanson examines the literature surrounding the wage rates in Mexico after the implementation of NAFTA. He concludes that, 'recent literature suggests that liberalizing barriers to trade and investment have contributed to changes in Mexico's wage structure. There is evidence consistent with tariff reductions having increased relative wages for skilled workers, increased foreign investment, having raised the relative demand for skilled labour...Mexico's economic opening thus appears to have raised demand for skill and reduced industry rents going to labour'. (Hanson, 14) He goes on to say that several larger messages can be found in the literature regarding this free trade agreement. The first is that Mexico's 'comparative advantage in low-skill activities is not as strong as one thought.' Mexico has reoriented itself form producing simple consumer goods to being a subcontractor for the North American economy. Mexico has clearly demonstrated a cost advantage in assembly services for the US economy.

CONCLUSION

At the time of the NAFTA signing, it was estimated that 500 jobs would be created in Mexico for every 100 jobs created in the US. (Orme, 109) Hanson states that there is a strong correlation between wage growth in Mexico and wage growth in the United States, as demonstrated in Figure 17.4 (Hanson, 23). Orme goes on to say that 'overall, NAFTA creates jobs in both the United States and Mexico. It allows employees on both sides of the border to specialize in doing what they are best at: producing goods and services that require more skilled, technology intensive manufacturing and services in the United States and making goods that are more labour intensive and does not require such educated workers in Mexico'. (Orme, 125) Furthermore, 'the evidence suggests that tariff reductions have increased relative wages for skilled workers, increased foreign investment has raised the relative demand for skilled labour, and tariff and quota reductions have altered inter-industry wage differentials. Mexico's economic opening thus appears to have raised the skill premium and reduced industry rents going to labour. It also appears to have increased wages in states along the US border relative to the rest of the country' (Hanson, p. 3). This is exactly what Samuelson predicted would happen. However, the correlation to the beginnings of NAFTA does not appear to be strongly apparent.

The fundamental basis for Samuelson's factor price equalization theorem has proven to be true, although with some hesitations. The main argument for the rise in wages in Mexico has been because of the movement of skilled labour. The world highly underestimated Mexico at the time of the signing of this agreement. In fact, Mexico has proven itself to be open to free trade and full of skilled labour. The FPE theorem can be proven in this case in part, but not in full. There has not proven to be a pure wage increase in Mexico and a decrease in the United States. This could be due to the many external factors. One cannot say that these wage increases are strictly due to the increase of free trade, since there is no pure correlation. It is impossible to say that this increase was due only to free trade and not because of some other reason such as the increase of technology, the proximity to the United States, or the increase skill level within the workforce. It can only be said that the employment of Mexican workers increased and migrated towards the US/Mexico border. Since the signing of NAFTA, trade between the three beneficiaries of NAFTA has increased. Yet how can one say this would not have happened in the absence of NAFTA? Trade was increasing before the agreement was signed and only continued after the signing. It is impossible to say that this occurred solely because of free trade. In short, Samuelson's theorem provided the basis of which we can examine this equalization of factors between two countries, yet it cannot be proven solely by the North American Free Trade Agreement. This agreement has far too many outside factors which influence the relationships between the countries involved. It provides minimal evidence to support the theorem.

REFERENCES

1. Bhagwati, Jagdish. 'Challenges to Doctrine of Free Trade'. *New York University Journal of International Law and Politics* 25 (1992-1993): 219-34. *Heinonline*. Web. 18 May 2010.

2. Bhagwati, Jagdish. 'Free Trade: Old and New Challenges'. *The Economic Journal* 104.423 (1994): 231-46. *Jstor*. Web. 18 May 2010.

3. 'CIA - The World Factbook'. *Central Intelligence Agency - World Fact Book*. CIA, 2010. Web. 20 May 2010. <https://www.cia.gov/library/publications/the-world-factbook/geos/mx.html>.

4. 'Country Statistical Profiles 2009'. *OECD Statistics*. OECD, 2010. Web. 21 May 2010. http://stats.oecd.org/viewhtml.aspx?queryname=18162&querytype=view(=en>.

5. Hamilton, Bob, and John Whalley. 'Efficiency and Distributional Implications of Global Restrictions on Labour Mobility'. *Journal of Development Economics* 14 (1984): 61-75. Web.

6. Hanson, Gordon H. What Has Happened to Wages in Mexico Since NAFTA? Implications for Hemispheric Free Trade. Working paper no. 9563. National Bureau of Economic Research, Mar. 2003. Web. 17 May 2010. <http://www.nber.org/papers/w9563>.

7. Krugman, Paul, and Anthony J. Venables. 'Globalization and the Inequality of Nations'. The Quarterly Journal of Economics 110.4 (1995): 857-80. Jstor. Web. 17 May 2010.

8. Kulkarni, Kishore G. *Reading in International Economics*. Delhi: Serials Publications, 2004.

9. Leamer, Edward. *The Heckscher-Ohlin Model in Theory and Practice*. Publication. Princeton: International Finance Section, Department of Economics, Princeton University, 1995.

10. Machlup, Fritz. 'Professor Samuelson on Theory and Realism'. *American Economic Association* 54.5 (1964): 733-35. *Jstor*. Web. 19 May 2010.

11. 'Mexico Country Profile'. *U.S. Department of State*. U.S. Department of State, 2010. Web. 20 May 2010. <http://www.state.gov/r/pa/ei/bgn/35749.htm>.

12. 'Mexico Data'. *Data | The World Bank*. The World Bank, 2010. Web. 20 May 2010. <http://data.worldbank.org/country/mexico>.

13. Montenegro, Claudio E. 'North American Integration and Factor Price Equalization: Is There Evidence of Wage Convergance between Mexico and the United States?' *Imports, Exports, and the American Worker*. By Ana L. Renenga. Washington, DC: Brookings Institute, 1998. 305-41. *Www. books.google.com*. Google Books. Web. 18 May 2010.

14. Morales, Isidro. *Post-NAFTA North America: Reshaping the Economic and Political Governance of a Changing Region*. New York: Palgrave Macmillan, 2008.

15. Moreno-Brid, Juan Carlos, Juan Carlos Rivas Valdivia, and Jesus Santamaria. *Mexico: Economic Growth Exports and Industrial Performance after NAFTA*. Rep. no. 42. Mexico, D.F.: United Nations Publication, 2005.

16. 'NAFTA'. NAFTA. Office of the United States Trade Representative, 2010. Web. 20 May 2010. <http://www.ustr.gov/trade-agreements/free-trade-agreements/north-american-free-trade-agreement-nafta>.

17. Orme, William A. *Understanding NAFTA: Mexico, Free Trade, and the New North America*. Austin: University of Texas, 1996.

18. Preston, Julia, and Samuel Dillon. *Opening Mexico: The Making of a Democracy*. New York: Farrar, Straus and Giroux, 2004.

19. Puttaswamaiah, K. *Paul Samuelson & the Foundations of Modern Economics*. New Brunswick: Transaction, 2002.

20. Rogoff, Kenneth. *Paul Samuelson's Contributions to International Economics*. Boston: Harvard University, 2005.

21. Samuelson, Paul A. 'International Trade and the Equalisation of Factor Prices'. The Economic Journal 58.230 (1948): 163-84. Jstor. Web. 17 May 2010.

22. Samuelson, Paul A. 'Ohlin Was Right'. *The Sweedish Journal of Economics* 73.4 (1971): 365-84. *Jstor*. Web. 18 May 2010.

23. Samuelson, Paul A. 'Prices of Factors and Good in General Equilibrium'. *The Review of Economic Studies* 21.1 (1953-1954): 1-20. *Jstor*. Web. 18 May 2010.

24. Sanchez, Manuel, and Nathaniel Karp. *NAFTA's Economic Effects on Mexico*. Working paper. 2nd ed. Mexico City: Economic Research Department, Av. Universidad, 2000.

25. Stiglitz, Joseph E., ed. *The Collected Scientific Papers of Paul A. Samuelson*. Vol. 2. Cambridge: M.I.T., 1966.

26. Weintraub, Sidney. *NAFTA at Three: A ProgressReport*. Washington, DC: Center for Strategic and International Studies, 1997.

27. Weintraub, Sidney. *NAFTA's Impact on North America: The First Decade*. Washington, DC: Center for Strategic and International Studies, 2004.

18 | Proving the Irrelevance of the Harrod-Domar Model in the 21st Century

Stephanie Dybsky

CHAPTER SUMMARY

Does a country's national savings rate correlate with its gross domestic product (GDP) growth rate? Similarly, does a country's national savings rate correlate with the amount of foreign aid it receives?

Every nation strives after development. Developed and developing countries alike endeavour to reach a high level of growth and achievement. So, when considering this goal, it is relevant to ask: what is the main driver of development? And further, has this 'driver of development' been formulated into a model or theory that can be applied to all countries worldwide?

Surely, economic progress is an essential component of development; but is it the only component needed? Today, most academics and economists have come to agree that, in order to achieve development, other factors need to be considered in addition to economic growth. In other words, development is not purely an economic phenomenon. Ultimately, development must encompass more than the material and financial side of peoples' lives. Considering this movement away from an exclusively economic focus, are older models that target economic growth as the key instrument to achieve development still relevant today?

One such model that is still used today to implement development strategies is the Harrod-Domar growth model. Developed over 50 years ago, the Harrod-Domar model was supposedly put to rest shortly after its emergence into mainstream theory. Nevertheless, economists working on development strategies still apply the model to calculate short-run investment requirements for targeted economic growth. Then, they calculate a "financing gap" between the requirement investment and the available resources, usually filling the financing gap with foreign aid. These calculations are meant to provide a model to apply to developing countries that are working to join the developed world.

This chapter examines the predictions of the Harrod-Domar growth model: a country's GDP depends directly on its national savings rates and inversely on the national capital-output ratio. Based on my literature review, I found that the Harrod-Domar/Financing Gap model did not hold true when applied to 88 different countries. Further, I discovered that the Harrod-Domar model did not hold true when applied to two different currently developing African nations, Ghana and Tanzania.

The following chapter is divided into four sections. Section I explores the development of the Harrod-Domar growth model. Section II provides a literature review of the Harrod-Domar model. Section III applies the Harrod-Domar model to two different sub-Sahara African countries: Ghana and Tanzania. Section IV offers conclusions and recommendations.

THE HARROD-DOMAR GROWTH MODEL

When interest in the poor nations of the world began to materialize following the Second World War, economists in the industrialized nations were caught off guard. They had no readily available conceptual apparatus with which they could the process of economic growth in largely agrarian societies characterized by the virtual absence of modern economic structures. On the other hand, they did have the recent implementation of the Marshall Plan, under which massive amounts of US financial and technical assistance enabled the war-torn countries of Europe to rebuild and modernize their economies in only a few years. Further, was it not relevant that all modern industrial nations were once undeveloped agrarian societies? Surely, their historical experience in transforming their economies from agricultural subsistence societies to modern industrial giants had important lessons for the developing regions of Asia, Africa and Latin America.[1]

The logic and simplicity of the two related strands of thought – the utility of massive injections of capital and the historical pattern of the now developed countries – were fully embraced by scholars, politicians and administrators in rich countries, despite their lack of evidence-based knowledge on Third World economic and social systems. Out of these strands of thought came the Stages-of-Growth model of development, advocated most strongly by American economic historian, Walt W. Rostow. According to what came to be known as the 'Rostow Doctrine,' the transition from underdevelopment to development can be described in terms of a series of steps or stages through which all countries must proceed: (1) the traditional society, (2) the pre-conditions for take-off into self-sustaining growth, (3) the take-off, (4) the drive to maturity and (5) the age of high mass consumption.

One of the principal components necessary for Rostow's 'take-off stage' was the mobilization of domestic and foreign savings in order to generate sufficient investment to accelerate economic growth. The economic mechanism by which more investment leads to more growth was then described in terms of the Harrod-Domar growth model. Developed independently by Sir Roy F. Harrod in 1930 and Evsey Domar in 1946, the Harrod–Domar model is used to explain an economy's growth rate in terms of the level of savings and productivity of capital.[2]

Previously ignored by economists preceding Harrod and Domar were the dynamic interactions among macroeconomic variables and the associated distinction between flows (e.g. saving and investment, measured in, say, US dollars) and stocks (e.g. capital, measured in US dollars at a point in time, such as the start of the year). To paraphrase Irving Fisher: a flow is as different from a stock as a waterfall is from sea level. Because of the continuous movement involved, the distinction between flows and stocks is an inherently dynamic problem most easily dealt with by mathematicians like Harrod and Domar.[3]

By definition, net investment equals the increase in capital stock less depreciation due to physical or economic wear. This explains why a high level of investment entails an increasing level of capital stock, and, therefore, why high levels of saving and investment are good for growth even if they are stationary, or not necessarily increasing. Of course, high and rising levels of saving and investment are still better for growth. The main point, then, is that – by continuously augmenting the capital stock – even stationary levels of saving and investment relative to output, drive the output higher and higher, thus generating economic growth.[4]

With zero net investment, the capital stock will remain unchanged so that, with given efficiency, economic growth will also be zero. Negative net investment – which signifies decreasing capital stock because gross investment is not enough to keep up with the depreciation of capital – entails negative economic growth. Additionally, rapid depreciation due to investments of low quality is an important source of slow or even negative economic growth over long periods in many countries, particularly in sub-Saharan Africa, as we will examine further in Section III.[5]

The link between efficiency and growth is a bit more complex. A high level of efficiency – for example, through intense foreign trade or high standards of education – stimulates growth by amplifying the effects of a given level of saving and investment on the rate of growth of output. An increase in efficiency will increase economic growth, *but* output growth does not require a continuous increase in efficiency. Instead, all that is required is a steady accumulation of capital through saving and investment. A given level of efficiency, including the state of technology, will then translate the capital accumulation into economic growth.

Harrod and Domar expressed the dynamic relationship described above in the following explicitly-explained equation, which formalized, simplified and summarized the essence of almost 200 years-worth of theorizing about economic growth:

(1) The Harrod-Domar growth model is based on the basic Keynesian Hypothesis: Consumption (C), which is the expenditure by consumers on final goods and services, primarily depends upon gross domestic product (GDP), which is represented by Y. Therefore:

$$C = cY$$

where c = consumption rate or average propensity to consume (apc).

(2) The model breaks down national savings, which is defined as the national income that is not consumed. Therefore:

$$S = Y - C$$

$$S = Y - cY = Y(1 - c) = sY$$
$$S = sY$$

where $s = 1 - c = 1 - apc$ or s = savings rate or average propensity to save (aps).

(3) The model explains investment (I) as the expenditure by producers on either:

(a) Machinery, tools, equipment (capital stock)

or   (b) Construction activities

or   (c) Increase in inventories (unsold goods)

All three of these (a, b and c) cause an increase in capital stock (K) of the economy. Therefore:

$$I = \Delta K$$

where Δ represents a change.

(4) Due to the equations shown above, the capital-output ratio is represented by:

$$K/Y = j$$

where the capital-output ratio is constant, which means the variables always have to compute to equal j. Therefore:

$$\Delta K/\Delta Y = j$$
$$\Delta K = j \times \Delta Y$$
$$I = j \times \Delta Y$$

(5) The model assumes that the interest rate (r) is flexible. Therefore:

$$I = S$$

For example, if $I > S$ then:

$r \uparrow$ (increases)

$I \downarrow$ (decreases)

$S \uparrow$ (increase)

then: $I = S$

Likewise, if $I < S$, then:

$r \downarrow$

$I \uparrow$

$s \downarrow$

then: $I = S$

As long as r is flexible, the model assumes:

$$I = S$$

or $j \times \Delta Y = sY$

or $\Delta Y/Y = s/j$

where s/j represents the percentage Δ in GDP or economic growth.[6]

Based on the above calculations, the Harrod-Domar theory of economic growth states simply that: *the rate of growth of GDP (ΔY/Y) is determined jointly by the national savings ratio (s) and the national capital-output ratio (j).*

More specifically, the model states that, in the absence of government, the growth rate of national income will be directly or positively related to the savings ratio (i.e. the more an economy is able to save, and invest, out of its given GDP, the greater the growth of their GDP will be) and will be inversely or negatively related to the economy's capital-output ratio (i.e. the higher *j* is, the lower the rate of GDP growth will be).[7] For example, in a country with a savings ratio of six per cent and a capital-output ratio of three, GDP will grow by two per cent each year.[8] However, in many developing countries, a GDP increase of two per cent is barely 'adequate' to keep up with the (usually high) population growth. Consequently, the net savings rate needs to be increased to about 15 to 20 per cent through increased taxes, foreign assistance and/or general consumption sacrifices.[9]

The difference between 'adequate investment' and a country's own savings is called the 'financing gap'. According to the Harrod-Domar model, private financing is assumed to be unavailable to fill this gap. The international community interpreted this part of the model to mean that the best way to fill the gap and help developing countries attain target growth is through foreign assistance. At the start, development economists were not clear on how long it would take foreign aid to help increase investment and, in turn, spur growth. Nonetheless, economists soon argued that the model was short-term (i.e. a year's aid will go toward that year's investment, which will go toward the next year's GDP growth).[10]

As the Harrod-Domar model gained attention as a useful teaching tool and easily-understood model in the 1950s and 1960s, numerous proceeding economic models were based on its conclusions. In addition, governments of many post-colonial developing nations – such as India, South Africa and Sri Lanka – implemented economic policies to deliberately mobilize resources, in order to achieve pre-determined objectives meant to raise their countries' national savings rates.[11]

Despite its strengths, the Harrod-Domar theory did not prove successful in all cases. Academicians and economists eventually realized that the 'tricks' of development embodied by the theory did not work because increased saving and investment – although necessary conditions for accelerated economic growth – are not the *only* drivers of development. Consequently, using the implicit assumptions of Western economic theory for the actual conditions in developing nations has not proved beneficial to many developing nations.[12]

The Marshall Plan worked for Europe because the European countries receiving aid possessed the necessary structural, institutional and attitudinal conditions (i.e. well-integrated money markets, an efficient government bureaucracy, a well-trained and educated workforce) to convert new capital effectively into higher levels of output. The Harrod-Domar model assumes the existence of these same attitudes and arrangements in underdeveloped nations which, instead, most lack. Furthermore, one simply cannot claim – as many economists did in the

1950s and 1960s – that development is merely a matter of removing obstacles and supplying various missing components such as capital, foreign-exchange, skills and management.[13]

LITERATURE REVIEW OF THE HARROD-DOMAR MODEL

Between 1950 and 1995, Western countries gave one trillion dollars (measured in 1985 US dollars) in foreign aid. Since virtually all of the Western aid advocates used the Harrod-Domar/Financing Gap model, this was one of the largest policy experiments ever based on a single economic model. To test if the two propositions of the model held true between the years of 1965 and 1995, renowned economist William Easterly ran two regressions that will be examined in the following literature review. [14]

Easterly first tested the aid-to-investment relationship for the years of 1965 to 1995. As shown in Table 18.1, the positive relationship between aid and investment – as prescribed by the Harrod-Domar/Financing Gap model – did not hold true for a majority of the countries examined. In fact, 36 countries, or 41 per cent of the sample, reflect a *negative* correlation between aid and investment.[15]

Easterly's second test, spanning the years of 1950 to 1992, assessed the investment-to-growth relationships. This experiment tested the model's prediction of growth with a constant capital-output ratio (j) being more than two but less than five. According to Easterly's interpretation of the model, the average *j* is supposed to be around 3.5; hence, most countries, if not all, should fall between two to five. As illustrated by Table 18.2 , only four countries had a positive and significant relationship between growth and investment and a capital-output ratio between two and five. Important to note, Easterly tested the short-term investment-to-growth relationship only; usually, there is a robust long-term relationship between investment and growth.[16]

Following his test findings, Easterly pointed out that the Harrod-Domar/Financing Gap model is still being used by the International Monetary Fund (IMF), World Bank and other regional agencies. These agencies use the model to measure foreign resource requirements, to allocate aid and to provide advice to developing countries on economic policy. Easterly argues that their use of this model is partly to blame for the high debt many developing countries have now accumulated. [17]

Further, Easterly emphasized the misconception inherent in the Harrod-Domar model – that foreign aid would go one and one into investments, leading to economic growth and the capacity to pay back the loans – did not come about as predicted. Nevertheless, several economists and scholars alike continued to argue for the potential foreign aid has to help developing countries grow and progress. For example, in the 1970s, developmental economist Peter Thomas Bauer argued that 'foreign aid is necessary to enable underdeveloped countries to service the subsidized loans under earlier foreign aid agreements'.[18]

Next, we will test the relevance of the Harrod-Domar model in a similar fashion as utilized by Easterly; however, we will apply the model to two countries striving for development in more recent years.

APPLYING THE HARROD-DOMAR MODEL TO GHANA AND TANZANIA

Ghana

Formed from the merger of the British colony of the Gold Coast and the Togoland trust territory, Ghana became the first sub-Saharan country in colonial Africa to gain its independence in 1957.[19] The country has a relatively diverse and rich natural resource base. Minerals – principally gold, diamonds, manganese ore and bauxite – are produced and exported. A major oil discovery off the coast of Ghana in 2007 has led to significant international commercial interest in Ghana. According to industry experts, within the following five years, Ghana is likely to be the third-largest producer of oil in West Africa. [20]

Ghana's industrial base is relatively advanced compared to many other African countries. However, additional scope exists for value-added processing of agricultural products. Industry – including mining, manufacturing, construction and electricity – accounts for about 30 per cent of the country's GDP. With higher commodity prices, gold and cocoa are the top two export revenue earning sectors for Ghana. On the other hand, the country's largest source of foreign exchange is remittances from workers abroad. [21] The domestic economy continues to revolve around subsistence agriculture, which accounts for 35 per cent of the GDP and employs 55 per cent of the work force, mainly small landholders. Public sector wage increases and regional peacekeeping commitments have led to continued inflationary deficit financing, depreciation of the local currency (the Cedi) and rising public discontent with Ghana's austerity measures. Additionally, according to the World Bank, Ghana's per capita income has barely doubled over the past 45 years. [22]

Over the 1990s, Ghana's macroeconomic performance was less consistent than that it attained in the first years following the initial launch of the Economic Recovery Programme in 1983. This is particularly evident in terms of the variability of GDP growth and inflation. Though external factors played a part, the relatively poor performance has been widely attributed to weak fiscal policy and consequent high deficits. The decade was characterized by high and volatile inflation and real GDP growth that was both unstable and relatively low (see Figure 18.3).[23]

From the point of view of living standards, the evolution of private consumption expenditure is more relevant in the short term. Official figures suggest that real private consumption increased each year except one in the 1990s, sometimes by quite large proportions (i.e. 21.5 per cent in 1997). However, the average magnitude (4.8 per cent per annum) is similar to that of real GDP, translating into a similarly modest increase in per capita consumption. Furthermore, the fiscal balance (fiscal deficits after taking account of grants) consistently exceeded five per cent of GDP over the period of 1992 to 1999, reaching over ten per cent in 1997.[24]

The consistently high fiscal deficits appear to be the main explanation for the poor macroeconomic performance over the 1990s. Revenue mobilization was weak or stagnant over much of the 1990s, while high levels of public spending were maintained. Fiscal slippages were particularly evident in 1992 and 1996, both of which were election years. In 1992, there was a sharp increase in the fiscal deficit associated with large salary increases in the public sector – not accompanied by significant retrenchment as had been intended – and a reduction in revenue collection efforts prior to the election. Also significant, Ghana experienced considerable liberalization in the 1990s. [25]

Applying the Harrod-Domar Model

First, using Easterly's analysis (Section II) as a guide, we apply the Harrod-Domar/Financing Gap model by testing the aid-to-investment relationship in Ghana using Ghana's national savings rate and Official Development Assistance (ODA) allocated to Ghana. Before doing so, though, the following notations are provided; due to a lack of available data on savings rates for Ghana, the savings rate assessed in this chapter includes the following types of deposits: time, savings and foreign currency deposits. Deposits are to commercial banks and other financial institutions that accept transferable deposits, such as demand deposits. Deposit money banks' data measure the stock of deposit money.

As illustrated in Figure 18.1, over the ten-year span of 1992 to 2002, Ghana's national savings deposits grew significantly each year. For example, in the first five years (1992 to 1997), national savings deposits grew from 214.6 to 1,585.7 – an increase of approximately 638 per cent or approximately 127 per cent per year if spread evenly across the five year span. Similar to the results of the first five year span, in the second five year span, national savings deposits grew significantly, from 1,585.7 to 6,909 – an increase of approximately 335 per cent or 67 per cent per year if spread evenly across the five years.

In keeping with the Harrod-Domar/Financing Gap model, we would assume that – because Ghana's national savings rate increased each year during the ten-year span assessed – ODA Ghana received during this same ten-year span increased as well. Figure 18.2 reflects ODA allocated to Ghana from 1988 to 2008; for our analysis, however, we are assessing the same ten-year span used to assess Ghana's national savings rate (1992 to 2002).

At the start of the 1990s, ODA to Ghana did, in fact, increase, peaking at approximately 900 million US dollars. Yet, from 1992 to 1994, ODA decreased dramatically to approximately 550 million dollars. In 1995, ODA increased slightly to a little over 600 million, but later dipped down again in 1996 and 1997 to about 500 million. By the late 1990s, ODA had increased again to approximately 700 million, and then dropped down and remained consistent at about 600 million from 2000 through 2002. Clearly, the fluctuating ODA allocated to Ghana does not correlate with its steadily increasing national savings (investment).

Second, we apply the Harrod-Domar model further by testing the growth-to-investment relationship in Ghana. The same ten-year span used to assess the aid-to-investment relationship (1992 to 2002) is also used to assess the growth-to-investment relationship. We should note here that the GDP data (see Figure 18.3) used for this assessment are based on constant prices (a common set of prices used to value the output of a firm or economy in successive periods. Changes in the real activity of an enterprise or an economy are measured by valuing its real inputs and outputs each year at the same, 'constant,' set of prices. The prices used may be those of some particular date, or average prices over a period).[26]

As illustrated by Figure 18.3, Ghana's economy grew and achieved an all-time high growth rate of approximately 8.6 in 1984. From that point forth, however, GDP growth decreased throughout the proceeding years, with the exception of the few high-point years of 1988 (7.9 per cent growth) and 1992 (16.2 per cent growth). Although Ghana's GDP gradually increased *overall* from 1960 to 2008 (see Figure 18.4), it was not until 2003 that the GDP began increasing *significantly* from approximately 15.3 per cent in 2003 to approximately 28.24 per cent in 2008. Furthermore, as reflected in Figure 18.1 , Ghana's national savings deposits increased most significantly in 1999 – increasing from 1,793.4 in 1998 to 2,332.3 in 1999. This significant increase trend does not correlate with Ghana's GDP growth rate over this same time period. In fact, from 1998 to 1999, the GDP growth rate decreased by 5.6 per cent.

In comparing Ghana's continuously increasing national savings rate to its fluctuating GDP growth rate and ODA allocations between 1992 and 2002, it is clear that the Harrod-Domar model does not hold for the Ghanaian economy; savings (investment) grew significantly, but neither the country's GDP nor the amount of ODA it received consistently increased over the same ten-year span.

Tanzania

Shortly after achieving independence from Britain in the early 1960s, Tanganyika and Zanzibar merged to form the nation of Tanzania in 1964. Tanzania's semi-autonomous status and popular opposition have led to two contentious elections since 1995, which the ruling party won despite international observers' claims of voting irregularities.[27]

Significant measures have been taken to liberalize the Tanzanian economy along market lines and encourage both foreign and domestic private investment. Beginning in 1986, the government embarked on an adjustment programme to dismantle state economic controls and encourage more active participation of the private sector in the economy. The programme included a comprehensive package of policies which reduced the budget deficit and improved monetary control, substantially depreciated the overvalued exchange rate, liberalized the trade regime, removed most price controls, eased restrictions on the marketing of food crops, freed interest rates and initiated a restructuring of the financial sector.[28]

In February 2007, the IMF completed the final review of Tanzania's second Poverty Reduction and Growth Facility (PRGF) arrangement and approved a three-year Policy Support Instrument as a successor to the PRGF. Tanzania had implemented a second three-year PRGF in August 2003. From April 2000 to June 2003, the Tanzanian Government successfully completed a previous three-year PRGF. The PRGF was the successor program to the Enhanced Structural Adjustment Facility Tanzania had from 1996-1999. Tanzania also embarked on a major restructuring of state-owned enterprises during the same period. [29]

Agriculture constitutes the most important sector of the Tanzanian economy, providing about

27 per cent of GDP and 80 per cent of employment. Cash crops – such as coffee, tea and cotton – account for the vast majority of export earnings. While the volume of major crops – both cash and goods marketed through official channels – have increased in recent years, large amounts of produce never reach the market. Poor pricing and unreliable cash flow to farmers continue to frustrate the agricultural sector. [30]

Despite Tanzania's unbroken record of political stability, an unattractive investment climate has discouraged foreign investment. Government steps to improve the business climate include redrawing tax codes, floating the exchange rate, licensing foreign banks and creating an investment promotion center to cut red tape. The most common complaints of investors, both foreign and domestic, are arbitrary courts' inability to enforce contracts and a hostile bureaucracy. [31]

Overall, Tanzania's real GDP growth has averaged about six per cent a year over the past seven years, higher than the annual average growth of less than give per cent in the late 1990s but not enough to improve the lives of average Tanzanians. The economy remains overwhelmingly donor-dependent. Tanzania had an external debt of approximately 5.311 billion US dollars (end of December 2008), down from approximately 5.36 billion dollars recorded as of the end of December 2007. During 2007, external debt service payments amounted to 42 million dollars compared with 90.3 million dollars paid in 2006. The drastic fall in the actual debt service is associated with the debt relief arising from the Heavily Indebted Poor Countries initiative and Multilateral Debt Relief Initiative and accumulation of arrears on non-serviced debts. [32]

Applying the Harrod-Domar Model

As assessed in section *Ghana*, first, we will apply the Harrod-Domar/Financing Gap model by testing the aid-to-investment relationship in Tanzania using Tanzania's national savings rate and ODA allocated to Tanzania. Again, the same notation is provided under this section; due to a lack of available data on savings rates for Tanzania, the savings rate assessed in this chapter includes the following types of deposits: time, savings and foreign currency deposits. Deposits comprise commercial banks and other financial institutions that accept transferable deposits, such as demand deposits. Deposit money banks' data measure the stock of deposit money.

Also similarly, our analysis of Tanzania assesses the country's national savings rate to from 1992 through 2002 (see Figure 18.5). Over this ten year span, national savings deposits grew significantly each year. For example, in the first five years (1992 to 1997), national savings deposits grew from 116.2 to 433.2 – an increase of 272 per cent or 54 per cent per year if spread evenly across the five year span. Like the results of the first five year span, in the second five year span, Tanzania's national savings deposits grew significantly, from 433.2 to 1,088.9 – an increase of approximately 151 per cent or 30 per cent per year if spread evenly across the five years.

In keeping with the Harrod-Domar/Financing Gap model, we would assume that – because Tanzania's national savings rate increased each year during the ten-year span assessed – ODA Tanzania received during this same ten-year span increased as well. Figure 18.6 reflects ODA allocated to Tanzania from 1988 to 2008. For our analysis, however, we are assessing the same ten-year span used to assess Tanzania's national savings rate (1992 to 2002).

At the start of the 1990s, ODA to Tanzania had increased from the previous decade to a total of just over one billion US dollars. Nonetheless, it decreased within just the first year to less than one million, but then jumped back up to about 1.25 billion by 1993. In the mid-1990s, ODA decreased substantially to 900 million and remained at that amount until jumping back up to one billion in 2001 and then to 1.25 billion in 2002. Undoubtedly, Tanzania's fluctuating ODA allocations does not correlate with its steadily increasing national savings (investment).

Second, we apply the Harrod-Domar model further by testing the growth-to-investment relationship in Tanzania. The same ten-year span used to assess the aid-to-investment relationship (1992 to 2002) is also used to assess the growth-to-investment relationship. Again, the GDP data used for this assessment are based on constant prices (see Figure 18.7).

As reflected in Figure 18.8, from 1991 to 1992, Tanzania had a significant negative growth rate (-71.8 per cent). In 1993, however, the growth rate increased considerably to 106.5 per cent. In 1994 it dropped to 29.9 per cent, but increased again considerably to 127.8 per cent in 1995. This same fluctuating pattern of GDP growth – decreasing one year and then increasing the following year – continued from 1996 through 2002, ending at a positive growth of 19.4 per cent. Although Tanzania's GDP gradually increased *overall* from 1998 to 2008 (see Figure 18.8), GDP growth did not *consistently* increase from 1992 to 2002 as its national savings did over the same ten-year span. Therefore, it is clear that Tanzania's fluctuating GDP rate does not correlate with its steadily increasing national savings (investment).

CONCLUSION AND RECOMMENDATIONS

Since the 1950s, many scholars have spent the majority of their careers creating, exploring and testing development models to assist underdeveloped nations. Most in the development field have since realized that creating and implementing a 'one size fits all' model is likely to be unsuccessful in all developing countries. Although the Harrod-Domar model is a noteworthy theory to keep in mind when assessing development – as our literature review and two-country case study evidenced – it is not the only model that should be considered. Rather, to assist the developing world, specialists need to devise models which take into considering the wide variety of components – economic, social and culture – that make up each unique nation.

APPENDIX

Table 18.1: Results of regressing Gross Domestic Investment/GDP on ODA/GDP country by country, 1965-1995

Coefficient of Investment on ODA	Number of Countries	Per cent of Sample
Total	88	100
Positive, Significant and > 1	6	7
Positive and Significant	17	19
Positive	35	40
Negative	53	60
Negative and Significant	36	41

Source: William Easterly, 'The Ghost of Financing Gap, How the Harrod-Domar Growth Model Still Haunts Development Economics,' 1997, Policy Research Working Paper 1807, The World Bank.

Table 18.2: Results of regressing GDP Growth on Gross Domestic Investment/GDP with a constant, country by country, 1950–1992

Coefficient of Growth on Investment/GDP	Number of Countries	Per cent of Sample
Total Sample	138	100
Positive, Significant, 'Zero' Constant* and 2<*j*<5	4	3
Positive, Significant and 'Zero' Constant	7	5
Positive and Significant	11	8
Positive	77	56
Negative	61	44
Negative and Significant	10	7

*A constant that is insignificantly different than zero
Source: William Easterly, 'The Ghost of Financing Gap, How the Harrod-Domar Growth Model Still Haunts Development Economics,' 1997, Policy Research Working Paper 1807, The World Bank.

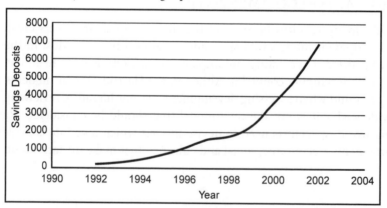

Figure 18.1: National Savings Deposits of Ghana, 1992–2002**

*Due to a lack of available data on savings rates for Tanzania, the Savings Deposits includes: Time, Savings and Foreign Currency Deposits. Deposits comprise commercial banks and other financial institutions that accept transferable deposits, such as demand deposits. Deposit money banks' data measure the stock of deposit money.
*Savings deposits are in billions of Cedi (end of the period).
Source: International Monetary Fund, *International Financial Statistics*, 2004, International Monetary Fund, Washington, DC.

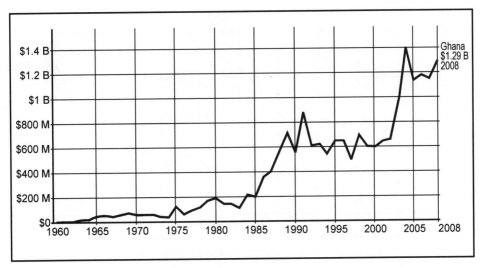

Figure 18.2: Official Development Assistance to Ghana, 1960–2008

Source: World Bank, World Development Indicators - Last updated 7 May 2010.

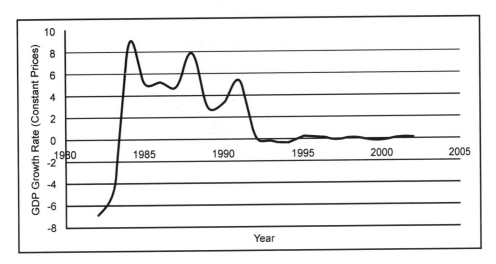

Figure 18.3: Gross Domestic Product Growth Rate of Ghana, 1992-2002

Source: Index Mundi, Ghana, May 2010.

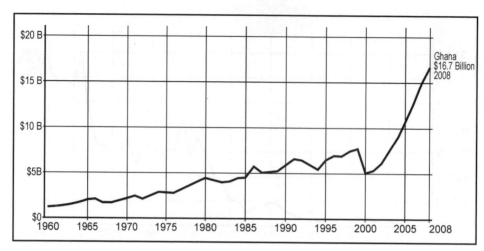

Figure 18.4: Gross Domestic Product of Ghana, 1960-2008

Source: World Bank, World Development Indicators - Last updated 7 May 2010.

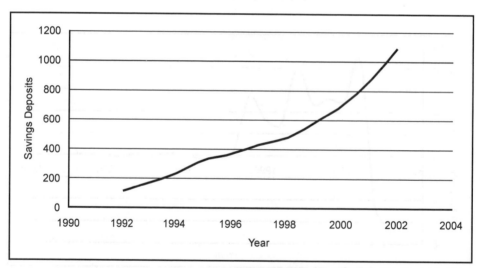

Figure 18.5: National Savings Deposits of Tanzania, 1992–2002**

*Due to a lack of available data on savings rates for Tanzania, the Savings Deposits includes: Time, Savings and Foreign Currency Deposits. Deposits comprise commercial banks and other financial institutions that accept transferable deposits, such as demand deposits. Deposit money banks' data measure the stock of deposit money.
*Savings deposits are measured in billions of Baht (end of the period).
Source: International Monetary Fund, *International Financial Statistics*, 2004, International Monetary Fund, Washington, DC.

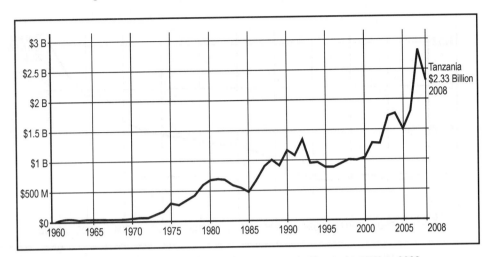

Figure 18.6: Official Development Assistance to Tanzania, 1960 to 2008

Source: World Bank, World Development Indicators - Last updated 7 May 2010.

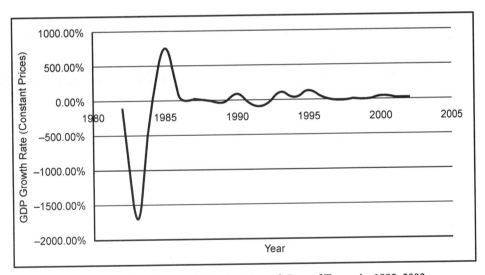

Figure 18.7: Gross Domestic Product Growth Rate of Tanzania, 1992–2002

Source: Index Mundi: Tanzania, May 2010.

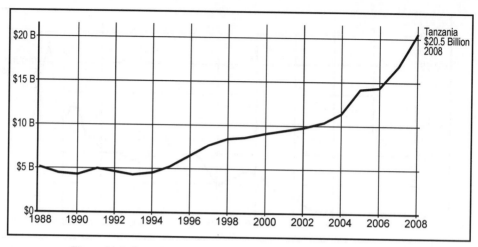

Figure 18.8: Gross Domestic Product of Tanzania, 1988–2008

Source: World Bank, World Development Indicators - Last updated 7 May 2010.

NOTES

1. Michael P. Todaro, *Economic Development*, Seventh Edition, 2000, Addison-Wesley Longman, Inc. New York, p. 79.
2. Todaro, pp. 79-80.
3. Thorvaldur Gylfason, *Principles of Economic Growth*, 1999, Oxford University Press, Oxford, pp. 24-25.
4. Gylfason, p. 25.
5. Gylfason, p. 25.
6. Kishore Kulkarni, 5 May 2010, Lecture.
7. Todaro, pp. 81-82.
8. A "normal" capital-output ratio is around 3.5 (Easterly).
9. The Rostow Doctrine defined the take-off stage of an economy in this way. Countries that were able to save 15 to 20 per cent of their GDP could grow at a much faster rate than those that saved less (Todaro).
10. William Easterly, 'The Ghost of Financing Gap, How the Harrod-Domar Growth Model Still Haunts Development Economics,' 1997, Policy Research Working Paper 1807, The World Bank.
11. Kulkarni
12. Todaro, p. 83.
13. Todaro, p. 83.
14. Easterly, p. 16.
15. Easterly, pp. 16-17.
16. Easterly, pp. 17-20.
17. Easterly, pp. 17-20.
18. Easterly, p. 20.
19. Central Intelligence Agency, The CIA World Factbook, May 2010 <*https://www.cia.gov/library/ publications/the-world-factbook/geos/gh.html*>.

20. US Department of State, Bureau of African Affairs, 5 March 2010 <*http://www.state.gov/r/pa/ei/ bgn/2860.htm*>.
21. US Department of State, Bureau of African Affairs, 5 March 2010 <*http://www.state.gov/r/pa/ei/ bgn/2860.htm*>.
22. US Department of State
23. The World Bank, *Growth and Poverty Reduction: Case Studies from West Africa,* World Bank Working Paper No. 79, The World Bank, Washington, D.C., pp. 10-11.
24. The World Bank, p. 11.
25. The World Bank, p. 11.
26. John Black, *A Dictionary of Economics*, January 2002, Oxford University Press.
27. CIA
28. US Department of State
29. US Department of State
30. US Department of State
31. US Department of State
32. US Department of State

REFERENCES

1. Bauer, P.T. *Dissent on Development: Studies and Debates in Development Economics.* November 1998. Harvard University Press.
2. Black, John. *A Dictionary of Economics.* January 2002. Oxford University Press.
3. Central Intelligence Agency (CIA). CIA World Factbook. May 2010 <*https://www.cia.gov/library/ publications/the-world-factbook/geos/gh.html*>. [Abbreviated 'CIA']
4. Easterly, William. 'The Ghost of Financing Gap, How the Harrod-Domar Growth Model Still Haunts Development Economics.'1997. Policy Research Working Paper 1807. The World Bank.
5. Gylfason, Thorvaldur. *Principles of Economic Growth.* 1999. Oxford University Press. Oxford, UK.
6. Index Mundi. May 2010 <*http://www.indexmundi.com/tanzania/gdp_real_growth_rate.html* >.
7. Talton, Bejamin. *Politics of Social Change in Ghana, The Konkomba Struggle for Political Equality.* 2010. Palgrave Macmillan. New York, NY.
8. The World Bank. *Growth and Poverty Reduction, Case Studies from West Africa.* World Bank Working Paper No. 79. The World Bank. Washington, DC.
9. Todaro, Michael P. *Economic Development.* 7th Edition. 2000. Addison-Wesley Longman, Inc.
10. US Department of State. Bureau of African Affairs. 5 March 2010 <*http://www.state.gov/r/pa/ei/ bgn/2860.htm*>.

19

'Fool's Gold?'

A Consideration of Immiserizing Growth and Dutch Disease on Economic Development in the Kyrgyz Republic

Stuart Thomas

CHAPTER SUMMARY

A pillar of its economic transformation after the disintegration of the Soviet Union, gold mining and production is an integral part of the Kyrgyz economy. Since commercial production began in 1997, gold's share in merchandise exports has grown quickly and considerably. The Kumtor gold mine, the country's largest, individually accounts for 45 per cent of industrial production, and in 2005, its production represented over 9 per cent of GDP. Gold's predominance in exports, however, raises questions over its sustainability and effect on other macroeconomic variables in the economy. Utilizing the theoretical frameworks of Bhagwati's Immiserizing Growth Hypothesis and Corden's Dutch Disease Model, this chapter critically examines how the inception of gold production in the Kyrgyz export economy can help us explain broader structural changes in the country's economy. We see that the Kyrgyz economy has become more dependent on gold-led export growth, and, amidst broader trade liberalization reforms, this development has had unintended consequences on the economy.

GOLD – THE MOST PRECIOUS NATURAL RESOURCE

Gold is the most precious natural resource of the Kyrgyz Republic. The flurry of gold mines to open in the country after the disintegration of the Soviet Union promised the Kyrgyz Republic access to wealth that no other resource could afford it. The discovery of reserves and development of the gold industry with international mining firms served as a pillar of the post-Soviet neoliberal economic and trade reforms in the country. At the heart of this development was the financing and commercialization of the Kumtor mine. The mine, which is majority owned by Centerra Gold INC and Cameco Corporation (Canadian), is the largest in the country, and one of the most important gold mines for any one country in the world. The mine's economic worth is an astonishing 9+ per cent of the Kyrgyz Republic's GDP. It provides the central government with around 3.5 per cent of the country's tax revenues annually (USD 30 million) [Sershen 2007; IMF Country Report 2009, 32]. The mine is representative of the hope of leaders in Bishkek that its reserves of natural resources will ultimately be a catalyst towards broader economic and social development.

The example of the Kyrgyz Republic is by no means a unique one. Developing countries have, for decades, placed the promise of economic growth and development on their ability and capacity to use and exploit their natural resource good fortune. Natural resources are a powerful symbol of hope and change, because their worth is tangible. They are important for developing countries, because their location is permanent; that is, they invoke a sense of nationalism and self-determination among citizens. In reality, though, natural resources are complicated. Evidence of natural resources serving as a boon to developing economies is mixed. Scholars continue to debate whether these resources are more of a blessing, or a curse.

To this end, a number of economists have sought to systematically and theoretically examine the potential of these resources. Two of the most important of these economists were Jagdish Bhagwati and W. M. Corden. As the developers of the formal models of Immiserizing Growth and Dutch Disease, they argued that countries that focused too heavily on one export sector of an economy to promote economic growth could, not knowingly, bring about more serious problems to the economy as a whole. Their arguments and theories bear significant importance and consideration, because each argues that even an expansion in the export sector can ultimately be deleterious to an economy.

This chapter develops each of these models and applies them to the case of the Kyrgyz Republic. It examines the relationship of the country's gold sector to the overall economy. The gold sector's size, contribution to the export sector, and ability to affect other economic variables are all considered. To date, little economic scholarship has been produced on the potential of Dutch Disease in the Kyrgyz Republic. Its size and relative obscurity in the global economy make a country seemingly overlooked by the academic world. Recent political turmoil in the country, though, has captured world attention and raised important questions in Central Asia about the cause of the unrest.

This chapter progresses as follows. The next section will develop Bhagwati's Immiserizing Growth Hypothesis and Corden's Core Dutch Disease Model. It examines the potential applications of each theory, as well as the recent attempts by scholars to test them empirically. These two theoretical frameworks will then be applied to the case of the gold sector of the Kyrgyz economy to empirically test their analyses. This chapter ends by examining the implications of the analysis on possible future policy prescriptions for officials in Bishkek.

DUTCH DISEASE AND IMMISERIZING GROWTH: THEORETICAL FRAMEWORKS DEVELOPED AND CONSIDERED

The term 'Dutch Disease' was first coined in a 1977 *Economist* article in response to the prolonged Dutch economic troubles following the post-OPEC recession [Economist 1977, 82-83]. The chapter describes how the development of significant new gas reserves in the country had helped exacerbate other economic problems in the Dutch economy. The chapter's author(s) carefully explained how the Dutch natural gas sector helped create distortions in the current account, the external and internal exchange rate, industrial costs and employment [Economist 1977, 82-83]. It also highlighted the use of gas revenues by the government to fund social programmes and increase deficit spending. In short, the chapter provided a simple example of the potential problems associated with the development of newly-found natural resources.

Netherlands's example caught the attention of a number of economists, who sought ways to explain its situation using more formal means. It was not, however, the first time that economists had sought to imagine a scenario similar to the Netherlands. In 1958, Jagdish Bhagwati developed a theoretical model that could explain situations similar to the experience of the Dutch. Bhagwati's Immiserizing Growth Hypothesis has since served as the foundation for other economists seeking to extend his theory and test whether export expansion in a developing country could have net negative effects on its economy. Here we develop his theory geometrically.

Bhagwati's premise was simple: under certain circumstances, export expansion may do more harm than good for a growing economy [Bhagwati, 1958, 201]. His hypothesis centres upon the argument that increased output in the export sector may lead to a severe deterioration in a country's terms of trade (TOT), thereby reducing real income and welfare in that country. The country's terms of trade (TOT) is defined as the ratio of its export price level to its import price level. Consider following Figure 19.1. Suppose initially that a country's consumption equilibrium is at point J and production equilibrium is at point T. To satisfy supply and demand needs, the country must export good x and import good y. In Figure 19.1, the country's initial

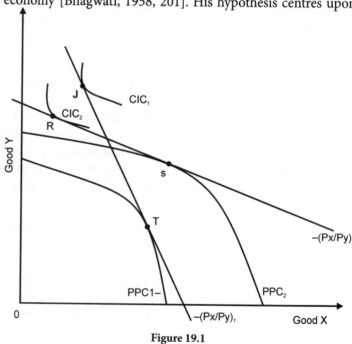

Figure 19.1

TOT is $(Px/Py)^1$, or the slope of the country's price line running tangential to its production possibilities curve (PPC_1) and its consumer indifference curve (CIC_1). Suppose now that a country's TOT deteriorates with concomitant expansion in the export sector. Prices of imports to the country increase faster than the price of its exports, which leads to the TOT deterioration $-(Px/Py)^1 \rightarrow -(Px/Py)^2$. The export sector has expanded ($PPC^1 \rightarrow PPC^2$). The domestic economy's production equilibrium (point S) shows that the economy has now increased the production of both good x and good y. However, the increase of import prices relative to export prices has hurt the real income of consumers in the country. Consumers now consume at point R, indicating a fall in welfare ($CIC_1 \rightarrow CIC_2$). So, despite the economic expansion, the economy is worse off.

Under what circumstances could a developing country see its TOT deteriorate so rapidly as to produce a negative net welfare effect on its economy? Economists give two possible explanations. First, export growth in an economy could lead to a deflation in the world price of that good, if that country's export growth was large enough to affect the world price of the good. Export prices would fall, leading to a deteriorating TOT and a decrease in overall economic welfare [Kulkarni 2006, 141]. Second, although the country has expanded its export sector, the prices of its imports may grow faster than its exports. Deteriorating TOT can occur over time in developing countries, it is argued, because the cost of production of exports, reflecting the standard of living of labourers, is related to the prices of exports in developed countries, but not in developing countries. Export prices from developed countries increase faster than export prices from developing countries, due to the price elasticity of the good in developed vs. developing countries. This price elasticity in developed countries keeps LDC export prices relatively lower, and as a result, developing countries' economic well-being remains below the developed world [Kulkarni, 2006, 141].

Corben (1984) extended Bhagwati's Immiserizing Growth Hypothesis to examine the effects of an expansion of *one* important export sector on exchange rates, *other* export sectors, inflation rates, unemployment and distortions in international payments accounts. His analysis is accepted and used here as the formal 'Dutch Disease' model. The model begins with an expansion of production in a specific export sector of the economy, what Corben labels as the 'Booming Sector' [Corben, 1984, 360]. This expansion could have occurred, because the sector had seen significant technological improvement, benefited from the discovery of new resources, and/or seen an exogenous rise in the price of its product [Corben, 1984, 360]. This boom increases wealth to the labour employed there, which leads to a rise in demand for all goods in that economy (including traded and non-traded goods) [Bruno and Sachs, 1982, 4]. Increased demand places upward pressure on prices of imports and domestically produced goods. The price of domestically produced 'non-tradable' goods rises faster relative to imports and other tradable goods, 'to preserve home-market equilibrium' [Bruno and Sachs, 1982, 4]. Factors and resources are drawn away from the tradable (usually light manufacturing and agriculture) sectors and into the non-tradable sectors due to increased demand and higher relative prices. Some of this demand will be satisfied by increased domestic production, with the rest disappearing as a result of the increases in prices. Increased demand for imports and tradables will be satisfied by increases of imports, because domestic production of tradables (excluding the booming sector) will fall as their factor inputs are drawn away into both non-tradables and the booming sector [Corben, 1984, 361-62; Bruno and Sachs, 1982, 4].

Inflows of foreign currency earnings resulting from the expansion of the booming sector, coupled with relative increases in the price of non-tradable goods associated with increased wealth and demand, leads to a real appreciation of the currency. Given the real exchange rate (RER)=ER(P*/P), where ER is the nominal exchange rate, P* is the foreign country price level and P is the domestic country price level, an increase in P relative to P* will cause the RER to fall (appreciate) [Kulkarni, 2006, 248]. Factor movements and real exchange rate appreciation can have debilitating effects on other tradable sectors. Increases in demand for non-tradables and boom sector products result in the re-allocation of resources away from other tradables into these two sectors as demand increases and price levels increase. Additionally, increased wealth from the expansion of the booming sector can drive up wages and the prices of domestic inputs faster than the price of exported goods [Kulkarni, 2006, 248]. This real appreciation can erode the profit margins of other export producers and force them to decrease production, thereby employing less people and/or paying them less. Put simply, the RER appreciation makes other exporters less competitive.

Increased foreign currency earnings from the booming sector increase the overall money supply, given by MS=D+R, where MS is the money supply, D is domestic supplies of money and R are foreign reserves [Kulkarni, 2006, 248]. Increases in the money supply drive up the domestic price level, exacerbating inflationary pressures and increasing the costs of production for all sectors of the economy. These myriad effects can severely strain the ability of other exporters to be competitive in world markets, given rising wages and input costs, as well as dwindling resources from resource/factor re-allocation.

As a result, the economy as a whole may not be better off from the expansion of a particular export sector. Although a country's TOT may improve in the short-run (from increases in booming sector export prices and exchange rate appreciation), this improvement may be short-lived. If the booming sector's export prices fall, or other tradable prices fall because of decreased production/supply, TOT will deteriorate as export prices fall relative to import prices. This might particularly be the case for a developing country, as it is much less able to affect the world price of its export goods. To maintain competitiveness, exporters of other goods might have to lower their export price, even in the face of rising input/wage costs and RER appreciation.

Developing economies may be more prone to the problems of Dutch disease, because they are less able to mitigate/deal with the problems which may arise from the nascent growth of an export sector. Developing countries can experience difficulties, especially in the short term, in re-allocating capital and labour away from other export sectors to the booming sector [Chang and Grabel, 2004, 65-66]. This can occur for several reasons. (1) There may be a lack of labour mobility in the country, whether for cultural, linguistic, or geographic reasons. (2) Labour may not be able to move easily into the booming sector if training or technological gaps exist. In the case of the Kyrgyz Republic, significant training is required for persons looking for employment in high-altitude gold mining. (3) The booming sector may simply not employ many workers. Oil export countries provide a good example of this phenomenon. Extracting oil or other natural resources usually does not involve a significant amount of labour, due to the advent and use of new mining technologies and equipment. In the Kyrgyz Republic, the Kumtor gold mine, which is responsible for 45 per cent of *all* industrial production in the country, employs only 2200 people [Kumtor, 2010]. We assume here that the boom sector has hurt other export sectors to the point that labour and resources are drawn away from those sectors, or that export firms are forced to cuts costs to maintain export competitiveness.

Dutch disease can be more difficult for developing economies in other ways as well. If the boom sector causes an increase of wealth in the country and/or leads to a wage increase, RER appreciation from an increase in domestic prices and inflation could force the developing country's government to make difficult fiscal or monetary policy decisions. If that country's central bank raises interest rates to combat inflationary pressures, it could lead to further appreciation of the home currency. This would place more of a burden on exporters' competitiveness and likely increase unemployment [Epstein and Yelden, 2008]. Developing country governments must also decide how to use natural resource earnings. Because developing countries are poorer and their governance systems usually weaker than developed countries, how developing countries use their natural resource wealth is of particular importance. Properly channeled earnings can help promote sustainable economic growth. However, these earnings often more easily find their way into the hands of corrupt politicians, rather than into social development programmes.

Actual experiences of developing countries are instructive in this regard. Nigeria, whose oil reserves are some of the largest in the world, has experienced numerous development and inflationary problems since the development of its oil fields in the 1960s and 1970s [Kulkarni, 2006, 246-254]. Mexico, Argentina, Russia and the DRC are just a few countries whose incredible wealth of natural resources has not translated into meaningful growth. OPEC nations have generally seen mixed results from the development of their natural resources. Countries such as Kuwait, Qatar and the UAE have prospered, while countries including Iraq, Yemen, Oman and to some extent Iran, have experienced economic and societal difficulties.

Specific to the mineral resources, concerns have been raised about how focusing on this particular sector can lead to a myriad of problems. Baldwin (1966) and Hirschman (1958) argued that focusing on mineral resources to fuel export growth could not benefit the overall economy because of the lack of technological and factor linkages with the rest of the economy [Davis, 1995, 3; Baldwin, 1966; Hirschman, 1958, 109-110]. Research on the environmental effects of mineral resource extraction is contentious and numerous. Indeed, large sections of empirics literature on Dutch disease and Immiserizing Growth are inconsistent. It is therefore very important to examine the possibility of Dutch disease against a backdrop of economic policies being pursued within a developing country.

IMMISERIZING GROWTH, DUTCH DISEASE AND THE KYRGYZ REPUBLIC

Background

The Kyrgyz Republic emerged from the dissolution of the Soviet Union with an uncertain economic future. After decades under a centrally planned economy, the disintegration of the Soviet Union resulted in the breakdown of *de jure* business and economic linkages with the rest of the former Soviet world. Policymakers in Bishkek no longer could rely upon Soviet organs to help integrate the Kyrgyz economy with the rest of the Soviet Union and the world [Broadman, 2006, 52]. Instead, the Kyrgyz Republic had to realign its economic policies and strategy to an increasingly open and integrated international economy. After a formal political transition to independence in 1991, the Kyrgyz Republic began transitioning to a market and rule-based economy [WTO Trade Policy Review Body (TPRB), 2007, 1].

A significant part of this transition has occurred in the mining industry. The discovery of significant gold reserves late in the 1980s provided hope for the newly independent Kyrgyz government that the country could benefit from the development of its natural resources. The new government sought out Western mining firms to help develop these reserves [Kumtor, 2009, 37]. Commercial gold production began in 1997 at the Kumtor mine in a joint venture of Kyrgyzaltyn, the state-owned mining company and Cameco, a Canadian uranium and gold firm [WTO TPRB, 2007, 89]. In its first year of production, the mine exported USD 184.8 million of gold [IMF Statistical Appendix, 2005, 18]. Kyrgyzaltyn has since undertaken a number of gold-mining, mining plant, and gold refinery joint ventures and other agreements with foreign companies from within Central Asia and around the world [WTO TPRB, 2007, 90]. Due to its significant size and importance to the Kyrgyz economy, Kyrgyzaltyn has remained a state-owned firm.

The nascent development of the gold industry in the Kyrgyz Republic deserves serious consideration. Commercial gold production began in 1997, and in just four years (2001), gold accounted for 47.2 per cent of all the country's exports. Until recently, gold has annually accounted for over a quarter or more of all exports. Annual revenues from gold exports have steadily risen since the inception of commercial gold production, from USD184.8 million in 1997 to USD 463.5 million in 2008 [IMF Statistical Appendix, 2005, 18; IMF Country Report, 2009, 29]. The rise of gold exports has had a significant impact upon where the country exports its merchandise goods. In 2005, two of its four largest export markets were Switzerland and the United Arab Emirates [WTO TPRB, 2007, 14]. With reserves dwindling and prices at all time highs, the government wants to gets as much benefit from the resources as it can. Gold production, then, has profoundly altered the structure of the Kyrgyz export market. Coupled with consumer spending, it is an important driver the Kyrgyz economy.

Analysis

The gold sector's considerable growth and importance to the Kyrgyz economy makes it an appropriate example to test Bhagwati's Immiserizing Growth Hypothesis and Corden's Dutch disease models. This section examines how the gold sector may have affected other economic variables in the country. Given that the majority of the country's gold resources are controlled by state-run Kyrgyzaltyn, this chapter examines whether policymakers have been too zealous in developing this particular sector of the economy. It analyzes the effects of the gold export sector on: inflation, the exchange rate, growth in foreign reserves, growth in real wages, effects on other export sectors, unemployment and fiscal and monetary balances. The growth of the gold industry is then placed within the larger economic and trade framework of the country to better understand the effects of the sector on other economic variables. (*Unless otherwise mentioned, all data presented from this section of the chapter come from the following sources: World Bank Trade and Development Indicators, the IMF, the National Bank of the Kyrgyz Republic, COMEX, and the WTO Trade Policy Review Body*)

Presented in the preceeding theoretical section, Corden argued that a case of Dutch disease begins with an expansion of a boom sector in an economy. Corden laid out three possible ways this could happen (increases in technology, discovery of resources, increases in world prices of the good). In this case, all three events occurred. Discoveries of gold reserves in the Kyrgyz Republic were followed by joint-ventures with Western firms and Kyrgyzaltyn to develop the finds. Western mining firms brought the highest levels of technology and expertise to the extraction and production of Kyrgyz gold. Discovery, extraction and growth have also paralleled historic changes in the price of gold. Following figure 19.2 charts the growth in the price of gold over the past 20 years.

Figure 19.2: Courtesy of Goldprice.org

Dramatic increases in the price in gold following the beginning of commercial production of gold in the Kyrgyz Republic indicate the possibility that subsequent growth in the gold sector could play a role in other economic variables in the economy. Although jumps in prices, increases in technology and the discovery of new reserves are not sufficient conditions to explain Dutch disease or Immiserizing Growth, they can serve as warning signs for the rest of the economy.

The gold sector became an important part of the economy immediately after production began in 1997. Figure 19.3 charts the growth in gold revenues and the gold sector's share in merchandise exports since 1997. From 1997-2001, the gold sector became the dominant player in the Kyrgyz export sector. Shares in the export sector fell as production at the Kumtor mine fell during the middle of this last decade, but production has begun to pick up again. Gold revenues have more steadily climbed over time, and the recent sharp increases in international gold prices have consequently led to spikes in gold revenue [IMF Statistical Appendix, 2005; WTO TPB, 2007; IMF Country Report, 2009].

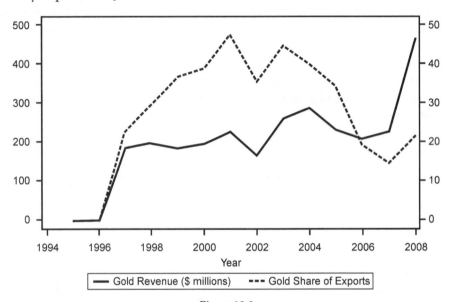

Figure 19.3

Effects on Selected Monetary Variables

As per Corben's Dutch disease model, increasing gold revenues and share of gold exports should have led to a quick and large inflow of foreign reserves. Figure 19.4 charts the inflow of gross international reserves into the country beginning in 1995. Spikes did not occur in gross international reserves until 2003, as the share in gold exports began to decline [National Bank of the Kyrgyz Republic, 2010; IMF Statistical Appendix, 2005]. It is possible that increases in gross international reserves could have experienced a lag effect with respect to the increases in gold market share and export share. Another possible reason for this weak correlation between the two variables could be explained by the way in which Kumtor and other gold mines were taxed. Gold sector firms were the beneficiaries of significant tax concessions and holidays from

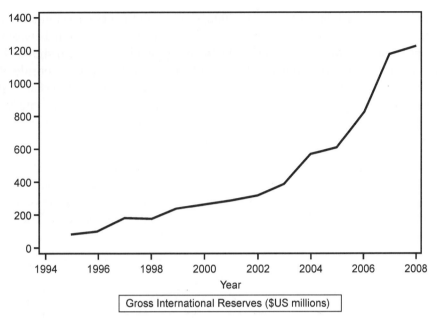

Figure 19.4

the inception of commercial production up until 2004, when the tax code was updated and the gold sector was subjected to a standardized tax regime.

Sequentially, inflows of international reserves would have had two effects on the economy. The country would have experienced inflationary pressures from the increases in wealth and the inflow of international reserves. Domestic inflationary pressures and the inflow of foreign reserves would have lead to an appreciation of the domestic currency. When gauging whether or not a country has experienced Dutch disease, these two particular factors are important, because revaluatory and inflationary pressures can cause significant pain in other areas of the economy. Figures 19.5 measures the annual inflation (GDP deflator) against per cent changes in gross international reserves. Figure 19.6 measures the exchange rate (som/USD) against total gross international reserves.

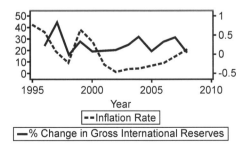
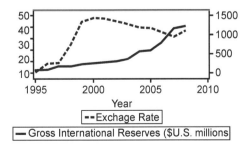

Figures 19.5 and 19.6

The picture here is mixed. From 1998 until 2002, changes in the price level mirrored, to some extent, per cent changes in gross international reserves. The correlation between the two variables has been less strong since 2002. On the other hand, Figure 19.6 shows clearly that as gross international reserves remained stagnant, the Som depreciated considerably. Only when reserves began to flow in more heavily did the currency begin to appreciate. This follows what is generally predicted to happen in an economy with a floating exchange rate regime, and confirms our hypothesis that that as foreign reserves begin to flow into a country, the exchange rate begins to appreciate.

However, upon closer examination, it is difficult to argue that the growing gold export sector caused an appreciation of the Som. Figure 19.7 charts growth in the gold export sector against the exchange rate. In fact, the opposite occurred. As the export sector of the economy began more heavily relying upon gold exports, the Som depreciated considerably. The relationship between rising gold exports and a depreciating Som appears strong.

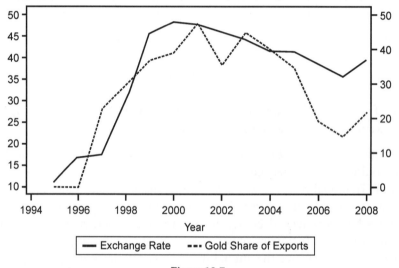

Figure 19.7

The relationship between gold shares and the Som/USD rate becomes stronger in the presence of other variables. Corben's model argues that the biggest determinants of exchange rate movement are growth in the boom sector, inflows of foreign reserves and inflation. Using an analysis of variance test, we can see how variations in the Som can be explained by the growth of the gold sector, gross international reserves and inflation. Data from 1995-2008 are used. The results are shown in Output 1 below. The results were statistically significant at all levels. Gross international reserves, gold shares of exports and the GDP deflator collectively explain nearly 85 per cent of the variance in the exchange rate ($R^2 = 0.845449$). Two of the three variables (gross international reserves and gold shares of export) are individually significant. Problems of multicollinearity appear not to be evident here, as gold shares of export seem to not have much of an effect on either gross international reserves (*see* Figures 19.2 & 19.3) or inflation.

OUTPUT 1

#Number of Observations Read	14
Number of Observations Used	14

Source	DF	Sum of Squares	Mean Square	F Value	Pr > F
Model	3	1691.663313	563.887771	18.23	0.0002
Error	10	309.242271	30.924227		
Corrected Total	13	2000.905583			

R-Square	Coeff Var	Root MSE	Exchange Rate Mean
0.845449	15.49768	5.560956	35.88250

Source	DF	Type III SS	Mean Square	F Value	Pr > F
Gross International	1	292.075232	292.075232	9.44	0.0118
Gold Share of Export	1	1090.423230	1090.423230	35.26	0.0001
Inflation Rate	1	38.932054	38.932054	1.26	0.2881

Nonetheless, given that Corben's model predicts that growth in the boom sector will ultimately result in the appreciation of the currency, it is difficult to make an argument that the Kyrgyz Republic has been victimized by Dutch disease. Proponents of the Corben model will argue, however, that movements in the *real* exchange rate must to determine whether or not the boom sector has caused real appreciation. Figure 19.8, taken from a most recent IMF study on the Kyrgyz Republic, shows the distinction between the nominal effective exchange rate and the real effective exchange rate.

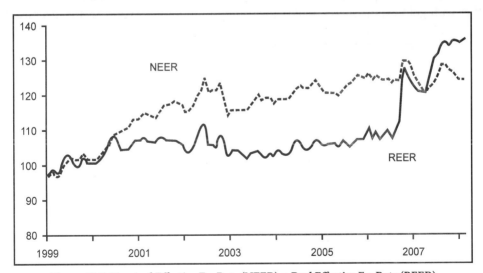

Figure 19.8: Nominal Effective Ex. Rate (NEER) v. Real Effective Ex. Rate (REER)

Source: IMF Country Report 2009, 18.

The real effective exchange rate (REER) indicates that appreciation of the currency since 2000 is less than it would appear otherwise. This would temper the relationship between the currency appreciation and the reduction in gold sector exports. Further, recent sharp REER appreciation in the currency (against NEER depreciation) coincides with a rebound in gold production, gold revenues, gold prices and the increases in gross reserves [National Bank of the Kyrgyz Republic, 2010; IMF Country Report, 2009]. Consequently, there is evidence to suggest that Dutch disease began to enter the economy starting in 2006.

Effects on Terms of Trade, Structure of Trade, and Trade Competitiveness

Recent real appreciation of the currency has had a deleterious effect on the country's terms of trade (*see* Figure 19.9) [IMF Country Report, 2009, 29; WTO TPRB, 2007, 4]. Nominally, appreciation of the currency since 2000 has led to recurring loss in terms of trade for the country. This development fits well with Bhagwati's Immiserizing Growth Hypothesis. Deteriorating terms of trade and rising real wages (wage growth has generally outpaced inflation growth, *see* Figure 19.10) have hurt export competitiveness. The ratio of manufacturing sector wages to per capita GDP (a proxy for unit labour costs) is higher in Kyrgyzstan than elsewhere in Central Asia [IMF Country Report, 2009, 19]. Recent data show that out of all CIS economies, the Kyrgyz Republic ranked lowest in competitiveness.

The Kyrgyz Republic's reliance on gold exports has hurt other export sectors of the economy. Agriculture's share of merchandise exports has fallen significantly, relative to gold exports, since commercial gold production began (*see* Figure 19.11) [World Bank: Trade and Development Indicators, 2009]. More broadly, increases in gold's share of exports have paralleled overall concentration in the export sector. Figure 19.12 shows the country's export concentration index together with gold export shares. Gold's inclusion in the Kyrgyz export sector has meant that

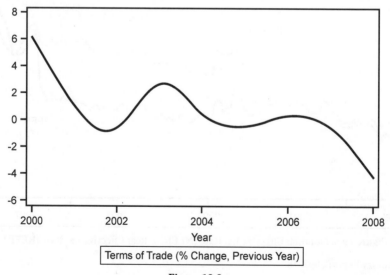

Figure 19.9

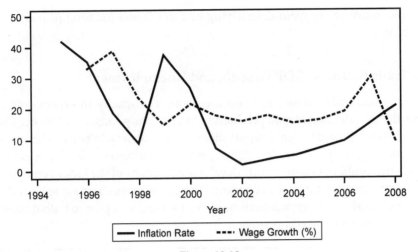

Figure 19.10

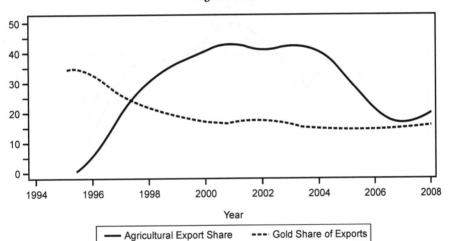

Figure 19.11

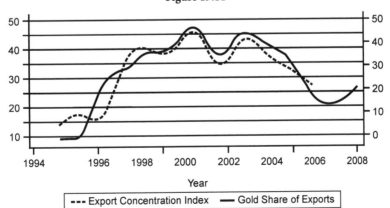

Figure 19.12

the country has moved away from diversifying its exports and focusing primarily on gold (as well as electricity).

Effects on Trade Balances, GDP Growth, and Unemployment

The country's goods trade balance rests on the country's capacity to export gold (*see* Figure 19.13). Since the introduction of gold production in 1997, the goods trade balance (as a per cent of GDP) has closely followed the gold export share in the economy. When gold exports dominate the export economy, the goods trade balance performs fairly well. Clearly, as gold shares fell, the goods balance could not recover. This development speaks of the lack of competitiveness in the merchandise export sector of the economy. As gold reserves continue to dwindle, and gold prices reach their peak, the Kyrgyz government must formulate a plan to both diversify exports, and make those exports more competitive.

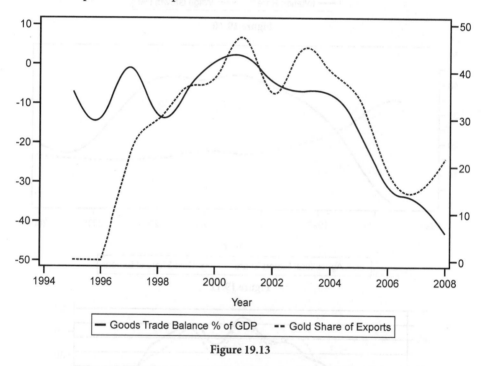

Figure 19.13

Concurrently, the country's current account has moved with the growth/recession of gold exports (*see* Figure 19.14). This kind of erratic movement in the current account is another problematic consequence of Dutch disease.

It should not be surprising then that gold has played a critical role in the total growth in the economy. Figure 19.15 plots gold revenue (USD millions) with GDP growth (annual per cent change). This gives us an indication of how overall GDP program has been influenced by the growth in the gold sector. The effect of gold on GDP growth is so strong that most statistical

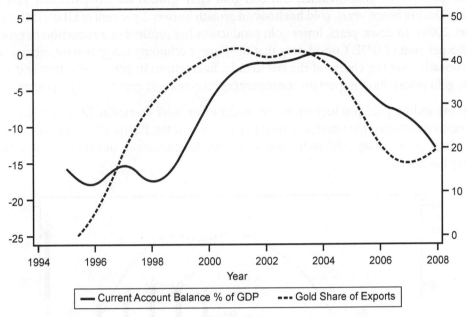

Figure 19.14

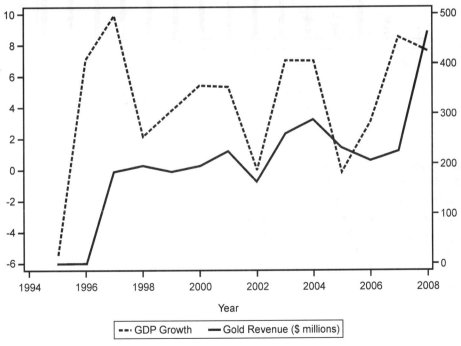

Figure 19.15

indices specify both gold-included and non-gold GDP growth for any particular year in the country. During boom years, gold has boosted growth by over 2 per cent of GDP [IMF Country Report, 2009]. In down years, lower gold production has resulted in a reduction of growth by over 2.5 per cent of GDP. Considering that the Kyrgyz economy has grown on average 4.8 per cent annually over the course of the last decade, fluctuations in gold production and sales, as well as gold prices, have important consequences on economic growth and prosperity.

Lastly, expanding gold production, in the midst of broader economic liberalization reforms, has negatively affected the unemployment rate in the country. Figure 19.16 illustrates that amid a backdrop of booming gold sector and economic liberalization, unemployment within the country has risen.

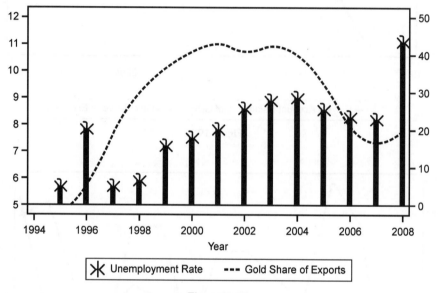

Figure 19.16

Certainly, there are many reasons why unemployment occurs in an economy, and this case is no different. However, the gold export sector employs relatively few people. Increasing export shares of gold and declining export shares of agriculture have played a role in the increasing unemployment. Additionally, the lack of competitiveness, high unit labour costs, and rising real wages contribute to the problem. Output 2 which follows is a correlation matrix comparing unemployment with other important variables we have considered thus far. For important statistical conclusions to be drawn from the data, more data will need to be gathered. With that said, initial data here indicates several interesting and important relationships to be considered for future policy prescriptions.

OUTPUT 2

Unemployment Pearson Coefficients with Selected Variables

Pearson Correlation Coefficients Prob > |r| under H0: Rho=0 Number of Observations	Exchange Rate	Wages Index (2005=100)	Inflation Rate	Agricultural Export Share	Export Concentration Index	Gold Share of Exports
Unemployment	0.56916	0.77944	−0.37832	−0.50409	0.51583	0.24873
	0.0336	0.0010	0.1823	0.0661	0.0860	0.3912
	14	14	14	14	12	14

Pearson Correlation Coefficients Prob > |r| under H0: Rho=0 Number of Observations	Gold Revenue ($ millions)	Terms of Trade % change	Gross International Reserves			
Unemployment	0.70688	−0.75310	0.40541			
	0.0047	0.0192	0.3669			
	14	9	7			

With regards to Dutch disease and Immiserizing Growth in particular, two particular relationships are important. Corben's model predicts that an appreciating currency will hurt non-gold export sectors' profit margins. It also predicts a structural shift in the economy, with labour and capital reallocating to other sectors (namely the boom sector and non-tradables). Unemployment would occur during this transition and structural reform process, especially if there is a significant skill-level gap between lagging sectors and other sectors of the economy. In our case, though, unemployment is related to depreciation in the currency. This clearly is a contradiction. In contrast, as per Immiserizing Growth predictions, declining terms of trade are associated with unemployment. This makes intuitive sense. Lagging export prices (in non-boom sectors) and rising import input prices place pressure on exporting firms to stay competitive. This price phenomenon, coupled with structural shifts in the economy away from agriculture could be a critical determinant in unemployment. Currency depreciation can hurt export industries that rely upon imported inputs in the production process. Coupled with declining terms of trade and rising wages, increasing import input costs can make export industries less competitive, regardless if currency depreciation by itself makes an export industry more competitive.

PLACING THE 'BOOM SECTOR' IN A WIDER ECONOMIC CONTEXT

Commercialization of the gold sector in Kyrgyzstan followed important concomitant economic and trade reforms in the country. In particular, the country pursued a rather extreme trade liberalization regime to integrate itself with the rest of the global economy. As a result, the

Kyrgyz Republic has 'one of the most open trade and investment regimes in the region and also among comparable developing countries' [WTO TPRB, 2007, 19]. The IMF's 2005 Trade Restrictiveness Index (IMF-TRI) ranks the country's trade regime as even more open than both the United States and the European Union [Allen, 2005, 17]. In 1998, the country became a WTO member. The Kyrgyz Republic's WTO accession is regionally unprecedented, as it is the only Central Asian state to have successfully entered into the organization. As a result, the country has eliminated virtually all protectionist measures in their attempt to tailor the country's trade regime to global rules and norms.

Pursuing such a quick and rigorous trade liberalization regime has resulted in the country becoming more and more reliant on trade. Indeed, its import and export integration policies have allowed the country to gain access to the world's imports and the world to its exports. No doubt, this development has aided the exporting gold sector as it reaches out to new markets. That Switzerland and the UAE have become vital export markets for Kyrgyz gold underscores this point. However, trade liberalization has exposed domestic producers to global competition. Considering that the country ranks 122nd out of 134 countries surveyed on competitiveness, it does not take long to realize the type of impact trade liberalization has had on export diversity and unemployment [IMF Country Report, 2009, 19].

CONCLUDING THOUGHTS AND IMPLICATIONS
FOR FUTURE RESEARCH

Regardless of how you define and interpret Dutch disease or Immiserizing Growth, pursuing an export strategy that relies heavily on natural resources or other primary export products can be precarious. Big mining projects are also a magnet of local and regional attention, because they are increasingly judged on their ability to bring wealth to local citizens. In the Kyrgyz Republic, these gold mines have been contentious. Protestors have blocked access to various mines across the Kyrgyz Republic in an effort to protest environmental and equity concerns [Sershen, 2007]. The government's intimate dealings with the gold sector are also a concern.

To gain a better understanding of how the gold sector in the Kyrgyz Republic affects other macroeconomic variables, and whether it is an appropriate example of Dutch disease or Immiserizing Growth, more time will need to pass and more data will have to be gathered. Commercial gold production has taken place in the country for just 14 years. With gold reserves dwindling, it will be appropriate to revisit this issue as policymakers in Bishkek seek alternatives to the wealth created through the export of gold. At first glance, while the gold sector has brought unquestioned wealth to the Kyrgyz economy, structural problems plague the economy. GDP growth is erratic, unemployment and inflation are increasing, and the country is as dependent on regional imports to sustain consumption as ever. The political coup earlier this year places focus and scrutiny on the government. It is up to the interim government now to assess the gold sector's place in the economy, and how wealth generated from these critical exports can bring gains in welfare to everyone.

REFERENCES

1. Allen, Mark (2005). *Review of the IMF's Trade Restrictiveness Index. Policy Development and Review Department: IMF.* 20 pages.

2. Baldwin, Robert E. (1966). *Economic Development and Export Growth: A Study of Northern Rhodesia, 1952-1960.* University of California Press: Berkeley, CA.

3. Bhagwati, Jagdish (1958). 'Immiserizing Growth: A Geometrical Note.' *The Review of Economic Studies.* Vol. 25 No. 3, pp. 201-205.

4. Broadman, Harry (2006). From Disintegration to Reintegration: Eastern Europe and the Former Soviet Union in International Trade. *International Bank for Reconstruction and Development/World Bank.* 440 pages.

5. Bruno, Michael and Jeffrey Sachs (1982). 'Energy and Resource Allocation: A Dynamic Model of the Dutch Disease'. *National Bureau of Economic Research Working Paper Series.* Working Paper No. 852, pp. 1-38.

6. Chang, Ha-Joon and Ilene Grabel (2004). *Reclaiming Development: An Alternative Economic Policy Manual.* Zed Books, 246 pages.

7. Corden, W.M. (1984). 'Booming Sector and Dutch Disease Economics: Survey and Consolidation.'*Oxford Economic Papers*, New Series. Volume 36, No. 3. pp. 359-380.

8. Davis, Graham A. (1995). 'Learning to love the Dutch disease: Evidence from the mineral economies.' *World Development.* Volume 23, Issue 10. pp. 1765-1779.

9. Epstein, G. and E. Yeldan (2008). 'Inflation Targeting, Employment Creation and Economic

10. Development: Assessing the Impacts and Policy Alternatives', *International Review of Applied Economics*, Vol. 22, No. 2 pp. 131-145.

11. 'Gold Price History.' *Goldprice.org. http://goldprice.org/gold-price-history.html*

12. Hirschman, Albert O. (1958). *The Strategy of Economic Development.* Yale University Press: New Haven, CT.

13. International Monetary Fund (2009). *Kyrgyz Republic: 2009 Article IV Consultation and First Review Under the 18-Month Arrangement Under the Exogenous Shocks Facility—Staff Report; Staff Supplement; Public Information Notice and Press Release on the Executive Board Discussion; and Statement by the Executive Director for the Kyrgyz Republic. IMF Country Report No. 09/209.* International Monetary Fund: New York (July 2009), 101 pages.

14. International Monetary Fund (2005). *Kyrgyz Republic: Statistical Appendix. IMF Country Report No. 05/31.* International Monetary Fund: New York (February 2005), 44 pages

15. Kulkarni, Kishore (2006). 'Has International Trade Benefited LDCs? – India's Case.' in *Readings in International Economics: Selected Writings of Prof. Kishore G. Kulkarni.* pp. 139-151.

16. Kulkarni, Kishore (2006). 'Impact of Dutch Disease on an Economy: A Case of Nigeria.' in *Readings in International Economics: Selected Writings of Prof. Kishore G. Kulkarni.* pp. 246-255.

17. 'Kumtor: Socio-economic Impact.' *Centerra Gold* (2010). *http://www.centerragold.com/properties/kumtor/impact/*

18. National Bank of the Kyrgyz Republic (2010). 'Gross international reserves.' *http://www.nbkr.index1.jsp?item=130&lang=ENG*

19. National Bank of the Kyrgyz Republic (2010). *Inflation Report: January 2010.* The National Bank of the Kyrgyz Republic: Bishkek, 43 pages.

20. Redmond, Dan, Tommaso Raponi & Jack Seto (2009). 'Technical Report on the Kumtor Gold Mine Kyrgyz Republic for Centerra Gold, INC. and Cameco Corporation.' 172 pages.

21. Sershen, Daniel (2007). 'Rethinking Kyrgyzstan's Gold Profits.' *Eurasianet.org. http://www. eurasianet.org/departments/insight/articles/eav030807a.shtml*

22. 'The Dutch disease.' *Economist* (1977), Volume 265 Issue 7004. *http://0-www.tlemea.com.bianca. penlib.du.edu/economist/results-view.asp?searchText=dutch%20disease&searchDate=1977&resperp age=10&respage=0&restotal=3&sort=aFDATE&resnumber=0&DocId=590669&Index=D%3a%5c database%5cuserdata%5cEcon2006&HitCount=11&hits=21+12a+12b+197+198+315+316+81f+8 20+10bc+10bd+&bhcp=1&lzm=M43*

23. Trade Policy Review Body (2007). *Trade Policy Review: Kyrgyzstan.* World Trade Organization. 119 pages.

24. World Bank (2010). 'Data and Statistics for the Kyrgyz Republic.' *http://web.worldbank.org/ WBSITE/EXTERNAL/COUNTRIES/ECAEXT/KYRGYZEXTN/0,,menuPK:305786~pagePK:14113 2~piPK:141109~theSitePK:305761,00.html*

25. World Bank (2010). 'World Trade Indicators: Benchmarking Policy and Performance.' *http://web. worldbank.org/WBSITE/EXTERNAL/TOPICS/TRADE/0,,contentMDK:22421950~pagePK:148956 ~piPK:216618~theSitePK:239071,00.html*

26. World Bank (2009). '2009 World Development Indicators.' *http://ddp-ext.worldbank.org/ext/ DDPQQ/member.do?method=getMembers&userid=1&queryId=135*

20 | Testing the Heckscher-Ohlin Theorem
Bilateral Trade Between South Africa and Zimbabwe

Stuart King

CHAPTER SUMMARY

Studies in international trade all lead to the same conclusion: countries that engage in foreign trade reap significant economic benefits. Adam Smith first popularized this topic by discussing the role of international trade in his most famous work *Wealth of Nations* (1776). As Smith pointed out, international trade results in an international division of labour and production specialization. Since that time, and given the confirmed benefits of international trade, economists have sought to define how and why countries engage in the types of trade they do. Multiple theories and models have been put forth to describe international trade, but the focus of this chapter is to elaborate on and test the popular Heckscher-Ohlin (H-O) theory of international trade. The research question of interest is whether the H-O theorem is an accurate model for modern trade, specifically in the case of trade relations between South Africa and Zimbabwe, and to what extent Paul Samuelson's extension of the model has been manifest in these two countries.

The Heckscher-Ohlin model of international trade states that for a mutually beneficial trade to occur, a country will specialize in and export that commodity that uses the country's abundant factor intensively. Using a set of simple assumptions, this theory has been a benchmark for many empirical studies regarding trade patterns and relations for nearly a century. Given the narrow parameters established by its assumptions, many have sought to disprove the validity and reliability of this economic theory. This chapter works to theoretically describe the H-O theorem, as well as compare and contrast the varying theoretical and empirical findings of past tests. In addition, attention is paid to the real-world manifestation of factor price equalization as proposed by Paul Samuelson.

Research into the bilateral trade between South Africa and Zimbabwe proves that even in the twenty-first century the Heckscher-Ohlin theory maintains a level of descriptive significance when evaluating trade flows. Throughout the study South Africa is assumed to be a capital-abundant country that exports capital-intensive goods to Zimbabwe, and Zimbabwe is assumed to be labour-abundant and export labour-intensive goods to South Africa. Analysis of each country's top ten exports confirms these assumptions, with slight variability observed in South Africa's trade to Zimbabwe. Thorough country studies reveal extreme domestic market distortion within Zimbabwe, and the corresponding greater demand for agricultural imports from South Africa. Economic and political turmoil within Zimbabwe has also contributed to high immigration to South Africa in search of wages above subsistence levels.

This chapter has been divided into three sections to aid in the understanding and test of the identified research topic: (1) theoretical section, (2) empirical section, and (3) conclusion. The theoretical section is designed to lay the foundation of the trade theory in question: the Heckscher-Ohlin (H-O) theorem. In this section, clear explanation of the model and its underlying assumptions will be discussed in detail to establish a working knowledge of the H-O theorem. In addition, attention will be paid to Paul Samuelson's extension of the H-O theorem to help identify the pre- and post-conditions of international trade and the supposed theory of Factor Price Equalization (FPE). This section will conclude with an elaborate literature review of past tests of the H-O theorem to help identify any holes in the theory's logic and to set the stage for its global significance in the twenty-first century. The empirical section will encompass the statistical analysis and test of the trade theory by examining the respective trade between South Africa and Zimbabwe. To test the theory, bilateral trade data will be referenced to see whether the H-O theorem holds true in the case of South Africa and Zimbabwe. This section will begin with country studies of each respective country to provide the reader with the necessary background information needed to perform a thorough analysis of each country's trade. This section will also detail the various trade unions between South Africa, Zimbabwe, and the surrounding countries, as well as highlight certain key economic indicators including Gross Domestic Product (GDP), GDP per capita, unemployment, and inflation.

Finally, the conclusion section will review several of the key topics described throughout the chapter and help draw some general conclusions for the validity of the H-O theorem as it pertains to trade between South Africa and Zimbabwe.

THEORETICAL EXPLANATION

Theory Defined

Swedish economists Eli Heckscher and Bertil Ohlin (Nobel Prize, 1977) proposed in 1912 that a country would specialize in the production of and export that commodity whose production uses that country's abundant factor intensively. Thus, a mutually beneficial trade will occur even if the technology of production of the same good across countries is the same due to differences in factor endowments. This theory is both an extension of the Theory of Absolute Advantage proposed by Adam Smith, and the Theory of Comparative Advantage put forth by David Ricardo. To more fully understand the significance of this model it is important to effectively define the various aspects that make this theory unique. As in most economic models, a series of key assumptions must be identified to help frame the H-O theorem:

- The theory is based upon a $2 \times 2 \times 2$ model of international trade – two countries, two goods, and two factors of production [capital (K) and labour (L)]
- There are no transportation costs, and both countries have free trade policies
- Perfect competition exists within each country, therefore indicating that firms in each market are price takers, not price makers
- All production occurs under increasing cost conditions, which implies that resources will have diminishing marginal productivity, resulting in incomplete specialization
- Prices are set according to the average cost of production, which means that long-run profits are equal to zero
- Demand conditions are similar across countries; consumer preferences are assumed to be homothetic
- Technology of production is the same across countries, but differ according to factor endowments; production frontiers are concave to the origin
- Only goods are traded between two countries, factors are immobile.

Regarding factor endowments, there are two ways used to determine a country's factor abundance: (1) factor quantities and (2) factor prices. It is important to note that factor abundance always refers to a country, not a good.

1. Factor quantities

Suppose two countries (A and B) have two factors of production [capital (K) and labour (L)]. Factor abundance can be determined by observing their respective capital labour ratios, where:

$(K/L)_A$ = capital labour ratio in country A

$(K/L)_B$ = capital labour ratio in country B

If $(K/L)_A < (K/L)_B$, then it can be said that country A has a larger stock of labour (L) in comparison to the stock of capital (K), and thus country A would be considered a *labour abundant* and country B by default a *capital abundant*.

2. Factor prices

Suppose for the two factors of production (K and L), the 'price' of capital (K) is represented by the rental rate (r), and the 'price' of labour corresponds to the wage rate (w) for that economy. Factor abundance can therefore be determined by observing each country's respective wage rental ratios, where:

$(w/r)_A$ = wage rental ratio in country A

$(w/r)_B$ = wage rental ratio in country B

If $(w/r)_A < (w/r)_B$, then it can be said that country A is *labour abundant* and country B is *capital abundant*. A greater wage rental ratio designates a country as capital abundant because the excess supply of labour in that country has driven the wage rate down, and therefore a low wage rate compared to another country's wage rate will suggest higher labour abundance.

The next step in explaining the model is to define factor intensity. Factor intensity always refers to a good (product or service), not a country.

Suppose two goods (X and Y) and two factors of production [capital (K) and labour (L)]. Factor intensity therefore be determined by observing each goods' respective capital labour ratio, where:

$(K/L)_X$ = capital labour ratio required to produce one unit of good X

$(K/L)_Y$ = capital labour ratio required to produce one unit of good Y

If $(K/L)_X > (K/L)_Y$ we can conclude that it takes a greater amount of capital in comparison to labour to produce one unit of good X than it does to produce one unit of good Y. Therefore good X production is said to be *capital intensive* and good Y production is said to be *labour intensive*.

Given these definitions of factor abundance and factor intensity the H-O theorem concludes:

If $(K/L)_A > (K/L)_B$ [or $(w/r)_A > (w/r)_B$], which means country A is capital abundant and country B is labour abundant, and

$(K/L)_X < (K/L)_Y$, which means good X production is labour abundant and good Y production is capital abundant, then international trade will be mutually beneficial if country A specializes in the production of good Y and exports it to country B, and country B specializes in the production of good X and exports it to country A, thus resulting in the conclusion that a country should specialize in and export that production which uses the country's abundant factor intensively.

In 1936, the H-O theorem received greater theoretical significance when an American economist Paul Samuelson (Nobel Prize, 1971) extended the H-O theory of international trade to summarize the pre-trade and post-trade situation in a country and explained the equilibrium volume of international trade between two countries. Samuelson's theory of Factor Price Equalization (FPE) is summarized by the following analysis:

Suppose before trade $(w/r)_A > (w/r)_B$ and $(K/L)_X > (K/L)_Y$, which according to the H-O theory means that country A is *capital abundant* and country B is *labour abundant*, and good X production is *capital intensive* and good Y production is *labour intensive*. As trade begins, according to the H-O theorem, country A will start specializing in the production of good X and export it to country B, and country B will start specializing in the production of good Y and export it to country A. Samuelson observed that under the assumption of full employment of resources, in order to produce more of a good, resources must come from lower production of the other good. In this example, for country A to increase its production of good X it must lower its production of good Y. However, lower production of good Y will release (free up) labour resources faster than capital resources because good Y production is labour intensive, and higher production of good X needs additional capital resources faster than labour since good X production is capital intensive. Therefore, with high demand and low supply, the rental rate (r) of capital in country A will begin to increase and the wage rate (w) will begin to decline as the labour supply increases due to lower good Y production. As country B begins to specialize in good Y production and export it to country A, the opposite will occur. For country B to produce more of good Y (the good that uses the country's factor abundance intensively), lower production of good X is necessary. However, lower production of good X releases capital faster than labour, and good Y production needs labour faster than capital. Therefore, the reciprocal effect occurs in country B, as the rental rate (r) of capital will begin to decline and the wage rate (w) will start to increase (Kulkarni, 2006: 305-306). Samuelson thus noted that after trade (w/r) $_A$ will start to decline, and (w/r)$_B$ will start to increase. It can then be said that international trade will reach an equilibrium trade volume when

$$(w/r)_A = (w/r)_B$$

This phenomenon is known as Factor Price Equalization (FPE) Theorem and can be used to explain the role of international trade in developing countries. Due to the theory of FPE, international trade is considered a perfect substitute for factor movement. Because the wage rental ratios will begin to equalize after trade begins, labour abundant developing countries will benefit from international trade by raising the wage rate, and the incentive for labour to migrate to higher wage paying countries will diminish. The opposite will occur in the capital abundant country, as capitalists will see a rise in the price of capital [rental rate (r)], and a decrease in the price of labour [wage rate (w)]. Therefore, according to the theory of FPE, it has been commonly accepted that international trade will benefit a country's abundant factor at the cost of its scarce factor. The FPE theorem also concludes that under less than the full employment of labour resources assumption, international trade would create more jobs in developing countries as labour specialization takes place. In addition, the import of capital intensive goods in developing countries is considered much more cost effective than through domestic production. The H-O-S (Heckscher-Ohlin-Samuelson) theorem therefore concludes that free trade can raise economic welfare and make economic development a reality.

As noted, the country's abundant factor will gain from trade and the scarce factor will lose. This results from the pattern of price changes (p* > p > p^a) [where p* = foreign market price, p = world market price, and p^a = domestic market price] according to the Stolper-Samuelson theorem. The marginal product of the abundant factor is lower in each country's abundant factor before trade; meaning its autarky 'price' equilibrium is lower without trade. Free trade allows the country to shift production towards the good that is intensive it that country's abundant factor, and export it, thereby absorbing the abundant factor without lowering its price (Feenstra, 2004: 35).

Literature Review

Quite possibly, the strongest case against the Heckscher-Ohlin theorem came from Wassily Leontief's 1953 study of US trade. Leontief used an input-output table for 1947 trade data to display the contributions by inputs to one unit of output for exported goods by the United

States, classifying exports by contribution of capital and labour. He quickly realized that US imports were arriving from many countries and/or sources and that it was impractical to test all goods from all different countries. He therefore used import substitutes (goods produced domestically) as a proxy for actual imports and tested the capital and labour contributions of these import substitutes. The use of import substitutes does not put the conclusion of the test in question, for according to the H-O theorem technology of production is the same across two countries. Under the assumption that the United States was a capital abundant country in 1947, Leontief expected to discover US exports to be capital intensive. Instead he found out that US exports were approximately 30 per cent more labour intensive than the import substitutes used to express foreign imports. This contradiction to the Heckscher-Ohlin theorem has been famously termed the 'Leontief Paradox'.

Since then economists have tried to rationalize Leontief's findings by using a series of explanations to account for this apparent paradox:

1. Leontief himself argued that US labour productivity in 1947 was most likely at least three times higher than labour productivity in the rest of the world. He contested that the United States' human capital (education, health, working habits) was much higher, and to arrive at a more accurate labour stock approximation, the labour force should be multiplied by a factor of three. In this case, the United States would become a labour abundant factor. However, other economists pointed out that US capital productivity is also higher than capital abroad, so Leontief withdrew his explanation.
2. Another explanation of Leontief's Paradox is the phenomenon known as Factor Intensity Reversal (FIR). FIR takes place when the same commodity is produced as a labour-intensive good in one country and as a capital-intensive good in another country. For example, sweater production in Bangladesh fits the H-O model of trade, as Bangladesh is a labour abundant country and sweater production in Bangladesh is labour intensive. If FIR does occur, then Leontief's use of import substitutes was a mistake, as sweater production would be a capital-intensive production in the United States. However, other studies have concluded that FIR takes place in only 16 per cent of all goods traded.
3. Others point out that the selection of 1947 was ill advised, for in 1947 to help create jobs for returning WWII veterans, the US congress placed heavy tariffs on labour-intensive imports. Researchers have used Leontief's method to test the H-O theorem in later years, discovering that the Leontief Paradox had indeed diminished, but had not disappeared completely (a topic discussed in greater details below).
4. In 1961, the Swedish economist Stephen Linder proposed that traditional trade theories assumed trade is dictated by the supply conditions of a country (price, cost of production, technology, etc.) are wrong, for in reality trade direction is mainly determined by demand conditions (tastes and preferences, expectations, incomes). Linder pointed out that in 1947, US consumers had a biased preference for capital-intensive goods such as cars, telephones, refrigerators, televisions, radios, etc.
5. Leontief's experiment only accounted for two factors of production, capital and labour. In reality, several factors of production are important to the division of labour. Robert Stern

and Keith Maskus repeated Leontief's study in 1981, with the inclusion of a third factor of production, and observed that that there was no longer a trade paradox (also discussed below).

In *An empirical investigation of the Heckscher-Ohlin theorem*, David Clifton and William Marxsen provide a new test of the H-O theorem by evaluating profit and wage content as an alternative to the classical capital and labour content described by the model, as this new data is perceived to be more reliable (1984: 33). In addition, to determine the factor abundance of a country, the GDP per worker was compared to the world's GDP per worker, concluding that a greater Gross Domestic Product to labour stock (GDP/L) ratio would suggest that country to be capital abundant. Using this GDP/L criterion, 1968 trade data for ten countries (Australia, Ireland, Israel, Japan, Kenya, Korea, New Zealand, the United Kingdom, and the United States) was used to evaluate trade pattern as they relate to the H-O theorem. Given that Israel, Kenya, and the United Kingdom failed the test, and that the chance of producing a similar result in favour of the H-O theorem was only 25 per cent likely, the study failed to confirm the theory at conventional significance levels; although the authors did identify several unusual circumstances within these three countries that could have significantly altered normal trade patterns (35-37). However, some empirical support was received for the H-O theorem from Richard Brecher and Ehsan Choudhri's study, in which the authors accounted for inter-industry factor price differences due to measurement errors, departures from long-run competitive equilibrium, and imperfect factor mobility (1993).

Adrian Wood feverously presents a study in favour of the H-O theorem in his paper *Give Heckscher and Ohlin a Chance!*. Wood points out that past studies of the H-O theorem have treated capital as if it were an immobile factor of production, when in reality it is extremely internationally mobile and thus should be excluded from the model. By comparing interest rates across countries, Wood contends that capital (other than infrastructure) is neither scarcer nor more expensive in developing countries as compared to developed countries (1994: 31). In his paper, Wood questions the application of the theory's assumptions arguing, 'The issue is simply whether or not they are sufficiently accurate to the H-O theory as a helpful description of (at least part of) reality, which is a matter of empirical evidence' (Milton Friedman's Positive Economics explanation) (31). A capital-output ratio (capital per unit of domestic value added) is presented as preferable to the capital-labour ratio to determine factor intensity, as a rise in the price of capital will effectively lead to a rise in the price of capital-intensive goods. Wood concludes that his skill-based H-O model from his capital intensity studies help explain North-South trade in manufactures, basing trade more on human, not physical, capital (39). However, Krugman and Obstfeld state Wood's findings on North-South trade should not be used to contradict the observation that the H-O theorem is not a good predictor of trade flows, because North-South trade in manufactures only accounts for 10 per cent of world trade (2006: 75).

As mentioned earlier, the Leontief Paradox was re-tested by Robert Stern and Keith Maskus in both 1958 and 1972 to determine if the paradox still held true. Using US factor endowments in physical capital, human capital, and unskilled labour, the authors compared the capital per man embodied in *net exports* compared to capital per man in *consumption*, and concluded that a reversal of the Leontief Paradox had taken place at some point between 1958 and 1972. The authors observed that the physical capital to labour ratio in the United States declined from 1.07 to 0.95 over this time period, and that the capital-labour ratio for net exports was less than in consumption (1981: 221).

In *Multicountry, Multifactor Tests of the Factor Abundance Theory*, Bown, Leamer, and Sveikauskas used a varied approach called the Heckscher-Ohlin-Vanek (HOV) theorem as a way to equate the factors embodied in a country's net exports to the country's excess supplies of factor endowments (1987: 791). The authors observed that a simultaneous relationship exists between trade, factor input requirements, and factor endowments, and it is too simplistic to rely on a generalized 2×2 model of trade. The study's methodology compared the amount of 12 factors embodied in the net exports of 27 countries in 1967 to the direct measures of factor endowments in each country to see if the theory held true. Test results did not support the hypothesis, as trade ran in the predicted direction less than 70 per cent of the time for two-thirds of the factors. The authors concluded that, 'The Heckscher-Ohlin model does poorly, but we do not have anything that does better. It is easy to find hypotheses that do as well or better in a statistical sense, but these alternatives yield economically unsatisfying parameter estimates' (805). It has been found that only when unlimited differences in productivities of factors across countries are allowed, do the HOV equations hold true. Therefore, exogenous and endogenous differences must be considered as underlying cause of varying trade patterns. Areas of additional study include geography and climate, colonial institutions, social capital, and labour efficiency (Feenstra, 2004: 60-61).

Similarly, Peter Schott's *One Size Fits All? Heckscher-Ohlin Specialization in Global Production* expands on the other determinants of trade such as technology differences, factor efficiency, and demand (2003: 686). In contrast to other H-O model studies, Schott provides a multiple-cone equilibrium that identifies countries that specialize in a particular subset of goods most appropriate given their factor endowments. Using 'H-O aggregates' and International Standard Industrial Classification (ISIC) industries Schott rejects the single-cone equilibrium and concludes that 'if high- and low-wage countries specialize in non-overlapping sets of goods, price-wage arbitrage may be reduced, or broken, depending upon the substitutability of goods' (705).

Daniel Trefler followed this study with an attempt to identify alternative models to the HOV theorem that prove statistically significant, as the HOV model had been repeatedly rejected. Trefler followed Leamer and Bowen by using data on technology, trade, and endowments, comparing the neutral technology differences between countries by assigning them a value less than one regarding estimated technology efficiency (Untied States = 1). From his study, he observed that technology differences with regard to efficiency do occur between countries (Bangladesh = 0.03; Panama = 0.28; New Zealand = 0.38; Belgium = 0.65; Switzerland = 0.79) (1037). Trefler therefore reached the conclusion that the HOV theorem does indeed perform poorly, but identified a somewhat meaningful alternative combining the Armington home bias with neutral international technology differences, causing many economists to drop the assumption that technologies are the same across countries (1995: 1044).

Paul Krugman and Maurice Obstfeld present yet another explanation of the lingering trade paradox in the United States by pointing out that the United States has an advantage by producing new, innovative products that may well be less capital-intensive than products whose technology of production have matured and become suitable for mass production. In essence, the United States might be exporting goods that use skilled labour (although still labour) very heavily, while it imports heavy manufactures (i.e. cars) that use large amounts of capita (2003: 73). In addition, 'while the Heckscher-Ohlin model has been less successful at explaining the actual patterns of international trade than one might hope, it remains vital for understanding the *effects* of trade, especially its effect on the distribution of income' (76).

EMPIRICAL STUDY

As can be seen from the theoretical explanation and literature review of the topic, the Heckscher-Ohlin theorem has an important place in the field of international economics. Whereas past studies of the H-O theorem are not in short supply and many economists have offered new extensions, explanations, and relevance to the model, the purpose of this chapter is to test its enduring applicability in the twenty-first century. To do so, an empirical study of the economies of South Africa and Zimbabwe has been conducted to test the validity of the H-O theorem as it pertains to these two countries' bilateral trade. Throughout this section we will be working under the assumption that South Africa is a capital abundant country that specializes in and exports capital-intensive goods, while Zimbabwe is a labour abundant country that specializes in and exports labour-intensive goods. By examining specific commodity trade between the two countries we will arrive at a conclusion as to whether the H-O theorem holds in the case of South Africa and Zimbabwe bilateral trade. Embedded in this study are the domestic characteristics of each economy that will further help explain why trade flows in the direction it does. We begin with a quick review of South Africa and Zimbabwe's respective political and economic histories, and the implications these events have had on the structure of each country's trade.

Historical Background

While under British rule, the country of South Africa formed a joint rule between the British ruling class and Afrikaners (formerly the Boers) in 1910, but did not gain full independence until 1961. In 1948, the elected National Party issued Apartheid rule (separate development of the races), benefiting the white minority at the cost of the black majority. Leading the opposition against the white minority Apartheid rule was the African National Congress (ANC). As internal unrest and foreign pressure mounted, the white-minority regime finally agreed to a peaceful transition to majority rule in 1994, when Nelson Mandela won the first multi-racial elections and officially ended the apartheid era. Since then, South Africa has sought to cure its national imbalances in housing, education, and healthcare, but these problems have proven more difficult than anticipated (CIA World Factbook, 2010). A country well endowed with agricultural land and mineral resources, South Africa owes its development from colonial status to the parallel investment in human and physical capital (Kowalski et al., 2008: 399-400). In many ways, the rise of precious metal prices can be contributed to South Africa's rise in world GDP, and has served as a platform to develop into a diversified, thriving economy. This, however, has caused a concern for over-reliance on one resource (Dutch Disease), as pearls, precious stones, and metals (diamonds, gold, and platinum) accounted for 21 per cent of South African exports in 2006.

Table 20.1: Inflation (%)

Year	Zimbabwe	South Africa	Year	Zimbabwe	South Africa	Year	Zimbabwe	South Africa
1965	2.50	4.07	1980	5.40	13.66	1995	22.59	8.68
1966	3.12	3.49	1981	13.15	15.25	1996	21.43	7.35
1967	2.37	3.54	1982	10.64	14.64	1997	18.74	8.60
1968	1.39	1.99	1983	23.12	12.30	1998	31.82	6.88
1969	0.37	3.24	1984	20.15	11.53	1999	58.52	5.18
1970	2.09	4.06	1985	8.49	16.29	2000	55.86	5.34
1971	3.03	5.71	1986	14.33	18.66	2001	76.72	5.70
1972	2.85	6.46	1987	12.47	16.16	2002	140.10	9.16
1973	3.11	9.59	1988	7.42	12.78	2003	598.70	5.86
1974	6.60	11.64	1989	12.88	14.73	2004	282.40	1.39
1975	10.01	12.52	1990	17.36	14.32	2005	302.10	3.40
1976	10.95	11.02	1991	23.34	15.34	2006	1097.00	4.64
1977	10.31	11.15	1992	42.07	13.88	2007	66212.00	5.00
1978	5.66	11.14	1993	27.59	9.72	2008	14.9 billion	11.30
1979	18.15	13.29	1994	22.26	8.94	2009	5.10	7.30

Source: International Futures; CIA World Factbook; DWCP - Zimbabwe.

Until the 1970s, trade policy was largely geared towards Import-Substitution Industrialization (ISI), but as economic objectives were not met, the country moved toward freer trade. After witnessing substantial growth in the 1970s, South Africa began to move back toward protectionist policies in the 1980s and 1990s due to domestic pressures and an ongoing debt crisis. Trade was gradually opened up throughout the remainder of the 1990s, but since 2000, this trade liberation has again been reversed, as the average tariff and duty rates have increased due to ongoing multilateral trade negotiations, preferential trading agreements, and industrial policy strategies with high protection (Kowalski et al. 2008: 398). South Africa's trade is quite dissimilar than other African countries based on its skill composition of labour as 9 per cent agriculture, 26 per cent industry, and 65 per cent services (2007 estimates). Even though South Africa has seen steady economic growth as a measure of GDP and is considered a middle-income country, it's unemployment rate remains high due to the disparate skill bases between the black majority and the capitalist white minority (24 per cent unemployment in 2009).

In 1923, the United Kingdom annexed Southern Rhodesia from the British South African Company. Independence was declared in 1965, but the United Kingdom refused to recognize this act due to the favouritism of white supremacy and inadequate voting rights for the black majority established by the 1961 constitution. The country's first free elections were held in 1979 and independence was finally granted in 1980, officially becoming the country of Zimbabwe. Between 1980 and 1990, Zimbabwe experienced positive economic growth of 2.9 per cent per annum through impressive agricultural yields, earning it the title of 'Breadbasket of Africa'. Robert Mugabe, Zimbabwe's one and only ruler, began his chaotic land redistribution campaign in 2000 in an attempt to equalize land holdings between black and white farmers. Unfortunately, Mugabe's campaign was riddled with corruption, abuses and injustices, proving to be the catalyst that threw Zimbabwe's economy into turmoil. As white farmers fled the country, Zimbabwe experienced a drastic reduction in food supply and a reversal of the positive economic growth which it had experienced during the 1980s. After another rigged election in 2002, President Mugabe launched Operation Restore Order in April 2005, resulting in the destruction of hundreds of thousands of homes and businesses mostly of the opposition party. In 2007, the government issued commodity price controls that ushered in a wave of panic buying and massive commodity shortages, plunging the country into even greater hyperinflation (see graph for annual inflation rates) (CIA World Factbook, 2010).

The recent crisis in Zimbabwe has been attributed to 'poor governance, economic mismanagement, and loss of support of the international community, all compounded by periods of drought' (Besada and Moyo, 2008: 2). In 2006, the portion of Zimbabweans living on less than USD1 per day was equal to 80 per cent. From the limited statistical figures available, we know that structural unemployment has been greater than 50 per cent since 2002 and even above 65 percent in 2005. An even more severe issue is the lack of economic opportunities for graduates, as only 10 per cent are effectively absorbed into the formal economy, resulting in 81 per cent of the total unemployed persons between the ages 15–29. Women also experience higher rates of unemployment than males, mainly due to historical discrimination and negative socialization in Zimbabwe (DWCP, 2009: 3). Dissimilar GDP and GDP per capita growth trends between South Africa and Zimbabwe can be observed by the following graphs.

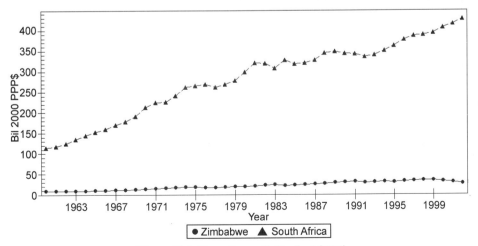

Figure 20.1: Gross Demestic Product (PPP)

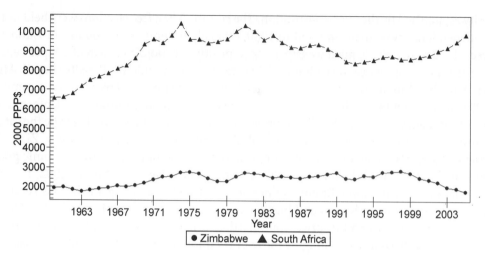

Figure 20.2: GDP Per Capita (PPP)

Source: International Futures.

Trade Between South Africa and Zimbabwe

South Africa has historically had a love-hate relationship with its surrounding countries. As noted, South Africa is by far the most developed of the southern African states and has experienced much higher levels of economic welfare. Southern African nations have resented South Africa's disproportional rise, and many believe apartheid South Africa to have stunted other countries' economic growth, resulting in a high level of animosity against South Africa. In addition, trade trends in southern Africa have historically followed a mercantilist framework, which is viewed to have served South Africa's interests because it is structurally dominant and able to find markets for its products, a characteristic absent from most neighboring countries. In 1992, the Southern African Development Community (SADC) was founded between Botswana, Lesotho, Madagascar, Malawi, Mozambique, Namibia, South Africa, Swaziland, Tanzania, Zambia, and Zimbabwe. Despite ill feelings, South Africa was welcomed into the SADC as the most developed industrial economy, believing that by opening up its markets to its neighbouring countries it would help solve the developmental asymmetries through technology transfer (Qobo, 2009: 54-55). The trade protocol signed in 1996 and implemented in 2000 was designed to establish a free trade area (FTA) through an asymmetric tariff phase-down process, but countries have been slow to engage in liberation policies and South Africa has maintained high levels of trade protectionism, two characteristics endemic to the region (Qobo, 2009: 55).

Besides both being members of the SADC, South Africa and Zimbabwe have a long history of bilateral relations. The bilateral trade agreement between South Africa and Zimbabwe was originally signed in 1964, but the newest version was normalized in 1996. The nature of this new agreement is a duty-free regime of preferential tariff quotas for dairy products, potatoes, birds and eggs, and woven fabric, subject to concessional tariff rates when meeting 75 per cent local (Zimbabwean) content (Qobo, 2009: 170). Due to Zimbabwe's recent political and economic collapse, much of the Zimbabwean economy has receded into the informal sector, as it is deemed as more reliable and lacks the bureaucratic corruption endemic to the formal economy. Even this informal trade provides insight into the relevance of the H-O theorem for trade between South Africa and Zimbabwe. Estimated informal imports into Zimbabwe from South Africa include electrical household items, motor vehicles and parts, industrial equipment and machinery spares, printers, industrial chemicals, cosmetics, pharmaceuticals, clothing, shoes, furniture, tires, bicycles, eggs, and cooking oil; while exports to South Africa include crafts, cane furniture, baskets, clothing, tie dye, bed and seat covers, reed mats, brooms and mops, agriculture goods, and whole and ground nuts (Qobo, 2009: 172). A quick analysis would suggest that goods such as industrial equipment, motor vehicles, and electrical household items are more capital intensive productions, while crafts, cane furniture, and agriculture goods are more labour intensive. Under the assumption that South Africa is a capital abundant country and Zimbabwe a labour abundant country, informal trade flows such as this lend support to the H-O model of international trade.

The following graph presents basic merchandise trade by commodity group and destination for both exports and imports for South Africa and Zimbabwe (2010). We see that exports by commodity group differ significantly for the two countries, as South Africa's top commodity is manufacturing exports with 54.5 per cent of its total exports, and Zimbabwe's most exported commodity group is agriculture with 44.4 per cent of total exports. Imports by commodity group also lend support to the H-O theorem, as Zimbabwe's top commodity group imported is manufactures (capital-intensive) as 54.4 of total imports. South Africa also imports and manufactures more than any other commodity group, and this could be due to its relative capital abundance compared to Zimbabwe, but labour abundance in respect to the rest of the world. In addition, it is clear that South Africa is a much more important trading partner for Zimbabwe than Zimbabwe is for South Africa, as 42 per cent of all of Zimbabwe's exports go to South Africa, and 62.1 of all of Zimbabwe's imports come from South Africa (WTO, 2010).

Table 20.2

South Africa 2008 - Merchandise Trade Exports By Commodity Group (%)		Zimbabwe 2008 - Merchandise Trade Exports By Commodity Group (%)	
Agriculture	8.7	Agriculture	44.4
Fuels and mining products	35.4	Fuels and mining products	24.3
Manufactures	54.4	Manufactures	31.1
By Destination (%)		By Destination (%)	
European Union	31.9	South Africa	42.0
Japan	11.0	European Union	22.1
United States	10.8	Bostswanna	9.3
China	5.8	Malawi	4.3
India	3.1	Zambia	4.1

Imports By Destination (%)		Imports By Destination (%)	
Agriculture	6.1	Agriculture	21.2
Fuels and mining products	25.7	Fuels and mining products	24.2
Manufactures	67.4	Manufactures	54.4
By Destination (%)		By Destination (%)	
European Union	31.3	South Africa	62.1
China	11.3	European Union	7.7
United States	8.0	Bostswana	7.6
Saudi Arabia	6.3	China	4.9
Japan	5.6	United States	4.0

Source: World Trade Organization.

Bilateral Trade

We now turn our attention to Zimbabwe's formal economy trade with South Africa, paying close attention to the top ten commodities traded according to trade statistics published by South Africa's Department of Trade and Industry for the years 2006–2009. Given the scarcity of trade data for Zimbabwe, we will use data published by South Africa for trade in both directions. The top export from Zimbabwe to South Africa for all four years was unwrought nickel. As the title describes, the nickel has not been worked into a finished condition (unwrought), indicating that this is purely a labour-intensive production. The same conclusion can be reached by examining the next two productions of unmanufactured tobacco and un-carded or combed cotton. The remaining commodities also represent labour-intensive productions, supporting our hypothesis that labour abundant Zimbabwe will specialize in and export labour-intensive goods to South Africa.

Table 20.3

Zimbabwe to South Africa			South Africa Imports (Rand '000)			
	Code	HS Title	2009	2008	2007	2006
1	7502	Unwrought nickel	376,434	878,609	1,581,761	851,499
2	2401	Unmanufactured tobacco; tobacco refuse	207,276	248,810	136,759	92,064
3	5201	Cotton, not carded or combed	207,032	168,856	115,877	169,930
4	2306	Oil-cake and other solid residues	60,856	63,539	36,518	12,034
5	5205	Cotton yarn (excl. sewing thread)	57,426	55,590	76,622	80,860
6	1207	Other oil seeds; andoleaginous fruits	51,581	8,890	6,594	6,168
7	4407	Wood sawn or chipped, slicled or peeled	41,042	75,254	83,588	115,375
8	2704	Coke and semi-coke of coal, of lignite or of peat	27,856	76,765	23,013	4,924
9	0602	Tea	24,429	19,925	18,175	26,841
10	6203	Men's or boys' suits, ensembles, jackets, blazers, trousers	23,747	33,109	34,680	27,640

Source: www.dti.gov.za

By comparison, South Africa does not initially appear to follow the pattern of trade strictly defined by the H-O theorem. Whereas the top commodity exported (petroleum) fits our assumption of capital-intensive production and export, the second most traded commodity (corn) would not suggest South Africa is solely exporting capital-intensive goods to Zimbabwe. One explanation for such trade flows is a direct result of Zimbabwe's ongoing political and economic instability. As previously mentioned, Zimbabwe's destructive land redistribution campaign resulted in a severe reduction in agricultural activity and massive food shortages. For this reason, it can be assumed that the rise in corn imports from South Africa do not follow the normal patterns of trade between the two countries, as Zimbabwe tries to manage its current food crisis with increased food imports. Other commodity groups that fit the H-O theorem include motor vehicles, structures, and various machinery, as each of these productions would be considered capital-intensive. Other exports to Zimbabwe that do not agree with the H-O model include sunflower seed, cereals, and cane sugar. Again, these trades can be explained by Zimbabwe's atypical domestic needs during this time of turmoil.

Table 20.4

South Africa to Zimbabwe			South Africa Exports (Rand '000)			
	Code	HS Title	2009	2008	2007	2006
1	2710	Petroleum oils and oils obtained from bituminous minerals	1,806,054	2,177,170	1,277,030	1,389,131
2	1005	Maize (corn)	614,936	2,531,271	66,052	480,264
3	8704	Motor vehicles for the transport of goods	441,131	819,097	469,855	290,489
4	1512	Sunflower-seed, safflower or cotton-seed oil and fractions	434,817	118,931	33,642	46,272
5	7308	Structures (excl. prefabricated buildings)	383,031	223,949	43,844	25,960
6	3401	Seep; Organise	360,987	177,521	56,341	33,284
7	3105	Mineral or chemical fertilisers	309,877	347,941	197,710	184,153
8	1103	Cereal groats, meal and pellets	271,470	111,075	1,937	4,507
9	8474	Machinery for sorting, screening, separating, washing, crushing	206,461	169,437	82,563	82,984
10	1701	Cane or beet sugar & chimically pure sucrose	202,958	26,402	464	241

Source: www.dti.gov.za

Factor Price Equalization (FPE)

Alexander Gerschenkron (1962) identifies a presumable 'catch-up advantage' for less developed countries, in the ability to apply and use technologies developed in other countries that would allow a country to pursue rapid development, suggesting international convergence of macro and micro economic fundamentals. Whereas the FPE theory states that international trade will move factor prices towards equality; theoretical, empirical, and historical aspects suggest that factor prices might not achieve complete *equality*, but move towards *convergence* as trade barriers fall (Rassekh and Thompson 1998: (4-5). Technology is a key issue in this debate, for only by importing improved technologies can a low-income country move towards price equality with a high-income country, an aspect in contrast to the basic assumptions of the H-O theorem.

Testing Samuelson's addition to the Heckscher-Ohlin theorem of Factor Price Equalization between South Africa and Zimbabwe is not easy, once again due to the lack of significant data and Zimbabwe's ongoing social, political and economic instability. On a purely macro level, per capita income trends do not suggest moves towards equality or even convergence for that matter. High levels of immigration from Zimbabwe to South Africa (mostly illegal) have occurred, with more than one million Zimbabweans estimated to have immigrated to South Africa over the past decade. Unavoidable to this trend is a high drain of skilled labour (brain drain) from Zimbabwe. By 2008, it was estimated that nearly one million skilled Zimbabweans had emigrated due to limited employment opportunities and a failing economy. More specifically, between January and April 2007, at least 4,500 teachers in Zimbabwe resigned due to poor wages and migrated to South Africa. 'For its part, South Africa is turning to Zimbabweans to fill its own severe shortage of mathematicians and physical science teachers at both the primary and secondary levels' (Besada and Moyo, 2008: 10). Salaries in South Africa are above the poverty level, which has drawn in Zimbabwean teachers, even to take up side jobs in construction and agriculture during school holidays to supplement their meager wages earned in Zimbabwe. This fact leads to the conclusion that FPE has not occurred between South Africa and Zimbabwe, as at the very most, only marginal levels of factor price convergence can be observed. Yet again, however, it must be noted that the interpretation of this trend (or lack thereof) can be attributed to Zimbabwe's internal distortion.

CONCLUSION

Rooted in Milton Friedman's theory of Positive Economics, the Heckscher-Ohlin theorem has had a major impact on economic theory and thought for the past century. Economists have struggled with the validity of the model in the face of its simplistic and narrow assumptions, with many refuting its applicability due to the complexity and multi-dimensional aspects of global trade and economics. However, as some researchers have worked to prove (Wood), the Heckscher-Ohlin model should not be judged based on the reality of its assumptions, but on its predictive nature of trade flows. Most scholars will tend to agree that the exclusion of differing technologies of production is not responsible in the evaluation of trade flows in the twenty-first century. Nevertheless, the concept of production specialization and export of good intensive in a country's abundant factor is still relevant and adds to the understanding of trade, even in an increasingly globalized world.

In this chapter we have worked to examine the bilateral trade between South Africa and Zimbabwe to test the validity and reliability of the H-O theorem in the twenty-first century. As observed, much of South Africa's trade, and even more so Zimbabwe's trade with South Africa, can be described according to factor endowments. South Africa on the whole is a much more developed and industrialized economy than any other country in the region, and as such, engages in higher levels of capital-intensive exports comparatively speaking. Zimbabwe on the other hand, is considered a labour abundant country, and it was proven that all of its top ten exports to South Africa perfectly fit the H-O model's conclusion of labour-intensive exports. However, it was observed that multiple exports to Zimbabwe from South Africa do not agree with the H-O theorem's conclusion, and at most, only slight factor price convergence has occurred, not equalization. The most logical explanation for these variances can be attributed to Zimbabwe's decade-long social, political, and economic instability. With the recent power-sharing agreement between President Mugabe and opposition leader Morgan Tsvangira, many believed Zimbabwe would get back on track, but political progress remains unacceptably slow (Mavhunga 2010).

Even amidst these uncertainties, however, it cannot be denied that elements of the Heckscher-Ohlin theorem are still applicable to modern-day trade between South Africa and Zimbabwe.

REFERENCES

1. Hany Besada and Nicky Moyo, *Zimbabwe in Crisis: Mugabe's Policies and Failures*, Working Paper (Waterloo: The Center for International Governance Innovation (CIGI), 2008).

2. Harry P. Bowen, Edward E. Leamer and Leo Sveikauskas, 'Multicountry, Multifactor Tests of the Factor Abundance Theory', *The American Economic Review* (American Economic Association) 77, no. 5 (1987): 791-809.

3. Richard A. Brecher and Ehsan U. Choudhri, 'Some Empirical Support for the Heckscher-Ohlin Model of Production', *The Canadian Journal of Economics* (Blackwell Publishing) 26, no. 2 (1993): 272-285.

4. Central Intelligence Agency, South Africa, April 28, 2010, https://www.cia.gov/library/publications/the-world-factbook/geos/sf.html (accessed May 20, 2010).

5. Central Intelligence Agency, Zimbabwe, April 27, 2010, https://www.cia.gov/library/publications/the-world-factbook/geos/zi.html (accessed May 18, 2010).

6. David S. Clifton and William B. Marxsen, 'An Empirical Investigation of the Heckscher-Ohlin Theorem', *The Canadian Journal of Economics* (Blackwell Publishing) 17, no. 1 (1984): 32-38.

7. Deparment of Trade and Industry: Republic of South Africa, South African Trade Statistics, 2010, http://www.dti.gov.za/econdb/raportt/rapmenu1.html (accessed May 13, 2010).

8. Robert C. Feenstra, *Advanced International Trade: Theory and Evidence* (Princeton, New Jersey: Princeton University Press, 2004).

9. Przemyslaw Kowalski, Ralph Lattimore and Novella Bottini, 'South Arica', in Globalization and Emerging Economies: Brazil, Russia, India, Indonesia, China and South Africa, ed. Raed Safadi and Ralph Lattimore, 397-453 (OECD, 2008).

10. Paul Krugman and Maurice Obstfeld, International Economics: Theory & Policy, 7th Edition (Boston: Pearson Education, 2006).

11. Kishore G. Kulkarni, Readings in International Economics: Selected Writings of Prof. Kishore G. Kulkarni, 2nd Edition (Darya Ganj, New Delhi: Serials Publishings, 2006).

12. Columbus Mavhunga, 'New Elections: Zimbabwe's Leaders Trade Positions', Time, January 23, 2010, http://www.time.com/time/world/article/0,8599,1956051,00.html (accessed May 25, 2010).

13. Mzukisi Qobo, 'Outlines of intra-state conflict in Zimbabwe and regional challenges', in *Regional Trade Integration and Conflict Resolution*, ed. Shaheen Rafi Khan, 165-180 (London: Routledge, 2009).

14. Mzukisi Qobo, 'Regional integration, trade and conflict in southern Africa', in *Regional Trade Integration and Conflict Resolution*, ed. Shaheen Rafi Khan, 45-68 (London: Routledge, 2009).

15. Farhad Rassekh and Henry Thompson, 'Micro Convergence and Macro Convergence: Factor Price Equalization and Per Capita Income,' 3, no. 1 (1998): 3-11.

16. Peter K. Schott, 'One Size Fits All? Heckscher-Ohlin Specialization in Global Production,' *The American Economic Review* (American Economic Association) 93, no. 3 (2003): 686-708.

17. Robert M. Stern and Keith E. Maskus, 'Determinants of the Structure of U.S. Foreign Trade, 1958-76,' *Journal of International Economics* (North-Holland Publishing Company) 11 (1981): 207-224.

18. Sub-Regional Office of Southern Africa, *Decent Work Country Programme for Zimbabwe: 2009-2011*, Country Study, International Labour Office (Harare: ILO SRO-Harare, 2009).

19. Daniel Trefler, 'The Case of the Missing Trade and Other Mysteries,' *The American Economic Review* (American Economic Association) 85, no. 5 (1995): 1029-1046.

20. Adrian Wood, 'Give Heckscher and Ohlin a Chance!,' *Review of World Economics* (Springer Berlin) 130, no. 1 (1994): 20-49.

21. World Trade Organization, Statistics Database, 2010, http://stat.wto.org/Home/WSDBHome. aspx?Language=E (accessed May 9, 2010).

21

Effects of Population Growth and Population Control Strategies

A Case Study of Bangladesh

Elizabeth Leighty

CHAPTER SUMMARY

'Effects of Population Growth and Population Control Strategies: A Case Study of Bangladesh' explores the effects of population growth through examining relevant theories, current trends, and future outlooks. The effects of population growth on economic development and the environment are debated topics, and this chapter seeks to explore the possible negative consequences of population growth, as well as means for controlling growth. The country of Bangladesh is used as an example as a country which has a high population density and a growing population to show some effects of population growth, as well as provide an example of a country that has adopted a relatively successful population control policy.

The first part of the chapter provides an overview of population growth, including an overview of population theories, a review of past and current literature on the topic, and population trends. Literature reviewed for this section includes relevant books, articles, reports and conferences relating to population.

The second half of the chapter focuses on Bangladesh. This section includes a review of the population control policy adopted by the Bangladeshi government in the 1970's, followed by an examination of the effects of population growth and challenges faced by the government to achieve population reduction and continued economic development.

Coupled with climate change and the depletion of natural resources and food and water shortages, overpopulation poses a significant threat to the state of the world. The challenges facing the world today will likely become enhanced as the population continues to grow, and resources that are already stretched thin could conceivably be pushed beyond capacity.

As discussed in December 2009 at the United Nations Climate Change Conference in Copenhagen (COP15), the prevailing scientific consensus suggests that current trends in population growth are not sustainable due to increased demand for limited natural resources along with potentially irreparable damages to valuable ecosystems as a result of pollution, global warming, and increased levels of atmospheric carbon dioxide (Denmakr.dk, 2009).

In 1750, the world's population was a mere 728 million. Today, the world population has reached approximately 6.9 billion and is continuing to grow. Given the current world growth rate of 1.2 per cent , it is estimated that by 2050 the world population will reach 9.2 billion (Todaro, Michael and Smith, 2007). It is unclear what the impact of this growth will be, however it is certain that it will change the dynamics of the world, as there continues to be less land and resources available to sustain the population.

This chapter explores the impact of population growth through a theoretical examination of past and current trends and future population outlooks. It will also examine the possible impact of continued population growth and explore methods of population control. The country of Bangladesh is presented as a case study to examine this impact and methods.

BACKGROUND ON POPULATION GROWTH

For the first part of human history, population growth was very slow. In the last half century, however, the population of the world has more than doubled, constituting what many refer to as the 'population explosion'. (Todaro et al.).

Population growth can be largely attributed to reductions in mortality rates and fertility rates. Mortality rates decrease significantly as a country begins to experience better healthcare and health facilities, vaccination campaigns, improvements in nutrition, access to clean water and education. Combined, these factors account for a 50 per cent reduction in mortality rates in Asia and Latin America and a 30 per cent reduction in mortality rates in parts of Africa (Todaro et al.).

Fertility is defined by the number of live births a women has, and the fertility rate is the number of live births per 1,000 in a population (Todaro et al.). Fertility rates today in the developed world are less then 15 per 1,000. In the developing world however, birth rates are much higher ranging anywhere from 15-40 per 1,000. Reaching replacement fertility (defined as having 2.1 children per women) is a goal that has been adopted by the international community as well as many developing countries as a means for slowing and eventually reversing rates of population growth. Developed countries have seen significant decreases in fertility rates, in many cases reaching lower than replacement levels, whereas in most developing countries birth rates remain high. Table 21.1 shows a selection of developed and underdeveloped countries and their birth rates.

Table 21.1

Country	Fertility Rate (children born per women)
United States	2.06
France	1.97
U.K	1.66
Bangladesh	2.65
Uganda	6.73
Guatemala	3.36

Source: CIA, 2010 A.

THEORIES OF POPULATION GROWTH

Debate over the effects of population growth still rages today. There are two sides of the argument: On one side are the policy makers and environmentalists, who consider the negative effects of population growth on the environment, natural resources, economic growth, and social problems such as poverty. Others argue that population growth is essential to economic development, and that with proper capacity, the growing population does not pose a large threat to the future of the world. Conversely, it will and it should, to further economic development in developing countries (Halfon, 2007).

This section of the chapter explores some of the theories about population growth and its effects.

British political economist and demographer Reverend Thomas Malthus, author of *An Essay on the Principle of Population*, theorized in the late 1820's that population growth, unless checked by dwindling food supplies, would continue exponentially. Malthus' position called for keeping the population in line through 'preventative checks' like postponing marriage. If these checks were not in place, population would be controlled through 'positive checks,' such as disease, starvation and natural disasters. His pessimistic view of overpopulation, which predicted the outbreak of wide-spread famine if his ideas were not incorporated, gained him a reputation as an enemy of the working class or a 'prophet of doom' (Heinberg, 2007, 116).

Though many disagree with Malthus' extreme viewpoint, noted author and educator Richard Feinberg suggests that 'global human carrying capacity' (the ability of the earth to sustain the growing human population), is without doubt reduced due to the contribution of fossil fuels and the expansion of population: their use in fueling machinery to clear land, pump irrigation water, fertilize soils and kill pests along with the transportation of crops to sustain people living in remote urban areas (Heinberg, 2007).

In the 1960's, after a series of famines devastated certain Asian and African countries, neo-malthiusts adopted a similar outlook on the effects of population growth. A 1958 report by demographers Ansley Coale and Edgar Hoover, suggested that the negative effects of economic growth and economic stagnation could lead to a 'malthian crisis.' Slowing population would lead to further economic development by decreasing demands for resources, which could then be utilized for investment purposes. They supported immediate action to curb the effects of population growth to support development in poor parts of the world. A similar view is also adopted by environmentalists, who consider population in terms of its effects on the land, including loss of land, food and water shortages and overall environmental degradation (Halfon, 2007).

The novel 'pro-natalist' approach emerged in the 1970s and informed the work of Julian Simon who, in 1981, proposed that increased population was a key factor in economic development. Simon suggested that increased standards of living would be reached through improved innovation, supported by a growing population. Pro-Natalist theorists argue that more people will lead to increased production and output and technological and economic innovations, all leading to an overall growth of Gross Domestic Product (GDP).

EFFECTS OF POPULATION GROWTH

'We already have the statistics for the future: the growth percentages of pollution, overpopulation, and desertification. The future is already in place.'

—Gunther Grass (BrainyQuote, 2010)

The effect of demographic change is a controversial and debated topic. Differences in a country's population density, economic policy, capacity, governance and its stage of development all impact and alter the effects of population growth, making circumstances in each country unique. Discussions on this topic generally focus on economic effects, effects on inequality and poverty, access to resources, and the environmental impact of population growth (Birdsall, Kelly and Sinding, 2007).

A lot of research focusing on population growth in the developing world concludes that without proper capacity, increasing populations will lead to negative outcomes. In their book *Population Matters*, Birdsall, Kelly, and Sinding continuously refer to the issue of capacity, asserting that collective action, which they define as *'the capacity of societies to develop the necessary policies, for example protection of property rights and the appropriate pricing of water.... and sustainable use of common property resources' (Birdsall et al. 2007, 18)* is the key to curbing negative effects of population growth.

Defining Overpopulation

According to the Environmental Protection Agency, overpopulation occurs when *'A population's density exceeds the capacity of the environment to supply the health requirements of an individual'* (CNN, 2007).

Scientists, demographers and environmentalists have made predictions for decades on the number of human beings that the earth can sustain: These numbers range anywhere from 5.5 billion to as high as 100 billion (Urban Habitat, 2009). The consensus is that there is no optimal population for the world. If the population is low, pro-natalists and supporting economists will argue that economic growth has declined as a result of insufficient population, whereas too high a population will result in resource depletion leading to a global incapacity to sustain world population, let alone support a growing one.

Six Criteria to Determine Optimum Population Size

1. It is not the same as the maximum number of people that could be packed onto Earth at one time.
2. Population is small enough to make it possible to provide the minimal physical ingredients of a decent life to everyone.
3. Population is of the right size to ensure basic human rights in the social sphere.
4. Population is large enough to sustain viable populations in geographically dispersed parts of the world.
5. Population is sufficiently large to support a 'critical mass' in each of a variety of densely populated areas where intellectual, artistic, and technological creativity would be stimulated.
6. Population is small enough to ensure the viability of biodiversity.

Figure 21.1

Source: Urban Habitat 2003.

In an Urban Habitat article 'Optimum Population Size', authors of *The Population Explosion* Anne and Paul Ehrlich (along with co-author Gretchen C. Daily) discuss the question of how to determine the optimal number of people to live on the earth, and suggest that current scientific evidence is available which defines possibilities. *'All optima must lie between the minimum viable population size, MVP and the biophysical carrying capacity of the planet. At the lower end, 50 to 100 people in each of several groups, for a total of about 500, would constitute an MVP,'* they write (Urban Habitat 2003).

The authors suggest six criteria to determine optimum population size, as seen in Figure 21.1. The article points out that population size becomes a matter of preference and that countries need to make realistic targets taking into account the distribution of resources. To reach target population size, countries must adopt social policies and change structures to influence fertility rates and incite demographic change (Urban Habitat, 2003).

While there is no concrete and accepted number for optimum population size, many agree that increased population in the world's poorest countries will contribute to and exacerbate the already strained situation. In marginalized areas, increased population poses a threat to economic growth by thwarting poverty eradication efforts, increasing problems of water and food scarcity, contributing to problems of health and sanitation and by leading to further environmental degradation.

Poverty Eradication

Poor, landless people in the developing world are the most affected by population growth. Not only do the negative effects of population growth hit them first, such as land degradation, but they are the ones contributing to the population problem. Poor households generally have more children for reasons relating to poverty, including the desire for social security in old age and work help to increase family incomes (Todaro et al.).

Water Supply

'If water goes, the species goes' Lawrence Smith, President of the Population Institute (CNN, 2007).

One of the biggest threats of population growth is access to clean water. According to the United Nations Water Assessment Programme, children that are born in a developed country consume 30 to 50 times more water annually then a child born in a developing country, but not for lack of need. This is mainly a problem of access: in developing countries, it is difficult to access clean water sources, and increasing populations in these already marginalized areas contributes to this problem. According to Smith, only 3 per cent of water in the world is usable by humans (CNN, 2007).

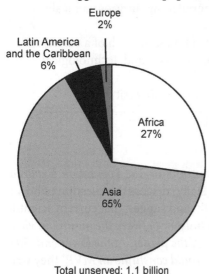

Total unserved: 1.1 billion

Figure 21.2: Water Access by Region

Source: Unesco 2010.

Increasing population, which leads to increased problems of water access also jeopardizes meeting the Millennium Development Goal (MDG): *'Reduce by half, by 2015, the proportion of people without sustainable access to safe drinking water.'*

There are approximately 1.1 billion people without access to clean water, regional breakdown as shown by Figure 21.2.

Sanitation

Lack of sanitation now affects about 40 per cent (2.4 billion) of the world's population and is expected to rise to 50 per cent by 2025 (Wateraid and Tearfund, 2010).

Sanitation issues pose a major problem, especially in growing urban areas of developing countries, where sanitation needs cannot keep up with the increasing population. Improper disposal of human waste leads to epidemic health issues, which according to the prediction of the scientists, could lead to massive outbreaks of diseases such as dysentery, cholera, typhus fever, typhoid, schistosomiasis, trachoma and numerous parasitic worm infections. Already, in Least Developed Countries (LDCs) 80 per cent of all diseases result from a combination of poor hygiene, contaminated water and poor sanitation.

GIT Dean Allen anticipates 'Huge outbreaks, fifty-thousand people dying over the summer. That's the kind of thing that in the developed world we no longer have problems with, but in the developing world are very, very real' (CNN, 2007).

Agricultural Production and Environmental Degradation

In the developing world, the livelihoods and the economic structures that characterize most rural societies are tied to agriculture. Therefore, the effect of increased population growth on land use is especially important when applied to developing countries, where poverty is a key factor. As populations increase in subsistence economies, the initial reaction is to increase agricultural productivity to support the additional people. The ability for this increase to occur, however, is difficult in many developing countries because of a lack of capacity. Land degradation, which is often exacerbated by poverty, since people lack the options to use resources and land in a sustainable way, has led to many developing countries having less agriculturally productive land. Population density must also be considered when trying to increase output: in densely populated countries, there is little land available per person to increase production. These restraints on land availability make increased food production a significant challenge to cope up with population growth (Birdsall et al., 2001).

Economic Development

All of the problems listed above contribute to difficulties in achieving economic growth. While there still a debate about whether more labour can contribute to increased productivity and economic development, many argue that rapid growth lowers per capita income in LDCs (Todaro, et al.)

CURRENT POPULATION TRENDS

Sue Halfon's 'Demographic Transitions Theory' evaluates the factors of fertility and mortality in explaining why decreased population growth occurs once countries have reached a certain level of social and economic development. According to this theory:

> As a population develops, mortality rates tend to fall somewhat faster than its fertility rate and the country experiences a rapid increase in population. Eventually, because of the social and economic changes that accompany development, the fertility rate decreases to a level that is equal to or below the mortality rate, producing a stable or shrinking population (Halfon 2007, p. 38).

Most developed countries have reached a stage in their development where population growth has stopped going any further and in some cases has actually begun to decrease.

Today, the vast majority of population growth is occurring in developing countries. It is estimated that between 2009 and 2050, the population of the developing world will increase by 2.3 billion people, compared to 0.05 billion in the developed world (CNN, 2007). There are several reasons why population growth rates in developing countries are continuing at elevated levels compared to developed countries.

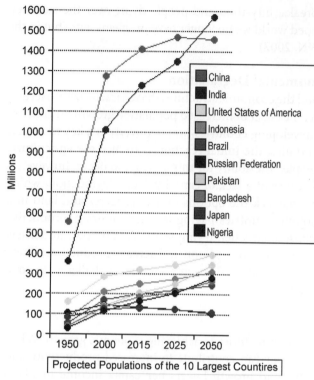

Figure 21.3: World Population Balance 2010.

Source: United Nations Population Division: World Population Prospects, 2000 Revision.

Youthful Population

In developing countries, the youth accounts for approximately 29 per cent of the population. These countries have a high population dependency ratio (the ratio of dependents- people under 15 and over 65- to working age adults- 16-64.) This puts a heavy burden on the economically productive sector of society. Consequently, these countries will see continued birth rates even if replacement fertility is reached. Once the youth reaches maturity and they begin reproducing, projections are made that they will contribute to increasing global population trends.

High Fertility Rates

Several factors contribute to high fertility rates. One important contributor is the trend of marrying young in most of the developing world. When women marry young, they have more years to reproduce, and the result is more children. Another important factor is that in many developing countries children are considered an asset, providing social security, and much needed agricultural work or other forms of income generation. When people are living in extreme poverty, having more children ensures more income for their family as well as security in old age. Today, fertility rates in most developed countries have either decreased or remained stable at 1.8 children per women.

Increased Life Expectancy

With the spread and advancement of medicine and improved access to medical care, life expectancy has increased in both developed and developing countries. In developed countries, life expectancy has raised from 60 in 1980 to 78 in 2005. Developing countries have seen respective rises in life expectancy from 48-62. Increased life expectancy in developing countries leads to a larger older population, which puts strains on poorly developed healthcare systems and puts further strains on resource management.

POPULATION CONTROL

A discourse on population control arouse in the 1950's when Western countries, the US in particular, determined that increased population growth posed a threat to both security and economic development. Since that time, numerous policies in independent countries and on an international level have outlined strategies for controlling these demographic changes. Earlier population control policies were more centered on demographics and a contraceptive-based strategy. Today, however, the world community has adopted an approach focused on women's empowerment. This approach, adopted at Cairo's 1994 International Conference on Population and Development, set forth a strategy linking sustainable development, sustained economic growth, reproduction, and population control. This change represented a more social response to the problem and helped curb criticism on earlier approaches, which leaders in many developing countries criticized for being inhumane and oppressive (Halfon, 2007, p. 3).

The policy of the United Nations Population Fund (UNPFA) policy supports this approach and identifies three areas as key to population control: The role of reproductive health and rights, women's empowerment, and population development strategies (UNFPA, 2010 A). This position recognizes that fertility rates are influenced by the choices made by women, and empowering women and focusing on reproductive health will enable them to make safe and smart decisions.

Many densely populated countries such as India, China, Sri Lanka and Bangladesh began adopting national population control strategies in the 1970's with the hope of slowing and eventually reversing population growth.

Bangladesh, one of the world poorest nations has seen a surprising amount of success with its population plan. Although widespread poverty is still prevalent, population control strategies have slowed the growth rate and if fertility rates continue to decline. The next part of this chapter explores the population problem in Bangladesh and the techniques used to combat it.

BANGLADESH

BACKGROUND INFORMATION

It is surprising that Bangladesh, a country slightly smaller then the state of Iowa, with a total area of approximately 143,000 km is the 7th most populous country in the world (CIA, 2010 B). The countries small size and increasing population have caused Bangladesh to have one of the highest population densities in the world – 948 people per square kilometer (UNFPA, 2010 B).

According to the World Bank figures, Bangladesh has experienced impressive economic and social success over the last decade. They have already met education related MDG's ensuring gender parity and increased primary school enrollment, and they are on track to meet the goal of halving extreme poverty by the 2015 deadline. Between 1990 and 2005, although 56 million still live below the poverty line, Bangladesh decreased poverty from 57 per cent to 40 per cent (World Bank, 2010). Economic growth in Bangladesh has been steady and the government adopted a pro-poor strategy, focusing efforts on creating safety nets and opportunities for impoverished people in rural and urban areas (UNDP, 2008). If growth rate can continue and social welfare is increasingly improved, Bangladesh may be able to become a middle-income country by the year 2021 (World Bank, 2010). Figure 21.2 gives an overview of country indicators in Bangladesh.

Table 21.2 Bangladesh Country Indicators

GDP	$242.2 Billion
GDP Growth Rate	5.6%
Unemployment Rate	2.5%
Life Expectancy	60.25 years
Literacy Rates	47.9%
Human Development Index	0.5453 (146th out of 182 countries)
Human Poverty Index	36.1% (112th out of 135 countries)
Urbanization	27% of population, 3.5% growth rate
Median Age	23.3 years

Source: CIA, 2010 B, (UNDP 2009).

This idealistic future, however, is a precarious one given the countries vulnerability to natural disasters and its large population, which exacerbates problems relating to poverty, economic growth and resource management. The ambitious goal of becoming a middle-income country is contingent upon the country's ability to control population and the problems associated with it through decreasing fertility rates by continuing with the promotion and adaptation of a comprehensive population control policy.

POPULATION CONTROL IN BANGLADESH

The population control policy in Bangladesh was adopted in the 1970's when Bangladeshi President Zaiur Rahman declared population growth as the biggest threat to the country. This policy was formed inline with the United Nations standards on population control, emphasizing family planning methods as a means of controlling fertility rates. The population control programme incorporated the following strategy:

- A strategy based on child and maternal health
- Network of service centers and field workers who were committed to the programme
- Collaboration between Government and NGO's
- Incorporation of religious leaders into programme planning and implementation
- Involvement of women and mass media (UNESCAP, 2010).

Since the implementation of this plan, Bangladesh has successfully incorporated population into development plans, and has seen remarkable success through this educational and culturally appropriate response (UNESCAP, 2010).

A revised plan, the Health Population Sector Programme (HPSP), emerged in 1998, which further incorporated health services into the population plan. The goal of this programme was to:

'Work with development partners and stakeholders to provide a package of essential health care services to the people and to lower the rate of population growth.' (Ministry of Health and Welfare, Bangladesh, 2005).

This involved reducing maternal and child mortality rates, continued reduction in fertility (with the overall goal of reaching replacement fertility by 2005), and to increase overall nutrition of the population. They used a grassroots strategy and built 3,290 care centers across the country. The implementation of this plan faced some problems including a tendency for families to discontinue family planning (FP) practices, inadequate care and low promotion of condom usage (Ministry of Health and Welfare, Bangladesh, 2005).

The most recent version of this plan, HNPSP: Health, Nutrition and Population Sector Programme, evolved out of the HPSP and addressed some of its major pitfalls. This detailed plan lays out a programme design in line with the MDG's to meet health, nutrition and population standards that will contribute to the growth and continued development of Bangladesh (Ministry of Health and Welfare, Bangladesh, 2005).

The population sub-sector of this plan has well developed and well researched goals that address the core issues behind population growth. These goals include aiming at decreasing the fertility rates through continuing the promotion of contraceptive prevalence rate (CPR), encouraging the use, and continuation of family planning methods, and discouraging young marriage and prevalence of giving birth at a young age, which will decrease 'population momentum.' It also recognizes the importance of improving the quality of care and also increasing access to this care (Ministry of Health and Welfare, Bangladesh, 2005).

These population control policies have seen significant success, however there are still challenges for the country to overcome to reach replacement fertility and slow population growth.

Positive Indicators

Bangladesh has seen a lot of improvements in population control since the government first adopted population control strategies in the 1970's. According to the World Health Organization, recent changes in demography have proven that these programmes are working. Between the years 1975-2007, CPR increased from 8 per cent to 56 per cent. During the same period, fertility rates decreased from 6.3 to 3.3, a significant decrease and the rates are continuing to fall. Antenatal care among women has increased from 49 per cent in 2004 to 52 per cent in 2007, and child mortality has declined from 250 deaths per 1,000 live births to 69 deaths per 1,000 lives births (USAID, 2010). Table 21.3 seen below lays out the past and also future predictions for total fertility, population change and population growth rates in Bangladesh and shows that experts predict a continuous decline in all aspects.

Table 21.3

Period	Total Fertility	Population Change in Thousands	Population Growth Rate (%)
1980-1985	5.92	2 519	2.61
1985-1990	4.89	2 528	2.32
1990-1995	3.96	2 491	2.05
1995-2000	3.30	2536	1.89
2000-2005	2.80	2471	1.68
2005-2010	2.36	2261	1.42
2010-2015	2.20	2158	1.27
2015-2020	2.10	2067	1.15
2020-2025	2.02	1892	0.99
2025-2030	1.95	1640	0.82
2030-2035	1.88	1343	0.65
2035-2040	1.85	1082	0.51
2040-2045	1.85	850	0.39
2045-2050	1.85	581	0.26

Source: United Nations Population Division, 2010.

Family Planning in Bangladesh

A recent policy brief by the Population Reference Bureau, focusing on the positive effects of family planning policies, highlighted the success of the Bangladeshi family planning and maternal and child health programme (FPMCH). Researchers surveyed areas that had been reached by the FPMCH, compared with those that were not. They found that in places where family planning was sustained, families were generally better off and had higher levels of education, higher incomes and improved access to food and water. Women who lived in the areas reached by this program had on average 1.5 less children per women. The researchers concluded that this decrease in children led to families having a higher quality of life because of better resource and wealth distribution (Population Reference Bureau, 2009).

CHALLENGES

Despite these positive indicators, Bangladesh still faces significant challenges related to reducing population growth and continuing economic gain. Challenges to reduced population growth in Bangladesh include the young age structure, tendency towards young marriage, and poor health services. Population growth, even as indicators show that it is falling, still poses a significant threat to issues such as food availability, and poverty reduction efforts, and the countries proneness to natural disasters threaten future economic development.

Young Age Structure

Like many developing countries, the age structure in Bangladesh is young. Approximately 40 per cent of the population is under the age of 15. This will cause what population experts call 'population momentum', meaning that even once replacement fertility rates are reached, a large percentage of the population will be between reproductive ages (15-49), which will cause population to continue to increase for some time. Figure 21.4 shows a population pyramid for Bangladesh, which demonstrates the young age structure of the country.

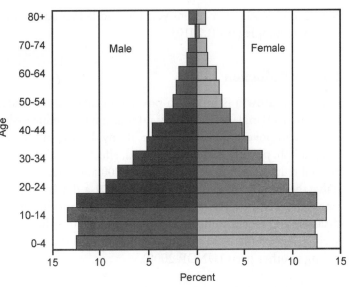

Figure 21.4: Population Pyramid Bangladesh 1999-2000

Source: WHO, 2010 A.

Young Marriage

Another challenge is the tendency towards young marriage. According to a recent report by the World Health Organization, 50 per cent of women in Bangladesh are married by the age of 15, and by age 19, 57 per cent of them have given birth a child (WHO, 2010). This tendency to marry young leads to women having many children during the reproductive period.

Poor Access to Health Care

The health care system in Bangladesh also needs to be improved to support the large population. Currently, the system does not have the capacity to support so many people, which affects the countries ability to fight poverty, hindering development (WHO, 2007). Maternal healthcare is an important factor in reducing population. In a 1999-2000 survey, 80 per cent of women indicated that they felt that adequate healthcare facilities not available close enough, and they also lacked confidence in the ability of the centers to address their needs. This hinders families' abilities to participate in family planning programmes, which is key to the countries population control policy. It is estimated that to reach the needs for family planning, the contraceptive prevalence rate needs to increase to 71 per cent, it is currently at 54 per cent (WHO, 2010).

Food Availability

According to the World Food Programme, approximately 65 million people, 45 per cent of the population of Bangladesh, do not have access to an adequate and nutritious food supply.

Rising food prices over recent years has added an additional 7.5 million people to the number of hungry people (WFP, 2010).

Poverty Reduction

Population growth is linked to poverty in that it contributes further numbers to the ranks of the poor. In Bangladesh, fertility rates among the educated people have fallen, whereas people who live in poverty have seen little, if any decline in fertility rates (*Financial Times*, 2010). In Bangladesh, poverty is still widespread, effecting mainly rural communities. With a 3.6 per cent annual reduction in poverty between 2000 and 2005, Bangladesh is in line to meet MDG 1: to halve the number of people living on USD1 a day by 2015, if they can continue this reduction rate. However, poverty eradication efforts in Bangladesh are continuously set back by natural disasters and recently affected by rising food prices. Because of these constraints, Bangladesh is seeing improvements in poverty reduction in certain areas of the country, while indicators are falling in other parts (UNDP, 2008).

Climate Change and Natural Disasters

'Bangladesh is nature's disaster laboratory, apart from volcanoes, we have every type (of disaster),' Professor Ainun Nishat

(D'Monte, Darryl, 2009).

Natural disasters in Bangladesh may pose the biggest threat to the countries' economic development and their continued accession towards becoming a middle-income country. At last December's COP15, the Bangladesh Delegation informed participants that despite the country's significant progress in population control and food production, climate change threatens to undermine this success.

Bangladesh state minister Hasan Mahmud called for a mandatory 'climate change adaptation fund.'

'More or less one billion people are affected in the world due to climate change and at least 15 per cent of them live in Bangladesh,' he said (Asiaone News, 2009).

It is estimated that by the end of this century, there could be up to 30 million climate refugees in Bangladesh. Many have already migrated into India, fleeing natural disasters. This has a high economic cost, and the countries ability to cope with frequent disasters is hindered by its high population and subsequent population density.

BANGLADESH WRAP UP

Bangladesh provides us with an interesting case study on how population growth can affect development, and provide an example of a population control policy that has seen success. Bangladesh is on a positive path to development, as indicated by falling poverty rates and economic growth, putting the country in line to meet several of the MDG's. Population density in Bangladesh and continued population growth threatens this path. Bangladesh has done a remarkable job of setting goals on population reduction and fertility rates, and the government seems to understand what needs to be done to follow this plan and meet these goals. Gaining control of population growth in Bangladesh still poses a threat to the future development of the country and is contingent upon continued promotion of family planning techniques and lowering fertility rates. Bangladesh can serve as an example to other densely populated countries to show both the effects of population growth, as well as a means to adopt a culturally appropriate strategy to combating it.

CONCLUSION

Population growth in developing countries exacerbates existing problems such as poverty, food and water access, land degradation, unemployment, and access to improved health services. While the debate is still taking place on the overall effects of population growth on economic development and land use, it is clear that by exacerbating these characteristics of underdeveloped societies, economic growth is going to be affected. Without proper capacity, these effects will take hold and have negative consequences on Developing countries. It is important for developing countries to recognize the ill effects growing population could have on their ability to develop, and adopt realistic strategies to combat these effects.

REFERENCES

1. Denmakr.dk. *The United Nations Climate Change Conference 2009.* Accessed May 2010.
2. Todaro, Michael and Stephen, Smith. *Economic Development.* Boston, MA: Pearson Education Inc. 2009.
3. CIA. *Country Comparison: Total Fertility Rate.* 2010. Accessed April 2010. *https://www.cia.gov/library/publications/the-world-factbook/rankorder/2127rank.html*
4. Halfon, Saul. *The Cairo Consensus.* United Kingdom: Lexington Books. 2007.
5. Heinberg, Richard. *Peak Everything.* Canada: New Society Publishers. 2007.
6. Brainy Quote. *Overpopulation quotes.* Accessed May 2010. *http://www.brainyquote.com/quotes/keywords/overpopulation.html*
7. Birdsall, Nancy, Kelly, Allen and Sinding, Stephen. *Population Matters.* New York: Oxford University Press. 2001.
8. United Nations Population Fund. *Linking Population, Poverty, and Development: Rapid Growth in Less Developed Regions.* Accessed April 2010. *http://www.unfpa.org/pds/trends.htm*
9. Hoevel, Anne. *Overpopulation could be People, Planet Problem.* CNN. May 2010. Accessed May 2010. *http://www.cnn.com/2007/TECH/science/09/25/overpopulation.overview/index.html*
10. Haput, Aurthur and Kane, Thomas. *Population Handbook: 5th edition.* Population Reference Bureau. 2004. Accessed April 2010.
11. Daily, Gretchen, Elrich, Anne and Elrich Paul. *Optimum Population Size.* Urban Habitat. 2003. Accessed May 2010. *http://www.urbanhabitat.org/node/955*
12. UNESCO. *World Water Assessment Program.* Accessed May, 2010. *http://www.unesco.org/water/wwap/facts_figures/basic_needs.shtml*

13. Wateraid and Tearfund. *The Human Waste: A Call for Urgent Action to Combat the Millions of Deaths Caused by Poor Sanitation.* Wateraid and Tearfund. Accessed May 2010.

14. World Population Balance. *The Global Population Situation.* 2010. Accessed April 2010. *http://www.worldpopulationbalance.org/global_population*

15. UNFPA. *Population Issues.* Accessed May 2010. A *http://www.unfpa.org/issues/*

16. CIA. *CIA World Factbook: Bangladesh.* April 21st, 2010. Accessed May, 2010. B. *https://www.cia.gov/library/publications/the-world-factbook/geos/bg.html*

17. UNFPA. *United Nations Population Fund, Bangladesh.* Accessed April, 2010. B. *http://www.unfpa-bangladesh.org/php/about_bangladesh.php*

18. World Bank. *Bangladesh Country Overview.* April 2010. Accessed May 2010. *http://www.worldbank.org.bd/WBSITE/EXTERNAL/COUNTRIES/SOUTHASIAEXT/BANGLADESHEXTN/0,,contentMDK:20195502~menuPK:295767~pagePK:141137~piPK:141127~theSitePK:295760,00.html*

19. UNDP. *Millenium Development Goals: Bangladesh Progress Report 2008.* UNDP. 2008. Accessed May 2010.

20. UNDP. *Human Development Report 2009: Bangladesh.* 2009. Accessed May 2010. *http://hdrstats.undp.org/en/countries/country_fact_sheets/cty_fs_BGD.html*

21. UNESCAP. *Population Program and Reproductive Health including Family Planning in Bangladesh.* Accessed May 2010. *www.unescap.org/esid/.../population/.../Bangladesh_country_report.doc*

22. Ministry of Health and Welfare, Bangladesh. *Health, Nutrition and Population Sector Programme, Revised Programme Implementation Plan.* November 2005. Accessed May 2010.

23. USAID. *USAID Bangladesh: Population and Health.* Accessed May 2010. *http://www.usaid.gov/bd/programs/pop.html*

24. United Nations Population Division. *World Population Prospects: The 2008 Revision Population Database.* United Nations. Accessed May 2010.

25. Population Reference Bureau. *Family Planning and Economic Well-Being: New Evidence from Bangladesh.* May 2009. Accessed May 2010. *http://www.prb.org/Search.aspx?q=bangladesh*

26. World Health Organization. *Bangladesh and Family Planning: An overview.* Accessed May 2010.

27. World Health Organization. *WHO Country Cooperation Strategy 2008-2013: Bangladesh.* 2007. Accessed May 2010.

28. World Food Program. *WFP in Bangladesh: Overview.* 2010. Accessed May 2010. *http://one.wfp.org/bangladesh/?ModuleID=181&Key=1*

29. Chowdhury, Mahfuz. *Population Challenge Before Bangladesh.* Financial Times. 2010. Accessed May 2010. *http://www.thefinancialexpress-bd.com/2009/08/16/76176.html*

30. D'Monte, Darryl. *Bangladesh: Community-Based Climate Strategies Are Key.* Terraviva. December 19th, 2009. Accessed May 2010. *http://www.ips.org/TV/copenhagen/bangladesh-community-based-climate-strategies-are-key/*

31. Daily Star/Asia News. *Bangladesh Demands Allocation of Funds for Population at Risk.* Asiaone News. December 13th, 2009. Accessed May 2010. *http://www.asiaone.com/News/Latest+News/Asia/Story/A1Story20091213-185611.html*

32. UNFPA. *World Population to reach 9 billion by 2050.* March 11th, 2009. Accessed April, 2010. *http://www.un.org/esa/population/publications/wpp2008/pressrelease.pdf*

22 | Limitations in Measurement of Economic Development and the Gross Domestic Product (GDP) Drawbacks

Teresa Manocchio

CHAPTER SUMMARY

Gross domestic product is the total market value of all final goods and services produced by an economy, and historically is the most widely used and accepted measure of economic development. This chapter seeks to challenge that notion by highlighting the constraints of GDP to measure development in the context of four largest GDPs in the world: the United States, China, Japan, and India. Alternative indicators are analyzed with respect to each of these countries in order to further illuminate what development really means and how to better measure it. Measures from all different sectors of society – economic, health, and social – are considered in this chapter and the data is collected and visually displayed for each measure in each country. The goal of this chapter is to bring awareness to readers regarding the shortcomings of GDP and to discourage the use of GDP as a singular measure of development while encouraging a broader, more in-depth and cross sectional analysis of development.

GDP – THE MOST TRADITIONAL MEASURE OF ECONOMIC DEVELOPMENT

Measuring, and more importantly, quantifying economic development has historically been a difficult task. The most traditional measure of economic development is gross domestic product (GDP), a dollar figure reflecting the total market value of all finals goods and services produced in an economy in a given time period. It is a measure of a country's overall economic output, and its calculations have come under much criticism as a true measure of actual economic development. The largest GDP in the world is the United States, with just over USD 14 trillion in output and a world-wide GDP of just over USD 60 trillion, so the first concern is clear: one country, of about 300 million people, is disproportionately responsible for nearly one fourth of the world's wealth.

The next three largest GDPs, in order, are China, Japan and India, collectively making up well over 2 billion people. When only taking GDP into consideration, it would appear as though the United States is the most developed country in the world, followed by China, Japan and India. This may seem counterintuitive, and it certainly is. Arguably, the United States is the most developed country in the world; but one would be hard-pressed to make the case that China or India is more developed than, say, Canada, or most of Western Europe. This would effectively argue that the general populace of China and India are better off than those that are usually considered the developed world. By just looking at the dollar figure of its GDP, a person might think that China's access to quality health care rivals that of the United States or that India's education levels rival those of Japan. These assumptions would be incorrect, as we will see later in the chapter, but without having more detailed access to other economic indicators, social indicators, and health indicators, GDP alone paints a rather incomplete picture of economic development in almost any given country. An examination of these four countries will help us better understand why, and in what ways other indicators are applicable and more useful than GDP alone.

BIGGER OR BETTER: CONSTRAINTS ON GDP

Gross domestic product can be measured in three different ways, but the most frequent expression is the expenditure method, or:

$$GDP = \text{Consumption (C)} + \text{Investment (I)} + \text{Govt. Expenditure (G)} + (\text{Exports} - \text{Imports})$$

Even at this stage of the definition, we begin to see problems with GDP as a measure of economic growth. 'This, economic wealth measured in this way, that is GDP, is purely market and monetary wealth. And growth is defined as the increase in GDP, that is the increase in the volume of goods and services that are sold or costed in monetary terms.'[1] Immediately, there are concerns about GDP being the tool of measurement and its applicability to development. There are different criticisms from different economists, which are summarized in this chapter, along with possible solutions to the problems of GDP and alternative measures. First, Oskar Morgenstern calls GDP a 'garbage-in, garbage-out' process which completely ignores individual demographics of a country. For example, if a country has a USD 3 trillion GDP, but a population of 1 billion people, there is a very different level of economic welfare and development for its people than a country that has a USD 3 trillion GDP and only 300 million people.

Second, GDP does not consider any non-market transactions, which are all of the transactions in any given economy that are not officially recorded as part of GDP because they are never officially bought or sold. This can result in under-estimating a country's GDP, and it happens much more frequently in developing countries than in developed countries. For example, 'if rich households pay servants to do their cooking and housework and child care and gardening, those services are counted as economic output. Why not when household members do the work for themselves and one another?'[2] Any sort of household work, yard work, or other type of volunteer or 'self' work is left unaccounted for in the equation for gross domestic product, underestimating output in all countries.

Third, the malicious side effects to production are left uncalculated in GDP, so these negative externalities may actually result in over-estimation of gross domestic product. Excess pollution, traffic, or increased risk of radiation are examples of cases where economic welfare is lowered; but there is no agreed upon dollar amount or way of measuring these externalities, which should ideally be deducted from overall GDP for a more accurate portrayal. In another example, 'the organized destruction of the Amazon rainforest is an activity that increases global GDP. Nowhere is any account taken of the resultant loss of natural resources, or the various effects on climate, biodiversity, the long term and the needs of future generations.'[3] 'As a result the GDP now only masks the breakdown of the social structure and the natural habitat upon which the economy – and life itself – ultimately depend; worse it actually portrays such breakdown as economic gain.'[4] This is one of the most commonly cited examples of negative externalities that are left unconsidered when calculating a country's development using GDP: loss of natural resources that are not subtracted or otherwise accounted for in any way.

Next, there is no consideration of quality when calculating GDP for a country, only quantity. Two similar GDPs may be reflections of two very different economies, for example, the difference between a largely agrarian society with production of USD 600 billion worth of mostly agricultural products as opposed to a country producing high technology luxury products valued at USD 500 billion. The larger economy is naturally considered the more developed country, but that is not necessarily true based on its production of mostly labour-intensive goods. Fifth, there is no consideration of equality of distribution of the total GDP: 'Does the fact of living in a society in which vast numbers of poor people coexist with a handful of very rich individuals have no impact at all on well-being?'[5] The answer must be 'NO'. A case where the GDP is smaller but better distributed may be considered less developed than a larger GDP with a much more concentrated distribution; however, larger numbers of people in poverty does not translate to a better developed society.

Lastly, there are significant problems with the measurement and data for calculating GDP to begin with. Reliability of data may be questionable, illegal activities are ignored, transparency in doubt, record keeping is not consistent across countries, and so on. For example, a cursory look at 2009 GDP numbers reveal different records: the International Monetary Fund (IMF) calculates India's GDP at USD 3.526 trillion, and the CIA records it at USD 3.560 trillion or a difference of about USD 34 billion. 'It remains the case that any comparative approach using statistics that attempt to cover every single country will inevitably come up against limitations with respect to relevance and reliability.'[6] Different sources place Japan in the second largest GDP spot, and others maintain that China is second place in the rankings. Even as other indicators of economic development are considered, this last issue will remain pervasive throughout any type of data collection. Cross-country comparisons are always problematic, not the least because different countries have different ways of measuring given indicators and one cannot be certain that they are truly making a comparison between the correct numbers, thus making a possibly incorrect assumption about the societies in question.

Highlighting the problems with using GDP to measure development levels are the four largest GDPs in the world in order, as seen in Figure 22.1: the United States, China, Japan, and India.[7] Gross domestic product has its place as an economic measure, but fails to provide a complete and accurate portrayal of what is happening within a country's borders, and these four countries are excellent examples of the differences in development levels. 'The GDP has been a touchstone of economic policy for so long that most probably regard it as a kind of universal standard…Actually, the GDP is just an artifact of history, a relic of another era.'[8] Each country and its corresponding economy will be discussed in more detail in the following section. I will not advocate for one particular indicator of development, but rather present a survey of alternative ways of measuring development in order to attempt a better, bigger-picture view of these four countries that may be applied to other countries when comparing levels of development.

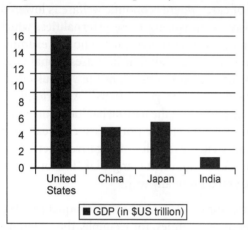

Figure 22.1: 2008 GDP

HEALTH OR WEALTH: OTHER INDICATORS OF DEVELOPMENT

There are several available solutions to handle the problems discussed in the previous section, and various alternative indicators that provide a more accurate and comprehensive vision of a nation's development level and overall economic welfare. There are the standard problems with using GDP as a measurement for each of these four countries, the most obvious of which is the fact that China and India together make up one third of the world's populations, but combined make up less than one-half of the United State's GDP. There are dozens of possible indicators that reveal more about the quality of life within a nation's borders, and several of them will be discussed later in this chapter, including life expectancy, research and development expenditures, and school enrollment levels. Many of these solutions will be examined shortly, but first, a quick background on each of the four economies that will be handled: the United States, China, Japan, and India.

The United States is the largest economy in the world, recording over USD14 trillion in GDP by most recent estimates. It is a highly industrialized society, with a large portion of its economy in the service sector and a very small portion, only about three per cent, still involved in agriculture. Its sheer size is an anomaly, and it is both a largest exporter and importer of goods and services, and plays a critical, leading role in international financial markets. Home to about 300 million people, it is the third-largest population and has the ability to cause great distress in the international markets when it slips into decline; seen in the most recent worldwide economic recession which was largely a result of the US economy tanking. The United States alone accounts for nearly one fourth of the global output, English is spoken all over the world, and the US dollar remains the most influential currency around the world.

China is home to the largest population within one country's borders, with over 1.3 billion people in an area of just over 9.5 million square kilometers. It became a sovereign country in 1949 and was largely a subsistence farming country at the time. China, under Soviet-style socialist economic modeling, quickly became a centrally planned economy with a focus on distributive justice and heavy industry,[9] although in more recent years, China has undergone certain structural changes with regards to its economy, namely its decentralization. China has also recorded some of the highest growth rates in history over the last twenty-five years, increasing real income per capita by over 5 times between 1980 and 1999, as a direct result of major decentralization policies and appropriate allocation of resources.[10] It is also home to the infamous 'one child' policy which prevents its citizens from having more than one child per couple, put in place a generation ago to control population growth. Not the most democratic of governments, China has displayed a unique willingness to liberalize its economy without necessarily liberalizing its politics or government.

Japan following World War II is one of the greatest economic success stories in history. Defeated, Japan's economy still 'grew rapidly (at or near double digit rates) throughout most of the post-war period and still managed to outperform Europe and the United States after the energy crisis slowed economic growth everywhere.' Reconstruction provided ample opportunity to gain from technology transfer, and culturally, the Japanese tend to be frugal people.[11] Made up of densely packed islands, the Japanese have surpassed the United States in per capita researchers and secondary school enrollment rates, and spend a larger portion of their GDP on investment in research and development. Clearly determined and fiscally responsible, it is unlikely that Japan will give up their edge in technology any time soon. Japan also has an aging population, which has seen its birth rate drop below replacement levels, which may be a key factor for production levels in the future.

India, a former British colony, became its own sovereign nation only two years before China, in 1947, and is the largest democracy in the world. Like China, at its independence, India was largely an agrarian society and agriculture comprised 73 per cent of employment in India in 1951.[12] Over the decades, India has also undergone several structural changes, seeing industrial production's share of the economy increase (although not at the rate of China), along with an increase in the service sector from 31 to 41 per cent of GDP.[13] India has developed somewhat differently from China, but similarly, its policies include an open economy, more market-focused, with a decreasing government role.[14] India, though, is 'smaller and poorer than China…and has had export success in textiles and clothing, and, given its abundance of unskilled labor, it seems almost bound to continue to sustain a competitive edge in these industries.'[15] India's economy remains slightly behind China's, while its level of democratization remains quite a bit in front of China's.

MACROECONOMIC INDICATORS

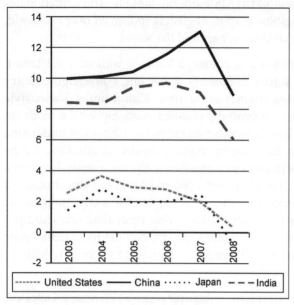

Figure 22.2: GDP Growth (%)

Apart from GDP, there are several other macroeconomic indicators that provide more valuable information about a given country. Examining the graph of GDP growth below, it is clear that India and China both have significantly larger GDP growth rates than either the United States or Japan, even though all of them have declined during the current world-wide recession, and Japan even dipped into negative growth rates. China and India 'have performed very strongly since 1995, especially when compared with other larger economies. China accounted for 13 per cent of the world growth in output over 1995-2004, and India accounted for 3 per cent.'[16] These are both large portions of world growth, but also further highlight the quicker pace of growth in China as opposed to India. Still, by housing over 30 per cent of the global population between the two countries, one might expect to see higher proportions of global growth, which is not the case quite yet.

The first problem (garbage-in, garbage-out) when we consider gross domestic product can quite easily be adjusted, by dividing the total GDP by the total population in order to arrive at the GDP per capita rate of each country. Consider the rates for the four largest GDPs previously displayed in this chapter. Now, with the per capita adjustment, the possible measure of development (at right) looks more like what one would truly expect to reflect on the conditions within each of these four countries: China and India with significantly lower GDP per capita numbers, the United States with the highest and Japan close behind. Japanese and US citizens are making more money collectively, and the United States with a very large GDP and much smaller population than India or China has fewer people amongst whom to distribute the

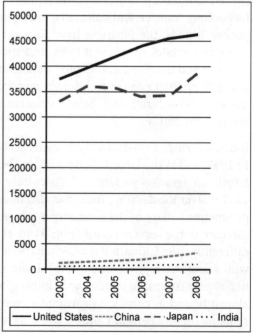

Figure 22.3: GDP per Capita ($US)

wealth. If one must use GDP in an assessment of economic development, the first step to truly make it relevant must be to convert it to per capita GDP, which in and of itself is a much better reflection of the standard of living within the country's borders than simple GDP alone.

Let's next consider other macroeconomic indicators, such as exports and imports as a percentage of their total GDPs. Every country ideally would like to have a positive current account balance, or export more than they import (which is clearly impossible for every country to do), but these are very large economies that can absorb large numbers of imports. Consider the table below: the United States remains the largest importer and exporter of goods and services in the world, and while its percentages may be smaller than others', their absolute numbers are still quite large – and so is their current account balance. A large negative current account balance would likely be a huge issue for a developing country (indeed, in many countries debt remains the number one expenditure), but the US can absorb these rates without too much discomfort. China and Japan, both of whose exports outweigh their imports, are in fairly good shape, trade-wise. India, slower to move to manufacturing than China was, has a negative current account balance as well, but not as large as the United States.

Table 22.1

Imports (% GDP)								
	2000	2001	2002	2003	2004	2005	2006	2007
United States	15.11	13.89	13.73	14.12	15.46	16.38	17.06	17.25
China	20.92	20.48	22.56	27.36	31.40	31.85	32.09	30.59
Japan	9.53	9.92	10.06	10.38	11.37	12.95	14.86	15.94
India	14.15	13.65	15.48	16.10	19.87	22.68	25.24	24.72
Exports (% GDP)								
	2000	2001	2002	2003	2004	2005	2006	2007
United States	11.23	10.25	9.66	9.54	10.17	10.60	11.23	12.10
China	23.33	22.60	25.13	29.56	33.95	37.43	39.94	39.68
Japan	10.99	10.56	11.36	12.00	13.30	14.30	16.11	17.61
India	13.23	12.76	14.49	14.80	18.07	19.85	22.20	21.16

Next consider the actual production and items being exported by each country. The United States' largest exports are capital goods (including aircraft, motor vehicle parts, computers and telecommunications equipment), industrial supplies, and agricultural products. China's top exports are electrical and other machinery, apparel, textiles, iron and steel, and optical and medical equipment. Japan's top exports are transport equipment, motor vehicles, semiconductors, electrical machinery, and chemicals. India's top exports are petroleum products, precious stones, machinery, iron and steel, and chemicals.[17] The high technology exports are the products that bring in big money, and require much more skilled personnel and capital to produce. The Figure 22.4 at right displays each country's high technology exports as a percentage of their GDPs: China surpasses the United States with a larger percentage of their GDP accounted for in high-technology exports, but in real dollar amounts, the United States is still the largest exporter of those goods. India, still a labour abundant country, seems to be more confined to producing more labour-intensive goods than the other top countries, but would undoubtedly like to move

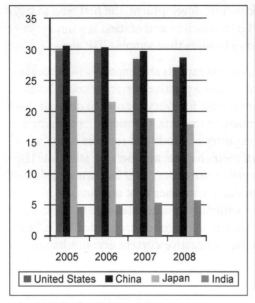

Figure 22.4: High Technology Exports
(% of Manufactured Exports)

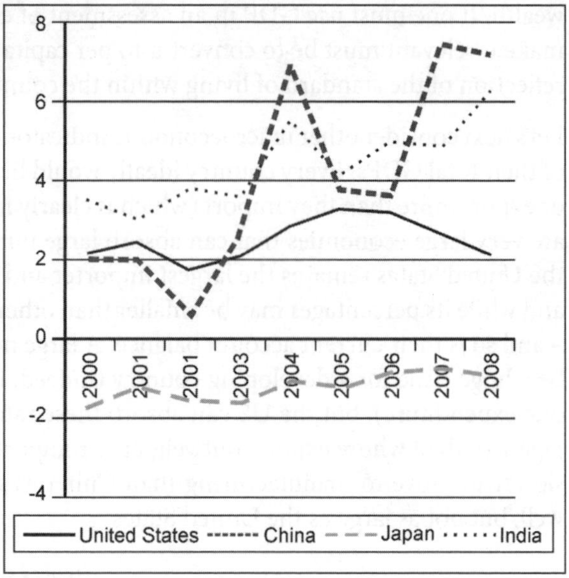

Figure 22.5: Inflation (GDP deflator %)

into these high-yield goods in the future. Here the United States and China come out on top as most developed with respect to exports.

It is irrelevant to talk about GDP without also considering inflation and its implications. Inflation is the measure of price increases from year to year, and keeps GDP calculations from mistakenly counting only an increase in prices (without considering quantity) as economic growth or expansion. It adjusts for the slight price increases in commodities that happen from year to year, and the more developed countries, the United States and Japan in this case, have much more stable, lower inflation rates than either India or China (See Figure 22.5). The latter have volatile rates that are currently on the rise, while Japan's inflation rate grows at a decreasing rate from year to year currently. They also have much higher growth rates, as seen previously, so the higher inflation rates are not actually unexpected. The United States' rate hovers between two and three per cent, and any larger number than that would be a huge macroeconomic shock to the US economy as a whole, which is unaccustomed to very high inflation rates as it does not grow at much more than three percent on a regular basis.

SOCIAL INDICATORS

By ignoring the social and demographic breakdowns of individual countries, GDP misses the majority of what development is truly about: quality of life, or raising standards of living everywhere. One single figure depicting a country's total economic output is irrelevant if its people are starving, dying young, or largely illiterate. In this section of the chapter, a necessary examination of certain indicators – urban and rural populations, school enrollment rates, women employed outside of agriculture, etc. – takes place, and 'social statistics are not only interesting, they are also most revealing of the quality of life'[18] in a country. The first indicator examined is the proportion of the population in each country that lives rurally and urban, with the United States at about 80 per cent urban population all the way down to India, at about 25 per cent in urban areas, as shown in the graph on the previous page. 'With successful development, countries tend to move toward commercialized agriculture...and

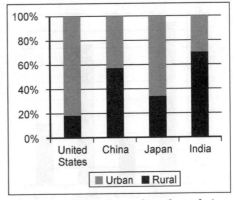

Figure 22.6: 2008 Urban and rural populations (% of total population)

some three-quarters of the world's extreme poor live in rural areas.'[19] The more industrialized a country becomes, the more mechanized agricultural production becomes and people migrate to the cities for jobs. Populations in urban centers have better access to health care, education, non-agrarian employment, plumbing and electricity, and in general, a better quality of life; overall, a higher percentage of the population living in urban areas tends to indicate higher standards of living. With such a large portion of its population living in urban centers, the United States takes the lead in this measure of development.

The next indicator is the one that almost always seems to have a huge impact on a society's development: education levels of the population, particularly tertiary education. Here in the graph below, the United States takes the top ranking again, followed by Japan. Secondary school rates are well over 50 per cent for all four countries studied, but the tertiary enrollment rates dip quickly in China and India, to at or below 20 per cent of the relevant age group enrolled. Higher education levels are critical to industrialized societies, who rely heavily on scientists, engineers and the like to continue to make technological advances in all kinds of fields that will keep them ahead. Higher education levels are also required to be upwardly mobile and employable in developed countries, as there is much less work for unskilled labour than in the developing world.

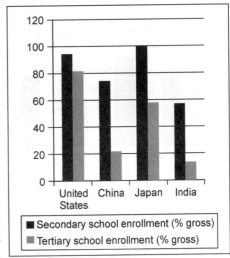

Figure 22.7: 2007 Secondary and Tertiary School Enrollment

Another social issue that sheds quite a bit of light on the development of a country has to do with the proportion of women in the work force. The overall condition of women in a society is almost always incredibly telling, and here, the specific indicator studied is the percentage

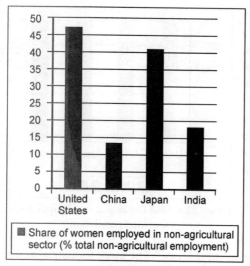

Figure 22.8: 2005 Share of Women in Non-agricultural Sectors

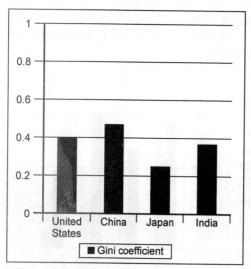

Figure 22.9: Gini Coefficient (from the United Nations Development Programme)

of women who are employed in non-agricultural sectors; the United States and Japan take the lead on this indicator by a fair amount in the graph at right. Women in the work force is a signal of a higher level of development because a country has reached a phase of not only better equality for its females, but also a place in their development where education and child care are much more readily available, so that women are not the sole caregivers while their husbands are at work. It is also indicative of more women staying in school, and for longer, and in the United States, women now outpace men in university attendance rates. Women in the United States and Japan now make up over 40 per cent (approaching an even 50 per cent in the US) of employment in the non-agricultural sectors, a clear indication of a more developed society.

The specific measure of the inequality of life in a country is the Gini coefficient, or a measure of the ratio of income held by both the wealthy and the poor. It is a measure between 0, or perfect equality (wealth is completely perfectly distributed amongst all), and 1, or perfect inequality. The Gini coefficient for 'countries with highly unequal income distribution typically lies between 0.50 and 0.70, while for countries with relatively equitable distributions, it is on the order of 0.20 to 0.35.'[20] Inequality is demonstrative of a few different things, and looking at these four countries' score on the Gini scale shows that Japan is really the only country who falls into the equitable distribution category, followed by India, the United States, and China – though none of them has surpassed the 0.50 mark into highly unequal. The higher the inequality, the more economic inefficiency exists, the lower the savings rate, the more social instability exists, and overall, it generally is regarded as unfair.[21] Japan is doing the best job at distributing its wealth more fairly, and the United States is notorious for income disparity between its richest and poorest, out-ranking India in this category and falling only slightly behind China. Japan takes the role of most developed nation by far in this measurement, as seen in the figure above.

Another indicator that is likely reflected in one of the previous categories (high-technology exports) is the level of focus on research and development in a country. Wealthier and more industrialized countries overall will have more funding to devote to this area, and it is reflected accordingly. Japan and the United States have higher per capita numbers of engineers in each of their populations. Consider the Figure on the following page, covering each country's expenditures on research and development: they both invest significantly more in research and development. Technology can spur growth, innovation, and raises the standard of living, so the ability to focus on this area can be considered as a key component to becoming a developed country. The sheer size of the US economy allows it not only to play a large role in the global economy but also allows for large amounts of technological innovation, maintaining its place at the forefront of developed countries.

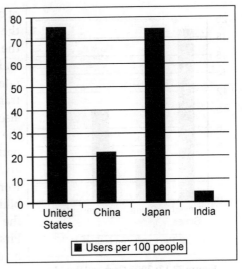

Figure 22.10: 2008 Internet Users

This next social indicator may be considered miscellaneous by many, but is likely an extension of some of the overall social indicators: more technological innovation, better infrastructure, and higher education levels. China actually has more internet users than any other country in real numbers, but below we see that the United States and Japan take over the category of internet usage per 100 people in each of those countries, at over 75 a piece, with China and India lagging considerably behind. Additionally, China is well-known for fairly harsh censorship and punishments for violators. Higher levels of internet usage means more access to information, and likely reflect higher literacy (and certainly, computer literacy) rates in the United States and Japan. Much more research is likely needed on whether this is a true correlation to development, but in the case of these four countries, it appears to be relevant when considered with all of the other social indicators.

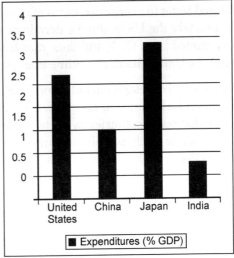

Figure 22.11: Research and Development Expenditures

The environment and the effects from growth on the environment are less-analyzed indicators, but should not be ignored. In the coming decades the planet will become more crowded and resources will only become scarcer, so the status of the world environment will become increasingly critical to mankind and its continued prosperity. The only indicator discussed here are emissions

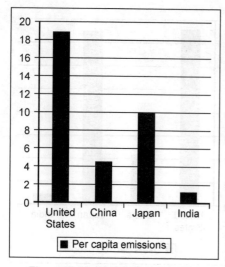

Figure 22.12: 2006 Carbon Dioxide Emissions

of carbon dioxide (CO_2) from each country, displayed in the figure above, and here again, the United States takes the lead – but in this case it is a negative connotation and certainly is not a lead to brag about. While this large rate means its citizens have reliable access to electricity, transportation, and other such energy consumption, it also means they are polluting at much higher rates than the rest of the world. The US far surpasses the other three nations in per capita CO_2 emissions, though as China and India's numbers rise, their potential to influence the world's environment will become larger. If their over two billion people combined polluted at the same rate that the United States does, the impact would be enormous. First, there are growing concerns about water and air quality, and second, '[India and China] are large enough to affect the global commons. Most significant in the long run are greenhouse gas emissions. Furthermore, [their increased] demand may put increased pressure on world energy markets.'[22] China, while it does not look like it in the figure, is second only to the United States in energy use, but is of course servicing a much larger population, and is expected to overtake the US in about a decade or so. Pollution is one of those externalities that are not discounted from GDP, and thus, may lead to over estimation of a country's GDP, in this case with the United States as a prime example.

These social development indicators provide a more in-depth look at what is actually happening in individual countries, and allow for a more thorough analysis of levels of development. It is clear that some countries by certain standards are far more advanced than others, and then an indicator such as pollution upsets the standards. While higher pollution levels may in fact reflect a higher development level, they also indicate large negative externalities that are unaccounted for in GDP. These are not intended to be used individually to gauge one country's level of development over another, but are meant to be applied in conjunction with economic and health indicators to better assess growth, progress, and development overall – not just in the macroeconomic sense.

HEALTH INDICATORS

Health indicators can clue us in to certain signs of development, or under-development as it may be. A high maternal mortality rate is certainly nothing to aspire to, with some of the worst rates in the world being countries that have fallen to the bottom of every index imaginable; for example nearly 2,000 deaths per 100,000 live births in both Afghanistan and Sierra Leone. Maternal mortality rates (MMR) tend to indicate certain other things, such as lack of skilled birthing attendants or less access to health care. Take a look at the graph to the left. India far and away has the highest MMR of the top-ranked (GDP) countries, with about 450 per 100,000 births. The US and Japan are considerably lower, both of them below 10, and China is also only at about forty-five. It is worth noting in China's situation, though, they have a unique population control solution in their one child per couple policy, resulting in what one would naturally expect to be far fewer pregnancies per woman than in India. There can be no speculation here about what China's population or demographics would look like it if not for that policy.

In addition to MMR, consider the following mortality rates in the graph at right, for children less than five years of age. A high rate of mortality of children less than five years of age has a similar correlation as the MMR above. The first few years of a child's life are some of the most vulnerable and a higher rate amongst that age group is indicative of several health disparities between developed and developing countries. Childhood vaccinations may be less available in developing countries, health care may be more readily available in developed countries, and citizens in the US and Japan may be more apt to take their children to a doctor quickly with less concern for the costs. A similar train of thought is probably also occurring in China, and is probably even more heightened by the same one child policy that may influence a lower MMR: they are likely particularly attentive to that one child and quick to act if there appears to be a health concern.

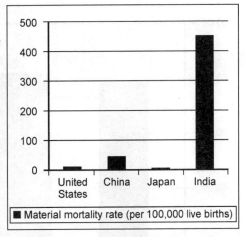

Figure 22.13: 2005 Maternal Mortality Rate

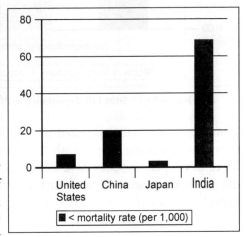

Figure 22.14: 2008 Under 5 Mortality Rate

Here as well we see India falling behind, by a fairly large margin, and Japan coming out on top with the lowest mortality rate for children under five years of age.

Life expectancy is one of the most basic health indicators, and one of the most revealing as well. It is included in the Human Development Index, an accepted alternative to GDP as a measurement of development. Socioeconomic status, which clearly will be lower in the development world, is linked quite consistently with health. 'Particularly noteworthy are social class differences in mortality, with persons lower in the social hierarchy having higher mortality rates than do persons in upper levels.'[23] In the Figure 22.13, Japan's life expectancy tops out at over 80 years old, followed closely by the United States at about 78, China at about 70, and India at just over 60. The longer life expectancies mean citizens are living longer, fewer are dying in childhood,

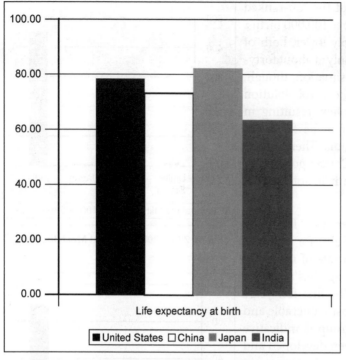

Figure 22.15: 2008 Life Expectancy at Birth (years)

and there is undoubtedly better access to health care. It is a critical component to look at when determining a given country's level of development, and often takes quite a bit of time to inch upwards. India has some catching up to do, but like most countries in the second half of the twentieth century, has made considerable progress from its rate fifty or sixty years ago.

There are many different health indicators that could be analyzed and applied to these four countries, but these are some of the most important and relevant to development status. The health status of women and children is indicative of access to quality care, as well as education levels and socioeconomic status. Women who are better educated tend to wait longer to have children, and have fewer of them, as well as take better care of both themselves during pregnancy and their offspring after birth. More developed societies have better medical technologies and access to care, and women die much less frequently in pregnancy or childbirth as they do in developing countries. Life expectancies are also indicative of similar trends: fewer children dying in childhood or infancy, and more people making it to older ages. Health and social development indicators have strong correlations between them, and are not unrelated to macroeconomic indicators.

CONCLUSION

It is unsurprising that gross domestic product is a very problematic economic measure of development. The GDP of a country provides limited information: the dollar amount of its outputs, and no more than that. It misses informal sectors, household work, volunteer work, population, quality, and the unreliability of data. In this chapter, GDP's constraints and problematic measurement have been detailed, along with alternative economic indicators for measuring economic development: per capita GDP, types of exports, inflation rates, and so on. An examination of each of these indicators with respect to the four largest GDPs in the world – the United States, China, Japan, and India – tells us a great deal about what actually needs to be considered when measuring development levels, and also tells us that there is no one correct answer, only several different, better options than GDP.

It is also clear that economic indicators alone do not suffice to explain a country's level of development, but social and health scores need to be evaluated as well. Social indicators can include everything from the status of female employment to school enrollment to pollution, and in conjunction with health indicators, provide a huge improvement on GDP as a window into a country's living standards and status of its population. Maternal mortality rates, child mortality rates, and life expectancy say a great deal about a country's access to quality health care; education, investment in research and development, and urban proportion of the population all say much about the opportunities available to its citizens, as well as their mobility and employment flexibility. These are all indicators that will vary slightly from country to country, so it is imperative to consider different measures when making any generalizations about development in a given country.

There is not one clear answer when measuring levels of economic development; instead, what is clear is that gross domestic product in and of itself tells us very little about a country or what may be happening within its borders. The answer then must require a more comprehensive, much broader analysis of indicators from all different sectors, including economic, health, and social development indicators. When studying the development of a country, looking at what its overall economy is doing is simply not sufficient. One must also look at what is happening to its people, and whether they are healthy, employed, or are pursuing education or not. I am not advocating one particular solution, rather, trying to illuminate the difficulties that lie in measuring development. I do support a comprehensive approach with at least one indicator, minimum, from each of the above mentioned sectors, as a vast improvement on GDP as a measure of a country's development. The United States may have the largest GDP and be considered the most developed nation in the world, but it is not the highest ranking in terms of per capita GDP or life expectancy, and it is the largest polluter in the world. Highlighted in this chapter is the fact that without snapshots of different sectors, an incomplete picture of development will be produced.

REFERENCES

1. Gadrey, Jean, 'What's Wrong with GDP and Growth?' in *A Guide to What's Wrong with Economics*, ed. Edward Fullbrook (London: Wimbledone Publishing, 2004), 264.
2. Stretton, Hugh, 'The Quarrelsome Boundaries of Economics,' in *A Guide to What's Wrong with Economics*, ed. Edward Fullbrook (London: Wimbledon Publishing, 2004), 11.
3. Gadrey, Jean, 'What's Wrong with GDP and Growth?' in *A Guide to What's Wrong with Economics*, ed. Edward Fullbrook (London: Wimbledon Publishing, 2004), 266.
4. Cobb, Clifford et al. 'If the GDP is up, Why is America Down?' in *The Atlantic Monthly*, online edition (October 1995), 3.
5. Gadrey, Jean, 'What's Wrong with GDP and Growth?' in *A Guide to What's Wrong with Economics*, ed. Edward Fullbrook (London: Wimbledon Publishing, 2004), 268.
6. Ibid., 270.
7. GDP table and all consecutive charts and graphs compiled from http://data.worldbank.org
8. Cobb, Clifford et al. 'If the GDP is up, Why is America Down?' in *The Atlantic Monthly*, online edition (October 1995), 4.

9. Majumdar, Badiul A., 'China and India: A Comparison of Their Development Experience,' in *China and India: Foreign Investment and Economic Development*, ed. Anant R. Negandhi and Peter Schran (Greenwich: Jai Press, 1990), 4.

10. Martinez-Vasquez, Jorge and Mark Rider, 'Fiscal Decentralization and Economic Growth: A Comparative Study of China and India,' in *Economic Development in India and China*, ed. Penelope B. Prime and Kishore G. Kulkarni (New Delhi: Serials Publications, 2007), 272.

11. Hulten, Charles R., *Productivity Growth in Japan and the United States* (Chicago: University of Chicago Press, 1990), 6.

12. Majumdar, Badiul A., 'China and India: A Comparison of Their Development Experience,' in *China and India: Foreign Investment and Economic Development*, ed. Anant R. Negandhi and Peter Schran (Greenwich: Jai Press, 1990), 12.

13. Ibid., 15.

14. Martinez-Vasquez, Jorge and Mark Rider, 'Fiscal Decentralization and Economic Growth: A Comparative Study of China and India,' in *Economic Development in India and China*, ed. Penelope B. Prime and Kishore G. Kulkarni (New Delhi: Serials Publications, 2007), 273.

15. Winters, L. Alan and Shahid Yusuf, 'Dancing with Giants,' in *Dancing with Giants: China, India and the Global Economy*, ed. L. Alan Winters and Shahi Yusuf (Washington DC: The World Bank, 2007), 19.

16. Ibid., 7.

17. Export data from https://www.cia.gov/library/publications/the-world-factbook/

18. Majumdar, Badiul A., 'China and India: A Comparison of Their Development Experience,' in *China and India: Foreign Investment and Economic Development*, ed. Anant R. Negandhi and Peter Schran (Greenwich: Jai Press, 1990), 9.

19. Todaro, Michael P. and Stephen C. Smith, *Economic Development* (Boston: Pearson Addison Wesley, 2009), 433.

20. Ibid., 214.

21. Ibid., 222.

22. Zmarak, Shalizi, 'Energy and Emissions,' in *Dancing with Giants: China, India and the Global Economy*, ed. L. Alan Winters and Shahi Yusuf (Washington DC: The World Bank, 2007), 137.

23. Friis, Robert and Thomas A. Sellers, *Epidemiology for Public Health Practice* (London: Jones and Bartlett, 2009), 170.

23 | Testing the J-Curve Hypothesis
The Cases of Malaysia, Ecuador, and Madagascar

Colleen Farr

CHAPTER SUMMARY

Theoretical treatments of currency devaluation generally conclude that it stimulates economic activity. The initial increase in the price of foreign goods relative to home goods is presumed to suppress demand for foreign imports and expand demand for exports of home goods. However, it is also argued that flows of export goods respond only with time lags to changes in the exchange rate. When plotted against time intervals, these lags produce a 'J' shape along the Balance of Trade curve (J-curve), reflecting an initial deterioration of the trade balance followed by a long-term improvement. This chapter will contribute to the literature on the effects of currency devaluation on the balance of trade with a test of the 'J-curve Hypothesis' on case studies from three developing regions: Southeast Asia, Latin America, and Africa. Specifically, this chapter finds evidence of the J-curve in the cases of Malaysia and Ecuador, but not in the case of Madagascar.

With the 1973 disintegration of the Bretton Woods international monetary system, governments were granted the power to independently control their monetary systems. Indeed, they were given the option to choose to let their currency values be determined on the international market, or to pick an arbitrary currency value. Most developed countries chose an open, floating exchange rate system, while most developing countries chose a fixed exchange rate regime.

Often, developing countries operating in fixed exchange rate systems are forced to lower the arbitrarily high value of their currencies. 'Devaluations' of this sort affect all aspects of an economy. Theoretical treatments of currency devaluation generally conclude that it stimulates economic activity. The initial increase in the price of foreign goods relative to home goods is presumed to suppress demand for foreign imports and expand demand for exports of home goods. However, it is also argued that flow of export goods respond only with time lags to changes in the exchange rate. These lags produce a 'J' shaped Balance of Trade (BOT) curve, reflecting an initial deterioration of the trade balance followed by a long-term improvement.

The J-curve is based more on empirical observation than actual theory. Studies of the effects of currency devaluation on trade balances have been conducted on individual countries, as well as multi-country panels. The results are mixed. This chapter will contribute to the literature on the effects of currency devaluation on the balance of trade with a test of the 'J-curve Hypothesis' on case studies from three developing regions: Southeast Asia, Latin America, and Africa. Specifically, this chapter will seek to find empirical evidence of the J-curve in the cases of Malaysia, Ecuador, and Madagascar.

The rest of the chapter is organized as follows. The next section will provide a theoretical overview of the J-curve Hypothesis and a brief literature review. Further, three case studies using annual statistics from the International Monetary Fund are presented in the next section. The final section, presents some general observations, conclusions, and policy implications in light of the evidence presented in previous section.

THEORETICAL SECTION

The J-Curve Hypothesis

Today, we define the exchange rate, in American terms, as the number of domestic currency units per unit of foreign currency (for example, $1.45/€). In this sense, an increase in the exchange rate defines a depreciation of the domestic currency, while a decrease in the exchange rate defines an appreciation of the domestic currency (Kulkarni, 2007, 42). In the case of a fixed exchange rate system, which is generally used in developing countries, 'devaluation' occurs when the government implements a policy to depreciate the currency. On the other hand, in the case of a flexible exchange rate system, which is generally used in the developed countries, the exchange rate is determined by the foreign exchange market.

Graph 23.1 depicts a 'demand for foreign exchange' curve and a 'supply of foreign exchange' curve. The demand curve is downward sloping because as the exchange rate increases, the domestic currency loses value. This causes the amount of imports into an economy to decrease, and leads to a subsequent decrease in demand for foreign exchange. As the domestic currency loses value, foreign residents are able to purchase more goods and services from the domestic economy. This increase in exports means that foreign residents supply more foreign exchange (Kulkarni, 2007, 43).

In a flexible exchange rate system, the exchange rate tends to remain at equilibrium (e). This is because of the 'Paradox of Flexibility'. The Paradox of Flexibility states that 'if a price (exchange rate in this case) is free to move up and down then it will stay at one level, namely at the equilibrium level' (Kulkarni, 2007, 43). In a fixed exchange rate system, however, a government can set its exchange rate at a level either above (e^2 e^2) or below equilibrium (e^1 e^1), as a change in the exchange rate has the effect of appreciating or depreciating the domestic currency. In most developing countries operating in fixed exchange rate systems, exchange rates are fixed below the equilibrium level at e^1 e^1. This effectively appreciates the currency. Most countries operating in fixed exchange rates choose to set their exchange rate below the equilibrium level because this allocates more

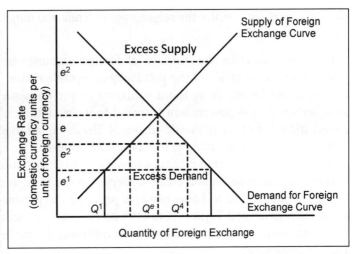

Graph 23.1

purchasing power to governments, who are generally the largest importers in an economy (Kulkarni, 2007, 44). Also, fixing the exchange rate necessitates trade tariffs, quotas, and other foreign exchange controls, which give some corrupt governments more administrative power. Pierre-Richard Agénor (1992) argues that an overvalued exchange rate in developing countries has been perceived as a symbol of economic independence, an inexpensive way to provide cheap imports to domestic consumers and producers that are seen as essential in promoting economic growth, and a way to foster the redistribution of income and economic activity from the tradable-goods sector to the nontradable-goods sector (Agénor, 1992, 11).

However, a fixed exchange rate can have negative consequences. Fixing the exchange rate creates both a shortage (from Q^1 Q^1 to Q^2 Q^2) of foreign exchange, and a deficit in the Balance of Trade (BOT). If a currency is fixed below its market-determined level, that currency is considered to be overvalued. The domestic country's exports become more expensive for foreign residents to purchase, and export levels decline. Because they are purchasing fewer domestic products, foreign residents supply less foreign exchange. To cover this shortage of foreign exchange, governments adopt policies that arbitrarily lower the quantity of foreign exchange demanded by domestic residents. Such policies include imposing tariffs or quotas on imported goods, limiting travel by domestic residents abroad, and banning or restricting purchases by domestic residents of foreign financial or real assets (Kulkarni, 1/11/2010). These policies often cause excess demand for foreign exchange among domestic residents. Excess demand for foreign exchange in a developing country can lead to the creation of black or 'parallel' currency markets (Agénor, 1992, 2). Indeed, parallel markets also have adverse effects, which include a high cost of enforcement to counteract illegal activities, a loss of tariff revenue as a result of smuggling, a loss of income taxes and domestic indirect taxes, and a reduced flow of foreign exchange to the central bank. Parallel markets also encourage rent-seeking behavior, which leads to the misallocation of scarce resources. Finally, the switch from domestic currency assets to foreign currency assets can reduce the seigniorage revenue accruing to the government (Agénor, 1992, 12).

When pressures from the shortage of foreign exchange become unbearable and when the trade deficit falls outside of the politically acceptable realm, 'the only option is to correct the exchange rate by accepting the devaluation of the domestic currency' (Kulkarni, 2007, 44). In other words, the government is forced to increase the exchange rate, which depreciates or lowers the value of the domestic currency. The devaluation effectively reduces the shortage of foreign exchange. For example, in Graph 23.1, an exchange rate shift from $e^1 e^1$ to $e^2 e^2$ should reduce demand for foreign exchange from $Q^3 Q^3$ to $Q^4 Q^4$ (Kulkarni, 2/23/2010). Also, in theory, currency devaluation should create a surplus in the BOT. Initially, an 'increase in the price of foreign goods relative to home goods is presumed to produce an excess of demand for home goods' (Krugman and Taylor, 1978, 445). As exports rise and imports decrease, the BOT should move into surplus. Therefore, currency devaluation should help developing countries facilitate BOT improvements.

However, a surplus in the balance of trade from currency devaluation depends on the response of export and import volumes to real exchange rates (Krugman and Obstfeld, 2009, 457). The Marshall-Lerner condition states that, 'all else equal, a real depreciation improves the current account if export and import volumes are sufficiently elastic with respect to the real exchange rate' (Krugman and Obstfeld, 2009, 457). Consider the following:

1. Real exchange rate (q)

$$Real\ Exchange\ Rate\ (q) = e\left(\frac{P^*}{P}\right)$$

   Where:
   - e = nominal exchange rate defined as the number of units of foreign currency
   - P* = price level in the foreign country
   - P = price level in the domestic economy

2. Elasticity of demand for imports (M) with respect to real exchange rate (q), $E_D^M E_D^M$

$$E_D^M = -\frac{\Delta M}{\Delta q} \times \frac{q}{M}$$

   Where:
   - M = amount of real imports

3. Elasticity of demand for exports (X) with respect to real exchange rate (q), $E_D^X E_D^X$

$$E_D^X = -\frac{\Delta X}{\Delta q} \times \frac{q}{X}$$

   Where:
   - X = amount of real exports

To derive the Marshall-Lerner condition, we must assume three things. First, the supply elasticities of exports and imports are infinite. This implies that there are no constraints or bottlenecks involved in supplying more or less exports or imports, thereby making all changes in the BOT a result of changes in demand (Kulkarni, 2007, 51). Second, there are no capital inflows or outflows, such that the capital account is always balanced. Therefore, at any given time, the Balance of Payment is defined by the BOT alone. Finally, it is assumed that at the time of the exchange rate change, the BOT is balanced. In other words, the value of all exports is equal to the value of all imports. Keeping in mind that the BOT is equal to exports minus imports expressed in foreign currency units, and, by assumption, the BOT is equal to 0, then:

$BOT = X - (qM) = 0$ $BOT = X - (qM) = 0$, which can be rearranged as:

$X = q \times M$ $X = q \times M$ or $M = \dfrac{X}{q}$ $M = \dfrac{X}{q}$

Now, considering the BOT equation with respect to changes in the real exchange rate (q), we have:

$$\frac{\Delta BOT}{\Delta q} = \frac{\Delta X}{\Delta q} - \left(\left(\frac{\Delta q}{\Delta q} \times M \right) \left(\frac{\Delta M}{\Delta q} \times q \right) \right)$$

Considering the equations for Elasticity of Demand for Exports, and Elasticity of Demand for Imports, and keeping in mind that the value of $E_D^M E_D^M$ is always negative, this equation can be simplified as:

$$\frac{\Delta BOT}{\Delta q} = M \left(E_D^X - 1 + E_D^M \right)$$

Then, to have a Balance of Trade with respect to the real exchange rate, $\dfrac{\Delta BOT}{\Delta q} \dfrac{\Delta BOT}{\Delta q}$, greater than zero, we need:

$\left(E_D^X - 1 + E_D^M \right) > 0 \left(E_D^X - 1 + E_D^M \right) > 0$ or $\left(E_D^X + E_D^M \right) > 1 \left(E_D^X + E_D^M \right) > 1$

The Marshall-Lerner Condition, then, states that:

$E_D^M + E_D^X > 1$ $E_D^M + E_D^X > 1$ For $\dfrac{\Delta BOT}{\Delta q} > 0$ $\dfrac{\Delta BOT}{\Delta q} > 0$.

If the current account is initially zero, a real currency depreciation 'causes a current account surplus if the sum of the relative price elasticities of export and import demand exceeds 1' (Krugman and Obstfeld, 2009, 458). Elasticities of demand for exports and imports, then, determine whether a balance of trade will be in surplus after currency devaluation.

One of the major determinants of the value of elasticity is the time that elapses after the change in the independent value (after the devaluation takes place) (Kulkarni, 2/23/2010). Indeed, it is widely accepted that the relationship between trade balance and real exchange rate varies over time, with short and long-run responses differing significantly. In the short-run, or immediately after devaluation, the elasticities of demand for exports and imports are too small

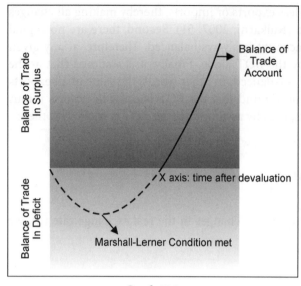

Graph 23.2

to fulfill the Marshall-Lerner condition, and the BOT immediately moves into (or toward) deficit. In the long-run, however, elasticities are higher and able to fulfill the Marshall-Lerner condition. In time, then, the BOT will move into surplus. In fact, the BOT may not reflect the new exchange rate for several months or years after the devaluation occurs (Krugman and Obstfeld 2009, 448). Some economists have found empirical evidence that supports lags of up to five years before the effects of exchange rate changes are felt on trade balances (Junz and Rhomberg, 1973, 414). If the current account initially worsens after devaluation but eventually moves into surplus, the BOT pattern is reminiscent of a 'J'. Indeed, economists have come to call this observation the 'J-Curve Hypothesis'. Graph 23.2 depicts a standard J-curve.

Literature Review

Since the early 1970s, scholars have studied the causes of the J-curve phenomenon, and have attributed it to several factors. Stephen Magee (1973) attributes the initial downward sloping section of the J-curve to a 'currency-contract' problem and a 'pass-through' problem. The 'currency-contract' problem deals with the brief period immediately following devaluation in which contracts negotiated prior to the change fall due. He finds that the currency in which the contract is denominated makes a difference. Indeed, if US trade contracts are denominated in, for example, US dollars, 'the immediate impact is to worsen the US deficit…because goods contracted for at pre-devaluation prices by US importers require more dollars in payment, and exports already in the stream of trade earn fewer dollars' (Magee, 1973, 312). The 'pass-through' problem refers to the behaviour of international prices on contracts agreed upon after the devaluation has taken place, but before it has effected significant changes in quantities (Magee, 1973, 305). Over time, new contracts made after the devaluation begin to dominate the market, and prices in the devaluing country begin to rise while prices in the upvaluing country begin to fall (Magee, 1973, 315). The result is an initial deterioration of the BOT.

In the same vein, Anne Krueger (1983) lists three factors that determine the *extent* to which the BOT pattern resembles a J-curve. First, the extent to which trade takes place under pre-existing conditions affects the shape of the BOT pattern. Second, the degree to which contracts are denominated asymmetrically in domestic and foreign currencies also has a significant effect.

Finally, the length of the lags in the execution of contracts can change the shape of the BOT pattern (Krueger, 1983, 40).

Paul Krugman and Maurice Obstfeld (2009) provide some specific examples of Magee and Krueger's 'lags'. In regards to the contract problem, Krugman and Obstfeld note that 'import and export orders are placed several months in advance. In the first few months after the depreciation, export and import volumes... may reflect buying decisions that were made on the basis of the old exchange rate' (Krugman and Obstfeld, 2009, 447). Also, even after the old export and import contracts are fulfilled, new shipments must adjust fully to the relative price change. For example, producers of exports may have to install additional plant and equipment and hire new workers to increase the volume of their exports (Krugman and Obstfeld, 2009, 448). On the consumption side, it may be necessary to build new retailing outlets abroad to increase consumption of products by foreign residents, which is a time-consuming process (Krugman and Obstfeld, 2009, 448). These issues create lags in the process between changes in exchange rates and their ultimate effects on real trade.

In 1973, Helen Junz and Rudolph Rhomberg categorized those lags into five types. The first type of lag is the *recognition* lag, which reflects the time it takes for buyers and sellers to become aware of the changed competitive situation. The second type is a *decision* lag, which reflects the time it takes for new business connections to be formed and new orders to be placed. Third is the *delivery* lag, which reflects the time it takes for goods to be delivered and payment to be recognized on published trade flows. This lag can vary from several months to several years, depending on the type of exported product. The fourth lag is the *replacement* lag, which reflects instances where inventories of materials must be used up or equipment allowed to wear out before any new materials or equipment can be purchased. Finally, there is a *production* lag, where producers who are convinced of a worthy profit opportunity will shift from supplying one market to supplying another, or they will add capacity in order to supply an additional market. In some extreme cases, suppliers decide to manufacture a new product, which takes time to design, market, and produce (Junz and Rhomberg, 1973, 413).

The J-curve hypothesis has been tested on many real world cases. Indeed, economists have found evidence to both support and reject the J-curve hypothesis in cases from Asia, Latin America, and Africa. For example, Mohsen Bahmani-Oskooee (1985) tested the J-curve hypothesis on three Asian economies: India, Korea, and Thailand. Each of these countries maintained different exchange rate regimes between 1973 and 1980, the period studied. India and Thailand pegged their currencies to the US dollar, while Korea had a fixed exchange rate with two devaluations between 1973 and 1979. Interestingly, during the period studied, the author finds both India and Korea showed evidence of the standard J-curve, but not Thailand (Bahmani-Oskooee, 1985, 502). Where India and Korea showed deteriorations in their trade balances within one year, in Thailand, the trade balance improved for five quarters immediately following devaluation and deteriorated thereafter.

Yu Hsing (2008) also tested the J-curve hypothesis on seven Latin American countries: Argentina between 1994 and 2007, Brazil between 1995 and 2007, Chile between 1980 and 2007, Colombia between 1995 and 2007, Ecuador between 1991 and 2007, Peru between 1992 and 2007, and Uruguay between 1993 and 2007. The author finds evidence in support of the J-curve for Chile, Ecuador, and Uruguay, where trade balances initially deteriorated, but improved in the long-run. However, his tests for Argentina, Brazil, Colombia, and Peru revealed little support for the J-curve hypothesis. In these countries, trade balances either improved initially (Argentina, Brazil, and Colombia), or initially deteriorated without long-run improvements (Peru) (Hsing, 2008, 9).

Other studies have tested the J-curve hypothesis in African countries. Eric Kamoto (2006), and Jacob Wanjala Musila and John Newark (2003) investigated the effects of currency devaluation on the BOT in Malawi. Kamoto, and Musila and Newark find that currency devaluation did lead to improvement in the BOT in the long-run (Musila and Neward 2003, 350). However, Kamoto does not find any evidence of a J-curve in which the BOT initially deteriorated (Kamoto 2006, 40). Conversely, Kishore Kulkarni (2007) does confirm evidence of the J-curve in the case of Egypt. Indeed, the devaluation of the Egyptian pound in 1988 led to a slight deterioration in the Balance of Payments in 1989, with significant improvement thereafter. By 1991, Egypt's Balance of Payments remained consistently in surplus.

Further, Kulkarni extends the J-curve hypothesis to explain cases where one devaluation is followed by another devaluation shortly thereafter. In fact, when countries allow their currencies to devalue several times, then a persistent balance of trade deficit is very likely. Consistent with the J-curve hypothesis, in the short run, elasticities of imports and exports are too small to meet the Marshall-Lerner Condition. So, if a second devaluation occurs before the Marshall-Lerner Condition is met, the J-curve is shifted to the right, creating persistent BOT deficits (Kulkarni and Clarke, 2009, 7). Kulkarni finds evidence of the Kulkarni Hypothesis in the case of Ghana, where progressive devaluations of the cedi led to a consistent deterioration of Ghana's BOT .

CASE STUDIES

Malaysia

The devaluation of the Malaysian ringgit (MYR) in 1997 stemmed from Malaysia's period of financial and trade liberalization throughout the late 1980s and early 1990s. Such liberalization created high levels of unstable capital flows, which effectively made Malaysia's economy vulnerable to economic shocks. This was the case for many countries in East and Southeast Asia during the early 1990s. In the end, devaluation did dramatically improve Malaysia's trade balance, which helped Malaysia move smoothly out of financial crisis and back on the track toward economic growth.

Graph 23.3 shows a progression of the Malaysian ringgit between 1980 and 2008. For the five years prior to 1997, the ringgit varied within the narrow band of MYR 2.70 to 2.53 per USD (IMF, 2010). During this short time, Malaysia registered consistently high levels of economic growth at around 8.8 per cent per year, increasing per capita income from USD 1,850 to USD

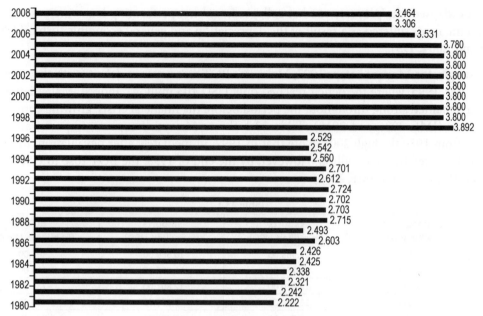

Graph 23.3: Malaysian Ringgit/USD

Source: IMF 2006 and IMF 2010.

4,425 (Yussof and Chin, 2004, 178). Indeed, by 1997, Malaysia was ranked number 35 in the world in terms of aggregate and per capita GNP (Varma, 2007, 207). Social cohesion was strong, unemployment was below 3 per cent per year, foreign exchange reserves were robust, and prices and the exchange rate remained stable (Meesook, 2001, 1).

During this time, Malaysia pursued a policy strategy aimed at raising economic growth by promoting rapid investment in export sectors. Policies included dramatic capital account liberalization and financial system deregulation (Varma, 2007, 208). Investment soared by 18.2 per cent of GDP between 1988 and 1996 (Doraisami, 2001, 167), and much of that investment went into electronics, machinery, manufacturing and other export-industries (Meesook, 2001, 4). As an open trading economy, stable exchange rates in Malaysia played a major role in attracting capital inflows and foreign investment to promote growth in the export sector. For this reason, Malaysia maintained its exchange rate within a narrow band. However, when the Thai baht came under heavy speculative attack in May 1997, the ringgit experienced heavy selling pressure (Yussof and Chin, 2004, 179). Capital outflows proceeded at rapid rates, and the Bank Negara Malaysia (BNM) attempted to defend the value of the ringgit by selling close to USD1.5 billion. However, the BNM was ultimately forced to give way to market forces in July 1997, and it allowed a devaluation of the ringgit. This devaluation is evidenced in Graph 23.3. The ringgit fell from MYR 2.47 per dollar in the first quarter of 1997 to its lowest at MYR 4.88 per dollar in January 1998, depreciating against the dollar by almost 50 per cent (Yussof and Chin, 2004, 179). The financial crisis subsequently turned into economic turmoil as the stock market collapsed, the property market collapsed, and nonperforming loans increased. In the short term, firms suffered as a result of the depreciation and general economic turmoil (Yussof and Chin, 2004, 179).

Interestingly, for 14 years before 1997, Malaysia's BOT was never in deficit (with the exception of one year, 1995, where the deficit reached only USD 103 million). Indeed, Malaysian export growth remained strong throughout the period before the financial crisis, growing consistently every year (IMF, 2006 and 2010). Table 23.1 shows Malaysia's exports, imports, and trade balance from 1980 through 2008. Note that in 1997, immediately after devaluation, Malaysia's trade balance fell by $338 million. However, by the end of 1998, the BOT rose to USD 17,505 million (IMF, 2006 and IMF, 2010).

Table 23.1

Year	Exchange Rate MYR/USD	Exports (in million USD)	Imports (in million USD)	BOT (in million USD)
1980	2.222	12,963.00	−10,569.00	2,393.00
1981	2.242	11,771.00	−11,886.00	−115.00
1982	2.321	12,070.00	−12,801.00	−731.00
1983	2.338	13,804.00	−13,366.00	438.00
1984	2.425	16,521.00	−13,590.00	2,931.00
1985	2.426	15,251.00	−11,677.00	3,573.00
1986	2.603	13,655.00	−10,441.00	3,214.00
1987	2.493	17,877.00	−12,093.00	5,783.00
1988	2.715	20,980.00	−15,553.00	5,427.00
1989	2.703	24,776.00	−10,498.00	4,277.00
1990	2.702	28,806.00	−26,280.00	2,525.00
1991	2.724	33,712.00	−33,321.00	391.00
1992	2.612	39,823.00	−36,673.00	3,150.00
1993	2.701	46,238.00	−43,201.00	3,037.00
1994	2.560	56,897.00	−55,320.00	1,577.00
1995	2.542	71,767.00	−71,876.00	−103.00
1996	2.529	76,881.00	−73,055.00	3,848.00
1997	3.892	77,881.00	−74,055.00	3,510.00
1998	3.800	71,883.00	−54,378.00	17,505.00
1999	3.800	84,098.00	−61,453.00	22,644.00
2000	3.800	98,249.00	−77,576.00	20,854.00
2001	3.800	87,981.00	−69,597.00	18,383.00
2002	3.800	93,383.00	−75,248.00	18,135.00
2003	3.800	104,999.00	−79,289.00	25,711.00
2004	3.800	126,817.00	−99,244.00	27,572.00
2005	3.780	141,808.00	−108,653.00	33,156.00
2006	3.531	160,916.00	−123,474.00	37,441.00
2007	3.306	176,433.00	−139,243.00	37,190.00
2008	3.464	199,733.00	−148,472.00	51,261.00

*Values reflect end-of-year averages
Source: IMF 2006 and IMF 2010.

Indeed, the negative impact of devaluation on Malaysia's BOT was small and short-lived. Graph 23.4 depicts Malaysia's BOT movements between 1992 and 2008. This graph does show evidence of a J-curve (magnified in Graph 23.5). Between 1996 and 1997, Malaysia's BOT deteriorated (minimally). This is the short period in which elasticities of demand for imports and exports did not sum to one. In other words, this is the period in which the Marshall-Lerner Condition was not yet met. In Malaysia's case, this period only lasted several months. Indeed, the Marshall-Lerner Condition was met before the end of 1998, when the BOT began its long-term improvement.

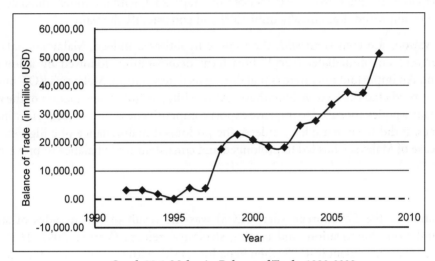

Graph 23.4: Malaysia, Balance of Trade, 1992-2008

*Values reflect end-of-year averages
Source: IMF 2006 and IMF 2010.

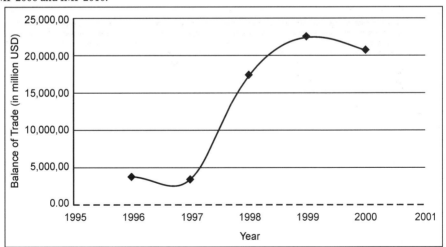

Graph 23.5: Malaysia, Balance of Trade, 1996-2000 (Magnified J-Curve)

*Values reflect end-of-year averages
Source: IMF 2006 and IMF 2010.

Malaysia's long-term BOT improvement, which began in 1998 and continues today, can be attributed to the long-term maintenance of an undervalued ringgit. In September 1998, Malaysia pegged the ringgit to the dollar at RYM 3.80. The IMF has argued that the fixing of the ringgit at that level 'has prevented the ringgit from correcting itself to its true market value. The IMF and the Malaysian Institute of Economic Research estimated that the ringgit remained undervalued by about 16 per cent to 18 per cent in 1999' (Mad et al., 2004, 187). This undervaluation, they argued, was instrumental in fostering Malaysia's export growth since it provided a competitive price advantage to Malaysia's exports against similar products and services of other Asian economies (Mad et al., 2004, 187). As evidenced in Graph 23.4, with an undervalued currency, Malaysia's BOT improved dramatically until 1999 and consistently thereafter.

These observations are consistent with the J-curve hypothesis. Indeed, Malaysia's Balance of Trade underwent an immediate, (very) short-term deterioration, followed by a long-term improvement. An important note here is that during its deterioration, Malaysia's BOT never fell into deficit, as predicted the J-curve hypothesis. Also, while the initial devaluation of the ringgit was not actually a policy tool used to improve export competitiveness, and subsequently improve trade balances, it did have that effect. Indeed, the prolonged maintenance of a high exchange rate, in the case of Malaysia, has led to prolonged and consistent trade balance improvements.

Ecuador

The devaluation of the Ecuadorean sucre (ECS) was the result of two decades of struggle with hyperinflation, dollarization, and lagging structural reform (Varma, 2007, 162). These vulnerabilities became evident in 1998 when Ecuador was hit with several shocks that threw the economy into deep recession, forcing several devaluations of the sucre. By 2002, however, the devaluations helped improve Ecuador's Balance of Trade and move Ecuador out of recession.

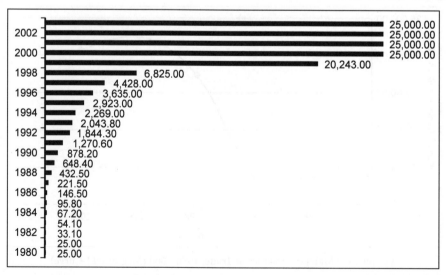

Graph 23. 6: Ecuadorean Sucres/USD

Source: IMF 2006 and IMF 2010.

Between 1990 and 1998, Ecuador maintained a slow but steady growth rate, averaging just over 3.5 per cent per year. This stable growth was fueled by an increase in oil and agricultural exports, which doubled during the same time. For several years, Ecuador's trade balance enjoyed a 'honeymood period' of consistent surplus and growth (Pérez, 2003, 458). In 1992, Ecuador also adopted a series of structural reforms, aimed at achieving greater macroeconomic stability. These reforms included an exchange-rate-based stabilization program based on a pre-announced crawling band to bring down inflation from 50 per cent annually (Jácome, 2004, 5). The stabilization program succeeded in reducing Ecuador's inflation to around 40 per cent per year (Jácome, 2004, 5).

However, financial deregulation and capital account liberalization in Ecuador's case led to a credit boom and an increase in imported products for consumption, rather than for investment. At the same time, a growing real estate and non-tradable goods bubble became evident. The sustainability of Ecuador's balance of payments was questionable (Pérez, 2003, 48990). Additionally, the adoption of several adjustments to the parameters of the exchange rate band (six between 1995 and 1998) slowly eroded the credibility of the new exchange regime (Jácome, 2004, 10). Beginning in 1995, the sucre depreciated several times, from ECS 1,844.30 per dollar in 1992 to ECS 3,635 ECS per dollar in 1996, and again to ECS 4,428 per dollar in 1997 (IMF, 2010).

Table 23.2 shows Ecuador's exports, imports, and trade balance between 1980 and 2009. Several devaluations between 1991 and 2000 correspond to deteriorations in Ecuador's trade balance. For example, a devaluation in 1992 corresponds to a USD 426 million deterioration in 1993. Another devaluation in 1996 corresponds to a USD 595 million deterioration in 1997. Yet another devaluation in 1997 corresponds to a USD1,593 million deterioration in 1998 and a shift into deficit. However, as is consistent with the J-curve hypothesis, these latter two devaluations also correspond with a significant improvement in the BOT between 1998 and 1999. Indeed, the BOT moved out of deficit and into a USD 1,665 million surplus. However, the long-term benefits of these devaluations were significantly eroded by a further, and much larger, devaluation of the sucre in 1998.

In fact, as the sucre depreciated throughout the second half of the 1990s, inflation soared. Investors lost confidence in the central bank's policy targets and shifted financial assets to foreign currencies as a means of hedging against inflation. High levels of dollarization, 'encouraged by the higher volatility of inflation vis-à-vis the exchange rate' added fuel to the fire (Jácome, 2004, 10). The dollarization process in Ecuador was fueled by the proliferation of offshore branches, which paid higher deposit rates and provided an expanded supply of financial services. This facilitated portfolio reallocations from sucres to dollars (Jácome, 2004, 10). By the end of 1997, foreign currency deposits reached to over one-third of total onshore deposits, and to more than 70 per cent of the Central Bank of Ecuador's net international reserves (Jácome, 2004, 10).

In the context of increasing financial liberalization, lax financial supervision, bad banking practices, and an unsustainable balance of payments, economic vulnerabilities were made

Table 23.2

Year	Exchange Rate ECS/USD	Exports (in million USD)	Imports (in million USD)	BOT (in million USD)
1980	25.00	2,520.00	-242.00	278.00
1981	25.00	2,527.00	-2,353.00	174.00
1982	33.20	2,327.00	-2,187.00	140.00
1983	54.10	2,348.00	-1,421.00	927.00
1984	67.20	2,621.00	-1,567.00	1,054.00
1985	95.80	2,905.00	-1,611.00	1,294.00
1986	146.50	2,200.00	-1,643.00	557.00
1987	221.50	2,021.00	-2,054.00	-33.00
1988	432.50	2,205.00	-1,583.00	622.00
1989	648.40	2,354.00	-1,692.00	662.00
1990	878.20	2,724.00	-1,715.00	1,009.00
1991	1,270.60	2,851.00	-2,208.00	643.00
1992	1,844.30	3,101.00	-2,083.00	1,018.00
1993	2,043.80	3,066.00	-2,474.00	592.00
1994	2,269.00	3,843.00	-3,282.00	561.00
1995	2,923.50	4,381.00	-4,057.00	324.00
1996	3,635.00	4,873.00	-3,680.00	1,193.00
1997	4,428.00	5,264.00	-4,666.00	598.00
1998	6,825.00	4,203.00	-5,198.00	-995.00
1999	20,243.00	4,451.00	-2,786.00	1,665.00
2000	25,000.00	5,137.00	-3,743.00	1,395.00
2001	25,000.00	4,814.00	-5,210.00	-462.00
2002	25,000.00	5,198.00	-6,196.00	-1,004.00
2003	25,000.00	6,446.00	-6,366.00	80.00
2004	25,000.00	7,968.00	-7,684.00	284.00
2005	25,000.00	10,468.00	-9,709.00	758.00
2006	25,000.00	13,176.00	-11,408.00	1,768.00
2007	25,000.00	14,870.00	-13,047.00	1,823.00
2008	25,000.00	19,147.00	-17,776.00	1,371.00

*Values reflect end-of-year averages
Source: IMF 2006 and 2010.

clear by several exogenous shocks in 1997 and 1998. El Niño floods destroyed vast amounts of agricultural products in 1997, and the Russian financial crisis and subsequent Brazilian crisis, which spilled over into Ecuador and the rest of Latin America in 1998, reduced Ecuador's ability to borrow on international markets. Oil prices also sank to less than USD 10 per barrel for Ecuadorean crude, which hurt public finances and foreign currency reserves (Jácome, 2004, 16). These shocks triggered banking and currency crises, and a large devaluation of the Sucre in 1998. Between January and February 1999, the Sucre depreciated another 50 per cent (Jácome, 2004, 20). As world oil prices continued to decline in early 1999, Ecuador's trade balance began to deterioirate.

Graph 23.7 depicts the movement of Ecuador's BOT between 1996 and 2007. On an important note, devaluations took place in 1996, 1997, 1998, and 1999, before the sucre finally stabilized in 2000. Consistent with the J-curve hypothesis, the 1996 and 1997 devaluations immediately led to a trade deficit in 1998. However, we would expect to see a further decline in the BOT after the 1998 devaluation. Instead, the BOT moves immediately into surplus between 1998 and 1999. This could be attributed to the 1996 and 1997 devaluations, whose long-term effects may have overpowered the short-term negative consequences of the 1998 devaluation. This could also be attributed to some other, external factor. However, the 'short-term' implications of the 1998 and 1999 devaluations seem to take effect after 1999, when the BOT again moves into deficit. This is consistent with a 'delayed' type of J-curve.

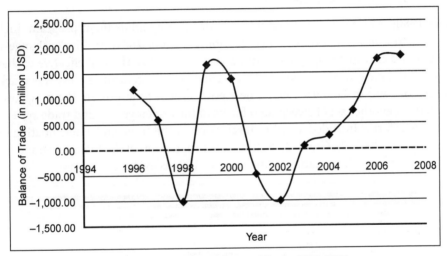

Graph 23.7: Ecuador, Balance of Trade, 1996-2007

*Values reflect end-of-year averages
Source: IMF 2006 and 2010.

Indeed, after the sucre stabilized with a peg to the dollar at ECS 25,000, the BOT began to slow its freefall. In 2002, two years after stabilization, the Marshall-Lerner condition was met. In other words, the short-term deterioration of the BOT, an effect of the 1998 and 1999 devaluations, lasted for two years. After 2002, Ecuador's BOT moved into surplus, and has consistently improved since then. This is consistent with the J-curve hypothesis.

Madagascar

The devaluation of the Malagasy franc (MGF) in 1994 was a policy included in a set of reforms used to mark a new government after several years of political turmoil. Between 1980 and 1994, Madagascar's balance of trade (barely) moved into surplus only two times, and even after the major devaluation in 1994, Madagascar's trade balance showed no improvements. As a result, Madagascar does not show evidence of the J-curve hypothesis.

In the late 1970s, Madagascar's government had a clear socialist leaning. It adopted a large public investment programme called the 'Investing to the Limit' policy. This programme called for massive investments in an effort to escape a prolonged spell of economic stagnation that had persisted since independence in 1960 (Razafimahefa, et al. 2005, 412). Increases in world coffee prices were supposed to generate domestic savings that would finance investments, but favourable coffee prices were actually short-lived, and investments did not bring about expected returns. "Ultimately, 'investing to the limit' dramatically increased imports of capital and intermediate goods, expanded foreign debt, and worsened the balance of payment deficit" (Razafimahefa et al., 2005, 412). This poor policy programme pushed Madagascar into a crisis from which the economy has never fully recovered. GDP actually fell by about 40 per cent between 1970 and 1994 (Azam, 2001, 2).

In the mid 1980s, Madagascar entered into a wide-ranging adjustment program, including a gradual move to a more market-oriented economy (Azam, 2001, 2). The exchange rate was managed under a crawling peg system, with a view to stabilize the real effective exchange rate to promote economic growth (Azam, 2001, 8). However, the reform process was marked with political turmoil, and in January 1993, a new government took power. The new government implemented yet another set of sweeping reforms of the exchange rate and trade system in May 1994. The new reforms included a major devaluation of the franc and a new floating exchange rate regime (Azam, 2007, 7). Graph 23.8 shows the progression of the Malagasy franc from 1980 to 2002. The significant depreciation of the franc in 1994 is evident.

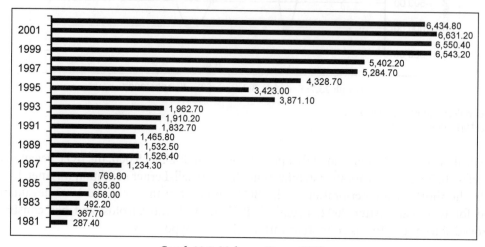

Graph 23.8: Malagasy Francs/USD

Source: IMF 2006 and IMF 2010.

Despite these reforms, however, the Malagasy economy resumed its downward slide throughout the 1990s. Under the independent floating regime adopted in 1994, the franc declined from MGF 1,962.7 per dollar in 1993 to MGF 3,871.1 per dollar in 1994. After 1994, the franc proceeded to decline slowly and consistently (IMF, 2006 and IMF, 2010). During Madagascar's structural adjustment period from 1980 to 2000, the franc depreciated by a factor of 32 per cent

(Razafimahefa et al., 2005, 426). Terms of trade also declined significantly for Madagascar's leading exports, rice and coffee, as the international prices of most commodities crashed on world markets (Azam, 2001, 3). This negatively affected Madagascar's BOT, preventing it from ever moving into surplus between 1993 and 2005. Table 23.3 shows Madagascar's trade balance from 1980 to 2005. In 22 years, the BOT only reached surplus two times (in 1987 and 1989). After 1994, the BOT progressively deteriorated (with the exception of a slight improvement between 2000 and 2001) (IMF, 2006 and IMF, 2010).

Table 23.3

Year	Exchange Rate FMG/USD	Exports (in million USD)	Imports (in million USD)	BOT (in million USD)
1980	225.80	436.00	−764.00	−328.00
1981	287.40	332.00	−511.00	−179.00
1982	367.70	327.00	−452.00	−124.00
1983	492.20	310.00	−378.00	−68.00
1984	658.00	337.00	−360.00	−23.00
1985	635.80	291.00	−336.00	−44.00
1986	769.80	323.00	−331.00	−8.00
1987	1,234.30	327.00	−315.00	11.00
1988	1,526.40	284.00	−319.00	−34.00
1989	1,532.50	321.00	−321.00	1.00
1990	1,465.80	318.00	−566.00	−249.00
1991	1,832.70	335.00	−446.00	−111.00
1992	1,910.20	327.00	−471.00	−144.00
1993	1,962.70	335.00	−514.00	−180.00
1994	3,871.10	450.00	−546.00	−96.00
1995	3,423.00	507.00	−628.00	−122.00
1996	4,328.70	509.00	−629.00	−120.00
1997	5,284.70	516.00	−694.00	−178.00
1998	5,402.20	538.00	−693.00	−154.00
1999	6,543.20	584.00	−742.00	−158.00
2000	6,550.40	824.00	−997.00	−174.00
2001	6,631.20	928.00	−955.00	−27.00
2002	6,434.80	486.00	−603.00	−117.00
2003	1,219.60	854.00	−1,111.00	−258.00
2004	1,869.40	990.00	−1,427.00	−437.00
2005	*3,087.00	834.00	−1,427.00	−592.00

*Indicates switch to Malagasy ariary
**Values reflect end-of-year averages
Source: IMF 2006 and IMF 2010.

The J-curve hypothesis would predict that, immediately after devaluation of the franc, Madagascar's BOT would deteriorate for a short period, but improve in the long run. This is not the case in Madagascar. Graph 23.9 shows Madagascar's BOT movements from 1993 to 2005. Indeed, immediately after devaluation in 1994, the trade balance deteriorated, but slowly and not significantly. The trade balance then continues to deteriorate every year thereafter (with the exception of 2001). This is inconsistent with the J-curve hypothesis, and could be attributed to the slow, steady decline of the Malagasy franc since 1994. Razafimahefa et al. estimate the size of Madagascar's elasticities of demand for exports and imports to verify whether or not the Marshall-Lerner condition is ever met. They find no statistically significant evidence that the elasticities are ever large enough to meet the Marshall-Lerner condition. Indeed, this is conducive to Madagascar's lack of J-curve.

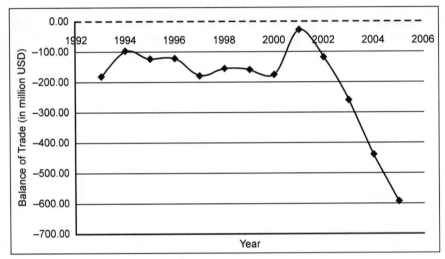

Graph 23.9: Madagascar, Balance of Trade, 1993-2005

*Values reflect end-of-year averages.
Source: IMF 2006 and IMF 2010.

CONCLUSIONS

This chapter tested the J-curve hypothesis on three countries: Malaysia, Ecuador, and Madagascar. It found evidence of the J-curve in Malaysia and Ecuador, but not in Madagascar. In Malaysia after the 1997 devaluation of the ringgit, the trade balance immediately deteriorated for a few short months then improved in the long-run. Interestingly, Malaysia's trade balance never moved into deficit after the 1997 devaluation. In Ecuador, several deteriorations of the sucre between 1996 and 1999 caused volatile shifts in the trade balance. However, the 1999 devaluation did immediately lead the BOT into deficit until 2002. Consistent with the J-curve hypothesis, Ecuador's trade balance improved after 2002. Finally, the 1994 devaluation of the Malagasy franc did lead to a slow, steady deterioration of Madagascar's trade balance. However, the BOT never moved out of deficit, and continued to deteriorate after 1994. This is inconsistent with the J-curve hypothesis.

In light of these results, we can draw two general conclusions. First, the initial cause of devaluation may have an effect on trade balances. Where banking or financial crises lead to devaluation

(Malaysia and Ecuador), countries may be more likely to see long-term improvements in their trade balances. Second, long-term exchange rate stability is consistent with long-term improvements in trade balances. Where the exchange rate was pegged after an initial devaluation (Malaysia and Ecuador), long-term growth ensued. Where the exchange rate was allowed to devalue further (Madagascar), long-term deteriorations of the trade balance ensued.

These observations have policy implications. While in some cases, devaluations lead to long-term improvements in trade balances, in some cases it does not. Therefore, a country considering using currency devaluation as a tool to improve trade balances should consider its unique situation carefully. Further, if that country's ultimate goal is a BOT improvement, it may follow devaluation with a currency peg to ensure stability. If that peg keeps the currency undervalued (like, for example, the Malaysian ringgit or the Chinese yuan), trade balances may dramatically improve in the long term. However, currency pegging and undervaluation may have serious negative implications, and should not be utilized without an in-depth, country-specific understanding of its effects.

REFERENCES

1. Agénor, Pierre-Richard. 1992. 'Parallel Currency Markets in Developing Countries: Theory, Evidence, and Policy Implications.' *Essays in International Finance* 188.

2. Azam, Jean-Paul. 2001. 'Inflation and macroeconomic instability in Madagascar.' Center for the Study of African Economies Paper Series: Berkeley Electronic Press: http://www.bepress/csae/paper140

3. Bahmani-Oskooee, Mohsen. 1985. 'Devaluation and the J-Curve: Some Evidence from LDCs.' *The Review of Economics and Statistics* 67 (3): 500-504.

4. Doraisami, Anita. 2001. 'The Malaysian Currency crisis: capital flows, policy response and macroeconomic stability.' In *Global Financial Crises and Reforms*. Ed. B.N. Ghosh, 157-183. London: Routledge.

5. International Monetary Fund (IMF). 2000. *International Financial Statistics Yearbook*. Washington, D.C.: International Monetary Fund Publication Services.

6. International Monetary Fund (IMF). 2010. *International Financial Statistics*. http://www.imfstatistics.org/imf/ (accessed May 28, 2010).

7. Jácome, Luis I. 2004. 'IMF Working Paper 0412: The Late 1990s Financial Crisis in Ecuador: Institutional Weaknesses, Financial Rigidities, and Financial Dollarization at Work.' New York: International Monetary Fund.

8. Junz, Helen and Rudolph Rhomberg. 1973. 'Price Competitiveness in Export Trade Among Industrial Countries.' In *The American Economic Review* 63 (2): 412-418.

9. Kamoto, Eric B. 2006. 'The J-Curve Effect on the Trade Balance in Malawi and South Africa.' http://economics.uta.edu/theses/Eric.Kamoto.pdf (accessed May 30, 2010).

10. Krugman, Paul R. and Lance Taylor. 1978. 'Contractionary Effects of Devaluation.' In *Journal of International Economics* 8 (1978): 445-456.

11. Krugman, Paul. R. and Maurice Obstfeld. 2009. *International Economics: Theory and Policy. 8th Edition*. New York: Pearson, Addison Wesley.

12. Kulkarni, Kishore G. 2007. 'The J-Curve Hypothesis and Currency Devaluation.' In *Readings in*

International Economics: Selected Writings of Prof. Kishore G. Kulkarni. 2nd Edition. New Delhi: Serials Publications.

13. Kulkarni, Kishore and Andrew Clarke. 2009. 'Testing the J-Curve Hypothesis: Case Studies from Around the World.' http://kulkarnibooks.com/assets/downloads/kishore_papers/paper_with_andrew_calrke_on_J-curve_and_kulkarni_hypothesis.pdf (accessed May 23, 2010).

14. Mad, Che Ani, Nik Kamariah bt. Kik Mat, Nasruddin Zainudin, Nor Hayati bt. Ahmad, and Engku Ngah Sayudin Engku Chik. 2004. 'Impact of Pegging on Malaysian Ringgit after the onset of the Asian Financial Crisis in July 1997.' In *Global Financial Markets: Issues and Strategies*. Ed. Dilip K. Ghosh and Mohamed Ariff, 187-205. Westport, CT: Greenwood Publishing.

15. Magee, Stephen P. 1973. 'Currency Contracts, Pass-through, and Devaluation.' Brookings Papers on Economic Activity 1973 (1): 303-325.

16. Meesook, Kanitta. 2001. 'Comparative Review of Policies and Performance, 1997-2000.' In *International Monetary Fund Occasional Paper 207: Malaysia: From Crisis to Recovery*. Ed. Kanitta Meesook, Il Houng Lee, Olin Liu, Yougesh Khatri, Natalia Tamirisa, Michael Moore, and Mark H. Krysl, 3-15. Washington, D.C.: International Monetary Fund.

17. Pérez, Pedro Páez. 2003. 'Financial Liberalization, Crisis and National Currency Destruction in Ecuador.' In *Regional Integration in Europe and Latin America: Monetary and Financial Aspects*. Ed. Pierre van der Haegen and Jose Viñals, 447-501. Burlington, VT: Ashgate.

18. Razafimahefa, Ivohasina Fizara, and Shigeyuki Hamori. 2005. 'Import Demand Function: Some Evidence from Madagascar and Mauritius.' *Journal of African Economies* 14 (3): 411-434.

19. Varma, Sumati. 2007. *Currency Convertibility: Indian and Global Experiences*. New Delhi: New Century Publications.

20. Wanjala Musila, Jacob, and John Newark. 2003. 'Does Currency Devaluation Improve the Trade Balance in the Long Run? Evidence from Malawi.' In *African Development Review* 15 (2-3): 339-352.

21. Yu Hsing, 'A Study of the J-Curve for Seven Selected Latin American Countries,' 2008, *Global Economy Journal*,8 (4):

22. Yussof, Mohammed B. and Lee Chin. (2004). 'Money, Exchange Rates, and Inflation: Evidence from Malaysia.' In *Global Financial Markets: Issues and Strategies*. Ed. Dilip K. Ghosh and Mohamed Ariff, 177-187. Westport, CT: Greenwood Publishing.

24

Effect of Globalization on India's Economic Growth

Kishore G. Kulkarni

CHAPTER SUMMARY

The wave of globalization appeared on India's shores only in 1991, much after China's and some other Southeast Asian countries such as Malaysia, Singapore and Hong Kong. Moreover the intensity of opening country's borders is much higher in other countries than in India where democratic political forces delay decision making significantly. Nonetheless, the Indian economy has broken the shackles of protectionism with great vigour which has led to some positive developments. This Chapter is an attempt to summarize the different policy making before and after the realization of gains from trade. In economic terms, one can undoubtedly prove that there are benefits realized, and the Indian economy is on a smooth sail partly because of the gains from trade. Of course any economy's real growth appears only with increased total factor productivity, greater and better use of her resources and public policy that understands and protects the private sector's interest. India still has a long way to go but major benefits already accrued from the right policies should serve as lessons to learn.

EFFECT OF GLOBALIZATION ON INDIA'S ECONOMIC GROWTH

As a new participant in the globalization wave, India went through several structural and policy changes only in early 1990s, even if the awareness of need for opening up country's borders was started in late 1980s, when Mr. Rajiv Gandhi was at the helm of policy design. With almost 20 per cent devaluation of the Indian rupee in 1991, the process began that for a while slowed down a little but rarely anyone was in doubt about its existence. The recent reports show that Indian economy grew at the record breaking and astonishing pace of 8 per cent growth in real GDP in 2003-2004. The real question is how did the economy that was an 'almost autarky' from 1950 to 1985 period, reached to such a realization that gains from trade are there to reap and the economic transition necessary for globalization is a pre-condition for wider economic growth? This chapter attempts to investigate if globalization is a cause of India's economic growth and if the new culture of trade policy change in India is there permanently or temporarily.

The present chapter is organized as follows: Section 1 makes the survey of trade policy in period 1950 to 1985, Section 2 summarizes the economic changes in period 1985 to 2005 with special focus on the liberalization attempt in 1991 and its after-effects. Section 3 summarizes results and makes a conclusion. In general, it is not very hard to prove that even a limited attempt of globalization has benefited Indian economy in the best possible way. As it is argued numerous times in other circles and by other economists (such as Prof. Jagdish Bhagwati and T. N. Srinivasan,) the drive of liberalization has to pick up the speed for better and faster gains for the economy.

The Big Move Toward Protectionist Posture

The Indian independence movement in 1940s, led by Mahatma Gandhi, was based on the general dislike of anything and everything 'foreign', especially the one originating from Britain. The public rallies to burn imported goods were famous. There was a strong belief that India can produce everything at home, can be 'self-reliant' and 'self-dependent' (popularly called 'Swadeshi movement'). Moreover, it was believed by strong nationalist movement that the import of any good was there to bring the 'foreign dominance'. As a result, foreign direct investment was seen to be a curse rather than blessing or a means of attracting higher investment. As a consequence, multi-national corporations were seen as the exploitative entities that merely benefit from cheap labour in the country, and were believed to be the ones that take the profits back home to better their lavish living and conspicuous standard of living.

Naturally, it was hard to convince the policy makers that import substitution was an expensive policy action in economic sense, even if politically it seemed to be a 'patriotic' thing to do. This 'extreme nationalism' was evident in blindly carried out economic planning process of early days. Leftists had an influence on each economic plan which increased tariffs on almost all imports, and economy resulted into almost 'autarky' stage. Table 24.1 makes the point clear. The export and import were so low that they formed less than one per cent of the total world trade. These low figures of trade were by the country that has had roughly 15 per cent of world population. The highest merchandise export figure was reached in 1980 (of USD 919.8 million) and they declined significantly in 1981 and 1982. For 6 years in a row (from 1979 to 1985) the merchandise exports were stagnant at roughly USD 700 to USD 800 million. The services sector did not fair any better. While the services exports were steadily increasing in this period the figures were less that USD 400.00 million. This was a period when computer technology services were unheard of and services sector in India was poorly developed so exports were not that attractive.

Merchandise imports were highest in 1981 (at USD 925.5 million) and with that exceptional year they were steadily increasing. One can see the giant jump in imports of merchandise in year 1974, thanks to the first oil price increase by the OPEC. India had not found any indigenous source of oil then and was primarily dependent upon the foreign oil. Nonetheless the total merchandise import bill never crossed USD1 billion, one of the primary reasons for that was the tremendous tariff rates and strict quotas on major imports. In 1974, the policy makers, when they were pointed out the tremendous increase in trade (im)balance from USD16.2 million (1973) to USD160.4 million (1974), efficiently blamed the oil price rise.

In general 1965 to 1985 was a turbulent time period. It witnessed the stagnation of the economy as well as that of Indian trade.

Table 24.1: India's Trade: 1965-1985

Year	Merchandise Exports	Services Exports	Merchandise Imports	Services Imports	Trade Balance
1965	129.4	62.1	125.3	57.5	4.9
1966	139.3	69.1	146.5	66.2	−8.6
1967	98.9	74.8	152.1	73.2	−57.3
1968	82.5	67.0	130.6	63.0	−51.2
1969	107.1	69.3	107.0	56.8	0.9
1970	146.2	85.1	143.5	71.3	2.1
1971	150.8	97.2	200.6	85.0	−49.0
1972	191.7	99.8	215.5	84.0	−25.8
1973	291.0	118.9	326.0	93.2	−16.2
1974	329.4	140.7	476.7	125.3	−160.4
1975	306.5	182.5	441.9	118.3	−102.7
1976	402.0	172.5	427.9	117.2	−22.8
1977	512.6	212.1	564.7	149.8	−48.3
1978	640.3	262.0	618.4	192.1	18.9
1979	779.6	2 92.8	754.1	253.5	−21.2
1980	919.8	279.8	899.9	262.8	−79.1
1981	896.4	302.8	925.5	282.0	−147.9
1982	685.5	340.6	837.6	308.5	−263.2
1983	742.0	342.5	721.6	280.7	−56.9
1984	743.2	347.1	756.6	310.9	−131.3
1985	814.0	394.3	814.3	362.9	−115.1

Source: International Financial Statistics Yearbook 1994, International Monetary Fund, Washington DC.

One of the reasons for this retarded growth in Indian trade was the disoriented trade policy. There was even a problem of assigning priority to industries for importing necessary parts and raw materials. As Bhagwati-Desai put it, 'It was not surprising, therefore, that the agencies involved in determining industry-wise allocation fell back on vague notions of 'fairness', implying pro rata allocations with reference to capacity installed or employment, or shares defined by past import allocations and similar other rules of thumb without any rationale' (see Bhagwati-Desai (1970) in bibliography, p. 290).

The hardship experienced by this virtual 'closed economy' was no more evident than in

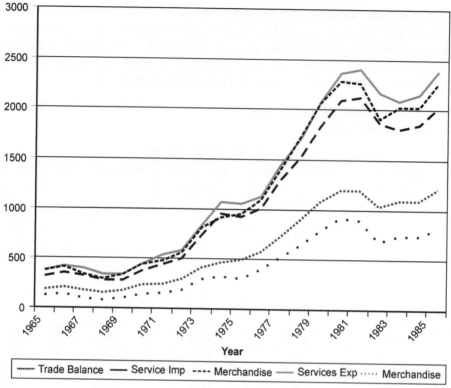

Graph 24.1: India's Trade: 1965-1985

early 1970s when the economy went through numerous shocks. The poor monsoons created agricultural production short-fall leading to severe droughts in some parts of the country. This put pressure on the industrial production which was not progressing very well in the first place. Due to the additional burden exerted by the Indo-Pakistan War of 1971, the economy started suffering miserably. Rationing of necessities was common and criminal elements made a heyday by hoarding. The political opposition parties made life miserable for Indira Gandhi government which had a little choice but to blame all starvation on foreign elements. In 1973, came the OPEC oil price shock and the things really went out of control. While country had no reserves to pay for imported oil, the import bill was growing very fast and export earnings were sluggish. See Table 24.1 figures for 1973 when imports increased from USD191.7 million to USD 291 million and again in 1976 went up to USD 402 million. Political parties were extremely active. But economically there was no way out. The protectionism was to the highest level. Consider the 350 per cent import tariff rate on automobiles and average tariff rate of 152 per cent. Domestic industries were well protected that they loved being monopolists and had no inclination for technological innovation. The maturity stage, that was supposed to have taken place according to the famous (?) Infant Industry Argument has never arrived. Strict foreign exchange controls were not only required but were very necessary to stop illegal foreign currency and gold smuggling transactions. It was an administrative nightmare where rent seeker made merry and black market constituted half of the official economy. Academicians learned several lessons of how protectionism can ruin the economy and policy makers watched economy reaching to a real low point while they searched for the solutions.

To top the political chaos, the ruling party (Indira Congress) declared emergency restricting many a freedoms and ruthlessly putting anyone in jail, who gave even a hint of 'anti-governmental activity'. The country definitely needed a magic for rapid economic growth which could have silenced the political 'trouble makers'.

In early 1980s, the monsoon god was nice to India. While agricultural sector that was in desperate need to prosper, received a big boost, the industrial sector invented few new technological advances and grew much more rapidly than before. India also realized that she can do much better in service sector. All in all, the economy started prospering at a slow rate but definitely much better than in 1970s. The need for opening up the economy was felt more keenly by Rajiv Gandhi's government and some reductions in tariff rates were activated in early 1980s. But the real support for globalization, liberalization and reduction in protectionism came in late 1980s.

The Wave of Globalization Arrived

In 1980s, there were some signs of policy change in Rajiv Gandhi's Prime Ministership, but the Macro-economy was already damaged by earlier faults. As Aggarwal (2004) puts it 'The Macroeconomic crisis reached its peak in 1990 with combined fiscal deficit of Centre and State governments standing at 10 per cent as percentage of GDP, current account balance at 3.3 per cent of GDP backed by a rate of inflation 9.9 per cent despite India's record economic performance measured in terms of rate of growth of GDP, 6.0 per cent, due to high rates of industrial growth of 5.9 per cent and domestic saving ratio of 21.9 per cent of the GDP.' (see Aggarwal, (2004) p. 47). Nonetheless this growth was accompanied by strange macro-imbalances that resulted into tremendous external borrowing, leading to heavy external debt of 28.7 per cent. As Joshi-Little (1997) pointed out, 'For the first time in her history, India was nearly forced to the prospect of defaulting on her international financial commitment'. Added burden of oil price shock due to Gulf War of 1991 put the country in such a precarious condition that foreign reserves of worth 'only 3 weeks of imports' were left in the treasury. Something drastic had to be done.

In June of 1991, when the current Prime Minister Dr. Manmohan Singh was the Finance Minister (and Mr. Narasinha Rao was the Prime Minister), country received first significant shock of globalization and liberalization. This was also the product of strong demand by some well known economists and policy planners for significantly changing the policy structure. While the declared plan reduced the Rupee value significantly by devaluating it by 21 per cent in one day, it also made it abundantly clear that the old ways of high tariff rates were almost completely over. The tariff rates were slashed, more foreign direct investment (FDI) was invited and import quotas were demolished. There were essentially 2 parts of the liberalization programme: Structural and Stabilization. Stabilization measures were supposed to be of short-term nature, including such policies as the 'austerity in governmental budgets', which was supposed to bring about the decline in aggregate demand and therefore lower the inflation rate. The structural adjustment was to be of a long-term nature with such measures as the convertibility on current account of the balance of payment, lower restrictions on domestic business and export promotion.

In words of Aggarwal, 'Far reaching meaningful changes in trade and exchange rate policies, viz., two bouts of devaluation of the Rupee, sweeping but phased reduction in import tariffs, quantitative restrictions, and quota except on consumer goods, the suspension of cash compensatory support of exports, trimming and rationalizing the structure of mounting export subsidies, full convertibility of the rupee on current account on balance of payment in 1993, moving from a dual exchange rate system in 1992 to a single market determined unified exchange rate system, have been made' (see Aggarwal, (2004), p. 48). These steps not only made a complete switch in the policy moves heretofore, but also showed policy makers' inclination to move to market oriented economy as the blunders of governmental controls were becoming more and more visible. All in all, these reforms aimed to achieve stability, curb the inflationary pressure and release the breaks on production and productivity. (Aggarwal, p. 49).

The post reform years showed quick and efficient recovery from the acute macroeconomic crisis of 1991. The real GDP in 1990s increased at an annual rate of 6 per cent which is even more impressive because the rest of the world was going through a minor recession. The highest increase in real GDP was experienced in 1996-1997 with 7.8 per cent (expected to be surpassed in 2004) Increased production had its effect on the prices. Inflation rate of 13.6 per cent in 1991 was reduced to 1.3 per cent in 2001-2002, a remarkable achievement by any standard. The monetary policy was carried out responsibly and the fiscal pressures were negative but much more manageable than earlier years. However the fiscal policy austerity programme was not totally effective, thanks to the crisis created by Iraq war as well as political troubles all over the country. In first 3 years of 1990s, the economic hardships continued partly due to the increased oil price and overall recessionary forces, coupled with political instability, lack of technological innovation, and poor monsoon. The recessionary trend did not last for a long time however. The increased international trade freer economy technological improvements prompted by tremendous growth in information technology combined to show the positive effects from 1994. Liberalization at least partially has become effective in attracting foreign direct investment, positive outlook for the Indian economy and overall excitement amongst producers and investors. Indian economy was on the move in a serious way.

As Table 24.2 shows, in 1994 while the real GDP increased by 5.9 per cent, the inflation rate declined from 13.7 per cent in 1992 to 8.4 per cent. While the interest was still very high, it had some downward pressure. The official unemployment number was very high (36.69 million) but it remained steady, a mild achievement in an increasing population. But as it is evident for several years, the Indian unemployment is beyond the reported figures of unemployed labor. It consists of heavy under-employment, it is marred by extreme poverty partly due to illiteracy. The so called 'full-time employment' in India is concentrated mainly in urban sector with very limited industrialization in rural or semi-rural areas of extreme backwardness. Added to those problems are the imperfections of labour market, the complications in collecting the data, the Indian labour employment (or unemployment) is as hard to report as its population survey results. But these imperfections notwithstanding, the economic growth in 1990s looks impressive, it does not matter how one calculates it.

Table 24.2: Macroeconomic Performance in Post 1991 Years

Year	Real GDP Growth	Inflation Rate	Interest Rate	Unemployment No. in Millions	Money Supply Billions of Rs
1991	0.96	8.9	17.88	36.3	1046.1
1992	2.3	13.7	18.92	36.75	1120.9
1993	1.5	10.1	16.25	36.27	1330.2
1994	5.9	8.4	14.75	36.69	1695.0
1995	7.3	10.9	15.46	36.74	1883.5
1996	7.3	7.7	15.96	37.43	2148.9
1997	7.8	6.4	13.83	39.14	2419.3
1998	6.5	4.8	13.54	40.01	2703.5
1999	6.5	6.9	12.54	40.37	3161.2
2000	6.1	3.3	12.29	40.34	3495.9
2001	4.0	7.1	12.08	41.99	3846.0
2002	6.2	4.7	11.92	42.36	4318.6
2003	5.5	5.1	11.50	43.10	4822.3
2004	8.0	4.5	10.60	42.50	5402.3

Source: Some figures are from Aggarwal (2004) and some are from IMF's Publication, International Financial Statistics Yearbook, 2003.

While the international trade policy was further liberalized, al beit, at a slower rate than many of the academicians argued for, there were signs for further opening up, by reduction in import tariff, convertibility on the current account transactions, freer availability of foreign reserves, and increased zest for inviting foreign direct investment. It appeared that policy makers by 1995 were convinced that globalization is what is needed for faster economic growth. Success sometimes breeds upon itself, and policy makers usually are fast learners especially when political benefits are high. However the growth of 1994-1997 was not perfectly matched by accelerated growth in 1997-2000 period. As Chitre (2003) points out, this sluggishness was due to the slow growth in agricultural sector, not because of industrial slowdown. The international trade as witnessed in Table 24.3 did not perform poorly either.

Better monsoons of years 2000 to 2004 helped not only the agricultural sector grow faster but also the manufacturing, trade and services sectors moved admirably. In 2004, it became official that Indian economy was second fastest growing in the world, second only to the Chinese economy. In fact, the Chinese economy's growth is also primarily explained by her newly found affection for openness. The Indian economy, much like the world economy, went through technological change. While the computer mega cities such as Bangalore (that now has 1500 foreign company offices), Hyderabad and Pune grew at unprecedented rates, the repercussions of this industrial growth was felt in many of the adjacent rural areas. In fact in April 2005, it was confirmed that India officially achieved 8 per cent growth in 2004 (*Times of India*, 28 April 2005)

Table 24.3: International Trade Performance Post 1991 Years

Year	Exports	Imports	BOT	Exchange rate
	(In billions of US dollars)			Rs/SDR
1991	18.09	21.08	4.01	36.95
1992	20.01	22.93	4.71	36.02
1993	22.01	24.1	3.48	43.10
1994	25.52	29.67	6.31	45.81
1995	31.23	37.95	10.21	52.29
1996	33.73	43.78	13.98	51.66
1997	35.20	45.73	13.36	52.99
1998	34.07	44.82	13.60	59.81
1999	36.87	45.55	11.44	59.69
2000	43.13	55.32	13.77	60.91
2001	43.82	50.53	5.97	60.54
2002	52.71	51.41	7.58	65.29
2003	63.45	61.42	8.69	67.27
2004	65.09	77.03	13.37	68.88

Source: IMF's International Financial Statistics Year book, 2003.
Website: www.rbi.org.in/statistics for figures after 1999.

Table 24.3 shows the drastic turn around of the economy in 1990s in terms of international trade patterns. While the exports increased drastically, the opening of the borders and reduction in tariff rates also allowed the imports to go up. The balance of trade figures were in a manageable amount (almost always less than USD 14 billion).

What is interesting to point out is that the 'non-oil' imports and exports showed a positive balance of trade for the Indian economy since year 2000. Hence oil imports formed the major drain on the foreign reserves and constituted the main reason for balance of trade deficit. While the Services sector picked the exports considerably, important raw material imports have also grown significantly. One of the major developments reported in April 2005 was that software exports from India's hi-tech hub, Bangalore rose more than 52 per cent to USD 6 billion (*Times of India*, 28 April 2005). However any economic spurt is not without a political controversy and Indian economic growth is not an exception. Political skeptics have pointed out the increased inequality of income as an unwanted result of the globalization. Some politicians (especially leftists and socialists) have also complained about the increased salaries of computer scientists and information technologists. The 'great digital divide' has become somewhat of a worry for some researchers. However, as Bhagwati (2004) has recently shown the globalization process has more benefits than costs and therefore needs to be supported to the fullest extent. In fact, the 'free trade for the whole world' scenario is based on the validity of globalization by all policy makers.

SUMMARY AND CONCLUSIONS

Main finding of this chapter is that India's economic growth has received a strong impetus in post 1991 era. This increased economic growth is mainly and directly is a result of country's better monsoons and the free trade movement that started in that year. Clearly the lethargic economic development was associated with greater protectionism and policy makers seemed to have learned an important lesson from 1950 to 1990 era. The data show that the free trade movement of 1990s has shown positive results in economic terms. The future economic growth therefore depends heavily on the speed of privatization and globalization. As Kulkarni (1996) points out, the country is ready to have a firm plan to get ready for the second wave of free-trade and liberalization movement.

REFERENCES

1. Aggarwal, M.R. 'Macroeconomic Adjustment, Stabilization and Sustainable Growth in India: Looking Back and to the Future', *The Indian Journal of Economics,* Vol. LXXXIV, No. 332, July 2003, pp. 45-67.
2. Bhagwati, Jagdish, 'In Defense of Globalization' Cambridge University Press, New York, 2004.
3. Chand, Satish and Sen, Kunal, 'Trade Liberalization and Productivity Growth: Evidence form Indian Manufacturing', *Review of Development Economics,* Vol. 6, No. 1, 2002, pp. 120-132.
4. Chitre, Vikas, 'Global Slowdown and the Indian Economy', The Eleventh D.T. Lakdawala Memorial Trust Lecture, February 8, 2003, unpublished manuscript.
5. Jain A. K. 'Challenges Before the Banking and Financial Sectors in the Context of Globalization', *The Indian Journal of Economics,* Vol. LXXXIV, No. 332, July 2003, pp. 183-186.
6. Joshi, Vijay and Little IMD, 'Reform on Hold', *Asian Development Review (by Asian Development Bank),* Vol. 15, No. 2, 1997.
7. Ketkar, Kusum W., Noulas, Athanasios G., and Agarwal Man Mohan, 'Liberalization and Efficiency of Indian Banking Sector', *Indian Journal of Economics and Business,* Vol. 3, No. 2, December 2004, pp. 269-287.
8. Krishna Pravin, and Mitra, Devashish, 'Trade Liberalization, Market Discipline and Productivity Growth: New Evidence from India', *Journal of Development Economics,* Vol. 56, 1998, pp. 447-462.
9. Kulkarni, Kishore, 'The Full Flexibility of Indian Rupee: Sooner the Better', *Asian Economic Review,* January 1996, pp. 346-352.
10. Panagariya, Arvind, 'India's Trade Reform', *India Policy Forum,* 2004, p. 9-68.
11. 'Cost of Protection: Where Do We Stand?', *American Economic Review, Papers and Proceedings,* Vol. 92, No.2, 2002, pp. 175-179.
12. Rao BSR, 'Indian Financial System: Emerging Challenges', *The Indian Journal of Economics,* Vol. LXXXIV, No. 332, July 2003, pp. 189-207.
13. Reserve Bank of India, Mumbai, website: www.rbi.org.in
14. Tripathi, G.C. and Mishra, S.K. 'Imp[act of Economic Liberalization on Employment in India', *The Indian Journal of Economics,* Vol. LXXXIV, Part IV, Issue No. 331, April 2003, pp. 557-569.

25

The Consequences of Child Labour on Developing Nations Economic Growth

The Case of Egypt

Cindy Ragab

CHAPTER SUMMARY

Child labour has been a topic of study for some time. However upon reaching a full understanding of the child labour's effects on developing economies it becomes clear that child labour plays an important role in many of the most substantial ills stifling economic development in the third world. Child labour drastically reduces the quality of state's human capital through its detriment to education outcomes and the physical and mental health of children. Unemployment is exacerbated both in the present and the future through increased competition for limited employment opportunities and with decrease in skill attainment in future employees. Child labour also plays a significant role in the underestimation of developing economies' Gross Domestic Product through increased illegal economic activity. Finally, child labour complicated international trade relationships as the movement to cut trade with nations where child labour is practiced and to the goods they create in the developed world gains strength.

Child labour is the result of many structural inequalities that hamper economic development. Poverty is the primary instigator for child labour, families that can afford to provide necessities for their children (food, water, clothing, shelter and education) rarely send their children to work. Over population – an integral input into child labour – continues to supply poor children who must work to sustain themselves and their families.

In Egypt, government initiatives have diminished the prominence of child labour. The proper government and civil society responses can drastically reduce the impact of child labour and decrease the number of children involved in dangerous economic activity. Solutions such as educational reforms, social education, increased regulation and legalization of child labour such as those implemented in our case study can lead to a decrease in the per cent of children in the labour force. Targeted regulations based on statistically significant research on the most vulnerable populations will enhance efforts to end child labour, freeing developing economies child labours negative effects and the world's poor of the vicious cycle it feeds.

Abject poverty has made the poor helpless and desperate for increased income. Many throw their lives into oceans and deserts in hopes of immigration and new chances, others sell their organs, and still others sell their children. The combination of increased poverty and population growth in developing countries has made families unable to feed their children. Child labour is only one symbol of the situation of the poor.

Child labour is one of the most abhorrent ramifications of poverty; its negative consequences extend into every aspect of the developing nations' economy. Child labour drastically decreases human capital, increases unemployment, risks trade relationships, and exacerbates the population growth crisis.

Children are the only actors in the third world who have no choice; their current situation is not of their own making. Children are often used as scapegoats and the pain of poverty is inflicted on them by guardians who could not bear the burden themselves.

CHILD LABOUR DEFINED

The definition of child labour has been a contentious issue for decades. Although differences in interpretation remain, the Worst Form of Child Labour Convention 182 of 1999 and the increase in inter-agency cooperation seen in Understanding Children's Work of 2000 have led to the creation of a standard definition of child labour observed by the World Bank (WB), International Labour Organization (ILO) and UNICEF. This definition of child labour is outlined in Table 25.1.

CHILD LABOUR IN PERSPECTIVE

The issue of child labour has traditionally been opposed from a human rights perspective. Horrendous human rights abuses occur primarily as a result of hazardous work and environments and employer abuse of children. These abuses are difficult to stem due to the illegal nature of child labour in the majority of the world's countries, including our case study of Egypt.

Not enough attention is given to the economic costs of child labour. Most of the literature considers child labour an economic benefit for families. Child labour is considered an economically positive or neutral activity. The inhumane treatment of children has been the primary vehicle for the fight against the practice. This understanding of child labour has led to a weak government and societal fight against child labour.

Maffie, Raabe and Ursprung provide a strong argument for the use of child labour as a form of political and social repression. They pose that the government and civil society fail to enforce

Table 25.1

Child work or children's work	A general term covering the entire spectrum of work and related tasks performed by children
Child labour	A subset of children's work that is injurious to children and that should be targeted for elimination
Hazardous work	- Physical, psychological or sexual abuse; 9 - Work that is underground, under water, at dangerous heights or in confined spaces; - Work with dangerous machinery, equipment and tools, or which involves the manual handling or transport of heavy loads; and - Work in an unhealthy environment which would expose children to hazardous substances, agents or processes, or to temperatures, noise levels, or vibrations which might damage their health.
(Unconditional) worst forms of child labour	'Children of any age below 18 who are involved in forms of slavery and forced labour, including forced recruitment for use in armed conflicts, commercial sexual exploitation (prostitution or pornography), illicit activities (particularly the production or trafficking of drugs) and hazardous work that jeopardizes their lives, health or morals.'
Ages	5-11: all children at work in economic activity; 12-14: all children at work in economic activity minus those in light work; 15-17: all children in hazardous work and other worst forms of child labour.

Source: Sakurai, 2006.

laws prohibiting child labour and support services designed to stem the practice in order to maintain their monopoly on resources in the state. If the poor are able to educate their children and provide stable environments for their development, elites fear that they will provide competition for their children for the limited jobs available. (Alessandro Maffei et al., 2006)

ECONOMIC COSTS OF CHILD LABOUR

The economic costs of child labour to developing countries are enormous. Many of the greatest economic problems faced in the lesser developed countries are further exacerbated by child labour. These include population growth, underestimated GDPs, unemployment, insufficient wage rates, limited human capital, and diminishing international trade. The solution to these problems is the key to the economic growth of the world's developing countries.

Human Capital

Child labour drastically reduces the quality of the state's human capital through its detriment to education outcomes and the physical and mental health of children. Human capital is the most important input into economic development. If one adopts Heckscher & Ohlin's theory and the view of Paul Samuelson that developing nations are to provide labour while developed nations provide capital in the international market, it is clear that a healthy and at least minimally educated population in necessary for economic growth. According to Paul Romer's theory that technological innovation is required for economic growth, education is a prerequisite innovation. In both scenarios the health and education of the population is necessary.

Education outcomes are greatly affected by child labour. Children who work are more likely to repeat grades. (Galal, 2003; Sassanpour, 2008; Yount, 2004) Children who work are forced to take time away from classes and homework. They are also more tired than their peers and are unable to concentrate. In addition, children who work often no longer prioritize school. Work brings much greater gains for them in the short term, thus, they chose to invest more time and energy in work, often with the encouragement of family.

Good health care is necessary for an effective work force. Child labourers' health is often compromised at work through malnutrition, dehydration, exposure to harsh chemicals, and dangerous equipment. (UNFPA, 2009) Abuse from employers through beatings and sexual harassment also compromises the children's health. The unhealthy environment leads to decreased productivity from the children in their present and future work. The treatment of the children's ills can become a gargantuan cost on the state where some public healthcare is provided. Illness is not only a cause of poverty and undignified work but it pushes children and families deeper into poverty creating a dangerous positive feedback loop. (Todaro, 2009)

Unemployment

Unemployment is exacerbated both in the present and the future as a result of child labour. Increased competition from children for limited employment opportunities in the state increases adult unemployment. Adult unemployment in turn exacerbates the need for children to work. Children are often preferred to adult employees because they are more obedient, are falsely perceived to be more efficient at certain tasks and are paid less. These perceived benefits to child labour have led to their mass employment in such activities as carpet weaving, silk production and agricultural work (especially the removal of pests). (Human Rights Watch, 2001)

Child labour not only increases unemployment rates in the short term for adults looking for work, in the long term, children are less employable due to their limited education, health restrictions and decreased skill attainment compared to those who have attended school or organized apprenticeships. Their peers also have the advantage of professional and academic degrees. While in some cases these degrees do not mean that those who possess them are more skilled, degrees and certificates are often appreciated by employers because they guarantee proficiency and are at times mandated by the government and unions for employment. Child labourers are at a disadvantage because of their inability to get these degrees as easily as those who stayed in school.

Underestimated GDP

The underestimation of gross domestic product (GDP) in developing economies is increased as a result of child labour. The GDP is measured through economic transactions that can be tracked by the government. Child labour being an illegal activity is not reported to authorities through tax receipts and other measures used by the government to track economic activity. The wages paid to children and their productions are not counted.

Child labourers often work in illegal markets in addition to the illegality of their employment in legal sectors of the economy. Children most often work on the streets, selling goods in sidewalk markets, to passing cars in the streets, and wiping windshields. Children are also often pushed into illegal work including prostitution and drug and arms smuggling. The illegitimate employment of children therefore enhances the black market in developing economies.

International Trade

In recent years, the developed world has been taking a stronger stance against child labour. Western governments are increasingly adopting measures which limit trade relationships with nations where child labour exists. More demure measures include the ban on imports that children play a role in producing. These policies have weakened trade relationships between developed and developing countries and, at times, created great tension.

In addition to government bans, consumers push corporations to eliminate products that children produce from their sales. Corporate responsibility policies have, in fact, decreased the export of goods which involve child labour. Boycotts of products produced by children and in sweatshops have been increasingly powerful in recent years.

These measures fail to eliminate or even decrease child labour in the developing world. As long as the poor need children to work to support the family, they will find work. The result of these changes is the increase of children working in illicit activities. Decreased child labour in legal sectors has decreased states export capabilities.

POSSIBLE SOLUTIONS

There are four preeminent approaches to child labour policy as conducted by developing countries and supported by international governing bodies. Many states including Egypt have adopted different policies at different points in time. Most countries enact parts of two or more approaches at any given time.

Bans on Child Labour

The first approach is pushed by the International Labour Organization (ILO), one of the most stringent attackers of child labour. The ILO sees child labour from a purely economic view and believes that it is likely that the ban of child labour will lead to the replacement of child labourers by adults. It considers child labour a substitute for adult labour because adults can do all of the tasks that children are given and studies show that they complete these tasks with greater efficiency. Thus child labour is the result of inadequate market wages for unskilled adults. This argument is supported by Wahba who provides evidence that increases in child labour can be directly correlated with decreases in the market wage for illiterate adults. (Wahba, 2006)

Supporters of a complete ban on child labour see unskilled labour supply to be highly elastic due to the pressures of poverty. In the graph produced by the economist Kaushik Basu depicting child labour as the result of a bad equilibrium (Figure 25.1), unskilled labour supply is perfectly elastic (A A') as is aggregate labour supply (T T') – adult labour added to child labour multiplied by the decreased productivity of child labourers. This approach sees demand as a product of poverty, thus if child labour were banned, the wage for adult unskilled labour would increase. This would increase family income, making child labour unnecessary.

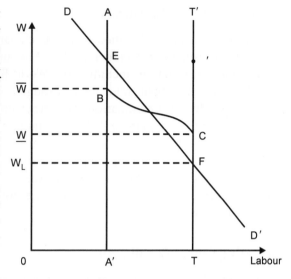

Figure 25.1

This theory makes several questionable assumptions. First, it assumes that impoverished families rely on the labour of unskilled adults. This is not the case in many developing nations where unemployment is a reality for well-educated and skilled adults. The theory proposed by Basu also falsely assumes that all unskilled labour is employed, pointing to inadequate wage rates as the cause of family poverty. Children are also forced to work because their guardians are unemployed. In this case increases in wages will exacerbate the problem because increased wages lead to decreased demand for labour.

Second, Basu assumes that child labour can be easily substituted for adult labour. While it may be statistically proven that children are not better employees than adults, tradition and faulty perceptions persist. The case of child labourers working in rug weaving is only one example where it is perceived that child labour is necessary and adults cannot take their place.

Third, it assumes that in all cases child labour is the result of parents' inability to provide for the family. While this may be true in majority of the cases, it is not uncommon for parents who work to force their children to work as well. As Wahba showed in her article that increases in local (province/region) income inequality, and a parent's history as a child labourer increase child labour rates. Traditions such as the use of children in Egypt to remove worms from cotton crops to avoid the use of harmful pesticides lead to child labour independently of parent's inadequate wages.

Due to faulty assumptions the belief that the economy will remain at the good equilibrium (where adults make enough money to provide for the family and keep their children out of work) once child labour is banned cannot be proven. Child labour exists in spite of some families' ability to provide due to social acceptability of the practice, broken families and unemployment which will increase with the increase in wages.

Poverty Reduction Measures

Child labour has been identified by most scholars who study the topic as the consequence of poverty. (Basu, 1999; Goldberg, 2004; Kanbur, 1994; Robinson, 2000) Many states and development organizations including the World Bank and the government of Egypt until the 1990s have chosen to fight child labour through poverty elimination strategies. These strategies focus exclusively on the elimination of poverty without supplementing these policies with direct measures targeting child labour. While it is more difficult to judge the successes of policies that do not directly address child labour, it is clear that there is a dramatic decrease in the per cent of children that are economically active. Measures of the per cent of children in the labour force have decreased dramatically since 1950 as seen in Figure 25.2 as poverty rates have increased internationally. The number of children in the labour force, however, has not decreased due to population growth.

Increasing School Enrollment

Many studies have pointed to child labour as a replacement to education. (Alessandro Maffei, 2006; Rammohan, 2007) Following this correlation, many have sought measures to increase

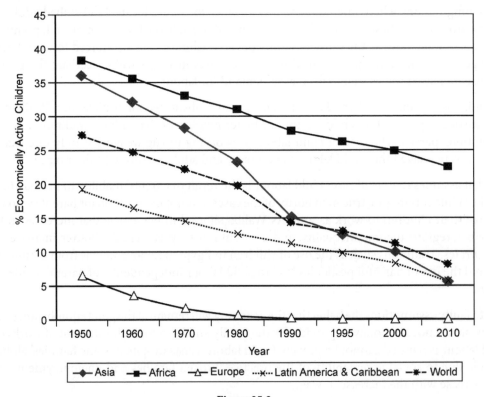

Figure 25.2

Source: Basu, 1999.

enrollment in schools and decrease drop out rates. These measures have proved effective in increasing the number of children in schools in some cases such as Mexico through its PROGRESSA programme. (Samuel L. Odom, 2003; Galal, 2003; Wells, Microeconomics, 2005) However, these measures have not been shown to directly decrease child labour rates.

Increasing enrollment further stretches resources in developing nations' education systems leading to a further diminished quality of education, which in the future may lead to greater grade repitition and unemployment rates for children in adulthood. (Sassanpour, 2008)

Protection of Child Labourers

The most pragmatic approach used to fight child labour is that of realists who recognize child labour as inevitable (at least in the short run). Those that accept child labour as a current reality focus their efforts on the regulation of child labour. UNICEF is the strongest advocate of this approach. (Bibars, 1998; United Nations Development Programme, 2005) As a result of acknowledgement of child labour and the legalization of child labour in some forms, child labourers are no longer excluded from unionization and legal protection in the workplace.

The legalization of child labour allows children the right to a minimum wage. The movement of child labour from illicit markets to legal sectors protects the children from abuses at the hands of their employers and guarantees for them a fair wage. Bans on child labour takes away the government's ability to control the work conditions of children. (UNICEF - Egypt Country Office, 2005) This technique is the greatest weapon against the increase of child labour in the black market, the trafficking of children and the underestimation of developing nation's GDPs. (UNICEF - Egypt Country Office, 2005)

CHILD LABOUR IN EGYPT

As children are left cold and alone in a country where they are voiceless, the Egyptian state has seemingly shirked its responsibilities by passing legislation to protect child labour without providing adequate support for the laws it enacts. The government also fails to protect children from many of the side-effects of child labour, particularly the protection of street children.

Many activists see child labour as a unitary problem with solutions which once again lead to the creation and revision of laws. Egypt has been one of the earliest signatories to the most important treaties applicable to child labour and its laws are not in the violation of any. However it is clear that the regulation of child labour as it stands today in Egypt is not enough to protect child labourers. The issue is not one-dimensional but complex and must be attacked in an equally multifarious manner. Destructive child labour will only be eradicated when the structural ills in Egypt which feed it are properly treated.

STRUCTURAL CAUSES OF CHILD LABOUR

Population Growth

Child labour is the result of many structural inequalities in the Egyptian state. The first is overpopulation. Over population is the result of poor social safety nets and inadequate wage rates which force families to have more children to help them financially through child labour in the short term and through support for elderly parents in the long term. Bad healthcare has made contraceptives difficult to obtain in some areas and high child mortality rates encourage families to have more children.

The population of Egypt was growing at a rate of 2.62 per cent in 1960, reached 2.75 per cent in 1987 and is currently at 1.82 per cent, see Figure 25.3.

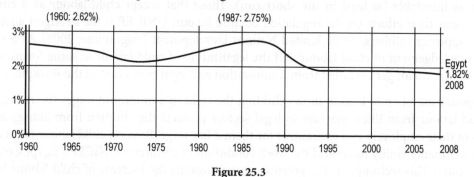

Figure 25.3

Source: World Bank, World Development Indicators - Last updated May 7, 2010

These rates have led to the growth of the Egyptian population from 27.8 million in 1960 (20th most populace state in the world) to 81.7 million (17th most populace). These figures have resulted in a decrease (taking inflation into account) in GDP per capita from USD 517 in 1950 (49th in the world) to USD 4,900 (136th in the world). (Nation Master, 2010) The increased need for resources has not been met with economic growth, which has led to the increase of child labour from a rare activity almost always characterized by the employment of children in family business' to rampant child labour in all sectors of the economy (minus the government sector) where children are abused and paid little in return.

Poverty

Poverty in Egypt is the instigator of child labour. Studies show that only children whose parents cannot afford to provide for them are forced to work. (Goldberg, 2004) In Egypt, increased unemployment rates and a minimum wage which has not increased since 1981 are to blame for the rapid increase in impoverished families. (Icon Group International, Inc., 2000) In the 1970's the government treated the youth bulge with a policy of guaranteed employment through the government which led to the creation of a gargantuan bureaucracy making the government more inefficient. (Iqbal, 2005) Corruption became a prominent problem for the Egyptian state as a result of the inability to pay a living wage to the surge of employees. (Sobel, 2006)

Unemployment

While official unemployment rates for Egypt hover around 10 per cent, real unemployment rates (including discouraged and underemployed workers) reside around 40 per cent. This means that not only does one out of every ten workers in Egypt have no income but that the majority of Egypt's workforce has failed to receive returns for the cost of their education. Egypt produces more than 400,000 university graduates every year. (Egyptian Ministry of Communications and Information Technology, 2010) Unemployment rates are a substantial incentive for children to shirk education and seek employment in traditional fields that are more likely to employ them in the future. The Egyptian economy continues to provide more employment for entrepreneurs, thus education that leads to employment in the government, academia, and large corporations in the private sector is considered a bad investment in comparison to skills such as car repair where the cost of starting one's own business is low.

This reality encourages children and parents to invest more in job training than education. While child labourers are employed more in their adulthood, their wages are stunted. (Robinson, 2000) While compulsory education can be a tool used by the state to curb child labour, if education is not valued by all sectors of society, especially the most impoverished and traditional it is not effective.

Societal Acceptance

Child labour has become an accepted norm in Egypt, beyond the labour of children in their parents shops or in the fields, children now work in every sector of the economy including construction, carpet weaving, tanning, agriculture, prostitution, and domestic labour. Upper classes which are educated and well travelled are fully cognizant of the inhumanity of child labour, creating a plethora of civil society organizations which seek to end the abuse of children. Nevertheless, child labourers are still visible in every corner of the country. (United Nations Development Programme, 2005)

Children are considered wonderful employees; they are cheap, easy to control and listen to directions. (United States Department of Labour, 2010) Children's employers legitimize their activities by claiming that if the children did not work for them, they would work for someone else. They risk leaving the child to someone who may not treat them as humanely as they do, who may not protect them from harm and give them an equally clean, safe and friendly environment to work in. This justification maintains the practice of child labour in light of government and civil society efforts decrease societal acceptance of the practice. (Maffie et al., 2006)

Inadequate Education System

While free education is guaranteed by the Egyptian constitution, the cost of uniforms, books, various fees and food are not included. The phenomenon of private tutoring is a major barrier to education as impoverished under-paid teachers do not teach material on the exams and at times force students to take lessons or fail.

Egypt's school system has proved an ineffective obstacle to child labour because it is not framed as labour's alternative. It costs money instead of generating it (present and future), punishment for evading education are not greater than those for partaking in illegal labour, and curricula are not considered valuable by parents and the community.

Curricula do not cater to various segments of society. Thus, poor children do not gain valuable work skills that they will need after graduation, instead they study information meant for children seeking university degrees. As a result, parents do not encourage their children to attend school if it will stand in the way of labour which will increase family income and training that will provide employment in the future.

In addition, the government of Egypt allots very minimal resources for education and this has made schools an unsafe environment for children. The lack of schools has been treated by the implementation of several shifts of children a day so that schools can absorb all children which are mandated to attend school. Morning, afternoon and night classes allow children to work and attend their classes simultaneously. Time for study and homework is limited for working children as a result of long hours and fatigue.

Allowing children to go to school and work leads to poor education and shorter work hours that lead to decreased learning on the job in apprentice positions, leaving children with neither a promising future in academia nor strong work skills.

Human Rights Abuses

Children routinely work for more than ten hours a day, are beaten and abused and do not receive adequate pay. Rarely are children paid in person, instead their income is sent to their families and the children remain financially dependent and do not receive adequate care. Some children are beaten for making too little. Many child labourers have unemployed parents or parents spend their money on mistress', alcohol, and drugs.

In Egypt, children work in a plethora of fields each posing different human rights abuses. In agriculture, children help their families harvest seasonal crops. The most common job for child labourers in Egypt remains the removal of worms that threaten cotton harvests. During their summer break, children work an average of eleven hours a day removing worm eggs from leaves and pieces of infected vegetation. Children face beatings for slow work, long hours often with only one to two water breaks in addition to their one hour break for lunch. Despite the fact that the 1956 law mandating that all farmers provide one labourer per season has been repealed, many farmers believe that the law still stands.

Leather tanning exposes children to dangerous chemicals. Construction and brick making threaten the safety of children and give them long-term injuries such as back problems. While these abuses are more dangerous than those faced by children working in cotton fields, they are illegal.

Street Children

Street children are almost always child labourers. Children, who are forced into labour due to family conditions of scarcity, no longer justify for themselves giving their income to parents, step-parents, aunts and uncles or other superiors in the case of domestic abuse. Thus the children run away due to their belief that they can sustain themselves on their own.

While they believe they can support themselves without family, the children often must beg for food, sleep on the streets and almost always travel through the cities barefoot. Street children are almost exclusively seen in the nation's biggest cities, mainly Cairo and Alexandria. Out on the streets the children are subject to abuse from civilians and police alike and are often sexually, physically and emotionally abused.

The children have created for themselves an underground society in which the children form packs and are known to other street children. This community dictates the superiority of children, rules of conduct and responsibilities of each child to the group. The older children are the leaders and abuse the young children often.

The Egyptian state has proven unable to provide a solution to the problem due to its complexity. It is difficult to know which children are at risk, to intervene in all situations, and once the children are on the street, their return to normal family life is next to impossible. Independence is difficult to give up for these children. The government currently has a policy of returning children to parents, fining parents for failing to take care of their children and putting the children in jail to encourage their homecoming. However this makes them vulnerable to police abuse and rarely encourages them to return home. In addition, parents often leave their children in jail because they cannot afford to pay the fines.

Children vend random toys and trinkets in the busy streets of cities. These are generally street children. Children working on the streets are at times trafficked children who were previously kidnapped, street children. These children are usually forced into work. Young and disabled children are preferred because they bring in sympathy money. Some children are disabled specifically for this purpose.

Children also work on the streets with their parents. These children help their parents sell fruits and vegetables in illegal sidewalk markets. Newspapers, Kleenexes, car accessories and other accessories are sold to passing cars often requiring children to weave through moving traffic. Children also wash windshields for cars stopped at traffic lights. This labour sets children up for abuse and injury.

Positive Consequences of Child Labour

Child labour has been proven to decrease educational results in the past, in addition to its negative effects on family cohesion, and social stability. However the illegality of child labour has not made measurable strides to decrease the phenomenon. Taken for granted in the discussion on child labour in Egypt are the positive effects it can have and the dire circumstances that lead to it.

Increased income that children make can make substantial changes to their standard of living. Earnings are often used for the purchase of food, clothing and the payment of school fees. If the children are properly protected, employment can lead to the accumulation of professional skills.

While child labour is defined as the negative forms of child economic activity, the transformation of these jobs into supportive and healthy labour can lead to enhanced development for the children. Organized trainings and tutoring, doctor's visits, nutritional meals and lessons in responsibility and work ethic are all possible benefits for working children. In order for these benefits to be realized, organized regulation and supervision is necessary. The government of Egypt has the opportunity to use child labour to distribute social services to children in need.

GOVERNMENT RESPONSE

Child's Law

Attempts to alleviate Egypt of child labour and to conform to the convention on the rights of the child-ratified by Egypt in 1990- have led to the passing of the child law in 1996. The law is an effective adoption of the strategy of engagement with child labour supported by UNICEF. The child's law dictates that all employment of children below the age of 14 is illegal with the exception of apprenticeships or occupational training which can start at the age of 12. Children between the ages of 12 and 15 may have seasonal jobs that do not harm their health or conflict with regular school attendance. Children below the age of 17 are prohibited from employment in hazardous occupations.

The regulation of child labour starting from the age of 14 includes many rules which are intended to deliver services to impoverished children. First, employers are required to pay for a yearly checkup at a doctor's office for their child labourers. This acts to provide some healthcare for the children, and to guard against work related injuries. Second, employers are to provide their child workers with 200 grams of milk per day of work. It is thought that the nutrients in milk will guard against the children's malnutrition. Third, children are only allowed to work between the hours of 7 am and 9 pm, cannot work for more than four consecutive hours and must receive at least one hour long break. A total of six hours of work a day cannot be exceeded. Children cannot work overtime or on official holidays or weekends.

While the laws in theory protect Egypt's approximately 2.5 million child labourers, even the government fails to implement these policies in the work of children employed by the ministry of agriculture in cotton fields during the summer months. (Galal, 2003) This labour falls under one of the three exceptions in the child's law of Egypt. First, domestic work is not considered labour. Second, children can work in family businesses at their family's discretion. Third, children below the minimum age can work during the summer months because this does not interfere with their schooling. These flaws in the child's law seem to have passed international labour standards because these exceptions have traditionally been upheld in developed countries as well. However, they greatly endanger children.

One of the most dangerous forms of child labour is domestic work which is one of the only three forms of child labour not protected by Egypt's child law. Child servants are traditionally sent to work for families in Egypt from very young age. Rural families often send their daughters to the city to work for elite families, alleviating them the cost of their education, food and clothing. The girl's employers send back their paychecks to the families. These girls are left vulnerable to beatings, sexual exploitation and the loss of education and family protection. The psychological effects of serving the spoilt children of their masters cannot be underestimated. While exact numbers of domestic servants are not available, girls comprise 71 per cent of Egypt's labour force, and the majority of them are domestic servants. (Goldberg, 2004)

RECOMMENDATIONS

Because child labour is mainly caused by family poverty, the government should push the increase of the minimum wage for adults in order to protect child labourers. The government of Egypt should pursue increased restrictions on child labour where it can be shown that adults will replace them. Note that child labour is a result of unemployment, thus focusing on the increase of opportunities for adults, will help alleviate child labour. Requiring employers to employ children for positions only when there are no adult applicants can help replace child labour with unemployed adults.

It is necessary to remove gaps between educational outcomes and market demands so that education is directly correlated with employment. In Egypt, it is not uncommon for a taxi driver to have completed postgraduate education with honors. With such developments, education fails to be seen as a priority for families who must choose between school and needed funds for family sustenance. Egypt has made progress towards access to education but no progress on quality of education. The costs of dropping out of school must be increased, however the majority of child labourers (64 per cent) are still in school, 16 per cent dropped out and 19 per cent never attended school. (Susan Hill Cochrane, 1990) Thus increasing the number of schools and ensuring that all school age children are enrolled may help decrease child labour.

The educational system needs to expand in areas where unemployment is relatively low. Different tracks for children who intend to stop school at the minimum requirement, intend to finish high school and those seeking university educations should be created so that all can find suitable work. This will encourage those who know that continuing in the education system is not possible to appropriately seek an education that will help them be easily employed upon graduation. It is only natural that a developing country does not need all of its students to have graduate degrees, but will need many labourers that are to highly educated. This may decrease the number of dropouts and increase the value of the education system to families. In addition, apprenticeship programs can be overseen by the government or other organizations so that students gain needed skills, have a certificate that ensures their mastery of the trade and protects them from exploitation.

CONCLUSION

Child labour is clearly a violation of the human rights of children. Over the years many have fought for the abolition of the practice for moral reasons and have failed. The reality is that child labour is the result of economic pressures, making social change ineffective. The economic nature of child labour is not only underestimated as an instigator of the crime, but the effects child labour has on economic growth have been severely underestimated. A full understanding of the effect that child labour has on retarding economic development is the only way for child labour to be eradicated.

Increases in unemployment rates, underestimation of GDPs, limiting of international trade relationships and retardation of human capital are all significant problems faced in the developing nations. These problems can be stemmed with the responsible alleviation of child labour in developing economies.

Child labour is a plague that has been enveloping Egyptian society for centuries. The government has repeatedly battled the disease, however child labour is still strong and a major deterrent to economic development for the state. The government of Egypt's efforts to fight inequality in its society is well noted and noble, however the methods utilized have been a failure. The desire to make detrimental traditions illegal is policy which has bred more negative externalities than results.

REFERENCES

1. Alessandro Maffei, N.R. (2006). Political Repression and Child Labour: theory and empirical evidence. *The Authors Journal Compilation* , 211-239.
2. Ali, A. A. Poverty in the Arab Region: a selective review.
3. Basu, K. (1999). Child Labour: Cause, Consequence, and Cure, with Remarks on International Labour Standards. *American Economic Association* , Vol. 37, No. 3, pp. 1083-1119.
4. Bibars, I. (1998). Street children in Egypt: from the home to the street to inappropriate corrective institutions. *Environment and Urbanization* , Vol. 10, No. 1, 201-216.
5. Dancer, A. R. (2008). Gender differences in intrahousehold schooling outcomes: the role of sibling characteristics and brith-order effects. *Education Economics* , Vol. 16, No. 2, 111-126.
6. Egyptian Ministry of Communications and Information Technology. (2010). *Egypt ICT Indicators Portal*. Retrieved 1 13, 2010, from http://www.egyptictindicators.gov.eg/default.htm
7. Fahmi, K. (2007). *Beyond the Victim: the politics and ethics of empowering Cairo's Street Children*. Cairo: The American University in Cairo Press.
8. Fahmy, N. S. (2002). *The Politics of Egypt: state-society relationship*. London: Routledge Curzon.
9. Galal, A. (2003). Social Expenditure and the Poor in Egypt. *The Egyptian Center for Economic Studies* , Wroking Paper No. 89.
10. Goldberg, E. (2004). *Trade, Reputation, and Child Labour in Twentieth-Century Egypt*. New York: Palgrave Macmillan.

11. Grimsrud, B. a. (1997). Child Labour in Africa: poverty or institutional failures? The cases of Egypt and Zimbabwe. *FAFO Institute for Applied Sciences* .

12. Handelman, H. (2009). *The Challenge of Thrid World Development.* London: Pearson Education.

13. Human Rights Watch. (2003). *Charged with Being Children: Egyptian police abuse of children in need of protection.* Washington: Human Rights Watch .

14. Human Rights Watch. (20 Jan 2001). *Egypt: cotton co-opt violate child labour laws.* Washington: Human Rights Watch.

15. Hussein, N. (2005). *Street Children in Egypt: group dynamics and subcultural constituents.* Cairo: The American University in Cairo Press.

16. Icon Group International, Inc. (2000). Executive Report on Stategies in Egypt. 106-111.

17. Iqbal, A.D. (2005). *Economic Growth in Egypt: constraints and determinants.* Washington: The World Bank.

18. Joan E. Spero, J.A. (2003). *The Politics of International Economic Relations.* Belmont: Wadsworth/Thomson Learning.

19. Kanbur, C.G. (1994). Child Labour: a review. *The World Bank* , 1-33.

20. Kozma, R.B. (2005). National Policies That Connect ICT-Based Education Reform to Economic and Social Development. *Human Technology* , Vol. 1, 117-156.

21. Mankiw, N.G. (2007). *Principles of Microeconomics.* Mason: Thomson Higher Education.

22. Mattar, M.Y. (2007, Oct. 20). *Child Labour in Egypt: scope and appropriate legal responses.* Retrieved 4 21, 2010, from Gozaar: http://www.gozaar.org/template1.php?id=800&language=english

23. Mehrez, S. (2008). *Egypt's Culture Wars: politics and practice.* New York : Routledge.

24. Nation Master. (2010). *Economy Statistics.* Retrieved 4 21, 2010, from NationMaster.com: http://www.nationmaster.com/graph/eco_gdp_pur_pow_par_percap-purchasing-power-parity-per-capita

25. Rammohan, D.D. (2007). Determinants of Schooling in Egypt: the role of gender and rural/urban residence. *Oxford Development Studies* , Vol. 35, No. 2, pp. 171-195.

26. Robinson, J.-M.B. (2000). Is Child Labour Inefficient? *Journal of Political Economy* , Vol. 108, No. 41, pp. 663-679.

27. Sakurai, R. (2006). *Child labour and education.* New York: United Nations Educational, Scientifiic and Cultural Organization.

28. Samuel L. Odom, M.J. (2003). *Early Intervention Practices Around the World.* Baltimore: Paul H. Brookes Publishing.

29. Sassanpour, M.H. (2008). *Labour Market Pressures in Egypt: Why is the unemployment rate stubbornly high?* Cairo: Arab Planning Institute.

30. Smith, M.P. (2009). *Economic Development, tenth edition.* Harlow: Pearson Education Limted.

31. Sobel, A.C. (2006). *Political Economy and Global Affairs.* Washington: CQ Press.

32. Susan Hill Cochrane, M.A. (1990). Education, Income and Desired Fertility in Egypt: A Revised Perspective. *The Universtiy of Chicago* , 1-27.

33. Todaro, Michael P and Stephen C. Smith. (2009). Economic Development. Harlow: Pearson Education.

34. Tzannatos, S.B. (1993). Child Labour: Waht have we learnt? *Social Protection Discussion Paper Series* , No. 0317, pp. 1-74.

35. UNFPA. (2009). *Healthy Expectations: celebrating achievements of the Cairo Consensus and highlighting the urgency for action.* New York: Population Referene Bureau.

36. UNICEF - Egypt Country Office. (2005). *Child Labour: what could be done?* Cairo: UNICEF.

37. United Nations Development Programme. (2005). *A Pro-Poor Vision for Egypt's Development*. New York: United Nations Development Programme.
38. United States Department of Labour. (2010). *Child Labour in Egypt*. Washington.
39. United States Department of Labour. (2009). *Egypt: overview: child labour in export industries*. Washington.
40. Wahba, J. (2006). The influence of market wages and parental history on child labour and schooling in Egypt. *Journal of Population Economics* , 19: 823-852.
41. Wells, P. K. (2006). *Macroeconomics*. New York: Worth Publishers.
42. Wells, P. K. (2005). *Microeconomics*. New York: Worth Publishers.
43. Yount, K.M. (2004). Maternal resources, proximity of services, and curative care of boys and girls in Minya, Egypt 1995-97. *Population Studies* , Vol. 58, No. 3, pp. 345-355.

Index